The Greek Economy and the Crisis

Panagiotis Petrakis

The Greek Economy and the Crisis

Challenges and Responses

 Springer

Prof. Panagiotis Petrakis
National and Kapodistrian
University of Athens
Department of Economics
Stadiou 5
10562 Athens
Greece
ppetrak@econ.uoa.gr

ISBN 978-3-642-21174-4   e-ISBN 978-3-642-21175-1
DOI 10.1007/978-3-642-21175-1
Springer Heidelberg Dordrecht London New York

Library of Congress Control Number: 2011938469

Printed on acid-free paper

Springer-Verlag is a part of Springer Science+Business Media (www.springer.com)

Contents

Introduction: The Responsibility of Knowledge, Challenges and Responses

Economic and social problems in Greece shook the worldwide economy in 2009. The consequences are multidimensional and develop through time. The crisis has affected almost all aspects of life of a society of 11 million people (and by extension the global economy). Similar crises have happened before in Greece and in various forms in many economies around the world.

Today, however, the social sciences are much stronger than they were during previous crises. Therefore, the key components of the problem (its emergence, pattern of repetition, functionality and impact) can be analysed to reveal its nature and thus prescribe methods for its management.

This, however, creates a **responsibility of knowledge**. In other words, no stakeholder (from ordinary citizens to decision makers in Greece and abroad) can continue to claim, to the extent that they are responsible for the crisis, that they are not aware of its key components. Certainly, this book and all of the knowledge produced on this topic demonstrate the complexity of the problem. Good will and readiness to manage the situation are insufficient. A major effort is required to understand the nature of the problem, the main asset in this effort is the substantial knowledge of the problem's components. Only once this effort is expended can we increase the certainty that the situation will not have devastating consequences for the economy on both domestic and global scales. However, it is not enough to appreciate knowledge and its bearers (intellect). Above all, we should conciliate ourselves with the implications of that knowledge in the conduct of routine economic policy.

The knowledge of the problem and the related responsibility are linked to social decisions on the course to be taken in the future. For reasons we will explain later, the actual development of the Greek economy will not head towards either end of the "rescue-catastrophe" spectrum. Under normal conditions, the real spectrum of the potential orientations of Greek economic and social development has development on one end, according to the relevant international indicators and scenarios, and problematic economic development on the other. Mistakes in social and economic policy might force the country to head towards "unsatisfactory" development. But it may ultimately be society itself that is responsible as it may not be

P. Petrakis, *The Greek Economy and the Crisis*,
DOI 10.1007/978-3-642-21175-1_1, © Springer-Verlag Berlin Heidelberg 2012

willing to move towards difficult development. In other words, the dominating social decision may not be the one that may lead to relative success but the one resulting in relative failure.

Easter Island, which is part of French Polynesia and is located in the middle of the Pacific Ocean (2,300 miles from Chile), is famous for its 397 complete and another 393 partially constructed huge anthropomorphic statues (each one weighing 10–270 tons). The statues have prehistoric origins (1,000–1,600 BC) and were built by a society of 15,000–30,000 people in a highly organised process. Few trees and few animals exist on the island today. Nearly three centuries after their discovery, a mystery remains about how these statues were made by a society that then virtually disappeared in the absence of external aggression or the negative consequences of climate change.

Anthropological science (Diamond 2006) now has the answer: it is perhaps the clearest example of a society that destroyed itself by overexploiting its resources, leaving behind monuments of its substantive decision to self-destruct.

Many find parallels in today's societies that do not ultimately make the decisions necessary for their rescue and development.

But what did the people of Easter Island think when they cut down the last tree on the island to use in the building of their monuments? In other words, how do societies make disastrous decisions?

We can distinguish five possible contributors to the process leading a society, or a decision-making group in general, to make disastrous decisions:

(a) The society may fail to anticipate the problem before it occurs. This may be due to a lack of previous experience with similar problems and a consequent lack of anticipation of the problem or the creation of false parallels so that the society is led to completely wrong conclusions.

(b) The society may fail to understand the problem after it has occurred. There are at least three reasons for this: (1) the actual causes of the problem are not immediately visible; (2) decision makers are far from the problem; and (3) the problem unfolds slowly, with peaks and valleys, obscuring the prospects for development.

(c) Although the society understands the problem, it fails to even attempt to solve it. The main reason for this is illogical behaviour deriving from a clash of interests between members of society. In particular, the solution to the problem will simply not lead everyone to a better state than their current one. A special category of such problems is the so-called "tragedy of common resources" (Ostrom 1999). It is very difficult to include common resources in management logic. A second special category of problems covers those related to the comparison of short- and long-term goals.

(d) Although a society understands the problem and tries to solve it, its system of values and stereotypes does not allow it to find a solution.

(e) Finally, a society may well have expected the problem and promptly and correctly tried to solve it, having overcome internal conflicts, but it nevertheless fails to apply the right solution simply because the problem is so large that it exceeds the society's capacity to solve it. In addition, its solution could be so expensive that it would not be possible for the society to allocate the necessary resources.

Considering the possible alternative situations created by these social decisions makes it clear that the future can become extremely complex.

The **challenges** associated with the Greek problem involve all organisational levels of society. They relate to the behaviour of the citizens of a society, as it is obvious that the present state of affairs relates to individual and collective attitudes and behaviours. However, they also concern specific categories of people, such as political representatives, entrepreneurs, intellectuals and social scientists. Each of these groups may have a different perspective on the state of affairs. In other words, this raises the question of the analysts; point of view. This should be determined by their Aristotelian ethics. Thus, their political view with reference to their field of operation is the "city". Of course, the city is not an abstract concept. It is made up of actors, operating structures and interests. Thus, the invocation of ethics is not sufficient to clarify the perspective of the analysis. The writer is required to declare his views on the contents of the city. The writer always has a personal opinion, but this book is written by basing the analysis on facts and data, making use of already developed social research. When subjectivity cannot be completely eliminated, observant readers may note it and choose to disagree if they wish.

This opens the path to the relation of challenges with policy and ultimately with the political system. The crisis of 2008–2010 exposed the weaknesses and opportunities of cooperation between the economy and politics, and especially political representatives. Essentially, we had the opportunity to tangibly comprehend the roles that the two fields of social organisation, economy and politics, can play.

The case of Germany is typical. In the early 2000s, the "Atzenta 2010" (2003), launched by Gerhard Schröder during his time as Prime Minister (1998–2005) and continued by the Christian Democratic Party and its allies after 2007 as part of a policy for the social state and globalisation, created the initial conditions for the miracle of German economic growth at the end of the decade. The adoption of this policy led the Social Democrats Party to a series of political defeats and decreased the disposable income of German citizens by 4.5% over the same decade (2000–2009), whereas disposable income rose by 8.6% in France and by 14% in Britain. At the worst point of the crisis in 2010, Germany had the lowest unemployment in Europe and the largest growth rate in the Western world. Essentially, their policy lent Germans the power to determine the future of Europe after 2010.

The Greek case is completely different. The Greek financial problem has been understood since 1930 (Zolotas 1926, Angelopoulos 1990). However, the Greek state (public and political representatives) never raised the issue (particularly after the regime change and especially after 1990) with the persistence and intensity needed to focus all efforts toward future growth prospects. Indeed, this book will shed light on the repetitive pattern of this economic and social crisis. From the birth of the Greek state in 1821 until today, Greece has suffered three other crises of national debt in addition to the most recent one (1830–1846, 1893, 1932–1950 and 2010). This pattern demonstrates the need to understand the endogenous production of systemic crises (and particularly national debt crises) in the Greek economy. It is obvious that a society that repeats behaviours for centuries (every 50–60 years) contains tangible forces that lead to this outcome irrespective of external conditions. To think about the future, we need to understand these forces. This indeed is the greatest challenge and the task of coming generations. However, as will be shown in the book, the lack of future orientation is a feature of Greek society. It is necessary to understand a society's goals when considering its problems; otherwise, the attempt to describe one (or more) future prospects for a society that does not care about them is only of historical interest for the future vindication of the proposer, if at all.

In conclusion, the question of the importance of the relation of policy with the economy and society has been repositioned in response to the present crisis and may constitute one of the key issues for the development of a society. While the global trend passed through a stage of market dominance over politics in the 1990s, we now appear to be entering a phase where the analysis of the importance of political relations coupled with the characteristics of the cultural background seems to play an important role in interpreting the future. This analysis concerns the rescue, functionality, and reorganisation of the political system, which organises the distribution of output. Indeed, these issues become extremely topical in light of a crisis of such magnitude that it affects the entire spectrum of social activity and particularly policy. This raises issues regarding the survival and change of political structures, such as the changes in domestic politics observed in many countries under international supervision or the structural political changes occurring today in the European Union. One of the most serious issues raised in a society arises when operations to rescue and change the political system capture the attention of society and use significant resources. However, the exact opposite may also happen; the demands of the political system may be ignored completely based on the belief that economic reforms will suffice for the reorganisation of the social model. In both cases, future developments may be problematic.

This line of reasoning reveals a new danger for the Greek economy when it exits the crisis. This exit may lead to the formation of a peculiar economic model that would result from the transformation of the existing model without acquiring the characteristics of the classic market model in which the allocation of resources is known to be effective, as required by the objectives of the adjustment programme. In this sense, for the Greek economy, the crisis of 2008–2010 could be an opportunity,–although this opportunity has already been lost to some extent. Although the political system had the courage to assume the costs to promote the new development model, a major problem was soon encountered because of the breadth and depth of the crisis in Greek society. Essentially, the very sustainability of the political system came into question. The politician who has to choose between preserving the welfare of the society and saving the political system may choose to save the political system because he believes that this will ensure the welfare of the state. However, the rescue of the political system contributes to reproducing the existing economic system, even if the political system itself is improved. Thus, in any case, it is preferable to renew the political mandate based on the setting of specific social targets.

This book took its final form in February 2011, when global economic developments focused on the construction of a permanent European monitoring mechanism, the rescue of European economies and the global financial crisis. The Greek economy was entering a very difficult 2 year of fiscal adjustment. If, however, the Greek economy is entering a period of strict supervision for the execution of a fiscal adjustment programme – which, of course, will last much longer than 2–3 years – is there any sense in writing a book aiming to find a developmental solution, like the one the reader is currently holding?

The answer is yes because this book details some concerns that are not affected by current events. The reason for their inclusion is simple. The current issue of economic policy is mainly associated with the fiscal problem. Nevertheless, no process of fiscal adjustment can solve the development problem of the Greek economy, and without addressing the fiscal problem, it is very difficult to formulate a development plan. Ultimately, the development problem remains unexplored.

Therefore, today it is imperative to think about the growth conditions of the Greek economy. Let us not forget that, now and in the foreseeable future, this issue will affect not only the Greek population and the Greek economy but also Europe and the world at large. The challenge of solving the Greek problem is international.

The key objective of this book is to define **answers** to the problems of the Greek economy, or at least for those arising as a synthesis of the conclusions of the analysis contained here. A key feature of the book is that it includes the outcome of an independent research effort, which was not funded by any third source, although: (a) the search for objectivity and truth requires resources; (b) resources are usually made available from several sources (particularly from government sources) to specific recipients, thus producing "concrete answers"; and (c) usually, the return on those resources is related to the produced and prescribed prospects for the study object, in this case the Greek economy and society. When, however, there is an intended aim in the organisation and specification of the future (i.e., the desired direction of affairs in society), it is clear that these solutions do not ensure better allocation of a society's resources and the achievement of maximal financial results. This result should be associated only with the ultimate goal of development, which is human happiness.

The most common cause of a deviation from the principle of maximising the availability of resources in a society is an orientation towards meeting the functional specifications of the system itself and not towards the effectiveness of their allocation. The above method controls the maintenance of the distribution of output and is expected (in theory at least) to yield the desired (maximum) result given the optimal functioning of the system. However, this method entails a visible risk of orienting efforts towards developing economic systems with a purpose of self-fulfilment (function for function's sake, not for the outcome). As indeed will be shown in more detail in the book, the Greek economy is noted for this deviation. The Greek economic system is largely oriented towards the control of the instrument (function) rather than towards the maximisation or improvement of the outcome. If, in forming the development prospects of the future social action, policy makers concentrate again on the organisation of (even a new) economic operation while yet again ignoring the result, we will only achieve another version of the Greek problem that will produce serious crises while retaining the control of wealth.

As this model will not seek to develop endogenous growth forces in its operation, it will reproduce serious functionality crises (Scenario 2 in the following figure, with repeated fiscal adjustments),[1] leaving open the prospect of a very serious crisis in 50 or 60 years (as can be foreseen based on historical data). On the positive side, however, its application would allow us to avoid a catastrophe bankruptcy today (Scenario 1 in figure) with all of the grave and disastrous consequences this would have on the lives of Greek citizens, due to lack of primary surpluses and the resulting economic (exclusion from international capital markets) and political implications (e.g., Greece's relationships with the European Union and the Eurozone). Such a scenario should not be excluded because society will abandon the effort to adjust (paying heed to those advocating an "easy" way out)[2] or because of some very important external event (e.g., large-scale war in the Middle East) whose "collateral" damage (along with many other similar losses in the world) would include the bankruptcy of Greece.[3] This sequence of events would bring about the greatest political risk that characterises the integration of an economy in a broader foreign rescue plan, which is the absence of elements of sovereignty and therefore of ultimate responsibility for the course of developments. Nevertheless, the same logic that supports the idea that an external event may adversely affect the domestic economic operations could also lead to a positive effect.

Thus, the challenge (to which the book devotes its final attempt at a solution) is to specify (Scenario 3 in figure) the development that aims to improve the welfare of society, of course within the real internal and external limitations, regardless of external developments in the future.

This book seeks to specify these development conditions, even though we believe that we are heading perhaps not towards the third but towards the second Scenario. This is because the mission of the social scientist is to describe and achieve goals that serve as points of orientation. This effort can help to shape the evolution of the (political and social) situation in Greece.

---

[1] A typical case is Portugal (Magone 2006), which, in the period of 2002–2005 (under J. Baroso), applied an identical adjustment plan (to that of Greece, 2010). Nevertheless, this did not stop it from finding itself in a very difficult position in 2010.

[2] A good example is the case of California, the eighth richest economy in the world, which has been in a state of "bankruptcy" since 2008 and still cannot operate a credible programme of fiscal stability.

[3] At this point we are referred to the "catastrophe bankruptcy" which is a rather different concept from other types of "friendly default", as the "debt reprofiling", which could take place in a rather friendly way to both (lenders–borrowers) sides.

Everyone would like to write and everyone would want to read a book that contains the magic formula for the future of the Greek economy and every economy and society. Such a book, though, has not been written and will never be. The reason is very simple: the role of randomness in the identification of the prospects of the economy and society is extremely important. But what can science do when it has already cited randomness as a determinant of the future? It can describe what

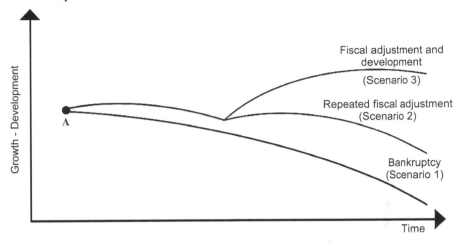

the human intellect can understand. Thus, we can understand the context of future developments in a highly accurate manner. We can comprehend, in other words, the background and the forces that determine the future as a necessary condition. Unfortunately, the description of all sufficient conditions will remain unfulfilled.

Moreover, a good forecast is not necessarily a "correct" forecast or, in any case, one that convinces us that we are on the right track. In contrast, it is that which identifies the issues of increasing interest and points to the facts that prepare us, mentally and organisationally, for different scenarios of the future and unexpected changes of fortune. In these alternative conceptions of future developments, the evaluation of each forecast is based on whether and to what extent it illuminates the unknown, calls into question our assumptions, forces us to clarify our thinking by motivating and organising difficult discussions, asks the right questions and leads us to make the tough choices about the management of future changes. A perception of the future is not necessarily good if it only predicts the future correctly, but it is certainly good if it prepares us well for a future full of uncertainty, as demonstrated by Gordon (2009).

The answers given by this book in an effort to clear the clouds of uncertainty about the future have a common denominator that sends a clear message to members of Greek society and its political representatives: In the distant future of global society, two expressions of human culture will play distinctive and important roles: history and corporate structures. Because of its historical presence, the Greek state has the unique advantage of being de facto present in that future. In order, however, for its members to survive in this future society, radical social changes are required today, for which the unique applicability criterion is their effectiveness. This means significantly changing and surpassing the political and social structures of power and the structures of all kinds of interests. To do so requires knowledge, sincerity, and determination at all decision-making levels.

Perhaps one of the most significant elements this book offers to readers is the methodology of the research per se. That is, the priority with which we approach the issues under study and the extent to which we choose to analyse each of these are unique. The book takes the view that the study of growth and development takes place through the investigation of the conditions for the accumulation of basic production factors of capital, labour, human capital, technology and the impact of certain exogenous variables (e.g., geography, strategic relationships) under the influence exercised by the political and cultural environment. An understanding of this development is achieved along three dimensions: (a) the structural, which covers the features of the current situation; (b) the longitudinal, covering the characteristics of change through time; and finally, (c) the comparison with similar financial entities (e.g., states or groups of states). These entities have either similar dimensions, i.e., economies with similar characteristics (Southeastern Europe), or serve as benchmark economies (Northern European countries). Hence, all research observations will be made based on this comparative analysis focusing on the current situation. In other words, the historical dimension is relevant to the extent that it reveals the active forces shaping today's and tomorrow's reality.

The book consists of 14 chapters and an Annex. Chapter 2 describes the changing world and the position of the Greek economy up to the 2008–2010 crisis. Chapter 3 describes the development conditions of the Greek economy up to the great crisis. Chapter 4 deals with the actual effectiveness of the economic development model in the Greek economy, i.e., human development by controlling the relation between happiness and development. Chapter 5 discusses issues of human capital (education, innovation and health), and Chap. 6 covers issues related to cultural background and the historical roots of Greek society. These are social elements that present little mobility and are therefore discussed, to a certain degree, for the purpose of shaping the future. Chapter 7 discusses the idiosyncratic situation of economic institutions, and Chap. 8 discusses the political institutions and the distribution of income and wealth. The notion that social engineering (i.e., the sole issuing of administrative acts, and laws) will determine the financial result for Greece reflects an unrealistic perception of the evolution of human society. What is of importance is how humans react and take action in these developments. Thus, Chap. 9 presents the shaping of incentives for human activity. Chapter 10 describes the crisis of 2008–2010 and the introduction of the European Stability Mechanism (ESM). Chapter 11 contains an analysis of the root causes of the Greek social problem. This analysis is to a certain extent conclusive in nature, based on the preceding analysis, while also serving as an introduction for the chapters that follow, particularly for the parts of the book concerning future analysis. Thus, Chap. 12 covers the economic situation in Greece in the post-May 2010 period, when the Greek economy was included in the Economic Adjustment Programme. The way in which the Greek economy entered the EAP will determine its short-term development. Thus, Chap. 13 discusses the effectiveness of economic adjustment interventions. Finally, the medium- and long-term prospects of the Greek economy are described in Chap. 14. This chapter describes the target conditions for the Greek economy, which will allow it to overcome the emerging trend in the long term. Finally, the Annex includes a dynamic sectoral development proposal for the Greek economy that is based on the long-term significant changes occurring in the wider environment.

The book discusses the political economy of the Greek social and economic problem. Political economy is the area of social sciences that analyses economic phenomena in a comprehensive manner, starting from how, where and when decisions are made, from production to distribution, consumption, savings and investment of the produced output. The methodology of such an analysis expands beyond the use of the analytical tools of economics. It also uses analytical tools from political science, organisational management, social and individual psychology. This approach is necessary as man stands at the core of the establishment of social phenomena. The human mind focuses its resources on organising its economic and social environment. If we do not understand that the ultimate object of our concern is exactly how the human mind works and, in particular, how it functions to organise its economic and social environment to meet its needs and ultimately achieve welfare, we are doomed to lose sight of our purpose as social scientists. The same is true, of course, for those who make and implement management decisions in this society.

This book follows the author's work: "The Greek Economy: Challenges (until 2010)", Athens, Papazisis Editions 2010. That book was based on the contributions of my collaborators; I would like to take this opportunity to thank them again.

This book was made possible thanks to the scientific assistance of P. Kostis, K. Stratis, A. Petrelli, D. Konstantakopoulou, J. Konstantakopoulou and the administrative assistance of K. Anomitri and L. Mantesou. The UOA also supported this effort. E. Giuli and the main partners at my office gave me the opportunity to dedicate myself to the completion of my research. My family supported me with of their patience. I thank them all.

P.E. Petrakis

February 2011

References

Angelopoulos E (1990) Conservatism and value relevance in the Greek financial sector. Department of Account Technology Institute of Patras, Greece

Diamond A (2006) The early development of executive functions. In: Bialystok E, Craik F (eds) Lifespan cognition. Oxford University Press, New York

Gordon A (2009) Future savvy. American Management Association Press, New York

Magone J (2006) Portugal. Eur J Pol Res 45:1247–1253

Ostrom E (2010) Governing the commons. Cambridge University Press, Cambridge

Zolotas X (1926) Greece in the stage of industrialization. Bank of Greece, Athens

The Changing World and the Greek Economy Before the Crisis

2

The worldwide economic and social environment is changing rapidly. The rate of economic and social developments is the main characteristic of the twentieth and especially the beginning of the twenty-first century. These changes concern all participants in the global economic process, whether they are national economies, organisational entities or workers. This chapter aims to introduce the reader to the dynamics of these changes and to enable the reader to place the Greek economy (as a small open economy and society) in the context of the wider global developments. To achieve this, it is necessary to identify the main components of global economic structuring and restructuring.

Which are the real forces that shape new value in the economy, and which are the forces that shape the increase of gross domestic product? In other words, what are the sources of growth in an economy? From one point of view, this question condenses the basic questions raised by classical economists, such as A. Smith (1776, 1977) in "Wealth of Nations," D. Ricardo (1817, 2001) in "On the Principles of Political Economy and Taxation" and K. Marx (1867) in the "Capital." It is not deemed necessary to discuss here the axiological approaches that ultimately shape philosophical differentiation in interpreting the creation of human wealth; we will simply accept that growth is created by the basic production factors, which are capital and labour and its improvement (i.e., investments in human capital), technology and others.

Section 2.1 of this chapter presents the basic sources of economic growth and the theoretical framework of the analysis. Section 2.2 presents the "uninterpreted" part of growth, not in the sense of the unknown but in acknowledgement of the importance and intricacy beyond the basic economic growth sources and the construction of the growth process. Section 2.3 discusses the relation between the size of the economy and growth. Section 2.4 presents the main global economic changes of recent years. Section 2.5 analyses developments in monetary economy, Sect. 2.6 the quantitative and qualitative evolution of population flows and Sect. 2.7 changes in technology and innovation. Section 2.8 analyses the field of energy and climate change and, more specifically, the depletion of resources and the demand for energy. Section 2.9 describes the process of configuring the national force of a

P. Petrakis, *The Greek Economy and the Crisis*,
DOI 10.1007/978-3-642-21175-1_2, © Springer-Verlag Berlin Heidelberg 2012

country. Finally, Sect. 2.10, analyses the relative position of Greece within Southeastern Europe.

2.1   Basic Sources of Growth

The main questions we will address are:
(a) What are the forces that influence a country's level of per capita income over time?
(b) What are the forces that create differences in the rates of growth of per capita income between different economies?

According to the neoclassical perception of economic growth (Solow 1957), the main source of long-run economic growth is exogenous technological progress, whereas short-run growth depends on the stock of capital, population growth, and the allocation of output among alternative uses (savings and consumption).

The improvement of the labour force, mainly through education, leads to the improvement of production capacity and thus the improvement of per capita production. Under the influence of Romer (1986) and Lucas (1988), technological progress, as a diffusion phenomenon in all levels of the economy, enters the equation, influencing the capacity of the labour force. However, as North and Thomas (1973) demonstrated, all of these factors referring to the accumulation of production factors (e.g., innovation, economies of scale, education) are not sources of growth; they are growth itself. To calculate the contribution of each factor to GDP, and thus the residuals from these factors, we should deduct the contributions of capital and labour, i.e., the product of the rate of change of capital and labour and the corresponding weight on total cost from GDP change.

Economists refer to this analysis as "growth accounting." Its exact development assumes a basic step: the calculation of the relevant costs shaping GDP in relation to the two basic factors of labour and capital. These calculations (Timmer et al. 2003, OECD – Factbook 2008) are presented for a series of countries in Table 2.1.

The results are based on the hypothesis of constant returns to scale, i.e., the hypothesis that the sum of the shares of labour and capital equals one. Below, we calculate the contribution of labour as the ratio of wages (and the income of the self-employed) to GDP (minus taxes and industries' operating costs). The subtraction of this percentage gives us the contribution of capital and vice versa. The adjustment of the methods to include the self-employed is achieved based on the hypothesis that their "wage" is similar to that of salaried employees (Timmer et al. 2003, p. 8).

Based on the data of Table 2.1, we see that in certain countries (some of which are very important, such as Germany and Japan), the factor of labour now, surprisingly, plays a negative role in shaping growth factors. On the contrary, in the USA it continues to play an important role, thus expressing the capabilities of the economy to widen the use of the labour factor, mainly because of immigration. Overall, it seems that labour continues to play a significant role in shaping the growth rate of GDP.

Table 2.1 Contributions to growth: average yearly growth (%), 1985–2006

	Labour (%)	Capital (%)	Uninterpreted part – remaining factors (%)[a]	GDP growth (%)
France	8.38	35.60	56.62	100
Germany	−23.25	45.95	77.61	100
Japan	−20.74	44.16	77.20	100
United Kingdom	16.89	39.32	44.47	100
USA	35.07	28.83	37.04	100
Spain	50.98	42.43	7.32	100
Portugal	11.96	35.68	52.97	100
New Zealand	37.49	36.28	27.07	100
Average	16.36	38.53	48.88	100

Source: OECD Factbook 2008 (p. 269) and OECD data (OECD Statistical Portal). Averages weighted by 2007 country GDP

[a]Usually, the "uninterpreted part" is presented as the Total Productivity Factor (TPF) in the sense that it is the product of the function of key production factors (capital, labour) under the influence of the overall environment in which they operate, i.e., their overall productivity. Here, this part of the contribution of growth is called the "rest," "uninterpreted part," "remaining inputs" or "Total Productivity Factor"

This topic can be examined from a pertinent and closely related perspective based on the econometric method of utilising the concept of constant returns to scale of the production function. In order to examine the effect of human capital on GDP growth, we calculate the parameters of Solow's augmented production function with the least squares method (Mankiw et al. 1992; Cohen and Soto 2007).

Mankiw et al. (1992) and Bernanke and Gurkaynak (2001) studied three groups of countries: non-oil (98 countries), intermediate (75 countries) and OECD members (22 countries) from 1960 to 1995. Their main assumption was that productivity levels are the same among all countries.

Easterly and Levine (2001) studied 64 countries under the assumption that production differs among the different groups of countries. According to the authors, OECD countries have higher production compared to the rest of the world. The results of these basic works are presented in Table 2.2.

We observe that, in all three studies, the contribution of labour ranges from 0.41 to 0.63, while the contribution of human capital ranges from 0.27 to 0.49. Finally, the contribution of capital ranges from 0.04 to 0.3, with an average level around 0.25.

It should be noted that the interpretability of the samples ranges from 28% to 83%. As a result, it is obvious that the "remaining factors," which are uninterpreted, exert a considerable influence. Combining all of the available data (Timmer et al. 2003, OECD-Factbook 2008, Mankiw et al. 1992; Easterly and Levine 2001; Bernanke and Gurkaynak 2001), it appears that in OECD countries, which include the countries Timmer et al. (Groningen)[1] studied, capital contributes about 30% to

[1] Groningen Total – Economy Growth – Accounting Database – http://www.ggdc.net.

Table 2.2 Literature findings concerning economic growth

Authors factors	Mankiw et al. (1992) period: 1960–1985			Easterly and Levine (2001) period: 1960–1995		Bernanke and Gurkaynak (2001) period: 1960–1995		
Database	Penn World Table 4.0			Penn World Table 5.6		Penn World Table 6.0		
Number of observations	98	75	22	126	90	72	21	
Countries	Non-oil	Intermediate	OECD	OECD, East Asia, West Asia, Sub-Saharan Africa, rest of Africa, Europe	Non-oil	Intermediate	OECD	
Capital contribution (a)	0.31	0.29	0.14	0.10		0.27	0.25	0.04
Contribution of human capital (b)	0.28	0.30	0.37	0.27		0.30	0.35	0.49
Contribution of labour (1 −a − b)	0.41	0.41	0.49	0.63		0.43	0.40	0.47
Interpretability of GDP growth	78%	77%	28%	81%		79%	83%	46%

GDP growth, labour about 25%, human capital[2] about 10% and "remaining factors" about 35%. Therefore, the proper study of growth sources in an economy should pay careful attention to the above-mentioned sources of growth. The political economy of development should be studied with special reference to the "remaining factors."

2.2 The "Unexplained Part" of Growth, or the Factors Shaping Total Productivity

Since the 1970s, researchers have been interested in the "unexplained part" of growth. Kuznets (1971) concluded that national differences in economic growth can be considered as the Solow residual (Solow 1957), which is simply differences in productivity that are characterised as exogenous in the simple neoclassical model. Abramovitz (1956) defined the residual as the "measure of our ignorance," a definition also supported by Dougherty and Jorgenson (1996). Today, thanks to extensive research on the topic, our relative ignorance on the subject has been reduced significantly.

The basic international empirical findings show that something else apart from the basic factors (capital and labour) plays a significant role in economic growth (Easterly and Levine 2001). This something else, the "total productivity" (TPF, Total Productivity Factor), is the basic factor that distinguishes the performances of

---

[2] The influence of human capital has been deducted from the effect of the "remaining factors".

economies in terms of space and time. In reality, it does not interpret but attributes or represents all of the factors that affect differential growth.

As a result, we now expand research to areas that including the history, culture, geography and political life of the economies studied. It is believed that differences in social structure are sufficient (Hall and Jones 1999) to interpret the greater part of an economy's growth rate.

A similar perception is used to interpret why different countries, with different economic institutions, structures and political institutions (Acemoglu et al. 2004), exhibit different economic growth rates.[3] Institutions are the political and financial "terms of the game" in a society (North 1990).

The "beginning of the world" (growth process) lies in the political institutions and the initial system of resource distribution in the economy. The redistribution of resources also has an endogenous character. The interactions of political institutions and the distribution of resources shape the means of exercising political authority. Political authority forms the concept of the state, with three distinct authorities: legislative, executive and judicial. This system consists of the structure and procedures that govern our everyday life and the functions of society. Economic institutions are formed under the influence of these terms and their procedures.

Economic institutions (e.g., the tax system, banking system, and financial system), like most other financial institutional organisations, are mainly products of endogenous processes. They are defined as society's collective choices and usually express contradictory interests and develop under the influence of historical process and cultural background. Generally favourable (for growth) economic institutions are those that offer secure property rights throughout the range of society's functions (Acemoglu et al. 2004, Ha-Joon Chang 2006). The relation between institutions and economic growth stems from three different sources: (a) their contribution to coordination and governance; (b) their influence on the process of development, knowledge and innovation; and (c) their effect on income distribution and the development of social coherence.

Economic institutions shape the structure of incentives (for individuals and businesses) that operate in the society, which shape transaction costs. The latter, of course, are affected by technological terms and finally shape the terms of operational contracts of financial transactions. This is how economic results and growth are formed in a society. Obviously, this brings us back to the "beginning of the world," meaning that financial results and economic growth (and its qualitative characteristics) affect political institutions and the distribution of resources in the society. This allows us to monitor the sequential process of growth at a higher (or lower) level (Fig. 2.1).

---

[3] Maybe the most important example of all of the empirically observed cases is the comparison between North and South Korea, which started from the same level of growth and development and today present a vast gap in growth and quality of life of their citizens.

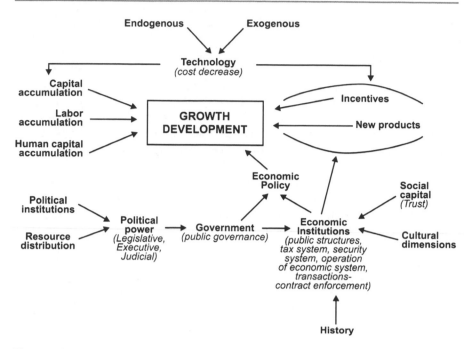

Fig. 2.1 Configuration of growth and development levels and rates

2.3   Small Open Economies and Development

According to Kuznets (1960), a small open economy is defined by two fundamental criteria. The first is a population of fewer than 15 m people. Sometimes, GDP or a country's size are used as indices of a small economy. Population, however, is highly dependent on a country's size and on GDP because of the possibly limited sources of raw materials in these countries.

The criterion for a small open economy is the country's limited international transactions. Its transactions are such that the country's policies do not put it in a position to influence global prices, interest rates or incomes. Consequently, countries with smaller open economies are price takers.

Under no circumstances does the fact that a small economy will not be able to compete with large economies or will have a balance of payments deficit constitute a rule. There is simply a greater danger because of lower transaction levels and because of the country's small population, both of which originate mostly from its low productivity. If, however, it manages to develop the appropriate skills, it will be able to reverse these conditions, increasing its productivity and competing on equal terms with large economies (Frankel and Romer 1999). This answers the question of whether size matters in economic growth; it does, but not as much as most think.

It is widely accepted that small economies rely mainly on the service sector and tourism and aim to increase the inflow of direct foreign investments. The increase of both inflow and outflow of direct foreign investments in a small economy is of significant help because it increases the spillover effect (Hogenbirk and Narula 1999).

2.4 Fundamental Global Economic Changes

The medium-term development of the worldwide economy involves two basic components: the up-and-coming Chinese economy and the USA's capacity to preserve positive levels of economic activity. The dynamic of the Chinese economy is based on three pillars: its capacity to export goods and services, export of its capital stock to the USA through the purchase of American debt and the improvement of standards of living domestically. China already carries half of the USA's relative position in global product production (10.8% versus 21.4% for the USA, Table 2.3). It has almost the same export rate (7.8% versus 9.6%) but has 20% of the world's population, versus 4.7% for the USA, with per capita income of $2,483 compared to $45,725 for the USA.

The Greek economy carries 0.5% of global GDP, 31% of EU-15 GDP and 2.1% of EU-27 GDP. Furthermore, Greece has 0.4% of total exports and 0.2% of the global population. Based on purchasing power parity (PPP), the per capita GDP of Greece was $28,152 in 2007, compared to $32,815 for the Eurozone (EU-15). Therefore, Greece is a very small economy with rather high output and income per capita.

Table 2.3 Gross domestic product, exports and population (2007 data)

	Country or region	GDP % of global GDP	Exports % of total exports	Population % of global population	GDP per capita US dollars, based on purchasing power parity (ppp)
Developed economies	USA	21.4	9.6	4.7	$45,725
	Eurozone	16.1	29.5	4.9	$32,815[a]
	Greece	0.5	0.4[b]	0.2	$28,152
	Japan	6.6	4.7	2.0	$34,296
Developing countries	Russia	3.2	2.3	2.2	$9,075
	China	10.8	7.8	20.5	$2,483
	India	4.6	1.3	17.5	$942
	Brazil	2.8	1.1	2.9	$6,938
	Mexico	2.1	1.7	1.6	$9,717

Source: International Monetary Fund (World Economic Outlook, April 2008)
[a]OECD stats (http://stats.oecd.org/wbos/default.aspx?datasetcode=SNA_TABLE1)
[b]UN data (http://data.un.org/Data.aspx?d=CDB&f=srID%3A29940)

Thus, at first glance we can characterise the Greek economy by taking into account the standard of living, exports and imports of capital. A strong relation exists between capital imports and growth. Of course, a similar relation could exist in any developing economy. Therefore, much deeper analysis is required to clarify the nature of the Greek economy.

Global growth, exchange rates, and interest rates largely depend on the relationship between the two giants of the global economy: the USA and China (Deloitte, Global Economic Outlook – 2008). More specifically, in order to preserve a low exchange rate for its currency against the US dollar, and given that it does not have any alternative placement outlets (i.e., markets with prospects) for its export-related income, China purchases American public bonds. However, it would be hasty to blame the Chinese funding for the "bubble" of the financial structure in the United States and the rest of the Western world. The actual capital flows from China are much smaller compared to the value of the monetary instruments generated in the West (see Sect. 2.5). This financing influx has kept interest rates in the USA, and consequently in the rest of the world, low and the exchange rate between the (depreciated) dollar and the (appreciated) Yuan more or less stable. At the same time, American and Chinese development continued while inflationary strain was exerted through demand for raw materials and oil in the global economy. This led to a relative improvement in the economies of developing countries, especially those with oil and raw materials.

This is how the second important development, which involved the formation of a strong growth rate among developing countries (emerging markets) in comparison to advanced economies (Fig. 2.2), emerged.

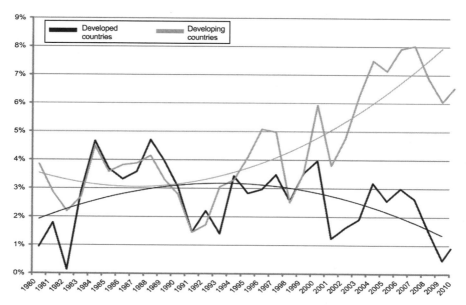

Fig. 2.2 Percentage growth of GDP and trend (Source: IMF data, estimates and data processing)

It is now obvious that the next long-term wave of growth[4] will be characterised either by the efforts of the developing countries to improve their standard of living in order to approach the levels of developed countries through the creation of a middle class (totalling 400–500 m people) in these societies or from the advent of one or more fundamental structural technological changes. The issue of the geographical origin of new sources of growth has also been expressed by the relative change of the global political scene as it has been portrayed by the creation of a new deliberation team, the G20, which has replaced the G7. The new core of the G20 is the BRIC countries, which are Brazil, Russia, India and China.

It should be noted that the smooth and gradual transition to a complex world where multiple major forces will play important roles and the centre of gravity will move to the East, presupposes that humanity will overcome, in a peaceful way, the turbulent transitional period that may last until the end of 2020.

External imbalances that appeared in the late 1990s exceeded 5% of the worldwide GDP in 2008 (from 2% in 1996). Most of these imbalances (total losses) came from the US, whose share in shaping the overall deficit exceeded 70% in 2002 (from 36% in 1996) but declined to 40% in 2008. Surplus countries are mainly China, Germany, the oil-exporting countries, and Japan.

Nevertheless, research (Cheung et al. 2010) has identified a series of partial equilibrium factors that play a role in shaping the current account deficits. Thus, there is a positive relation between fiscal balances and current account deficits (Chinn and Ito 2008; Gruber and Kamin 2007; Bussiere et al. 2005) (twin deficits). More specifically, the impact of budget deficits on the current account balance depends on how fiscal expenses are allocated. Higher social spending could reduce savings (through an increase of imports) in developing and emerging economies. In addition, their funding through higher levels of taxation and the redistribution of incomes across households with different consumption trends lead to reduced savings and thus to the need to import goods. Figure 2.3 presents the budget surplus or deficit as a percentage of GDP for the same groups of countries depicted in Fig. 2.4. An increase in the fiscal deficit – unless offset by an increase in private savings – leads to an increase of the current account deficit and generates a threefold deficit: current account deficit, budget deficit and a deficit of savings in relation to investment.

Moreover, under the life-cycle hypothesis, agents borrow a lot when they are young, save a lot during the productive years of their lives and end up consuming their savings after retirement. This hypothesis implies that societies with large numbers of young and elderly people should show larger fiscal deficits (Chinn and Prasad 2003; Gruber and Kamin 2007; Chinn and Ito 2008). The stage of economic development plays an important role as well. The outflow of capital to emerging economies is expected to be smaller than anticipated due to factors in local societies (e.g., underdeveloped financial systems, weak institutions) that

---

[4] If we accept that the previous is marked by two major recessions (around 1980 and 2008).

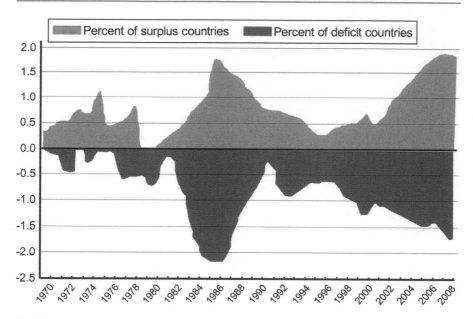

Fig. 2.3 Fiscal deficit and surplus (% of GDP) (Source: OECD, Economic Outlook, No. 88, 2010/2. Note: Values are weighted based on population per year for both groups of countries)

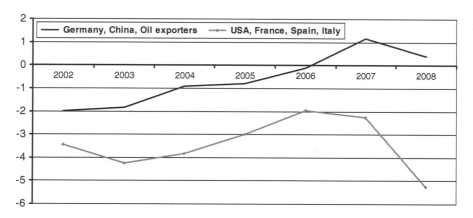

Fig. 2.4 Global current account balances (% of worldwide GDP) (Source: OECD, Economic Outlook No. 87 database)

reduce risk-adjusted returns on capital (Lucas 1988). Furthermore, the level of financial development and integration also seems to play a role. One explanation for the large global external imbalances may be that emerging economies with inefficient financial markets export their surplus capital to more efficient economies (Ju and Wei 2006), contributing to the growth of a global savings saturation. If the above suggestion is correct, countries with deep financial markets will reduce levels of saving and thus develop a negative relation between financial development and the current account balance. However, the opposite relation can be seen as traditional economic development encourages savings, reduces transaction costs and facilitates risk management.

The net foreign assets of a country affect the balance of net investment and hence the movements of current account transactions. Weak institutions in a society reduce the risk-adjusted return on equity of developing countries (Alfaro et al. 2005). In addition, the quality of institutions affects levels of financial development (Levine et al. 2000). Depending on whether a country imports or exports oil and on the extent of the impact of this action on the economic result, the current account balance is affected. More specifically, the greater the dependence on an oil importer is, the slower the adjustment of demand to changes in oil prices and the greater their effect on the current account balance become. Countries with higher growth in productivity attract more international capital flows and are expected to achieve higher returns. Finally, a country with highly developed trade, which is therefore more globalised, is expected to pursue trade and transaction policies that affect the current account balance.

From the perspective of national accounts, the result of the current account balance equals the difference between national savings and investment. Therefore, countries with positive results in the current account balance will present a positive savings minus investment balance, while the opposite is true for countries with a negative external balance (Fig. 2.5).

However, the basic imbalances of economies (current account balance, fiscal balance and balance of savings and investment) usually enclose a further threefold imbalance: that of the relation between the balance of trade in goods and services, that of the net movement of investment and that of net capital transfers (Fig. 2.6). What has been confirmed in a significant number of cross-layer longitudinal observations, however, is the existence of the so-called twin deficits, external and fiscal, which are not necessarily accompanied by other types of deficits. However,

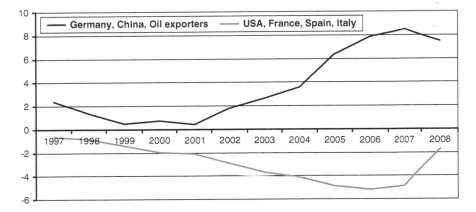

Fig. 2.5 Savings minus investments (% of GDP) (Source: World Bank database. Note: Values are weighted based on population per year for both groups of countries)

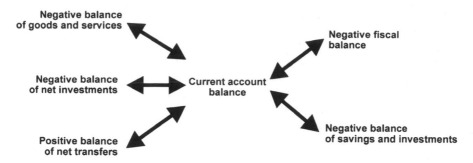

Fig. 2.6 Global imbalances

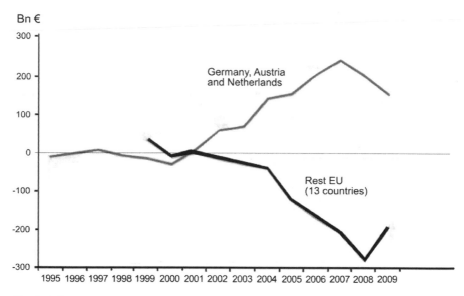

Fig. 2.7 Current account balances in the European Union (Source: Hans-Werner Sinn, CESifo, Volume 11 [August, 2010])

we could say that the emergence of the next two imbalances (savings-investment and trade balance) are particularly characteristic of the present crisis.

Imbalances between the balance of goods and services and capital transfers (either as investments or in the form of net transfers) were evident, even within the European Union. Thus, Northern European countries, especially Germany, Austria and the Netherlands, have developed significant external current account surpluses, which correspond precisely with the deficits of other European countries (Fig. 2.7).

In 2007, these countries developed a surplus of the external current account balance of €244 bn (Germany alone presented €185 bn), while the rest of Europe had a corresponding deficit in the current account balance of €280 bn in 2008. Thus, in 2007, Germany was the second largest capital exporter in the world after China.

2.5   The Monetary Economy

The global financial system over the past two decades has been characterised by the systematic expansion of monetary output.

The 2007 global GDP was \$54.5 tr. In the same year, the capitalisation of financial markets, public and private securities and banking system assets reached 4.2 times the global GDP. However, if we add to this figure the "value" of OTC products and derivatives, then this figure is 16.6 times. It is worth highlighting that the excessive expansion stems from OTC products – that is, derivatives – and not from the derivatives exchanged in the markets. Of course, the relation of the real economy (GDP) and monetary values is indirect. This comparison, however, still provides us with an idea of the rate of growth of financial expansion, which, in the end, was largely responsible for the 2008 crisis.

The relation between the monetary and real economy in Greece is similar to the global relation. The ratio between the banking system's assets and GDP was 1.60 in Greece, 0.90 in North America, 2.75 in Europe and 1.55 globally. The comparative indices for the EU and North America portray the different role of the banking systems in these economies (see below): in North America, in contrast to the EU, the financing of the economy passes mainly through non-banking channels. In Greece, however, the banking system's assets expanded more conservatively compared to the EU. This is probably due to the smaller role that the banking plays has in funding the Greek economy, mainly because of the delay in development and the role of the parallel (shadow) economy. Negotiable instruments, bonds and bank assets as percentage to GDP display an approximately equal relation to GDP in all regions (Greece included), except for developing countries, where this is 2.53 (almost half).

Globally, at the end of 2007, OTC derivatives were interest rate "debts" (66%), foreign currency derivatives (9.5%) and associated with bankruptcy risks (9.7%). The rest concerned equities, merchandise, and so on. Moreover, 23% of financial products had durations of longer than 5 years. The above formulation shows that this large volume of financing tools is still an instrument of debt, which excessively expands monetary variables.

During a period of prosperity, those responsible for the Western financial system demonstrated, in essence, procyclical behaviour. That is, during periods of growth, they were inclined to undertake continually higher risks, pushing the monetary economy to greater expansion and thus grossly increasing systematic risk.

It should also be noted that global reserves amount to 12% of GDP in developed countries and 28% in developing ones. The value of this relation in developing countries is mostly due to the smaller issuance of (mostly) public and private debt securities.

2.6   Population Flows

The main feature of population trends today is the observed change in the structure of age groups. The impact of baby boomers is due mainly to their increased life expectancy. Birth rates are declining as a result of efforts to raise the per capita income and of a change in lifestyle characterised by the increased participation of women in production. The absence of structured measures for protecting mother-hood has resulted in decreasing birth rates and an upward bulge in the age pyramid.

The changes in the population pyramid are straightforward. From 1960 to 2006, the under-15 age group lost about 10 percentage points of population participation. The share of the population in this age group decreased from 28.6% in 1960 to 19.1% in OECD countries and from 23.6% to 15.9% in the EU. The same change is observed in the Mediterranean countries and the Greek economy, but not in Northern European countries. In the latter, a decrease in the participation of this age group is observed, but it is not that significant (at least in Denmark and Sweden). Obviously, this difference is due to the development of systems for the social protection and promotion of motherhood in these countries.

The decreasing share of the population in this age group resulted in the increased share of dependent individuals (i.e., those who depend on social funds) aged over 65. As a result, the participation of this age group increased in the OECD from 8.5% to 14% and in the EU from 10.1% to 17.5%. In the Mediterranean countries, there is a clear increase of 10 percentage points: in Greece from 8.1% to 18.5%, in Italy from 9% to 19.6%, and in Spain from 8.2% to 16.7%. The same holds for the Balkan countries.

These trends are universal and longitudinal in nature and follow the improve-ment of the per capita income. Thus, the youthfulness of the population that today is a striking feature of China, India and many African countries will tend to decrease over time as living standards improve.

At the same time, another important change is observed. In certain countries, there is a significant increase of the net inflow of people born in other countries (i.e., immigration). In 2006, 12% of the total population of OECD countries was born in another country. This value is 20% more than it was in 2000. The countries with the biggest increases in the percentages of people born in other countries were Ireland, Finland, Austria and Spain. The countries with the biggest outflows of population were China, Poland and Romania. More specifically, in 2006, 60% of migratory inflow in Europe came from Europe itself (Table 2.4).

2.7   Technology and Innovation

Technology and innovation constitute a key source of growth in economic activity and improved living standards. It is obvious that the future change and development will emanate from the capability to produce and use technology and innovation.

Table 2.5 portrays indicative data concerning two basic indices of the role of technology in the productivity of the economies, which testify to the importance of

Table 2.4 Population data

		Population (in thousands)		Rate of increase 2005–2006 (%)	Distribution of population by age groups (percentage of total population)						Population of individuals born in other countries – Percentage of total population		
					Under 15 years old		15–64 years old		65 years old and up				
		2006	1996		2006 (%)	1960 (%)	2006 (%)	1960 (%)	2006 (%)		1960 (%)	2006 (%)	1996 (%)
Mediterranean countries	Greece	11,149	10,709	0.4	14.3	26.1	67.1	65.8	18.5		8.1	5.3	2.8
	Italy	58,435	56,826	0.5	14.2	23.4	66.3	67.6	19.6		9.0	5.0	2.0
	Spain	44,068	39,479	1.5	14.5	27.3	68.8	64.5	16.7		8.2	11.9	3.0
	Portugal	10,586	9,866	0.2	15.5	–	67.2	–	17.3		–	6.1	5.4
Balkan countries	Bulgaria	7,699	8,363	–0.5	13.5	26.1	69.3	66.4	17.2		7.5	–	–
	Romania	21,588	22,619	–0.2	15.5	–	69.7	–	14.8		–	–	–
	Turkey	72,974	62,909	1.3	28.1	41.2	66.0	55.1	6.0		3.7	–	1.9
Northern countries	Denmark	5,435	5,263	0.3	18.7	25.2	66.1	64.2	15.3		10.6	6.6	5.1
	Netherlands	16,346	15,531	0.2	18.2	30.0	67.4	61.0	14.4		9.0	10.6	9.2
	Sweden	9,081	8,841	0.6	17.1	22.4	65.5	65.9	17.3		11.8	12.9	10.7
EU (15 countries)		388,200	371,983	0.5	15.9	23.6	66.6	63.2	17.5		10.1	–	–
OECD (30 countries)		1,175,344	1,096,466	0.7	19.1	28.6	66.9	61.6	14.0		8.5	–	–

Source: OECD in figures, 2008 (Eurostat), (http://epp.eurostat.ec.europa.eu/portal/page?_pageid=0,1136184,0_455572595&_dad=portal&_schema=PORTAL)

Table 2.5 The role of technology (2006 data)

		Exports as a percentage of imports (%)		Share of high tech exports as a percentage of the member countries of OECD (%)
		High-tech industries (1)	Medium-tech industries (2)	(3)
Northern countries	Denmark	106.2	85.2	1.0
	Netherlands	105.1	122.7	6.1
	Sweden	134.0	121.5	1.8
Mediterranean countries	Greece	23.0	19.7	0.1
	Italy	68.6	123.0	2.5
	Spain	44.3	76.9	1.3
	Portugal	45.9	65.4	0.3
BRIC	Brazil	44.2	98.0	0.6
	China	116.4	91.1	20.5
	India	25.9	61.1	0.4
	Russia	16.6	37.2	0.2
	USA	81.0	69.5	19.5
	Japan	133.1	366.9	9.3

Source: OECD, OECD in figures, 2008

this factor: the relation of exports to imports for high- and medium-technology industrial products and the industry share in exports of high-technology products.

The United States exports 70–80% of the volume of its high- and medium-technology imports. Japan, which is clearly export oriented, exports more technologically advanced products (133% for high-technology products and 366% for medium-technology products). The countries of Northern Europe also have high ratios. On the contrary, Mediterranean countries (Greece included) are clearly importers of technology. The same does not hold for China, which, despite the prevailing perception, has a remarkable performance in exporting high- and medium-technology products that is clearly superior to that of the United States. On the contrary, the rest of the BRIC countries are definitely technology importers.

The USA, Japan and China export 50% of all high-technology products exported globally (column 3). On the other hand, countries such as those of the Mediterranean have a much smaller (or even minimal) effect on shaping high-technology exports.

Measuring the global innovation of economies is not an easy task, especially when we want to derive useful conclusions, as estimating certain measures is very difficult. We will use two different methods of measurement, each with its own unique characteristics. These are the European Innovation Scoreboard – EIS, formulated in relation to the EU and the Global Innovation Index (2008) and produced by INSEAD and the Indian Confederation of Industries. The European Innovation Scoreboard EIS 2008 evaluates three innovation fields: (a) businesses and their production (indices such as patents and entrepreneurial R&D as a percentage of GDP), (b) investments in human capital (e.g., graduates of tertiary education or published articles), (c) structures and absorption capability (ICT expenses, broadband networks and public R&D). The shaping and the theoretical background of innovation indices show that it is now widely accepted that innovation is not unidimensional. Primarily, two-dimensional structures of human capital and real high-tech material (e.g., broadband networks) play an important role in promoting research.

Table 2.6 presents a ranking of 45 countries using the EIS innovation indices (European Innovation Scoreboard, 2008). Based on their total rankings (which include corporate influence, influence caused by the changes in human resources and the effect of the situation of infrastructure), the United States ranks 6th, Japan 5th and the EU-27 20th. Northern European countries hold the first ten places; Mediterranean countries rank between the 20th and 30th positions; and Balkan countries hold the next ten places. BRIC countries are in the last ten places.

It should be noted that Mediterranean and BRIC countries (except for Russia) show significant positive changes in their relative positions. The improvement of Greece's position is due exclusively to the improvement of human capital, contrary to the deterioration that is observed in corporate activity.

On the contrary, the improvement of BRIC countries is due to the improvement of the innovative activity of corporations and infrastructure.

In the same table, the first column presents a ranking produced by the Global Innovation Index, which follows a different methodology and is probably more comprehensive than the EIS index. It ranks 130 economies but is rarely calculated (twice at the time of this writing).

Its main methodological difference is that it evaluates the roles of inflows in the production of innovation (such as institutions and policies, human capability, infrastructure, levels of market and business development) and of outflows (knowledge, competitiveness and wealth) to rank the countries. According to this index, the US, Japan and Northern European countries form the top ten. Italy and Spain are in the top 30, Portugal in the top 40 and Greece in the top 50. Of the BRIC countries, China makes it to the top 30. India is in the top 40, Brazil in the top 50 and Russia in the top 70.

Obviously, the potential of economies and the consequent improvement of the living standards stem and will continue to stem mostly from the improvement of innovation. According to all evidence, China shows rapid rates of improvement, Russia lags behind, and Northern Europe preserves high rates of innovation.

2.8 Energy and Climatic Change

In the future, the global economic and social system will face limitations in its growth due to the availability of resources – mainly energy, food, water, and the environment. These constraints will lead to limitation of these resources' consumption and increase their usage price. Figure 2.8 describes the global demand for energy by type. Oil remains the most important source of energy production.

Table 2.6 Country rankings based on innovation indices

| | | Global innovation index 2008–2009[a] | European innovation scoreboard 2008[b] | | | | | | | |
| | | Total ranking 2008/2009 | Total rankings | | Corporate activity | | Human resources | | Infrastructure and absorption capability | |
			2005 ranking	Change from 1995	2005 ranking	Change from 1995	2005 ranking	Change from 1995	2005 ranking	Change from 1995
Mediterranean countries	Greece	54	31	4	43	-8	24	8	35	-2
	Italy	31	26	2	26	-3	32	-4	22	3
	Spain	28	24	6	28	0	15	10	24	4
	Portugal	40	30	7	35	3	31	8	26	3
Balkan countries	Bulgaria	74	38	-5	47	-11	33	-3	37	-7
	Romania	69	48	-12	44	-19	41	-8	45	-1
Northern countries	Denmark	8	7	3	10	3	8	1	4	7
	Netherlands	10	11	-4	9	1	20	-1	6	0
	Sweden	3	1	0	4	-3	4	-2	1	1
EU-27		–	20	-3	16	-1	19	-4	21	-2
USA		1	6	-3	8	-2	6	-1	7	-6
Japan		9	5	-1	1	2	13	-3	9	-4
BRIC	Brazil	50	42	5	34	11	46	2	32	10
	China	37	34	8	25	7	48	-3	31	9
	India	41	46	1	36	11	42	0	38	7
	Russia	68	29	-2	27	-1	11	2	42	-3

[a]Global Innovation Index, 2008 (Confederation of Indian Industries and INSEAD)
[b]European Innovation Scoreboard, 2008

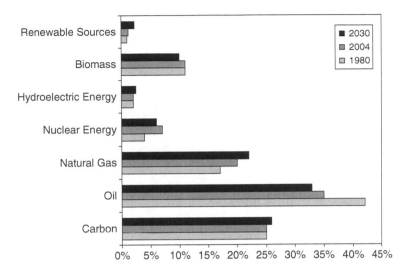

Fig. 2.8 Global structure of primary energy demand (percentage) (Source: International Energy Agency, World Energy Outlook, 2006)

In the long term, the use of oil diminishes as natural gas and coal, especially the latter, demonstrate particularly rapid growth of use.

In addition, nuclear energy (third-generation nuclear reactors) together with renewable energy sources claim a market share. Renewable energy will grow rapidly and will surpass natural gas after 2010. It will be the third most common energy source after oil and coal (IEA 2008).[5]

The much-expected new technology that will inexpensively replace traditional energy sources seems likely to appear in about 15 years (NIC 2008).[6] If this happens and the price of oil decreases, if they do not change their production orientation, the countries depending on oil (especially in the Middle East and Russia) will see their positions change dramatically in the new circumstances.

Nowadays, the EU-27 generates 37% of its energy from oil, 24% from natural gas, 18% from coal, 14% from nuclear energy and 7% from renewable sources (Eurostat).

The energy security of the European Union is a crucial objective for the maintenance of economic growth and the living standards of its citizens. According to all scenarios, in 2002 the dependence of the EU on energy imports will have increased to 56%, assuming that the energy policy of the EU will have taken effect and that the barrel price will be around $100.

These scenarios assume the implementation of some vital infrastructure projects, including: (a) the linking of the Baltic with the EU; (b) exploration of the possible

---

[5] International Energy Agency, World Energy Outlook 2006.
[6] National Intelligence Council (2008). Disruptive Civil Technologies Six Technologies with Potential Impacts on US Interests out to 2025.

supply of liquidated natural gas (LNG), which is of vital importance for countries with unique natural gas suppliers; (c) the completion of a Mediterranean energy network, which will connect Southeastern Europe with the rest of Europe and include solar and wind energy potential; and (d) the development of linkages of Northern and Southern Europe with Central and Southeastern Europe (Second Strategic Energy Review 2008).

Today, total Greek energy consumption consists of 64% oil, 23% coal, 8% natural gas, 4% hydroelectric energy, and 1% renewable sources. Oil imports come from Iran, Saudi Arabia, Russia, Libya, and Kazakhstan. Greece purchases 80% of its natural gas from Russia. The known coal reserves are in the US (28.6%), Russia (18.5%), and China (13.5%), among others (BP Statistical Review of World Energy, June 2008).

Based on the above policy framework for the development of networks, Greece falls into a broader organisation that is vital for European interests on one hand and suppliers on the other.

Thus, it is understood that the Greek economy has limited energy capabilities as Greece is nearly entirely an energy importer. It acts as a transit point for energy transport, especially from the Caspian region to Europe, through three main projects: the Bosphorus-Alexandroupolis gas pipeline, the interconnection with Turkey and further connecxions of these regions with Italy. A good depiction of the extent of the involvement of the Greek area in this international transport network – mainly for natural gas and oil – is shown in Map 2.2, including the smaller map of Greece (Map 2.1). This image, however, clearly shows that the "energy hub" definition usually attributed to Greece is not accurate; Greece has a relation of proximity with the areas of energy transportation. More specifically, the developments in the relations between Russia and Turkey (Map 2.1) concerning the construction of the Samsounta-Tseihan pipeline, which, in a way, rivals the Bourgas-Alexandroupoli pipeline, supports this opinion.

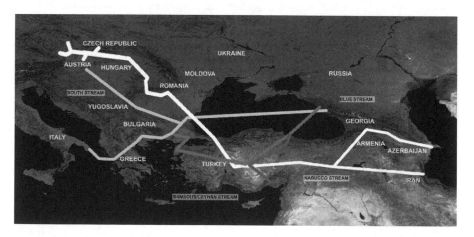

Map 2.1 Natural gas pipelines and Greece

Internationally, growing energy consumption leads to environmental pollution. If the current rate of gas emissions continues, in the long term, it will increase average global temperature up to 6°. These changes will affect the entire world, including the specific area of the Southeastern Mediterranean. These changes will involve decreased volumes of available drinking water, rising sea levels and the opening of areas in the world that are currently inaccessible, such as Siberia, certain areas of Canada and the Arctic.

The opening of these areas may affect global economic geography as it will increase the potential energy production of the countries who own these territories, such as the United States, Russia, Canada, Denmark, and Norway.

In the Southeastern Mediterranean, climate change will primarily lead to rising sea levels, which will affect population movement, while also leading to an extended summer season, which will affect the most important industry for these regions, tourism. At the same time, there will be greater demand for energy consumption during those months.

2.9   The Formation of National Power

Although a country's economy reflects all aspects of the development process, these are not the only conditions for establishing the living standards of its citizens. The reason is very simple: An unfortunate military adventure with a neighbouring country could have a devastating effect on the standard of living. It is very important, therefore, to see what fields affect the development of forces in the international front, always in reference to the country under observation (in our case, Greece).

Power, in strategic terms, is the capacity to kill and protect oneself from being killed. After this, the abilities to exploit, enforce financial terms, and inspect come naturally. Power is not only exerted when one kills, but also when one threatens to kill.

National power is the comprehensive expression for all of the capabilities a nation has at a specific moment in time in order to promote internally and internationally the conquering of national goals, regardless of the difficulties that may be faced (Kelly 1994).

The geostrategic environment in which these changes take place involves the exercise of power and international influence, which is founded on the availability of military force (i.e., the possible use or threat of use). The Greek economy and society neighbour parts of the world where international influence does not yet have a definite shape, the so-called "Eurasia" (continuous line, Map 2.2), which creates a large zone of instability (dotted line, Map 2.2). If to that we add the tension with Greece's eastern neighbour (Turkey), the international environment in which the Greek economy operates becomes turbulent. This is not a situation that is shared with most other EU countries.

The prevalence of a globalised capitalistic system has led to the collapse of the dividing lines of international political influence. As a result, the simplistic declaration of integration in the "West" under a capitalistic system is void of meaning

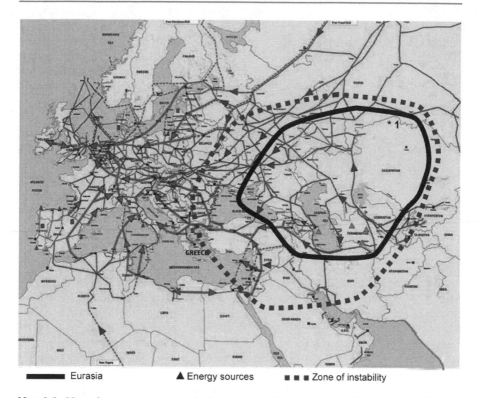

■■■■■■ Eurasia   ▲ Energy sources   ■ ■ ■ Zone of instability

Map 2.2 Natural gas transport routes in Europe, Central and South Asia (Caucasia) and disputed geographical areas: composite view (Source: Ramsay [2006] and Brzezinski [1997])

because this social system has established global dominance. As a result, new problems concerning strategic choices arise. In essence, we are called upon to locate the new or upcoming international centres of influence and to decide how much and in what ways we will connect with them. It should be noted that Greece, geographically and historically, neighbours one of the major uprising players of the international scene: Russia. As a result, questions of orientation have a special character.

The debate surrounding the development of quantitative indicators that can reflect the term "national power" begun in the eightieth century with emphasis on the strength of nations as stemming from the size of their population. This led to the development of an entire body of research that continues to expand today, especially around the topics of international relations and politics. Since the beginning of the twentieth century, the indicators measuring national power have included population, steel production and energy production. Military expenses, the value of external trade, and other indicators were added later. The main protagonists in this debate originated from the United States, China, India and Russia, which are the most important of the countries claiming primacy in the global rankings.

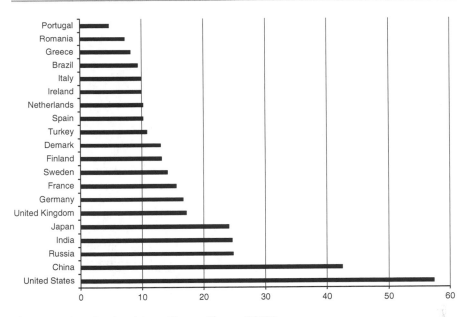

Fig. 2.9 Index of national force (Source: Hwang [2008])

Kumar (2008) describes the Indian index, the National Security Index (NSI), as follows: 25% financial power, 25% defence capability, 20% energy security, 15% technological force and 15% active population. The model used by the National Intelligence Council of the United States (the International Futures Computer Model) produces an index based on GDP, military forces, population and technology (NIC – Global Trends 2025, 2008).

Figure 2.9 shows the calculation of national force by the German Institute of Global and Area Studies (Hwang 2008). Hwang's ranking is shaped based on the following basic weights: 6.25% economic figures, 6.25% life expectancy, 6.25% education, 6.25% level of society's dignity (corruption), 25% energy production, 12.5% defence expenses, 12.5% weapons production and 25% nuclear weapons.

The total classification of power depicted in Fig. 2.9 shows a world image that is different from that achieved through the simple examination of economies and production structures. We see that BRIC countries are very close to the USA. Northern European countries are in satisfactory positions (22nd to 43rd), as is Italy. Turkey has an even better ranking (28th). Greece is in 52nd place, and Portugal, Bulgaria and Romania hold similarly low positions.

The conclusion from the above analysis in terms of "national power" indicates that the temporal dynamics of this index are not in favour of Greece, and the resolution of certain long-standing issues over time (especially with Turkey) does not seem to be favoured by the evolution of active forces unless the emerging trend of this indicator is reversed. In any case, the present value of a future agreement under uncertainty increases as the time of agreement approaches.

With regard to global developments, the findings of the U.S. National Intelligence Council (NIC), which were included in its study of developments by the year 2025, are characteristic:

1. The entire international system, as established after World War II, will be re-established. Not only will new players appear (Brazil, Russia, India and China) in the international scene, but they will be the ones to determine the new rules of the game.
2. Wealth will continue to move from West to East.
3. The entry of 1.5 bn people on the international scene will put pressure on resources, especially energy, food and water, and increase global purchasing power.
4. The danger of conflict will increase, especially in the greater Middle East.

If we take into account that the NIC represents the concern of the community of the security services of the US and that this concern does not seem to be positive for the US, then these conclusions are of greater value.

It is obvious, then, that there is a tendency for the development of a world with a wider distribution of economic and political power. Such a world will require more effort to come to an agreement. Fortunately, communications have been improved faster than the distribution of the governance centres has widened.

2.10 Southeastern Europe and Greece

Throughout human history, Southeastern Europe[7] has been characterised by strong economic and cultural convergences and conflicts. The network of relationships that have developed in Southeastern Europe could be a source of economic development.

Today, as shown in Table 2.7, there remain significant ethnic and cultural tensions, although the area demonstrates economic development and diffusion of economic interests.

This tension has caused Greece to keep a military presence – albeit in some cases purely symbolic – in many areas of the broader region.

Meanwhile, the existing tension with Turkey complicates Greece's economic development as it imposes increasing pressure on spending for defence. This tension fluctuates depending on the broader political and geographical rearrangements and influences on all sides. The supposed existence of oil deposits in Southeastern Europe, including Cyprus, is a typical example. It highlights the issue of the continental shelf and the economic zone of 200 miles. These matters could cause a new round of mid-term tension. Possibly, however, they could constitute an opportunity for the re-exploration of the deposits in the region, as

---

[7] It concerns the following countries: Albania, Bosnia-Herzegovina, Bulgaria, Croatia, Montenegro, FYROM, Romania, Serbia and Turkey. The region includes Black Sea countries such as Ukraine and Georgia.

Table 2.7 National
tensions in Southeastern
Europe and neighbouring
areas

Serbia – Kosovo
FYROM – Greece
Greece – Turkey
Greece – Cyprus – Turkey
Ukraine – Russia
Georgia – Russia
Turkey – Kurdish population
Middle East – Suez

resources are located (North and South Cyprus) in NA edge of the region, where the economic areas of Greece, Cyprus, Israel, Egypt and Turkey meet.

Between 2000 and 2008, the economies of Southeastern Europe recorded strong growth of around 6% per year on average. In the first half of this period, the development in the region was promoted by supply, particularly the rehabilitation of unutilised labour capacity, and hence by productivity growth that was a result of structural reforms. Until the crisis of 2008, the increase of domestic consumption and investment demand, combined with the increase of exports, constituted strong advancement factors. Credit expansion and net inflows also played important roles.

Greece is the largest direct foreign investor in Albania, Serbia, and the Former Yugoslavic Republic of Macedonia (FYROM), and the second largest foreign investor in Romania. Greek companies have invested more than €630 m in Albania. This amount corresponds to about 27% of Greece's total foreign investments in neighbouring countries. There are about 270 Greek businesses and businesses with Greek interests in Albania, creating 9,000 jobs. Greece is also first in direct foreign investments in FYROM. The 251 companies with Greek interests that operate in FYROM have invested €1 bn in FYROM and have created 20,000 jobs. In Serbia, the total Greek invested capital amounts to €2.5 bn. There are 150 mixed Greek-Serbian companies as well as 120 solely Greek ones, which together employ 20,000 people. The Greek banking sector has a strong presence in Serbia, with branches of Alpha Bank, Piraeus Bank, EFG-Eurobank and National Bank. In Romania, Greece is the second largest foreign investor, with over €3 bn invested. The Greek banking sector is now in second place (with 16.5%) among foreign investors, after Austria. From the existing data, one can conclude that the sum of current assets of the seven Greek banks has increased by 81% and reached €11.5 bn in 2007. Together with the Greek banks, 800 businesses are in operation. Finally, Greece ranks third in the list of foreign investors in Bulgaria, having invested over €1.5 bn, which translates into 10% of total banking investments. Greek banks hold 23.6% of total bank capital, and 1,500 Greek enterprises are also active. Table 2.8 shows Greece's economic presence in the countries of Southeastern Europe. It is characteristic that 68.87% of the claims of Greek financial institutions abroad are located in Southeastern European countries.

The Balkans and Southeastern Europe constitute a preferential region for the development of external trade for the Greek economy. It should be mentioned that

Table 2.8 Claims of Greek financial institutions abroad

Country	Claims of Greek banks abroad (millions of dollars)	Percentage of the total claims of Greek banks abroad (%)
Turkey	20,823	20.58
Romania	18,689	18.47
Bulgaria	10,358	10.24
Cyprus	8,605	8.50
Serbia	4,703	4.65
FYROM	1,834	1.81
Albania	1,737	1.72
Russia	1,041	1.03
Ukraine	999	0.99
Egypt	413	0.41
Total of Southeastern Europe	69,681	68.87
Grand total	101,177	100

Source: Bank of International Settlements (http://www.bis.org/statistics/consstats.htm#)
Note: Also includes other countries in the area with very low participation

in 2007, Greek exports to the Balkans constituted 18.7% of total exports, whereas imports from the area amounted to only to 3.6%.

Because of the existence of so many Greek banks in Southeastern Europe, the region constituted a source of financial instability for the Greek economy during the crisis of 2008. This was due to the decrease of exports caused by the consumption inability of those countries and to the threat to the stability indices of the Greek banking system. The support package amounting to €24.5 bn that was designed for the banking sector in Central and Eastern Europe by the European Bank of Restructuring and Development (EBRD), the European Investment Bank (EIB) and the World Bank (WB), was aimed at the reinforcement of the real economy and the provision of support for the survival of small and medium enterprises (SMEs) in Eastern European countries.

In conclusion, Greece is geographically situated in a broader environment that remains under development. The Greek economy is currently in the middle of a rather serious economic fluctuation that initially originated from the operation core of the global economic system and is supported by its internal weaknesses. It should be seriously examined whether the national capability (economic standard of living, military forces, human capital and the innovation environment) can be preserved. Furthermore, external relations should take into account the actual possibilities and future prospects generated. In any case, sufficient thought should be given to the quality that the concept of national status and power should assume, considering that the deterioration of national financial conditions leads to a decrease in political choices.

Observing the development of Greek economy compared to the economies of Southeastern Europe, it becomes apparent that this is a region of tension and wealth production. The case of Turkey is illustrative because Turkey is the biggest debtor of the Greek financial services system, while at the same time Greece's relationship with Turkey is the most important reason for preserving the spending on defence.

At the same time, though, Southeastern Europe is a large market of 141 m (if we include only the Balkan countries) to 193 m consumers if we include Ukraine, Georgia and Armenia. The level of its development promises catching-up effects, i.e. high growth, due to the effort of the countries to approach higher levels of per capita product and income.

What does this practically mean for developmental politics in the Greek economy? It is vital for an economy to be adjacent to large areas that are entering periods of strong growth. This process, though, demands large national investments across the region, which entail a significant social (public and private) cost.

References

Abramovitz M (1956) Resource and output trends in the United States since 1870. Am Econ Rev 46:5–23

Acemoglu D, Johnson S, Robinson J (2004) Institutions as the fundamental cause of long-run growth. C.E.P.R. Discussion Paper 4458

Alfaro L., Kalemli-Ozcan S., Volosovych V (2005) Why does not capital flow from rich to poor countries? An empirical investigation. National Bureau of Economic Research, 11901

Bernanke B, Gurkaynak R (2001) Is growth exogenous? Taking Mankiw, Romer and Weil Seriously. NBER Working Paper 8365

Brzezinski Z (1997) The grand chessboard. Nea Synora, Athens

Bussiere M, Fratzscher M, Müller G (2005) Productivity shocks, budget De.cits and the current account. ECB Working Paper No. 509

Chang Ha-Joon (2006) Understanding the relationships between institutions and economic development. Eur. Invest. Bank, Econ Financ Stud DP 2006/05

Cheung C, Furceri D, Rusticelli E (2010) Structural and cyclical factors behind current account balances, OECD, Working Paper No. 775

Chinn MD, Ito H (2008) Global current account imbalances: American Fiscal Policy versus East Asian savings. Rev Int Econ 16(3):479–498

Chinn MD, Prasad ES (2003) Medium-term determinants of current accounts in industrial and developing countries: an empirical exploration. J Int Econ 59(1):47–76

Cohen D, Soto M (2007) Growth and human capital, good data, good results. J Econ Growth 12(1):51–76

Dougherty C, Jorgenson D (1996) International comparisons of the sources of economic growth. Am Econ Rev 2:25–29

Easterly W, Levine R (2001) It's not factor accumulation: stylized facts and growth models. Central Bank of Chile, Working Paper 164

Frankel J, Romer D (1999) Does trade cause growth? Am Econ Rev 89:379–399

Gruber JW, Kamin S (2007) Explaining the global pattern of current account imbalances. JIMF 26:500–522

Hall R, Jones C (1999) Why do some countries produce so much more output per worker than others? Q J Econ 114(1):83–116

Hogenbirk A, Narula R (1999) Globalization and the small economy: the case of Netherlands. Res. Memo. 002. Maastricht Econ Res Inst Innov Technol

Hwang K (2008) New thinking in measuring National Paper. German Institute of Global and Area Studies

Ju J, Wei S-J (2006) A solution to two paradoxes of international capital flows. NBER Working Papers 12668, National Bureau of Economic Research

Kelly PL (1994) Geopolitical themes in the writing of general Carlos de Meira Mattos of Brazil. J Lat Am Stud 16:439–461

Kumar S (2008) India's national security: annual review 2007. Knowl World, New York

Kuznets S (1960) Economic growth of small nations. In: Robinson EAG (ed) The economic consequences of the size of nations. Macmillan, London

Kuznets S (1971) Economic growth of nations: total output and production structure. Harvard University Press, Cambridge

Levine R, Loayza N, Beck T (2000) Financial intermediation and growth: causality and causes. J Monet Econ 46:31–77

Lucas R (1988) On the mechanics of economic development. J Monet Econ 22:3–42

Mankiw G, Romer D, Weil DN (1992) A contribution to the empirics of economic growth. Q J Econ 107:407–437

Marx K (1867) Das Kapital. Hamburg, Germany

North D (1990) Institutions, institutional change and economic performance. Cambridge University Press, Cambridge

North D, Thomas P (1973) The rise of the western world: a new economic history. Cambridge University Press, Cambridge

Ramsay W (2006) Security of gas supplies in Europe. Paper presented in international energy agency workshop in Vienna

Ricardo D (1817, 2001) In: Kitchener (ed) On the principles of political economy and taxation. Batoche Books, Ontario

Romer P (1986) Increasing returns and long-run growth. J Polit Econ 94(5):500–521, 1002–37

Sinn HW (2010) Rescuing Europe. Cesifo Special issue. Vol. 11, August

Smith A (1776, 1977) An inquiry into the nature and causes of the wealth of nations. University of Chicago Press, Chicago

Solow R (1957) Technical change and the aggregate production function. Rev Econ Stat 39:312–320

Timmer M, Ypma G, Van der Ark B (2003) IT in the European Union: driving productivity divergence? Res. Memo. 200363, Groningen Growth and Development Centre, University of Groningen

The Pre-Crisis Growth of the Greek Economy

3

This chapter describes the basic components involved in the development of the Greek economy. We identify and explain the factors that have contributed to the growth of the Greek economy, focusing on the last two decades. Based on the information in the preceding chapter, we adopt the view that the GDP results from the inputs of physical capital, human capital and other factors contributing to growth. More specifically, we will delve further into whether and to what extent this development is due to the increase of inflows (quantity increase), to the improvement of their productivity (quality improvement), or to both. GDP could be estimated based on production, final expenses, or the income that growth factors experience. At the same time, we examine the importance of every branch of the economy in the production process.

In the Greek economy, the "shadow economy" accounts for a significant part of economic activity (approximately 20–27% of GDP). This activity "escapes" statistical measurements and any other analysis. Consequently, it is important to realise that this loss changes our analysis and conclusions. We describe the consequences of the shadow economy and reveal its structure. Finally, we present the characteristics of entrepreneurship in the Greek economy.

The comparison of the basic macroeconomic figures of the Greek economy with various country groups (Mediterranean, Balkan and Northern European) allows us to formulate a better image of the developmental model of the country.

The chapter has the following structure: Sect. 3.1 presents an analysis of the terms for economic growth. Section 3.2 presents the issue of growth and wealth accumulation, while Sect. 3.3 describes the organisation of production. Section 3.4 presents data on consumer behaviour, and Sect. 3.5 presents Greece's imports and exports. Section 3.6 presents the issue of competitiveness and productivity in the Greek economy. Subsequently, Sect. 3.7 examines the evolution of GDP in relation to the formation of active demand conditions. Next, Sect. 3.8 defines the concept of the size of the shadow economy and the concept of the parallel financial system. Finally, Sect. 3.9 presents the form, structure, characteristics and evolution of Greek companies.

P. Petrakis, *The Greek Economy and the Crisis*,
DOI 10.1007/978-3-642-21175-1_3, © Springer-Verlag Berlin Heidelberg 2012

Table 3.1 Rate of growth of real per capita GDP

Year	1999	2002	2005	2007	Average 1999–2007
European Union					
EU-27	2.8	1	1.5	2.5	2.08
Mediterranean countries					
Greece	3	3.1	2.5	3.6	3.79
Italy	1.4	0.1	−0.2	0.8	0.94
Spain	4.2	1.2	1.9	1.8	2.34
Portugal	3.4	0	0.5	1.7	1.20
Balkan countries					
Bulgaria	2.9	5.1	6.8	6.2	6.01
Romania	−1	8.1	4.4	6.6	5.26
Northern countries					
Denmark	2.2	0.1	2.1	1.2	1.59
Norway	1.3	0.9	2.1	2.1	1.73
Sweden	4.5	2.1	2.9	1.8	2.80

Source: Eurostat, national accounts: tsdec100
Note: The annual rate of GDP growth is calculated as the percentage change of the per capita output produced, in constant prices, in relation to the immediately previous period

3.1   Growth in the Greek Economy

In the last decade, the Greek economy has grown at an average yearly rate of 3.8%. It should be noted that this rate is almost double the averages of both the EU-15 and the EU-27. Moreover, it has greatly exceeded the performance of the rest of the Mediterranean countries and most of the Northern European countries (Table 3.1).

On the other hand, Greece had a lower growth rate than Bulgaria and Romania did. The higher rates of growth of these economies are mostly due to the fact that they began the convergence process with the rest of Europe much later than Greece. As a result, they are currently assimilating the "catch-up" effects, as defined by the OECD (OECD 2004, p. 16).[1]

The biggest part of gross fixed capital in the Greek economy was in the construction sector[2] (averaging 82% of the total) and in low-technology equipment (averaging 10% of the total). As a result, the Greek economy's growth was mostly supported on the traditional branches of the economy (Timmer et al. 2003, p. 1).

Table 3.2 shows that the gross configuration of fixed capital in Greece as a percentage of GDP is higher than that of the Northern European counties, at the same level as that of the Balkan countries and slightly lower than the average of the Mediterranean countries.

Concerning the active population and the population in general, the rates of growth of the population in the Mediterranean and Northern European countries are

---

[1] OECD (2004) Understanding Economic Growth.

[2] The index does not include the construction of houses.

Table 3.2 Gross fixed capital (percentage of GDP)

Year	1999	2002	2005	2007	Average 1999–2007
European Union					
EU-27	20.4	19.6	20	21.3	20.3
Mediterranean countries					
Greece	–	22.5	21.6	22.5	22.2
Spain	24.6	26.3	29.4	31	27.8
Italy	19.6	20.9	20.7	21.1	20.6
Portugal	26.8	25	22.2	21.8	24.0
Balkan countries					
Bulgaria	15.1	18.2	24.2	29.8	21.8
Romania	17.7	21.3	23.7	30.4	23.3
Northern countries					
Denmark	19.8	19.6	19.5	22.2	20.3
Norway	21.9	17.9	18.8	21.3	20.0
Sweden	17	16.8	17.4	19	17.6

Source: Eurostat, national accounts: p. 51

positive for all years between 1999 and 2007. This increase is due to the natural rates of population increase (positive birth-death balance), the massive inflows of immigrants and the limited migration of the populations of these countries to others. On the contrary, the populations of Romania and Bulgaria have decreased because of the migration of their populations to other countries. These may be the reasons for their increased per capita GDPs.

The percentage increase of the population (workforce) causes a decrease in the average productivity of capital (capital to labour ratio) as the existing capital is allocated to a greater number of workers.

Moreover, although, over time, unemployment rates in Greece have fallen, they remain higher in general compared to the other countries (except Spain). The average unemployment rate for the period of 1999–2007 was 10.13% for Greece, compared to 8.3% for the EU-27. In general, Mediterranean countries have higher unemployment rates compared to Northern European countries. Moreover, given their easy access, the main host countries of immigrants from Asia (the most densely populated continent, with the highest migration rates) are the Mediterranean countries.

According to Eurostat, the lowest employment rates in Greece are found among young people under 25 years old (22.9% of unemployed in 2007), women (12.8% of unemployed in 2007) and workers aged 55–64 (all close to retirement), while the long-term unemployment rate (longer than 12 months) reached 4.1% in 2007. On the contrary, employment rates for men (ages 25–54) exceeded the EU average (OECD-Factbook 2007, p. 31). This group forms a pool of inactive labour.

In an effort to assess the availability of human capital in each country, Arnold et al. (2007) used a variable that captures the average number of years dedicated to education. This variable ranks Greece first among Mediterranean countries, but not among Northern European countries. More specifically, for the population group

Table 3.3 Percentage contribution to the development of growth rates: 1985–2006. For the Greek economy: 1990–2004

		Labour inflows (%)	Inflows of technological capital (%)	Inflows of non-technological capital (%)	Remaining factors (%)[a]	GDP growth (%)
Greece	1990–1995	59	2	38	0	100
	1995–2000	24	3	24	49	100
	2000–2004	30	3	25	42	100
Mediterranean countries	Italy	19	15	32	35	100
	Spain	51	12	31	7	100
	Portugal	12	15	21	53	100
Northern countries	Denmark	7	27	23	43	100
	Netherlands	35	15	14	36	100
	Sweden	11	24	16	50	100

Source: OECD-Factbook (2008), Timmer et al. (2003) and Groningen Growth and Development Center, Total Economy Growth Accounting Database
[a]Effect of human capital included

aged 15–64 years, the average number of years of education for Greece is 10.33, compared to 8.83, 9.70 and 11.90 years for Spain, Italy and Portugal, respectively.

The key question to be raised at this point concerns the identification of the sources of growth of the Greek economy. The effect of the remaining inflows is similar to the effect globally (around 40–50% when the effect of human capital investments is included, which is about 15%, see Sect. 1.1) (Table 3.3).

Concerning work hours for the period of 1999–2007, workers in Greece were employed for more hours compared to workers in the other countries considered, with the exception of Romania. The average for the Greek economy amounted to 1,889 h, whereas the averages for the EU-15 (1999–2002), Mediterranean countries and Northern European countries were 1,573, 1,692 and 1,531 h, respectively. That is, we end up with a labour market balance with relatively low but intense employment of those in the labour market.[3]

3.2   Financing of Growth and Wealth

Table 3.4 shows the historical development of savings and lending as a percentage of the produced output. Regarding savings, Greece is far behind other countries for all years and shows on average the lowest percentages of the groups of countries examined. Possible reasons for this behaviour are the basic characteristics of individuals' attitudes toward savings, the large share of GDP that corresponds to businesses' profits, the low returns of savings (difference between bank deposit and loan interest rates) and the increase in consumption. Consequently, the low

---

[3] See also Giannitsis (2008), p. 125.

Table 3.4 Gross savings and lending as percentage of GDP

Average 1999–2007	Gross savings as a percentage of GDP[a]	Net lending (+)/net borrowing (−) as a percentage of GDP[b]
European Union		
EU-15	20.45	0.25
Mediterranean countries		
Greece	9.5	−11.03
Spain	22.1	−5.13
Italy	20.3	−0.43
Portugal	15.15	−7.50
Balkan countries		
Bulgaria	15.13	−9.98
Romania	17.6	−3.43
Northern European countries		
Denmark	23.35	2.60
Norway	34.1	12.53
Sweden	23.9	5.80

Source: Eurostat, national accounts, b8g. b9
[a]Gross savings = Gross available national income − final production
[b]Net lending (+)/net borrowing (−) = Gross savings − Fixed capital consumption + Capital transfers received from abroad − Capital transfers paid abroad − Gross capital configuration − Purchases minus nonmonetary sales, non-produced property assets

inclination towards savings signifies that Greece imported capital from abroad to finance its investments.

Concerning Greece's lending, it is apparent that for the period between 1999 and 2007, Greece borrowed a significant amount, as a percentage of GDP, to cover its financing needs. Note that only Bulgaria had a higher debt level than Greece during 2005–2007.

Table 3.5 presents the deficit (debt) of the state budget for 1999–2007. Clearly, although Greece's deficit declined until 2007, it remains quite high. This deficit led to further accumulation of public debt.

Another analysis of Table 3.5 demonstrates very simply that there has always been a "Keynesian" fiscal policy in the Greek economy. Obviously, Greece's relatively weak productive capacity and the specific characteristics of its active population have oriented the economic policy towards the preservation of high levels of employment to preserve a high fiscal deficit in a continuous "expansionary intervention". This has the corresponding dilatant consequences on the balance of payments, affecting the competitiveness of the Greek economy (see Sect. 3.5), and exhausts the possibilities of invoking an expansionary policy when necessary (economic crisis in 2008–2009). In effect, the preservation of the short-term conditions of the present level of activity contrast with the medium- and long-term needs of the economy.

The next issue raised is whether the produced GDP and the inflow of lending capital in the Greek economy have shaped wealth in true values in Greek society. This wealth is described in Table 3.6.

Table 3.5 Deficit/surplus of public budget and general government debt (percentage of GDP)

Year	Deficit (−)/surplus (+) of government budget					Debt of government budget				
	1999	2002	2005	2007	Average 1999–2007	1999	2002	2005	2007	Average 1999–2007
European Union										
EU-27	−1	−2.5	−2.4	−0.9	−1.7	65.9	60.3	62.7	58.7	61.90
EU-15	−0.8	−2.3	−2.4	−0.8	−1.58	67.2	61.6	64.1	60.4	63.33
Mediterranean countries										
Greece	–	−4.7	−5.1	−3.5	−4.43	105.2	100.6	98.8	94.8	99.85
Spain	−1.4	−0.5	1	2.2	0.33	62.3	52.5	43	36.2	48.50
Italy	−1.7	−2.9	−4.3	−1.6	−2.63	113.7	105.7	105.9	104.1	107.35
Portugal	−2.8	−2.8	−6.1	−2.6	−3.58	51.4	55.6	63.6	63.6	58.55
Balkan countries										
Bulgaria	–	−0.8	1.9	0.1	0.40	79.3	53.6	29.2	18.2	45.08
Romania	−4.5	−2	−1.2	−2.6	−2.58	21.9	25	15.8	12.9	18.90
Northern European countries										
Denmark	1.5	0.3	5.2	4.9	2.98	57.4	48.3	36.4	26.2	42.08
Norway	–	9.3	15.1	17.4	13.93	–	36.1	43.7	52	43.93
Sweden	1.3	−1.2	2.4	3.6	1.53	64.8	52.6	50.9	40.4	52.18

Source: Eurostat, gov_dd, indicators GD and EDP_B9

Table 3.6 Total assets of Greek individuals

	Absolute amounts	Percentage composition (%)
Real estate[a]	1,177,200	62.55
Stocks[b]	30,200	1.60
Deposits[c]	127,000	6.75
Bonds[d]	8,700	0.46
Rent	0	0.00
Human capital[e]	538,943	28.64
Total of accumulated investments	1,882,043	–
Private/household debt (loans)[f]	79,955	–
Net worth of individuals	1,811,088	–

Source: Publication by L. Stergiou in the "Kathimerini" newspaper, March 23, 2009; Bank of Greece (Governor's annual reports, Bulletins of Conjunctural Indicators, Intermediary monetary policy reports); government budgets of various years; Central Securities Repository; Athens Stock Exchange; annual publications of the Capital Market Commission; National Bank of Greece; and EFG Eurobank-Ergasias

The figures correspond to the year 2005 (in bn euros)

Notes – Assumptions:

[a]It is estimated that 80% of the total value of real estate belongs to individuals

[b]According to the levels of diversification published by the Central Securities Repository

[c]Deposits of individuals are defined as the total amount of bank deposits

[d]Banking officials believe that less than 5% of the bonds of the Greek state are owned directly by Greek citizens. Participation in mutual funds, insurance-investment or other investment-saving products is not included

[e]Investments in human capital are calculated as follows: For every level of education, we divide the average income (based on data from the Hellenic Statistical Authority) by the rate of return to education, as calculated by pertinent studies (Psacharopoulos and Patrinos 2002). This offers an estimate of the average investment (per student) in every educational level. We subsequently calculate the total investment in every level of the educational system by multiplying the average amount of investment per student by the number of graduates at every level of education. Finally, in order to calculate the total investment in human capital in the Greek economy, we sum the amounts previously calculated for every level of education

[f]OECD-National Accounts of OECD countries, vol. 2007

The per capita net wealth of Greece, as a percentage of GDP, has exceeded the Eurozone average since 2002 and has approached the corresponding level of Northern European countries and the richest countries of the Mediterranean, Italy and Spain. According to Davies at al. (2008), for the year 2000 and not including investments in human capital, the per capita net wealth of households based on purchasing power parity (ppp) was $72,825 for Greece, compared to $119,704, $92,253 and $53,357 in Italy, Spain and Portugal, respectively, and $66,191, $120,086 and $80,091 in Denmark, Netherlands and Sweden, respectively.

The biggest part of the created wealth is accumulated as real estate. Apart from investments in human capital, the contribution of real estate to the wealth of Greek households ranges between 80% and 90%, compared to 40–50% in the Eurozone and 20–30% in the USA.

The burden of Greek households, compared to that of the Mediterranean and Northern European countries, in relation to GDP is very interesting (Table 3.7).

Table 3.7 Debt of households as percentage of GDP

		1995 (%)	1999 (%)	2004 (%)	2008 (%)
	Greece	5.84	10.22	29.68	49.72
Mediterranean countries	Italy	18.17	21.60	27.59	34.24
	Spain	31.48	42.78	64.43	83.47
	Portugal	26.92	56.89	79.67	95.99
Northern countries	Finland	34.67	30.83	40.64	49.42
	Sweden	45.89	48.90	61.05	74.35
	Netherlands	59.14	83.06	107.80	120.00

Source: Eurostat, Financial Accounts, Indicator F4 (loans), Sector S14_S15 (households; non-profit institutions serving households)

The exponential increase in the borrowing of Greek households (compared to output produced) after 1995 is obvious. The levels of lending appear to be higher than those of Italy but lower than those of Spain and Portugal. It is worth mentioning that in Northern European countries, which have historically shown a higher borrowing burden of their households, the corresponding rate is not especially high, with the exception of the Netherlands. However, the borrowing burden of Greek households has been relatively moderate.

3.3   Production and Income

Table 3.8 presents the total gross value added per sector plus taxes, minus subsidies, as a percentage of GDP.

Based on the analysis of Table 3.8, we establish that the contribution of the industrial and energy sectors (mines, quarries, manufacturing, electricity, natural gas and water) to the total gross value added for Greece is stable and the smallest among the countries examined.

The Greek economy had the highest share of construction, compared to the European average, for 2002 and 2007 (before and after the 2004 Athens Olympics). We observe, however, that the percentage of construction is small (at least in the official economy) and consequently cannot be considered as the basic source of value in the Greek economy. On the other hand, trading, transportation and telecommunications (wholesale and retail trade, repairs of vehicles and household products, hotels and restaurants, transportation, storage and communications) top the list (32.6% for 2007). These activities have, for the period in question, the greatest weight in the country's production activity. Business activities and financial services (financial intermediaries, asset management, leasing) also play an important part (average of 19.6%). This sector, however, is in third place in terms of its contribution to the creation of gross value (19.4% for 2007).

Finally, the same table presents the contributions of other services to GDP for the examined countries (public governance, national defence, education, mandatory social insurance, health and social care, other social services, private households that engage staff). Greece is ranked first in this sector (23.9% for 2007).

Table 3.8 Gross values of market prices for six basic sectors (percentage of the total)

Year	Primary sector (agriculture, fishery, hunting)			Secondary sector (mining, manufacturing, energy)			Construction			Trading, transportation, telecommunications, hotels			Business activities, financial organisations			Other services (public governance, national defence, education)		
	1997	2002	2007	1997	2002	2007	1997	2002	2007	1997	2002	2007	1997	2002	2007	1997	2002	2007
European Union																		
EU-27	2.8	2.2	1.8	23.3	21.1	20.1	5.6	5.7	6.5	21.3	21.8	21.2	24.8	26.6	28.1	22.3	22.6	22.4
EU-15	2.6	2.1	1.6	23.1	20.9	19.7	5.5	5.6	6.4	21.1	21.5	20.8	25.2	27.1	28.7	22.5	22.8	22.7
Mediterranean countries																		
Greece	–	5.9	3.8	–	13.3	13.3	–	6.2	7	–	32.1	32.6	–	19.8	19.4	–	22.7	23.9
Spain	5	4	2.9	22.2	19.5	17.5	7.1	9.4	12.3	26.4	26.1	24.4	18.3	20.5	22.1	21	20.5	20.9
Italy	3.2	2.6	2	24.4	22.4	20.8	5.1	5.4	6.3	23.9	23.9	22.5	22.8	25.6	27.6	20.6	20.2	20.8
Portugal	4.6	3.3	2.5	22	19.2	18	7	7.6	6.5	24.2	24.5	24.3	19.7	20.5	22.4	22.5	25	26.4
Balkan countries																		
Bulgaria	26.2	12.2	6.2	26.4	24.3	24.1	2.7	4.4	8.2	17.5	23.1	24.4	18.8	20.3	22	8.4	15.7	15.1
Romania	–	12.6	6.4	–	30	27	–	6.3	10.1	–	22	26.6	–	15.8	18.3	–	13.3	11.6
Northern European countries																		
Denmark	3.2	2.2	1.2	20.9	20.4	20.3	4.8	5.1	6.1	22.5	21.8	21.3	21.8	23.2	24.7	26.8	27.3	26.4
Norway	2.4	1.7	1.4	27.4	27.3	26.2	4.7	4.5	5	21.4	19.2	17.5	16.8	18.5	17.9	22.2	22.6	20.5
Sweden	2.5	1.9	1.4	25.1	23.1	23.4	4	4.4	4.9	19	19.3	19	24.2	24.6	24.8	25.1	26.7	26.4
Finland	4.1	3.3	3.2	32.5	33.4	37.7	4.9	5.2	6.4	21.8	22.6	21.6	19.3	20.3	21.1	22.7	21.2	21.4

Source: Eurostat (tables b1g_a_b, b1g_c_d_e, b1_g_f, b1g_g_h_i, b1g_i_k, b1g_l_to_p)

Table 3.9 Final private and public consumption expenses as a percentage of GDP

Average of 1999–2007	Final expenditures of private consumption	Final expenditures of public consumption
European Union		
EU-27	58.1	20.8
EU-15	58.0	20.5
Mediterranean countries		
Greece	71.8	16.5
Spain	58.3	17.7
Italy	59.1	19.4
Portugal	64.2	20.1
Balkan countries		
Bulgaria	70.4	17.4
Romania	69.9	16.2
Northern European countries		
Denmark	48.5	26.0
Norway	44.4	26.6
Sweden	48.5	20.8

Source: Eurostat, national accounts (nam_gdp_c), indicators p31_s14_s15_, p3_s13

3.4   Consumer Expenditures

The consumption of Greek households as a percentage of GDP (>70%) greatly exceeds that of Mediterranean and Northern European countries for the period of 1999–2007, with rates similar to those of Balkan countries. Southern countries in general (Mediterranean and Balkan) have higher consumption expenditures as a percentage of GDP compared to Northern countries, a fact that demonstrates both their position towards consumption and savings and differences in consumption norms. The expenditures of Greek households focus mostly on health, clothing and footwear, education and hospitality (Eurostat national accounts data).

Table 3.9 describes the average private and public consumption as a percentage of GDP for 1999–2007. The highest private expenditures, as previously mentioned, are observed in Greece, Bulgaria and Romania (about 70% of GDP), whereas the percentages are lower in the Northern European countries (roughly 47% of GDP). Concerning public consumption expenditures (central government), Greece is in the last position, together with Bulgaria and Romania. Furthermore, the Northern European countries have higher public consumption expenditures compared to Mediterranean and Balkan countries.

3.5   Imports, Exports and Balance of Payments

The Greek economy engages in limited exports (Table 3.10) when compared with the rest of the countries (around 21% of GDP), which mostly export services, groceries, oil products, textile industry products, chemicals, machines and

Table 3.10 Exports, imports and balance of payments as a percentage of GDP

Year	1999			2002			2005			2007		
	Exports[a]	Imports[a]	Current account balance[a]	Exports	Imports	Balance of payments	Exports	Imports	Balance of payments	Exports	Imports	Balance of payments
European Union												
EU-27	32.5	31.7	–	35.4	33.9	–	37.4	36.7	–	40.3	39.8	–
EU-15	32.2	31.1	–	34.8	33.1	–	36.4	35.5	–	39.1	38.2	–
Mediterranean countries												
Greece	–	–	-1.8	21.1	34.6	-5.5	22	30.9	-6.4	23	33.5	-12.3
Spain	26.7	28.5	-1.8	27.3	29.5	-2.2	25.7	31	-6.5	26.5	33.3	-9.6
Italy	24.5	22.6	0.9	25.7	24.8	-0.8	26	26	-1.6	29.2	29.5	-2.2
Portugal	27.9	38.1	-6.4	28	36.3	-6.6	28.5	37.4	-8.3	32.6	40	-8.1
Balkan countries												
Bulgaria	44.6	50.3	-5.1	51.5	59.9	-5.6	60.2	76.4	-11.3	63.4	85.5	-27.2
Romania	28	32.9	-3.9	35.4	41	-3.1	33.1	43.2	-7.9	29.5	43.5	-12.8
Northern European countries												
Denmark	40.7	35.7	2.6	47.2	41.4	2.6	49	44.1	4.5	52.3	50.2	0.7
Norway	39.4	32	6.0	41.1	27.7	12.7	44.6	28.2	16.2	45.8	29.8	15.9
Sweden	43.2	36.7	3.0	44.6	37.8	4.9	48.7	41	7.0	52.6	44.9	8.5
Finland	38.8	28.7	6.3	40.4	31	8.9	41.8	37.4	3.8	45.7	40.7	4.2

Source: Eurostat, Indicators p6, p71, D, 993, 994, B1GM

[a] Includes elements of trade balance and services balance

appliances (EL. STAT. data for external trade). The largest importers of Greek products are EU countries (about 70% of the total of Greek exports for the period of 1998–2001), especially Germany and Italy. Greece imports about 35% of its GDP, mostly from EU countries (about 80% of the total for the period of 1998–2001), mainly Germany and Italy. Imports include cars, machines, groceries, chemicals and plastic, oil products, textile industry products, clothes, and metals. Its extensive imports combined with limited exports have driven Greece to a large deficit (12.3%) similar to that of Romania and much greater than that of the Mediterranean countries. On the other hand, Northern European countries constantly demonstrate a high surplus in their balance of payments.

Over the last 15 years, the Greek economy has shown internal and external imbalances that have been presented internationally (see Sect. 1.4). The external current account balance has grown (Table 3.10), linked to the widening budget deficit and the savings-investments deficit (Fig. 3.1). Furthermore, the balance of goods and services has continued to deteriorate (Fig. 3.2), as has the net investment balance, and only the balance of net transfers supports the two previous figures, mainly because of transfers from the EU.

3.6   Competitiveness and Productivity

The issues of competitiveness and productivity in an economy – in this case, that of Greece – are critical as they trigger issues of economic policy and politics. Given the importance of these indicators, an economic policy is developed, essentially as a horizontal management approach to improve these in key areas: labour conditions, investment conditions and conditions of employment remuneration and capital. The

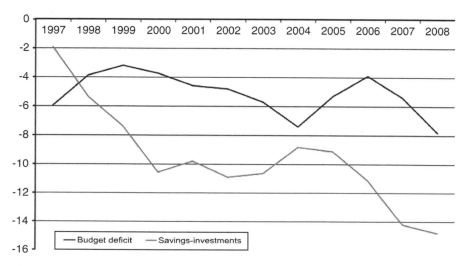

Fig. 3.1 Budget deficit and savings-investments (% of GDP) (Source: World Bank database)

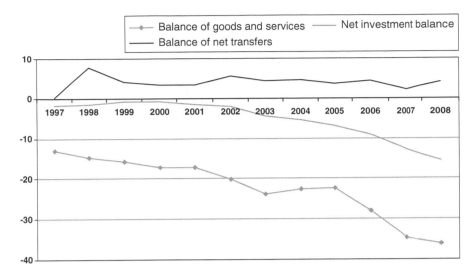

Fig. 3.2 Balance of goods and services, balance of net transfers and net investment balance (in millions of dollars) (Source: OECD Economic Outlook, No. 88, 2010/2)

success of these policies is always related to the accuracy of diagnosing the underlying problems.

A series of indices and methodologies from several national agencies and international organisations is usually used to assess a country's competitiveness. The use of these specific indices to measure concepts such as competitiveness entails several methodological issues, of course. The three basic methodological approaches used to quantify the concept entail: (a) the choice between a one-dimensional index and complex indices; (b) the choice of the appropriate reference field (e.g., time, size of geographical reference field); and (c) the choice between quantitative amounts and qualitative subjective indices.

Here, we use two groups of indices: (a) indices based mainly on the comparative development of prices and costs in a country in comparison with its competitor countries and (b) indices that have a broader view, including a series of elements which, to a great extent, describe the growth and development capacity of an economy. This expresses its ability to compete in the international economy. Specifically, this second category of indicators has a strong endogeneity problem. In other words, if the economy has a growth problem, its individual competitiveness indicators will obviously be reduced. In parallel, as long as it has reduced competitiveness indicators, it will continue to present problematic growth. In other words, these indicators are, to a certain extent, "reflective" and do not explain the process of growth.

The competitiveness indicator based on the effective exchange rate aims to capture changes in the country's competitiveness in international markets based on changes in exchange rates and price levels in a given country (whether the prices are of consumer goods, production or labour costs) compared with those of competitors. The most commonly used indicators are the Nominal Effective Exchange Rate (NEER)[4] and the Real Effective Exchange Rate (REER).[5]

The NEER index is calculated by comparing the change in the exchange rate of each country compared to U.S. dollars with a weighted average of the changes in the exchange rates of the country's competitors (also compared to U.S. dollars). The weighting is performed at the level of trade, as reflected by the current account balance with each partner with which that country does business. Consequently, the NEER index can be used to calculate the change in trading conditions with a large number of countries. The drop of the NEER is a positive sign for the state of competitiveness of this country as it shows that imports of all goods and services are cheaper in relation to the past and that their exports – or a combination thereof – are more expensive.

The real effective exchange rate (REER) constitutes an improved approach to the nominal effective exchange rate (NEER) because it is especially useful and important to understand the comparative changes in the real economic conditions of a country. The relative consumer price index, the relative producer price index and the index of unit labour cost can be described as REER computation indices. Unlike the NEER, these indices take into account not only the weighted changes in the market's exchange rates but also the changes in the relevant price levels (using consumer prices, producer prices, and unit labour cost, respectively). A country's relative consumer price index is calculated by comparing the change in a country's consumer price index (after conversion to US dollars) to a weighted average of changes of the consumer price index of its competitors (also expressed in US dollars). This ratio is multiplied by the NEER. The changes to the relative producer's price index and to the relative unit labour cost index are computed in the same way.

At this point, we should emphasise that an increase in the indices implies deterioration of the country's competitiveness. More specifically, an increase in a country's REER relating to the consumer's price index, the producer's price index and the unit labour cost leads to a decrease in its competitiveness and a worsening of the current account balance. Furthermore, it should be emphasised that the indices demonstrate changes only relating to each country's competitiveness on an international level over time and that changes between countries on the level of indices have absolutely no meaning.

Based on Table 3.11, we observe that the REER index for the Greek economy is increased, a fact that hinders Greece's competitive position, while 2008 shows a remarkable adaptation reaction (bending) of the Greek economy to the crisis that began in 2008. Sweden presents the most competitive picture of the examined countries.

---

[4] NEER: Nominal Effective Exchange Rate.
[5] REER: Real Effective Exchange Rate.

Table 3.11 REER index prices – relative index of unit cost

Year	1995	1998	2000	2001	2002	2004	2005	2006	2007	2008
Greece	88.35	96.79	97.33	93.50	100.65	100.57	102.45	102.33	104.40	104.96
Denmark	93.69	98.60	99.11	101.07	102.52	102.51	103.68	105.25	109.09	112.42
Netherlands	99.44	99.13	101.97	104.87	107.81	108.29	106.78	106.83	107.65	107.34
Sweden	91.12	101.67	108.43	101.61	100.99	98.58	96.05	95.31	98.40	94.28
Italy	84.39	99.54	99.19	100.03	101.36	105.57	107.37	108.95	109.30	110.75
Portugal	90.01	98.48	103.13	104.41	105.49	107.17	109.22	109.11	108.57	108.78
Spain	96.48	99.32	101.50	102.18	102.56	105.03	107.17	109.74	112.29	113.73

Source: Eurostat (1999 = 100), ert_eff_ic_a

The overall evaluation of the competitiveness of various economies at a global level is usually based on the reports of two international institutes (WEF and IMD)[6] and three organisations (World Bank, IMF, and OECD). The WEF and IMD reports adopt different approaches relevant to the ranking of countries, while the reports of the World Bank, the IMF and the OECD focus on individual aspects of economic function with no absolute reference to competitiveness.

Based on WEF rankings, Greece ranks relatively low in the global competitiveness index, dropping year after year; from the 36th position in 2000, it fell to the 67th position in 2008. Northern European countries are very high in the global rankings, demonstrating a steadily increasing trend in competitiveness, whereas Mediterranean countries steadily dropped in global competitiveness rankings.

Table 3.12 presents the ranking of each country based on the global competitiveness indices of the WEF and the IMD for 2008 and 2009 as well as each country's score for overall competitiveness. The numbers in parentheses indicate the position of each country in the previous year.

Northern European countries are highly competitive, as demonstrated by the fact that they are consistently positioned at the top of the rankings at both the EU and the global level under both competitiveness measurement systems. On the other hand, Mediterranean countries rank low in both the WEF and IMD rankings, and Greece's competitiveness is very low, both in the EU and in the world rankings.

The above analysis demonstrates that the cost competitiveness of the Greek economy is not satisfactory compared to other European countries, although in all countries with similar levels of development (and others), these indicators move in the same direction. Sweden and Germany (not shown) present a contrasting picture.

---

[6] The WEF (World Economic Forum), headquartered in Switzerland, has published since 1979 annual reports for 131 countries dedicated to countries' competitiveness, through which it attempts to trace the factors that allow the national economies to achieve rapid development and increased levels of prosperity.

The IMD, headquartered in Lausanne (Switzerland), has published annually since 1989 the Yearbook of International Competitiveness, aiming to assess the overall competitiveness of over 60 countries in the world.

Table 3.12 Rankings of countries based on the global competitiveness indices of the WEF and IMD

Country	WEF EU ranking (2008–2009)	Global ranking (2008–2009)	Score	IMD EU ranking (2008–2009)	Global ranking (2008–2009)	Score
Denmark	1 (1)	3 (3)	5.58	1 (2)	5 (6)	91.74
Sweden	2 (2)	4 (4)	5.53	2 (3)	6 (9)	90.52
Netherlands	5 (5)	8 (10)	5.41	4 (4)	10 (10)	87.75
Spain	12 (12)	29 (29)	4.72	18 (17)	39 (33)	57.85
Portugal	17 (16)	43 (40)	4.47	16 (18)	34 (37)	62.59
Italy	20 (19)	49 (46)	4.35	21 (21)	50 (46)	52.06
Greece	24 (24)	67 (65)	4.11	22 (22)	52 (42)	50.78

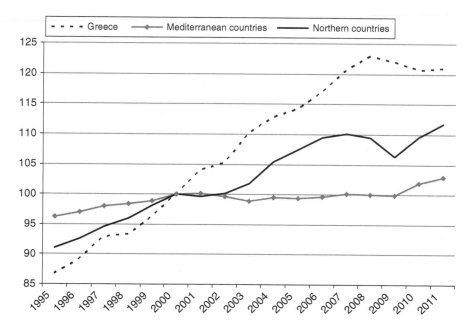

Fig. 3.3 Index of labour productivity per employee (base year 2000 = 100) (Source: Eurostat. Note: The values of the productivity index for the Mediterranean (Italy, Spain and Portugal) and Northern European countries (Denmark, Sweden, the Netherlands) are weighted based on the number of workers and the index price for these countries)

Meanwhile, the overall productivity indicators of the Greek economy have improved significantly since 1995. It is noteworthy that labour productivity in the Greek economy has grown continually from that year onwards (Fig. 3.3).

It is worth noting that productivity growth in Greece seems to originate mostly in sectors that are not associated with high technology (Giannitsis 2008, p. 23). Indeed, Table 3.13 shows that transport and trade have given impetus to the growth of labour productivity (37%). The zero contribution of the public sector to the increase of productivity – although its work hours account for 16% of total labour

Table 3.13 Gross added value and productivity at work: 2000–2008

| | Mean annual change rates, % | | | |
	Gross added value	Gross added value per employee	Mean share of total work hours	Contribution to growth of labour productivity in all industries
Total sectors	3.4	2.7	100	2.7
Electrical equipment and communication	9.2	7.5	1.7	0.1
Manufacturing, excluding electrical	1.4	2.5	15.7	0.4
Energy, construction, mining, agriculture, fishing, hunting	1.5	3	24.7	0.8
Wholesale and retail trade and transport	5.6	4.5	22.1	1
Financial and business services	6	1.9	8.4	0.1
Hotels, restaurants and social services	4.8	2.7	11.5	0.3
Public administration and defence, education and health	2	0	15.9	0

Source: EUKLEMS database, http://www.euklems.net/

resources in the economy – is noteworthy and may be due to increased employment in the public sector.

Of course, the loss of competitiveness and the productivity improvement observed in the Greek economy are related to the development process that is ongoing in Greece. The causes, therefore, of this "paradox" are the following:

1. We are facing a typical manifestation of the Balassa–Samuelson phenomenon. The growth of productivity differs between sectors, whereas wages do not differ much. Given that productivity is growing faster among sectors producing tradable goods and services compared to industries producing non-marketable products, growth increases the price level in all areas by increasing the general price levels of the economy.

2. The development of oligopolistic situations and the existence of transfer pricing (see Chap. 6) provide a second interpretation. Given the very limited exports and the general import orientation of the economy, the pricing policy reflects the targeting of the internal market and serves transfer pricing policies. The overall result is inflationary and ultimately results in reduced competitiveness.

3. The unique organisation of Greek production is based on SMEs. In each case, the average numbers of employees employed in both services and productive sectors are the smallest among the countries being compared (see Chap. 7). This fact, combined with the relation of SMEs with the shadow economy, reveals that industry is turning productivity gains into losses in the shadow economy by keeping prices high and thus reducing competitiveness (Table 3.14).

Table 3.14 REER index values – consumer price index

	1995	1998	2000	2001	2002	2003	2004	2005	2006	2007	2008
Greece	97.34	99.05	98.09	99.13	100.93	105.89	107.82	108.68	110.41	112.50	115.82
Denmark	103.78	100.76	96.13	98.08	99.40	103.06	103.87	103.37	103.73	105.29	108.26
Netherlands	105.18	100.23	98.47	101.79	104.12	108.29	108.17	108.29	108.80	109.59	111.29
Sweden	100.27	101.48	98.06	90.29	92.38	97.76	98.82	96.10	95.85	96.71	95.19
Italy	89.96	101.41	96.61	98.14	100.92	106.82	109.13	109.16	110.42	112.56	115.29
Portugal	101.14	99.97	98.19	99.80	101.84	106.06	107.30	107.68	108.74	110.45	111.93
Spain	102.12	100.30	97.75	99.87	102.04	107.13	109.90	111.17	113.07	115.81	119.24

Source: Eurostat (Base year 1999 = 100), ert_eff_ex_a

3.7   Growth and Demand in the Greek Economy

Thus far, the analysis has approached the issue of development from the perspective of supply conditions of its basic factors (capital, labour, human capital, overall productivity factors). Furthermore, we have analysed the basic description of the product according to the basic categories of its configuration. As a result, demand for the output produced is formed in each economy and is crucial for its development. Once product demand factors begin exerting an effect, their final influence is a result of the specific weight they allocate to the output produced and of the rate of their change. Such an analysis for the Greek economy during the period of 2001–2008 is presented in Table 3.15.

We realise that the basic advancement force of demand, and hence of the conservation of growth rates, was internal, not external, demand (whose contribution is minimal or even negative). We thus see that the forces advancing demand were endogenous. The most essential advancement factor of internal demand was gross, especially private, investments. Private consumption plays an important and stable role. The economy's management model for this entire period remains almost stable. Two time periods should be emphasised: the public investments of 2003 in improvements necessary for hosting the 2004 Olympic Games and the increase of private investments in residences in 2006. In essence, both of these types of investments played similar roles. This analysis implies that if the levels of internal demand are negatively affected for any reason, economic growth rates will be affected extremely negatively.

Table 3.15 Growth and demand in the Greek economy: 2001–2008

	2001	2002	2003	2004	2005	2006	2007	2008
1. Gross domestic product	4.3	3.8	4.9	4.7	3.7	4.5	4	2.9
(1.1) Private consumption	3	3.1	4.2	4.6	3.7	4.8	3	2.2
(1.2) Government consumption	−3.2	8.3	−1.3	2.5	−0.5	0	7.7	3.2
(1.3) Gross investments	6.5	5.7	13.3	5.8	0.2	9.2	4.9	−11.5
Residences	–	–	–	–	–	29.1	−6.8	−29.1
Business investments	7.4	7.9	13	5.5	1.8	−2.4	14.5	−4.4
Government investments	2.4	−5.4	15.9	8.5	−13.5	9.1	2.6	−32.1
(1.4) Stock/reserves	−0.4	−0.2	−0.3	−0.1	−0.1	−0.2	1.6	1.4
2. Total internal demand	2.4	4.2	5.1	4.5	2.3	4.8	5.1	0.7
(2.1) Exports of products and services	−1	−7.7	4	7.5	3.7	10.9	3.1	2.2
(2.2) Imports of products and services	−5.2	−2.9	−4.9	5.6	−2.11	9.7	6.7	−4.4
3. Net exports	1.7	−0.9	−0.7	−0.3	1.3	−0.3	−1	2.2

Sources: 2006–2008 OECD, Economic Surveys, Greece, Vol. 2009/15, July 2009
2006–2008 OECD, Economic Surveys, Greece, 2007
2006–2008 OECD, Economic Surveys, Greece, 2005

3.8   The Size of the Shadow Economy and its Effects

Many researchers, in an effort to measure the shadow economy, must complete the difficult task of defining it. A simple definition could be the following: "The shadow economy includes the production of goods and services, legal or illegal (e.g. drug trafficking), which escapes detection, and consequently is not calculated in the official Gross Domestic Product" (Smith 1994, p. 18). It is apparent that the nature of the shadow economy itself make its measurement and recording very difficult. Numerous methodological approaches have been developed to define the size of the shadow economy. In order to calculate the size of the shadow economy in Greece, the present study uses a method based on the definition of the function of money demand, also known as the method of the research team of Leicester University (Bhattacharyya 1990). According to our estimation, the size of the shadow economy in Greece for 2008 was roughly equal to 20.97% of GDP.[7] Table 3.16 presents the diachronic tendency of the size of the shadow economy in Greece resulting from our calculations.

The shrinking of the shadow economy in recent years is due to its partial inclusion in the official GDP. Table 3.17 presents Schneider's (2002) estimations for Greece and various OECD countries. Schneider's (2002) calculations were based on a methodology known as the "method of money demand" (Cagan 1958; Tanzi 1980, 1983). This method is based on the hypothesis that transactions in the shadow economy are effected mostly with cash to avoid detection by the authorities. Thus, by calculating the effects of taxation (direct and indirect) and of other factors that are thought to affect the size of the shadow economy on the quantity of money reserves observed and considering that the circulation speed of

Table 3.16 Estimation of the size of the shadow economy in Greece

Year	Shadow economy (% of GDP)	Year	Shadow economy (% of GDP)	Year	Shadow economy (% of GDP)
1973	12.37	1985	18.62	1997	22.61
1974	12.84	1986	18.46	1998	24.3
1975	12.93	1987	18.95	1999	25.69
1976	13.76	1988	18.38	2000	27.45
1977	14.05	1989	17.35	2001	25.95
1978	14.25	1990	18.77	2002	24.24
1979	14.28	1991	19.23	2003	23.04
1980	13.61	1992	19.87	2004	22.87
1981	13.39	1993	20.86	2005	22.29
1982	16.47	1994	21.31	2006	21.56
1983	18.06	1995	22.01	2007	20.89
1984	18.96	1996	21.98	2008	20.97

---

[7] OECD Vol. 2009/15 July 2009, p. 60 estimates the equivalent measure to 25%.

Table 3.17 Estimated size of the shadow economies in the considered countries (% of GDP)

	Mean value 1989/1990	Mean value 1991/1992	Mean value 1994/1995	Mean value 1997/1998	Mean value 1999/2000	Mean value 2001/2002
OECD countries (21)	13.2	14.3	15.7	16.7	16.8	16.7
Greece	22.6	24.9	28.6	29	28.7	28.5
Mediterranean countries						
Spain	16.1	17.3	22.4	23.1	22.7	22.5
Italy	22.8	24	26	27.3	27.1	27
Portugal	15.9	17.2	22.1	23.1	22.7	22.5
Northern European countries						
Denmark	10.8	15	17.8	18.3	18	17.9
Finland	13.4	16.1	18.2	18.9	18.1	18
Sweden	15.8	17	19.5	19.9	19.2	19.1

Source: Schneider (2002)

money is the same in the official and unofficial economies, we can measure the size of the shadow economy as a percentage of GDP.

Greece seems to have the largest shadow economy among the examined countries. Its estimated size increases over time.

Transactions in the shadow economy mostly use cash. Thus, the expansion of the shadow economy leads to an increased demand for money reserves and to a decrease of the elasticity of money demand to the exchange rate.[8] This development decreases the effectiveness of monetary policy.

Furthermore, the shadow economy also affects the monetary system through another channel: an increase in the size of the shadow economy leads to an expansion of the "parallel monetary market", which includes loan sharking, illegal foreign currency sales, circulation of counterfeit money, the "unsealing" of post-dated checks, and other consequences.[9]

This unofficial money market, in turn, conserves and reproduces the parallel market of products as those who are mainly active in the shadow economy find it difficult to secure sources from the official credit system.

The decrease of tax income caused by the shadow economy limits the government's capacity to make public expenditures. This has a negative effect on

---

[8] The demand for money reserves (otherwise known as money demand) refers to the quantity of money that individuals retain. Retaining money results in the resignation from the exchange rate that certain financial products offer (e.g., bonds, deposits). Thus, the percentage change of money demand, which is caused by a percentage change in interest rates (elasticity), is negative. The sensitivity degree of money demand on exchange rate decreases because of the increased need for money that transactions in the underground economy require.

[9] The term "breaking" of post-dated checks refers to the borrowing of money that takes place with the relinquishment, on the part of the borrower, of a check that registers an issue date after the actual date of issuance as a form of guarantee to the lender. Usually, the height of this loan is a percentage of the check's value from about 90% (maximum), and it keeps decreasing as the precarity of the issuer and of the underwriter of the check increases.

the effectiveness of the exercised fiscal policy as smaller levels of public revenues and expenditures as a percentage of GDP have a limited capability of affecting GDP and other macroeconomic indicators using the "tools" of fiscal policy. Furthermore, the decrease of tax income caused by the growth of the shadow economy leads to the further growth of the shadow economy through the following cumulative process. The decrease in tax revenues because of the increase in tax evasion causes an increase in the relative tax burden on the official economy, resulting in increased tax evasion, and so on. This vicious cycle renders fiscal policy means ineffective.

Data on the extent of tax evasion in Greece are disheartening. We calculated that undeclared tax income amounted to 4.9% of GDP for 2005 and to 4.7% of GDP for 2008.

The growth of the shadow economy deprives the insurance system of the resources that secure its viability. More specifically, the revenue loss of insurance organizations due to social security contribution evasion limits the resources available for pensions. Moreover, the payment of much smaller contributions than those corresponding to real earnings impedes the collection of the necessary number of duty stamps to ensure a dignified pension. On the other hand, in order to support a minimum level of living, the government is compelled to pay in full non-redeeming pensions in the form of Social Solidarity Subsidies of the retired. All of the above lead in turn to the preservation and expansion of the vicious cycle of uninsured work.

The data on the extent of contribution evasion in Greece are quite enlightening. We estimated the extent of contribution evasion as a percentage of GDP was 3% in 2005 and 2.8% in 2008. Consequently, the overall effect of fiscal needs should be calculated at 7–8% of GDP or €18 bn.

The extended shadow economy absorbs a significant percentage of the unemployed workforce through the creation of new positions (usually part-time). Thus, shadow economic activity contributes to the employment of an additional number of people who would otherwise be unemployed. Furthermore, the shadow economy can absorb the shocks caused by a financial system crisis. For example, the "unsealing" of post-dated checks can lift obstacles of credit limitations in the official sector of the economy because of a financial crisis and ensure the necessary market resources that will lead to a gradual exit from the recession. All of the above often lead to the conclusion that there is a positive aspect of the shadow economy and that shadow economic activity could function as a "security valve" in times of recession and increased unemployment (Carter 1984).

The issue of the shadow economy, however, becomes explosive when its socioeconomic benefit (contribution to employment) is smaller than its socioeconomic cost (tax evasion), mostly because of fiscal needs (fiscal and insurance expenses).

According to Schneider (2007), the main factor leading to the creation of shadow economies is the increase of taxation and social insurance contributions. The increases of the cost of labour and of the tax burden, as well as the rigidity of the regulatory frame, reduce companies' competitiveness in both the international and domestic markets. As a result, companies are forced to participate in the shadow economy to overcome the state's obstacles and develop some competitive advantage.

The financial systems are divided into those based on the banking system and those based on capital markets (i.e., market-based systems vs. stock-based systems). However, since 2006, the IMF (World Economic Outlook, 2006) has made a much more interesting distinction. It distinguishes between those systems based mostly on publicly available information (i.e., their organisational core is the capital markets) and those that are based mostly on trust among contracting partners (i.e., their organisational core is the banking system).

In general, European countries (Greece included) rely more on systems that carry the resources of capital through the banking systems. According to measurements taken in 2006 (i.e., before the 2008 crisis), 30% of all capital handled in the European economies (except inter-bank transactions) was transferred through the banking system, while in the US the corresponding rate was 15%.

During a recession, it is very important to understand whether capital is circulated by an organisation based on publicly available information or based on mechanisms that rely on intra-business (lender–borrower) relations. Businesses that operate in economies where lender–borrower relations dominate are expected to more easily adapt to developments based on the long-term relationships they have with their lenders. In the event, however, that the recession is inextricably linked to liquidity issues in the banking system (as in the present crisis), systems based on publicly available information could possibly realise the evolutions more quickly and be able to manage more quickly and effectively the new distribution of resources, ignoring the difficulties of the banking system.

In the Greek economy, as in the rest of the world, there is a parallel financial system based on the issuance of checks and for the contractualisation of intra-business transactions. At the same time, because of the legal framework of their circulation, it seems to constitute a form of transaction insurance. To some degree, these checks "ensure" credits from the banking system equal to 80% of their value (today). In essence, they take the form of a guarantee and have no further value for our analysis.

The Greek economy had about €250–300 bn in checks, of which €100–120 bn[10] are anticipated (before their maturity) by the banks. If they bounce, their last holder bears responsibility, so they do not really constitute an added means of financing the economy.

It is obvious, however, that the remaining €165 bn does not entirely constitute financing for the economy because checks usually have a mean maturity time under 1 year. That is, if a real yearly transaction of €100 is financed by three four-monthly checks, then there is a nominal size of financing of €300. We cannot directly and clearly ascertain the average duration of the checks in circulation. The only data at

---

[10] Source: Clearing Office, Interbanking System, L. Stergiou, Kathimerini (22/2/2009).

our disposal concern "bad checks" and bills of exchange, which are recorded in the Tiresias.[11]

The other element at our disposal is the insolvency rate of Greek businesses from 2003 to 2008 (column (4), Table 3.18), which arises from the relevant study of ICAP[12] in 170,301 businesses that cover all of the basic sectors of activity and almost all of their forms. We see that this percentage is around 3%, with an increasing tendency. A bad cheque or bill of exchange is almost always connected with bankruptcy or difficulty paying off debt. It could reasonably be assumed that the same percentage applies to checks and bills of exchange. We could actually accept that this percentage became slightly elevated from 2008 to 2009 because of the crisis. Columns (5) and (6), which show two possible levels of circulating checks and bills of exchange in the Greek economy, are based on these assumptions. If we accept that the mean duration of checks and bills of exchange is 4 months, then we reach the annual adjusted amounts in columns (7) and (8) of the same table.

It should be noted that €165 m of circulating 4-month checks yields a similar size to that which arises from the table's calculations. This finding confirms our estimates.

We discover (column 9 of the table) that the financing of businesses in the bank sector is almost the same as that of businesses in the non-bank sector. This is an extremely important feature of the Greek economy (e.g., for SMEs) that can shed light on many points of the economy. First, it is apparent that the specific non-banking relationship that is supported on checks concerns lending relationships based on the quality of information produced through the specific relationship and is not based on the information's public availability. In order for our examination to move forward, we should clarify the degree to which the two forms of financing are complementary or substitutes.

The issue of financing from the banking sector raises a series of questions. We could further assume that when interest rates increase (which leads to a shrinking of the banking sector financing), there is a greater use of these credits. If this assumption holds, however, the followed monetary policy loses part of its strength. Maybe here lies an interpretation of the Greek economy's relative strengths (or weaknesses) during the credit crisis? What is the relation between non-banking financing and the shadow economy? We already have enough (research-related) indications that the two sides are quite close.

---

[11] Tiresias is an inter banking company that processes data that reflect the economic behaviour of individuals and companies as well as data that contribute to the prevention of fraud in financial transactions. The distributed data contribute to the protection of credit, the reduction of credit risk and the improvement of financial transactions, to the benefit of individuals and the banking system in general.

[12] ICAP Group is one of the most successful regional Business Services Groups in Southeastern Europe. It provides a wide range of services grouped in the following six business practices: Business Information, Business Directories, Management Consultants, Contact Center, HR Outsourcing, and Receivables Management.

Table 3.18 Bad checks, percentage of checks' inconsistency in circulation and banking financing (in millions of euros)

Year	Checks[b]	Bills of exchange[b]	Total[c]	Inconsistency percentage[c]	Probable height of checks and bills of exchange[d]		Checks' and bills' of exchange adjustment on a yearly basis[e]		Loans to businesses from domestic monetary financial institutions[f]
					3–5%	5–7%	$(7) = (5)/(3)$	$(8) = (6)/(3)$	
	(1)	(2)	(3)	(4)	(5)	(6)	(7)	(8)	(9)
2005	1,464	180	1,644	3.04%	54,800	32,880	18,267	10,960	5,716,6
2006	1,202	188	1,390	4.02%	46,333	27,800	15,444	9,267	5,376,9
2007	921	177	1,098	3.57%	36,600	21,960	12,200	7,320	13,095,3
2008	1,291	170	1,461	3.73%	29,220	20,871	9,740	6,957	13,761,3
2009 (q1)	712	59	771	–	11,014	8,567	3,671	2,856	–
2009[a]	2,848	236	3,084	–	44,057	34,267	14,686	11,422	–

[a]The estimate for 2009 arises through reduction of the resulting data for the first 3 months of the year (without seasonal restructuring)

[b]Source: Statistical data from Tiresias

[c]Source: ICAP, February 2009, "Evolution of the credit capability of Greek businesses, 2003–2008". It concerns a sample of 170,301 businesses (92,009 PLC-LTD and 78,292 GP-LP and individual businesses in the industry, trade and services sectors)

[d]The numbers of bad checks and bills of exchange that are taken into account in the relevant scenarios concern the years 2005–2007 and 2008–2009, respectively

[e]We assume that the mean duration of the checks is 4 months. Also see a study by the SMB GCPHMG (Small Businesses Institute – General Confederation of Professional Handcrafters and Merchants of Greece) from 8/2009, where the duration of post-dated checks is estimated by 30% of the businesses to be longer than 6 months and by 55.5% to be 2–5 months

[f]Source: Bank of Greece Bulletin, February 2009

More specifically, Petrakis and Eleftheriou (2009) ascertained, based on a co-integration model (Engle and Granger 1987; Johansen 1988), that the 2 monthly time series (parallel financing activity and official business financing) for the period of 2004–2008 are mutually influenced and, more specifically, that checks and bills of exchange constitute a substitute for bank loans. Consequently, when interest rates decrease in the official financial system, both the real and official sectors of the economy are favoured. When, however, the cost of money increases during a crisis because of segmentation (low interbank trust and low levels of trust between the banking system and the enterprises), the business sector substitutes the absence of official financing with non-official financing means (checks). This confirms the opinion of the International Monetary Fund (IMF 2006)[13] that economies with financial systems based less on public information and market procedures (arm's-length systems) and more on intra-business relationships might have less negative consequences. The opposite applies for a broadened banking sector (as in Greece).

3.9   Entrepreneurship

Of the 900,633 businesses operating in the Greek economy, 74.63% (size notwithstanding) operate in the tertiary sector, 23.06% in the secondary sector and only 2.23% in the primary sector. In the services sector, the leading industries are trade, which accounts for 34.81% of businesses, asset management (14.01%) and hotels and restaurants (11.29%). The most important sectors in manufacturing are construction (12.12%) and manufacturing-related businesses, which amount to 10.68%.

In the tertiary sector, trade (wholesale and retail) accounts for 43% of the total sector turnover and industry for 23%. Moreover, the annual number of new businesses (PLC and LTD) founded in the Greek territory shows fluctuations, accompanied by an important and simultaneous change to the initially invested capital, which decreases at a constant rate. The new businesses founded are ever smaller.

Essentially, the estimation of the relative contributions of the retail and wholesale trade sectors to activity can be better appreciated if the contribution of these sectors to total value added for the period of 2000–2007 is examined.

Greece has a contribution rate of 18%, which is among the highest in the EU-15. Obviously, this reflects the higher profitability conditions (gross profit level), which, before the crisis, reached 9.7% versus 6.7% in the Eurozone (NBG, Nov. 2010).[14]

The vast majority of Greek businesses are SMEs; micro (0–9 employees) and small (10–49 employees) businesses account for 98.09% and 1.57% of the total,

---

[13] IMF (2006) World Economic Outlook, Financial Systems and Economic Cycles.

[14] National Bank of Greece (2010) Unleashing Greece's medium-term growth potential.

respectively (HEL. STAT. data for the year 2002). Consequently, medium-sized (50–249 employees) and large companies comprise only 0.32% of total businesses. This pattern is mirrored in the legal shape of businesses, with sole proprietorships accounting for 81.2% and public limited companies for only 3.2% of the total. In other words, in Greece, 96% of businesses have 0–4 employees, 2% have 5–9 employees and the remaining 2% more than 10 employees. The mean number of employees in Greek businesses is two, the smallest in the EU, where the mean is six employees.

Thus, most businesses are SMEs in the form of LTD, GP, LP or PLC, with small capital adequacy. This is due to the fragmentation of economic activity and the structure of the economic and production system. Contrary to other European countries, there is no concentration in large economic units due to the specific characteristics of the Greek economy (e.g., unit fragmentation, small industrial production, low-risk financial investments by entrepreneurs, close collaboration with the Greek state or bureaucracy). Apart from construction, the same applies in the primary sector of agricultural production, i.e., many very small business units that cause agricultural production to be counterproductive. The same model seems to apply in tourism, supplementary services, and other services.

According to data gathered for this book, Greece has 1,641 medium and large enterprises. These businesses have an average of 423 employees, and the total number of employees constitutes an extremely important figure in reference to employment in medium and large businesses (a total of about 700,000 employees).

In order to study the evolution of medium-sized and large businesses in Greece, we analyse the data of the sample to detect trends concerning the founding of new businesses. Figure 3.4 analyses the development of medium-sized and large companies by country of origin (domestic or foreign). The study of the establishment of new Greek businesses compared to foreign companies or subsidiaries in Greece underlines that the domestic environment similarly affects both groups of companies. The trend lines of the two groups, however, reveal a more dynamic development of Greek compared to foreign firms.

The development rates of Greek businesses started to increase in 1969, whereas the development of foreign businesses becomes more evident only after 1991, a year coinciding with both the establishment of the collective European market and the deregulation of the banking system.

These data also highlight the fact that the vast majority of medium and large companies operating in the country – about 82.8% – were created during the period of 1975–2005. Most of these were founded during the 1980s and 1990s, which shows that there is no important tradition of big businesses in Greece. After 2000, the establishment of medium and big businesses decreased significantly, while the 2004 Athens Olympic Games gave a small boost to new businesses (mostly foreign).

Another interesting observation in the context of the above analysis is the indication that the foreign medium and large enterprises operating in Greece today are very new (with an average age around 15 years). Foreign businesses in Greece do not grow after their entrance in the country. They operate exclusively in the tertiary sector (e.g., trade, supermarkets, and department stores). As a result,

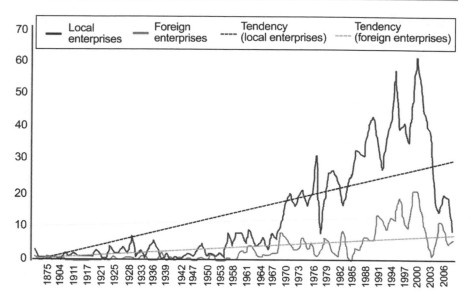

Fig. 3.4 Founding year, number of enterprises and company ownership (2009 data) (Source: ICAP data (2009))

they do not participate in networks of knowledge and technology transportation or in primary production structures.

The observation of the non-growth of foreign firms suggests vertical integration compared with the corresponding structures of origin abroad. For foreign firms (Chap. 6), the domestic economy is an area of economic activity to achieve higher levels of profitability (compared to Greek firms), to create long-term capital and possibly to implement transfer price policies. Moreover, this conclusion is consistent with the argument that the Greek economy is an area with high transaction costs (see Chap. 6) and a bank-based model, which leads firms to a greater degree of vertical integration; the question, however, relates to the direction of vertical integration (Acemoglu 2009).

The studies of Global Entrepreneurship Monitor (GEM) offer an image of the total entrepreneurial activity, depicting the number of businesses and measuring the business spirit and business activity in different stages of a business's development (Ioannidis and Tsakanikas 2008, pp. 101–102).

The basic index of the GEM is the level of "early stage entrepreneurial activities", which are demonstrated in every country and include two categories of individuals: prospective entrepreneurs and new entrepreneurs. Based on the FEIR's[15] (Foundation for Economic and Industrial Research) (2008)[16] latest

---

[15] The FEIR (IOBE) is the agency responsible for the compilation of the specific report of GEM for Greece.

[16] IOBE (2008) Entrepreneurship in Greece, 2007–2008.

Table 3.19 Participation in business activity

	Prospective entrepreneurs (%) (1)	New entrepreneurs (%) (2)	Early stage entrepreneurship (%) (3)	Established entrepreneurs (%) (4)	Total entrepreneurial activity (%) (5)
Sweden	1.9	2.4	4.2	4.7	8.8
Netherlands	2.7	2.6	5.2	6.4	11.3
Spain	3.5	4.3	7.6	6.4	13.4
Italy	3.6	1.5	5	5.6	10.4
Europe (average)	3.6	2.9	6.4	5.6	11.7
Finland	4.4	2.7	6.9	7.6	14
Greece	4.6	1.1	5.7	13.3	18.7
Portugal	4.8	4.1	8.8	7.1	15.4
GEM countries (average)	4.9	4.4	9.1	6.6	15.3

Source: FEIR (2008)
Note: (1) + (2) $\approx$ (3) and (3) + (4) $\approx$ (5)

published research, in 2007, 5.71% of the population aged 18–64 (i.e., 388,000 individuals) were in the initial stages of entrepreneurial activity (self-employment included) (Table 3.19). This category included all of the entrepreneurial activities, ranging in duration from newly formed businesses to 42 months, in which these businesses employed individuals.

Concerning the performance of the initial-stage entrepreneurship index, we observe that its increasing trend since 2004 stopped in 2007, which marked a low point for the period of 2003–2007. This decrease affected early-stage entrepreneurship. More specifically, whereas, in 2006, 7.9% of the population (aged 18–64) were prospective or new entrepreneurs, the equivalent number for 2007 was 5.7%. This, combined with the expansion of established entrepreneurship from 8.2% in 2006 to 13.3% in 2007, confirms the hypothesis of the appearance of entrepreneurship in waves, as concluded in the FEIR's previous research. When increased rates of early-stage entrepreneurship are seen during a given year, even though not always in a continuous manner, the established entrepreneurship is gradually fuelled.

More than 13% of the population aged 18–64 partly or wholly controls a business that has been operating for at least 3.5 years. Table 3.19 depicts Greece's performance in relation to countries with the same characteristics and with countries that could be developmental targets, such as Finland, Sweden and Netherlands.

The best performances in terms of opportunity entrepreneurship are observed in the Northern European countries and in the highest-income countries in general. On the other hand, high necessity entrepreneurship in Europe is observed in Serbia, Russia, Turkey and Croatia (more than half of all attempts).

In total, Greece shows high rates of both prospective entrepreneurs and total entrepreneurial activity. The percentages of new entrepreneurs and early-stage entrepreneurship, however, are especially low.

In terms of its performance in initial entrepreneurship stages, Greece is 7th in Europe (among 22 countries) and 11th among the countries with a high standard of living (income). In particular, the decrease of the percentage of entrepreneurs in initial stages in 2007 saw Greece drop to the 26th position internationally (among 42 countries).

The above finding confirms the special relation between a country's economic development and the initial stages of entrepreneurship. The relation between this index and the per capita GDP is depicted through the convex curve of Fig. 3.5 as it was recorded in GEM's previous research.

As we can see in Fig. 3.5, neighbouring countries that share traditions with Greece are relatively close, creating uniform clusters of countries. Many of the EU-15 countries show low early-stage entrepreneurship levels and lie below the convex curve. Of the EU countries, only Ireland seems to deviate, as it can be seen on the right side of the above figure. Under the curve are also the countries of the former Eastern Bloc and of Central Asia (left side of the figure). Latin American countries with an equivalent per capita GDP to these groups of countries demonstrate increased business activity. Finally, we observe that the richest and most industrialised countries lie above the curve (on the right).

The historical, cultural and institutional parameters of countries affect the relation between the level of economic development and early-stage entrepreneurship, as verified by Fig. 3.4.

Countries with low per capita income, which are in the development stages, usually achieve high early-stage entrepreneurship levels, mostly because of the

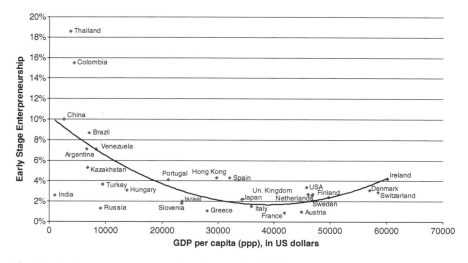

Fig. 3.5 Early-stage entrepreneurship and per capita GDP

large number of small businesses that characterises them. Development, however, and more specifically industrialisation and economies of scale, requires larger and more established business units that can respond to increased demand. Consequently, the decrease of early-stage entrepreneurship in low-income countries could constitute a sign of development and of a transition to a higher standard of living. Nonetheless, after a long developmental process, the search for new entrepreneurial opportunities is allowed because the established businesses have significant and increased roles. In any case, it is observed over time that certain countries demonstrate a certain stability in relation to the convex curve.

Today in Greece. early-stage entrepreneurship is close to the bottom of the convex curve of Fig. 3.5. When per capita output begins to grow, we expect increased business initiative. But as long as per capita GDP stands near its current levels, the operative force for the development of early-stage entrepreneurship will remain low. Therefore, the coincidence of the current economic crisis (see Chap. 10) with the current point in the evolution of early-stage entrepreneurship is rather unfortunate, aggravating (with respect to the recession) this weakness in taking business initiatives.

References

Acemoglu D (2009) Introduction to modern economic growth. Princeton University Press, New Jersey

Arnold J, Bassanini A, Scarpetta S (2007) Solow or Lucas?: Testing growth models using panel data from OECD countries. OECD Economics Department Working Paper 592

Bhattacharyya DK (1990) An econometric method of estimating the hidden economy: United Kingdom (1960–84): estimates and tests. Econ J 100:703–717

Cagan P (1958) The demand for currency relative to the total money supply. J Polit Econ 66(4):308–328

Carter M (1984) Issues in the hidden economy – a survey. Econ Rec 60:209–221

Davies J, Sandstrom S, Shorrocks A, Wolff E (2008) The world distribution of household wealth. Working Paper DP2008/03, World Institute of Development Economic Research (UNU-WIDER)

Engle R, Granger C (1987) Co-integration, and error correction representation, estimation and testing. Econometrica 55(2):251–276

Giannitsis T (2008) In search of Greek development model. Papazissis, Athens

Ioannidis S, Tsakanikas A (2008) Entrepreneurship in Greece 2007–2008. Global Entrepreneurship Monitor – Entrepreneurship Obs. FEIR

Johansen S (1988) Statistical analysis of cointegration vectors. J Econ Dyn Control 12:83–85

Petrakis P, Eleftheriou K (2009) Informal financing of the small and medium enterprise sector, the case of Greece. J Serv Sci Manag 2(4):378–383

Psacharopoulos G, Patrinos H (2002) Returns to investment in education: a further update. World Bank Policy Res. Working Paper 2881

Schneider F (2002) Size and measurement of the informal economy in 110 countries around the world. The World Bank, Rapid Response Unit, Washington, DC

Schneider F (2007) Shadow economies and corruption all over the world: new estimates for 145 countries. The Open Access J No. 2007–9

Smith P (1994) Assessing the size of the underground economy: the Canadian statistical perspective. Can Econ Obs 7(5):16–33

Tanzi V (1980) The underground economy in the United States: estimates and implications. Banca Nazionale del Lavoro 135(4):427–453

Tanzi V (1983) The underground economy in the United States: annual estimates, 1930–1980. IMF Staff Pap 30(2):283–305

Timmer M, Ypma G, Bart Van der Ark B (2003) IT in the European Union: driving productivity divergence? Res. Memo. 200363, Groningen Growth and Development Centre, University of Groningen

The Question of Growth

4

This chapter focuses on the development of the Greek economy and particularly on the quality of life in Greece. The question of the level of growth of the Greek society and therefore the efficiency of the economic model in terms of human happiness is approached through three perspectives. The first is based on an examination of indicators that represent the levels of "happy life years"; the second on the examination of the convergence of basic socio-economic indicators with their respective levels in groups of target countries; and finally, the third approach makes use of some research findings concerning the perception of the future and consumer trust.

This chapter is organised as follows: Sect. 4.1 addresses the issue of human development and the measurement of happiness and life satisfaction. Section 4.2 presents the convergence of the Greek economy with the goals of the Lisbon Strategy in comparison with the EU-27 and Northern European countries. Finally, Sect. 4.3 discusses the key question of this chapter and summarises some conclusions.

4.1   The Issue of Human Development

The exclusive focus on indicators of economic growth obscures the true picture of an economy's performance as regards its actual purpose, which is to enable a certain standard of living.

In the 1990s, the United Nations Development Programme (UNDP) created the Human Development Index (HDI) in order to clearly and precisely measure development levels because the per capita GDP presents some shortcomings in quantitative measurements. The complete HDI used considers the years of life expectancy, the literacy level, the education level and, of course, the per capita GDP.

Based on this index, in 2007 Greece held the 24th position out of 177 countries. This result is quite satisfactory when we consider the process of growth and

P. Petrakis, *The Greek Economy and the Crisis*,
DOI 10.1007/978-3-642-21175-1_4, © Springer-Verlag Berlin Heidelberg 2012

development of the Greek economy that had to occur to achieve this result. Indeed, Greek society is very close to highly developed countries, and its position, at least until 2007, has shown significant improvement. Its ranking presents a notable distance from neighbouring Balkan countries, rendering Greece a particularly attractive example for these countries.

We should take these conclusions seriously as objective evidence when evaluating the course of economic policy and growth of the Greek economy.

We wonder, however, if these conclusions apply when happiness is linked with growth (Sen 1999). We should note that the measurement of pessimism and confidence in the future in Greek society seem to be approaching an all-time low, which raises some concern. The key question is whether the economic model applied in the Greek economy in the post-war (after 1953) and especially the post-junta period (after 1974) has helped to improve the quality of life (happiness) of people living in Greece.

This discussion covers what Easterlin (1995, 2005) termed the "Easterlin paradox," according to which per capita growth of production does not always improve or maintain quality of life, although average happiness has shown no remarkable increase in recent decades. Perhaps this paradox relates not only to per capita GDP but also to the HDI, mainly if we take into account the criticism that it essentially fails to consider the qualitative dimensions of life. Research on this possibility has been conducted mainly by two institutions.

The first is the OECD, which has developed what it terms "social cohesion indicators" that include several items relating to quality of life: for example, life satisfaction, job satisfaction, crime rates and suicide rates. These indices are compiled based on the Gallup World Poll. The "life satisfaction" index is shown in Fig. 4.1, and its change in the period of 2000–2006 is shown in Fig. 4.2.

On this basis, we find that:

(a) Life satisfaction is higher in richer OECD countries and notably (in order of priority) in Denmark, Finland, the Netherlands and Norway. Italy, Portugal, and Greece ranked below average.

(b) Life satisfaction improves over time. In particular, in the years 2000–2006, the countries showing remarkable improvement were Turkey, Finland, the Netherlands, Italy, and Greece.

The second institution studying this issue is the Erasmus University of Rotterdam, and in particular R. Veenhoven.[1] The university has developed a World Database of Happiness from 1946 to the present. The overall conclusion of Veenhoven and Hagerty (2003, 2006) is that average happiness shows a slight increase, but it certainly has grown in rich nations, as well as in many of the poorer nations for which data are available.

---

[1] The OECD states Veenhoven's database as the source of its variables (World Database of Happiness, Distributional Findings in Nations, Erasmus University Rotterdam) (http://worlddadabaseofhappiness.eur.nl).

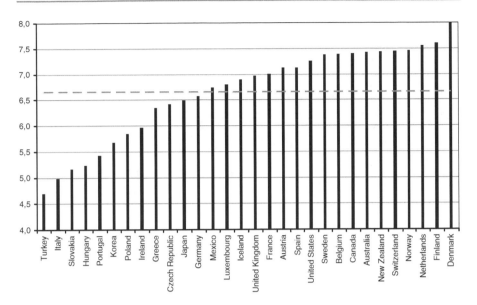

Fig. 4.1 "Satisfaction with life" in OECD countries (2006) (Source: OECD, Society at a Glance, 2009)

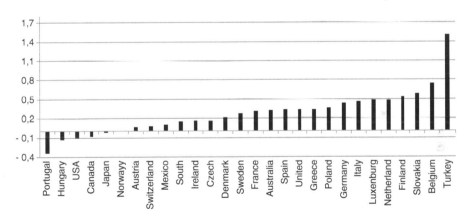

Fig. 4.2 Change of "life satisfaction" (Source: OECD, Society at a Glance, 2009)

In particular, data on human happiness are gathered based on the question: "Taking into account all issues, would you say you are very happy or less happy?" Citizens answered the question on a scale from 1 to 10. The data were collected from the Gallup World Poll and are available until 2008.

The rankings of countries based on their responses are shown in Table 4.1, column (1). We can then calculate the variable "Happy life years," which combines the concept of life satisfaction and life expectancy (life satisfaction multiplied by

Table 4.1 "Life satisfaction" and "happy life years"

	Level of "life satisfaction," 2000–2008 (ranking of 144 countries) (1)	"Happy life years" (2000–2009) (2)	Mean change of "happiness" (until 2006) (3)
Denmark	2	65	Steady state (since 1975)
Greece	48–53	51.5	Small increase (since 1982)
Spain	21–24	58.8	Increase (since 1981)
Italy	34–37	54.4	Small increase (since 1981)
Norway	8–11	62.4	Small decrease (since 1985)
Netherlands	13–15	60.6	Small increase (since 1976)
Portugal	72–78	44.6	Small increase (since 1990)
Sweden	8–11	62.8	Steady state (since 1972)

Source: Veenhoven (2009-2d). http://www.worlddatabaseofhappiness.eur.nl/index.html.

life expectancy). The results appear in column (2) of the same table. Finally, based on available comparable data, we estimated the average change in "happiness" as shown in column (3) of the same table.

Table 4.1 reveals the following:

(a) The level of happiness in Northern European countries is very high, ranking them in positions 2–15 (the highest worldwide), while the level of happiness in Mediterranean countries is around the middle of the rankings, in positions 21–78; of this group of countries, Spain is in a relatively better position and Portugal in the worst.

(b) The indicator "happy life years" (column 2) gives similar messages to those inferred from the level of satisfaction with life. Northern European countries have from 60.6 to 65 "happy life years," whereas Mediterranean countries vary from 44.6 (Portugal) to 58.8 (Spain).

(c) The average happiness between 1973 and 2008 shows fluctuations. Northern European countries (except Norway), as well as Italy, Spain and Portugal, have improved their positions. The situation of Greek society has shown little improvement since 1982, in line with OECD data. We know that both sources of information use data from the Gallup World Poll. Of course, the Veenhoven index refers to "happy life years," and the third column of Table 4.1 shows the average change in the "happiness" of countries, whereas the OECD refers to "life satisfaction." These may be relatively different concepts, with the second being less "ambitious" than the first. Considering that the HDI index marks a positive change in the same period, we accept that "life satisfaction" has increased in Greek society, albeit moderately, although we have seen that the relevant OECD index score appears to be lower than the average score of OECD countries (OECD-Society at a Glance 2009).

The indices monitored by the Eurobarometer also relate to the issue of people's satisfaction with their lives, focusing on their expectations. Clearly, the continual pessimism of individuals and, by extension, of their society, is a sign of poor quality of life.

Portugal presents the highest pessimism about the future of the three Mediterranean countries (Greece, Spain, Portugal). In contrast, Northern European countries, namely Denmark, show the most positive expectations of all countries, even during 2008, a year dominated by pessimism in all areas. Typically, as can be seen in Table 4.2, the Netherlands and Denmark are among the most optimistic countries on questions relating to expectations about the economy. On the contrary, in Greece and Portugal, the mood is generally pessimistic. Especially for Greece, the drop in the indicators from 2000 to 2010 is impressive.

Moreover, the evaluation of the personal financial situation is very positive in Northern European countries, in contrast to the Mediterranean. In general, the prevailing view in Northern European countries is that the national financial situation is better than the European average. The opposite happens in Mediterranean countries.

Important conclusions can also be derived from the Consumer Confidence Index (CCI), arising from the data of the European Directorate General for Economic and Financial Affairs (DG ECFIN), for the period from 1985 onwards. It can be considered that this index provides the same information as these that count the optimism/pessimism.

The consistently positive growth rates of the Greek economy in the period from 1994 onwards, which rely heavily on private consumption, were expected to lead to increased optimism of consumers/households. However, according to the CCI index, this is not the case.

Figure 4.3 shows the time series of the index for Greece and the Eurozone and the trend in the Greek economy, in combination with the periods of economic slowdown or recession in both regions. The index is calculated based on expectations about the economy and the overall economic situation of households and levels of unemployment and savings in the following 12 months. The intention of consumption concerns the consumption of durable goods rather than simple consumer essentials in the following 12 months.

The main conclusion of the above figure is that, in the examined period, Greek households were consistently more pessimistic than those of the Eurozone. The long-term trend in the Greek economy is clearly negative, whereas no clear long-term downward trend is observed in the Eurozone, although it appears that EU households are more pessimistic (rather than optimistic) as CCI balances are negative for the examined period. Thus, almost throughout the 25-year period, the CCI index for Greece is lower than that for the EU, with a difference of up to about 34% points. The difference between the two regions appears to increase slowly, but steadily (by around 0.05% per month). However, the CCI index of Greece seems to converge over certain short periods with that of the EU (1993–1994, 1996–1997, and 2004–2005). Finally, it appears that in times of recession, the CCI index shows a downward trend in the Eurozone, whereas a similar trend is not clear in Greece.

Table 4.2 Positive expectations for the next 12 months

	Life in general						National economy						Personal finances					
	1995 (%)	2000 (%)	2004 (%)	2008 (%)	2009 (%)	2010 (%)	1995 (%)	2000 (%)	2004 (%)	2008 (%)	2009 (%)	2010 (%)	1995 (%)	2000 (%)	2004 (%)	2008 (%)	2009 (%)	2010 (%)
EU-27	33	34	35	24	26	24	19	23	19	15	28	24	22	27	25	18	21	19
Netherlands	34	31	27	22	28	27	31	23	20	13	42	32	30	30	20	16	19	21
Denmark	32	32	39	34	32	34	25	18	21	21	45	42	30	26	28	29	26	26
Greece	36	43	37	28	29	11	18	28	14	7	24	8	28	34	22	13	24	7
Spain	36	38	41	26	31	26	23	25	23	18	27	26	25	27	30	22	27	21
Portugal	35	29	23	10	15	15	29	17	12	7	18	15	26	22	15	7	13	13

Source: European Commission, Public Opinion, Eurobarometer

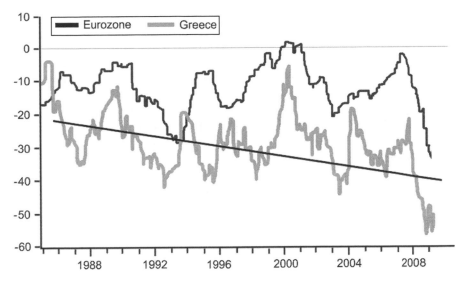

Fig. 4.3 Consumer confidence index in the EU and Greece. (Source: EFG Eurobank Research (September 2009))

4.2   Examination of the Greek Economy's Convergence with the European Union

The debate at the European level regarding the formulation of what is termed the Lisbon Strategy (2008) determined the indices that are to be used to assess the convergence of European economies.[2] These indicators are representative of the level of economic growth of economies and, in particular, of the economic, social, educational and environmental standards in each country. Consequently, they are representative of the most important aspects of an economy's growth.

---

[2] The convergence or divergence of financial indices from the target and the speed of adjustment to this are examined using an appropriate econometric model. The basic form of regression used for the purposes of this analysis is $\left[\frac{x_t^i}{avg\,\bar{x}_t} \times 100 - 100\right] = \gamma\left[\frac{x_{t-1}^i}{avg\,\bar{x}_{t-1}} \times 100 - 100\right]$, which is adjusted each time to the needs of the study, depending on whether the achievement of the target concerns its approach in relation to Northern European countries or in relation to all EU members. In the analysis of variables, where xit are the variables referring to the Lisbon economic indicators (LI), for targets we have set a value of 100. The rate or speed of convergence (v) – which is the object of our research - is extrapolated from the relation $v = -\ln\gamma$. If the result of this relation is negative, this implies that we find the annual rate of divergence, while a positive result means that we calculate the annual rate of convergence. This relation is valid if we assume that the variables are subject to constant change in the time vector examined. The methodology developed is based on the work by Meliciani and Peracchi (2006).

Indicators L1–L12 are the convergence criteria indicators derived from the Lisbon Treaty. The other indicators (L13–L22) derive from the Lisbon goals for education.

The conclusions drawn from the study of these indicators on the state of Greece in relation to the average of the EU-27 and the Northern European countries are summarised below. For the sake of brevity, in the ensuing analysis, these indicators will be presented followed by the abbreviation L (Lisbon) and the code number 1–22, depending on the index. The variables describing the indicators and targets come from the Eurostat database.[3]

Among the key indicators that reflect the economic performance and progress of a country is per capita GDP (L1). Apart from the index of the average (absolute) level of wealth in a society, it also serves as an approach to quality of life. Greece, despite lagging behind in absolute per capita income, shows a strong trend towards convergence. Greece's divergence from Northern European countries is much greater than its divergence from the EU-27 average. It is noteworthy that for the last year for which data are available (2007), Greece almost fully converged with the EU-27 average. The speed of convergence with the EU-27 average is much greater than the speed at which Greece approaches the performance of Northern European countries.

Regarding the indicators on employment, we focus on the following: "labour productivity (broken down by gender)" (L2), "levels of employment (broken down by gender)" (L3), "employment of older people" (L4) and "percentage of long-term unemployed (broken down by gender)" (L10). Regarding "labour productivity" (L2), Greece made rapid progress over the last decade. Specifically, since 2002 it has converged with the productivity levels of the EU-27 and actually surpassed them after 2003. Moreover, despite the shortfall in previous years compared with Northern European countries, in 2008 Greece reached their productivity levels, a striking and potentially promising achievement if combined with similar development initiatives with the potential to exploit such a comparative advantage.

In "employment levels" (L3), Greece presents a declining course compared with other EU-27 members. Specifically, while in the 1990s it showed employment levels much higher than the EU-27 average, the negative performance recorded over the last decade of the twentieth century made it fall under the EU average, and, by 2007, it had not been able to surpass this. Furthermore, compared with Northern European countries, Greece's course is stagnant, as it has shown no significant fluctuations in the period of 1992–2007 for which data are available. However, a more thorough examination of the data shows that both the divergence from Northern European countries and its negative trend in relation to the EU-27 are due solely to the rapidly deteriorating position of women's levels of employment. Thus, the main conclusion arising from the study of this index is that Greece falls significantly short in employment compared with the two groups of countries only for women.

---

[3] http://epp.eurostat.ec.europa.eu.

The "employment of older people" (L4) indicator reflects the active involvement of older individuals in the economy, when this involvement diminishes or stops, but perhaps also the capabilities and efficiency of these individuals, which, if low, renders the older population less competitive and less preferable in the working environment. The importance of this indicator, however, may be twofold. People who are retired or near retirement age may not be working because society has no need for them to do so. For example, in Greek society, the institution of the family sometimes replaces or supersedes such needs. The older generation usually support the younger generation in starting a family and in the upbringing of their children (and thus, their economic activity remains in the shadow) and in return may not receive a salary but other necessary material considerations (care, medication, nursing home). Greece's performance in this index shows a decline after 1995. Significantly, this was the year when Greece reached the target level of the Northern European countries for the employment of older persons. As noted for the variables analysed above, the deviation from Northern European countries is significantly greater than the deviation from the EU-27 average.

The last convergence index using employment as a criterion is "the percentage of long-term unemployed (broken down by gender)" (L10). Greece has the highest percentage of long-term unemployed compared with both groups of countries used as reference points. Specifically, the data reveal a greater deviation from Northern European countries than from the EU-27 average. It is noteworthy that during the period of 2000–2004, Greece deviated significantly and increasingly from the levels of long-term unemployment in Northern European countries. As regards unemployment in men, although the pace is very slow, Greece could theoretically reach the level of European countries by 2010, while absolute convergence with Northern European countries is estimated to occur by 2022. Compared to men, the calculation of the convergence rate for long-term unemployment among women in Greece is disproportionately pessimistic. Compared with both groups of countries, this index diverges systematically.

Regarding the indicators reflecting the state of the economy and how it develops, compared with the two examined groups of countries, we also analyse the courses of three additional indicators. The index L7 concerns convergence in relative price levels, as calculated by the variable "purchasing power parity." The relevant data show that Greece is in the process of convergence with both groups of countries. Convergence with Northern European countries is taking place at almost the same speed as convergence with the EU-27 average. However, as expected, the absolute distance to the first group of countries is greater.

"Private investment" (L8), a key indicator of growth and development, is calculated as the gross fixed capital formed by the private sector as a percentage of GDP. The pattern observed is quite different from that of the previous variables. Specifically, Greece shows better performance than the European average. Although, compared to Northern European countries, Greece's lag is evident, it is converging steadily.

The last of the economic indicators of increased importance, however, is the "population percentage at the threshold of poverty" (L9). Based on available data,

Greece diverges significantly from both the European average and that of Northern Europe. The statistical analysis shows that Greece may soon fully converge with the EU-27 average, whereas the corresponding convergence with Northern European countries is expected to need at least another two decades.

The crucial contribution of training and education in general to the formation of human capital and, through that, to the economic development and growth of a society, requires the careful consideration and study of these issues to understand the direction and potency of their influences. Below, we analyse the indicators relevant to education and its performance in Greece compared to European and Northern European countries.

The first indicator we examine is L5, the "percentage of population aged 20–24 having completed at least secondary education," which shows Greece's favourable position over the two comparison groups of countries. This observation also applies to the separate categories of men and women.

The next indicator concerns the "percentage of people leaving the educational process early" (L13). According to the objectives of the Lisbon Treaty, this percentage should not exceed 10%. Although this figure for Greece was 25% in 1992–1993, the steady process of convergence and the positive performance of students brought Greece close to the target (13%) by 2004–2007. Thus, its performance is slightly better than the EU-27 average and slightly worse than that of Northern European countries.

Regarding the indicator L14, which refers to "persons who have knowledge of reading, mathematics and science" (Lisbon Treaty objective: 15%), we observe that Greece fares better than both reference groups (EU-27 and North European countries). Specifically, for the whole of the examined period (1995–2007), Greece has shown a decline of around 3% points, from 30% at the beginning of the period; however, other countries stand at 22% (EU-27) and 19% (Northern European countries).

Due to the different classifications of the two groups of indicators (main indicators L1–L12 and educational indicators L13–L22), the indicator L5 is repeated as L15 in the educational category. For this reason, an analysis of L15 is not considered appropriate at this point.

The next considered convergence indicator regarding education is the "percentage of adults participating in lifelong learning" (L16). The aim of the Lisbon Treaty was to exceed 12.5% in 2010. The picture presented by Greece in this context is daunting. Unlike the 25% for Northern European countries and the 9% EU-27 average, in 2007, Greece barely succeeded in demonstrating positive rates for participation in lifelong learning. These rates hardly exceeded 1%!

The next indicator is that of "linguistic skills" (L17). Greece's performance is ahead of the two groups of countries, with a large difference from the EU-27 average. In this index, Greece has by far surpassed the target of the Lisbon Treaty.

Concerning convergence in "skills in new technologies" (L18), Greece's performance falls short. In fact, it appears that, since 1995, its performance has been continually decreasing at a rather accelerating rate. Especially compared to the EU-27 average, while Greece was far above the target in the middle of the last decade of the twentieth century, in 2001, it fell below the target for the first time during this period and continued its downward trend. This downward trend explains not only its poor performance but also its expected further divergence.

The next indicator examines convergence in "university graduates" (L19). This indicator is based on the percentage of the population that is expected to complete studies in higher education. The data show that, during the years 2002–2005, Greece exceeded the EU-27 average, although its performance then decreased to the target level. Compared to Northern European countries, Greece increasingly converged until 2004, but later its performance in this area declined significantly.

As regards the "cross-border mobility of students" (L20), calculated as the percentage of students studying in another EU country besides their country of origin, we observe that Greece exceeds the goal of absolute convergence compared to both Northern European countries and the EU-27. This means that a higher percentage of Greek students study at universities of European Union countries compared with other European citizens. However, tellingly, this indicator shows a steady downward trend.

The "educational level of the population" (L21) is calculated based on the percentage of people aged 18–24 who were students in the years 1992–2007. The results of the empirical analysis suggest Greece's convergence with the EU-27 average and the corresponding Northern European average. Thus, despite the initial poor educational attainment of the population, there is a gradual improvement in relation to EU and Northern European countries.

The latest available education indicator refers to "investment in education and training" (L22). The analysis of the relevant data shows that although Greece has improved its position in relation to the two groups of countries, it still lags in the process of absolute convergence.

Generally, we observe in relation to education indicators that Greece presents a relatively better image in contrast to its performance in economic indicators. Specifically, regarding the indicators "knowledge of reading, mathematics and science" (L14), "completion of secondary education" (L15), "language skills" (L17), and "transborder student traffic" (L20), Greece ranks higher than both reference groups.

The convergence indicators we examine include three that do not belong to two categories discussed above. First, we analyse the indicator "expenditure on research and development" (L6), calculated as a percentage of GDP. According to Eurostat, Greece lags significantly in this category in relation to both the EU-27 and Northern Europe. The study of the data highlights Greece's poor position and its slow convergence. According to calculations, it requires 60 years to reach full convergence in research and development.

The next indicator concerns "greenhouse gas emissions" (L11). We note that Greece diverges from the levels of pollutants of EU and Northern European countries; the gap is greater in relation to Northern European countries than to the EU-27 average.

Finally, we examine convergence on "energy intensity" (L12). This indicator is calculated as the "percentage of each kilo of oil per 1,000 Euro." In the field of energy intensity, Greece ranks well below the two groups of comparison countries. In particular, Greece uses much less energy, which may, to a certain degree, be due to its limited heavy industry.

Table 4.3 presents estimates based on Eurostat data for the convergence of Greece in individual convergence indicators in relation to EU-27 and Northern European countries. These estimates do not take into consideration the global crisis of 2008 and the ensuing events, including the developments in 2010 and the CSM measures.

The conclusion from the study of the above as regards Greece's convergence in the relevant indicators is that regardless of the classification category of the indicators, first, Greece diverges more in relation to Northern European countries than it does in relation to the EU-27 average. Namely, its performance is much lower compared to Northern Europe than it is in relation to all other EU countries. Secondly, the speed of convergence with Northern European countries is lower than that observed with the EU-27 average. Thirdly, Greece's shortfall is noted especially in terms of economic and environmental indicators, while the performance of education in Greece is satisfactory and, as mentioned earlier, in many cases, its indicators surpass those of both groups of reference countries.

4.3   The Question of Quality of Life and Development

The question of quality of life, which emerges in this chapter as the final aim of the process of economic development, leads to some new questions and conclusions:

1. We can distinguish (Table 4.4) between two distinct reference fields in the examination of convergence: one presenting remote convergence and one presenting divergence. The two groups of indicators, however, forming the two reference fields, share a feature. They bring to light the weaknesses in the development process, which is exactly what society seeks to reveal.

   The reference field (remote convergence) includes indicators such as women's employment, expenditures on research and development, the overall poverty rate and the percentage of unemployed men. The second reference field (divergence) covers the total employment of people aged 55–64, the employment of women aged 55–64, the percentage of both men and women living in poverty, the overall percentage of unemployed people, the percentage of unemployed women, the emission of greenhouse gases and energy intensity.

2. The OECD indicator on "life satisfaction" shows an improvement in the Greek economy, although Greek society is placed below the average of the OECD countries.

3. The Veenhoven "happy life years" indicator of 1981 also shows a slight improvement in the "happiness" of the Greek society.

4. Indicators of expectations and optimism for the future show a systematic – and impressive – deterioration in Greece.

5. Consumer confidence, as shown by the CCI, presents a negative trend from 1985 onwards, indirectly reflecting the structural problems of the Greek economy.

Table 4.3 Conclusions on convergence regarding the Lisbon indicators (economic, educational, others)

Group of countries	Variable	Available years of data	Year of convergence (based on the same speed of convergence)	Group of countries	Available years of data	Year of convergence (based on the same speed of convergence)
EU-27	GDP per capita (L1)	1998–2008	2009	Northern European countries	1996–2008	2014
	Labour productivity (L2)	2003–2008	Achieved target		1996–2008	Achieved target
	Total employment rate (L3)	1993–2007	2008		1993–2007	2013
	Employment rate, men (L3)	1993–2007	Achieved target		1993–2007	Achieved target
	Employment rate, women (L3)	1993–2007	2026		1993–2007	2031
	Total employment rate, 55–64 (L4)	1993–2007	2008		1993–2007	Deviation
	Employment rate, men 55–64 (L4)	1993–2007	2008		1993–2007	2008
	Employment rate, women 55–64 (L4)	1993–2007	2011		1993–2007	Deviation
	Total level of education, 20–24 (L5)	1993–2007	Achieved target		1993–2007	Achieved target
	Level of education, men 20–24 (L5)	1993–2007	Achieved target		1993–2007	Achieved target
	Level of education, women 20–24 (L5)	1993–2007	Achieved target		1993–2007	Achieved target
	Expenditure on research and development (L6)	1991–2006	2068		1991–2007	2080
	Relative price levels (L7)	1996–2007	2012		1996–2007	2014
	Private investments (L8)	2004–2007	Achieved target		1992–2007	2014
	Total poverty rate (L9)	2003–2006	2007		1996–2007	2028
	Poverty rate, men (L9)	2003–2006	2007		1996–2007	Deviation
	Poverty rate, women (L9)	2003–2006	2007		1996–2007	Deviation
	Total unemployment rate (L10)	1995–2007	2023		1993–2007	Deviation
	Percentage of unemployed men (L10)	1995–2007	2010		1993–2007	2022
	Percentage of unemployed women (L10)	1995–2007	Deviation		1993–2007	Deviation
	Greenhouse gas emissions (L11)	1997–2006	Deviation		1991–2007	Deviation
	Energy intensity (L12)	1991–2005	2017		1991–2007	Deviation

(continued)

Table 4.3 (continued)

Group of countries	Variable	Available years of data	Year of convergence (based on the same speed of convergence)	Group of countries	Available years of data	Year of convergence (based on the same speed of convergence)
EU-27	People leaving education early (L13)	1992–2007	2010	Northern European countries	1992–2007	2012
	Knowledge of reading, mathematics and science (L14)	1995–2007	Achieved target		1995–2007	Achieved target
	Percentage of young people who have completed at least secondary education (L15)	1992–2007	2009		1992–2007	2009
	Adult participation in lifelong learning (L16)	1992–2007	2017		1992–2007	2065
	Language skills (L17)	1995–2007	Achieved target		1995–2007	Achieved target
	Skills in new technologies (L18)	1995–2007	2009		1995–2007	Deviation
	Graduates of higher education (L19)	1998–2006	Achieved target		1998–2006	2009
	Transborder student traffic (L20)	1995–2007	Achieved target		1995–2007	Achieved target
	Educational level of the population (L21)	1992–2007	2009		1992–2007	2012
	Investment in education and training (L22)	1992–2007	2009		1992–2007	2020

Essentially, the above data show that the achievement of improved material living standards in Greek society was financed through credit. This general conclusion about the modern proportionate change in per capita production and the subjective perception of happiness in Greek society is consistent with earlier work (Stevenson and Wolfers 2008) that finds a clear, positive relationship between the two variables and their changes. However, as Greek society began to approach the limited capacity of the economic model that had been followed since the 1980s at breakneck pace, Greece passed into a period of pessimism and failure to "incorporate" material happiness.

The social awareness that critical indicators expressing substantial elements of social cohesion (e.g., employment of older people, poverty, and total unemployment rate) showed a remote convergence or divergence trend compared to societies that were considered as reference points contributed to this pessimism. It should also be noted that these findings do not include the real effects of the 2008–2010 crisis, which would magnify the differences and divergences.

Therefore, the development model followed by the Greek economy has expressed its finite nature in a variety of manners. In socio-economic terms, the Greek society seems to accept a change to the terms of its economic operation

Table 4.4 Convergence

	Convergence	Remote convergence or divergence
Convergence with the EU-27	Per capita GDP	
	Labour productivity	
		Employment of women (remote convergence)
	Total employment rate	
	Level of education	
		Expenditure on research and development (very remote convergence)
	Relative price levels	
	Private investment	
	Poverty rate	
		Total unemployment rate (remote convergence)
		Unemployed women (divergence)Greenhouse gas emissions (divergence)
Convergence with Northern European countries	Per capita GDP	
	Labour productivity	
	Total employment rate	
		Employment of women (remote convergence)
		Total employment from 1955 to 1964 (divergence)
		Employment of women 55–64 (divergence)
	Total educational level	
	Level of education, men 20–24	
	Level of education, women 20–24	
		Expenditure on research and development (very remote convergence)
	Relative price levels	
		Poverty rate (remote convergence)
		Poverty, men (divergence)
		Poverty, women (divergence)
		Total unemployment rate (divergence – relatively remote convergence)
		Unemployed women (divergence)
		Emissions of polluting gases (divergence)
	Energy intensity	

model provided that the conditions for a substantial improvement in quality of life are created. A change that would promise confidence in the future and optimisation of human happiness, provided, of course, that it also promises to expand the improvement of per capita GDP, would be embraced. This view is based on the simple observation that the continued deterioration of the relevant indicators in recent decades can only give way to an improvement, but not necessarily immediately.

References

Easterlin R (1995) Will raising the income of all increase the happiness of all? J Econ Behav Organ 27:35–48

Easterlin R (2005) Feeding the illusion of growth and happiness: a reply to Hagerty and Veenhoven. Soc Indic Res 74:429–443

Meliciani V, Peracchi F (2006) Convergence in per-capita GDP across European regions: a reappraisal. Empir Econ 31:549–568

Sen A (1999) Development as freedom. Alfred A. Knopf, New York

Stevenson B, Wolfers J (2008) Economic Growth and Subjective Well-Being: Reassessing the Easterlin Paradox, CESifo Working Paper Series 2394, CESifo Group Munich

Veenhoven R (2009) Distributional findings in nations. World database of happiness. Erasmus Univ., Rotterdam

Veenhoven R, Hagerty M (2003) Wealth and happiness revisited – growing national income does go with greater happiness. Soc Indic Res 64:1–27

Veenhoven R, Hagerty M (2006) Rising happiness in nations 1694–2004: a reply to Easterlin. Soc Indic Res 79:421–436

Human Capital: Education, Innovation and Health

5

The evolution of economic thought from the 1950s onwards underlines the need to give due attention to the issue and the importance of human capital. Human capital, although intangible, is an important contributor to growth and incorporates a variety of features, such as knowledge, education, health and innovation. This Section of the book approaches the concept of human capital through the examination of the quantitative and qualitative production of the educational system, the relation between the produced result and innovation, the degree of utilisation of human capital by the economy, the innovativeness of the production system and, finally, its robustness.

Section 5.1 presents quantitative data on participation in education, while Sect. 5.2 presents the qualitative results for the educational system. Section 5.3 describes the relation between levels of education and the labour market, while Sect. 5.4 addresses the second major problem of the Greek higher education system and the relation between research and innovation. Section 5.5 presents the sources of education funding, followed by an evaluation of the degree of utilisation of human resources by the productive system (Sect. 5.6). Section 5.7 examines the innovative activity of Greek companies, and Sect. 5.8 presents some measurements of the views of citizens of various countries about their physical and mental health.

5.1 The Quantitative Dimension of Education

The OECD figures for the mid-2000s reveal a significant shortfall of the Mediterranean countries in the education of their overall populations as compared to Northern European countries (OECD-Education at a glance, 2009).

Two main issues that cause a bias in the indicators are noteworthy. On one hand, Greece enjoys high percentage of the population with primary and secondary education. On the other hand, a relatively small percentage of the population has completed higher education, representing the second lowest rate compared to other countries. Thus, Greece's problem compared to other Mediterranean countries and, to a much greater extent, to Northern European countries, seems to be the generally low education level of the entire population.

P. Petrakis, *The Greek Economy and the Crisis*,
DOI 10.1007/978-3-642-21175-1_5, © Springer-Verlag Berlin Heidelberg 2012

Greece and other Mediterranean countries – with the exception of Spain – fall short especially regarding the percentage of the population aged 25–64 with a high level of education. Tellingly, in 2007, the corresponding rate for Greece was 19.2%, while the average was 27.86% for Northern European countries and 12% for Italy and Portugal (Eurostat-Labour Force Survey, 2008). The higher rates of education of the countries of the Scandinavian Peninsula lead to long-term comparative advantages and confirm the higher average education and training levels enjoyed by these countries. Therefore, the Northern European economies have a significant competitive advantage that is incorporated in labour productivity.

This finding highlights the weak position of Greece, which, despite benefiting from a marked increase of the rate by 5% age points over the period of 2000–2007, still has one of the lowest percentages of the population with a high level of education.

However, as regards the rates for participation in education of the 20- to 29-year old age group, Greece has made spectacular progress compared to other Mediterranean countries. In 2007, it was first among Mediterranean countries and higher than the EU-19 average, exceeding 25% (OECD-Education at a Glance, 2009). It is also worth noting the gap in participation rates compared with the countries of Northern Europe, especially Finland and Denmark. Although Greece has made great progress in education participation rates for the 20- to 29-year old age group, it lags significantly behind Northern European countries, more so in absolute figures than in terms of growth rates.

Based on recent trends, the characteristics of the education level for the entire population in Greece are not expected to change dramatically until 2025. According to the projections in Table 5.1 and the actual figures for 2005, we observe that the percentage of tertiary graduates is low compared with the Northern European countries and Spain, whereas they remain at low levels in Italy and Portugal. The percentage of graduates in the total population is expected to increase over the next 15 years; however, the deviation from Northern European countries for the 25- to 64-year-old age group is also expected to increase. These forecasts are not very

Table 5.1 Percentage of tertiary graduates in total population, 2005 and 2025 (projected)

	2005					2025 (20-year trend)				
	25–64[a]	25–34	35–44	45–54	55–64	25–64	25–34	35–44	45–54	55–64
Denmark	34	40	35	32	27	48	47	58	47	41
Finland	35	38	41	34	27	49	43	59	48	47
Ireland	29	41	30	22	17	46	59	53	42	31
Netherlands	30	35	30	30	24	39	40	43	40	34
Sweden	30	37	28	28	25	35	45	40	33	24
Greece	21	25	26	19	12	27	32	29	24	23
Italy	12	16	13	11	8	17	21	23	17	13
Spain	28	40	30	22	14	45	58	52	44	33
Portugal	13	19	13	10	7	18	27	22	15	10

Source: OECD-Education at a Glance, 2009
[a]Age groups

Table 5.2 Actual and projected participation in tertiary education according to recent trends

	Tertiary education				Indicator (base year 2004)		
	2005	2015	2020	2025	2015	2020	2025
Denmark	208	289	296	285	139	142	137
Finland	224	237	225	221	106	100	99
Ireland	169	158	179	215	94	106	128
Netherlands	515	640	681	726	124	132	141
Sweden	295	389	325	333	132	110	113
Greece	647	593	605	639	92	94	99
Italy	2,015	2,236	2,402	2,566	111	119	127
Spain	1,678	1,393	1,409	1,589	83	84	95

Source: OECD-Education at a Glance, 2009
Note: On the left, the base year is 2000 = 100, and on the right, the base year is 2004 = 100

encouraging as we observe that Greece appears to be ill-situated to meet future needs; if verified, these forecasts are expected to have an immediate impact on the economy's potential for growth and development.

Regarding projections for participation in tertiary education, recent trends and evidence suggest that a decrease in the absolute number of students should have been expected, whereas in all other comparison countries (except Spain) presented in Table 5.2, the forecasts are more optimistic, and the expected increase is significant. The comparison can be better understood by using the indicator shown in the last three columns of Table 5.2, which sets 2004 as the base year. The size of the indicator shows the percentage change in tertiary education participation in relation to the base year.

In contrast to the characterisation of Greece in terms of the indicators previously presented, secondary education graduation rates appear to have improved significantly. Among the examined countries, Greece ranks first for men and second for women after Finland and, on the whole, ranks second, with a difference of just one percentage point from the top-ranked county, Finland. This feature, if studied in conjunction with the graduation rates from tertiary education given below rather than in isolation suggests that the problem of the relatively low educational level of the entire population does not apply to secondary education.

The issue, therefore, of encouraging the completion of education in an effort to improve the educational attainment, expertise and skills of the overall population of Greece is reduced mainly to a problem related to higher education, its orientation, and – mainly – the three points that are analysed below: (a) the completion of studies by students, (b) the implementation of a timeframe for the completion of their studies and (c) the almost complete absence of lifelong education.

Tellingly, Greece occupies the last position in the ranking of tertiary graduation rates among European countries,[1] according to OECD data (OECD-Education at a

---

[1] This concerns the sum of tertiary education graduates in 2007 as a percentage of the expected number of graduates (based on enrolments) for the same year.

Table 5.3 Percentage of participation of the 25- to 64-year-old age group in lifelong learning

	2001	2006
Denmark	18.4	29.2
Finland	17.2	23.1
Ireland	–	7.5
Netherlands	15.9	15.6
Sweden	17.5	32.1
Greece	1.2	1.9
Italy	4.5	6.1
Spain	4.4	10.4

Source: Eurostat (tsiem051)

Glance, 2009). Greece's great problem in taking measures to encourage the completion of academic studies is obvious. Of the students who were expected to complete their studies in Greece in 2007, only 18% managed to do so, whereas the target proposed by the EU was 40%. Greece lags in performance mainly compared with Northern European countries, which present rates of 40% to 48%, but it also lags significantly behind other Mediterranean countries with rates of 32% to 43%.

The Greek problem of divergence between enrolling and graduating students is probably largely due to the method of admission to higher education. Interested secondary school graduates are required to declare up to 30 or 40 Technological Educational Institutes (TEI) or University departments in which they are interested, in order of preference. Thus, commonly, they enrol in departments that they are not especially interested in and hence have no particular interest in graduating.

The situation is similar for lifelong learning. Participation in lifelong learning, as described in Table 5.3, is defined as the percentage of interviewed people who stated that they participated in some form of education in the last 4 weeks, before the research. Northern European countries present the highest rates for participation in lifelong education and Mediterranean countries the lowest. Greece has the lowest rates among the examined countries (Table 5.3).

5.2   The Qualitative Results of the Education System

This chapter highlights the need for careful analysis of the issue of education not only in quantitative terms, as partially undertaken in the previous part of the chapter, but also from a qualitative viewpoint, because these two criteria – quantity and quality – neither require nor ensure each another. The indicators usually used include, among others, the evaluation of university production, adult life skills and students' skills in using new technologies. It is very important to consider the results of similar secondary education competitions at an international level. Based on their results (test scores), in addition to comparing participation rates, which could relate to ineffective educational systems, these competitions

Table 5.4 Scores of
15-year-old pupils in an
international reading,
mathematics and science
competition in 2009

	Reading	Mathematics	Applied sciences
Sweden	497	494	495
Denmark	495	503	499
Finland	536	541	554
Greece	483	466	470
Italy	486	483	489
Spain	481	483	488
Portugal	489	487	493

Source: PISA, 2009 (OECD (2009). PISA 2009 Results: What
Students Know and Can Do.)

(e.g., PISA[2]) enable the comparison of individual educational processes at a
transnational level (Table 5.4).

However, we note that there is a clear positive correlation between per capita
income and student performance at all three levels of analysis: reading, mathematics
and science (Fig. 5.1). Though causality cannot be established, the correlation
raises suspicions about its bi-directional existence. It is likely that the higher per
capita income that accompanies higher living standards and, according to scientific
studies, is associated with a higher educational level encourages student performance. On the other hand, populations that are characterised by higher levels of
education and specialisation boast more skills and higher productivity, which could
lead to higher per capita income.

Thus, we see that although the results of the PISA survey on the efficiency of
secondary education rank Greece in a relatively low position, when taking into
account economic growth, it appears that, for all three indicators (reading, mathematics, sciences), Greece is in a proportional position. It should be noted that the
indicators measure the productivity of the education development level, which
means that they describe the education gained in both formal and informal (private
tuition support centres) secondary education. This is a particular issue for concern
given the magnitude of the informal education system in Greek society. Essentially,
it appears that the combination of the two systems produces a minimum acceptable
result.

In higher education, relevant performance indicators can include research production (i.e., publications), citations or the overall evaluation of university
institutions. It is significant that of the 29 developed countries (Table 5.5) for
which data are available, Greece holds the 21st position for the indicator of
"scientific articles" per million inhabitants. It is worth noting that Greece is in the
25th place among the same countries in terms of the total annual salaries of
researchers and academic staff of universities. Relating the production cost (salaries
of academic staff) to scientific article production yields a picture of the unit labour
cost of scientific production in the Greek economy. According to this index, Greece
rises to tenth place.

---

[2] PISA: Program for International Student Assessment through common tests.

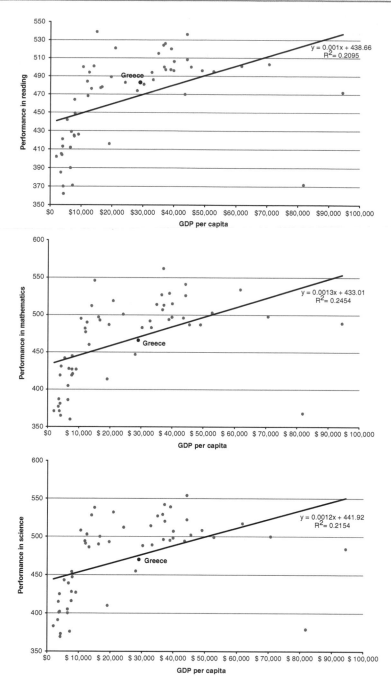

Fig. 5.1 Performance in reading, mathematics and applied sciences in terms of per capita GDP (Source: PISA 2009)

Table 5.5 Cost per publication (unit labour cost)

Annual pay after taxes and social contributions in ppp[a]			Scientific articles per million inhabitants, 2003[b]			Productivity: scientific articles per million inhabitants/pay for researchers		
1	USA	62,793	1	Switzerland	1153.54	1	Finland	0.0272
2	Australia	62,342	2	Sweden	1142.78	2	Sweden	0.0242
3	Japan	61,991	3	Israel	1037.57	3	Denmark	0.0224
4	Austria	60,530	4	Finland	997.89	4	Iceland	0.0207
5	Switzerland	59,902	5	Denmark	981.63	5	Switzerland	0.0192
6	Israel	59,580	6	Netherlands	830.61	6	Norway	0.0174
7	Netherlands	56,721	7	UK	810.83	7	Israel	0.0174
8	Belgium	55,998	8	Australia	791.24	8	UK	0.0153
9	Germany	53,358	9	Norway	731.43	9	Netherlands	0.0146
10	UK	52,776	10	USA	725.60	10	Greece	0.0138
11	Ireland	49,654	11	Iceland	701.76	11	Slovenia	0.0127
12	France	47,550	12	Belgium	636.59	12	Australia	0.0126
13	Sweden	47,143	13	Austria	604.35	13	Italy	0.0125
14	Denmark	43,669	14	Germany	536.90	14	USA	0.0115
15	Norway	41,813	15	France	516.22	15	Belgium	0.0113
16	Spain	38,873	16	Slovenia	485.54	16	France	0.0108
17	Slovenia	37,970	17	Japan	470.34	17	Spain	0.0103
18	Czech Rep.	36,950	18	Ireland	440.49	18	Germany	0.0100
19	Finland	36,646	19	Italy	428.72	19	Austria	0.0099
20	Italy	34,120	20	Spain	400.58	20	Slovakia	0.0095
21	Iceland	33,801	21	Greece	342.00	21	Hungary	0.0089
22	Portugal	33,334	22	Czech Rep.	289.17	22	Ireland	0.0088
23	Hungary	27,692	23	Portugal	251.41	23	Poland	0.0082
24	Turkey	26,250	24	Hungary	247.10	24	Czech Rep.	0.0078
25	Greece	24,668	25	Poland	177.25	25	Japan	0.0075
26	Poland	21,591	26	Slovakia	175.29	26	Portugal	0.0075
27	Slovakia	18,282	27	Turkey	88.02	27	Romania	0.0033
28	China	13,755	28	Romania	45.44	28	Turkey	0.0033
29	Romania	13,489	29	China	22.59	29	China	0.0016

Notes

Assumption: Salaries for Greece are reduced by 20%

Articles are attributed to countries by the author's institutional affiliation at the time of publication. A paper is considered to be co-authored only if its authors have different institutional affiliations or are from separate departments of the same institution (OECD-Science Technology and Industry Scoreboard, 2007, p. 92)

[a]European Commission, Research Directorate-General, Remuneration of Researchers in the Public and Private Sectors, 2007:43 (April)

[b]OECD, Science Technology and Industry Scoreboard, Innovation and performance in the global economy, 2007

Essentially, the production cost of publications in Greece one of the lowest among the examined countries. Thus, these data reveal a highly productive and efficient system of organising research in the Greek higher education system.

The evaluation of effectiveness is slightly different when taking into account the international rankings of universities according to the Times Higher Education (www.timeshighereducation.co.uk). Here, the evaluation is based only partially on research results (33% of the total score), while it takes into account issues such as the attraction of capital from the private sector, the evaluation of teacher and student performance and multi-ethnicity, in which Greek higher education falls short. In Greece, only the University of Athens is included in the list of the top 200 universities in the world from 2007 onwards. More specifically, in 2007 it held the 247th position, 1 year later the penultimate position (200, in a tie with the University of Twente), and, in 2009, it climbed 23 positions (177).

Obviously, the "isolated" Greek language and the legal obligation of hiring teachers who speak Greek plays a major role in the failure to attract foreign students and hence the low score, at least in this evaluation.

Using the evaluation data for 2009, we note that, as shown in Table 5.6, the top 200 universities list includes universities in 32 countries.

Figure 5.2 reveals a positive correlation between the level of a country's development and the number of universities participating in the evaluation per million population. Greece is ranked low on this measure, obviously due to the factors taken into account by the evaluation, as mentioned above, in which Greece probably falls short. It is worth noting that if we limit the analysis (see Fig. 5.2, EU Line) to EU countries, Greece's position is above the trend line.

Table 5.7 shows the percentages of tertiary graduates by field of study for the year 2005. From this table, we see the following:

(a) The percentages of Greek graduates of humanities and arts and social, economic, and legal sciences do not show major differences from other countries or from the average, although an analysis of individual disciplines would be of particular importance.
(b) Greece is significantly ahead in science, mathematics and technology, in which it boasts the highest percentage of graduates after Ireland, with a 5-percentage-point deviation from the average.
(c) In engineering, mechanics, architecture and health and welfare, Greece lags in comparison to all countries in the table. Specifically, it is far below the average, although again the analysis of individual disciplines would be of particular importance. This result confirms that there is now an oversupply of doctors and a great shortage of nurses.
(d) In agricultural and veterinary professions, Greece has the most graduates and the largest deviation from the average compared to other countries.
(e) Finally, in services, Greece presents very high graduate percentages and a 4-percentage-point (upward) deviation from the average.

Thus, all indications point to a noteworthy problem in the orientation of higher education that is linked to the historical roots of educational demand for specific disciplines and the inability to interpret signs that demand should be adjusted (e.g., although there is an oversupply of lawyers, the discipline is in very high demand amongst student applicants). The analysis we have already performed gives several indications that the current graduate production model does not meet the

Table 5.6 Number of universities in the Times Higher Education's top 200 by country

Countries with at least one university in the top 200 list	Number of universities
United States	54
UK	29
Netherlands	11
Japan	11
Canada	11
Germany	10
Australia	9
Switzerland	7
China	6
Belgium	5
Sweden	5
Hong Kong	5
France	4
Korea	4
Denmark	3
New Zealand	3
Israel	3
Ireland	2
India	2
Russia	2
Singapore	2
Norway	2
Austria	1
Greece	1
Spain	1
Italy	1
Finland	1
Thailand	1
South Africa	1
Mexico	1
Malaysia	1
Taiwan	1

Source: Times Higher Education (www.timeshighereducation.co.uk)

requirements of the existing production model, although this conclusion would require a more detailed analysis of the supply and demand for graduates.

An interesting question that arises is whether the new generation of students "corrects" the observed inconsistencies. For this reason, we studied the distribution of students during the year 2005 (Table 5.8).

(a) We note an improvement in Greece's position regarding engineers and architects. The percentage of students in this class is 16.5% of the total, just half of a percentage point from the average.

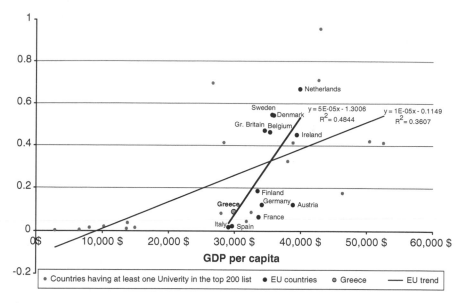

Fig. 5.2 Number of universities in the top 200 list per million population in relation to per capita GDP (Sources: Times Higher Education (www.timeshighereducation.co.uk) and OECD-World Economic Outlook 2010)

(b) Although Greece already had increased graduate percentages in agricultural and veterinary professions, the trend to pursue such studies does not drop but actually rises, approaching 6%.

(c) Although Greece is lagging behind in health and welfare graduates as compared to other countries, the percentage of students in these disciplines is even smaller, 7 percentage points below the average of Mediterranean and Northern European countries.

(d) Finally, as regards services, we note a decrease in the percentage of students in relation to graduates (on the whole), which raises concern.

The above-discussed findings are also important for another reason. According to Baroso (2005), the percentage of graduates per field of study directly affects transaction costs in society. Baroso (2005) concludes that a large percentage of graduates in social sciences, management science and law increases transaction costs and slows economic growth.

5.3   Education and Labour Market

The data on the employment of higher education graduates in Table 5.9 show that Greece holds the fourth highest position for men in relation to scientific or administrative positions, after Finland, the Netherlands and Portugal. For women, the picture is even better, as Greece is in the second position, after the Netherlands.

Table 5.7 Percentage of tertiary graduates by field of study

	Humanities and arts	Social, economic and legal sciences	Physical sciences, mathematics and technology	Mechanics, engineers, architects	Agricultural and veterinary professions	Health and welfare	Services
Denmark	14.2	30.0	8.0	10.0	2.0	24.0	4.0
Ireland	23.3	30.0	16.7	11.7	0.0	10.0	1.7
Netherlands	7.5	37.4	7.5	8.4	1.9	16.8	2.8
Finland	12.8	23.1	7.7	20.5	2.6	17.9	5.1
Sweden	6.9	24.1	8.6	19.0	1.7	24.1	1.7
Greece	13.3	28.3	15.0	11.7	3.3	10.0	8.3
Italy	16.1	39.6	6.7	16.4	1.7	12.1	2.7
Spain	9.0	29.2	10.4	16.7	2.1	14.2	7.6
Portugal	10.0	30.0	11.4	15.7	2.9	21.4	7.1
Average	12.6	30.2	10.2	14.4	2.0	16.7	4.6

Source: Eurostat, Labour Force Survey (data extracted July 2008)

Table 5.8 Percentage of tertiary education students by field of study (2005)

	Humanities and arts	Social, economic and legal sciences	Physical sciences, mathematics and technology	Mechanics, engineers, architects	Agricultural and veterinary professions	Health and welfare	Services
Denmark	15.0	29.8	8.2	10.3	1.4	22.0	2.0
Ireland	16.9	21.8	12.3	10.3	1.3	11.5	4.2
Netherlands	7.9	39.8	7.6	7.9	1.6	15.8	3.0
Finland	14.5	22.3	11.6	26.4	2.3	12.9	4.7
Sweden	12.9	26.5	9.5	16.4	0.8	16.9	1.7
Greece	11.6	31.9	15.7	16.5	5.9	6.9	5.0
Italy	15.7	36.7	7.7	15.9	2.3	12.5	2.5
Spain	10.5	32.2	12.2	17.6	2.3	10.9	5.4
Portugal	8.6	31.4	7.6	21.8	2.0	14.5	5.5
Average	12.6	30.3	10.3	15.9	2.2	13.8	3.8

Source: Eurostat, Labour Force Survey (data extracted July 2008)

Table 5.9 Employment of tertiary education graduates by type of occupation and sex, 2007

		Greece	Spain	Portugal	Italy	Ireland	Netherlands	Denmark	Sweden	Finland
Scientists/business executives	Men	65.5	44.0	70.4	65.4	58.4	69.1	60.4	61.4	69.0
	Women	61.8	45.7	60.2	51.2	56.9	65.2	40.9	52.2	47.1
	Total	63.8	44.8	64.4	58.2	57.6	67.3	50.4	56.2	56.7
Technical professions	Men	15.7	20.2	16.0	23.2	10.1	18.2	23.1	23.1	18.2
	Women	18.7	20.4	24.2	32.3	10.2	19.1	44.8	34.4	31.6
	Total	17.1	20.3	20.8	27.8	10.1	18.6	34.2	29.5	25.7
Clerks/sales staff	Men	11.4	12.6	–	7.6	15.0	7.9	6.7	6.6	4.5
	Women	16.0	27.2	13.5	13.6	28.7	13.9	11.8	11.1	17.9
	Total	13.5	19.6	11.0	10.6	22.1	10.6	9.3	9.1	12.0
Workers	Men	7.3	23.3	–	3.8	–	–	9.1	8.7	8.2
	Women	–	6.6	–	–	–	–	–	–	3.4
	Total	5.6	15.3	–	3.3	9.6	3.4	5.7	5.0	5.5

Source: Eurostat, Labour Force Survey (data extracted July 2008)

Against this background and taking into account the employment percentages of university graduates in other job categories, we see that Greece has a comparatively small percentage of people employed in jobs where their work requirements do not coincide with their qualifications. Only in the third category (clerks, sales staff and services) do we observe relatively higher employment rates of higher education graduates than in Northern European countries.

Therefore, Greece has a particular problem in the employment of tertiary education graduates per employment category compared to countries in the Mediterranean and Northern Europe.

An analysis of Table 5.10 shows that, additionally to age, the second most crucial factor in finding and securing employment in EU countries is qualifications. For example, the employment rate for people with tertiary education is significantly higher than the rate for those with fewer qualifications and a lower educational level. In the 25- to 39-year-old age group, the employment percentage was 20 percentage points higher for university graduates compared to peers with fewer years of education. These differences are even greater among the 40- to 64-year-old age groups with and without higher education.

The analysis of Table 5.10 leads to three main conclusions:

(a) Regarding the employment rates of young people aged 25–39 years in the lowest educational category, we see that, with 72.3%, Greece stands close to the average of other countries, equal to Spain and higher than Sweden, Finland and Ireland.

(b) For secondary school and post-secondary non-university graduates, Greece's shortfall is significant in absolute and relative terms in both age groups as it has the lowest employment rates in both categories compared to all countries in the table. The deviation from the maximum rate reaches 13 percentage points for those aged 25–39 years and approximately 18 percentage points for those aged 40–64 years.

(c) We see two remarkable phenomena concerning the employment rates of higher education graduates. For the younger group (25–39), employment rates are significantly lower than in all other countries in the table other than Italy, and, compared with the Northern European countries, Greece is between 5 and 10 percentage points behind. On the other hand, for the 40- to 64-year-old age group, Greece does not seem to lag considerably as the employment rate is just 1.5 percentage points lower than the average and the maximum deviation does not exceed 6%. The phenomenon of unemployment amongst younger graduates of higher education may be linked to the phenomenon of self-employment and the staffing of the small and micro enterprises that form the backbone of the Greek economy. It is known that the involvement of young people in self-employment and small businesses is linked with an average age of around 31–33 years. It is also known that the structure of employment in the Greek economy (Table 5.11) is unbalanced in favour of this population group. Thus, the phenomenon of unemployment among new graduates affects and is affected by the extent of the population's self-employment.

Table 5.10 Employment rates by age group and educational level in 2007

	Age group (years)	Greece	Spain	Portugal	Italy	Ireland	Netherlands	Denmark	Sweden	Finland
ISCED 0-2	25–39	72.3	72.3	80.8	65.7	63.5	74.5	75.7	67.2	68.8
	40–64	55.5	54.7	66.8	47.5	56.9	57.6	63.8	66.4	56.1
ISCED 3-4	25–39	75.2	79.8	81.7	76.5	80.7	87.9	87.9	86.3	80.2
	40–64	63.6	72.7	76.8	72.6	73.3	75.2	79.3	81.3	73.8
ISCED 5-6	25–39	83.2	85.4	86.4	76.7	88.8	93.8	90.8	88.8	87.4
	40–64	82.8	83.0	85.3	83.9	83.5	83.4	85.5	88.3	83.8

Source: Eurostat, Labour Force Survey (data extracted July 2008)

Notes

ISCED 0–2 includes the following educational levels: preschool (0), primary (1) and mandatory (2)

ISCED 3–4 includes the following educational levels: secondary (3) and post-secondary non-tertiary education (4)

ISCED 5–6 includes the following educational levels: tertiary education (5) and advanced research education (PhD) (6)

Table 5.11 Employment by age and educational level in the Greek economy

Years	Self-employed		Employment relationship	
	All levels of education	Tertiary education	All levels of education	Tertiary education
25–49	552,600	115,800	235,500	54,800
50–64	356,100	46,200	127,800	30,800

Source: Eurostat (Ifsa_esgaed)

The effect of education on the prevention of unemployment is more evident in men than in women. According to the statistics in Table 5.12, compared with men, women with the same education and expertise are much more likely to be unemployed, although the disparity in unemployment rates for the same level of qualifications is significantly lower for the more skilled and educated women. In Greece, the differences in unemployment between men and women at all levels of education are much larger than they are in Northern and other Southern European countries.

Table 5.12 highlights the magnitude of the unemployment problem for women at all levels of education, especially in the countries of Southern Europe. A brief analysis of the data reveals that the differences between Northern and Southern countries are considerable. In Northern European countries, women in the highest education group present few differences in unemployment rates compared to men, while only small unemployment differences are noted at other educational levels and do not exceed 1.5%.

In contrast to Northern European countries, all Mediterranean countries present gender-related differences in unemployment biased against women, per educational level, of up to 7–8 percentage points. We note that that the Southern countries are characterised by an inability to use the skills and education of women in the labour market, a fact that may be partly attributable to discrimination and inequality between the sexes. In the EU-27, Greece has the highest unemployment rates for women in the two lowest education categories (compulsory and secondary), while male unemployment rates do not differ significantly from the average for the corresponding education levels.

The education level is directly related to unemployment rates in each age category of the population. Specifically for young people aged 25–34 years, the data of the OECD (Education at a Glance, 2009) highlight the chronic unemployment problem faced by Mediterranean countries compared to Northern countries as regards tertiary – and even compulsory – education graduates, while it is noteworthy that, in some cases, there are no differences between the two categories. In particular, Greece, like other Southern European countries, shows higher rates of chronic unemployment (i.e., in the total number of unemployed workers), with Spain in a slightly better position than the rest, whereas there are no particular differences between the two education levels. In Greece, Italy and Portugal, 60% of unemployed higher education graduates are chronically unemployed. Obviously, this category mainly concerns higher education graduates with specialties and skills that are not related to the production model. Unlike the Mediterranean countries, Northern European countries, except Ireland, present much lower

Table 5.12 Unemployment rates by gender and level of education, 2007

		Greece	Spain	Portugal	Italy	Ireland	Netherlands	Denmark	Sweden	Finland
ISCED 0-2	Men	4.5	6.5	6.5	5.0	6.4	3.3	3.4	6.0	8.3
	Women	11.9	13.3	9.8	9.1	5.5	4.9	5.1	8.6	9.7
ISCED 3-4	Men	4.6	5.0	5.9	3.0	3.5	2.3	2.0	3.9	5.5
	Women	12.9	12.9	7.8	5.6	3.6	3.2	3.0	4.7	6.9
ISCED 5-6	Men	4.1	3.8	5.1	3.1	2.3	1.7	2.9	3.8	3.3
	Women	8.2	5.9	7.6	5.2	2.3	1.8	3.0	3.1	3.8

Source: Eurostat, Labour Force Survey (data extracted July 2008)

chronic unemployment rates amongst the unemployed with tertiary education; compared to Greece, the difference reaches approximately 35 or 45 percentage points for Denmark and Sweden, respectively. Finally, in Greece, the rates of the chronically unemployed with obligatory or higher education and in the total unemployed for each educational level are much higher than in the countries of Northern Europe.

5.4   The Relation Between Research and Innovation as a Serious Problem in the Greek Educational System

The next major problem of the higher education system for the Greek economy is the relation between the educational system and innovation – that is, the extent to which research produces results that can be incorporated into the production process. It should be noted here that this section of the book links the issue of knowledge/research with innovation, not innovation with production, as the latter is the subject of Sect. 5.8. We should highlight the negative methodological impact of confusing the use of these three concepts. Of course, the issue of the orientation of studies is linked directly to the production of innovation.

We found previously that the Greek scientific community is particularly active in the production of publications and citations and that their production costs are very low. However, the conversion of research into production results is disappointing. Of course, the overall production of new technology is disappointing, as shown in Table 5.13.

Table 5.14 shows the significantly higher production of innovation by the developed countries of Northern Europe. Typically, these countries present very satisfactory research results on a global scale, surpassing the U.S. (which, in 2005, had about 53 patents per million population) but behind Japan (more than 110 patents per million population in 2005).

Table 5.13 Patent applications and their sources by year in Greece, 2002–2009

	Patent applications	Natural persons	Legal entities	Universities	Research centres
2002	560	446	114	0	13
2003	539	442	97	3	9
2004	514	420	94	3	13
2005	632	548	84	5	14
2006	709	630	79	3	9
2007	788	696	92	7	7
2008	828	730	98	3	9
2009	720	598	122	3	3

Source: Greek Industrial Property Organization
Notes
The categorisation "natural person/legal entity" is based on the capacity of the first applicant
The numbers of submissions by universities and research centres can be subsets of columns NP or LE, depending on the number of applicants

Table 5.14 Number of patents per million population, 1985–2005

	1985	1990	1995	2000	2001	2002	2003	2004	2005
Greece	0.15	0.45	0.16	0.69	0.53	0.73	0.88	0.77	1.00
Italy	8.98	11.32	10.65	11.63	12.25	11.65	12.44	12.49	12.44
Spain	0.89	1.83	2.02	3.48	3.76	3.78	3.72	4.40	4.55
Portugal	0.15	0.07	0.32	0.38	0.55	0.55	0.64	0.63	1.07
Denmark	15.94	24.04	35.22	43.21	41.05	40.86	39.82	41.06	42.24
Sweden	51.06	50.82	83.57	77.24	74.86	77.19	74.79	77.97	80.85
Finland	11.28	30.01	60.77	67.26	61.52	48.30	50.88	52.34	53.03
Netherlands	38.03	39.03	48.09	67.67	80.99	69.67	68.38	68.81	66.96
Ireland	4.92	7.57	7.94	12.22	13.98	12.78	14.26	15.19	15.01

Source: OECD, Science Technology and Industry Scoreboard, 2007 edition, IMF World Economic Outlook database (last update April 2009), data processing

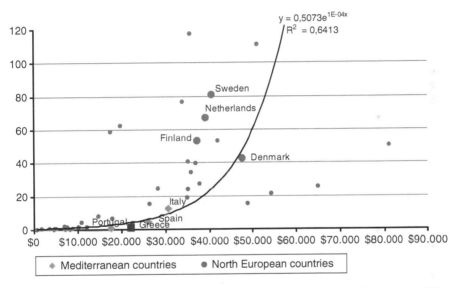

Fig. 5.3 Relation between GDP per capita (*horizontal axis*) and the number of patents per million population (Source: OECD, Science Technology and Industry Scoreboard, 2007 edition, IMF World Economic Outlook database (last update April 2009), data processing)

When the production of technology (registration of patents) is reduced to terms of per capita product, however, we see that the relation between patent registration and per capita product is non-linear and, in fact, exponential. The gross domestic product of Greece is in the lower part of the curve. Obviously, the improvement of the development of the Greek economy is linked to (causes and is caused by) the growth of innovation (Fig. 5.3).

The number of registered patents is a key indicator of innovation activity. However, it concerns primarily the ability to produce results of applied research activity without adequately reflecting the results of primary research. Clearly, there is a significant difference between being able to produce research results and utilising them in the further development of research or in production. The first version of the examination of the research results system relates to the so-called citations system, whereas the latter is related to the creation of spin-off companies.

We should thus consider the relative importance of scientific papers as indicated by their number of citations in other papers. According to the Science Citation Index of each country, Greece (with a score of 0.47) lags behind the other Mediterranean countries of the European Union (with scores between 0.60 and 0.70). This result is perhaps indicative that although Portugal has a significantly smaller quantity of scientific research, its results appear to be recognised by the international scientific community at a -albeit marginally- higher rate (0.51). Northern European countries, as expected, achieve the highest scores according to the Science Citation Index, with scores of 0.83–0.97.

The conclusion is obvious. Primary – and perhaps even applied – research produces results in the Greek economy. However, these results are not recognized satisfactorily and are not translated into production.

5.5   The Financing of Education

Table 5.15 shows that, despite the gradual increase in educational expenditure (both in absolute terms and as a percentage of GDP) over the last 5 years, the amount of public investment in education is still considerably below 5% of the domestic product, the percentage often cited as the objective of the educational policy. Moreover, we observe that its relative size over time remains at lower levels than those of the Mediterranean states of the European Union. It is particularly interesting, perhaps, to note that Portugal seems to maintain the highest levels of investment in education amongst Mediterranean countries, consistently above 5% of GDP. Furthermore, Northern European countries spend a much larger percentage of their income on education. Particularly with regard to Scandinavian countries, the presence of the welfare state is clearly reflected in the size of the investment in

Table 5.15 Public funding of education (GDP percentage)

	2001 (%)	2002 (%)	2003 (%)	2004 (%)	2005 (%)	2006 (%)
Greece	3.5	3.6	3.6	3.8	4.0	–
Italy	4.9	4.6	4.7	4.6	4.4	4.7
Spain	4.2	4.3	4.3	4.3	4.2	4.3
Portugal	5.6	5.5	5.6	5.3	5.4	5.3
Denmark	8.4	8.4	8.3	8.4	8.3	8.0
Sweden	7.1	7.4	7.3	7.2	7.0	6.9
Finland	6.0	6.2	6.4	6.4	6.3	6.1
Netherlands	5.1	5.2	5.4	5.5	5.5	5.5
Ireland	4.3	4.3	4.4	4.7	4.8	4.9

Source: EC, Key data on Education in Europe 2009

Table 5.16   Public funding of education by educational level (2006 data)

	Preschool education (%)[a]	Primary (%)	Secondary and post-secondary (%)	Tertiary (%)	Total (%)
Greece	–	1.1	1.4	1.4	4.0
Italy	0.5	1.2	2.2	0.8	4.7
Spain	0.6	1.1	1.7	1.0	4.3
Portugal	0.5	1.6	2.1	1.0	5.3
Denmark	0.9	1.9	3.0	2.3	8.0
Sweden	0.6	1.7	2.7	1.8	6.8
Finland	0.3	1.3	2.6	1.9	6.1
Netherlands	0.4	1.4	2.2	1.5	5.5
Ireland	–	1.6	2.1	1.1	4.9

Source: EC, Key data on Education in Europe 2009
[a]The financing of preschool education includes costs that cannot be categorised

human capital production. Finally, a substantial increase in public investment in education over 5 years was noted in Ireland, consistent with the shift of its economic activity towards innovation and technological development in recent years.

We will subsequently analyse public investment in education at every level of the education system to identify the individual education levels where the lack of funding is most pronounced. Based on Table 5.16 below, we draw interesting conclusions about the funding of the Greek educational system. We note that in the lower educational level, public expenditure is similar to that of other Mediterranean countries (with the possible exception of Portugal, which seems to spend a much higher percentage of its income on primary education). In secondary and postsecondary education, however, the relative (as a percentage of GDP) expenditure in Greece is obviously lower. Finally, Greece appears to invest the greatest part of its domestic product in higher education compared with other Southern European countries.

Greek investment in human capital cannot, of course, be compared with that of Northern Europe as these countries (especially those in Scandinavia) spend a much larger percentage of their disposable wealth on each level of education. The preceding brief analysis seems to justify the approach of further strengthening investment in education starting from the lower levels, which seem to lack resources for investment.

The analysis up to now has focused on the size of the investment in human capital in relation to the produced product. This approach, however, ignores the relative size of the educational system of each country. Table 5.17 shows the expenditure of public educational institutions per learner at each level, separately.

Table 5.17 once again highlights the low level of investment in the Greek educational system. The expenditure per learner is much lower than in both the developed countries of Northern Europe and other Mediterranean countries. It is indicative that this situation also applies to higher education, although, as we saw previously, the total investment at this level is much higher (as a percentage of

Table 5.17 Expenditure of public educational institutions per pupil (for primary, secondary and post-secondary education) and tertiary education student, 2006

	Total	Primary	Secondary and post-secondary	Tertiary
Greece	4,600	3,800	4,900	5,200
Italy	6,800	6,400	7,100	7,000
Spain	7,100	5,600	7,700	9,500
Portugal	5,200	4,300	5,700	8,100
Denmark	8,300	7,700	8,300	12,800
Sweden	7,400	6,400	7,000	14,400
Finland	6,400	4,900	6,300	11,000
Netherlands	7,000	5,300	7,100	12,400
Ireland	6,800	5,300	7,100	10,400

Source: EC, Key data on Education in Europe 2009
Notes
All values are given in euros
The first column shows the corresponding figure obtained for the entire education system
The column presenting higher education expenditure applies to active students

Table 5.18 Allocation of funding for infrastructure, salaries and operating costs (data 2006)

	Infrastructure (%)	Teacher salaries (%)	Other operating expenses (%)
Greece[a]	21.7	67.3	11.0
Italy	7.2	71.9	20.9
Spain	9.8	73.5	16.7
Portugal	3.6	86.2	10.2
Denmark	5.3	74.1	20.7
Sweden	6.6	65.0	28.4
Finland	7.0	60.9	32.1
Ireland	8.4	74.2	17.3

Source: EC, Key data on Education in Europe 2009
[a]Data for Greece for the year 2005

GDP) compared with other Mediterranean countries. The difference in the two tables regarding higher education is obviously due to the expansion of higher education observed in Greek society after 1997–1998, which inflated funding costs. This assumption is confirmed by Table 5.18. Finally, the table confirms the particularly high investments in human capital by the developed countries of Northern Europe.

Our analysis so far has touched on measurements of the size of investment in the creation and accumulation of human capital, without referring to the more qualitative characteristics of such expenditures. The method of their utilisation, however, is of particular importance as it directly affects the returns on investment in human capital. Table 5.18 shows the percentage distribution of investments in educational infrastructure funding, teacher fees and other operating costs. It is readily apparent that Greece is striving to tackle the problem of educational infrastructure. Infrastructure funding receives over 20% of investments in education; more than double

Table 5.19 Total public expenditure for the support of pupils and students as a percentage of total public education expenditure (2006 data)

	Primary and secondary (%)	Tertiary (%)	Total (%)
Greece[a]	0.2	1.4	0.6
Italy	1.7	16.6	4.5
Spain	1.8	7.9	3.0
Portugal	1.6	11.6	2.6
Denmark	10.5	29.5	17.5
Sweden	6.3	26.1	11.2
Finland	3.0	16.2	7.2
Netherlands	7.2	29.5	11.6
Ireland	9.0	14.4	10.7

Source: EC, Key data on Education in Europe 2009
[a]Data for Greece for the year 2005

that of any other Mediterranean or Northern European country. It can safely be concluded that the increased investment in education in recent years is mainly directed at the financing of educational infrastructure.

Given the low total investment in education shown above, funding for infrastructure projects in the education system diverts resources from other equally important objectives. Perhaps the most striking example of the deprivation of education funding due to the need for infrastructure is that of financial aid to pupils and students. Table 5.19 shows that aid (e.g., scholarships, grants, student loans) financed from public funds accounts for a minimum percentage of total education expenditure, in contrast to the practices of other European Union countries.

The issue of support for learners at all levels is of major importance as it cuts back attendance costs at all educational levels. This affects the incentives for people to stay in education longer through participation in higher level educational programs and allows people who would otherwise drop out to continue their education. Support for learners implements the requirement for equal opportunities, enhances participation in the educational process and, therefore, leads to lower dropout rates. In this critical issue of support for learners, which facilitates the accumulation of human capital and simultaneously promotes social cohesion, Greece brings up the rear among the 25 member states of the European Union (Key data on Education in Europe, 2009).

Concluding this brief analysis of the financing of the Greek educational system, we should note that, until now, we have only examined the public funding of education. In EU countries, private investment in education represents only 12.5% of total education expenditures. In particular, in the developed countries of Northern Europe, with the exception of the Netherlands, private investment in education is very low, a fact attributed to generous public funding. Greece is below the level of public investment of other Mediterranean countries (see previous tables) while also lacking the corresponding private investments. According to the European Commission (EC, Private Household Spending on Education & Training), private investment in education for the accumulation of human capital in Greece accounts for around 0.2% of GDP (Table 5.16). Therefore, the total investment in human capital is expected to be even lower. It is notable that, in Greece, private expenditure accounts for 6% of total expenditure on education (EC, Key data on Education in Europe, data 2005). The corresponding figures for Italy, Spain and Portugal are 7.7%, 11.1% and 8%, respectively (data 2006). Extremely low levels of private expenditure are presented by Sweden and Finland (2.7% and 2.5%, respectively).

Indeed, private investment in education in Greece appears to be aimed mainly at primary and secondary education (90.2%) and is obviously associated with the need for tutorial support for high school students wishing to proceed to tertiary education. Second, a significant proportion of investment in human capital concerns post-secondary education (Institutes of Vocational Training) (7.2%). On the contrary, private funding of higher education still represents an extremely low percentage of the total education expenditure of Greek households (2.7%), whereas in other Mediterranean countries and in the developed countries of Northern Europe, the associated costs – despite more adequate public funding – range from 48.5% (Italy) to 97.3% (Portugal).

The efficiency of public expenditure on higher education has been examined carefully by Aubyn et al. (2009) for the 1998–2005 period using Data Envelopment Analysis and Stochastic Frontier Analysis. These methods are reliable mainly because they use physical input and output indices, although the significance of various parameters remains an important issue. According to the findings of this research, the efficiency of public expenditure on Greek higher education is very low.

5.6   Summary of Problems in the Education System

The key problems associated with the Greek educational system can be summarised as follows:
1. Expenditure on public secondary and tertiary education is low.
2. Pre-school education is extremely limited.
3. The effectiveness of secondary education is comparable to that of other countries, taking into account the level of economic development, if considered as a single knowledge provision system (private and public).
4. The percentage of tertiary education graduates in productive age groups (>29 years) is low, and lifelong education is very limited.
5. The future production of tertiary education graduates is declining.
6. We note high youth unemployment rates, especially amongst graduates of secondary education, which are mainly related to the production structure of self-employment.
7. We note a large discrepancy between the number of students enrolling in tertiary education and the number of tertiary education graduates.
8. The tertiary education system draws few students from other EU countries, mainly because of the mandatory use of the Greek language.

9. There is a problem in the production structure of higher education. There may also be a problem within specific courses of study that could not be detected using the available data. Thus, while mathematics could be considered a production-oriented course, the way in which they are taught in higher education renders them irrelevant to the production requirements of applied research.

10. There is a fundamental problem concerning the interconnection of higher education with production.

Any intervention in the education system should prioritise the management of these problems.

5.7   The Development of the Human Capital

So far, this chapter has analysed the importance and features of the education system, which generates human capital. The major question raised concerns the utilisation of human capital by the productive system in macroeconomic terms.

The human capital index can be calculated based on the methodology used by the Lisbon Council (Ederer 2006; Ederer et al. 2007). The index assesses countries' ability to exploit and develop their workforces. The size of the human capital of a country is calculated based on the cost of its formal and informal education system, weighted by population. A kind of depreciation is applied to this size to take into account the effect of time. This is done in order to redefine the value of knowledge and skills based on both their usefulness in light of developments and new conditions and the limited capacity of the human mind to store data. Essentially, this index focuses on countries' ability to develop their human capital according to four concepts: resources, utilisation, human capital productivity and, finally, estimates on demographic developments. The measurements obtained from different groups show the position and the relative progress of each country's international ranking in relation to the strategies for the development of its human capital. The index was calculated for Greece, Portugal, Finland, Denmark, Sweden and Norway.

Human capital resources are defined as the sum of knowledge, expertise and skills of a person or the whole population, and they provide the best description of the production coefficient usually known as "human capital". Human capital resource figures are obtained using five basic characteristics, which were measured for the years 1999–2005 for each country:

- Education by the family: This characteristic refers to the education and skills acquired by children directly from their parents and is calculated on the basis of the lost opportunity cost of parents (lost wages). Its calculation assumes that parents spend 1 h per day on the education of their children during primary school, half an hour during secondary school and none at all after their children complete secondary education. This assumption is common for all six countries. The opportunity cost is calculated based on the hourly wages of employees for the respective times by level of education.

- Primary and secondary education: This characteristic refers to the skills children acquire through primary and secondary education. These are measured based on public expenditure for these levels of education. These skills include reading, writing and suitable preparation for active entry into society.
- University education: This characteristic refers to the skills that students acquire during tertiary education. It is calculated based on public expenditure on higher education.
- Adult education outside of work: This characteristic includes skills acquired by adults outside of their working environment. The opportunity cost for adult education is measured as the cost per employee multiplied by the number of employees for the years 1999–2005.
- Education at work: This characteristic includes skills acquired as part of daily work to allow employees to respond to new demands. This type of education was also calculated as the opportunity cost (wages), with the common assumption that employees spend 2 h per week on training at work.

Some depreciation is applied to these coefficients, either because the knowledge has been forgotten or because it has become obsolete. The depreciation periods applicable to the above costs are 40, 30, 20, 10 and 10 years, respectively, while the maximum depreciation after these periods is 30%, 30%, 75%, 75% and 25%, respectively.

The human capital index is calculated for the six examined countries: (a) for each age year (from 15 to 64); (b) for the age groups 15–24, 25–54 and 55–64, as a weighted average by age group; and (c) per capita (human capital endowment per capita). These calculations are followed by an assessment of the utilisation of human capital.

The utilisation of human capital concerns the active workforce which is equal to the sum of human capital per age group divided by the total human capital per age group. Its difference from traditional employment indices lies in the fact that this measure is weighted based on different age groups. The sub-optimal utilisation of human capital leads to inefficiencies throughout the economy as the productive coefficient of human capital is not fully utilised. At the individual level, absenteeism excludes the possibility of participation in training offered at work, resulting in the deterioration of human capital resources. Failure to timely update knowledge and skills, combined with their depreciation, increases difficulties in re-employment.

In Greece, about 25% of people in the 15- to 24-year-old age group, 70% of the 25- to 54-year-old age group and 40% of the 55- to 64-year-old age group are in the active workforce. All other countries present higher employment rates by age group, led by Northern European countries. Denmark ranks first in employment rates for the 15- to 24-year-old age group (approximately 62%), Norway for the 25- to 54-year-old age group (approximately 85%) and Sweden for the 55- to 64-year-old age group (approximately 69%).

As an index, human capital productivity examines the economic output for every euro invested in human capital. It is the ratio of the GDP of a country to the total workforce employed. This index, unlike others, includes the training of human resources instead of the total hours of work.

Economic, demographic and immigration issues are considered to calculate employment levels for the year 2030. Our calculations are based on the assumption that employment levels as a percentage will remain the same as today but the workforce will increase in absolute numbers as a percentage of the population. To calculate the growth of the workforce in 2030 compared to the years of the examined study, we used population projections from 2005 until 2060.

Figure 5.4 shows the relationship between human capital resources and their utilisation (1999–2005 average). We observe that Greece holds the lowest position in both indices. Sweden is indisputably first in human capital resources, while Norway leads in human capital utilisation.

Figure 5.5 presents the averages of the indices of productivity and human capital utilisation for the six examined countries. We note that Greece is by far the leader in

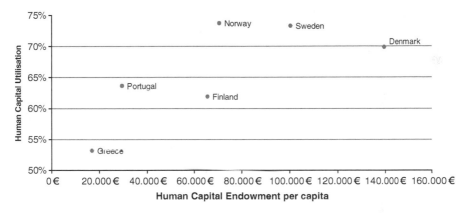

Fig. 5.4 Human capital resources and their utilisation

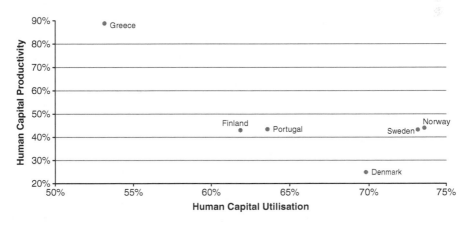

Fig. 5.5 Productivity and human capital utilisation

Table 5.20 The human capital index

	1999	2000	2001	2002	2003	2004	2005
Denmark	14	14	14	14	14	14	14
Greece	19	19	19	19	19	19	19
Portugal	14	14	14	14	16	17	18
Finland	19	19	18	19	17	16	16
Sweden	9	9	9	9	10	10	9
Norway	9	9	10	9	8	8	8

the human capital index of productivity, mainly due to a combination of a marked decline in per capita human capital and an increase in the GDP.

The human capital index consists of the four indices presented above. The classification of the countries for the period under review is used to calculate the index. For each measure, the countries are ranked from 1 (best) to 6 (worst). Therefore, the best score a country may get is 4 and the worst 24. The results of the human capital index for each year are presented in Table 5.20. We note that Greece consistently ranks last among the countries and throughout the 7 reviewed years without showing signs of improvement in its rankings.

Table 5.20 shows Greece's weak rankings on the human capital index compared to the rest of the countries in the table and also shows that, over time, the country exhibits no sign of the expected improvement and/or convergence.

The general conclusion of this analysis is entirely consistent with what has been noted so far: The utilisation of human capital by the Greek economy is very poor. This finding demonstrates another aspect of the development problems of the Greek economy.

5.8   Innovative Activity of Enterprises

Surveys conducted in the EU on the innovative activity of enterprises in its member states are summarised in the reports of the Community Innovation Survey (CIS). The enterprises involved in these community surveys necessarily include those enterprises employing over ten people, while enterprises employing fewer than ten employees are included optionally (EC, Regulation No. 1450/2004).

According to the results of the latest published CIS report (2006) for Greece, 40.85% of companies in the target population demonstrated innovation activity in 2004–2006, showing an upward trend, and for the period 2002–2004 (CIS4), the figure was around 35.8% (Table 5.21). This percentage is higher than the respective figures of the Netherlands, Italy and Spain (35.51%, 34.61% and 33.60%, respectively), although it falls short compared to Finland, Denmark, Sweden and Portugal (51.44%, 46.89%, 44.57% and 41.28%, respectively).

The issue that is of particular importance concerns the fact that only 2.6% of Greek enterprises participate in the CIS. Therefore, the 40.85% of Greek enterprises generating innovation refers only to the target population drawn from the 2.6% of

Table 5.21 Enterprises that produce innovation

Country	Population target (%)	Innovative businesses in population target (%)	Total innovating companies (%)
Sweden	14.20	44.60	6.30
Finland	16.00	51.50	8.30
Denmark	27.70	46.90	13.70
Netherlands	25.50	35.50	9.10
Average of Northern European countries	20.85	44.60	9.35
Italy	17.40	34.60	6.00
Spain	22.00	33.60	7.40
Portugal	19.70	41.30	8.10
Average of Mediterranean countries	19.70	36.50	7.20
Total average	20.30	40.60	8.25
Greece	2.60	40.85	1.10

Source: Community Innovation Survey, CIS 2006

all Greek enterprises with more than 10 employees and does not include very small enterprises, which represent the remaining 97.4%.

The extent of the difference in innovation generation between Northern European and Mediterranean countries and Greece is also shown in Table 5.21. It is easy to understand the vast difference in the target population, i.e., enterprises participating in the CIS, between Greece and the other countries reviewed. More specifically, while only 2.6% of Greek enterprises participate in the community survey, the rates for Northern European and Mediterranean countries are 20.85% and 19.70%, respectively.

Table 5.21 shows one of the main reasons for Greece's high competitiveness deficit compared to Northern and Mediterranean countries. More specifically, Greek enterprises generating innovation represent only 1.1% of Greek enterprises. For Northern European countries, this percentage reaches 10%, and for Mediterranean countries it exceeds 7%.

Figure 5.6 illustrates the above information for Northern European and Mediterranean countries for the period from 2004 to 2006. According to this figure, it is obvious that within the CIS enterprises, the Greek enterprises show higher innovation rates than Spain, Italy and the Netherlands in all employment size classes, whereas the differences compared to Portugal are very small. The rest of the Northern European countries exhibit higher innovation activity in comparison to Greece. It is also confirmed for all countries reviewed that the larger (in employee headcount) the enterprise is, the more innovative it is.

Essentially, Greece operates a two-tiered enterprise system. On one hand, there is a very small minority of medium and large innovative enterprises that appear to be competent in meeting the demands of an ever-changing and demanding global market, and on the other hand, there is a vast majority of very small enterprises characterised by non-innovative activities. In accordance with the references made in the operational program, "Competitiveness and Entrepreneurship 2007–2013",

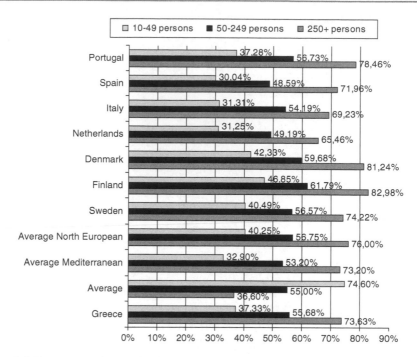

Fig. 5.6 Percentage of enterprises by employment size class that demonstrated innovative activity for the period of 2004–2006 (Source: Community Innovation Survey, CIS 2006)

the lack of innovation activity in very small enterprises comes mainly from their limited capability to implement high-volume investments in new technological equipment and the inability to invest in human capital and expertise that shall evolve to create the foundations for developing innovation in all its aspects.

This is the conclusion reached by, among others, Komninos and Tsamis (2008), who argue that innovation is a systemic process (Tsipouri and Papadakou 2009). Success in innovation is directly related to the flow of expertise and interactions as defined by mutuality and feedback mechanisms, with continued coexistence of cooperation and competition between operators.

Besides, it is easily understood from the data of Table 5.22 that Greek enterprises over the years (1997–2006) have featured the lowest participation rate in gross domestic expenditure in the private sector on research and technological development (RTD) as compared to the whole European Union and also to the averages of Northern European and Mediterranean countries. These findings broadly confirm why Northern European countries, according to IMD and WEF surveys and reports, exhibit high competitiveness, placing them in the top positions in world rankings.

The percentage of investments of the Greek public sector is exceptionally high, while the respective percentages with which the public sector participates in the European Union and the Northern European countries are much lower. Similarly, the participation rates of external resources in Greek enterprises' innovative

Table 5.22 Gross domestic expenditure on RTD, averages for the period of 1997–2006

Country or region	Gross domestic expenditure on RTD		
	Participation (%) of private sector	Participation (%) of public sector	Participation (%) of external sources
EU-27	55.02	34.76	8.03
Sweden	67.32	24.42	5.4
Finland	67.73	27.07	4.14
Denmark	59.42	29.27	7.96
Netherlands	52.58	35.85	11.11
Average of Northern European countries	61.79	29.25	7.13
Italy	34.68	51.94	9.19
Spain	47.87	40.73	6.4
Portugal	29.45	62.02	5.18
Average of Mediterranean countries	37.39	51.56	6.87
Greece	28.09	48.03	21.15

Source: Eurostat (2006)

Table 5.23 Expenditure of private and public sectors on RTD per capita and as a percentage of GDP (2006 data)

	Private sector – € RTD per capita	Public sector – € RTD per capita	% GDP total RTD
Sweden	857.20	58.60	3.60
Finland	740.30	99.90	3.48
Denmark	642.50	60.70	2.46
Netherlands	317.00	74.60	1.72
Italy	134.40	46.20	1.09
Spain	127.40	40.40	1.12
Greece	32.20	21.10	0.58
Portugal	43.90	16.70	0.81
Average	361.86	52.28	1.86

Source: Eurostat (2006)

restructuring is almost three times higher than that of all other countries. The necessary boost to the Greek innovation system is not provided by the weak (in terms of innovation) private sector. On the contrary, the public sector and particularly the external resources try to stimulate demand for innovation and to drag the enterprises along, investing greater amounts over time in expenditure on research and development than do the enterprises themselves.

Table 5.23 shows, in absolute monetary terms (€ per capita), the participation of the private and public sectors in expenditure on research and technological development (RTD). Particularly striking are the data showing the GDP percentage spent by other European countries on research and technological development compared with the Greek figure.

Table 5.23 clearly shows that Greece lags behind – in absolute terms – compared to other countries in the field of investment expenditure on research and techno- logical development, mainly in the private sector. In particular, Greek companies spend only €32.20 per person for internal RTD, while Sweden spends €857.20 and Italy €134.40. Portugal alone, with private sector expenditure of €43.90 per capita and public sector expenditure of €16.70 per capita, has similar investment research characteristics to those of Greece, as reflected in the similar rankings for innovation and competitiveness of these two countries on both the European and worldwide lists. Greece, therefore, spends only 0.58% of its GDP on research and technologi- cal development, when the target limit, as professed in the Lisbon Agreement, is 3%.

The large inflow of external resources that is necessary for Greek enterprises to become innovative comes from EU funds. More specifically, as shown in Table 5.24, in 2004, 19.7% of external resources came from the EU, and a similar percentage of external resources was received for research and development in 2006 (19.05%).

From Table 5.24, it is also evident that the percentages of large Greek enterprises receiving funding from the EU (from 12.1% to 22.33%) and from the central government (from 11.2% to 27.44%) for research activities have increased.

According to OECD, the main categories of innovative activities and techno- logical development (RTD) are internal and external. Tables 5.25 and 5.27 illustrate the development over time of Greek enterprise activities and the comparative analysis between Northern European and Mediterranean countries and Greece.

Table 5.25 shows that, in Greece, rates for all activities related to the creation or acquisition of innovation, except for the "acquisition of knowledge", have dropped over time. Such activities are certainly important steps in technological evolution, but if enterprises fail to generate independent research and development departments (through which a continuous flow of expertise through the appropriate processes achieves innovative results), the situation is not expected to change drastically. The goal is to have a constant increase in demand for innovative activities, which in turn will lead to further use of new technologies to achieve competitive advantage by increasing their productivity. The even more staggering fact is that although an external expertise market is observed, it does not seem to result in better training of enterprise staff. This may create a diseconomy of

Table 5.24 Funding of research and development for Greek firm

	Funded by local or regional authorities		Funded by central government		Funded by the European Union	
	2006	2004	2006	2004	2006	2004
Total (%)	7.07	5.5	17.96	19.9	19.05	19.7
Small 10–40 (%)	8.98	5.9	15.97	17.8	18.47	18.7
Medium 50–249 (%)	0.31	4.4	23.54	31.2	20.42	25.9
Large 250 + (%)	4.19	3.2	27.44	11.2	22.33	12.1

Source: Eurostat, CIS4, CIS6

Table 5.25 Activities related to innovation: percentage of actively innovative Greek enterprises that engaged in the following innovation activities

	Internal RTD		Continuous internal RTD		External RTD		Purchase of machinery, equipment, software	
	2006	2004	2006	2004	2006	2004	2006	2004
Total (%)	47.93	51.00	27.10	30.20	23.60	32.00	82.20	92.30
Small 10–40 (%)	48.17	48.50	26.08	26.30	21.14	27.20	79.58	91.20
Medium 50–249 (%)	46.35	62.30	27.60	44.60	29.27	48.00	91.04	97.60
Large 250+ (%)	50.23	53.50	42.33	47.30	40.47	63.70	87.91	91.80
	Acquisition of other external knowledge		Training of employees		Introduction of innovations in the market		Other ways to obtain innovation	
	2006	2004	2006	2004	2006	2004	2006	2004
Total (%)	21.00	14.70	68.64	72.30	60.07	54.00	35.80	25.80
Small 10–40 (%)	18.39	13.80	63.27	68.10	36.46	49.70	33.87	24.50
Medium 50–249 (%)	28.96	18.40	83.96	86.80	50.42	70.00	38.33	32.20
Large 250+ (%)	30.23	16.00	92.09	96.40	55.81	72.70	57.21	24.20

Source: Eurostat, CIS5, CIS2006

scale in an enterprise as from the time that expertise develops through acquisition, it should be disseminated to employees to increase their effectiveness.

Table 5.26 shows that Greek companies present similar data to companies in Spain and Portugal for almost all categories and that, generally, their performance is encouraging. However, we should not ignore the fact that the percentage of the target population in the case of Greece covers just 2.6% of all Greek enterprises.

Furthermore, the innovative Greek enterprises proceed to purchasing new technology (e.g., machinery, equipment and software) to a much greater extent than do enterprises in other countries, particularly the Northern European countries, whose main development pillar is generating innovation. This disparity shows the will of Greek enterprises to achieve a competitive advantage that will increase their market share, a measure that, in the long term, may prove costly and inefficient. This finding supports the fact that the vast majority of Greek enterprises are interested primarily in the short-term impact of the investment movements they undertake. A lack of appropriate structural interventions that will yield benefits in the long term is noted.

Komninos and Tsamis (2008) report that, in Greece, the most innovative sectors of economic activity have very small shares in the overall economy and that the most innovative sector of the Greek economy, information technology, participated in 2006 with just 0.3% of total added value (at current prices). This contribution of the information technology sector to innovative activity in Greece is more than six times smaller than the corresponding European average. Therefore, the overall benefits are severely limited because the interactions and cooperations for the

Table 5.26 Percentage of actively innovative enterprises that presented activities related to innovation

	Internal RTD (%)	Continuous internal RTD (%)	External RTD (%)	Purchase of machinery, equipment, software (%)	Acquisition of other external knowledge (%)	Training of employees (%)	Introduction of innovations in the market (%)	Other ways to obtain innovation (%)
Denmark	48.86	35.20	34.86	61.13	33.67	38.97	39.99	52.78
Greece	47.93	27.10	23.60	82.20	21.00	68.64	40.07	35.80
Spain	31.78	22.22	17.29	36.78	2.81	11.25	14.46	6.58
Netherlands	63.55	45.69	29.81	54.29	14.53	44.10	35.54	17.10
Portugal	47.72	21.14	28.11	81.89	24.46	71.03	41.81	40.35
Sweden	64.64	34.29	26.84	62.19	35.62	67.42	36.40	31.00

Source: Eurostat (CIS 2006)

Table 5.27 Significant barriers to the innovation activities of actively innovative enterprises (%)

	Greece				Spain	Portugal	Netherlands	Sweden
	10–49	50–249	250+	Total				
Lack of funding within enterprises or groups	19.20	12.60	32.09	18.46	25.7	26.82	8.51	15.53
Lack of funding from external sources	14.86	20.31	20.93	16.20	23.34	26.15	4.71	7.21
Exceedingly high innovation costs	6.18	19.38	23.26	9.52	34.83	36.63	7.56	11.53
Lack of skilled personnel	24.95	27.50	40.47	26.16	16.63	13.3	7.01	15.89
Lack of information on technology	28.96	30.83	56.74	30.54	11.13	5.53	2.62	2.33
Lack of information on markets	35.57	31.88	52.09	35.60	8.52	6.87	2.71	3.27
Other companies dominate the market	23.81	24.69	27.44	24.15	18.66	15.14	4.8	14.41
Uncertain demand for innovative goods or services	23.41	20.00	33.49	23.19	18.81	16.25	3.95	4.08
No demand for innovation	30.66	22.50	28.84	28.98	10.04	5.76	1.1	0.9
No demand for innovation because of earlier innovations	23.68	19.17	37.21	23.39	6.11	4.49	0.9	0.7

Source: Eurostat (CIS 2006)

transfer of expertise are not able to dynamically disseminate innovation throughout the economy.

There are some significant obstacles to the transition from the creation and development processes to continuous innovation generation. Sometimes these obstacles dampen the increase in demand for technological progress and contribute to a reduction or stabilisation of innovative activity. Table 5.27 presents the major problems faced by innovatively active enterprises in Greece and other countries (Spain, Portugal, Netherlands, Sweden).

Table 5.27 reveals that the greatest obstacles faced by innovatively active Greek enterprises are the lack of information on the markets (35.60%), the lack of information on technology (30.54%), the lack of skilled personnel (26.16%) and zero demand for innovation (28.98%). What makes the above findings even more surprising is the fact that very large enterprises exhibit higher response rates than smaller ones. Therefore, very significant obstacles to the technology development of enterprises derive from the demand.

In addition, differences exhibited by enterprises in Greece compared to other countries become evident. Significant differences also appear in the lack of market information, the lack of information on technology and the lack of qualified staff, highlighting the traditional organisational structure of Greek enterprises.

5.9   Population Health

The level of population health is expected to be closely linked to magnification. Indeed, the accumulation of health status and the level of health itself are also expected to be linked to magnification. The link is made through the endogenous theory of human capital improvement. It has been found (Aghion et al. 2009) that a higher initial level and a higher rate of improvement of life expectancies have a positive effect on the magnification of per capita gross national product.

The comparison between countries with regard to citizens' views about their own health should be made with some reservations as to the subjective judgments, which are generally affected by a number of factors. These include culture, the income and educational levels and the structure of the survey questionnaires, which may vary from country to country. However, the results of such a survey may be very important for forecasts of future public health and mortality rates of societies.

Figure 5.7 shows the percentage of citizens over age 15 years who believe they are in good physical health. For Greece, 78% of the population over 15 years believe themselves to be of good physical health compared to the overall average of 69%. The highest percentage of citizens who are satisfied with their health is found in the U.S. (89%), while the lowest percentage is found in Portugal and Japan (only 39%).

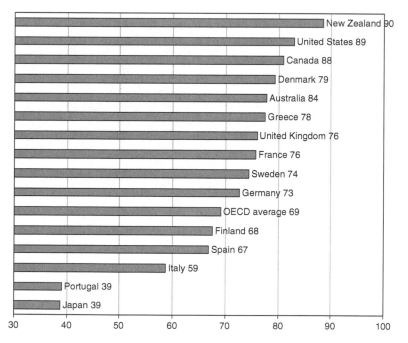

Fig. 5.7 Percentage of citizens who believe themselves to be in good physical health (Source: OECD-Society at a Glance 2009)

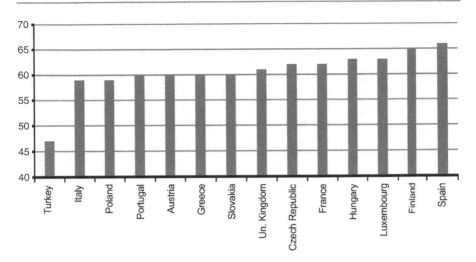

Fig. 5.8   Index of mental health (Source: OECD, Society at a Glance 2009)

Mental health includes anxiety and mood disorders, impulsivity control and disorders due to use of alcohol and various illegal substances. Figure 5.8 presents the results of mental health indices for various European countries in 2007. High index values indicate good mental health. The lowest index values are observed in Turkey, Italy and Portugal and the highest in Finland and Spain. The value for Greece is quite low (60%).

The "health reserve" with which one starts one's adult life is impaired with age, may increase with investments in childhood health and nutrition and is maintained or eroded depending on the experiences of working life. The mental, emotional and biological human capital health reserve is an important indicator, and, according to Grossmann (1972, 2004), maintaining it has a positive effect on productivity.

However, a specific reference to occupational stress impairing the human capital health reserve should also be made. This type of stress is of major importance for the human resources of health and productivity because its symptoms do not subside at the end of the day when the individual leaves the workplace, affecting the broader psychosocial status of individuals (Schwartberg and Dytell 1996). This influence is reflected in the cost of occupational stress to society through the financial claims and compensations for disease and disability resulting directly from the professional environment (Byrne 2002). There are many reasons for occupational stress, but the main reason constitutes competition experienced by an employee in his professional environment and the increasing need to keep working or to climb the career ladder. Additionally, when a person perceives a discrepancy between the demands a situation poses and his or her reserves (biological, psychological, social) available to meet it, he or she experiences stress.

Occupational stress is manifest in various forms, such as increased tension, lack of job satisfaction, professional burnout and depression. These signs of burnout have an impact on the personal and social lives of employees and ultimately weaken their performance, leading to decreased productivity. Maslach et al. (2001) argue that professional exhaustion is divided into:

- Emotional exhaustion, referring to feelings of mental fatigue and rendering the employee unable to concentrate;
- Depersonalisation, referring to the development of neutral and negative feelings; and
- Reduced sense of personal achievement, referring to a reduced desire for and seeking out of a sense of professional satisfaction from work.

Professional burnout is associated with various consequences for employment, such as withdrawal or/and absenteeism from work. However, for those who remain at work, professional burnout leads to lower productivity and efficiency. Consequently, it is associated with reduced job satisfaction and reduced commitment to the job or organisation (Maslach et al. 2001).

At a micro-economic level, human capital is approached in financial and business terms as a fixed "property" element of the organisation or enterprise that should be maintained and improved by taking measures to protect health and safety (Schultz 2002, WHO 2004).[3] When the employee's health is improved, the efficiency of the organisation is also increased, as reflected by increased employee productivity or/and reduced health or time costs due to productivity failure (Goetzel et al. 1998, 2008). Pelletier (2001) and Goetzel et al. (2002) demonstrated that employees who are depressed or feel stressed "cost" employers much more in health costs compared to the employees with no such risk factors. Jacobson et al. (1996) stressed the positive relation between occupational stress and absenteeism.

Apart from the potential resources saved by undertaking health and safety policies at the workplace, Dejoy and Southern (1993) emphasise the improvement of the employee's productivity as a result of such policies. Characteristically, according to Johansson et al. (1991), the addressing and improvement of health risk factors reduce accidents and injuries in the workplace. In order to help promote employee health and safety, enterprises are required to introduce and implement procedures for the prevention of occupational hazards. The Presidential Decree 17/1996, "Measures to improve safety and health of employees in compliance with the Directives 89/391/EEC and 91/383/EEC", defines the obligations of employers to their employees' safety in the Greek area, while its amendment by the Presidential Decree 159/99 provides a clearer assessment of occupational hazards. Measures to protect the health and safety of human resources have the following goals:

- To promote and maintain the highest levels of physical, mental and social well-being of employees in all occupations;
- To prevent adverse effects of working conditions on the health and safety of employees;
- To adapt the work to human capabilities and

---

[3] World Health Organization (2004) Health systems: concepts, design & performance. www.emro.who.int/mei/mep/Healthsystemsglossary.htm

• To protect the employees from occupational hazards.

In addition, it is worth noting that the health and safety programs adopted and introduced in the workplace may be approached from the perspective of innovative public health measures (Leviton 1996). Regulatory provisions, public health policies and social marketing can help to change the processes on an enterprise level to improve the employees' health and safety. It should be noted that, at the European level, EU member states have agreed on a list of social issues related to quality of life, including issues such as health, control over the provision of goods and services, work and the quality of life at work (Yfantopoulos and Gitonas 2004).

References

Aghion P, Howitt P, Murtin F (2009) The relationship between health and growth: when Lucas meets Nelson-Phelps. OFCE/ANR, No. 2009–28, 1–30

Aubyn St, Pina M, Garcia, Pais JF (2009) Study on the efficiency and effectiveness of public spending on tertiary education, European Economy, Economic paper no. 390

Baroso R (2005) Transaction costs, higher education preferences and economic development. Social Science Research Network Working Paper Series 831727

Byrne DG (2002) Occupational stress, occupational structure and occupational morbidity. Int Congr Ser 1241:151–154

DeJoy D, Southern D (1993) An integrative perspective on worksite health promotion. J Med 35:1221–1230

Ederer P (2006) Innovation at work: the European human capital index. Lisbon Council Policy Brief, Belgium

Ederer P, Schuler P, Willms S (2007) The European human capital index: the challenge of central and Eastern Europe. Lisbon Council Policy Brief, Belgium

Goetzel RZ, Jacobson BH, Aldana SG, Vardell K, Yee L (1998) Health care costs of worksite health promotion participants and non-participants. J Occup Environ Med 40(4):341–346

Goetzel RZ, Ozminkowski RJ, Sederer LI, Mark TL (2002) The business case for quality mental health services: why employers should care about the mental health and well-being of their employees. J Occup Environ Med 44(4):320–330

Goetzel RZ, Ozminkowski RJ, Bowen J, Tabrizi MJ (2008) Employer integration of health promotion and health protection programs. Int J Workplace Health Manag 1(2):109–122

Grossman M (1972) On the concept of health capital and the demand for health. J Polit Econ 80 (2):223–255

Grossman M (2004) The demand for health, 30 years later: a very personal retrospective and prospective reflection. J Health Econ 23(4):629–636

Jacobson BH, Aldana SG, Goetzel RZ, Vardell KD, Adams TB, Pietras RJ (1996) The relationship between perceived stress and self-reported illness-related absenteeism. Am J Health Promot 11 (1):54–61

Johansson G, Johnson JV, Hail EM (1991) Smoking and sedentary behavior as related to work organization. Soc Sci Med 32:837–846

Komninos N, Tsamis A (2008) The system of innovation in Greece: structural asymmetries and policy failure. Int J Innov Reg Dev 1(1):1–23

Leviton LC (1996) Integrating psychology and public health: challenges and opportunities. Am Psychol 51(1):42–51

Maslach C, Schaufeli WB, Leiter MP (2001) Job burnout. Annu Rev Psychol 52:397–422

OECD (2009) Education at a glance. Education and Skills. 17:i–475

Pelletier KR (2001) A review and analysis of the clinical- and cost-effectiveness studies of comprehensive health promotion and disease management programs at the worksite: 1998–2000 update. Am J Health Promot 16(2):107–116

Schultz TP (2002) Wage gains associated with height as a form of health human capital. Yale University, Economic Growth Center, Discussion paper 841 http://www.econ.yale.edu/growth_pdf/cdp841.pdf (11-01-2010)

Schwartberg NS, Dytell RS (1996) Dual-earner families: the importance of work stress and family stress for psychological well-being. J Occup Health Psychol 1(2):211–223

Tsipouri L, Papadakou M (2009) Profiling and assessing the Greek innovation governance system: the contribution of Greece to the OECD MONIT project. Centre of Financial Studies, University of Athens

Yfantopoulos GN, Gitona M (2004) Measurement of quality and utility in heath services. In: Kyriopoulos J, Lionis C (eds) The quest for quality in health and health care. Casus Sanitatis – Health Services in Greece, Papazisis, Athens

Cultural Values, Stereotypes and Historical Evolution

6

The institutions in a society and an economy are human constructs that function as rules and restrictions in shaping human behaviour. As a result, they frame the motives of individuals' transactions, irrespective of whether these take place at a political, social or economic level. In essence, the institutional framework decreases the uncertainty that accompanies everyday life, offering a structure (albeit not necessarily an effective one) for its operation. The institutional background of transactions mostly includes the issue of property rights and the contract terms concerning transactions (North 1990). Cultural background constitutes a determining element of the institutional construct and originates from a basic generator of behaviours and structures: the human mind. The human mind processes information and comprehends situations. However, its information is deficient, and its processing abilities are limited. As a result, there is no single point or level of balance but only multiple levels or points of reference that also take into account the cost of information processing and the operation of transactions.

Cultural background affects economic results mostly through two channels: Initially, it can affect the motives and the desire of individuals to engage in certain activities of employment, market organisation and the desire to accumulate physical and human capital. The second channel concerns the cooperation and trust levels in the economy.

Institutional ⟶ Rules of the ⟶ Motives ⟶ Transactions ⟶ Economic
framework   game   performance
Cultural
background

There is a close relation between institutions and cultural background. Both concepts affect and are affected by human behaviour and motives. However, there is an important difference between these two constructs: The first (institutions) is directly under the influence of the society's members, meaning that by changing the allocation of resources, the constitution, laws and policies might lead to a change of societal institutions. On the contrary, cultural background is long lasting, although

P. Petrakis, *The Greek Economy and the Crisis*,
DOI 10.1007/978-3-642-21175-1_6, © Springer-Verlag Berlin Heidelberg 2012

it should be pointed out that education affects, to a certain degree, the organisation of cultural background. At the same time, institutions could be considered as representing a point of societal balance; however, the same does not hold for cultural background.

Acemoglu et al. (2004) demonstrated that institutions have greatly influenced the performance of today's economies. In effect, the authors introduce the question of whether improved institutions favour development or whether development helps institutions to improve. They conclude that historical institutions improve first; consequently, they affect economic development.

Historical development   ⟶   Cultural background   ⟶   Economic development

Cultural background is certainly (in the long term) an endogenous phenomenon of economic development, and thus it is more difficult to isolate its effects.

Analysing the global financial crisis of 2008, Akerlof and Shiller, in their book "Animal Spirits" (2009), underlined the importance of powerful internal human forces, explaining that these forces are responsible for the evolution of the wealth of nations. As the authors themselves mention in their introduction: "to understand how economies work and how we can manage them and prosper, we must pay attention to the thought patterns that animate people's ideas and feelings, their animal spirits. We will never really understand important economic events unless we understand the fact that their causes are largely mental in nature".

In essence, the specific approach introduces the concept of cultural background in the operation and growth of the economy. What we call "cultural results", meaning depictions of the cultural background and of culture itself, are basic elements of the cultural background. These are made up of society's "common knowledge" and the cultural syndromes created throughout time.

The chapter develops as follows: Sect. 6.1 describes the evolution of and the negative events affecting the Greek economy and describes the levels of risk since 1985. Sect. 6.2 contains an analysis of risk, the time of commitment and the production model of the Greek economy. After the description of the concept and content of cultural background (in Sect. 6.3), we present a description of empirical evidence for the structuring of cultural values (Sect. 6.4). Section 6.5 features an analysis of the concept of social capital in the Greek economy, together with the role of family networks (6.6). Finally, in Sect. 6.7, we demonstrate the economic and social reflections of the cultural model.

6.1   The Evolution of the Greek Economy

Since the birth of the Greek state, economic growth has been accompanied by serious national, social, and macroeconomic crises. This process involves the factors of accumulation of capital, labour and all growth factors. As a result, economic growth is responsible for the quantitative and qualitative characteristics of these factors and consequently for the social behaviour in and stereotypes of Greek society.

Figure 6.1 presents the evolution of the Greek per capita GDP in US dollars, using 1990 as the base year, based on purchasing power parity (PPP). It appears that income was almost stagnant before 1953. This figure begins to improve, almost aggressively, after 1953.

The structure of GDP in the main sectors of economic activity – primary, secondary and tertiary production – followed the same trend (Fig. 6.2). The Greek economy, which was traditionally agricultural (1833), evolved into an economy of services (2008) and broadened its monetarisation (Thomadakis 1981).

The stagnancy of the extroversion of the Greek economy is impressive, as evaluated based on the exports-to-GDP ratio. For 2008, this is comparable to that for 1930 (Fig. 6.3)[1]!

The evolution of Greece's society and economy can be divided into two important sub-periods: Before and after 1940. To facilitate presentation, the period before 1940 can be further divided into two equal sub-periods: 1827–1878 and 1879–1940.

Figures 6.4–6.6 (and the explanatory Tables 6.1–6.3) present the major negative events in the Greek economy and society; these include wars, revolutions and serious international crises. They are presented based on whether they have an endogenous or exogenous origin, i.e., if they originated inside or outside Greek

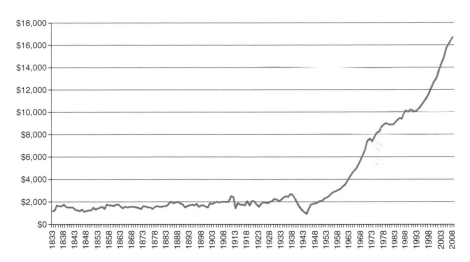

Fig. 6.1 The evolution of per capita GDP (1833–2008) (Source: Kostelenos et al. (2007) and Groningen, Growth and Development Centre, Total Economy Database)

---

[1] If we take into account that exports in 1928 (20%) were mostly product exports, while the corresponding export production in 2008 was evaluated at 7% of GDP, the image of the commercial extroversion of the Greek economy and its evolution appears bleak.

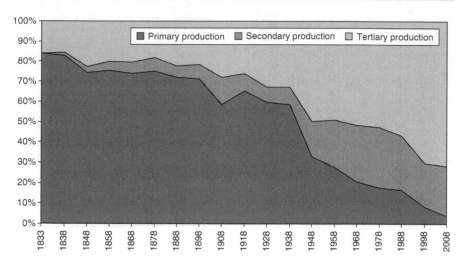

Fig. 6.2 Percentage participation of each sector of economic activity in GDP for 1833–2008 (Source: Kostelenos et al. (2007) and HEL. STAT. Statistical Bulletins)

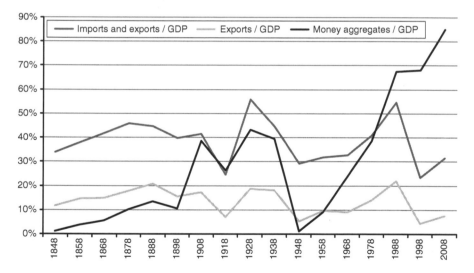

Fig. 6.3 Imports, exports and money aggregates (M3 quantity except for monetary circulation, M0) as percentage of GDP (Source: Kostelenos et al. (2007), HEL. STAT. Statistical Bulletins and Economic Bulletins of the Bank of Greece)

territory. The frequency of negative events in Greece is particularly high. The cumulative frequency of endogenous and exogenous events leads to increased inconsistency in the economic and social settings.

The appearance of important negative events in the Greek economy and society throughout the period under observation is remarkable; the most important

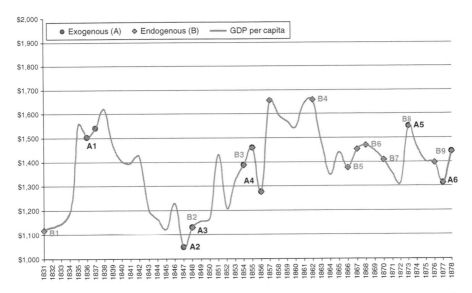

Fig. 6.4 Negative events in the Greek economy and society: 1831–1878 (Note: Dollars in 1990 ppp)

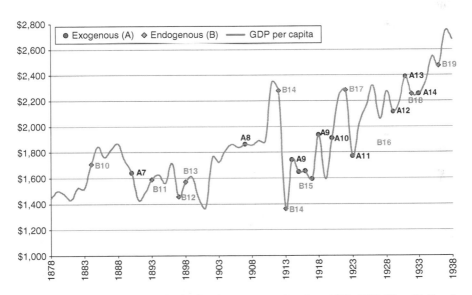

Fig. 6.5 Major negative events in the Greek economy and society: 1879–1938 (Note: Dollars in 1990 ppp)

exception is the period after 1974. Wars, insurgencies and social crises were experienced to an extent that is inconceivable today. It should also be noted that these events transpired under a much weaker economic structure of an almost

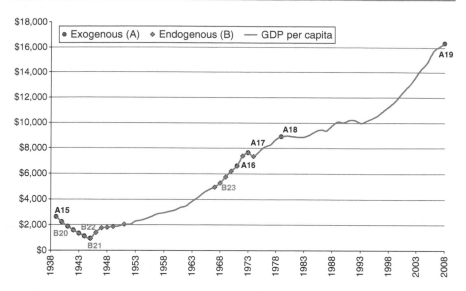

Fig. 6.6 Major negative events in the Greek economy and society: 1939–2008 (Note: Dollars in 1990 ppp)

Table 6.1 Years: 1831–1878

Year	Exogenous (A)	Endogenous (B)
1831		Murder of the Governor of Greece, Kapodistrias (B1)
1836	Anglo-American capital	
1837	market crisis (A1)	
1847	Agricultural crisis and railway bubble (A2)	
1848	Revolutions in France,	First mandatory circulation of the drachma (B2)
1854	Germany and Austria (A3)	
1855	Crimean war (A4)	Occupation of Piraeus by Anglo-French (B3)
1856		
1857		
1862		Fall of King Othon (B4)
1866		Cretan revolution (1866–68) – dynamiting of the
1867		Monastery of Arcadion, 1866 (B5)
1868		Second mandatory circulation of the drachma (B6)
1870		Massacre at Dilesi and international slander of the country (B7)
1873	Financial crisis in England, Italy and Germany (A5)	Lavreotika (B8)
1876		1877: Third mandatory circulation; recession in the
1877	Russian–Turkish war;	commercial centres of the country, especially
1878	bankruptcy of Egypt: 1878 (A6)	Hermoupoli (B9)

Table 6.2 Years: 1879–1938

Year	Exogenous (A)	Endogenous (B)
1884		Economic crisis (B10)
1890	Bankruptcy of Argentina, i.e., the baring crisis (A7)	
1893		Bankruptcy; crisis in raisin exports (B11)
1897		Defeat in the war against the Ottomans (B12)
1898		International financial control (B13)
1907	Financial and credit crisis in New York (A8)	
1912		Balkan Wars (B14)
1914		
1916	World War I (A9)	The height of national division (B15)
1918		
1920	Plunge of the N.Y. and London stock exchange	Economic embargo (B16)
1922	markets (A10)	Destruction of Asia Minor (B17)
1923	Hyperinflation in Germany (A11)	
1929	Crash of the New York stock exchange (A12)	
1931	Britain abandons the "gold standard" (A13)	
1932		Abandonment of the "gold standard"
1933	USA abandons the "gold standard" (A14)	(B18)
1936		Dictatorship of (B19)

closed nature. After 1940, World War II and the civil war had destructive effects on the course of the Greek economy.

We measure the risk levels of the Greek economy during 1985–2009 using the data of the International Country Risk Guide (ICRG).[2] The available indices constitute measurements of the political, economic, financial, and composite risk of each country. Each of these indices is the weighted average of the individual statistical data that depict the dominant political, social, and economic conditions that affect the shaping of a stable environment of economic development.

The following Fig. 6.7 depicts the evolution of the relevant risks of the Greek economy since 1985. The simple graphic depiction of the data reveals a significant improvement of all indices during the 1990s. After 2000, however, the relevant indices[3] seem to recede, without taking into account the crisis after 2008, during which, obviously, the relevant indices collapsed.

Concerning the ranking of Greece in terms of individual and composite risk levels among the EU-27, we note a definite deterioration of the Greek economy based on all of the measurement indices of the individual risks examined.

---

[2] http://www.prsgroup.com.

[3] In order for the data depicted in the following figures to be clearly understood, it should be mentioned that the individual indices are measured on different scales.

Table 6.3 Years: 1939–2008

Year	Exogenous (A)	Endogenous (B)
1939		
1940		
1941		
1942	World War II (A15)	The war of 1940; occupation (B20)
1943		
1944		
1945		
1947		Continuous depreciations of the drachma; the gold
1948		sovereign is substituted for the national currency, while
1949		the drachma is limited to small transactions (B21);
1950		1946–1949: Civil war (B22)
1951		
1952		
1953		
1967		
1968		
1969		
1970		
1971	Dollar depreciation – End of the	Dictatorship (B23)
1972	Bretton Woods era (A16)	
1973	First oil crisis (A17)	
1974		
1979	Second oil crisis (A18)	
2008	Financial crisis (A19)	

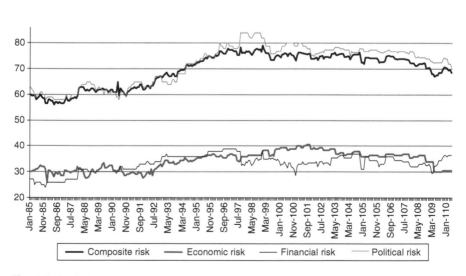

Fig. 6.7 Evolution over time of political, economic, financial and composite risk in the Greek economy (Source: PRS Group, ICRG historical data)

In conclusion, tellingly, since the beginning of the twentieth century (110 years), only 25 years could be said not to be under the influence of severe inflationary pressures or periods of high risk (e.g., wars). These periods are 1953–1970 and 2000–2007. It is obvious that the course of the Greek economy since the beginning of the previous century has been anything but stable. The intense uncertainty, risk and various disturbances affected the establishment of the modern production model of development of the Greek economy.

6.2 Risk, Commitment Time of Investment Funds and Productive Model in the Greek Economy

The discussion of the role of macroeconomic experiences in the investment behaviour of individuals and, by extension, of societies began because of the effects of the Great Depression of 1929 (Friedman and Schwartz 1963) on the investment behaviour of individuals and investment directors in the US. During the last two decades, however, it has developed with the evolution of psychology and social psychology. It originated in the acknowledgment that individuals do not engage in stable behaviours against risk. Instead, their behaviours are shaped according to their economic experiences (Hertwig et al. 2004).

In their effort to define the degree to which previous experiences affect individuals making investment decisions, Malmendier and Nagel (2008) concluded as follows: households with more experiences of high returns in the capital market have a lower aversion to risk and participate to a higher degree in investments in the capital market, which is where they invest the biggest part of their wealth. Moreover, households that have experienced periods of higher inflation tend to invest a smaller percentage of their reserves in bonds while holding more reserves.

As a result, willingness to take risks also depends on personal microeconomic history. Human behaviour could be interpreted through the shaping of an endogenous development of preferences, where risk depends on the performance of risky investments in the past (Palacios-Huerta and Santos 2004), or through knowledge, in which case present perceptions depend on the real experiences of the past.

According to all data from its beginning until recently, the evolution of the Greek economy was characterised by events that mainly contributed to the growth of its systemic risk. Numerous pieces of evidence support this claim. The most serious indication should be sought in the financing conditions of the private and public sectors.

The financing conditions reflect high risk in two ways: (a) high interest rates and (b) credit allocation or selective administration of credit that is not based on the applicant's interest rate capacity. That is, normal interest rate levels do not necessarily indicate that there is no risk in the transactional relations. It might simply mean that there is no financing with "normal" interest rates. The financing conditions could, however, conceal the "recognition" of high risk levels, even if loans with "normal" interest rates were issued. This can be incorporated as follows:

(a) in the difference between the nominal and real debt capital and (b) in the required guarantees of all types.

There are indications that the nominal interest rates of financing in the Greek economy were higher than those of other European economies. The data on the evolution of certain Greek state loans from 1867 to 1924 are enlightening. Most of them are bond loans, meaning that they were mostly purchased (funded) by foreigners (over-the-counter financing). Their nominal interest rate was between 5% and 9%, with most ranging between 8% and 9%. During the period of 1825–1913, the interest rates in France were around 3–4% (Bourguignon and Lévy-Leboyer 1984). Dritsa (1990, p. 245) mentions that until 1840, the interest rates of the National Bank ranged between 30% and 50%, while during the interwar period they did not increase but never fell under 15% (Zolotas 1927).

Maybe the most important indication for the prevalence of high risk is the manner of the evolution of public borrowing, mostly as regards the difference between the nominal capital used to calculate sinking payments.

At the same time, the emerging production model reflected all of the characteristics of "lightness". The productive industrial organisation of 1917, 1930 (Dritsa 1990) and 2008 is indicative. The main characteristic of the Greek economy is the prevalence of very small businesses. Finally, the low innovation rates in the Greek economy could also be linked to the lack of mid- and long-term investments.

6.3   Cultural Values and Stereotypes

In "The Achieving Society", McClelland (1961) convincingly proved that the cultural indices capturing motivation for achievement could forecast the future economic growth in developing countries for a 25-year period. Numerous other studies have also quantified the "dimensions" of the cultural background and provided measurements for a large number of countries (Hofstede 1980, 2001; House et al. 2004; Savig and Schwartz 2007). The literature includes aspects such as cultural complexity, austerity of cultural background (Triandis 1994, 2009) and orientation to values (Kluckhohn and Strodtbeck 1961). Georgas and Berry (1995) and Inglehart (1997) have located groups of countries that seem to share similar cultural values. The strong correlation of the research results with developmental growth indices and their aptness in forecasting important variables such as the GDP per capita demonstrate that culture measurements could be of significant value (Minkov and Blagoev 2009).

Hofstede's research (1980, 1991) presented a group of characteristic values that could be used to measure the cultural background of a society. He claims that these aspects[4] concern basic problems of humanity that every society faces. Each

---

[4] In the research, the terms "cultural dimensions", "cultural values" and "cultural attitudes" are used alternately. For the sake of simplicity, we can accept that the concept of "stereotypes" is

country's different performance in every aspect demonstrates that different societies face these problems in a different manner (Hofstede 1980, p. 313).

An equally important and much more recent study, the GLOBE (Global Leadership and Organizational Effectiveness – 2004), added to the domains of Hofstede's culture. This study aimed to explore the relations between social culture, practices and organisational leadership (House et al. 1999, 2004). It presented nine domains of social culture that reflect the views of mid-level directors on the present societal situation and their preferences concerning its desirable situation. The aspects presented were: Power Distance, Uncertainty Avoidance, Institutional Collectivism (Collectivism I), In-group Collectivism (Collectivism II), Gender Egalitarianism, Assertiveness, Future Orientation (Confucian Dynamism), Performance Orientation, and Humane Orientation. These aspects of social culture shape a relatively comprehensive image of a society's cultural background that can be described in terms of five domains.

The domain of Power Distance signifies the degree to which a society accepts the unequal distribution of power among its members. Inequality could exist in connection with wealth, capacities or prestige. This inequality is reflected in the values of both the weaker and the stronger members of a society and is cultivated through basic relations of early socialisation, such as those of parent with child or teacher with student.

The domain of Uncertainty Avoidance refers to the lack of tolerance of uncertainty and doubt shown by a society. This lack is expressed through higher concern for the future and the release of more energy, a greater need for rules and absolute truth and less tolerance towards individuals or groups with ideas and behaviours deviating from the usual. The most active cultures tend to apply more specialisation, formalism and standardisation, and they attribute greater value to uniformity than to different ideas. Their main characteristics are bureaucracy and increased resistance to change. Furthermore, they avoid high-risk decisions. On the contrary, less active cultures place less importance on typical rules and specialisation; they demonstrate no interest in uniformity and show tolerance towards many different ideas and behaviours. The lack of formalism allows a quick response and adaption to changes. Finally, individuals from these cultures undertake the risk of personal decisions with greater ease.

The domain of "individualism/collectivism" describes the relationship between the individual and the group or society as a whole. It depicts the degree to which the individuals of a country learn to act more individually as opposed to as members of a society. In countries where collectivism is strong, greater emphasis is placed on social, friend or family bonds. In such societies, people have a collective mindset

---

similar to that of "values" and "cultural dimensions" and "attitudes". This equalization of the concepts might be daring, but it allows us to connect, in a manner that is easy to understand and helpful, the accepted concepts developed in social psychology with the concepts developed in organizational psychology. These common tools are useful, in the end, for understanding the cultural background of the process of development and growth.

and strive for the good of the group, often demoting their personal goals for the good of the group. The members of such groups present signs of codependence and believe that the preservation of the group's prosperity is the best guarantee for their own prosperity. On the other hand, in individualistic societies, the bonds between individuals are loose, and people mostly act on their private interests. Individual achievements and freedom are of great importance. People are self-sufficient and do not feel the need to seek support from others. They see their personality as a separate entity and prioritise the fulfilment of their personal goals, not those of the group.

The domain of "masculinity/femininity" captures the degree to which "masculine" values, such as good performance, success and competition, dominate over "feminine" values, e.g., quality of life, preservation of good personal relationships, convenience, care for the feeble and solidarity. In a masculine society, the family guides children towards ambition and competitiveness, imposing different roles on men and women. The society is interested in results, and compensation is distributed according to performance. On the other hand, "feminine" societies emphasise social relationships and helping one another, as might be reflected in public policies that favour income redistribution and increased social spending.

In a later study, Hofstede and Bond (1988), identified a fifth domain, which they named "Confucian Dynamism" or, later, "Future Orientation". This domain separates short-term-oriented from long-term-oriented cultures. Future orientation entails persistence, breakdown of relationships according to social status, maintenance of this order, saving and a feeling of shame. Short-term orientation is connected with personal stability, price protection, respect for tradition and exchanges of greetings, favours and gifts. In this framework, the GLOBE research refers to future orientation, which is defined as the degree to which members of a society engage in future-oriented behaviours, such as planning, future investments and delay of pleasure. This domain is based on the domain of orientation towards the past, present or future of Kluckhohn and Strodtbeck (1961).

"Performance orientation" refers to the degree to which a society encourages and rewards its members for the improvement of their performance and for their superiority. Additionally, "human orientation" refers to the degree to which people in a society encourage and reward others for their justice, truthfulness, friendliness, generosity, care and politeness.

The role of religion in shaping the basic system of societal values is integral to the previous analysis. Many researchers support the idea that religion creates and affects personal values and attitudes (Tayeb 2000). For instance, according to Weber (1958), individualism, preference for personal choice and autonomy and the willingness to achieve personal goals constitute characteristics of Protestantism. On the contrary, Confucianism is characterised by family and group orientation, respect for age and hierarchy, preference for harmony and avoidance of confrontations and competitiveness.

Furthermore, religion (apart from individualistic behaviour) also affects a society's activities. The change of the economic structure in England from feudalism to capitalism and private property in the seventeenth century is a characteristic example. According to Weber, one of the factors that contributed to this change was the particularly Protestant "morality" that emphasised the tireless, continuous procurement of goods. Weber believed that Protestantism was the cradle of the modern economic human, and Calvinism in particular accentuated individuality, personal capabilities and initiatives. Even though modern capitalism was a result of the special social structure of the Western world, it would have been inconceivable without Calvinism, which contributed to the liberation of the procurement of goods from the inhibitions of traditional morality (Tayeb 2000).

The cultural values stemming from the influence of Orthodox Christianity that are connected with economic activity have not been sufficiently studied, even though they concern populations (about 200 m people globally) which, almost in their totality, have been under their full influence for almost two millennia. One of the very few sources is the study by Oikonomou, "Axioms and virtues of entrepreneurship in Orthodoxy" (Ed. Petrakis 2008). The author's approach that "as holistic religious beliefs, also include the values that produce or inspire the economic theory and practice" is characteristic. A basic element of the Orthodox Christian approach is that man is not the master of the physical world but its user and manager, while all the goods that need to be managed (knowledge and materials) come from the outside (from God) and are given for free; that is, they are "God's trust".

Based on the previous point, it is apparent that the Orthodox Christian worldview does not place ownership, and consequently the process of wealth accumulation and economic growth, in the highest position of its hierarchy of values.

6.4 Empirical Facts on the Hierarchy of Cultural Values

Table 6.4 presents Greece's rankings, as well as those of certain other Mediterranean and Northern European countries, for every one of the domains of social culture based on Hofstede (2001) and the GLOBE study (Koopman et al. 1999). The Mediterranean countries examined were Spain, Italy and Portugal, and the Northern European countries were Denmark, the Netherlands, Norway, Sweden and Finland.

Based on the data in Table 6.4, we arrive at two basic conclusions:
Greece can be considered a typical Mediterranean country in terms of its cultural values.
There is an obvious differentiation between the cultural characteristics of Mediterranean and Northern European countries.

The two studies reached similar conclusions concerning the rankings of the two groups of countries. However, a comment is required on the ranking of uncertainty avoidance: Mediterranean countries present a lower ranking compared to Northern European countries, meaning that the former avoid uncertainty to a lesser degree. A possible explanation for this finding is that the comparison of the results of the two studies is problematic as Hofstede's research did not include countries from Central and Eastern Europe. Moreover, the two studies used different measures to

Table 6.4 Rankings of Greece and Mediterranean and Northern European countries according to social culture domains, based on Hofstede (2001) and GLOBE

Domains/countries	Greece	Mediterranean countries	Northern European countries
Power distance (acceptance of inequalities)	27 (H)	24–34 (H)	40–51 (H)
	21	15–20	47–60
Uncertainty avoidance	1 (H)	2–23 (H)	31–51 (H)
Individualism vs. collectivism	30 (H)	7–33 (H)	4–17 (H)
Institutional collectivism	61	46–56	1–20
In-group collectivism	35	26–41	54–60
Masculinity vs. femininity	18 (H)	4–45	47–53
Gender egalitarianism	27	15–52	5–31
Assertiveness	9	11–46	1–18
Confucian dynamism/future orientation	51	37–56	4–14
Performance orientation	61	37–55	19–48
Human orientation	59	41–60	14–38

Note: H indicates Hofstede's elements and indicates that these rankings concern "values". The GLOBE elements concern "practices"

analyse this domain (Koopman et al. 1999). In general, the two studies present similar rankings of societies, with the exception of "uncertainty avoidance". In the present work, we adopt Hofstede's measurement for this domain, mostly because it is compatible with the risk measurements that prove that, through time, Mediterranean countries have been systematically dominated by increased risk levels, which explains the history of intense uncertainty avoidance. Consequently, it is reasonable to accept the measurements that demonstrate that practices of risk avoidance are followed rather than those that show the opposite.

The cultural values model described in the two groups of countries is, in general, the following: Mediterranean countries accept the existence of inequalities more than Northern European countries do and present increased (according to Hofstede) uncertainty avoidance. The value of individual achievements is not greatly esteemed, but, at the same time, organisationally and socially established rules and practices are not accepted. Individuals, however, express pride, faith and closeness with their families and the specific organisations to which they belong. Feminine values, such as quality of life, caring for the feeble and solidarity, play a minor role and are a main characteristic of Northern European countries. Consequently, it does not seem that the values of enforcement and confrontation dominate.

Mediterranean countries are not future oriented. On the contrary, a short-term view, with limited use of programming and long-term planning, dominates. Performance orientation and orientation to humanity are also decreased.

The very important observation that the cultural model of Greek society is the same as that of the other Mediterranean countries and has specific differences from that of the Northern European countries may be largely due to the geographical

Table 6.5 Comparison of cultural models (Hofstede)

	Power distance	Individualism	Masculinity	Uncertainty avoidance
Northern European countries (Norway, Sweden, Finland)	24	65	9	38
Greece	60	35	57	112
Italy	45	70	63	70
Spain	52	45	38	80
Portugal	58	20	25	98
Turkey	60	30	40	80
Arab countries (Egypt, Iraq, Kuwait, Lebanon, Saudi Arabia, UAE)	80	38	52	68

Source: www.geert-hofstede.com

locations of the countries. Greece is strategically positioned in the midst of technological and innovative developments, between Western and Central Europe, the
Arab nations (to the south) and Turkey (to the east). More specifically, in the Balkan
region, there are strong mutual influences with the Arab nations, and the cultural
differences are sometimes minimal. The last two centuries have seen important and
stable changes to the degree of influence between countries and to the determination of geographical borders (e.g., repeated raids, piracy in the Mediterranean).

Table 6.5 presents a comparison of cultural models between Greece, Turkey, and
the Mediterranean, Northern European and Arab countries according to Hofstede's
computations (Hofstede 2001).

The analysis of Table 6.5 shows that the Turkish cultural model is very similar to
that of Mediterranean countries. Moreover, the Mediterranean countries' model is
much closer to that of Arab countries than it is to that of Northern European
countries. The exogenous factors shaping the cultural background of the Mediterranean and Arab countries are similar, even though it appears that the effect of these
factors somehow decreases for the Mediterranean countries over time. These factors
seem to be those that shape Western civilisation, such as religion and climate.

Comparing the Greek cultural model with that of the Northern European
countries, we observe that the sum of the four cultural values is 264 for Greek
society and 136 for Northern European countries.

In effect, the societies of the Mediterranean can be characterised as "old"
(increased sum of values), presenting strong subconscious bonds with older
societies. In contrast, Northern European countries could be characterised as
"new", lacking an extensive cultural background (low sum of values), which allows
them to cultivate modern values and offer their citizens increased satisfaction and
happiness.

Based on the above, we conclude that the cultural model dominating the
Mediterranean is not a result of conflicts and controversy between nations but of
the blending of the broader cultural models of the area, which arose from the
interconnection of common fundamental forces. For Greek society (which is
similar to societies of other Mediterranean countries), this difference indicates

Table 6.6 GLOBE's results for Greek culture

Domains of social culture	Society – practices Scores	Ranking Rank	Society – values Scores	Ranking Rank	Practices – values Scores
Power distance	5.40	21	2.39	52	−3.01
Uncertainty avoidance	3.39	57	5.09	17	1.70
Institutional collectivism	3.25	61	5.40	5	2.15
In-group collectivism	5.27	35	5.46	42	0.19
Gender egalitarianism	3.48	27	4.89	16	1.41
Assertiveness	4.58	9	2.96	57	−1.62
Future orientation	3.40	51	5.19	48	1.79
Performance orientation	3.20	61	5.81	40	2.61
Human orientation	3.34	59	5.23	50	1.89

that there is an active Greek cultural background that can lead to growth and development. However, the exact opposite could happen if the cultural background does not favour this change.

Table 6.6 presents the results of the GLOBE research on Greek culture. Specifically, it presents the average scores and rankings for the aspects of culture that correspond to Greek society's current situation (practices). Furthermore, it shows the desired cultural aspects (values) and the difference between the current and the desired situations. Based on the table, we conclude that the differences between the current and desirable situations of Greek society are quite important. Bourantas et al. (1990) realised that the differences between the real and the desired states reveal the desire of members of Greek society for cultural change. This table may allow us to envision the dynamic change of the cultural model, even though it is known that culture changes very slowly.

In the first domain, power distance, Greece has a relatively high ranking (21st among 61 countries), as well as the largest difference between the present and desired situations.

Concerning the degree to which Greek society favours collective over individual behaviour, the research reveals the individualistic nature of the Greeks. In institutional collectivism, Greece is at the bottom of the list. Greeks find it difficult to operate as a team. However, the research participants would like more collectivism in action as well as in the decisions that are made.

On the contrary, in in-group collectivism, which relates to family or organisational ties, the research reveals a different picture. Greece ranks 35th, and the degree of the present societal situation is two points higher than that for institutional collectivism. These results agree with Hofstede's findings, based on which Greece ranks near the middle of the individualism scale. Greece has the second lowest score of any Mediterranean country, after Portugal. The bonds of the Greeks with their families remain quite strong. Despite an intense urban pull, which tends to alienate and disrupt relationships, the family maintains its importance as the core of education, security and protection of its members.

The aspect of in-group collectivism relates to the different treatment of members of a group versus individuals who do not belong to it. This also constitutes a characteristic of Greek society (Triandis 1995). In-groups could include family, relatives and friends, and in-group members enjoy protection, trust and support while providing faith, devotion and sacrifice in exchange. On the other hand, individuals who do not belong in this group are treated with suspicion and animosity.

The participants' perceptions of gender egalitarianism demonstrate that there is extensive inequality between men and women in Greek society. They also express the wish for greater equality between the sexes. According to Table 6.4, Greece holds one of the highest rankings for assertiveness. Assertiveness is an attribute of members of a society that mainly relates to their assertiveness in social relationships and their ability to survive in a competitive environment (e.g., extraversion).

Greece ranks 51st in future-oriented behaviour. This ranking suggests that there is, in general, a short-term view of things, with decreased use of programming and long-term planning. This specific aspect is connected with the future orientation of Hofstede and Bond (1988), who emphasise the importance of savings and patience, contrary to the values of entertainment and immediate pleasure.

Finally, in performance orientation and human orientation, Greece ranks last among the 61 examined countries. This result signifies that the prevailing concept in Greece is that society does not encourage or reward its members enough and according to their performance, while the higher score of the desired situation shows that greater recognition is sought. According to Papalexandri (2007), there is a general trend of distrust towards individual achievements and increased success. Competitiveness is usually combined with individualism, a disposition towards disbelief, difficulty in allocation of responsibilities or combination of efforts for the achievement of a common goal and continuous conflicts and altercations over events or ideas. The lack of performance and human orientation is remarkable, indicating the absence of goals.

6.5 Social Capital

In the middle of the 1980s, the concept of social capital began to gain more and more importance in social theory and research (Paraskevopoulos 2007). In general, the term refers to benefits that are strengthened by participation and incorporation in social networks (Portes 1998). Besides this basic approach, however, many significant alternative definitions of the concept of social capital have been put forward (Adler and Kwon 2002).

Bourdieu (1986), one of the founders of research on social capital, dissociates social from economic and cultural capital, defining the first as the sum of the real and conditional sources creating a stable network of mutual familiarity. Coleman

(1990), approaching the subject from a sociological point of view, defined social capital not based on the resources arising from being part of networks but as the networks themselves, which facilitate the actions of their members. Putnam (1995) extended Coleman's approach, defining social capital as those characteristics of the societal organisation that "facilitate coordination and cooperation towards the common good". These characteristics include three concepts: networks, rules and trust.

The common characteristic of these approaches is the view that participation in social networks carries benefits in the forms of resources and support. Networks could thus be characterised as the basic providers of social capital between individuals, groups and society (Franke 2005). Social networks can include many individuals or groups of individuals. The benefits of coexistence depend on those involved and include increased access to priceless information and ideas, chances for shaping new relationships and strengthening of individual efforts through common action (Adler and Kwon 2002).

Social capital, as the property of either individuals or groups, has been associated with many important outcomes. On the part of the individual, social capital could be considered as a significant sum of secondary resources that increase the individual's power and facilitate the achievement of goals. They could include not only economic targets but also ultimate personal and relative intermediate goals (Snijders 1999).

Recent studies have shown that Greece ranks in one of the lowest positions for social capital among the European and other OECD member countries. One such study (Christoforou 2005) gathered all of the scores from the European Community Household Panel (ECHP) for 1999 and found that among the EU15, the four southernmost countries, i.e., Spain, Portugal, Italy and Greece, had the lowest percentages for citizen participation in groups. Of these countries, Greece had the lowest percentage (8.9%) compared to the mean of the rest of the countries (32.4%). It should be noted that these four countries also had the lowest per capita incomes among the 15 countries, which further supports the argument that there is an important correlation between social capital and economic development.

Using citizen scores from 23 European countries collected for the European Values Survey (EVS) for 1999/2000, Van Oorschot et al. (2006) concluded that Northern European countries (Sweden, Finland and Denmark) had the highest scores on most of the variables used to calculate social capital. Southern and Eastern European countries presented less trust towards institutions. Greece ranked just above Portugal (12.3%) with the lowest level of trust among the 23 countries (23.7%) towards institutions per se. Spain and Italy had generalised trust towards institutions of 38.6% and 32.6%, respectively. At the same time, the active and passive participation of Greeks in organisations was generally higher than that of citizens of many other countries, especially those of Eastern and Southern Europe.

Analysing the results of the European Social Survey (ESS) of 2002, Paraskevopoulos (2007) confirms that social capital, in the form of trust and participation in groups, is lower in the countries of Southern and Eastern Europe compared to other regions of Europe. Greece ranked lowest among 18 countries, with a score of 3.6 on a scale from 0 to 10 (0 = no trust, 10 = absolute trust). Spain, Italy and Portugal had scores of 4.9, 4.5 and 4, respectively.

Concerning probable changes in social capital through time, Adam (2008) claimed that according to the EVS results, from 1981 to 1990, there was an increase of generalised trust in most European countries that participated in the research. From 1990 until 1999, however, generalised trust decreased in more countries than it increased. During the same period, there was an increase in participation in volunteer organisations in most European countries participating in the research. The lack of data for Greece in the EVS before the 1999/2000 wave makes it impossible to compare possible changes to those observed in other countries for this period.

Although the last decade has seen an increase in research concerning the fundamental measurement of social capital in Greece, there are still many gaps. The half-yearly Eurobarometer and the biannual European Social Survey (ESS) provide useful data concerning trust towards institutions, interpersonal trust and social networking. Unfortunately, however, the questions in the Eurobarometer study seem to focus exclusively on the attitudes of European citizens towards the EU and not towards levels of interpersonal trust or trust towards national institutions or volunteer organisations. As for ESS, valuable information emerged concerning trust in Greece from the first (2002) and second (2004) measurements; unfortunately, though, Greece was not included in the third measurement (2006), so changes in measures of social capital in Greece from 2002 to 2006 cannot be determined based on the ESS.

Table 6.7 highlights significant correlations. One of these is the low participation in teams as compared to the average of all countries participating in the European Values Survey of 1999–2000 already mentioned.

Table 6.7 shows that trust in public institutions is higher, by far, in many European countries, especially those in the North, compared to Greece. Another noteworthy element is that trust towards institutions decreased significantly in 2007 and 2008. Furthermore, trust in the Greek government decreased by 12% from 2007 to 2008. These variables show that trust in institutions, one of the basic measures of social capital, has recently decreased in Greece. It is characteristic that Cox (2003) positively correlates the lack of trust in political institutions with the lack of interpersonal trust.

The modern history of Greece reveals possible reasons for the feeble institutional and generalised trust of the country in relation to other European countries. Lyberaki and Paraskevopoulos (2002) propose the causes to be the traditional presence of an autocratic Greek state as well as the difficulties in organising the institutions during the transitional period to democracy (from 1974 until the mid-1990s). These difficulties contributed to the creation of indistinct limits between the government, the markets and society, as well as to the dominant position of the government and political parties in the relationships between the government and society. This led to the development of a weak volunteer sector, with a minimum strengthening of relationships with existing volunteer organisations or other organised groups of individuals. Similarly, Christoforou determined two basic factors that contributed to the low social capital in Greece. The first is the economic

Table 6.7 Measurements of relationships, interpersonal trust and trust in institutions in Greece

Networks	1999–2000 EVS[a]	2001–2002 ESS	2004 ESS	2007	2008
Participation in teams	8.9%[c] (32.4%)[b]	26.3%[d]	26%[e] (45%)	–	–
Passive participation in teams	1.0 (0.7)	–	–	–	–
Active participation in teams	0.8 (0.5)	–	–	–	–
Ages of team participation, 15–24	–	37.4%[f] (50.1%)	–	–	–
Family relationships	2.2 (2.1)	–	–	–	–
Relationships with friends	2.7 (2.4)	–	–	–	–
Relationships with friends and family	–	4.2 (5.0)	3.8 (4.9)	–	–
Trust towards					
Other individuals	1.2	3.6 (4.7)	3.8 (4.5)	–	–
Institutions	12.1[g] (14.6)	34%[h] (35%)	–	–	–
Parliament	–	4.8 (4.6)	4.7 (4.5)	52%[i] (35%)	49% (34%)
Parliament	–	–	–	81[j]	51
National government	–	–	–	22 46% (34%)	12 34% (32%)
Legal system	–	6.3 (5.1)	5.4 (4.9)	–	–
Police	–	6.4 (6.1)	6.0 (5.7)	–	–
Politicians/political parties	–	3.5 (3.6)	3.6 (3.4)	22[j]	10

Source: Mavris, 2007 and 2008 (Greek Indicators of Confidence in Institutions (GICI), 15 May 2009.)

[a]The letters in the columns show the initial source of the data contained in each column. EVS: European Values study 1999/2000; ESS: European Social Survey, 2002 and 2004. The exceptions to the sources are signified with numbers in superscript

[b]Where data are available, the means of all countries participating in the research are included in brackets

[c]Data from the European Community Household Panel, 6th wave, 1999 (European Union)

[d]Data from research for a specific work, Athens: Kapa Research, 2002 (reference from Lyberaki and Praskevopoulos 2002)

[e]Data from the special Eurobarometer 223 (reference from European Commission 2007 – European Social Reality. Spec. Eurobarom. No. 273)

[f]Data from the European Commission, Directorate-General for Education and Culture, department of Youth (reference from Lyberaki and Paraskevopoulos 2002)

[g]Combination of trust in the parliament, the system of social insurance, the health system, the justice system, the police and public services (Van Oorschot et al. 2006)

[h]Combination of trust in the national government, parliament, public services and political parties (Source: Eurobarometer 55)

[i]Source of data (in this row) for 2007 and 2008: Eurobarometer 69

[j]The numbers in this row for 2007 and 2008 are the Greek indices for trust in institutions (GICI), calculated by dividing the number of individuals questioned who said that they trust an institution by the number of those questioned who do not trust it and multiplying the result by 100

and political instability prevailing in modern Greek history. The country became vulnerable to economic turbulence and urban society faltered, contributing to the advancement of the second factor, which is rules and networks based on customer protection relations, nepotism and corruption (see Jones et al. 2008). Christoforou (2005) also calls attention to the fact that research in EU member states demonstrates that income and education could be connected with low levels of social capital in Greece.

6.6   The Role of Family Networks in Greece

Family networks in Greece play a crucial role. The absence of an extended social state and its services is, in essence, compensated for by family care, leading to an important decrease in the demand for public services such as kindergartens, old-age homes and unemployment coverage. This structure broadens social coherence and intra-family social capital to the degree that trust and the mutual accommodation of family members increase while offering grounds for the exercising of family entrepreneurship based on autonomous intra-family planning. However, family networks also engage an important part of the active workforce, such as women, who are severed from the labour market, leading to multiple social and financial consequences.

The basic forms of pre-school childcare in Greece are municipal day nurseries and day-care centres (for children aged 8 months to 4 years) and public kindergartens for children aged 4–6 years. There are many private kindergartens and day nurseries. Even though it is generally accepted that it is extremely difficult to find specific data as there is no systematic record or official documents (Karamessini 2005), according to certain estimates, the existing positions in public childcare institutions cover 4–5% of the needs of children up to 3 years and 65–70% of the needs for children aged 3–6 years, while private institutions cover 2% of the needs of children aged 8 months to 5 years (European Childcare Strategies, Statistical Annex).

We should mention the important deviation from the targets set by the European Council concerning the participation of women in the labour market and the presence of institutionalised care for pre-school children that is directly dependent thereon. The suggested target by 2010 was to cover 90% of the required positions for children older than 3 years up to the age of compulsory school entrance and 33% of the required positions for children under age 3 (EU Expert Group 2005).

In addition, the state officially obliges businesses with more than 300 employees to have kindergartens (L. 1483/1984 and P.D. 193/1988). In reality, however, very few companies have such facilities (Stratigaki 2006). The significant deviation between the available positions in municipal childcare institutions and the number of children whose parents both work (and who, consequently, require some sort of care) is largely covered by family members. According to a HEL. STAT. study from 2006, friends, family or household members (mostly grandmothers) took care of 80.5% of children up to age 2 and 56.8% of children aged 3–5 years (Stratigaki 2006, Karamessini 2005). Consequently, in Greece, mostly for cultural reasons relating to the strong structure and presence of the family, there is a definite preference for children up to the age of 3 to remain at home with some caregiver instead of enrolling in a day nursery. Besides, the operating hours for day nurseries and the extended vacations (2 weeks during Christmas and Easter and 1 month during the summer) are incompatible with the work schedules of employed parents. Therefore, in reality, even when these childcare institutions are used, there is still a need for some other person (usually relatives) to take care of the children from time to time.

The existence of two official childcare institutions for pre-school children constitutes a basic prerequisite for the free access of women to the labour market and for the reconciliation between work and private life, which is one of the cornerstones of employment policies in the EU. In Greece, the large discrepancies in welfare policies between the private and public sectors concerning maternity and nursing leave create two different realities for women working in the private and public sectors (Stratigaki 2006): the percentage of women leaving work in the private sector after having a child, especially in low-salary positions, is particularly high because of the high "cost" of caring for children at home (Karamessini 2005), while in the public sector, the assurance of maternity leave rights creates a definite and improved regime.

Finally, the welfare scheme prevailing in Greece is cited in the literature as the "family care model" (Antonnen and Sipila 1996, Abrahamson 1999, Esping-Andersen 1990). The family bears a significant part of the cost of caring for its dependent members, whether they are children or elderly, and the financing of the corresponding care institutions by the government is weak. Thus, the existence of care institutions is not only dictated by obvious economic criteria such as the unencumbered and equivalent access of women to the labour market, especially those in socially vulnerable population groups and who are negatively affected by the absence of such childcare institutions, but also by social cohesion criteria (Stratigaki 2006).

6.7   Economic and Social Reflections of the Cultural Model

We have determined that Greek society presents social and cultural characteristics similar to those of other Mediterranean countries. The primary forces that shaped the social models of various Mediterranean countries (e.g., geography, evolution, history) share certain characteristics, as do those that shaped the social models of Northern European countries (which are different from the Mediterranean countries).

6.7.1   The Basic Description of the Model

The cultural model of Greek society consists of a mixture of priorities. Thus, power distance (wealth, income power) is largely accepted, even though wishes have been expressed to the contrary. Tellingly, the GNI indices in Greece and other

Mediterranean countries are significantly higher (i.e., there is more unequal distribution of income) than in the Northern European countries.

The level of uncertainty avoidance is increased, as are the risk levels experienced by the social model. Indeed, all risk indices, namely, composite risk, political risk and economic risk (Table 6.9, rows 2, 3 and 4, respectively) are higher in Mediterranean compared with Northern European countries. The fear of crime experienced in Mediterranean countries (see Table 6.9, rows 5, 6) in comparison with the Northern European countries is also noteworthy.

Greece presents low future orientation. This finding indicates a short-term view of things and decreased use of programming and long-term planning.

Individualism and promoting individual achievements are low priorities. Society does not encourage or reward its members enough and according to their performance, although this is desired (as indicated by high "values" scores).

The lack of performance orientation is worth mentioning. Characteristically, to date, the introduction of evaluation procedures to ensure quality and transparency in all levels of education of Greek society has not been completed. In addition, the acceptance of entrepreneurship by the public seems to be much lower in Mediterranean than in Northern European countries, except for Denmark (Table 6.9, row 14).

In addition, trust in institutions and participation in collective procedures are particularly low in Greece and other Mediterranean countries (see Table 6.9, row 7).

In-group collectivism, a concept that is mainly relevant to family, constitutes a very important index in Greece, assuming high values. The extraordinary importance of family for Greeks is also supported by Eurobarometer's research on European social reality, in which 100% of the individuals questioned considered family to be one of the most important institutions in their lives (European Commission, European Social Reality, 2007). For this reason, the average participation of children in organised nursery care is extremely limited in Mediterranean countries in comparison with Northern European countries (Table 6.9, row 9). The aspect of in-group collectivism captures a different way of dealing with the groups of a society and constitutes an important element that determines the strength of the sense of collectivism and social cohesion.

Greek society's organisation is highly "masculine", distanced from social solidarity and caring for the feeble. A world full of uncertainty and limited collective trust leads to the procurement of individual wealth as a last measure of security. Tellingly, the level of individual wealth in Greece is higher than that of Denmark and comparable with that of Norway (Table 6.8, row 8)! Obviously, the citizens of Northern European countries live more "happy life years" (Table 6.9, row 1) using services that improve their quality of life and do not necessarily depend on their levels of individual wealth. Nevertheless, in Greece, the value of assertiveness is denied, and competitiveness in social relationships is not greatly encouraged. Furthermore, "feminine" values are weak in Mediterranean countries. The objectively much higher greenhouse gas emissions in Mediterranean compared to Northern European countries is indicative of this situation (see Table 6.9, row 17).

Table 6.8 Economic and social indices

Variable	Annual data	Mediterranean countries				Northern countries				
		Greece	Italy	Spain	Portugal	Netherlands	Denmark	Norway	Sweden	Finland
1. GDP per capita growth (%)	Average 1999–2007	3.8	0.9	2.3	1.2	1.3	1.6	1.7	2.8	2.0
2. Equality index (Gini coefficient) (%)	2000	32.1	35.2	31.9	38.5	27.1	23.2	27.6	23.4	26.9
3. Public debt (GDP %)	Average 1999–2007	99.9	107.4	48.5	58.6	54.8	42.1	43.9	52.2	42.7
4. Private consumption (GDP %)	Average 1999–2007	71.8	59.1	58.3	64.2	48.7	48.5	44.4	48.5	51.1
5. Gross formation of fixed capital (GDP %)	Average 1999–2007	22.2	20.6	27.8	24.0	20.1	20.3	20.0	17.6	19.1
6. Exports (GDP %)	Average 1999–2007	22.0	26.4	26.6	29.3	68.7	47.3	42.7	47.2	41.7
7. Size of shadow economy (%)	Average 2001–2002	28.5	27.0	22.5	22.5	13.0	17.9	19.1	19.1	18.0
8. Wealth per capita ($)	2000	72,825	119,704	92,253	53,357	120,086	66,191	72,254	80,091	38,754

Table 6.9 Developmental indices

Variable	Year	Mediterranean countries				Northern countries				
		Greece	Italy	Spain	Portugal	Netherlands	Denmark	Norway	Sweden	Finland
1 Happy life years[a]	2008	50.4	54.4	57.8	44.0	59.1	65.4	61.7	62.2	69.0
2 Composite risk[b]	2007	72.2	77.2	77.5	77.5	85.0	86.5	92.2	87.2	88.2
3 Political risk[c]	2007	77	79	80	83	84.5	85.5	89.5	88.5	94
4 Economic risk[d]	2007	35.5	39.0	39.5	35.5	45.0	44.0	48.0	46.0	46.0
5 Crime[e]	2004	12.3	12.6	9.1	10.4	19.7	18.8	15.8	16.1	12.7
6 Fear of crime[f]	2004	42	35	33	34	18	17	14	19	14
7 Trust in institutions (%)[g]	2006	−16.0	−31.0	−8.0	−23.0	1.0	7.0	–	3.0	30.0
8 Participation in a team (%)[h]	1999/2000	8.9	23.8	24.5	18.0	44.8	65.1	–	40.9	55.2
9 Percentage participation of children (<3 years old) in organised infant care (%)[i]	2005	7.0	6.3	20.7	23.5	29.5	61.7	43.7	39.5	22.4
10 Corruption index[j]	2008	4.7	4.8	6.5	6.1	8.9	9.3	7.9	9.3	9
11 Home ownership (%)[k]	–	≈ 80	≈ 72	≈ 80	–	≈ 50	≈ 65	–	≈ 65	–
12 Employment (%)[l]	2007	61.5	58.7	66.6	67.8	74.1	77.3	77.5	75.7	70.5
13 Entrepreneurship acceptance (%)[m]	2007	65.9	68.5	61.0	67.2	68.8	79.1	56.6	67.4	84.8
14 Acceptance of entrepreneurship by public opinion (%)[n]	2007	43.4	43.9	45.5	51.2	61.1	35.5	69.5	62.8	68.3
15 Classification of the frame of business activity[o]	2009	96	65	49	48	26	5	10	17	14
16 Governance effectiveness[p]	2007	70	65	81	80	95	99	100	98	98
17 Gas emissions (millions of equivalent tons CO_2)[q]	2007	131.85	552.77	442.32	81.84	207.5	66.64	55.05	65.41	78.35

[a]Estimate of how many happy years the citizens of every country will live on average (Veenhoven 2009)

[b]The composite risk index constitutes a computation of individual risk indices (e.g., economic, financial, political) and assumes values from 0 to 100. An increase of the index signifies a decrease of a country's risk levels and vice versa. Source: PRS Group, ICRG database

[c]The political risk index is the weighted average of individual measurements of political risk (e.g., internal and external conflicts, quality of public governance, estimates concerning corruption) and assumes values from 0 to 100. An increase of the index signifies a decrease of the political risk in a country and vice versa. Source: PRS Group, ICRG database

(continued)

[d]The economic risk index is the weighted average of individual indices of the economic situation of a country (e.g., rate of growth, levels of inflation, balance of current transactions and budget, levels of public debt) and assumes values from 0 to 50. An increase of the index signifies a decrease of the economic risk in a country and vice versa. Source: PRS Group, ICRG database

[e]The index indicates the percentage of the population that reports criminal activity. Source: OECD, Society at a glance, 2009

[f]The index expresses the percentage of the population that reports being afraid to walk in the street after sunset. Source: OECD, Society at a glance, 2009

[g]Positive minus negative opinions concerning national institutions. Source: Eurobarometer 66 (2006)

[h]European Values Study 1999/2000

[i]OECD, Society at a glance, 2009

[j]The Corruption Perceptions Index is the weighted average of the individual indices from two answers to questionnaires completed by people knowledgeable about these subjects. Source: Transparency International, 2008

[k]French statistical service (www.insee.fr)

[l]OECD, Society at a glance, 2009

[m]Percentage of positive answers to a question concerning recognition of and respect towards people who successfully create a new business. Source: FEIR, 2008

[n]Percentage of positive answers to a question concerning the promotion of stories of successful new businesses by the media. Source: FEIR, 2008

[o]The index constitutes an indication for the facilitation of businesses and arises from the computation of individual indices (e.g., ease in starting new businesses, recruiting new associates or securing credits). Source: World Bank, Doing Business

[p]The effectiveness of the governance index arises from the statistical processing of answers to questionnaires of individuals working in businesses and specialists in the relevant sector. It assumes values from 0 to 100, with the highest values signifying greater governance effectiveness and vice versa. Source: World Bank, Governance Indicators, 2007

[q]Eurostat, env_air_emis, GHG

6.7.2   Temporal Orientation and Relationship with the Future

The pessimism observed in Greek society is connected to the lack of future orientation. Specifically, a significant pessimism towards the future is observed in Greece, as expressed through the predominance of bleak opinions about the financial situation and unemployment (European Commission, European Social Reality, 2007). As portrayed in Eurobarometer's research between 2000 and 2008, the percentage of Greeks expecting a better outcome in all issues has decreased steadily.

It is extremely difficult to understand whether the lack of future orientation and pessimism are connected through a causal relationship or if they simply coexist as two situations with probably common origins. These values obviously discourage individuals from saving and investing and consequently from growth of their personal wealth, accentuating the value of consumption (see Table 6.8, row 4). Consumption as a percentage of GDP is definitely higher in Mediterranean compared to Northern European countries, even though, surprisingly, Greek households have shown a steadily declining course of (consumer) optimism since 1985, and for over 20 years the percentage of pessimistic households in Greece has remained greater the Eurozone average. The lack of future orientation is thus related to a more general political and social trend. The inflated fiscal deficit and public debt, which are definitely higher in Mediterranean countries (see Table 6.8, row 3), constitute prevalent examples of these trends. Another negative characteristic of the Greek administration is the lack of strategic long-term planning (Myloni et al. 2004). This is mostly due to Greeks' great uncertainty about the future, the frequent changes in legislation and unforeseen events that force Greek managers to limit themselves to short-term planning (Makridakis et al. 1997).

6.7.3   Self-Employment and the Shadow Economy

The degradation of the value of individual achievements, together with the difference between the principle of competitiveness and the lack of faith towards collective activity, have created a strong tendency in the Greek society towards self-employment, although creative entrepreneurship is not promoted. On the other hand, the strong support of the society for "masculinity" is expressed through individualism and thus self-employment. This line of reasoning provides a sufficient explanation for the very high levels of self-employment in the Greek economy (see Table 6.9, row 12), which are also due to the lack of future orientation and trust in the future.

Culturally, the enlargement of the shadow economy is the result of the coincidence of a number of aspects of Greek culture: Denial of institutional collectivism and decreased trust towards institutions combined with the dominance of in-group collectivism (family-immediate environment) play the most important roles. At the same time, however, the low future orientation, including pessimism, which discourages long-term resource commitment, also plays an important role.

References

Abrahamson P (1999) The welfare modeling business. Soc Pol Admin 33(4):394–415

Acemoglu D, Johnson S, Robinson J (2004) Institutions as the fundamental cause of long-run growth. CEPR Discussion Paper 4458, C.E.P.R Discussion Papers

Adam F (2008) Mapping social capital across Europe: findings. Trends and methodological shortcomings of cross-national surveys. Soc Sci Inf 47(2):159–186

Adler P, Kwon SW (2002) Social capital: prospects for a new concept. Acad Manag Rev 27:17–40

Akerlof GA, Shiller RJ (2009) Animal spirits: how human psychology drives the economy, and why it matters for global capitalism. NJ: Princeton University Press, Princeton

Antonnen A, Sipila J (1996) European social care services: is it possible to identify models? J Eur Soc Pol 6(2):87–100

Bourantas D, Anagnostelis J, Mantes Y, Kefalas AG (1990) Culture gap in Greek management. Organ Stud 11(2):261–283

Bourdieu P (1986) The forms of capital 241–58. In: Richardson JG (ed) Handbook of theory and research for the sociology of education. Greenwood Press, New York

Bourguignon F, Lévy-Leboyer M (1984) An econometric model of France during the 19th century. Eur Econ Rev 25:107–141

Christoforou A (2005) On the determinants of social capital in Greece compared to countries of the European Union. Fondazione Eni Enrico Mattei Note di Lavoro Series No 68–2005

Coleman JS (1990) The foundations of social theory. Harvard University Press, Cambridge

Dritsa M (1990) Industry and banking in Greece during the inter-war period. Historical Archive of the National Bank of Greece, Athens

Esping-Andersen G (1990) The three worlds of welfare capitalism. Polity Press, London, Cambridge

Franke S (2005) Measurement of social capital: reference document for public policy research, development, and evaluation. Document Prepared by the Policy Research Initiative Project: Social Capital as a Public Policy Tool, Canada

Friedman M, Schwartz A (1963) A monetary history of the United States 1867–1960. NJ: Princeton University Press, Princeton

Georgas J, Berry JW (1995) An ecocultural taxonomy for cross-cultural psychology. J Cross Cult Res 29:121–157

Hertwig R, Barron G, Weber E, Erev I (2004) Decisions from experience and the effect of rare events in risky choice. Psychol Sci 15:534–539

Hofstede G (1980) Culture's consequences: international differences in work-related values. Sage Publishers, Beverly Hills, CA

Hofstede G (1991) Cultures and organisations. Harper Collins Publishers, London

Hofstede G (2001) Culture's consequences – comparing values, behaviours, institutions and organisations across nations, 2nd edn. Sage Publications, London

Hofstede G, Bond M (1988) The Confucius connection: from cultural roots to economic growth. Organ Dyn 16:4–21

House RJ, Hanges PJ, Ruiz-Quintanilla SA, Dorfman PW, Javidan M, Dickson M et al (1999) Cultural influences on leadership and organisations: project GLOBE. In: Mobley WF, Gessner MJ, Arnold V (eds) Advances in global leadership, vol 1. JAI, Greenwich, CT, pp 171–233

House RJ, Hanges PJ, Javidan M, Dorfman PW, Gupta V (2004) Culture, leadership and organisations – the GLOBE study of 62 societies, thousand oaks. Sage Publishers, CA

Inglehart R (1997) Modernization and postmodernazation: changing values and political styles in advanced industrial society. Princeton University Press, Princeton NJ

Jones N, Malesios C, Iosifides T, Sophoulis CM (2008) Social capital in Greece: measurement and comparative perspectives. S Eur Soc Polt 13(2):175–193

Karamessini M (2005) Reconciliation of work and private life in Greece. EGGSIE/ EWERC, The University of Manchester

Kluckhohn F, Strodtbeck F (1961) Variations in value orientation. Harper Collins, New York

Koopman PL, Den Hartog DN, Konrad E et al (1999) National culture and leadership profiles in Europe: some results from the GLOBE study. Eur J Work Organ Psychol 8(4):503–520

Kostelenos G, Vassiliou D, Kounaris E, Petmezas S, Sfakianakis M (2007) Gross domestic product 1830–1939. Centre for Planning and Economic Research (KEPE)

Lyberaki A, Paraskevopoulos CJ (2002) Social capital measurement in Greece. Paper presented at the OECD-ONS International conference on social capital measurement, London, U.K., September 25–27

Makridakis S, Caloghirou Y, Papagiannakis L, Trivellas P (1997) The dualism of Greek firms and management: present state and future implications. Eur Manag J 15(4):381–402

Malmendier U, Nagel S (2008) Depression babies: do macroeconomic experiences affect risk-taking? NBER Working Paper 14813

McClelland DC (1961) The achieving society. Van Nostrand, New Jersy

Minkov M, Blagoev V (2009) Cultural values pedict subsequent economic growth. Int J Cross-Cult Manag 9(1):5–24

Myloni B, Harzing A-W, Mirza H (2004) Human resource management in Greece: have the colours of culture faded away? Int J Cross-Cult Manag 4(1):59–76

North D (1990) Institutions, institutional change and economic performance. Cambridge University Press, Cambridge

Palacios-Huerta I, Santos T (2004) A theory of markets, institutions, and endogenous preferences. J Pub Econ 88(3–4):601–627

Papalexandri N (2007) Greece, from ancient myths to modern realities. In: Chhokar JS, Brodbeck FC, House RJ (eds) Culture and leadership, across the world: the GLOBE book of in-depth studies of 25 societies. Lawrence Erlbaum Associates, New Jersey, pp 767–802

Paraskevopoulos CJ (2007) Social capital and public policy in Greece. Hellenic Observatory Papers on Greece and Southeast Europe GreeSE Paper No. 9

Petrakis PE (ed) (2008) Entrepreneuriship. 2nd edn, Publisher P.E. Petrakis, Athens

Portes A (1998) Social capital: its origins and applications in modern sociology. Annu Rev Sociol 24:1–25

Putnam R (1995) Bowling alone: America's declining social capital. J Democr 6:65–78

Savig L, Schwartz SH (2007) Cultural values in organisations: insights for Europe. Eur J Int Manag 1(3):176–190

Snijders ABT (1999) Prologue to the measurement of social capital. The Tocqueville Rev/La Rev Tocqueville 20(1):27–44

Stratigaki M (2006) The gender of social policy. Metaixmio, Athens

Tayeb M (2000) National cultural characteristics. In: Tayeb M (ed) International business theories, policies and practices. Pearson Educ. Ltd, Harlow, pp 309–335

Thomadakis S (1981) Credit and monetization of the Greek economy. Discount Credit and the National Bank of Greece (1860–1900), Athens

Triandis HC (1994) Culture and social behaviour. McGraw-Hill, New York

Triandis HC (1995) Individualism and collectivism. Westview Press, Boulder, CO

Triandis HC (2009) Ecological determinants of cultural variation. In: Wyer RW, Chiu C-y, Hong Y-y (eds) Understanding culture: theory research and applications. Psychology Press, New York, pp 189–210, Chapter 10

Van Oorschot W, Arts W, Gelissen J (2006) Social capital in Europe: measurement and social and regional distribution of a multifaceted phenomenon. Acta Soc 49(2):149–167

Veenhoven R (2009) World database of hapiness. Distributional Findings in Nations, Erasmus University Rotterdam

Weber M (1958) The protestant ethic and the spirit of capitalism. Charles Scribner's Sons, New York

Zolotas X (1927) Greece in the stage of industrialization. Bank of Greece, Athens

Idiosyncratic Economic Institutions

7

North (1990) defined institutions as the rules of the game in society or otherwise as the organisation of restrictions of human origin that define human relationships. He also defined the most serious consequence of economic institutions as the shaping of incentives for all kinds of human relations: political, social and economic.

Economic institutions can be described in terms of three main concepts: property rights, the quality of market functioning (i.e., good, moderate or poor) and contractual organisation methods. There are two types of economic institutions: contracting institutions and property rights institutions. The first type of institutions in particular facilitates the establishment of relations between lenders and borrowers, of which the financial system is the most typical example. The other type concerns the institutional structures that limit the imposition of the government and powerful oligarchies and their exploitation of the less powerful. These institutions protect property rights. The first group of institutional structures could be described as horizontal in the sense that they oversee relations between ordinary citizens. The second is rather more vertical in nature as it covers the relations between authorities and the people they govern.

The institutional structures that protect property rights are more important than those governing contracting procedures. Essentially, weak financial intermediation institutions can affect financial flows, but weak protection of property rights prohibits such investments. Under these conditions, those involved in the financial market either will not invest or will mask their investments (black economy). Yet, we should keep in mind that often these two characteristics coincide in the same institution.

Similar characteristics surround the tax and insurance system. It is clear that extensive redistributive policies remove property rights from individual wealth and transfer it to others. The same applies to the insurance system, which involves the transfer of property primarily through time and, secondarily, among members of society.

This chapter is organised as follows: Sect. 7.1 presents the main characteristics of financial transactions involving the concepts of visible and invisible transaction costs, while Sect. 7.2 explains ownership rights in the Greek economy. Section 7.3 focuses on the description of the oligopolistic situation in Greece, and Sect. 7.4

focuses on the activities of domestic and foreign firms in the Greek economy. Section 7.5 examines the structure of the financial system. It thus analyses the extent to which different financial systems are based on the mediating function of banking institutions or on a decentralised market mechanism. Section 7.6 describes the main features of the Greek financial system. Finally, Sect. 7.7 presents general aspects of the tax and insurance systems, and Sect. 7.8 describes the insurance system of the Greek economy in particular.

7.1   Characteristics of Transactions

To understand how transaction costs emerge from a behavioural viewpoint, i.e., the assumptions underlying their existence, we must analyse their origin as an effect of individual characteristics. These characteristics, as reported in the literature on transaction costs and as mentioned by Williamson (1981), are twofold: (a) the recognition and admission that those involved in the financial market are subject to bounded rationality; and (b) the assumption that at least some people are motivated by the search for opportunities (opportunism).

In general, transaction costs can be divided into two broad categories: visible and invisible. Visible costs include transaction costs such as contracts, fees for professional licensing and other expenses for the execution of tasks, which are known, legitimate and in many cases determined by law. Invisible transaction costs may relate to corruption or invisible transactions.[1] In cases of corruption, transaction costs may relate to either legal or illegal procedures. This cost represents the sum paid by the interested party to facilitate a process (e.g., acceleration or deceleration, bypassing of bureaucratic obstacles), or, in severe cases, the promotion of specific interests (e.g., appointment to a specific position, exemption from obligations or charges/offences). Invisible transactions usually involve illegal transactions and interrelated interests, i.e., activities that combine the black economy and corruption. This category usually includes more severe cases within the scope of criminal law. In any case, the cost per transaction is important for both the method of execution and the feasibility of the transaction.

The basic features of transaction costs are frequency, uncertainty and asset specificity.

7.1.1   Visible Transaction Costs

The creation of a specific terminology for transaction costs is not an easy task. Two definitions that can give a general understanding of transaction costs are "the costs

---

[1] Includes the following types of transactions: (a) black market transactions, (b) agreements, exchanges without direct financial return, and (c) opportunity costs for allocating resources.

of exchanging property rights" and "the costs for the appropriation of gains from specialisation and division of labour".

According to Wallis and North (1986), economic activities are divided into those relating primarily to transactions and those relating to the production and manufacturing of goods. All resources used to complete transactions form the transaction sector. The transaction costs include the value of labour, land and capital used in transactions. At this point, it should be noted that, apart from the costs incurred through the purchase mechanism (e.g., legal costs), the realisation of a transaction also entails other types of costs (e.g., costs corresponding to the waiting time at public services), which cannot be measured. Therefore, not all transaction costs are captured by measurement.

Below, we present the results of the measurement of transaction costs in member countries of the OECD and the EU-27 (Table 7.1). The period under review includes the years 2002, 2004 and 2006. More specifically, this analysis focuses on transaction services that result from the use of the market, for which official statistics exist. The transaction sector includes costs associated with the realisation of the transactions and costs that are required for the protection of property rights. Results are expressed as a percentage of GDP to allow direct comparison between countries.

As shown in Table 7.1, in 2002, the countries with the largest transaction sectors were Switzerland (54.22%), Slovakia (53.96%), Slovenia (50.95%), the United Kingdom (45.34%), and the Netherlands (43.05%). For the same year, Iceland (9.13%), Turkey (9.16%), Bulgaria (12.19%), Romania (13.16%) and Mexico (14.93%) were ranked low.

The situation did not appear to vary considerably in 2004, apart from some small changes in certain countries. In particular, the share of transaction costs in Portugal increased by 2.6% compared with 2002, reaching 20.23% of GDP, while in Turkey it increased from 9.61% in 2002 to 13.23% in 2004. On the contrary, the Slovenian economy demonstrated a significant reduction in the transaction sector from 51% to 32%, while Korea and Sweden marked drops of 6.5% and 2.5%, respectively. The remaining countries in 2004 showed no major differences, remaining around the same levels as in 2002.

Finally, in 2006, we observed that, in many cases, countries where the transaction sector as a percentage of GDP dropped in 2004 returned to or exceeded the 2002 rates. Two typical examples are Sweden (22.29% in 2002, 26% in 2006) and Lithuania (18.14% in 2002, 19.37% in 2006). We should also note that there were countries where transaction costs fell in 2006 compared to 2002. Some of these countries are Belgium, Luxembourg, Norway, the United Kingdom and Cyprus. In 2006, the Greek economy showed a fairly high percentage of measurable transaction costs (27.07%).

7.1.2 Invisible Transaction Costs and Business Development

The analysis so far has offered a picture of visible transaction costs. However, some transaction costs are invisible. Given this invisibility, they cannot be measured directly but only approached indirectly. Thus, we can understand "invisible"

Table 7.1 The transaction sector as a percentage of GDP

Country	% GDP		
	2002	2004	2006
Australia	29.95	29.44	31.20
Belgium	12.52	11.32	11.54
Finland	31.60	33.66	32.96
Hungary	20.17	21.09	21.98
Japan	–	21.42	20.77
Luxembourg	16.28	15.57	14.08
Netherlands	43.05	42.38	–
Norway	36.95	35.48	32.24
Portugal	17.63	20.23	20.33
Spain	21.39	21.67	22.46
Switzerland	54.22	55.30	54.56
UK	45.34	45.54	44.66
Austria	29.28	–	–
Canada	30.17	29.77	30.14
France	–	13.70	14.05
Greece	–	–	27.07
Iceland	9.13	8.48	14.75
Korea	4.32	4.49	4.83
Mexico	14.93	14.29	13.93
New Zealand	30.48	32.30	34.45
Poland	22.52	22.13	22.73
Slovakia	53.96	53.10	55.97
Sweden	22.29	19.73	21.54
Turkey	9.16	13.23	–
Bulgaria	12.19	13.64	14.34
Estonia	29.09	27.52	27.76
Cyprus	16.16	9.62	9.80
Latvia	26.72	25.35	26.03
Lithuania	18.14	17.93	19.37
Malta	4.65	3.19	2.52
Romania	13.16	14.08	11.14
Slovenia	50.95	31.73	31.68

Source: Processing of the International Labour Organization Database (ILO)

transaction costs by assessing the quantitative indicators of the "functioning" of the economic system.

The study of the World Economic Forum (WEF) for 2008 reveals a number of problematic factors related to the exercise of business activities and their individual gravity. The relevant rankings showed that the majority of respondents stated that the most problematic factor when doing business in Greece is "inefficient government bureaucracy" (26.5%), followed by "tax regulations" (15.6%), "prohibitive

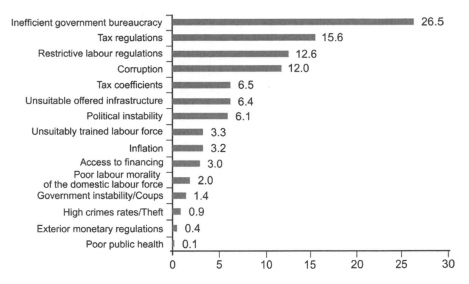

Fig. 7.1 Factors hindering business transactions in Greece (Source: World Economic Forum)

labour regulations" (12.6%) and "corruption" (12.0%). The responses are presented in detail in Fig. 7.1.

The obstacles to entrepreneurship created by domestic government bureaucracy are being dealt with very gradually. The tentative and limited changes that have been promoted have not brought about dramatic changes in the country's performance. According to the World Bank,[2] Greece's business-friendliness ranking has improved from 106th in 2008 to 96th in 2009. This improvement is due largely to the streamlining of the required procedures for establishing and running a business.

Below we present Greece's performance on the relevant indicators compared to other European countries. We note the division between the countries of Northern and Southern Europe, with the latter lagging in business-friendliness (see Table 7.2).

Based on the table below, it is evident that the Greek economy is remarkably rigid in terms of government bureaucracy for the licensing of new businesses and establishment costs in general. The study of the cited data reveals two main

---

[2] Since 2003, the World Bank has been preparing a research project to measure the impact of the institutional environment on business. The methodology adopted concerns quantitative indicators that illustrate the relationship between businesses and government bureaucracy. It does not thus record the personal evaluations of respondents, as in the case of the World Economic Forum. Overall, it uses 43 indicators, which are divided into 10 topics: (1) Establishment of the company, (2) Dealing with licenses, (3) Employment of staff, (4) Registration of property, (5) Reception of credit, (6) Investor protection, (7) Payment of taxes, (8) Cross-border trade, (9) Imposition of contracts and (10) Business closure. For the limitations and weaknesses of the methodology adopted in the "Doing Business" surveys, see National Competitiveness and Development Council, Annual Competitiveness Report, 2007, pp 113–114.

Table 7.2 Doing business in southern and northern European countries (2009 rankings)

Indicator	Country						
	Greece	Portugal	Italy	Spain	Denmark	Netherlands	Sweden
Establishment of the company	133	34	53	140	16	51	30
Dealing with licenses	45	128	83	51	7	94	17
Employment of staff	133	164	75	160	10	98	114
Registration of property	101	79	58	46	43	23	10
Reception of credit	109	109	84	43	12	43	68
Protection of investors	150	38	53	88	24	104	53
Payment of taxes	62	73	128	84	13	30	42
Cross-border trade	70	33	60	52	3	13	6
Enforcement of contracts	85	34	156	54	29	34	55
Business closure	41	21	27	19	7	10	18
General classification	96	48	65	49	5	26	17

Source: World Bank (data)

facts: Greece's backwardness in terms of the speed and ease of closing paperwork and the slight improvement that has been noted over the last 2 years, which is not sufficient to improve the image of the Greek economy.

7.1.3 Invisible Transaction Costs and Corruption

Corruption is a (non-registered) transaction cost in the financial system. The international literature features many studies analysing corruption, but their diversification complicates the selection of a single definition to fully explain the concept. In general, corruption is defined as the abuse of public power for private gain. It is used by journalists and politicians as a general concept that encompasses all forms of abuse of power, both public and private. It also includes nepotism or self-serving policies that allow companies, politicians, civil servants or managers to avoid accountability.[3]

Below, we present statistics and findings regarding the level of corruption in Greece according to three different indicators of Transparency International: (a) the Corruption Perceptions Index (CPI), (b) the Global Corruption Barometer (GCB) and (c) the Corruption Index (CI). For this measurement, the organisation draws on views of experts, entrepreneurs, academics, economists and sociologists; questionnaires sent to citizens concerning issues of corruption and transparency; and the willingness of foreign companies to engage in bribery to serve their interests.

Table 7.3 lists the sizes of the index for Mediterranean (Spain, Italy, France, Portugal) and Northern European countries (Sweden, Denmark, Finland) and their

---

[3] Labelle, Kathimerini (13/1/2008).

Table 7.3 Corruption perception index for Mediterranean and Northern European countries

Country	Corruption perception index	Position	Standard deviation
Greece	4.7	57	0.6
Spain	6.5	28	1.0
Italy	4.8	55	1.2
Portugal	6.1	32	0.9
France	6.9	23	0.7
Sweden	9.3	1	0.1
Finland	9.0	5	0.8
Denmark	9.3	1	0.2

Source: Transparency International

positions in the global rankings on the basis of six surveys.[4] It is characteristic that Greece is in last place compared to the rest of the table, while the fact that Italy is the only other country with a score under five suggests the existence of common cultural roots.

According to studies by Transparency International Greece (2006, 2007, 2008),[5] if Greece scored one point higher on the CPI, this would increase capital inflows by €1.2 bn, while citizen incomes would increase by 4%.[6]

In contrast to the CPI, the GCB clearly reflects the opinion of citizens on specific issues relating to corruption and transparency.[7] The qualitative measurements of the GCB show no significant differences between the countries of the European Union. They do, however, reveal an obvious difference between Greece and other countries.

7.2   Property Rights

The protection of property rights in the Greek economy and society is peculiar. In the relevant world indices of the World Bank, Greece ranks very low based on the "vesting ownership" variable, while based on the "facilitation of contracting" variable, it ranks approximately in the middle of the list (Table 7.4).

In fact, the whole situation concerning property rights is even more problematic than shown in Table 7.4. The discrepancy between the statistical measurement of the index and reality is due to the fact that the index is based on a static display of the operation of the protection system without measuring the exact nature of this protection, and, in particular, its effectiveness. If, for example, there is a law on the protection of real estate that specifies its ownership but there are another eight or ten

---

[4] EIU 2008, IMD 2008, IMD 2007, MIG 2007, WEF 2007, GI 2008.

[5] Source: http://www.transparency.gr/Content.aspx?page=43 (2006, 2007, 2008).

[6] Enet (24.09.2008).

[7] http://www.transparency.gr/Content.aspx?page=50.

Table 7.4 Rankings among 183 countries based on the "vesting ownership" and "facilitation of contracting" variables

	Vesting ownership	Facilitation of contracting
Greece	153	88
Spain	54	52
Italy	95	157
Portugal	31	24
France	142	7
Sweden	15	52
Finland	26	11
Netherlands	46	29
Denmark	30	30

Source: The World Bank, Doing business, June 2010 (www. doingbusiness.org/rankings)

legal provisions that set the legal basis for challenging the interpretation of the main legal provisions, then, prima facie, there is a functional system for the protection of property rights. However, in reality, this obfuscates the property system, as shown by the fact that in "Doing Business 2011" (World Bank 2010), Greece ranked amongst the ten countries with the most property vesting procedures in the world (11, compared to a maximum of 14 procedures).

The beginning of this obfuscation of property rights in Greek society should be sought in some key phenomena pertaining to the birth of the Greek state. In particular, these concern the peculiar status of "heritage" of "national lands" that, for one hundred years after the birth of the Greek state, constituted the only productive resource of the country and the essential means for extending its public finances. Essentially, the configuration of land ownership after the end of Ottoman rule was the first key mechanism for the modulation of private wealth in Greek society. These lands covered 35–50% of the arable land of the Greek Kingdom. Indeed, a very peculiar situation prevailed regarding their ownership status as they belonged to the state. Consequently, the state mortgaged them, requiring 15% of gross production as rent, while farmers also had inheritance and expropriation rights on the land (they distributed the land, sold ownership rights and decided on the method and type of cultivation).[8]

The management of the complex property issue that developed required numerous management mechanisms, lawyers, notaries, public officials and other parties. Thus, a mechanism for all types of professions, which were initially useful for solving and processing all of these complex ownership system issues, gradually became a pressure group, which could reproduce the conditions that would allow it to maximise its social usefulness by maximising processing needs. Subsequently, of course – and this should be stressed – the obfuscation of ownership rights grew independent of its initial root cause and the interests of lobbyists and became an inextricable part of these rights as perceived by society. The further use of the property later gave birth to

---

[8] Meleti and Xanthopoulou (Monthly Review 26/8/2010).

similar peculiar management mechanisms (e.g., post-war land exchanges in urban areas), which concurrently contributed dramatically to the cultivation and expansion of the parallel economy. At the constitutional level, Greek law recognises the protection of property as an individual right. In constitutional law, the term "property" is a broader concept than that of ownership in civil law as the former includes all absolute rights over any object, movable or immovable. Apart from ownership of property, it includes intellectual property rights, even those, such as copyrights, that refer to an object with which the holder has a close relationship. The Greek legal framework of real estate has inherent weaknesses, such as complexity, an inability to provide a binding method for determining the limits of property, the ineffective implementation of the principle of legality, incomplete disclosure, transaction uncertainty and a lack of an accurate picture of proprietary relations for a particular property. These shortcomings lead to information asymmetry, which limits the rationality required for economic activity while increasing the risk of opportunism. The confusing picture of proprietary relations in the context of real estate requires very careful transactions because of the possible revocation of improperly executed transactions, which entails a time-consuming and costly examination of title deeds. There is also a visible risk of increased legal costs as the definite safeguarding of rights can only be achieved through the courts, through recognition of ownership or through the rebuttal of attacks thereon.

However, the confusion over property rights is not limited to personal property but spreads across the whole spectrum of economic activity. Five other critical cases of confusion over property rights contribute to the current Greek social and economic reality:

(a) The establishment of a restricted number of jobs (numerus clausus) for certain professions in a society essentially leads to the formation of property rights on those posts by persons, who, for whatever reason, were given access to them. Examples include public transport (taxis and public use trucks for the domestic and international transport of goods). The organisation of property rights in these areas is formed based on a system - parallel to the formal economy – that sets a price for each "restricted job", which, under certain circumstances, is transferred to whoever is willing to pay this price. It is characteristic that the price of a taxi license in Athens (where there are about 15,000 taxis) is approximately €180,000. Very recently, this price fell to €110,000 after an announcement (in March 2010) of the prospect of the deregulation of registration number restrictions. Such transfers are contracting acts that take place only in the parallel economy.

(b) Areas of deliberate obfuscation of property rights are also created in contemporary Greek society. The most typical case is that of Greek television stations after 1989. It should be noted that the television sector is critical to the functioning of Greek society. The fact that, in Greece, television stations, which make up a market of €1 bn annually, have operated under lawful conditions, albeit illegally, for 20 years, is definitely unique and unprecedented in the global political, economic and television reality. The contradictory operation system of private television, based on the institutional conception of "temporary legitimacy", launched for political reasons in 1989 and grew into a labyrinthine net where the concept of "interwoven interests" was just a single episode in a sensational history. Overall, the landscape of illegally operating media, which is complicated by the powerful laws of the interwoven interests between media and political powers, was set and evolved under the "control" of 30 Greek legislative acts.

(c) Over the last few years, copyright infringements have assumed threatening dimensions. The term "infringement" (or "piracy") is generally used to describe the deliberate infringement of copyright on a commercial scale. Piracy represents an organised form of black economy and is directly and demonstrably linked to other forms of organised crime.

For example, in the computer software market, the global value of unauthorised (pirated) software reached $51.4 bn in 2009. Table 7.5 presents percentages of the use of pirated software compared to the overall use of computer software. It is characteristic that Greece ranks first among the examined countries.

(d) Frequent changes and difficulty in transactions with the tax system. The tax system in Greece is characterised by frequent restructuring and complicated transaction methods (Table 7.6). The frequent changes (usually increases) of the tax rates for natural and legal persons are perhaps the simplest form of "expropriation" of income rights. It is obvious that this frequent change is a major negative factor for any form of planning and organisation of economic activity. Indeed, it attacks the core of wealth and value production and therefore is of special significance for the development of attitudes in the cultural background.

(e) The development of legal entities of public jurisdiction. This is one dimension of economic institutions in Greece that was formed by the political and social system. It concerns the creation of legal entities under private and public law (public entities and private entities under public law) or of other types and forms, such as autonomous independent civil services and many other related forms that are essentially linked to and belong to the basic administration system, namely the ministries.

Table 7.5 Percentages of use of pirated software

	Piracy percentage 2009 (%)
Greece	58
Spain	42
Italy	49
Portugal	40
France	40
Sweden	25
Finland	25
Netherlands	28
Denmark	26

Source: Business Software Alliance (BSA) and IDC Global PC Software Piracy Study, May 2010

Table 7.6 Rankings based
on the ease of tax payments
among 183 countries

	Ease of tax payments
Greece	74
Spain	71
Italy	128
Portugal	73
France	55
Sweden	39
Finland	65
Netherlands	27
Denmark	13

Source: The World Bank, Doing business, June
2010 (www.doingbusiness.org/rankings)

Table 7.7 Entities of the wider public sector

Authority	Total
Ministry of regional development and competitiveness	
Public entities	6
Private entities under public law	9
Limited companies	26
EOMMEX subsidiaries (SA)	26
Ministry of education, lifelong learning and religion	
Independent (autonomous) government departments directly under the minister	9
Public entities (except higher educational institutions and libraries)	35
Private entities under public law	16
General secretariat for research and technology, technological development directorate, supervised technological entities	9
Research institutions supervised by the general secretariat for research and technology, research institutions supervision department	12

Notes: The Ministry of Labour supervises three agencies OAED (Labour Employment Office),
OEK (Workers' Housing Organisation) and OEE (Welfare and Recreation Centre), two limited
liability companies (P.A.E.P., Olympic Village 2004) and the National Centres E.KE.PIS. and
EKEP. Finally, with regard to the Ministry of the Interior, municipalities across the country
operate about 6,000 public entities, private entities under public law, and municipal enterprises

Examples of these for some typical ministries are given in Table 7.7. The need of
economic institutions to "produce" these organisations stems from the need to
consolidate the efficiency of public spending through the enlargement of the
division of work and the development of executives who would represent long-
term choices for the management and implementation of specific projects.

The number of these entities expanded rapidly upon the need to manage the
allocation of European Structural Funds, i.e., after 1980. Today, these entities are
fully controlled by the ministers of their supervising ministries, which means that,
in most cases, any political changes – not just the alternation of parties in power, but
even simple changes of ministers within the same government – bring about large-
scale changes in these organisations. In reality, therefore, political changes cause

confusion regarding the results of the activities of such organisations, as their losses are usually socialised, while the resulting profits are of a questionable nature (e.g., public or private). The continuing question of the nature of the results of such organisations has always been a source of confusion over property rights. These problems are magnified in cases of management by public funds agencies, particularly in the case of funds originating from the European Structural Funds. Essentially, this confusion has led to the development of mechanisms for the management of funds outside of public control. Obviously, the result is confusion over the nature of the generated property rights. This confusion extends to the management of these organisations' own resources. Thus, when seeking specialised staff, we typically see a growth of employment other than through the formal recruitment process (Supreme Council for Civil Personnel Selection – ASEP) in these organisations, causing a swelling of public expenditure.

This situation only partially achieves the initial need for increased efficiency of public spending through the independence of specialised public services and the development of expertise of a more permanent staff. In reality, the system feels the negative effects of frequent political changes in administration, the capacity for managing public funds from the budget and European Structural Funds and the certainty of the socialisation of losses.

7.3   The Oligopolistic Situation in Greece

The market share of a company is interpreted in relation to its industry. In economic theory, firms with a very large market share are called dominant. The law uses other similar concepts, such as dominance and significant market power (Vettas and Katsoulakos 2004).

By applying the sectoral concentration ratio CR4[9] to data of companies operating in the Greek economy, we observe a high concentration in sectors of industry (tobacco, tobacco products, petroleum products and coal, liquefied petroleum bottling, drinks, footwear), in the trade of minerals and ores, postal services, energy, telecommunications, entertainment (cinemas, theatres), radio-television companies and the banking sector.

Table 7.8 shows the values of the concentration ratio in the sectors of the Greek economy where the CR4 exceeds 50%, which, according to their size, are considered as "narrow oligopolies".

Table 7.8 shows that 34 sectors of the Greek economy present a narrow oligopolistic structure. Importantly, the necessities sectors of the industry and commerce of fuel and ores present a high concentration of over 50%. They are followed by the groceries sector (i.e., supermarkets and hypermarkets) and the pharmaceutical industry, with concentrations of 40.38% and 34.27%, respectively. It is noteworthy

---

[9] Concentration ratio: It measures the degree of concentration of a market. The number 4 refers to the 4 largest firms in the industry.

Table 7.8   Sectors of high concentration in the Greek economy

Sector description	CR4 (%)	Percentage of the largest business in industry sales (year 2007) (%)
1. Factoring	99.98	43.58
2. Industry (tobacco products)	99.74	63.25
3. Industry (oil and coal products)	99.65	66.11
4. Gambling – casinos	98.47	87.85
5. Trade (minerals – ores)	96.21	75.87
6. Industry (bottling of LPG)	90.82	49.3
7. Venture capital firms	87.8	34.06
8. Telecommunications	87.66	32.32
9. Air transport	87.45	76.56
10. Portfolio and investment companies	87.38	28.48
11. Energy	86.89	60.01
12. Post	86.59	63.48
13. Shipping	79.9	26.17
14. Cinemas – theatres	79.76	33.77
15. Trade (leather – fur)	79.72	53.94
16. Industry (tobacco)	75.87	29.03
17. Mutual funds	72.77	25.2
18. Industry (leather – fur)	71.76	34.69
19. Investment services companies	67.35	27.19
20. Leasing	66.51	20.38
21. Banks	63.6	23.92
22. Trade (books – newspapers – magazines)	63.5	19.68
23. Radio – TV enterprises	63.41	28.36
24. Industry (beverages)	61.73	32.35
25. Industry (metal products)	60.71	19.86
26. Industry (electric appliances – lighting)	60.6	41.91
27. Financial brokers	59.17	19.51
28. Holding companies	58.57	29.21
29. Football – basketball	56.54	22.58
30. Industry (mining – pits – saltworks)	54.12	18.66
31. Tourism (yachting – cruising businesses)	52.79	26.04
32. Trade (representations – imports – exports)	51.4	14.05
33. Industry (footwear – leather goods)	50.71	17.69
34. Trade (fuel – lubricants – LPG)	49.45	16.99

Source: ICAP data for the purposes of this study

that the concentration of 99.65% in the fuel industry (oil and coal products) is evidence of an extremely narrow oligopoly.

The oligopolistic concentration in the fuel industry, which has serious effects on the economy, may be related to the rising prices in the Greek economy. In the first quarter of 2006, while the price of gasoline in the EU-25 dropped, in Greece it rose by 5%. In Greece, two refineries control 100% of refining and market supply, thus imposing their own prices. The increase of their profits by 77% in the first quarter of 2008 and by 90% in the fourth quarter of 2007 is only one example of the consequences of this oligopolistic structure.

7.4   Greek and Foreign Companies

The bulk of foreign companies in Greece are active in industry and commerce. Greek businesses, on the other hand, operate in construction, metals and the food industry. Of greater interest, however, are the differences in performance between Greek and foreign firms and the factors affecting them.

The performance of companies, evaluated based on either total sales or profit, plays an important role at the micro- and macro-economic levels. At the micro-economic level, the performance of foreign firms highlights important structural differences between domestic and foreign companies. These differences (both in business performance and in how they operate in the domestic market) should be analysed as they prove crucial in the low competitiveness of domestic compared to foreign firms, in differences in productivity and the quality of goods offered, and in the use of technology, innovation, capital intensity, the use of financial resources, and so on.

On the other hand, significant differences that reveal a comparative advantage of foreign compared to Greek companies exert effects on the overall structure of the economy. Low profitability and low sales volumes reduce tax revenues. The low competitiveness of Greek compared to foreign firms creates a disadvantage for the potential of Greek exports and therefore the trade balance. The lagging profitability of domestic firms directly affects the volume of income reinvestment and the incentives for innovation, research, and development.

More specifically, the analysis of the financial performance of the two groups highlights differences in capital structure between Greek and foreign firms. These findings were based on a comparative analysis of 140 domestic and 140 foreign companies operating in the Greek economy. The sample was drawn based on the structural features of 140 foreign firms in ICAP's archives.

Differences in funding between foreign and Greek companies can be summarised in the following points:

- In the case of foreign companies, their size plays an important role in their short-term financing. However, for Greek companies, the size of total assets is positively correlated with long-term and total borrowing. For Greek companies, there appears to be no relation between size and short-term borrowing.
- Growth (measured as the increase of total assets) leads to higher long-term loans for foreign companies. For Greek companies, there appears to be no significant correlation between the two variables.
- While, in foreign firms, there is a positive correlation between stocks and short-term leverage in Greek companies, the correlation is negative. Banks appear

reluctant to grant loans to Greek companies, considering high stocks of products as evidence of ineffective management.

- Higher profit margins (according to net profit to gross profit and net profit to net sales ratios) lead to increased short-term and long-term borrowing for the Greek, but not for foreign, companies.
- Management capacity (based on the ratios of net value to long-term capital and the creditors' index multiplied by 360 to net sales) affects all of the financial obligations of the Greek, but not foreign, companies.
- Productivity (as the ratio of total sales to the number of employees) is not a statistically significant factor in determining the allocation of capital for Greek, as opposed to foreign, firms.

The above estimates allow us to draw some conclusions: domestic companies appear to have considerable untapped resources; the most typical example is their non-intensive exploitation of their assets. They are also noted for their high precarity rates due to their limited organisational structure and a lack of schedules for the recovery and repayment of short-term obligations. Failure to recover receivables prior to the payment of obligations in order for the former to be used as working capital is an important indication of ineffective management. Finally, domestic firms with sufficient liquidity do not reinvest their capital but leave it relatively untapped.

Regarding the percentage of profit, there is strong evidence for the existence of differences between Greek and foreign companies. Foreign companies on average present much higher levels of profitability than Greek firms do, in addition to smaller performance fluctuations. Simultaneously, according to the empirical study of the timeframe of borrowing, foreign companies have access to more long-term capital, whereas the Greek companies secure loans for shorter periods.

These data, in conjunction with the findings obtained from Eurostat for the average cost of workers and the added value of work, strengthen the hypothesis of the existence of transfer pricing from Greece to the countries of origin of foreign firms.

According to Barry (2005), the volume of outflows through transfer pricing can be approximated by subtracting the average cost of workers from the added value per worker. In this study, reference is made to Ireland, where the value added per worker is about double the EU average while the average cost of workers is less than half of the EU average! These data clearly indicate the existence of transfer pricing in favour of Ireland as the profit margins for companies that exploit the increasing gap between average costs and added value through work are many times higher than those seen in other countries. The low corporate tax in Ireland compared with the U.S., for example, makes it obvious why Ireland has a large influx of capital from America in the form of investment.

According to Agrawal (2009), transfer pricing has multiple effects. Initially, it has an impact on public finances as valuable tax revenue is lost. This loss of tax revenue leads to an additional burden on the rest of the population as it increases the relative burden to be borne or leads to additional government borrowing. Thus, the additional burden is borne by taxpayers and renders income distribution more unequal.

Furthermore, transfer pricing causes distortions in the balance of payments between the countries of origin of the companies involved. The inflows/outflows in the form of transfer pricing give the wrong impression as regards trade between two countries as these inflows and outflows are merely transfers from a subsidiary to its parent company and do not reflect actual economic activity.

Moreover, foreign firms may worsen income distribution in a country if they happen to operate in typically oligopolistic industries; they may therefore entail harmful consequences for society, as outlined above for oligopolies. More specifically, in Table 7.5, we observe that some of the sectors that present low values of the capital inflows index (relative to the figure for Ireland) have an oligopolistic structure (e.g., postal service and telecommunications, air transport, maritime transport). In these cases, it is obvious that the oligopolistic power of the company and the sector's structure favour the accumulation of profits, whereas if ownership is foreign, the funds flow abroad.

Barry's (2005) findings and conclusions are confirmed by Table 7.9. The greater the positive (negative) difference between these two variables, the greater the volume of inflows (outflows) of capital from (to) abroad. In Ireland's case, we see the highly positive values assumed by the capital inflows ratio, which underline the placement and capital investment conditions that are highly attractive for foreign companies because of the low corporate taxes, which enhance transfer pricing.

Based on Eurostat's data for Greece compared with other countries in the Mediterranean (Italy, Portugal, Spain) and Northern Europe (Denmark, Netherlands, Finland, Sweden and especially Ireland), we observe large differences in the capital input index, suggesting the existence of transfer pricing practices in the Greek economy. More specifically, we observe high values of the index both for Ireland and for the rest of Northern Europe, in contrast with Greece and other Mediterranean countries that exhibit weak performance. In some cases (e.g., inland and air transport, restaurants and hotels, research and development), the index assumes negative values for Greece, stressing the outflow of capital to destinations promising more attractive profit margins. It should be noted that in 14 of the 17 sectors shown in Table 7.9, the ratio of capital inflows to transfer pricing assumes the lowest price compared with the countries of Northern Europe and even other Mediterranean countries.

The capital inflows index of Greece (especially in comparison with the countries of Northern Europe), in combination with empirical findings regarding the favourable treatment of foreign firms seeking loans (in terms of volume of capital and repayment period), suggest that foreign firms are able, through transfer pricing practices, to transfer funds abroad and take advantage of the conditions of long-term financing. By doing this, they benefit at three levels: they reap the surplus of the consumer, benefit from the long-term financing provided to them by Greek banks and finally avoid taxation by transferring funds abroad.

Table 7.9 Capital inflows ratio and oligopolistic structure by economic sector (year 2007)

Sector	Ireland	Greece	Spain	Italy	Portugal	Denmark	Finland	Sweden	Netherlands	CR4[a] for Greece (%)
	Index of capital inflows through transfer pricing by the method of Barry (2005)									
Other business activities	15.8	6.3	6.2	8.3	4.0	7.6	8.9	3.2	6.8	–
Research and development	0.1	−2.5	11.9	−7.3	0.5	−33.7	−3.4	–	7.8	–
IT and related activities	31.5	10.4	7.1	6.6	9.9	15.1	16.1	2.1	11.7	26.93
Rental of machinery and equipment without operator and personal and household goods	111.4	49.5	43.9	57.8	47.6	76.4	87.2	–	123.3	–
Real estate management	36.4	20.5	47.8	23.4	23.4	175.7	104.7	120.4	108.3	–
Activities related to real estate management, renting and business activities	25.2	7.4	14.1	10.1	7.4	33.1	21.9	20.3	14.6	–
Postal service and telecommunications	54.4	66.4	91.9	69.1	79.4	37.5	34.7	26.6	58.9	86.59 and 87.66
Supporting and auxiliary transport activities	33.0	4.6	21.9	14.0	35.9	39.3	18.7	9.1	35.6	–
Air transport	–	−11.4	16.2	57.3	–	16.8	35.8	3.8	–	87.45
Shipping	–	19.1	48.0	61.7	–	158.8	38.8	11.1	–	79.9
Inland transport	8.4	−6.4	8.5	2.2	7.4	11.2	10.8	7.1	10.9	25.96
Transport, storage and communications	39.8	8.5	24.2	22.2	27.4	34.5	20.9	12.4	32.2	32.68
Restaurants and hotels	4.7	−2.1	2.3	0.8	2.6	5.8	5.9	2.4	6.0	16.13 and 5.23
Retail trade, except vehicles, repair of personal and household goods	9.7	0.7	4.8	−1.3	4.1	7.7	11.0	3.5	7.5	–
Wholesale trade and commission trade, except vehicles and motorcycles	54.5	15.5	15.3	15.1	11.7	26.9	32.3	17.1	35.4	–
Vehicle trade, maintenance and repair	14.6	4.7	11.8	3.0	5.0	12.9	12.7	7.9	12.7	18.19
Wholesale and retail trade, repair of vehicles and personal and household goods	23.3	5.9	8.8	4.4	6.7	15.4	17.6	9.2	17.4	–

Source: Eurostat, 2007 data, and ICAP (2007) for the purposes of this study

[a]In the case of two sectors, the concentration ratio in the cell CR4 refers to the first and second sectors, respectively

7.5   The Structure of the Financial System: Banks or Financial Markets?

In Anglo-Saxon countries (typical examples are Great Britain and the USA), historically, the market's functioning is the heart of economic activity. For decades, the financing of projects for the development of the business world has been based on capital markets with free trading of various kinds of securities (e.g., equities, bonds). Furthermore, the existence of an efficient market allows households to invest their savings, contributing to the profitability of the productive sectors of the economy and creating an investment profile (in terms of performance and risk) that suits them.

On the other hand, countries like Germany and Japan are the most common example of countries that base the funding of their investments and development projects on the banking system. Although the production model of the two countries differ in significant ways, it cannot be disputed that the intermediary function of economic institutions in Germany and Japan was not limited to providing funds but included the participation of banking institutions in the management of production units.

The organisation of the financial system and the relative importance of the mediation process in funding through arm's-length transactions presents a number of advantages but also, under certain conditions, raises important issues about the smooth functioning of economic activity.

In economies where the mediation process of the banking system is the main source of financing for the business sector, there has been a closer relation between credit institutions and the funded production units. This relation has historically been proven (Gerschenkron 1962) to reduce the information costs of banking institutions, increasing their ability to supervise and exercise control over the enterprises they finance. This renders the financing of investment projects of productive units of the economy easier (and cheaper). Especially in economies in which contract enforcement is not easy, the efficiency of the banking sector is much higher than that of the market mechanism (Gerschenkron 1962; Rajan and Zingales 1998).

Cooperation between firms and mediators provides productive units of the economy with financing when they need it most: during financial turbulence and financial crises. During these periods, finding funding through the market mechanism (e.g., issuance and distribution of new securities) is possible only for prosperous businesses (which are most likely to be able to finance their investments in other ways, e.g., by retaining profits) because of negative investor psychology and investors' refusal to undertake higher risk. Moreover, even companies that, in times of instability and uncertainty, maintain their ability to raise funding from the market mechanism manage this by paying significantly higher costs. Because of all of the above, economies that rely less on a decentralised market mechanism experience fewer turbulence effects (IMF, World Economic Outlook 2006).[10]

---

[10] IMF (2006) World Economic Outlook, Financial Systems and Economic Cycles.

On the other hand, economies that rely to a greater extent on the "invisible hand" of the money market are better equipped to respond to major technological changes and adopt innovations. In such cases, investors can more easily be released from financial sectors with an uncertain future (with whatever political, social and other effects this attitude can have) while providing funding to sectors with higher growth. Typically, these economies are more dynamic and enjoy higher growth rates because of their ability to invest in more promising technologies and adopt innovations, often changing the structure of their productive activity.

The organisation of the financial system, apart from the business world, can greatly influence the consumption of households. In general, in economies where the majority of funding takes place through the intermediation of the banking system, consumers are more strongly affected by income shocks. On the contrary, the ability to make arm's-length transactions allows households to smooth their level of consumption (e.g., allowing them to borrow by mortgaging their home or taking advantage of periods of welfare in the real estate market). At the same time, these economies present a greater dependence of private wealth on the assets held, which are traded freely in markets. In this way, the wealth of households is directly linked to the climate in the respective markets, so their welfare is exposed to sudden changes in asset prices (IMF-World Economic Outlook 2006).

From the above it follows that no form of financing of economic activity is a necessary and sufficient condition for economic growth (Rajan and Zingales 1998; Levine 2002). Moreover, in most developed countries, the money market and bank lending jointly provide, to one degree or another, the liquidity necessary for the productive fabric of the economy. However, in recent years, there has been a trend towards the enhancement of the relative importance of the money market in relation to the banking system.

The study by the International Monetary Fund for 2006, which was mentioned above (IMF-World Economic Outlook 2006), presents the methodology for the assessment of an index that reflects the structure of the financial sector of the economy, i.e., the relative role of the banking system and money market in financing investment opportunities. The value of the index, as the weighted average of individual indicators, shows the relative importance of the market mechanism, bank financing and brokerage by other (not purely banking) institutions. Higher index values signify the greater presence of the market mechanism, while lower values signify economies where mediation plays a more important role in financing economic activity.

The findings of the IMF, as depicted in Fig. 7.2, show that the relative importance of money market transactions (in relation to transactions where mediating institutions play a key role) in the decade of 1995–2004 increased in all of the examined economies, with the exception of Greece.

The observation concerning the increased importance of the role of money market transactions can be attributed to, among other things, the increase in the wealth presented by the respective economies in the decade under investigation.

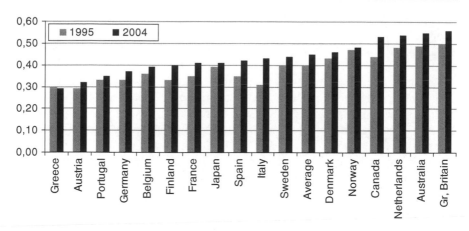

Fig. 7.2 Ranking of countries according to indicators reflecting the extent to which economies are based on the funding of financial markets as opposed to mediation (Source: IMF-World Economic Outlook (2006))

Beck et al. (2000) documented an increasing trend of the relative importance of markets (compared to bank financing).

The above observation of the enhanced role of the market is probably associated with the dominance of the neoclassical ideology in recent decades, which was accompanied by the imposition of (neo-) liberal policies in every aspect of economic activity. This trend is most evident in the processes of transaction de-intermediation and market liberalisation.

In conjunction with the belief that markets are able to adjust without external interference, the adoption of new, innovative financial products has rendered the boundaries between the market mechanism and the banking system less clear. The lifting of the ban[11] on the investment activity of commercial banks in the U.S. contributed to this end.

Furthermore, there was a trend towards boosting the relative size (and hence the role) of a series of non-purely banking institutions (e.g., insurance companies, private funds and other institutions involved in over-the-counter transactions) that assume a mediator role but participate in arm's-length transactions. In this way, the dividing lines between each area of the modern financial system become even more blurred.

---

[11] The ban on investment activity had been imposed by the legislation of the democrats Glass and Steagall (Glass-Steagall Act, 1933) as a result of the crisis of 1929 in an effort to protect depositors from the speculation of banking administrations and the corresponding market risk. The decisive lifting of the ban took place in 1999 with the voting for the bill of the Republicans Gramm, Leach and Bliley (Financial Services Modernization Act).

Perhaps the most striking example of the convergence between banking and "market" funding in recent years was the possibility for the securitisation of receivables arising from the assets of banks and their disposal to interested investors.

What was not immediately understood, however, was the distortion of the incentives of participants in the financial system and the difficulty of assessing and measuring the level of risk posed by exposure to complex products (e.g., securitised products, derivatives). The problems created by the modern structure of the financial system were noted in time (a good example is the prophetic article by Rajan 2005), but without receiving the necessary attention during the euphoric climate of recent years (2001–2007).

7.6   Key Features of the Greek Financial System

If we wanted to study the particular characteristics of the Greek financial system, we could easily conclude that the Greek economy is based almost exclusively on the intermediary function of the banking system and much less on the "invisible hand" of the market.

As mentioned earlier, past years were marked by an international trend towards market liberalisation and an effort to de-mediate the financing process (even in countries where financing was traditionally based largely on the banking system). This trend was recorded in the study of the International Monetary Fund as an increase of the average value of the index (from 0.4 to 0.45 in the decade under consideration, Fig. 7.2). Moreover, as already mentioned, empirical studies confirm that as economies grow, the relative importance of the money market compared to the banking sector tends to increase.

In 1995, Greece, along with Austria, recorded the lowest rates in the sample of the 18 developed economies under consideration. This finding is indicative that the value of the index for Greece is lower than it is for countries like Germany and Italy, where the banking system plays an important role in economic activity. Of course, as was expected, the numerical value of the index for Greece was significantly lower than the values in the Anglo-Saxon countries, where traditionally the market mechanism is central to economic activity.

We would expect, given the growth of the last 10 years and the trend observed internationally, that the value of the relevant index would show a substantial increase for Greece, especially as it started from the lowest position on the international rankings. In reality, what happened was exactly the opposite. Greece is the only economy of the countries under investigation that showed a decrease of the index in 2004 compared with 1995. In other words, the role of the banking system (relative to the money market) in providing financing to the Greek economy was strengthened between 1995 and 2004.

The above study of the IMF confirms the common belief that the banking system is present in every aspect of the Greek economy, and its role seems to increase over time despite the contrary international trends.

Simultaneously, the Greek banking system presents a high degree of concentration. The concentration of the assets of the five largest banks (along with that of Portugal) is significantly higher than that in other Mediterranean EU member states and comparable with that of developed countries in Northern Europe (Table 7.10).

Furthermore, Greek banking groups control a number of alternative forms of financing for the business sector from non-purely banking sources (e.g., factoring, leasing). The strong presence of economic institutions through subsidiary companies coincides with the high degrees of concentration of these sectors. More specifically, in leasing, the five largest firms, all of which are members of banking groups, collectively account for 75% of turnover (data processed by ICAP), while in factoring, four companies, all of which are subsidiaries of banking institutions, account for the total turnover (99.99%, data processed by ICAP).

Moreover, a very high percentage of non-purely banking institutional investors (mutual funds, investment trusts, and newly created real estate investment companies) and securities firms are linked to banking. Examples include the mutual funds sector, where the five largest companies (all members of banking groups) account for 77% of turnover (data processed by ICAP). This finding raises questions of moral risk regarding the quality of assets that may be channelled by banks to fund investors.

The organisation of the financial system affects the decisions of those involved in the financial system and thus the structure of the total economic activity. The difficulty of ensuring the proper financing of the private sector, especially for small and medium enterprises, forces businesses to look elsewhere for the necessary support. Hence, the financial system devises new procedures, such as the use of checks and bills, not only as mediums of exchange but also as credit instruments, as became more evident through the increased delays in repayments with the outbreak of the credit crisis. This process, however, extends the operational risk of a business unit to its customers and suppliers, increasing the risk levels for the entire industry in which it operates.

Table 7.10 Degree of concentration of the Greek banking sector compared to other Mediterranean and Eastern European countries

	2001 (%)	2002 (%)	2003 (%)	2004 (%)	2005 (%)	2006 (%)	2007 (%)
Greece	67.0	67.4	66.9	65.0%	65.6	66.3	67.7
Italy	28.8	30.5	27.5	26.4	26.8	26.2	33.1
Spain	44.9	43.5	43.1	41.9	42.0	40.4	41.0
Portugal	59.8	60.5	62.7	66.5	68.8	67.9	67.8
Finland	79.5	78.6	81.2	82.7	82.9	82.3	81.2
Sweden	54.6	56.0	53.8	54.4	57.3	57.8	61.0
Denmark	67.6	68.0	66.6	67.0	66.3	64.7	64.2
Netherlands	82.5	82.7	84.2	84.0	84.5	85.1	86.3
Ireland	42.5	46.1	44.4	43.9	45.7	44.8	46.1

Source: ECB-EU Banking Structures (2005, 2007, 2008)
Note: The concentration of the Greek banking sector is calculated as the share of the total assets of the five largest credit institutions in the total assets of the banking system

Furthermore, this usual market practice facilitates shadow economic activity and makes it more difficult to identify the origin and use of venture capital. According to the estimates presented in Chap. 3 (Sect. 3.8), the size of the shadow economy is many times larger compared to official business lending and to the funds raised each year by Greek companies from the domestic market. Therefore, if (even a small) part of the profits originating from shadow trade are (re)directed to the financing of businesses, then this source of capital is likely to constitute alternative financing and not standard bank loans.

Of course, the shadow financing of businesses becomes more difficult as their size increases. However, the vast majority of the manufacturing sector consists of very small business units. Therefore, it is not unlikely that a significant proportion of economic activity could depend on financing from funds derived from shadow activities and thus feed back into the huge parallel economy.

Perhaps a good example of the importance of the proper functioning of the financial system in economic activity is the process of creating new businesses and finding the necessary funding for their initial stages.

The inability of the Greek money market to absorb new and innovative business ventures does not permit the release of part of the funds invested in a short time. Therefore, the market discourages potential investors from providing capital to finance start-up business structures. Bank lending is not conducive to such funding as new ventures entail very high risk and new businesses are rarely able to provide physical collateral to lenders.

The inability of the Greek financial system to channel funds to finance the most dynamic part of the business sector is confirmed by a recent study (The Foundation for Economic & Industrial Research – IOBE 2008, p. 25)[12] in which 30% of the prospective entrepreneurs responding highlight the difficulty of finding funding as one of the major problems when starting a new business venture. This percentage is far higher than the values recorded for barriers to entrepreneurship such as bureaucracy and the amount of tax and social security contributions,. The void left by the financial system is usually covered by the friends and relatives of the prospective entrepreneur (IOBE 2008, p. 9).

7.7 The Tax and Insurance System

The tax and insurance systems affect the preferences of those involved in every facet of economic activity and thus form the incentives for work, consumption, saving, avoiding or not avoiding taxes and/or insurance charges, and other actions.

Of course, the way in which these systems are organised and operate is not incidental. On the contrary, it largely reflects the cultural background of society in a dynamic way. The current provisions of the tax and insurance system in Greece are

---

[12] IOBE (2008) Entrepreneurship in Greece 2007–2008, Athens, November.

influenced by historical factors and have thus acquired political and social dimensions.

Furthermore, we should clarify that we shall consider the two systems together because the accumulated pathologies of decades and the modern challenges they face are largely shared. The most serious of these relate to the complexity of their operations, particularly the increased costs of operation and the expansion of the shadow economy (informal sector).

The shadow economy diverts resources from both the Treasury and insurance organisations. It is no coincidence that, in a recent analysis of the Greek economy, the OECD (OECD-Economic Survey: Greece 2009) recommends the establishment of a united front to combat the evasion of taxes and social security contributions.

On the other hand, largely because of the fight against the evasion of taxes and social security contributions, the Greek tax and insurance system is characterised by a particularly high degree of complexity. The level of bureaucratic complexity does not solve the problem of revenue leakage. On the contrary, bureaucratic complexity often impedes revenue management and complicates the provision of services to the transacting public. Furthermore, the complexity of the system impedes any effort to enact transparent and rational control and significantly increases the operating costs of the insurance agencies and the tax administration.

Figure 7.3 shows the relative cost of tax administration in Greece, which stands at a significantly higher level than in other European countries and is the third highest among OECD member countries after Belgium and Poland. This cost is

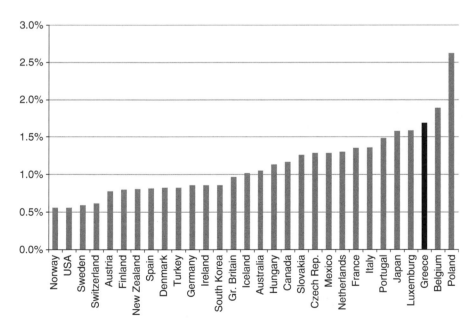

Fig. 7.3 The operational cost of the collection mechanism as a percentage of net tax revenue (Source: OECD-Economic Surveys, Greece, Volume 2009/15)

inevitably passed on to all financially active individuals and burdens every legal transaction between them.

The fact that the taxation (including contributions) of salaried services as a percentage of total labour costs is very high, and in fact the highest among OECD member countries, is indicative of this burden. Below are the relevant tax and insurance charges incurred for an unmarried employee without children (Fig. 7.4) and a married employee with two children (Fig. 7.5) as a percentage of total labour costs.

Regarding the total labour cost for an unmarried employee without children, we note that the cost in Greece is higher than the average of OECD member countries and at the same level as the EU-15 average (about 42%). The total labour cost for a married employee with two children in Greece is much higher than the averages of both groups of countries. Given these results, various issues can be raised regarding the competitiveness of the Greek economy. Certainly, the issue of the shadow economy may have distorted this image. If we accept that the average size of the shadow economy in Greece is around 20% and that in France is 12%, the percentile tax and insurance charges on the total labour cost for an employee with two children in Greece (Fig. 7.5) will drop from 43% to 35.8% and in France from 42% to 37.5%.

Moreover, apart from shaping the incentives of the financially active population, the structure of the tax and social insurance systems affects the distribution of resources. The progressiveness of the tax system and the distributional characteristics of social security,[13] among other goals, aim to achieve more equal redistribution of disposable income and to reduce the percentage of the population living below the poverty line. The latter is achieved by the financing (through tax revenue) of social transfers to individuals/households with lower incomes.

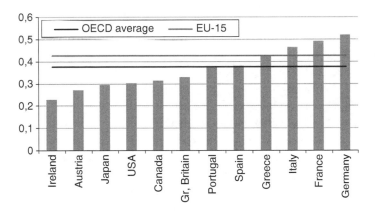

Fig. 7.4 Percentile tax and insurance charges on total labour costs for an unmarried employee without children (2007) (Source: OECD, Taxing wages database (2008))

---

[13] Here, we use the term "redistribution" to mean the transfer of resources between individuals of the same generation.

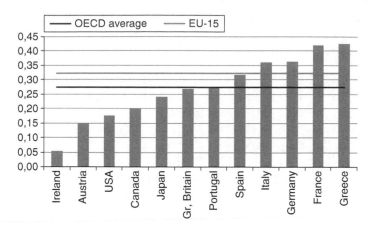

Fig. 7.5 Percentile tax and insurance charges on total labour costs for a married employee with two children (2007). (Source: OECD, Taxing wages database (2008))

Table 7.11 shows the risk of poverty before and after the redistributive effects of the social insurance system and after inclusion of all social transfers financed by state revenue.

Table 7.11 reveals that, in the Mediterranean countries, the social insurance systems play a key role in social policy. In these countries, the insurance system dramatically reduces the risk of poverty. It is evident that this reduction is greater than in the developed countries of Northern Europe. In Northern European countries, however, the strong presence of the welfare state (outside of the insurance system) reduces the ultimate risk of poverty to considerably lower levels.

In other words, it is concluded that in Mediterranean countries (including Greece), much desirable social policy is implemented by the insurance system. On the contrary, Northern European countries, which apply substantially higher tax charges to economic activity, are able to finance an effective social policy without passing on the corresponding costs to the social insurance system.

7.7.1   The Structure of the Tax System

Figure 7.6 shows the sources of tax revenue for the Greek government for the period of 1995–2007. It is evident that, over time, most of the revenue (about 60% of total tax revenue) is covered by indirect taxes (VAT and other taxes on consumption and production).

This finding raises obvious issues of social injustice. In contrast to the progressive nature of personal income tax, indirect taxation of transactions accords the same tax rate to all taxpayers regardless of their economic status and thus their actual ability to pay taxes. As the poorest people/households generally spend most of their income on consumption, they are required to pay disproportionately high taxes compared to their actual tax-paying ability. The predominance of indirect

Table 7.11 Risk of poverty before and after the effects of social insurance and all social transfers

	Risk of poverty (%)	Social insurance			Other social transfers		
		Risk of poverty (%)	Improvement (%)	Percentile improvement (%)	Risk of poverty (%)	Improvement (%)	Percentile improvement (%)
	(1)	(2)	(3) = (2) − (1)	(4) = (3)/(1)	(5)	(6) = (5) − (2)	(7) = (6)/(2)
Greece	41	24	17	41.5	21	3	12.5
Italy	42	22	20	48.6	19	3	13.6
Spain	40	22	18	45.0	19	3	13.6
Portugal	avg	26	–	–	19	7	26.9
Sweden	45	29	16	35.6	11	18	62.1
Finland	40	28	12	30.0	11	17	60.7
Denmark	38	32	6	15.8	12	20	62.5
Netherlands	36	22	14	38.9	12	10	45.5
Ireland	36	31	5	13.9	21	10	32.3

Source: Eurostat, Income poverty and social exclusion in the EU25, 13/2005, data processing

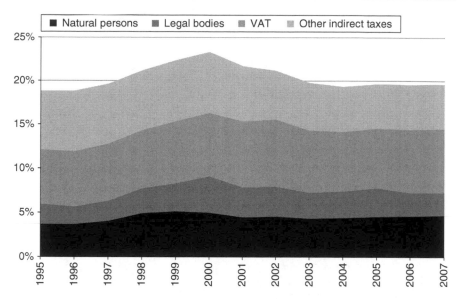

Fig. 7.6 The sources of tax revenue for the Greek government. Data shown as a percentage of GDP (Source: European Commission (Taxation trends in the European Union, 2009))

taxation burdens those with lower incomes with a higher average tax rate[14] compared to individuals/households with higher incomes, virtually nullifying or reversing the progressive nature of the tax system.

The question raised here is where a tax system that seeks the progressive taxation of citizens based on their actual standing leads if it assumes the above inverse progressive features and thus promotes social injustice. The explanation should be sought in the diachronic prevalence of the shadow economy in a wide range of activities.

It is perhaps characteristic that the only country with a similarly high contribution of indirect tax revenue in the treasury is Portugal, which suffers similar shadow economy and tax evasion problems. As evident from the data in Table 7.12 the revenue from indirect taxes in Greece and Portugal amounts to more than 60% of total tax revenue, a level significantly higher than that of other Mediterranean countries (where the corresponding figure is less than 50%).

Undoubtedly, more extensive support of the tax system for direct (and progressive) taxation would be socially equitable and therefore desirable. However, it would have a limited impact unless accompanied by a corresponding expansion of the tax base achieved by minimising the concealment of taxable income.

---

[14] The average tax rate is defined as the total tax burden to the total household income. In a progressive tax system, the average tax rate increases with personal/household income.

Table 7.12 Division of tax system income (as a percentage of GDP) into direct and indirect taxes (2007 data)

	Total (%)	Indirect (%)	Direct		
			Total (%)	Natural persons (%)	Legal entities (%)
Greece	20.4	12.3	8.1	4.7	2.6
Italy	30.2	15.0	15.2	11.4	3.2
Spain	24.9	12.0	13.4%	7.7	4.8
Portugal	25.1	15.3	9.8	5.7	3.7
Sweden	36.1	17.0	19.0	14.6	4.0
Finland	31.1	13.3	17.8	13.0	3.9
Denmark	47.7	18.0	29.8	25.2	3.6
Netherlands	25.4	13.1	12.3	7.4	3.5
Ireland	26.3	13.5	12.8	7.3	3.4

Source: European Commission (Taxation trends in the European Union, 2009)

In other words, the relatively large emphasis placed on indirect taxation is only one rational response of the tax administration to the practice of concealing taxable assets that is engaged in by a significant proportion of citizens.

Despite the justified (given the extent of tax evasion) effort to enhance revenue through indirect taxation, the overall result is not as desired. The Greek tax system manages to collect meagre revenues, certainly lower than expected given the size of domestic economic activity. Comparing the corresponding figures of Greece and other Mediterranean EU member states, we conclude that the total tax revenue should be higher by about 5 percentage points compared to the value obtained. Of course, the difference in tax revenues is significantly larger when compared with the developed Northern European countries.

Furthermore, a shortfall in tax revenues is observed in each taxation category (e.g., direct or indirect taxation and natural and legal persons) and is irrefutable evidence of the size of the shadow economy, confirming the weakness of the relevant mechanism to collect a sufficient part of the corresponding taxes. Greece thus heads the list for tax evasion and tax avoidance among developed countries (OECD-Economic Survey: Greece 2009).

This shortfall in tax revenues is not a recent phenomenon but concerns the entire period from 1995 (and probably even prior to that) until today. Indeed, during the extreme fiscal effort before joining the Euro area, the difference in tax revenue for the Greek government compared to other Mediterranean EU countries decreased significantly (but was not nullified) for a period of about 5 years. Then, after the peak observed in 2000, tax revenues (as a percentage of the product obtained) dropped and in 2002 returned to pre-1996 levels of 20% of GDP.

Obviously, the relative size of tax revenue in the developed countries of Northern Europe (around 40% of GDP, about double the rate of Greece) is a distant target for the domestic tax mechanism.

Apart from the shortfall of income from public funds and the social injustice resulting from the excessive taxation of those who are unable to conceal taxable income, the ability of certain groups to avoid the tax charges raises major issues regarding incentives. It is commonly accepted that the ability to hide taxable income applies almost exclusively to the self-employed (OECD-Economic Survey: Greece 2009). Therefore, it is likely that incentives would arise in the Greek society for working in freelance professions over choosing dependant employment. Therefore, it is no coincidence that Greece has a disproportionately high percentage of self-employed entrepreneurs compared with other EU member countries.

7.7.2 Organisation and Operation of Social Insurance Schemes

Individual insurance schemes reflect the economic conditions and social requirements during the period in which they were established and entered into force. They are affected by the economic, historical and social aspects and reflect the culture of a society.[15] In addition, the insurance schemes of individual sectors of activity (e.g., secondary, professional insurance) reflect the specifics of each sector. Therefore, the classification of social security schemes in individual categories is not easy and may never be absolute. However, we will attempt a categorisation of social security schemes based on their key individual characteristics. These parameters of the insurance scheme contribute to the development of incentives for all parties involved (employers, employees and pensioners) and therefore may constitute a helpful or limiting factor in the development dynamics of economy.

The first key aspect of social insurance schemes involves financing of pension costs and dividing of social insurance schemes into redistributive (pay as you go, PAYG) and funded.

A redistributive social insurance scheme implements a social contract between different generations. Under this scheme, current employees accept their burden of social insurance contributions, which are used to fund the payment of pensions to current beneficiaries (pensioners). Meanwhile, employees acquire the right (when they reach retirement age) to receive in the form of pensions capital that will consist of contributions from future employees. It is easy to conclude that the proper functioning of such a scheme requires the confidence of employees (and future beneficiaries) in the scheme's ability to pay their pensions in the future (when they secure their pension rights). It is no coincidence that for the vast majority of redistributive schemes, the state is the guarantor of their smooth functioning and sustainability.

On the other hand, in a funded insurance scheme, employees' contributions are invested during their working lives to accumulate sufficient capital to fund their

---

[15] A typical example is the difference between the Anglo-Saxon world and continental Europe. In the first case, the role of government in social security is significantly smaller than in the second, where people expect the "social contract" of the state to guarantee the smooth functioning of the social security scheme.

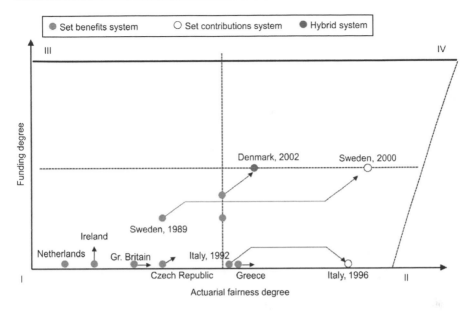

Fig. 7.7 Degree of redistributive fairness (Classification of social insurance schemes based on the degree of actuarial fairness (horizontal axis) and funding (vertical axis). We see that redistributive schemes with some degree of actuarial fairness (quasi-actuarial) offer performance equal to the economy's growth rate, while funded schemes exhibit performance equal to the rate of the economy. As this rate is usually higher than the rate of economic growth, point II presents a lesser degree of actuarial fairness than IV (Nectarios 2008; Lindbeck and Persson 2003). The interrupted arrows indicate the direction of major insurance reforms implemented in the respective countries.) (Source: Werding (2003))

pensions after their retirement. This scheme usually uses personal accounts (where paid contributions and any returns from past investments are credited) and is therefore easier to operate in the private sector as well.

Based on the financing of benefits (redistributive or funded system) and the degree of redistributive fairness, insurance schemes may be classified as depicted in Fig. 7.7. This figure depicts schemes with lower (points I and III) and higher degrees of redistributive fairness (II and IV). The same figure shows the most recent large-scale insurance reforms undertaken in various countries. We observe that all reforms are implemented with the goals of greater redistributive fairness and introduction of more funded features.

7.8   The Insurance Scheme in the Greek Economy

The issue of social insurance returns to the fore after the publication of every scientific report on the redistributive deficits of the funds and the studies related to viability (or, more correctly, non-viability) of the existing scheme and the

Table 7.13 Estimation of pension payment cost by the year 2060 as a percentage of GDP for each social insurance institution

	2007 (%)	2020 (%)	2030 (%)	2040 (%)	2050 (%)	2060 (%)
Civil servants	2.0	2.2	2.7	2.9	3.2	3.4
IKA-ETAM	3.3	3.7	5.0	7.1	8.6	8.5
OGA	1.6	1.1	1.0	1.1	1.1	0.9
OAEE	0.9	1.6	2.3	2.9	2.9	2.5
Other carriers (TAP-OTE TSMEDE, NAT, etc.)	3.9	4.6	6.1	7.5	8.3	8.8
Total	11.7	13.2	17.1	21.4	24.0	24.1

Source: European Commission, Pension schemes and pension projections in the EU-27 member states, 2008–2060 (2009)

required measures.[16] The fact is that the accumulated redistributive deficit makes obvious the issue of the survival of insurance funds. Indicatively, the cost of paying pensions amounts to nearly 12% of GDP, but this percentage is expected to rise to 24% of GDP in the year 2060 (Table 7.13).

A large subset of the problems with social insurance schemes originate in demographic factors (e.g., increased life expectancy, population aging and consequent aggravation of the employees to pensioners ratio) that are evident throughout the developed world. The situation presents a challenge for social insurance schemes of the developed world that came into force in periods with very different social and demographic characteristics, including that of Greece.

However, not all developed economies face problems to the same extent as a result of population aging. Table 7.14 shows the level of expenditure (for the year 2007) and the expected increase by the year 2060 due to population aging.

It is significant that while, in the other expenditure categories, Greece falls behind other European countries, it is expected to record higher costs (as a percentage of GDP) of social insurance benefits than the corresponding European averages. In other words, a more efficient management of the insurance scheme's resources would allow the release of significant funds and their investment in development projects and infrastructure projects.

The predictions made about future developments in costs are also noteworthy. The estimate for the necessary increase in spending excluding pension payments (e.g., health care and long-term care costs) is similar in magnitude to the respective averages of the European Union and the Eurozone (see Table 7.14). Nevertheless, pension needs over the coming decades in Greece are expected to increase, on average, at rates three times higher than the rates estimated for the European Union and the Eurozone. These estimates raise the cost of the Greek social insurance scheme to 25% of GDP for the year 2060.

---

[16] Significant contributions to the insurance scheme were made under the Economic Reconstruction Program in 2010, whose effect is examined in Chap. 11 of this book.

Table 7.14 Public expenditures related to population aging for the period of 2007–2060 as a percentage of GDP

		Greece (%)	EU-27 (%)	Eurozone (%)
Pensions	2007 level	11.7	10.2	11.1
	Change to 2035	7.7	1.7	2.1
	Change to 2060	12.4	2.4	2.8
Healthcare	2007 level	5.0	6.7	6.7
	Change to 2035	0.9	1.0	1.0
	Change to 2060	1.4	1.5	1.4
Long-term care	2007 level	1.4	1.2	1.3
	Change to 2035	0.8	0.6	0.7
	Change to 2060	2.2	1.1	1.4
Unemployment benefits	2007 level	0.3	0.8	1.0
	Change to 2035	−0.1	−0.2	−0.2
	Change to 2060	−0.1	−0.2	−0.2
Education	2007 level	3.7	4.3	4.2
	Change to 2035	−0.3	−0.3	−0.3
	Change to 2060	0.0	−0.2	−0.2
Total	2007 level	22.1	23.1	24.3
	Change to 2035	9.1	2.7	3.2
	Change to 2060	15.9	4.7	5.2
Total without pensions	2007 level	10.4	12.9	13.2
	Change to 2035	1.4	1.0	1.1
	Change to 2060	3.5	2.3	2.4

Source: Stability and Growth Programme (January 2010)

This unbearable cost of the insurance scheme is, in addition to demographic developments, a result of the way in which the benefits are administered and financed. In particular, many of its provisions are considered particularly generous.

The case of Greece, however, is characterised by the specificity of further differentiation between employees of the public and private sectors. While one would expect a socially fair system to even out the differences in the treatment of different groups of employees to the benefit of the least favoured, in the case of the Greek insurance scheme, it appears that the situation is reversed. Thus, the highly favourable treatment of employees of the larger (including, e.g., public utilities, public entities) public sector by the insurance scheme supports and explains, in part, the formulation by Greek society of a clear preference for employment in the public sector.

The Greek social insurance scheme, despite its complicated breakdown into individual funds, each with different characteristics and operating parameters, is a redistributive scheme with defined benefits and a low degree of actuarial fairness.

The scheme's redistributional characteristics make it particularly vulnerable to adverse demographic developments. Currently, about two employees account for every pensioner, whereas, for the scheme to be considered viable, the ratio should be about 4 to 1. Figure 7.8 shows predictions from the Center for Planning and Economic Research (CPER) of the development of the pensions-to-employees ratio.[17] Apart from demographic developments, this deterioration will depend largely on the ability of the Greek economy to create new jobs. The predictions describe a bleak future as the current ratio is expected to deteriorate significantly in the coming years.

Of particular importance is the finding about the impact of immigration on the demography of social insurance scheme. Under the assumptions adopted by CEPR (2009), migration flow is not sufficient to solve the problem of actuarial deficits as it seems to improve the ratio of employees to pensions, in the best case scenario, by 5%; the dashed lines in Fig. 7.8 reflect possible variations due to different levels of immigration. According to this analysis, the flow of immigrants from neighbouring countries will not necessarily be maintained at the levels of the recent past due to the gradual development of local economies. Therefore, these findings, in conjunction with the social problems arising from the continuing inflow of immigrants, make it necessary to find different solutions for the continued funding of the social insurance scheme.

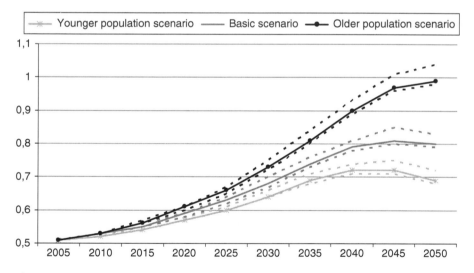

Fig. 7.8 Scenarios for the development of the pensions-to-employees ratio (This ratio for the year 2050, according to the most probable scenario, is 0.8, according to the most positive scenario (younger population scenario) 0.7, and according to the most negative scenario (aged population scenario) is 1! *Dashed lines* show possible variations of the three scenarios, depending on the pace of migration in the Greek economy.) (Source: Athanasiou et al. 2009)

---

[17] It is difficult to convey the exact number of pensioners as many pensioners receive pension benefits from more than one fund. It is clearly easier to assess the ratio of pensions to employees.

References

Agrawal KM (2009) Transfer Pricing: A beginner's perspective. Available at: http://www.scribd. com/doc/19883573/Transfer-PricingBeginners-Perspective.

Athanasiou L, Zervou F, Kotsi A (2009) Economic and demographic sustainability of the social insurance system, CEPR, Report 57

Barry F (2005) FDI, transfer pricing and the measurement of R&D intensity. Res Pol 35(5):673–681

Beck T, Demirgüç-Kunt A, Levine R (2000) A new database on financial development and structure. World Bank Econ Rev 14:597–605

Gerschenkron A (1962) Economic backwardness in historical perspective. A book of essays. Harvard University Press, Cambridge

Levine R (2002) Bank-based or market-based financial systems: which is better? J Fin Interm 11:398–428

Lindbeck A, Persson M (2003) The gains from pension reform. J Econ Lit 41(1):74–112

Nektarios M (2008) Pension reform with consensus and transparency. Papazisis, Athens

North D (1990) Institutions, institutional change and economic performance. Cambridge University Press, Cambridge

Rajan R (2005) Has financial development made the world riskier? Proceedings Federal Reserve Bank of Kansas City, issue August, pp 313–369

Rajan R, Zingales L (1998) Which capitalism? Lessons from the East Asian crisis. J Appl Corp Finan 11:40–48

Vettas N, Katsoulakos C (2004) Competition and regulatory policy: the financial deregulation in monopolistic markets. Typothito-George Dardanos, Athens

Wallis JJ, North CD (1986) Measuring the transaction sector in the American economy, 1870–1970. With a comment by Lance Davis. In: Engerman SL, Gallman RE (eds) Long-term factors in American economic growth. University of Chicago Press, Chicago

Werding M (2003) After another decade of reform: do pension systems in Europe converge? CESifo DICE Report Ifo Institute for Economic Research at the University of Munich 1(1), pp:11–16

Williamson O (1981) The economics of organization: the transaction cost approach. Am J Sociol 87:548–577

Political Institutions and the Distribution of Income

8

Political institutions are a way of accumulating or otherwise assembling the individual preferences and conflicts throughout the social fabric. Different political institutions shape and are shaped by different winners and losers and therefore represent different balances of forces. Thus, social tension constantly surrounds the formation of institutions. Political institutions govern the processes by which decisions are made, including control over the ruling structures (e.g., governments, administrations) and the systems of election of representatives.

The initial allocation of resources, the basic cultural background and some basic characteristics of transactions shape the present characteristics of transactions, the cultural background, the political institutions and the allocation of resources. These basic conditions of society have de jure and de facto political power. Ultimately, the entire framework shapes the financial institutions (through property rights and contracting procedures). Financial institutions, in turn, are shaped by and shape relative prices in the economy and thus shape the incentives for the operation of those individuals and businesses that are active in the economy. The shaping of incentives ultimately shapes the economic performance of the entire system. The system is dynamic, so the description of its performance captures only one moment of its development over time.

Based on the above analysis, it is understood that the process of allocating resources and creating incentives is crucial for the development of the system. This is not only the case because it determines the performance level of the economic system, as one would expect. More importantly, this process shapes the future conditions of resource allocation and the new political institutions. These two elements constitute a new starting point for the system that essentially determines its future (Fig. 8.1).

After discussing the political institutions in Greece (Sect. 8.1), this chapter presents the evolution of the quality of political institutions (Sect. 8.2). Section 8.3 analyses problems regarding the operation of the public sector, its size, effectiveness and its influence on the market. Section 8.4 records the extent of bureaucracy in the Greek state and presents the basic quantitative data reflecting the current situation. Section 8.5 addresses the issue of public enterprises that have either been

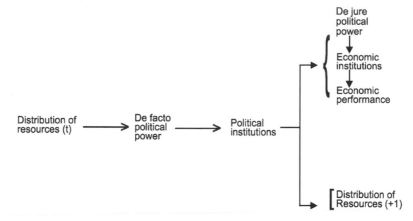

Fig. 8.1 Distribution of resources and political institutions

privatised in recent years or still belong to the Greek state, while Sect. 8.6 describes the regulatory interventions and the regulatory framework that has been promoted or is implemented by the Greek state in relation to public administration. Section 8.7 examines the issue of pressure groups in Greek society, presenting their categories and the manners in which their action may affect the distribution of income. Finally, Sect. 8.8 presents the concepts of inequality and poverty and the mechanisms of distribution and redistribution of income and wealth.

8.1   Political Institutions in Greece

The following analysis focuses on key dimensions of issues related to the basic features of the political system in Greece and their influences on economic growth, the manner in which domestic political institutions affect the welfare of the population and the distribution of the social product and the types of incentives for economic action that are formulated in the context of specific political institutions. More specifically, we will attempt to highlight the relation between the political and institutional environment that has established itself in the Third Greek Republic (since 1974) and the economic performance that has been achieved.

The post-junta institutional changes after the collapse of the dictatorship (in 1974) launched a period of stability that was unprecedented in Greek history. The restoration of democratic institutions, the adoption of a new Constitutional Charter (1975), the smooth transition of governments (1981), the further deepening of democracy and the country's accession to the European Union provided a stable system of political institutions during the Third Greek Republic (Lyrintzis et al. 1996; Kontogiorgis et al. 2004).

Political institutions in Greece present characteristics that are associated (positively or negatively) with economic growth. Institutional checks and balances of power that would restrict state power do not exist. The typical, for a liberal state, distinction between the powers is noted by the primacy of the executive power (government), which creates significant institutional problems, particularly if the function of the domestic party system is taken into account. The degradation of the parliament (legislative power)[1] and weaknesses regarding the function of the justice system (cases of corruption or biased decisions) constitute an unbalanced institutional reality with significant effects on the equitable distribution of political power.

The primacy of the executive power, which was requested by the pre-junta National Radical Union (ERE)[2] and implemented with the Constitution of 1975,[3] developed under the umbrella of a decision-making system centred around the prime minister. This model, which was strengthened after the constitutional revision of 1986 and the restriction of the powers of the President of the Republic (Manesis 1989), had important effects on a wide range of fields of economic, social and political life. It is summarised in a model of decision making centralised around the Prime Minister. The imbalance in the distribution of political power and its impact on decision making increases if the weak nature of the domestic "civil society" (Sotiropoulos (ed.) 2004), the limited presence of truly independent administrative authorities and the partisanisation of all institutional expressions of collective action (real syndicalism) are taken into account.

The weakness of domestic political institutions and their negative impact on economic growth become more pronounced in the context of the party system. The structure and function of the latter gradually leads public opinion to form a trend to depreciate policies, which hinders all necessary reformatory efforts. The operation of the partisan and the broader political system is associated with images and perceptions of the political world as disconnected from social and economic needs, with its own specific interests that it assiduously promotes.[4] Two main factors contribute to this perception: first, the partisanisation of the entire social fabric, and second, the gradual isolation of citizens and lack of dissemination of meaningful political information on the capacities of the state and its politicians.

The collapse of the junta and the start of the political changeover gradually led to the establishment of a bipolar party system. On one pole are the two "power parties" (PASOK and N.D.), alternating in positions of government and converging on similar ideological and political positions. On the other pole, we find the smaller, in terms of electoral influence, political parties, which do not affect the formation of

---

[1] As only the MPs of the ruling party suffice to vote for a bill, with a positive or (often) negative effect, which the government itself is required to implement.

[2] For the proposal on a "radical change" in the Constitution of 1952, which was submitted in 1963 by the ERE without being implemented, see Charalambis (1985).

[3] See e.g., Venizelos (1980).

[4] The law "on ministerial accountability" has often been the focus of such criticism, as have the salaries of MPs.

Table 8.1 Percentage of "power parties" in Greece in general elections (1981–2007)

Year	N.D.	PASOK	Total
1981	35.88	48.07	83.95
1985	40.84	45.82	86.66
1989 (June)	44.28	39.13	83.41
1989 (November)	46.19	40.67	86.86
1990	46.89	38.61	85.50
1993	39.30	46.88	86.18
1996	38.12	41.49	79.61
2000	42.73	43.79	86.52
2004	45.36	40.55	85.91
2007	41.83	38.10	79.93
2009	33.48	43.92	77.40

Source: Ministry of Interior (Results File)

governments and are characterised by divergent, clear, ideological and political positions.[5] Table 8.1 shows that the dominance of the two "power parties" as regards the monopolisation of governmental power has remained unchallenged throughout the political changeover period. More than three quarters of the electorate support both "power parties".

The reproduction of the dominant positions of the two power parties is favoured by the electoral system. With the exception of the highly proportional electoral system of the 1989–1990 elections, all other adopted systems have complied with the rationale of a powerful government as a fundamental condition for a smooth and stable political life.

The electoral law contributes to the reproduction of the electoral-political dominance of the two "power parties" without, however, determining it. Their political power is mainly due to their close connection to the state and the sequential distribution of economic resources. In fact, despite their initial theoretical differentiations, the two "power parties" consolidated their dominance through clientelism by managing the state resources towards which they are constantly oriented

---

[5] The internal criteria composing the two poles (ability to hold government positions and ideological-political character) are the basic patterns of different typologies that have so far been proposed on the character of the Greek party system. When emphasis is placed on the ideological and political character of parties, the domestic party system appears as a "polarized and asymmetrical tri-partisanship". See Mavrogordatos (1984), vol. 7, issue 4, pp. 156–169 and Nikolakopoulos (1989). When emphasis is placed on this issue of the ability to hold government positions, it appears as typical bipartisanship. See Pappas (2001), issue 17, pp. 71–102. For related theoretical discussions, see Sartori (1976).

(Lyrintzis 1984; Spourdalakis (ed.) 1998).[6] Their gradually increasing influence and prevalence are not the result of clear ideological and political plans designed to express specific class and social interests but of their ability to handle public funds. This fact, which to some degree interprets the ideological-political convergence observed in the two "parties of power" (Metaxas 1998), is evidenced by the amplitude of partisanisation in the social fabric. The domains of syndicalism, education, public administration, and local administration are indicative examples. The absence of distinct political plans that are promoted consistently by candidates and party staff creates a twofold effect. On one hand, the electoral costs continually expand, thus potentially creating the conditions for irregular practices to the point that the evaluation of candidates is connected predominantly to their "visibility". Their visibility is effectively promoted by television. On the other hand, this battle of promotion and controversy over minor issues enhances the distrust of public opinion towards politics.

In these circumstances, the incentives leading to the formation of real reformatory political goals fall into disuse or disappear altogether. The only element that remains is the dispute about the need for reformatory plans, indicating the very prominence that now occupies the communicative picture at the expense of political substance. To the extent that the electoral influence of the two "parties of power" depends primarily on the distribution of state resources and benefits, there is no strong reason to divert these resources to promote a particular political and economic direction. Their actions are directed mostly at balancing conflicting interests, providing "solutions" for the majority of the population rather than methodically planning and implementing reformatory plans, which involve costs for some social groups and thus political costs for power parties themselves.[7] It is characteristic that the think tanks of the two "parties of power" have very little involvement in shaping policy. Often, though not usually, they handle only the ways to justify the policies developed at the top of the party hierarchy. The reformatory plans, to the extent that these exist, represent the top of the party hierarchy rather than collective projects formed in conditions of political participation. The personalisation of politics, which is enhanced by modern "telecracy" (Papathanassopoulos 1997; Kominou 1996, pp. 219–246), culminates in the case of political leaders, who traditionally enjoy a hegemonic position within the two "parties of power" in Greece.

The establishment of PASOK and N.D. as the "parties of power", i.e., as the political formations alternating exclusively in positions of governmental authority, is connected to the developments within their structures. These developments generally refer to the descriptions of such theoretical shapes as the "pluriform"

---

[6] For the transformation of PASOK as a "state party", see Vernardakis (2004), pp. 154–175. It is characteristic that, at least until recently, all key positions for the functioning of public administration, such as those of General Secretaries, complied patiently with the choices of the party nomination (appointment) without any claim of institutional transparency and meritocracy, with whatever it involves functionally for the state apparatus.

[7] For the case of PASOK, see Givalos (2005), pp. 86–127.

and "cartel" parties. Their convergence, which has been properly pointed out (Metaxas 1998), is characterised, among else, by the continuing weakening of the ideological and political character of the party, the eminence of the party leadership compared to the ordinary party members, the development of links with specific interest groups, the party's conversion into supporters of government policy, "professionalisation" and an ever-growing connection to the mass media to disseminate positive images, making it easier for them to win and maintain government authority.

These trends, however, comply with the electoral support of the two "parties of power". Despite its rhetorical condemnation, bipartisanship continues to have expectations because of its strong engagement with the state. However, this oxymoron continually highlights the ongoing detachment that clearly exists between the political system and society, thus resulting in the cancellation of any reformatory perspective. The vice of distorting expectations, whose grip becomes ever tighter, includes the inability of the state and its mechanisms to implement any (often minor) reformatory efforts, as there are no safeguards requiring or ensuring their implementation, and, on the other hand, the (usually) unrealistic expectations of the majority of the public, who are uninformed and disconnected from the political process public. Table 8.2 illustrates the creeping doubt over executive institutions (ministries, courts, police) and representative institutions (parties, governments, parliament, prefectures, municipalities).

8.2   The Effectiveness of Political Institutions

The above discussion suggests the hypothesis that political institutions in Greece are of relatively poor quality. The measurement of the quality of institutions conducted by organisations like the World Bank is carried out using indicators such as "voice-accountability", "political stability", "government effectiveness", "regulatory quality", "rule of law" and "control of corruption" (Kaufman et al. 2009). More specifically, "accountability" measures the extent to which citizens of a country are involved in the government selection process and the degree of freedom of expression of the press and associations. "Political stability" measures the probability of the government's destabilisation by constitutional or violent means, including terrorism. "Government effectiveness" measures the quality of public services, politicians' ability to provide services and independence from political pressures. "Regulatory quality" measures the government's ability to design and implement reforms and policies that can strengthen and promote the development of the private sector. "Rule of law" measures the extent to which citizens trust the laws of society, including the quality of property rights, policing and justice. Finally, "control of corruption" measures the extent to which public power is exercised with a view to promoting the government's own interests, including both small- and large-scale corruption. These indicators can capture a

Table 8.2 Social trust in institutions (2009)

	Ranking 2008	Index 2008	Ranking 2009	Index 2009	Change 2008–2009	Trust +	Distrust −
National Weather Service	2	1517	1	1840	323	92	5
Fire department	1	1840	2	1517	−323	91	6
President of the Republic	3	880	3	978	98	88	9
Athens Academy	5	483	4	590	107	59	10
Ombudsman	4	486	5	507	21	71	14
Army and armed forces	7	375	6	494	119	79	16
Olympic	16	166	7	444	278	71	16
New technologies and IT companies	9	250	8	290	40	61	21
Universities	10	246	9	275	29	66	24
European parliament	8	267	10	260	−7	65	25
National Statistical Service	6	394	11	219	−175	59	27
Radio	11	233	12	204	−29	57	28
OTE	15	167	13	197	30	63	32
European Union	12	203	14	188	−15	60	32
Private hospitals and clinics	14	184	15	184	0	59	32
Non-governmental organisations	17	158	16	181	23	56	31
ASEP	25	93	17	157	64	55	35
National Intelligence Service	18	130	18	155	25	48	31
Bank of Greece	21	110	19	138	28	51	37
Data Protection Authority	19	130	20	138	8	51	37
Internet	13	192	21	131	−61	46	35
PPC	24	98	22	123	25	53	43
Police and Security Forces	26	93	23	120	27	49	41
Church	22	107	24	119	12	51	43
Schools	32	76	25	96	20	43	45
Municipalities	20	115	26	91	−24	43	47
Justice and Judges	29	83	27	91	8	42	46
Prefectures	23	102	28	83	−19	39	47
Colleges and Vocational Studies Centres	33	69	29	75	6	33	44
Parliament	36	57	30	74	17	39	53
Construction businesses	30	80	31	71	−9	34	48
ADEDY	27	89	32	63	−26	32	51
Mobile phone companies	38	56	33	60	4	33	55
Competition Commission	35	57	34	60	3	28	47
GSEE	28	87	35	58	−29	31	53
NHS	37	56	36	57	1	34	60
SEV	39	55	37	54	−1	28	52

(continued)

Table 8.2 (continued)

	Ranking 2008	Index 2008	Ranking 2009	Index 2009	Change 2008–2009	Trust +	Distrust −
Insurance funds	34	63	38	53	−10	32	60
Newspapers	31	79	39	52	−27	28	54
Advertising businesses	40	53	40	50	−3	30	60
Food manufacturers	45	27	41	39	12	25	64
Banks	41	44	42	37	−7	25	68
Ministries	44	31	43	34	3	22	64
TV	42	37	44	32	−5	22	68
Insurance businesses	43	36	45	29	−7	20	69
ASE	46	16	46	22	6	15	69
Parties	48	10	47	15	5	12	79
Governments	47	12	48	14	2	11	81

Source: Public Issue (January 2010)

country's performance in a historical and comparative perspective and thus allow us to draw useful conclusions about the quality of political institutions.

Studying the evolution of Greece's performance from 1996 to 2008, we observe that the quality of all domestic political institutions progressively worsened in recent years. Only the political stability index shows an improving trend, while regulatory quality deteriorated significantly. This conclusion is confirmed by examination of the findings. The high state interventionism in many sectors of the economy, which hinders the promotion of healthy private initiatives and their contribution to the country's economic growth, is also demonstrated statistically. Overall, most indicators suggest that the quality of political institutions has gradually deteriorated, especially since Greece's entry into the EMU.

Greece's position as regards the quality of political institutions in 2008 compared to other EU countries shows that, in 2008, Greece presented worse quality indicators for political institutions in relation to other countries. The exception is Italy, which shows similar scores to Greece, sharing the last position on the list of the 11 EU countries examined (Austria, Belgium, Greece, Cyprus, Czech Republic, Denmark, Estonia, Finland, France, Italy and Germany). By contrast, Scandinavian countries (Denmark and Finland) showed the best quality of political institutions in 2008, in most cases receiving an excellent score (100).

As already noted, the quality of political institutions has a significant impact on economic growth. Policies that channel the social product to groups with disproportionate political influence over others contribute to the devaluation of the political system. This effect annuls any efforts to reform the economy to allow it to adjust to the demands of international competition. The possibility of long-term growth is restricted. This vicious cycle is completed by the formulation of incentives for counterproductive and shadow economic activity as positive expectations are lacking. A key point, however, of the negative effects of political institutions on growth is the redistribution of the social product.

8.3 Size and Efficiency of the Public Sector

The size of the public sector is very difficult to measure accurately. These difficulties stem mainly from the complexity and often the uniqueness of services provided to citizens by the state. They also relate to the productivity of the state's operation and the efficiency of the services offered. The rapid technological developments of recent years, in conjunction with the improvement of social welfare and the improvement or creation of new and costly infrastructure, have generated new questions and concerns about the role and size of the public sector under these new conditions.

Table 8.3 General government expenditure as a percentage of GDP

Year/country	2000	2001	2008	Avg. 2002–2008
EU-27	45.2	46.2	46.8	46.4
Denmark	53.7	54.2	51.9	53.3
Netherlands	44.2	45.4	45.9	45.6
Finland	48.3	47.8	49.0	48.9
Sweden	55.6	55.5	53.0	55.0
Average of Northern European countries	50.5	50.7	50.0	50.7
Spain	39.1	38.6	41.1	39.0
Italy	46.2	48.0	48.7	47.9
Portugal	43.1	44.4	46.0	45.5
Average of Mediterranean countries	43.0	44.0	45.0	44.1
Greece	46.7	45.3	48.3	45.2

Source: Eurostat

Table 8.4 General government revenue as a percentage of GDP

Year/country	2000	2001	2008	Avg. 2002–2008
EU-27	45.4	44.8	44.6	44.6
Denmark	55.8	55.4	55.4	55.9
Netherlands	46.1	45.1	46.6	45.2
Finland	55.2	52.7	53.4	53.0
Sweden	59.3	57.2	55.5	56.6
Average of North European countries	54.1	52.6	52.8	52.7
Spain	38.1	38.0	37.0	38.8
Italy	45.3	44.9	46.0	45.0
Portugal	40.2	40.1	43.2	42.0
Average of Mediterranean countries	41.2	41.0	42.1	41.9
Greece	43.0	40.9	40.6	40.0

Source: Eurostat

The main indicators used for calculating the size of the public sector are spending – primarily – and general government revenues as a percentage of GDP. Tables 8.3 and 8.4 analyse the rates of general government expenditures and revenues, respectively, as percentages of GDP, as an indication of the size of the public sector in Northern European and Mediterranean countries and Greece.

The analysis presented in these tables reveals that Northern European countries, especially those in Scandinavia, have very large public sectors because their expenditures as a percentage of GDP are very high (above 51%). The size of the public sector in Greece is similar to that of other Mediterranean countries and to the EU average. This means that Northern European countries have significantly larger public sectors than Greece does. However, when comparing the two tables, an interesting difference appears. Despite their magnitude, the expenditures of Northern European countries are approximately 12% less than their revenues. In Greece, – despite smaller expenditure, revenues are 5% less than the expenditure of the central government.

The size of the public sector is directly related to the tax system that should be implemented to allow the offsetting of public expenditure – which is the most important indicator for determining the size of a state – by the revenue generated. The main source of revenue for a state is taxation, and, consequently, the greater the role of the state, the higher tax rates are expected to be. Both indirect taxes and income and capital taxes can create distortions.

General government expenditure, however, is often confused with the state's contribution to GDP. This is not correct because expenditure includes transfer payments – wages, pensions – that are not included in the calculation of GDP. The governments' respective contributions to GDP in Greece and Northern European and Mediterranean countries are shown in Table 8.5.

Table 8.5 shows that, in Mediterranean countries, the public sector contribution to GDP is around 18%, with the lowest participation rate – 16.5% – in Spain and a maximum of 19.6% in Portugal. In Greece, the public sector contributes around 18.5%. In contrast, in Northern European countries, it contributes around 25%.

Table 8.5 Contribution of general government to GDP

Year/Country	2000	2001	2007	Avg. 2000–2007
EU-27	18.2	18.5	18.6	18.7
Denmark	26.7	27.3	27.2	27.5
Netherlands	18.4	18.9	18.9	19.2
Sweden	27.6	28.1	27.2	28.0
Finland	23.2	23.8	24.2	24.4
Average of Northern European countries	24.0	24.5	24.4	24.8
Spain	16.2	16.6	17.0	16.5
Italy	17.7	17.9	18.3	18.3
Portugal	20.1	19.8	18.7	19.6
Average of Mediterranean countries	18.0	18.1	18.0	18.2
Greece	19.1	18.9	18.2	18.5

Source: Eurostat

8.4   Bureaucracy

The prevailing perception of the Greek state is of an overgrown organisation that has employed an excessive number of public officials since its beginning (Tsoukalas 1981). This perception is accompanied by views that the operation of public administration is governed by overregulation, a lack of rationality and cooperation between authorities and discrepancies in substance and form between formal and informal practices (Spanou 1996). It is supported, more generally, that bureaucracy is closely linked with the parties alternating in positions of governmental authority. This system leads to clientelism that weakens it while creating centres of corruption and misrule.[8]

The Netherlands Central Planning Bureau estimated the cost of the administrative burden as a percentage of GDP for all European Union countries.[9] Their results are shown in Table 8.6.

Table 8.6 Administrative burden per EU country (GDP percentage)

Austria	4.6
Belgium-Luxembourg	2.8
Czech Republic	3.3
Germany	3.7
Denmark	1.9
Spain	4.6
Finland	1.5
France	3.7
UK	1.5
Greece	6.8
Hungary	6.8
Ireland	2.4
Italy	4.6
Netherlands	3.7
Poland	5.0
Portugal	4.6
RE	6.8
Slovakia	4.6
Slovenia	4.1
Sweden	1.5
EU-25	3.5

Source: Kox (2005)
Note: BL includes Belgium and Luxembourg; RE includes all Baltic countries, Malta and Cyprus; the result for the EU-25 is a weighted average based on GDP

---

[8] See, for example, Lyrintzis (1984), pp. 99–118, and Sotiropoulos (1995).

[9] Commission of the European Communities Staff working document (Brussels, 24/1/2007).

Table 8.7 Number of civil servants (2006)

Agencies	Employment relationship		
	Permanent	Open-ended	Total
Public services	83,723	8,456	92,179
Public entities	109,191	7,788	116,979
Local authorities[a]	75,918	7,611	83,529
Public legal bodies under private law	–	77,830	77,830
Total:	268,832	101,685	370,517
Others serving in the public sector			
Military	55,000	–	–
Security forces	62,155	–	–
Teachers	191,416	–	–
Judicial	3,755	–	–
Doctors	13,500	–	–
Total	325,826	–	–
Grand total	696,343		

Source: Secretary of Public Administration and e-Government, Ministry of Interior, Department of Electronic Data Processing, Annual Statistics from Census 2006 (10/02/2009)
[a]This includes persons employed by public entities who are supervised by local authorities

Table 8.6 shows that the largest administrative burdens appear in Greece and Hungary and the smallest in Denmark and Finland.

No data on the number of employees in public administration services are kept (Operational Program "Administrative Reform" 2007). According to data (dated 10-2-2009) of the General Secretariat of Public Administration and Electronic Governance of the Ministry of Interior (Department of Electronic Data Processing), based on the annual census of 2006, the number of civil servants with permanent or open-ended employment contracts, without taking employees employed under fixed-term and project contacts in the narrow and broader public sector into account, amounts to 696,343 people (Table 8.7). According to the census of the National Statistical Service (NSS) for the fourth quarter of 2008, these workers represent approximately 15.3% of the workforce (4,553,600 people).[10]

The number of civil servants in the annual census of 2006 certainly falls short of the actual number currently employed in the public sector. According to the quarterly census conducted by the Department of Electronic Data Processing of the General Secretariat of Public Administration and Electronic Governance of the Ministry of Interior, the number of government officials on December 31, 2008, is estimated at 735,294 people. Nevertheless, even this figure does not reflect the sum of public employment. The category of legal persons does not include the staff of hospitals and universities and colleges as they are paid from the regular budget; the Department of Public Utilities does not monitor public utilities such as the Post

---

[10] For related information see http://www.gspa.gr/(4512188387384214)/eCPortal.asp?id=1479&nt=19&lang=1&pID=235&p2ID=236.

Table 8.8 Number of
public officials (31-12-
2008)

Authority	Number
Central administration	391,800
Public entities	46,887
Local authorities	82,665
Public enterprises	23,584
Various enterprises[a]	55,369
Security forces	69,189
Clergy	10,800
Military	55,000
Total	735,294

Source: Secretary of Public Administration and e-Government,
Ministry of Interior, Department of Electronic Data Processing,
Inventory of Public Sector Personnel, Fourth Quarter 2008
[a]The category "Various enterprises" includes those listed on the
Stock Exchange (PPC, Hellenic Petroleum, EYATH, Water Authority,
Thessaloniki Port Authority, PPA, IGME) and their subsidiaries

Office and the ERT (National TV) or public entities such as the NOM, the Tourist
Organisation (EOT) and the OEDB; and clergy and military are only roughly
estimated (Table 8.8).

However, the main problem in estimating the total number of civil servants in
Greece is the number of fixed-term contracts, which is roughly estimated at more
than 550,000 people.[11] In other words, this constitutes a "public sector within the
public sector", bringing the number of employees to approximately 1,250,000
(27.4% of the workforce based on the NSS census for the fourth quarter of 2008).
In addition to the major questions this figure raises concerning the organisation and
functioning of the domestic bureaucracy, it also raises insurmountable obstacles to
its comparative valuation. The issue of the exact number of public employees
remains unclear. Tellingly, Alpha Bank's financial statement in February 2010
stated that expenditures for the payment of public sector employees in 2009
amounted to €30.44 bn, up from €14.27 bn in 2000, recording an average annual
increase of 8.8% in the 2000–2009 period, while the corresponding increase in
inflation was 3.4% and that of GDP 6.3% at current prices. Finally, in 2009 the
Greek government retired 14,000 employees but recruited 29,000 new permanent
staff. The development of the public sector workforce is shown in Table 8.9.

Given this peculiarity of the domestic public sector and taking into account, for
the sake of data comparability, the permanent and semi-permanent personnel as
recorded in the annual census of 2006, it could be argued that, contrary to popular
belief, the number of civil servants in Greece is not significantly greater than in
other European countries. It is true that from the end of the war onwards, the

---

[11] Posted on the website www.in.gr on 26/5/2009.

Table 8.9 The evolution of state-paid employees

	Total	Public services	Public entities, public organisations	Local authorities	Government ownedcorporations	State banks	Enterprises controlled by the state	Clergy
1998	857,301	375,587	212,677	74,915	116,775	57,084	10,168	10,095
1999	860,399	435,434	164,829	70,550	96,704	44,367	39,751	8,764
2000	862,634	414,162	182,105	87,374	90,019	44,396	36,237	8,341
2001	858,762	437,571	168,226	85,214	83,340	34,437	42,065	7,909
2002	886,583	455,418	174,370	100,371	70,347	32,761	44,842	8,474
2003	912,399	476,148	171,558	102,739	70,748	39,771	43,914	7,521
2004	997,810	499,700	225,968	106,486	75,228	37,845	42,097	10,486
2005	967,259	480,600	216,826	112,925	68,060	38,325	40,848	9,675
2006	1,013,531	507,063	221,375	126,418	73,435	35,865	40,717	8,658
2007	1,025,653	527,966	225,561	123,773	69,570	30,396	40,735	7,652
2008	1,031,213	519,649	223,845	127,021	73,486	33,762	44,358	9,092
2009	1,014,047	518,031	217,659	136,263	64,223	32,493	36,756	8,622
Average annual change	1.9%	3.3%	5.0%	5.4%	-4.5%	-5.1%	15.9%	-1.0%

Source: Alpha Bank Economic Bulletin, February 2010, No. 111 (quarterly)

number of civil servants has increased in absolute numbers,[12] as has the number of ministries.[13] This change is evident in government spending as a percentage of GDP.[14]

However, even if the larger estimate of the number of domestic public officials is considered (27.4% of the workforce if project contracts are included), this does not necessarily mean that the size of the bureaucracy is the cause of its problems or, therefore, that its restriction will act as a panacea. In other words, the performance of the public sector cannot be evaluated solely on its quantitative size. As noted, the Northern European countries have high percentages of civil servants in total employment, but we will see below that they rank best in the world in the quality of public services. What is needed, therefore, in terms of the role of bureaucracy in economic development, is to examine its qualitative characteristics and general operating framework as an institutional infrastructure rather than its quantitative size per se.

The available data included in the Operational Program "Administrative Reform, 2007–2013" show that, in the period of 2000–2004, the public workforce aged. This finding is particularly important considering the need for cognitive ability and awareness of new technologies to maintain productivity. Indeed, a survey by the Observatory for the Information Society found that older general managers have clearly inferior skills in information technology. They do not regard these skills as particularly important for their career development.[15] Table 8.10 reflects the changes in the age distribution of public administration personnel in the period of 2000–2004.

The educational level of civil servants is another critical variable affecting quality. Again, data from the Operational Program "Administrative Reform, 2007–2013" show a slight increase in the percentage of executives with university or vocational education and a reduction in the percentage of executives with compulsory education in the period of 2000–2004. This change, however, is undoubtedly linked to the gradual spread of information technology in the public sector and the upgrading of standards for the recruitment of staff; it does not indicate an alteration in the basic distribution of the educational levels of civil servants, most of whom are secondary or compulsory school graduates (Table 8.11).

---

[12] According to data of what was then known as the Ministry of Interior, Public Administration and Decentralization (2000), the number of government employees rose from 106,000 in 1961 to 200,000 in 1981 and to 290,000 in 1999. See also OECD (2001), p. 42 (note 4). However, in the period 2000–2004, the number of government employees decreased by 9.5%. See Operational Program "Administrative Reform", OECD (2001), p. 64.

[13] The number of ministries rose from 32 in 1973 to 57 in 1988. See Makridimitris (1992), p. 105.

[14] According to the OECD, the related expenditure rose from 21% in 1976 to 51% in 1988. See OECD, Economic Surveys. Portugal 1988–1989, Paris 1989, p. 45.

[15] See Operational Program "Administrative Reform", OECD, Economic Surveys. Portugal 1988–1989, Paris 1989, p. 36.

Table 8.10 Distribution of public administration personnel based on age (%)

Year	Ages (%)			
	≤34	35–44	45–54	≥55
2000	11.0	33.0	42.0	14.0
2004	11.0	25.0	42.0	22.0

Source: Operational Program, "Administrative Reform, 2007–2013"

Table 8.11 Distribution of public administration personnel based on level of education (%)

Year	University	Vocational	Secondary	Mandatory
2000	16.0	12.0	51.0	21.0
2004	18.0	13.0	51.0	17.0

Source: Operational Program, "Administrative Reform, 2007–2013"

Table 8.12 Distribution of public administration personnel (Census 2006) based on educational level (%)

Authority	Educational level			
	University	Vocational	Secondary	Compulsory
Public services	31.1	9.4	49.7	9.8
Public entities	11.3	24.6	47.3	16.8
Local authorities	17.6	12.2	45.3	24.9
Legal bodies under private law	13.5	8.3	60.1	18.1
Total	18.1	14.6	50.1	17.2

Source: Secretary of Public Administration and e-Government, Ministry of Interior, Department of Electronic Data Processing, Annual Statistics from Census 2006 (10/02/2009)

Based on the annual census of 2006, the education levels of the 370,517 workers (see Table 8.7) in public services, public entities, local authorities and private entities are distributed in Table 8.12.

As is clear from the table, those with university education constitute the majority in public services, while those with vocational education more often work in public entities. In contrast, the majority of those with secondary education work in private entities and those with compulsory education at local authorities.

8.5 Public Enterprises

Public enterprises are directly related to the active role played by the state in the economy and society. In particular, public enterprises were established mainly to address the inefficiencies and failures of the free market. However, a wave of privatisations launched in Britain in the early 1980s under Prime Minister Margaret Thatcher spread to many countries worldwide. This phenomenon took a heavy toll in the 1990s with the collapse of socialism in the countries of Eastern Europe. As we can see from Table 8.13, the largest privatisations in the last two decades

Table 8.13 Activities of public enterprises as a percentage of GDP

Ranking of countries according to income	1980	2000	Change
Low income	15	2.5	−12.5
Middle income	11	4	−7
High income	6	4	−2

Source: Sheshinski and Lopez-Calva (2003)

Table 8.14 Revenue from privatisation by category

Category	Revenue (%)
Financial services	34
Telecommunications	33
Services	12
Public utilities	7
Oil	7
Processing	5
Transportation	1
Trade	1

Source: Rapanos (2009)

took place in low-income countries, where, as expected, the percentage owned by the state was higher.

In the Greek economy, privatisation proceeded either through direct sales (e.g., the Olympic Games, use of the port of Piraeus) or through conversion to limited companies and listing on the stock market (PPC, OTE, DEYAP). Since the early 1990s, over 40 total or partial privatisations have taken place; the state still holds various stakes in these, and they have generated revenues of around €25 bn. The largest proceeds from privatisation – about €3.5 billion per year – were received in 1999 and 2006. On the contrary, a total of around €1 bn was received from privatisations in 1991, 1993, 1996 and 2001(Table 8.14).

The privatisation of financial services and telecommunications accounts for over two thirds of total revenues from privatisations over the last two decades.

Privatisation alone will have no positive effect on the growth of a country if it is not accompanied by improvements in the overall institutional framework (Shirley and Walsh 2000; Kikeri and Nellis 2002; Nicoletti and Scarpetta 2003).

The companies that have undergone privatisation do not include public transport or rail companies. Particular reference is made to these public enterprises – especially public transport – because, despite recording losses continuously over a period of many years, they execute a social service. Consequently, their situation requires particularly delicate management because, for obvious reasons, the fares must remain very low.

The state has full responsibility for 47 public enterprises, all of which record losses. Even the profits of profitable public enterprises are too small to offset the huge losses of loss-making public enterprises, especially urban transport enterprises and the railway (OSE) and its subsidiaries. Each year, these enterprises receive 70% of all government subsidies, while 47% of state losses come from the OSE and its subsidiaries and 38% from urban transport (ETHEL, ISAP, ILPAP).

As Rapanos (2009) explains, loss-making enterprises charged with the maintenance of social responsibility are not necessarily bad, provided that they are effective in maintaining their resources and that their losses are due to a protective pricing policy for the benefit of society. However, no attempt has ever been made – or at least published – to analyse whether any of these public enterprises effectively meet the set objectives. In addition, no existing research has focused on the following important issues: the reasons for their continued and increasing losses, the productivity of any investments made, their utilisation of human resources, whether they employ on merit and are consistent with their professional obligations, their productivity or their quality of services.

According to Law 3429/2005, public enterprises are required to follow certain rules for measuring efficiency in order to demonstrate that their operation is acceptable and can lead to maximum productivity and efficiency. Under that law, enterprises are required to publish annual financial results to verify the achievement of their objectives. This law, however, has certain shortcomings if compared to the law proposed by the OECD for the measurement of efficiency. Under this law, public enterprises' administrations should operate freely and independently of the desires of governments; they should set economic, quantitative and qualitative targets and see if they have been achieved at the end of the year. They should also find methods to measure, tackle and minimise corruption and achieve greater transparency in their operations.

Table 8.15 Financial results of public enterprises by sector

Enterprises	2007 Financial result	2007 Public subsidies	2008 Financial result	2008 Public subsidies
Rail (3)[a]	−887.88	0.00	−877.79	0.00
Urban transport (5)	−577.61	114.7	−641.85	−118.35
Port authorities (10)	*4.41*	0.00	*4.98*	0.00
Urban planning (5)	*43.73*	22.22	−23.4	44.70
Health-pharmaceuticals (3)	−2.89	2.20	−2.20	2.26
Central markets (2)	*1.19*	0.00	*0.96*	0.00
Certification-training (3)	−1.64	2.05	−0.98	2.10
Development (5)	−12.28	10.00	−4.47	10.00
Silver processing (5)	*0.32*	0.00	*0.11*	0.00
Other (6)	−35.46	2.65	−50.54	2.60
Revenue	100.81	–	82.46	–
Expenditure	−1,568.92	–	−1,677.64	–
Total	−1,468.11	16,5.22	−1,595.18	184.51

Source: Processed data presented in Rapanos (2009)
The italics in the table indicate profits
[a]Number of enterprises in parentheses

It would be of particular interest to observe the financial results for all 47 unlisted public companies, whose operation burdens the overall functioning of the state, over a number of years. The analysis of the above data leads to a very interesting result: although, in 2008, 26 of the 47 companies were profitable and only 21 made losses, these losses were enough to create a deficit of over €1.5 bn.

The analysis summarised in Table 8.15 shows that the average annual revenue from public enterprises in the 4 years from 2005 to 2008 was €88 m, while the corresponding expenditures reached €1.5 bn annually. The cumulative damages for these 4 years were more than €5.5 bn.

8.6   The Influence of the State on the Functioning of the Economy and Society

The state can affect the way in which infrastructure companies operate even if the latter are purely private or the public has only a small stake therein. This influence takes place through regulatory interventions and may affect economic growth. Although such regulatory interventions are difficult to measure, the creation of specific indicators has allowed a first attempt to measure the scope of these regulations. These indicators were developed based on a numerical scale in a lower score indicates that the state intervenes less in a particular market. This numerical scale ranges from zero (0), indicating that there is no state intervention, and reaches up to six (6), indicating that there are no limits to state intervention in a particular market. It is particularly interesting to assess the influence of the public sector on network companies and, especially, companies producing and supplying electricity, telecommunications and transport as they are the most basic forms of infrastructure, strongly affect the daily lives of citizens and contribute significantly to social welfare and economic development.

Before we begin this analysis, we present a comparative view of state regulatory interventions in all businesses, regardless of industry, operating in Greece, in other Mediterranean countries and in Northern European countries.

In Fig. 8.2, we note the magnitude of state regulatory interventions in product markets; despite a marked decrease from 1998 to 2003, Greece still tops the list of Mediterranean and Northern European countries.

In 2003, the interventionist policy of the Greek state in the electricity sector was the strongest in the EU-15. In particular, we note that Greece and Portugal appear to be the only countries examined whose regulations create barriers to entry in the electricity sector.

The deregulation of this sector in Greece is considerably slower than it has been in the rest of the EU15 and the OECD. According to OECD's figures (2007), the openness of the Greek market – as defined by the percentage of electricity consumed by those consumers who are given the choice to choose their electricity

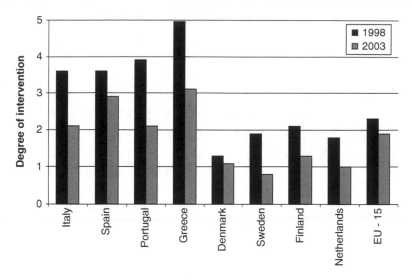

Fig. 8.2 Regulations in the product market (Source: OECD, national accounts of OECD countries, 1995–2006 (2007))

supplier – was 62% in early 2005, whereas the corresponding percentage for the EU-15 was 88%.

8.7   Pressure Groups in the Greek Society

The Greek society is a typical Western organised society with a strong presence of pressure groups at all levels (economic, social, political, and cultural). These groups are organised and consistently exert pressure towards their desired outcomes.

It is necessary at this point for the reader to understand the impossibility of recording and reporting on all pressure groups in Greek society because of both their abundance and their non-obvious and widely known presence. Therefore, the first problem concerns the impossibility – in the context of this book – of gathering information on all pressure groups. The second problem concerns groups that, despite actively exerting pressure in particular directions, do not define themselves, making it impossible to know precisely their constituents, origin, and often their final aims.

One of the major institutional pressure groups in any society are the clergy. The representatives of any religion are rightly considered to be critical factors in the implementation of policies both at the domestic level and in the international relations of a country. Apart from purely religious interests, the clergy also have strong economic and political interests. Because of its role in Greek society and the traditionally strong religiosity of the Greeks, the clergy have gained extensive power as a social institution. This power is commonly accepted by the majority of the Greek people, and this makes the clergy's work more acceptable to the public, lending it more legitimacy.

A second very important constitutional pressure group whose interests are strongly represented is the military. The military can be divided into subgroups according to sectors, corps, specialties, and other categories. The basic division, however, splits the military into the Army, Navy and Air Force. The funds intended to equip the armed forces are perhaps the key concern of the respective interest groups. In addition to equipment issues, each pressure group may express other political or broader economic and social interests.

Table 8.16 shows the number of clergy in the period of 1998–2009 in Greece and the number of employees in the armed forces for the period from 1998 to 2008. The year 2004 marked a great increase in the size of the military of around 20,000 people because of the recruitment of permanent professional soldiers. The average annual change in their number is about −0.4%.

Academics (13,143 people) gained particular sectional power with the establishment of the first universities in Western Europe. The two dominant issues for academics are academic freedom and independent university administration. It should be noted that the exclusive control academics have over admission to their profession offers them additional power that is difficult to bypass.

Another important pressure group is the judiciary (approximately 2,100 persons). Both the institutionalised hierarchy and the autonomous and independent functioning of the judiciary give them special statutory powers, institutionalised or not, through which they are able to exert pressure to protect their rights, to promote changes to the functioning of their body, or to ensure their position within their body.

Table 8.16 Number of clergy and employees of the armed forces in Greece

Year	Clergy[a]	Armed forces[b]
1998	10,095	45,200
1999	8,764	38,900
2000	8,341	41,100
2001	7,909	39,900
2002	8,474	41,600
2003	7,521	39,300
2004	10,486	60,600
2005	9,675	59,900
2006	8,658	55,700
2007	7,652	59,200
2008	9,092	55,700
2009	8,622	–

[a]Alpha Bank Economic Bulletin, February 2010, No. 111 (quarterly).
[b]Eurostat (ec.europa.eu/eurostat)

8.7.1 Professional Organisations

Greek society has many professional organisations, which can be divided into some basic categories. These are the employers' organisations, trade unions, farmers, professionals, pensioners, the unemployed and certain other pressure groups.

At the highest level, the world of employers is represented by organisations such as the "Hellenic Federation of Enterprises" (SEV), the "Hellenic Confederation of Professionals, Craftsmen and Merchants" (GSVEE), the "National Confederation of Greek Commerce" (ESEE) and the Chambers, led by that of Athens (ACCI). These employers' organisations have separate histories and development and diverse degrees of influence on public consultation and decision making. However, despite their individual differences, a common denominator of their action is that they seek to represent the largest possible number of SMEs, which are the dominant type of business in the country.

As already noted, the recognition of the important role of employers' organisations in the public debate, with the institutional upgrade that enabled it, reflects their substantial political weight. Aside from the de jure power surrounding their public action, employers enjoy a strong de facto power. The strength of employers' interests has become particularly evident in recent decades, when political, economic, and social events have encouraged their further empowerment. A network of developments in this direction relates to the deregulation of the broadcasting media. The loss of the state monopoly in television from 1989 onwards did not only open up a new field of economic action for economic factors that had influenced the sector since the early post-junta period. Primarily, it created the possibility of using the political influence of television to promote a variety of business pursuits. The (political) influence of television became an instrument to strengthen the political influence of business interests.

A second set of developments that increased the substantial political weight of employers' interests concerns the leading position of the construction industry in the Greek economy. Its development in the context of EU support in recent decades, as well as during the preparation for the Olympic Games in Athens in 2004, provided multiple opportunities for entrepreneurial action, which further strengthened the construction industry's political weight.

Finally, a third set of developments concerns the prevalence of neo-liberal policies in the economy, which strongly favour employers' interests. Privatisation, public-private partnerships (PPPs) in construction and project management, the deregulation of labour relations by introducing flexible forms of employment and favourable tax provisions create a network of state policies that further enhance employers' interests.

In the country's political system, where two "parties of power" manage the resources of the state to perpetuate their political influence, the use of these developments – which are favourable for employers' interests – is not always affected in a transparent manner. The extensive debate on corruption, which has intensified in recent decades, does not only suggest overt attempts to influence policy and serve specific interests. It is also indicative of the strong connections between the institutional voices of political power and multifarious business interests. The term "vested interests", introduced into the public vocabulary in the 90s, precisely describes these complex and largely opaque transactions intended to promote specific objectives. The provisions in the recent revision of the Constitutional Charter (2001), which regulated a set of relations between business activity and government function, document these very complex relations, which have intensified in recent decades. Provisions such as those on the media, their ownership and operation (see paragraph 5 of the revised Article 14) strive to prevent corruption and irregular transactions between government and business.

The question of the "interweaving" of political and financial power is one of the most controversial and explosive issues in today's society; at a global level, the main example is Wall Street and the American political leadership. J.K. Galbraith was amongst those who had raised the issue beginning in 1954 (Galbraith 2000). Referring to the crash of 1929, he gave the apt ironic title, "In Goldman Sachs we trust", to the relevant chapter of his book.

The same issue was observed to a much greater extent during the 2008 crisis, when, one after another, Washington's economic policy managers were found to originate or to be linked to the financial capital. The tradition started with R. Rubin, who took over as the 70th U.S. Secretary of the Treasury (1995–1999) after having served 26 years at Goldman Sachs and then became director and senior counsellor of Citigroup until 2009.

He was succeeded by L. Summers until 2001, who had also been criticised for his potential strong relationship with Wall Street and who, in January 2009, took over as the Director of the Eighth National Economic Council in the Obama administration. He was the target of considerable criticism for his proposals, mainly by Krugman and Stiglitz, who do not participate in the formulation of the economic policy in the Obama administration. Perhaps the most representative case of the link between policy and financial capital is H.M. Paulson, U.S. Secretary of the Treasury (Republican) in 2006–2009. He handled the largest part of the financial crisis of 2008. Before making the move to the Treasury Department, he had served, since 1974, as President and Chief Executive Officer of Goldman Sachs.

G. Epstein, in a recent interview (13/10/2010), noted that of the total of 19 major and "independent" economists in the U.S., most of whom comprised two important pressure groups for the formulation of the standards reform platform after the crisis of 2008–2010 and who make regular appearances in the press and media, 13 are paid by banks and private funds, 8 were board members of banking and private equity firms, 6 work for two or more financial companies, 2 are co-founders of private capital, 2 are consultants, and 1 of them works for two banks as a chairman and a manager. In Greek society the 4/5 of financial analysts who appear in the mass media, are directly or indirectly related to economic and political authorities.

8.7.2 Freelance Professionals Unions

Freelance professionals have their own organisations, which are primarily charged with defending their own interests. They exert pressure on the state both to maintain their rights and to acquire new rights that will enable them to expand their power in society, affecting the country's economic activity. Because of the comparatively high participation rate of freelance professionals in total employment, their importance is crucial in shaping social dynamics. Typical cases for the Greek society are all kinds of engineers, who form the Technical Chamber, lawyers, whose concerns are voiced through local bar associations, doctors, who are represented mainly through medical associations, and the road transport industry.

As stressed in the literature, professional unions of freelancers are distinguished by the features of their craft guild (e.g., doctors, lawyers) where the state grants extensive autonomy. Thus, the group itself may regulate, outside of the influence of the state, the rules governing its operation, and many of the professional rights, responsibilities and obligations of its members, such as mandatory registration, that are necessary to exercise the profession. These professional organisations oversee their members in a strict way and have control over their entering and leaving the profession.

The legalisation of these institutions and their monopoly in each sector accords both groups and their members special powers. In addition, the hierarchy accompanies this convention, so within the confines of the professional group, there may be a clear separation of authority and power between colleagues. Professional associations (e.g., medical associations, bar associations) primarily aim to defend professional rights, to promote economic (e.g., tax, insurance) interests, and generally to influence issues of concern to group members.

In Greece, although trade associations have the form of unions, it would be more correct to consider them as institutional pressure groups, mainly because of their organisation into structures such as chambers. The organisation and operation of trade unions in Greece incur great economic and social costs due to their uncontrolled autonomy and monopoly status. It is striking that the Technical Chamber and bar and notarial associations have been successful in establishing minimum fees for their transactions that are indeed paid (minimum) through the banking system. In this way, they ensure that there are no negotiations to determine the amount of payment.

One of the strongest chambers in the Greek society and economy is the Technical Chamber. The Technical Chamber represents graduates of higher education whose productive activity is directly linked to large-scale infrastructure projects (roads, bridges), conveyances for commercial and passenger purposes (ships, tankers, ferries) and buildings for commercial and personal purposes (businesses, homes). Building all of these structures requires measurements, designing, supervision and active participation of Technical Chamber members. This fact alone shows the dynamics of this particular productive class and its increased bargaining power to exert pressure on the state. Table 8.17 shows the numbers of registered members in the Greek Technical Chamber in recent years.

Another very important pressure group in Greece has always been the Bar. The purpose of the Bar is to protect the interests of its members, who are lawyers. In Table 8.18, we see the numbers of lawyers and notaries who are members of the Bar.

Table 8.17 Number of technical chamber members by specialty in 2004 and 2006

Specialties	2004	2006
Civ. Eng.	23,579	26,704
Archit.	15,505	17,245
Mech.	11,234	13,264
Elec.	12,076	14,295
Mech. Elec.	2,696	2,372
Agron. Topog.	5,574	6,076
Chem.	7,345	8,554
Metal. Eng.	1,980	2,193
Nau.	93	80
Naut. Eng.	1,301	1,521
Elect. Eng.	2,178	2,860
Total	82,561	95,164

Source: Technical Chamber of Greece (2007)

Table 8.18 Number of bar members

Year	Lawyers	Notaries	Total
2009	43,500	3,250	46,750

Source: Athens Bar (2009)

Table 8.19 Number of notaries

Country	Notaries	Population (m)	Inhabitants/Notaries ratio
Greece	3,250	11.2	3,446
Austria	463	8.3	17,926
Belgium	1,411	10.7	7,583
Bulgaria	525	7.6	14,476
France	8,741	63.7	7,287
Spain	2,863	45.3	15,822
Italy	4,766	57.3	12,022
Portugal	708	10.4	14,689
Estonia	79	1.4	17,722

Source: Council of EU Notaries (Conseil des Notariats de l'Union Europeene)

It is notable that of the 43,500 lawyers currently registered in the Greek Bar, almost half (21,131) are professionally active in Athens and are members of the Athens Bar Association (ABA). According to official ABA data, 11,000 of its member lawyers did not record any activity during 2008. According to the same source, the constantly increasing number of law school graduates has greatly depressed lawyer fees, particularly those of new entrants in the labour market. These facts have weakened the strength of the bar association because the primary concern of its members – particularly its younger ones – is to strive for personal survival, not to dynamically assert new rights. As concerns notaries, their number in Greece is much higher (notaries per population) compared with other EU states. As seen in Table 8.19, notaries in Greece are at least 2½ to 20 times more common in relation to the size of the population.

Another important pressure group in Greek society are doctors. The members of the medical association are medical school graduates. The Medical Association exhibits similar characteristics to the bar association. In Greek society, there is an oversupply of doctors – although there is a disparity in their distribution in metropolitan areas compared with the countryside; this problem contributes greatly to reducing the bargaining power of the medical association because finding work for its members is a priority.

The road transport industry in Greece is the most important industry for freight transport. Over the last decade, the contribution of this particular industry to intercity transportation work amounted to 98% of the total. According to the FEIR, this industry helps to implement 46.3% of the value of exports and 42.9% of the value of imports. At the same time, while the market has expanded significantly – with an average annual increase for the period of 1990–2005 of 5.7% compared to 3.8% for the EU15 – the share of Greek transporters in national transport has declined gradually from 84.4% to 78.8%. The main reasons for this decline are deregulation of road freight transport in EU countries combined with continued efforts to improve road safety and enact environmental protection policies and the spread of the trend for fast and flexible transportation.

An important point is that while the fleet of heavy vehicles in Greece increased significantly in size from 1998 to 2007, only 15% of the vehicles are for public use – a fixed number for the last 25 years – and the remaining 85% are for private use (Table 8.20).

Another major pressure group that has gradually been losing its power is taxi drivers. Although in recent years there has been a freeze on issuing new permits for taxi drivers, there are about 15,500 taxis in circulation in Attica alone. According to the International Road Transport Union (IRU), the ratio of taxis to population should be 1 taxi per 1000 inhabitants. In Greece, the ratio today is 3.65 taxis per 1000 inhabitants, nearly four times the number of taxis that should be in circulation in order to meet the citizens' needs according the IRU's estimate. If we also include in these data the dramatic improvement during the last decade in the quality of services rendered by public means of transport – busses and trolley busses with

Table 8.20 Number of trucks with a gross weight exceeding 3.5 t (heavy) by year

Years	Total heavy trucks	PUFT	%PUFT
1998	140,831	36,495	25.91
1999	148,767	36,495	24.53
2000	157,739	36,495	23.14
2001	169,073	36,495	21.59
2002	181,312	36,495	20.13
2003	194,947	36,495	18.72
2004	206,393	36,495	17.68
2005	215,785	36,495	16.91
2006	226,209	36,495	16.13
2007	238,939	36,495	15.27

Source: Ministry of Transport and Communications

reduced emissions, trams, and the subway – and increasing private car traffic, the diminishing bargaining power of taxi drivers over the last decade is understandable.

8.7.3 Trade Unions

Whereas employers' organisations gradually increase their bargaining power in the (political) distribution system of (financial) resources, trade unions follow the opposite course. Their relatively strong position in the 1970s and 1980s gradually began to decline from the 1990s onward. The reasons for this decline, which no doubt are manifold, are recorded in the historical development of the trade union movement of workers as well as in the particularity of the domestic business structure. The associations of private and public sector employees in Greece may not have the same social weights as they do in most European countries, where paid employment is more common than self-employment.[16] Also indicative of the particularity governing the domestic organisation of workers' interests is the fact that the leading role in labour struggles has at times been played by professional groups that were considered anything but pure labour groups. The position of tobacco workers, the vanguard of the labour movement before the war, was assumed by construction workers after the war and by bank employees after the junta (Mavrogordatos 1984).

This is not, however, the main reason for the gradual social decline of labour unions in Greece. This development was due to three main factors. First, unions' suffocation by the state and party was clearly indicated by their direct economic dependence on the state and the apparent sectional divisions and frictions. Second, there were multiple disunions characterising the representation of interests of public and private sector employees, combined with the failure to represent important sectors of paid employment both for institutional reasons and for reasons related to changes in the structure of domestic production. Third, there has been growing dissatisfaction, due to the above factors, among the public regarding the role of trade unions, which has combined since the 1990s with a state policy that, in line with relevant European policies, opts for consent rather than conflict and highlights aspects of production (e.g., flexibility, productivity) rather than distribution. The consequence of all of these developments was, as we shall see, the abetment of labour unions' legalisation, which is reflected in the drastic reduction of their organisational density (Table 8.21), and thus the loss of their power to influence the distribution of (financial) resources.

Inherent with multiple disunion is the unbalanced representation of paid employment at the tertiary level. For 2004, employment in the public sector accounted for only 35% of paid employment compared with 65% of the private sector, but a union represented 56% of public workers compared with 18% of workers in the private sector (Kouzis 2007). Also indicative of the importance of public employment in

---

[16] On this point, see also Kouzis (2007).

Table 8.21 GSEE and
ADEDY union density
(1983–2004)

Year	Union density	
	GSEE (%)	ADEDY (%)
1983	43	27
2004	23	55

Source: Kouzis (2007)

the representation of paid employment is the evolution of union density, as shown in Table 8.21 for GSEE and ADEDY[17] during the period of 1983–2004.

As Table 8.21 shows, union density in public employment as reported by ADEDY doubled in 20 years, whereas the density for GSEE was reduced by almost half. The special significance of public employment in union representation of paid employment becomes clearer in the case of GSEE. Although employment in the public sector represents only 28% of the union's power, the rates of unionism in the broader public sector reach 70%, while those in the private sector are limited to about 20%. Mostly, however, the corresponding representation in union leadership bodies is composed – mostly, if not entirely, by public sector representatives.

However, the main problem in paid employment representation arises from the rapid changes in employment structure in recent years. Flexible forms of employment in the private and public sectors (e.g., uninsured semi-employment, contract agents, hired staff), increased employment of women, emergence of new professions (e.g., IT)[18] and a growing migrant population have created categories of workers that are not represented in unions (Kouzis 2007).

The attacks on the legitimacy of paid employment unions intensified beginning in the 1990s, when emerging governments began to promote consensus models of social dialogue while paying attention to issues of competitiveness, productivity, and flexibility of labour. These policies are in line with the prevailing problems at the EU level, as reflected in L. 1876/1990, which revokes the state's compulsory arbitration and establishes structures of social dialogue (ESC). Thus deprived of the political environment that, in the 1970s and 1980s, offered them vast initiatives, and remaining introverted organisations without wider European relationships, labour unions are gradually losing their social influence and importance in the public debate over resource distribution.[19] The marked decrease in the number of strikes and the number of workers participating therein is indicative of the current climate of consensus. The following table, despite possible objections to the validity of relevant measurements, reflects these developments.

In Table 8.22, we observe that in 2007, strike activity reached its highest level (52) since 2002, while the largest number of strikers since 1992 is noted in 2008. It should

---

[17] GSEE: General Confederation of Greek Workers.ADEDY: Senior Management of Unions of Public Servants.

[18] On this point, see also Soumeli (http://www.inegsee.gr/enimerwsi-76-doc4.htm).

[19] On this point, see also Tsakiris (2005).

Table 8.22 Numbers of strikes and strikers (1974–2008)

Year	Number of strikers	Number of strikes	Year	Number of strikers	Number of strikes
1975	46,374	142	1992	969,484	166
1976	300,759	947	1993	501,274	83
1977	559,858	569	1994	226,155	56
1978	471,305	616	1995	210,250	43
1979	1,262,443	588	1996	233,674	31
1980	1,407,821	726	1997	216,799	36
1981	401,757	466	1998	214,546	38
1982	354,315	968	1999	94,500[a]	21
1983	224,265	585	2000	144,000[a]	32
1984	155,318	280	2001	144,000[a]	32
1985	785,725	456	2002	306,000[a]	68
1986	1,106,420	214	2003	175,500[a]	39
1987	1,609,175	249	2004	211,500[a]	47
1988	449,441	320	2005	49,500[a]	11
1989	795,744	207	2006	713,300	37
1990	1,405,497	200	2007	744,800	52
1991	476,582	161	2008	954,813	28

Source: Ministry of Labour (1975–1998), INE GSEE–ADEDY (1999–2007)
[a]Estimates

Table 8.23 Development of union density in Greece (1983–2004)

Year	Union density (%)
1983	39.3
1986	42.9
1989	40.7
1992	37.1
1995	31.8
1998	29.1
2004	28.0
2006	27.0

Sources: Paleologos (2006); Kouzis (2007), INE GSEE–ADEDY (2008)

be noted that 96% of the strikes that took place concerned services and organisations in the public sector. On the other hand, 2005 is the year with the fewest strikes.

As already noted, these factors contributed to the gradual reduction of labour unions, which is clearly reflected in the decline of union density.[20] This development, which undoubtedly reflects broader trends in Europe,[21] is reflected in Table 8.23.

---

[20] For the difficulties of calculating the union density at local and European levels, see Paleologos (2006), issue 24.

[21] See, indicatively, Ebbingbaus and Visser (1999), Vol. 15, No. 2, pp. 135–158.

Table 8.24 Course of union density in various EU countries (various years)

Country	Year			
	1970 (%)	1980 (%)	1990 (%)	2000 (%)
Portugal	–	59	30	31
Italy	36	49	39	41
Spain	–	31	17	16
Denmark	60	77	80	83
Netherlands	37	35	25	24
Sweden	68	80	86	87

Source: Kouzis (2007)

Table 8.25 Employment rate in agriculture in the total workforce, 1961–2007

1961	1971	1981	1991	2001	2007
56.0	39.8	27.5	22.2	16.1	11.5

As already noted, the situation in other European countries looks different. Table 8.24 depicts the development over time of union density in different EU countries. We conclude that trade unions in the Northern European countries are overwhelmingly stronger than similar organisations in the Mediterranean countries.

8.7.4   Farmers

The percentage of domestic workers in the agricultural sector is shrinking. In 1961, agricultural workers constituted 56% of the working population; in 1971, this percentage dropped to 39%, and in 1981, to 28%. This trend, which continued throughout the 1980s, intensified in the 1990s. The decline of the rural population is, of course, is not the same for all regions of the country, nor uniform in its effects; because of the scant opportunities for multiple jobs in some regions (e.g., Epirus), the decline is particularly noticeable in recent years (Table 8.25).

Greek farmers have been the subject of numerous complaints, protests and demands, especially in the provinces where sustainability and development is based mostly on agricultural occupations. Farmers, like other professionals, are classified according to certain characteristics. We can classify the farmers into (a) farmers with large or small farms; (b) farmers involved in agriculture or raising livestock; (c) farmers involved with crops or markets; (d) farmers divided by regional, religious and ideological differences; and (e) farmers separated in unions, associations and chambers.

8.7.5   Pensioners

Pensioners, just like the unemployed, who will be discussed below, represent a unique pressure group in that the pressure they can exert is limited. These are either people who have ceased to work and maintain their particular professional identity or other categories of people who get a pension for a parent, spouse, or due to health problems that prevent them from working. The first category of pensioners can exert more pressure as, thanks to their profession, they may be associated with the respective professional body and receive support from fellow workers who want to defend the interests of the pensioners because they themselves will become pensioners in the future. For members of the second category, the capacity for pressure is very limited. It is hard both to exert pressure and to find supporters for their claims because the pensioners in this category are not distinguished by clear and specific characteristics. It is therefore difficult for a specific community to identify with them and support them.

The very large differences between different groups of pensioners and the fragmentation of different pension arrangements are proof that the more powerful pressure groups have managed to make progress in pursuing their goals, whereas other pensioner groups have not been able to improve their position even a little. The numerous insurance funds, on the other hand, out of submission to political parties governing individual organisations and private selfishness, which is the main motive for claims in Greece, have acted as a catalyst to divide members of various pressure groups and to make it difficult to defend common objectives and interests.

8.7.6   The Unemployed

The unemployed, as a pressure group, do not differ from pensioners in their structural characteristics. Essentially, they do not belong to a particular entity with an inherent incentive to support them, and, like pensioners, they do not have in their hands the tool of strike action that may be used to exert pressure towards a certain objective. The unemployed generally belong to different groups with no particular common characteristics. Their power and consistency are low due to lack of motivation, which separates them into two informal but essentially different groups. The first consists of the unemployed who are actively looking for work. The second includes those who are content to rely on the unemployment benefit and the difficult-to-identify and often generously paid "black" labour, which creates disincentives. Therefore, the unemployed in Greece cannot easily mobilise and support as one body any group claims because they do not have common aims and requests.

8.8   Political Institutions and Income Distribution

The fundamental understanding of the relation between politics and the economy is a key point in formulating a comprehensive understanding of political economy, development and growth. The initial distribution of resources creating a de facto political power, and hence its political institutions, ultimately leads to a new distribution of resources in a specific economic system through the configuration of financial institutions.

8.8.1 Distribution of Income

The issues of distribution of income and resources are linked directly to the system of political institutions that operates in the economy, whose main product is the observed distribution of income and resources.

Income inequality in a geographic area is quantified by various methods (Atkinson 1970; Sen 1973; Cowell 1977). The most accepted and commonly used indicators are: the Gini coefficient,[22] the Hoover index, the Theil index and the Atkinson index.

In Fig. 8.3, we see the values of the Gini coefficient for a range of Mediterranean and Northern European countries. We note that Northern European countries are characterised by lower values of the Gini coefficient and hence more equal distribution of income. In contrast, Mediterranean countries exhibit higher inequality levels. In addition, we note that Ireland has more Mediterranean than Northern European values. Among the Mediterranean countries reviewed in Fig. 8.3, Greece and Spain occupy have the most unequal distributions of income, with a negligible difference between them. However, these countries are also the only ones among the countries reviewed where the Gini index has decreased significantly in the last decade, marking a major effort to achieve a more equal distribution of income.

In Fig. 8.4, we observe the range of levels of income from the poorest 10% of the population to the richest 10% of the population. So, for Greece, we see that the poorest 10% of the population has an average per capita income of less than $10,000 (based on purchasing power parity), while in Northern European countries the minimum income is never less than $10,000. The Mediterranean countries have a lower minimum income, a lower average per capita income, and greater income variability in the population compared to the countries of Northern Europe.

For most developed European countries and Canada, the Gini index values are between 0.24 and 0.36 (Sutcliffe 2004). In contrast, for the United States and Mexico, the index average values are over 0.40,[23] indicating higher levels of inequality. The worldwide Gini index has been estimated at between 0.56 and 0.66.[24]

Looking back, namely in the period of 1950–1970, the golden era of global economic advancement, we observe that the steady global economic growth was

---

[22] The index represents the percentage of total income attributable to a specific percentage of the population. The lower the value, the more equal the distribution of income. A key advantage of the Gini coefficient is that it estimates the equal distribution of income, taking into account not only the GDP but also the way in which this is distributed as a percentage to the population. The Gini coefficient is independent of personal characteristics, measurement units of the economy and population size and is based on the principle of transfer. The most important disadvantage is that it may not be calculated properly if the areas of values that it takes are taken into account without considering the overall figures, even if the calculation included all areas. Moreover, it may be proven to be a non-optimal way of measuring the uneven distribution of income because the Lorenz curve does not reflect the effectiveness of the use of income. Finally, it fails to take into account the age and stage of each individual in society.

[23] http://hdr.undp.org/docs/statistics/understanding/resources/HDR_2003_2_2_global_income_inequality.pdf.

[24] United Nations Development Programme.

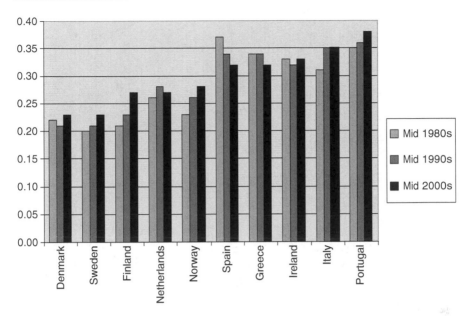

Fig. 8.3 The values of the Gini coefficient for selected OECD countries in the middle of each of the last three decades (Source: OECD statistics)

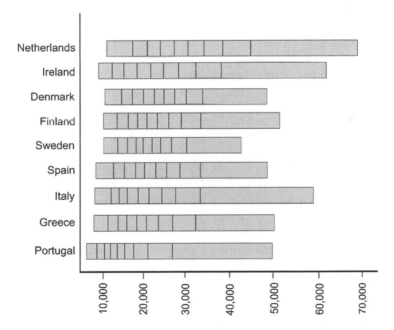

Fig. 8.4 Distribution of per capita income, mid-2000s (Source: OECD, www.oecd.org. Note: The above figure shows the level of income in each tenth of the population (10%). Each separating line in the *blue vertical bar* for each country represents 10% of the population. The *blue diamond* within each bar represents the average per capita income in each country)

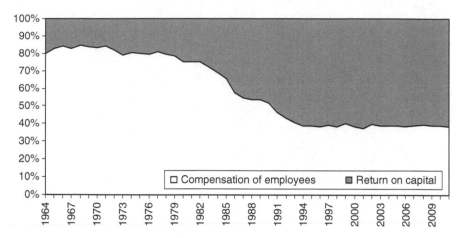

Fig. 8.5 Estimates of the amount of gross operating surplus (return on capital) and compensation of employees in the Greek economy (Source: European Committee (http://ec.europa.eu/economy_finance/ameco/user/serie/SelectSerie.cfm))

accompanied by a reduction in income inequality in most countries (with some exceptions). This trend reversed in the next few decades, when there was a rise in income inequality (Cornia and Court 2001).

The issue of uneven distribution of income at the expense of the labour coefficient in the Greek economy has been also noted from a different perspective: that of distribution of produced income between capital and labour. Indeed, we find that the share of labour coefficient is undervalued and that the adjustments for the parallel economy do not make it comparable with the values of the comparison countries.

Figure 8.5 shows the percentage of work and capital compensation throughout the period from 1965 to 2009. We note that from the mid-1960s until the early 1990s, the relative size of the gross operating surplus constantly increased, indicating the change of Greek production from labour intensive to capital intensive and the change of the social balance of power at the expense of the labour coefficient, noted principally from 1989 onwards. It should be noted that the conclusion on the validity of the latter reason derives from the fact that it is not reasonable to believe that the intensity of change (abrupt change) resulted from a rapid change in the economy's production organisation in the period of 1987–1993. Therefore, it is obviously a result of the rapid formation of "new" conditions for the distribution of wealth in terms of the social correlation of forces. Furthermore, we note the stabilisation in their relation over the past two decades.

8.8.2 Redistribution of Income

Income redistribution is affected by different mechanisms included primarily in the tasks of fiscal policy. More specifically, these mechanisms are divided into:

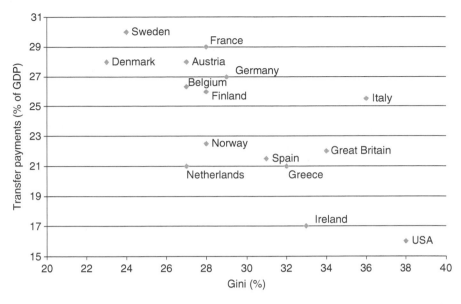

Fig. 8.6 Transfer payments and Gini coefficients, 2005 data (Source: OECD statistics)

1. Transfer payments: unemployment benefits, disability benefits, social security schemes, pensions.
2. Progressive taxation, whereby higher incomes correspond to higher tax levels.
3. Public provision of social services: the main examples of social services in Greece are education and health care.

Although taxes and social transfers have a direct effect on income distribution, public provision of social services is an indirect method of redistribution and is of a more long-term nature.

The correlation between social transfers and inequality has a negative sign. According to a study by the International Institute for Labour Studies (IILS), the correlation coefficient between the two ratios is -0.75 for a sample of 64 countries. This means that the countries having more resources in transfer payments have lower levels of income inequality.

The above conclusion is confirmed by Fig. 8.6. We note that the Northern European countries (Finland, Denmark and Sweden) and Central European countries (Germany, France and Austria) have higher levels of social transfers as a percentage of GDP and comparatively lower levels of uneven distribution of income (Gini < 0.30). Social transfers in these countries exceed 25% in the first category and 20% in the second. Greece, in relation to other European countries in the table, has a highly uneven distribution and lower social spending. The difference is significantly greater in the countries of Northern Europe than it is in the Mediterranean countries (Spain and Italy). Strong similarities can be seen between the characteristics of Greece and Spain.

8.8.3 Key Features of Poverty in Greece

Despite high growth rates observed during the period of 1994–2007, Greece still has one of the highest poverty rates in the European Union. Additionally, the percentage of the population below the poverty line has been relatively stable over the past 14 years, ranging between 20% and 23%. More specifically, for the year 2007, 832,975 households with 2,186,869 members were at risk of poverty.[25] This figure indicates that high growth rates over the last decade have had little impact on both the levels and the risk of poverty and on the uneven distribution of income in Greece. Some key features of poverty concerning Greece derived from the NSSG survey are presented below[26]:

- The income limit that constitutes the poverty line is €6,480 per person per year and €13,608 per year for households with two adults and two dependent children.
- Based on income levels for 2008, 20% of the Greek population was below the poverty line.

Figure 8.7 shows the percentage of the population below the poverty line in Greece from 1994 until 2008. We note a steady situation with the poverty rate at an average of 21%.

Figure 8.8 compares the percentage of the population at risk of poverty in Greece to the corresponding percentages in other European countries for the year 2008. In

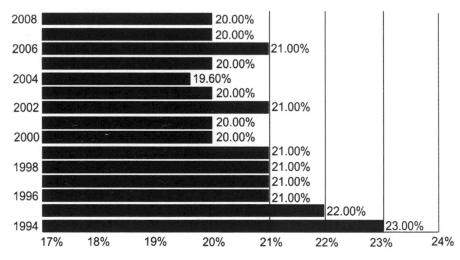

Fig. 8.7 Percentage of population below the poverty line in Greece (Source: HEL. STAT (Hellenic Statistical Authority) (2008))

[25] Source: Statistics on Income and Living Conditions, General Secretariat of the National Statistical Service, 2008.

[26] All results relate to the sample survey on Household Income and Living Conditions conducted by the NSSG in 2008 (data 2007).

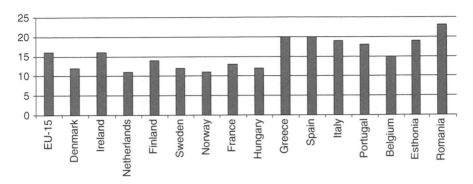

Fig. 8.8 Population at or below the poverty line for the year 2008 (%) (Source: Eurostat)

Northern European countries, the proportion of the population living at or below the poverty line reaches 11–14%, in contrast with the Mediterranean countries, whose rates are 19–20%. The value for Greece is similar to those of other Mediterranean countries, but Greece's poverty rate remains the highest in the Eurozone. In more detail, in the 15 Eurozone countries, the average risk of poverty after social transfers is 16%, ranging from 11% in the Netherlands to 20% in Greece and Spain.

Based on recent (2010) figures published by Eurostat, the poverty rate is higher among women (21%) than among men (20%).

- The poverty rate for people aged over 65 years amounts to 22%, while for those aged 18–24 years it is 23%.
- The poverty rate stands at 14% for employed people (16% for males and 12% for females), 26% for non-employed and 37% for unemployed. The relative risk of poverty for employees in full-time employment is 14%, versus 26% for part-time employees.
- The poverty risk for households with dependent children and no employed members is 44%, while the corresponding rate for households without children and with no employed members is 29%.
- The risk of poverty for households with one parent and at least one dependent child is 27%, while the index for households with two parents and one dependent child is 22%.
- Households living in privately owned residences have a 19% risk of poverty, while those living in rented residences have a rate of 25%. The corresponding figures for the elderly (75 years and over) are 15% and 29%, respectively.

One of the useful qualitative conclusions from these data is the role of education. Of the population living in poverty, 72.1% completed only compulsory education, in contrast to 43.1% of the total Greek population. Furthermore, 42% of all illiterate people and people who did not complete primary education are threatened by poverty. The corresponding figure among those who have completed higher education (e.g., technical colleges, universities, post-graduate studies) is only 7%. Table 8.26 shows the temporal evolution of poverty levels in Greece taken from successive surveys of household income. The data are shown for one-person

Table 8.26 Evolution of the poverty threshold (in Euro) in Greece, 1995–2006

Year[a]	One-member household (annual amount in euro)	Household with 2 adults and 2 children under 14 years (annual amount in euro)
1995	3,125	6,563
1996	3,279	6,886
1997	3,535	7,424
1998	3,847	8,079
1999	3,810	8,001
2000	4,154	8,723
2001	4,264	8,954
2002	–	–
2003	4,922	10,337
2004	5,306	11,143
2005	5,650	11,866
2006	5,910	12,411

Source: Eurostat (ECHP, EU-SILC)

[a]The year refers to the year of the survey; the income used to assess the risk of poverty corresponds to the previous year

households and households with two adults and two children under 14 years. The poverty limit is 60% of average income.

References

Atkinson AB (1970) On the measurement of inequality. J Econ Theory 2:244–263

Charalambis D (1985) The army and political power: the structure of power in post civil war Greece. Exantas, Athens

Cornia GA, Court J (2001) Inequality, growth and poverty in the era of liberalization and globalization, vol 4, WIDER Policy Brief. UNU-WIDER, New York

Cowell FA (1977) Measuring inequality. Philip Allan, Oxford

Ebbingbaus B, Visser J (1999) When institutions matter. Union growth and decline in Western Europe, 1950–1995. Eur Sociol Rev 15(2):135–158

Galbraith JK (2000) The Great rash of 1929. Nea Synora, Athens

Givalos M (2005) Transformations and differentiations of PASOK during the decade 1990–2000. Comparisons of political governments and. leaders. In: Vernadakis C (ed) Public opinion in Greece. Election political parties, interest groups, space and society. Savalas, Athens, pp 86–127

Kaufman D, Kraay A, Mastruzzi M (2009) Governance matters VIII, aggregate and individual governance indicators 1996–2008. The World Bank, Dev. Res. Group, Macroecon and Growth Team

Kikeri S, Nellis J (2002) Privatization in Competitive Sectors: The Record to Date. World Bank Policy Res. Work. Pap. 2860

Kominou M (1996) The role of the media the third Hellenic democracy. In: Lyrintzis C, Nikolakopoulos H, Sotiropoulos D (eds) Society and politics: aspects of the Third Hellenic Republic, 1974–1994. Themelio, Athens, pp 219–246

Kontogiorgis C, Lavdas K, Mendrinou M, Chryssochoou D (2004) Thirty years of democracy, the political system of the Third Hellenic Republic, 1974–2004. Kritiki, Athens

Kouzis J (2007) The characteristics of the Greek syndicalistic party. Similarities and differences from the European region. ςθήνα, Gutenberg

Kox H (2005) Intra-EU differences in regulation-caused administrative burden for companies. CPB Memo. 136, CPB Netherlands Bureau for Econ. Policy Analysis

Lyrintzis C (1984) Political parties in post-junta Greece: a case of "bureaucratic clientelism". West Eur Polit 7:99–118

Lyrintzis C, Nikolakopoulos H, Sotiropoulos D (1996) Society and politics: aspects of the Third Hellenic Republic, 1974–1994. Themelio, Athens

Makridimitris ς (1992) The organization of the government. Matters of cohesion and differentiation. Sakkoulas, Athens

Manesis ς (1989) The constitutional revision of 1986. A critical assessment of its political and legal importance. Paratiritis, Thessaloniki

Mavrogordatos G (1984) The Greek party system. A case of "limited but polarized pluralism". West Eur Polit 7(4):156–169

Metaxas ς (1998) Senator political parties and opposed political forces. Sakkoulas, Athens

Nicoletti G, Scarpetta S (2003) Regulation, productivity and growth: OECD evidence. World Bank Policy Res. Work. Pap. 2944

Nikolakopoulos H (1989) Introduction to the theory and practice of the electoral systems. Sakkoulas, Athens-Komotini

Paleologos N (2006) Labor and trade unions in the 21st century. Meletes, Athens

Papathanassopoulos S (1997) The power of television. The logic of the instrument and the market. Kastaniotis, Athens

Pappas T (2001) Party system and political competition in Greece, 1981–2000. Greek Rev Polit Sci 17:71–102

Rapanos V (2009) Size and range activities of the public sector. Found. for Econ. & Ind. Res. Work. Pap.

Sartori G (1976) Parties and party systems: a framework of analysis. Cambridge University Press, Cambridge

Sen A (1973) On economic inequality. Oxford University Press, Oxford

Sheshinski E, Lopez-Calva F (2003) Privatization and its benefits: theory and evidence. CESifo Econ Stud 49:429–459

Shirley M, Walsh P (2000) Public versus private ownership: the current state of the debate. World Bank Policy Res. Work. Pap. 2420

Sotiropoulos D (2004) The unknown civil society. Social mobilization, voluntary and state in modern Greece. Potamos, Athens

Sotiropoulos D (1995) The remains of authoritarianism: bureaucracy and civil society in post-authoritarian Greece. Instituto Juan March de Estudios e Investigaciones, Estudio

Spanou C (1996) Penelope's suitors: administrative modernization and party competition in Greece. West Eur Polit 19:97–124

Spourdalakis M (1998) PASOK: Party, State, Society. Patakis, Athens

Sutcliffe B (2004) World Inequality and Globalization. Oxford Rev Econ Policy 20(1):15–37

Tsakiris A (2005) Trade unions and labour relationships. From the crises to the non trade union organizing. In: Vernardakis C, Givalos M, Menelaos A, Koukourakis G, Black I, Symeonides C (eds) The public opinion in Greece 2004. Elections, political parties, lobbing and society. Savvalas, Athens, pp 385–408

Tsoukalas K (1981) Social development and the state. The formation of the public sector in Greece. Themelio, Athens

Venizelos E (1980) The logic of the political system and the structure of executive power in the Constitution of 1975. Paratiritis, Thessaloniki

Vernardakis C (2004) PASOK: The foundation, the development and the transformation from the "party of the mass" to the "state party". In: Kontogiorgis C, Lavdas K, Mendrinou M, Chryssochoou D (eds) Thirty years of democracy, the political system of the Third Hellenic Republic, 1974–2004. Kritiki, Athens, pp 154–175

Human Incentives

9

Understanding the social structure and the operation and development of theoretical constructions facilitating the explanation thereof requires, directly or indirectly, adopting certain assumptions about human behaviour and the incentives of human action.

The "revelation" of human behaviour, or the knowledge of factors defining individual behaviour and thus social behaviour, is a key step in understanding past economic systems' results, in comprehending the present and in predicting future efficiency.

This chapter is organized as follows: Sect. 9.1 discusses the importance of incentives in shaping economic output, while Sect. 9.2 specifically determines the formation of incentives depending on the targets set. Section 9.3 includes an analysis of the influence of key cultural aspects on the incentives of economic behaviour. Section 9.4 presents the basic mechanisms of incentives, while Sect. (9.5) comments on the impact of the structural expressions of economic institutions (financial system, tax system, etc.) in shaping incentives. Section 9.6 discusses the importance of the duration of commitment of investment capital and the assumption of risk. Section 9.7 presents the results of measurements of the Greek society, regarding the needs of the population. The incentives arising from the investment in human capital and its returns are explained in Sect. 9.8. Section 9.9 addresses the issues of incentives relating to the financial, tax and insurance systems and the issues of the parallel economy, tax evasion, evasion of social security contributions and the return on capital. Finally, Sect. 9.10 presents the relationship between incentives and business activity.

9.1 Incentives and Economic Results

When the nineteenth century Polish sociologist Leon Winiarski was mixing J. Lagrange's mathematics theories (Lagrange 1797), the views on thermodynamics from the study of physics and the equation system of Walras to create a theory of social behaviour engineering, he could never have imagined that a simplified version of his views would be adopted (albeit not expressly stated) by many administrators, i.e., the political executives. These individuals have adopted Winiarski's views as a concept refusing the importance and the value of the human role and of human behaviour in the operation of the society and in exaggerating the capacity of discipline in social processes by administrative decisions.

However, the social mechanic cannot exist as a way of administration and even more as a way of managing the social change. In an economy, the economic and political institutions form the structure of behaviour incentives by organising the public and the shadowy relative prices. In this way, we may understand the points of change in human behaviour and comprehend the overall social structure of incentives. Usually, societies differ from one another based on their incentive structures.

When members of a society are involved in the formation of the equilibrium price of a product, which is formed by the mutual influences of the offer and demand curbs of this product, then everyone (businesses and consumers) has an identifiable remunerative incentive to form a new balance point (price and quantity) for the product and the society.[1]

At this point, it is worth noticing the following three important considerations: First, prices may be public (to be able to be public and registered), but they may also be shadowy, i.e., not precisely evaluated or not able to be registered. Two examples can illustrate this point. The first concerns the labour market. For someone who has the ability to choose between work and unemployment, the difference in remunerative incentives is defined by comparing the salary to the unemployment allowance. However, in the parallel economy, the possibility to work modifies the prices and the incentive system in a way that is not directly registered by the system The second example concerns the price of a plot of land, which is dependent not only on the actual value fixed by the tax authorities and the market value but also on the value of the information about the future potential to construct on the land. Consequently, the actual relative prices (the comparative prices between plots or the comparative prices of alternative investments – for instance, investment in a plot of land or investment in human capital) are very different from those formed at first glance.

The second point concerns the assessment that incentives are not necessarily remunerative (of material remuneration: e.g., salary, profit, compensation). They may be moral or emotional. Indeed, very often these incentives may be much stronger that the remunerative incentives are. This phenomenon is mainly due to the complexity of human nature. Finally, there is a system of "forced incentives" related to punishment and obligation. This third point relates to identifying the

---

[1] This is Walras' classical analysis on offer and demand.

importance of the incentive system existing in a given society, mainly as compared to the perception of engineered guidance of human societies' behaviour.

The kind of incentive mixture existing within a society is very important for the efficiency of the economic system; however, an in-depth analysis of the importance of this point would be beyond the scope of this book. Nevertheless, an important question that could be raised relates to whether certain societies are more or less prone to the influence of the human incentives system's operation or to an administrative decision system. The answer to this question could explain the capacity of implementing the economic policy. It is obvious that the profound analysis of this question lies within the scope of political sciences and social psychology. However, some simple thoughts may be expressed:

– It seems that the more developed a society is, in the sense that there have been stable incentive systems for a long period of time in an efficient socio-economic environment, the greater the role of an administrative decisions system becomes. Under similar circumstances, ceteris paribus, the administrative decisions system is expected to be characterised by the scarcity of changes and intensive interventions.
– The more a society is characterised by high levels of confidence and the more the population respects and evaluates positively the state and the administration, the more the administrative systems play a more significant role compared to the incentive systems.
– The more a society is characterised by density of cultural values – in other words, in societies with a strong presence of cultural dimensions (stereotypes; as measured by the total cultural values rating) – the more this society is expected to be prone to the influence of incentives rather than to the issuing of regulatory decisions.
– The more the cultural background of a society is characterised by "regulatory" knowledge as compared to "declarative" knowledge, the less the incentive system seem to be important as compared to the administrative decisions system. In other words, the more a society has organised its stereotypes in such a way that repetition and regularity play a part by definition, the more important the influence of the administrative actions will become.

For the above four reasons, Greek society presents the characteristics of a socio-economic situation where the incentive systems play a bigger role than the administrative decisions do. When incentives are opposed to the sought targets, then the results can be extremely negative. Thus, when the individual is called upon to decide whether he/she will work in the parallel economy, the aspects taken into consideration are as follows: (a) the net financial profit the decision will yield, and (b) the uncertainty he/she feels when engaging resources and time in formal procedures of the economy and a much less important part if this leads him/her to a tax evasion situation, ignoring something that is prohibited by many administrative decisions, will play a much greater part.

In conclusion, it was found that in the Greek economy the importance of incentives plays, proportionally, a bigger part as compared to a behavioural system that is influenced by a variety of administrative acts. This point was particularly obvious during the phase when financial discipline measures were introduced in the Greek economy in the first months of 2010. When the political administration called on the patriotic feelings of people for help in "rescuing" the country, positive response incentives were mobilised in the society. However, when each citizen was faced with the individual measures concerning him, he responded with particular discontent. This contradiction in human behaviour is based in the different responses created within a person by the predominance of specific kinds of incentives as driving forces of behaviour. Those contradictions could constitute a determining factor for the success of a financial stability program. Thus, starting from the positive attitude of the population towards the need to "rescue" the country, one could end up in an action plan based on the philosophy deriving from the need to establish this action plan. In this way, the extraordinary "fiscal" measures should have been expressively dissociated from the "new development" measures. Thus, the extraordinary "fiscal" measures would not have touched on the issue of "uncertainty" because they would "promise" stability, and consequently, the incentives for a positive response to the budget problem would have remained unaltered. But when the incentive of forecasting and ensuring the future leads to conclusions comprising some kind of threat, the conditions for contradictory human behaviour are created.

9.2   Formation of Incentives

The formation of behaviour incentives and consequently of the predominance of a specific incentive mixture in a society is defined by the goals set. Incentives activate human behaviour in order to achieve those goals.

The two main schools of incentive creation, which concern the incentives' content (Maslow 1954) and the procedure of understanding reality (Vroom 1964), also form a creation framework within a society. In this way, people's orientation to satisfying their basic needs pyramid (beginning from physiological needs and ending at self-esteem and self-actualisation), to predicting their future by creating a comprehensive expectations framework or to institutionalising procedures constituting behaviour incentives based on the research on "justice" can finally influence the creation of an incentive structure for individual and social behaviour.

In societies where the basic subsistence needs prevail, there are more dense incentives corresponding to a lower level of human activity that is equivalent to a lower level of social development. It is quite obvious that a society influenced by people facing subsistence problems "thinks" very differently from a society in which individuals are trying to achieve self-actualisation. This disparity impacts a series of sectors, such as entrepreneurship. In the first society, the predominant need for recourse to business activity is to cover the basic subsistence needs, so the business activity will be small in size, with no long-term investments, while in the second society, there will be much greater participation rates in innovative business activities.

There are indications that in Greek society, the meeting of basic subsistence needs and of security and safety needs plays a significant part in the formation of human incentives. Thus, the need satisfaction portfolio is based 50% on the above basic needs and 50% on the needs for perspective and social inclusion, self-esteem and self-actualisation. Societies dominated by the incentives of the basic needs group find it hard to analyse and to manage complex objectives and goals that will upgrade their social operations, even though the desire to meet their needs is much more intense, creating "catch-up effects" in economy and society.

However, similar societies (i.e., with similar mixtures of behaviour incentives) in a globalised world where innovation and creativity prevail may find it rather difficult to survive. And this makes sense! The Europe of 2020 (characterised by intelligent, innovative development) requires populations that will have incentives favouring, for instance, the accumulation of human and innovative capital; this need is inconsistent with the mixture of incentives in a population with needs related to basic subsistence.

This kind of population may set goals related to general economic and social development. But if the populations do not develop similar mixes of incentives, is it possible to impose them through external interventions?

In fact, the question posed relates to whether the overall cultural background contains elements that may be transformed into goals and thus form incentives related to economic development and growth. In addition, if the culture does not contain such elements, how can it acquire them? But even if it contains or acquires such elements, the next question concerns the extent to which the procedures of their appeal can finally activate the expected human behaviour. It is obvious that the purposes link the cultural stereotypes with the individual behaviours and consequently play a very important part in the social and economic processes and in economic development and growth.

Consequently, we may understand much more about the incentives existing in a given society by examining its cultural stereotypes.

9.3   Impact of Cultural Stereotypes on the Formation of Incentives

According to the foregoing discussion, it is obvious that societies with different mixtures of needs create different incentive models that in turn form different goal incentives, which ultimately determine different models of human activity.

However, in the previous part, we ascertained that the goals are components of the cultural model, i.e., of the stereotypes, and that goal formation is dependent on the cultural model. Evidently, the relations among incentives, goals and cultural stereotypes are bidirectional.

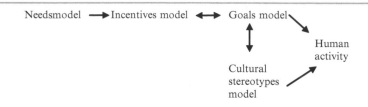

Greek society is characterised, among other cultural dimensions, by uncertainty avoidance, orientation towards the present, projection of collectivism to the detriment of privacy, acceptance of power distance, masculinity and, of course, lack of confidence. Certainly, as ascertained, the existence of this set of stereotypes does not mean that the Greek cultural background lacks contradictory dimensions (e.g., preference for the future, confidence). However, the above dimensions seem to prevail in terms of values in the cultural background of the members of Greek society.

Indeed, the presence of uncertainty avoidance seems to be confirmed by the exploration of the incentives found in the Greek society because 50% of the incentives are linked to this factor. However, what kind of impact may be found in the formation of the goals model in the Greek society?

The orientation towards the present indicates, of course, denial about the future. When there is denial about the future, pessimistic models are created, indicating a *lack* of goals and an overall shortage of incentives.

On the other hand, uncertainty avoidance is linked to the expression of the need to predict the future. Because there is no future horizon, the combination of preference for the present and future avoidance leads to forming a type of goal that is linked to specific models of investment behaviour: for example, preference for consumption, investment in real estate property, denial for educational investments.

The above example provides an opportunity to better understand the fact that because goals link the individual and the collective entity with the future, if there is no future horizon, then there are no goals. But if, in the above chart, we remove the presence of goals, then there is also a *pause* of the interaction between cultural stereotypes, goals and incentives. In this scenario, the only promoter of incentives appears to be the needs model, isolating, to a large extent, its impact from the evolution and the development of the cultural environment.

During times of international economic and social improvement, such an assessment may prove particularly negative because, in substance, it isolates the external environment (which is positive) from the possibility of influence by the internal incentive model. On the contrary, in times of recession, the basic hierarchal systems of the needs do not necessarily produce behaviours that may separate the difficulties of the recession and evolve into basic determining factors.

However, a society whose members' goals are significantly formed by the impact of their personal needs depends on the mixture of those needs. If this mixture is at the bottom of their hierarchical pyramid, then the goals set will be mainly linked to the needs to resolve subsistence issues and to deal with problems in the face of uncertainty. When, however, such a society is compared to another whose members' needs are at the top of the hierarchical pyramid, then the derived human behaviours produce an economic result of higher value.

Besides, the dispersed lack of confidence is linked with the projection of the value of the individual's microcosm, a small scope of economic activity and the lack of confidence in the society's institutions. This kind of situation sets goals whose scope is not positively linked to the development needs because it does not allow the expansion of contracting procedures for economic relations and the development thereof.

Finally, the projection of collectivism to the detriment of privacy sets goals that are linked to the incentives depriving the individual from activating to improve his or her economic situation. The responsibility of individual improvement to collective action requires a working knowledge of efficient collective activity, which is not always found in societies projecting collectivism to the detriment of privacy.

9.4 Basic Incentive Mechanisms

The issue of incentives' formation of behaviours aimed at consumption and investment should be of particular interest because, in the Greek society, it appears to have significant weight. In particular, savings as a percentage of the available income are particularly low. In fact, this percentage is lower than in the countries of Southern Europe and, of course, in the Northern European countries. This situation has a significant negative impact on the balance of payments and, of course, on the Greek economy's self-financing capacity. From one point of view, the income percentage placed in savings could be one of the key factors with important potential for explaining both the Greek economic problem and its future development.

Of course, the issue of the income level in relation to the basic (relative) subsistence and living needs is a matter that may provide an explanation of this behaviour in the Greek economy.

Coming back, however, to the basic theoretical specifications of investment behaviour (life cycle hypothesis, Ando and Modigliani 1963), we realise that the perception of the future plays an important role. If this perception is limited, then the need for normalising consumption during the individual's life span does not seem to be significant. The impressive thing about the Greek economy is that consumption has been maintained at high levels for several years, as if the income increases that occurred in the previous years were stable and permanent (permanent income hypothesis, Friedman 1957) and there were no reason for "proactive savings". Private households in Greece ensure stable, positive cash flows because the loans covering the differences between income and consumption took the form of financial debt that was later passed on to the economy as a stable positive financial flux. Nonetheless, Greek households' borrowing was kept at rather low levels.

This savings behaviour may, of course, be explained mainly on the basis of the preference for the present and the existence of high uncertainty levels in Greek society. Under these circumstances, saving for the future makes no particular sense. Besides, the perception about the ever-present collective entity ensuring the present and the future eliminates the need for worrying about the future. Thus, the preference for collectivism to the detriment of privacy has a substantial manifestation in savings behaviour as well. If, of course, the confidence in the power of the collective entity wavers, then it is most likely that the individual and the society will be led to increase their savings behaviour.

The need for assurance against future developments is covered to some extent through the particular preference of the Greek society for a specific investment form: housing. This is why there are very high percentages of owner-occupied dwellings in Greece, and, of course, a great part of personal wealth takes the form of investments in housing.

Certainly, the liquidation possibilities of this kind of investment are rather restricted. However, in time, the change in land value is reflected in the continuous and almost timeless value increase of this specific investment.

On the contrary, investments in human capital are a more complex option. Such investments ensure cash returns and also contribute to personal satisfaction.

Based on the estimations calculated for the Greek economy, it is ascertained that from secondary education until the master's degree or doctoral degree level, the investment returns in human capital accumulation increase according to the level of studies. In fact, as far as higher education is concerned, the relative return exceeds (under normal circumstances) the respective returns of the Greek public sector securities (10-year bond). This assessment confirms, for Greece, similar conclusions to those that have been found for most developed countries. It has to be noted that the inclusion of unemployment risk in our calculation enhances the positive image of investment in human capital and is usually provided by some mass media.

It shall be underlined that this picture contradicts an artificial image of over-production of degree holders in the Greek economy that is supposed to be based on the non-return of the relevant investments in human capital.

Generally, it is known that in times of economic recession, when unemployment rises and the production schemes are being restructured, the demand for education services increases.

But what happens when high financial deficits, and thus over-production of public sector bonds linked to high returns, are combined with unemployment and, consequently, a fall in human capital returns? This question applies under the circumstances of year 2010 (when this book was written) and is particularly important because it entails a lack of demand for educational investment.

A first answer relates to the fact that the same conditions do not apply all over the world. Because the dilemma concerns one productive factor that is changeable, it is highly possible that investments in human capital may not be efficient in an economy with high deficits and high unemployment; it will be efficient in other economies with low deficits. Thus, the issue is raised of movement of populations from the former economies to the latter. This is why economies like that of Greece attract a work force with low investment in human resources and experience an outward flux of the population with developed investments in human capital.

This issue raises a matter of particular importance for Greek society: the attitudes (incentives) of Greeks towards space and time.

It may be stated that Greeks present a remarkable space and time immobilisation mainly the last 40 years, when was observed an improvement in the standard of living in Greece. A typical example of space immobilisation is the unease about considering changing one's place of residence as a means of improving working conditions, specifically by moving outside of Greece to elsewhere in Europe. There are two factors influencing the formation of this kind of behaviour. The first is intra-group collectivism, the family environment that is particularly strong in the Greek economy. The second, of course (for migration outside of Greece) is the language barrier. The impact of the "isolated" Greek language extends not only to communication difficulties but also to generalised isolating cultural models.

A typical example of time immobilisation is the delayed response to the modifications of education opportunities. For instance, it is quite clear that medical (not nursing) studies produce degree holders who, due to over-production, are hard to absorb under the circumstances of the Greek market. Nonetheless, the pressure to enter similar schools is particularly high. In other words, even though, for years, there has been a communication signal stating that this particular choice entails many difficulties, this signal is not transformed into a guiding force that would change the model of educational services demand. Thus, the Greek society, given that it has no future horizon and is characterised by time immobilisation, uses the projection of the past as an exclusive substitute for predicting the future.

The explanation of this behaviour relies on the perseverance on the present and on the predominance of uncertainty for the future. In such a context, the past becomes a valuable source of information because it bears, above all, the element of certainty.

9.5   Incentives and Entrepreneurial Behaviour

The analysis of business incentives in the Greek economy in relation to the compared countries brings, on the surface, the basic features already identified that concern business activity; it also brings about new evidence related to Greek cultural background and the facts of the Greek economy.

The first particularly noteworthy element is the entrepreneurship deriving from the incentive to create or to maintain income in the Greek economy, which is particularly low (12.9%) compared to the EU average (20.8%) and to the countries with similar development rates, i.e., Portugal (22.7%) and Spain (21.1%), as well as more developed countries, such as Italy (20.7%) and the Netherlands (20.1%). On the contrary, the incentive of increased income plays a much more important role in Greece than it does on average in the EU (39.7% versus 27.1%). At this point, it is obvious that business activity in the Greek economy is perceived as an activity for boosting income that also remits benefits in the parallel economy.

The second particularly interesting element concerns the differences found in the role of incentives for employment independence. Thus, while 23.7% of business efforts in Greece evoke this incentive as the creative force for adopting a business initiative, the respective rate in the EU appears to be 33.5%, while in the developed countries it is very high ($\approx$40%). Based on these figures, we return to the hierarchy of primary needs as an incentive creator for economic behaviour. The observed immobilisation in the incentives pyramid's base is also reflected in the incentives for undertaking entrepreneurial activity. However, this is not a unidimensional process exclusively linked to the establishment of a business. When the entrepreneurship behaviour activation needs are not driven by the inner ambition of personal actualisation, the individual does not feel the need to expand upon his or her personality through education that he/she might receive and thus acquire the necessary knowledge to become active in sectors of advanced entrepreneurship. Exploiting the opportunities presented (i.e., through development of business opportunities) possibly relates to opportunities presented at lower levels of business activation.

This conclusion is in fact confirmed if we consider the extent to which the undertaken economic activity has business features. As regards entrepreneurship in Greece and in Portugal, it is typical that three out of four customers of the companies do not believe that the offered products bear an innovative dimension. On the contrary, in Denmark and in Italy, the average customer believes that the offered products do have an innovative dimension. Only 5.4% of business efforts in the Greek economy enter a truly new market when there is no other competitor, while the corresponding rate for Denmark is 19.4%.

Certainly the realisation of business is one component of the macroeconomic conditions, in addition to the cultural background, knowledge, and so on. But the issues of time perception and of the predisposition to commit resources also play a significant role. Research conducted in SMEs shows that the desirable ideal fund commitment duration in Greek society is around 5.5 years. So, in fact, it is ascertained that there is a short term perception as to what business activity means.

Of course, this kind of time spectrum limits the possibility of creating investment initiatives with innovative background. Besides, in order to have innovative initiatives, there should also be production of innovative ideas, which does not seem to be a focus of Greek society. It is typical that in an economy where a comparatively large part of innovative ideas is produced in research and university institutions (as in the rest of the world), there is no provision for remunerating natural persons who innovate. So, there is Law 2083/92 that, in essence, provides that no matter how important the innovation (invention) of a university professor or a researcher may be, he may receive from the sales thereof an amount as high as the salary he receives from the state. Alternatively, he could, based on the Law on spin-off creation (L.2919/2001), become a businessman, which requires extremely complicated procedures, decisions by collective bodies and so on, in a particularly unfavourable environment for such an initiative. We have also ascertained, in Chap. 5

of this book, that the transformation of research results to innovative results in Greece is extremely limited. However, the fact that the Greek state has no intention to deregulate the process of innovation indicates a broader social choice that lacks interests and refuses to provide incentives for processes creating new value.[2]

9.6   The Importance of Investment Funds' Commitment Duration and of Risk Taking

The risk entailed by an investment constitutes a determining factor for the decision to become involved with it, as well as the decision for the size of the investment. However, the risk entailed by the investment equally affects the duration for which funds are committed that may be tolerated by an investor. The time dimension of an investment plan is of primary importance for the decision concerning this specific plan, mainly because of the uncertainty involved.

Previous studies have shown the importance of time preferences during the process of making decisions about investments for the utilisation of available resources. The importance of time preferences of economically active persons has been proven using at least three different approaches. First, this importance has been demonstrated in the neoclassical example (Epstein and Zin 1989, 1991; Weil 1990), where the time preferences affect the discount coefficient of future against current cash flows. Additionally, as regards the investment evaluation criterion according to the payback method of invested capital (payback period) (Lefley 1994, 1996), the fund commitment duration becomes the most important criterion in evaluating investments. More specifically, Lefley underlines the value of investment evaluation based on the payback period of the capital as a widely used, useful, simple and traditional criterion for classifying available investment plans. Finally, during the evaluation of investment plans, in addition to the information on the calendar dimension, time as perceived by businessmen/investors (intrinsic time of investors) (Derman 2002) becomes equally important.

Even during the evaluation of investment plans using the criterion of internal rate of return, the time distribution of cash flows is equally important. This criterion is based on subjective estimations of the level of risk undertaken; another important factor affecting the acceptance of a plan is the return expected or required by the investor. However, even in this case, the distribution of cash flows during the investment period affects the numerical results during the calculation of the internal rate of return and, consequently, the acceptance of an investment plan or its relative ranking among the available investment proposals.

According to Bird and West (1997), the business action in terms of the distribution of investment resources over time is directly linked to the three dimensions of perception, evaluation and action. Perception concerns the businessman's ability to comprehend the current conditions and to make decisions in order to exploit

---

[2] This administrative "ankylosis" was lifted with a new legislative regulation in June 2010.

possible opportunities presented to him. Additionally, the businessman's capability to evaluate the possible future conditions plays an important role. By extension, the size and the overall value of the company are directly associated with the businessman's goals as well as with his preferences on the time distribution of cash flows.

After identifying the business opportunities and compiling and processing the relevant information follows the evaluation and the discounting of future flows. At this point, the businessman's attitude regarding time is critical for the choice and the use of the right discount rate, expressing his relevant preference for the present in relation to the future. However, it is easily understood that the importance of the time preferences is much more significant than in the previous stages of evaluation of investment opportunities.

As previously stated, any form of investment initiative and organisation of business activity bears an important time dimension that is defined to a large extent by the existing economic, business and often social environment. When a society shows a significant preference for the present in relation to the future, it does not make sense to expect intense long-term investment activity. Besides, in these cases, the specialised capital markets that will assist the businessman in implementing his plans are usually nonexistent.

Das and Teng (1997) present an interesting analysis of the relation between risk and time; they separate the types of risk into short range, when the decision's result becomes evident in a short period of time, and long range, when the result of a decision becomes evident after a longer period of time. Human behaviour may be substantially different when making short-term compared to long-term decisions. Moreover they highlight that most risk-seeking, opportunist businessmen may be identified by their short-range conservative (low-risk) behaviour.

The person undertaking a business action may combine a more long-term or short-term orientation with a risky or conservative attitude in taking risks. Consequently, there are four different combinations on the level of undertaken risk and time preferences:
1. Short-range orientation and conservative attitude towards risk.
2. Long-range orientation and conservative attitude towards risk.
3. Short-range orientation and inclination to undertake more risk.
4. Long-range orientation and inclination to undertake more risk.

Additionally, we may classify the overall economic activity into two main categories (Petrakis 1997): (a) balancing entrepreneurship, which mainly concerns servicing the current needs and contributes to balancing supply and demand, and (b) innovation entrepreneurship, which concerns the production process, promoting the development of new products. The will to undertake risks is compatible with the nature of business activity, while risk as well as time commitment (orientation to the future) of invested capital increase with the innovative nature of the activity. The balancing of offerings and demand and the immediate time demands (orientation to the present) to cover the market needs are part of the balance required for entrepreneurship.

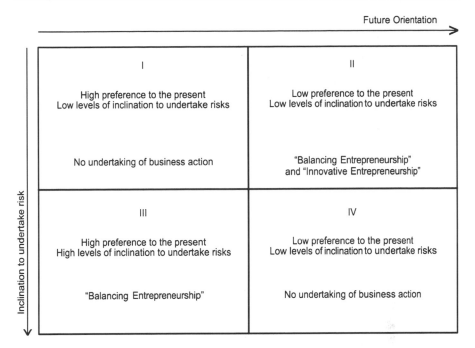

Fig. 9.1 The businessmen's preferences in relation to the investment time dimension, the undertaken risk and the different activity categories

Thus, innovative activity is linked to a clear orientation towards the future among businessmen. Given that the innovation results are not immediately perceived, the businessman should have a certain interest in the future, when the results of the present business actions will become visible. At the same time, individuals engaged in innovative business activities are expected to undertake reasonable levels of risk.

On the contrary, the personal inclination to undertake high risk (risk-seeking) combined with an orientation towards the future is not expected to lead to the undertaking of any business activity. The lack of inclination to undertake even smaller risks combined with an orientation towards the present does not favour undertaking any business action. On the other hand, the combination of the inclination to undertake risk with an orientation towards the present favours undertaking business action with no special innovative features. This combination seems to favour business activity aiming at balancing offer and demand, as described above. The above reasoning is shown in Fig. 9.1.

According to the evidence stemming from the responses to questionnaires given out to 120 businessmen of SMEs active in the Greek economy (Petrakis 2005) and based on their preferences for time and risk, we classified the businessmen[3] in the

---

[3] The sample of businesses is structured as follows: 20% of businesses are active in industry, 44% in trade and 36% in the services sector. 31% of those businesses employ own funds below

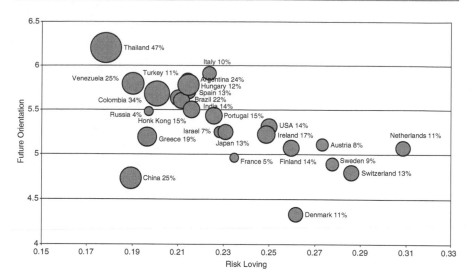

Fig. 9.2 Entrepreneurship, risk-loving and future orientation in the form of cultural values (Note: All variables derived from House et al. (2004) (GLOBE))

four quadrants of Fig. 9.1. It is impressive that 48% of business activities incorporate behaviours having no business features, i.e., inclination to undertake risk and orientation towards the future.

The analysis above is particularly important because entrepreneurship constitutes a factor that significantly affects an economy's growth rates and development levels. Consequently, depending on the type of the prevailing business activity, it is expected that the structural elements of the overall economic activity would be different. At the same time, adopting a different type of business action may bring significant changes in the productive process as a whole, impacting directly the growth rates and the development levels of the economy.

Based on Fig. 9.1, it is ascertained that there is a negative relation between orientation towards the future and inclination to undertake risk. Additionally, it is ascertained that the extension of the entrepreneurship time dimension expands the possibility to show innovative entrepreneurship.

If we combine the GEM data on the density of appearance of business activity, on the inclination to undertake business risk and on the orientation towards the future (House et al. 2004), we may see that they are correlated for a series of countries for which data are available (Petrakis 2007). In Fig. 9.2, it is indeed ascertained that there is a negative correlation between risk preference and the future orientation. It is quite typical that the Greek economy is positioned rather low

€150,000, 39% of businesses use own funds between €150,000 and €1 m, while the remaining 30% have own funds between €1 m and €10 m.

as regards its "appetite" for the future and comparatively to many examined countries rather low as regards presence of the future.

Consequently, a change in the future orientation in the cultural background of a society would be accompanied by much more long-range and more innovative investments in the undertaken business efforts. It should be noted that the degree of future orientation in a society (with greater confidence in the future) will not change with a reduction of risk levels because it seems that these two issues do not relate to one another.

9.7   Psychological Needs and Incentives

According to Maslow's theory (1954) on the human needs (i.e., basic subsistence needs, need for security and safety, need for personal and social inclusion and need for self-actualisation and self-esteem), individuals enter the process of incitement and create incentives in order to satisfy their various needs, always using as a criterion the significance of the need and starting from the subsistence need.

We conducted research in the Greek reality on the degree to which these needs are sought in the Greek population[4] (Fig. 9.3).

The needs sought today are concentrated at 55% on the needs for basic subsistence, security and safety. This result shows that the general population has issues that remain unaddressed to a great extent. The remaining 45% of the population is split into 19% citing the need for personal and social inclusion and 26% the need for self-esteem and self-actualisation.

9.8   Returns of Investments in Human Capital

The investment in human capital is activated by the following incentives:
(a) Individuals maintain and increase their personal value through education, while at the same time they enhance their personal comparative advantage.
(b) The investment in human capital often provides moral and psychological satisfaction. In this way, individuals, through the increase of personal satisfaction combined with personal development and improvement, are led to moral strengthening and to the increase of the prestige they feel within society (Tay 2008).

---

[4] We addressed 800 participants in the Program of Complementary Education of the National and Kapodistrian University of Athens via email. 386 people responded. 59% of the participants were women. 53% were university degree holders, 13% technical education degree holders, 14.5% were holders of a master's degree and 13.5% were graduates of secondary education. 41% of the people questioned belonged to the age group of 20–30 years, 34% belonged to the age category of 30–40 and 20% to the age category of 40–50.

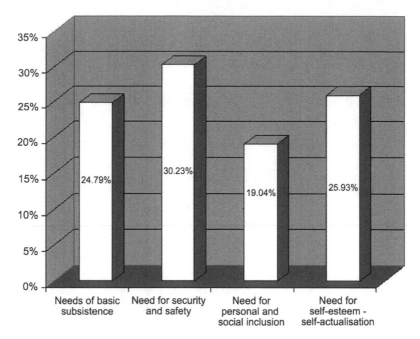

Fig. 9.3 Needs currently sought (total population)

(c) Education is, for many employed people, a way to preserve their employment position. In financially unstable periods, individuals are trained to improve their knowledge on the topic of their work or to find a job with relatively less difficulty.

(d) In the labour market, competition is very intense, and those seeking a position in those markets should, among other characteristics, be specialised. This means further education, i.e., investment in human capital.

The issue of incentives for economically active people in their decision to invest in education is closely linked to the expected return of this investment. The increased possibilities to find a job and/or to earn higher future income creates incentives of constant participation and development in the field of education and specialisation, which means investment in human capital.

Investment in education and, through this, in the process of accumulating human capital has significant private returns, mainly deriving from the expected higher future income and the lower unemployment risk. At the same time, investment in education includes (other than the cost of attendance, which varies according to the country and the type of educational institution) the opportunity cost due to the abstinence from the labour market during the period of studies.

The high private returns from the investment in human capital are due to the post-development of the production organisation system observed during recent years. Thus, the economic activity where land, labour and capital were of primary importance has been replaced by the modern economy of knowledge, technology and innovation (Schleicher 2006). In this modern economy, human capital is already – and will be to a greater extent in the future – the major production component. Consequently, investment in education is expected to bring about further higher returns. So far, the returns of the investment in tertiary education for the entire developed world are higher than the real interest rates of their respective economies (Schleicher 2006).

Of course, education is a special case of investment activity. It offers, beyond the expected purely financial returns, rewards concerning exclusively participation in it. In other words, education carries both intrinsic and extrinsic incentives that mobilise human behaviour.

Nonetheless, at this point we will only touch on the extrinsic incentives influencing the decision to invest in human capital. In other words, we will analyse the economic incentives developed around education issues and formed by the expected returns of this investment. The additional internal human need for education may only strengthen the above incentives and increase the demand for investments in education.

At this point, we will try, using simple calculation methods, to determine indicative measurements of the returns of the investments in human capital for Greece. Table 9.1 shows the returns of the investment in education (Rates of Return of Education, RORE) resulting from the "short-cut" Psacharopoulos method (Psacharopoulos 1994, 2008; Psacharopoulos and Patrinos 2002) and the Groot and Oosterbeek method (1992). In both cases, the calculation of education return concerns the percentage difference in income received, on average, by graduates of two consecutive education levels for every year of studies they complete.

Thus, we observe that from secondary education until the level of the master's or doctoral degree, the investment returns in human capital accumulation increase according to the level of studies. More specifically, for higher education, the relative return exceeds the respective returns of the Greek public sector securities in the period of 2001–2006. This assessment confirms, for Greece, the image observed in a series of developed countries (Schleicher 2006).

At this point it should be noted that, as previously pointed out, the investment in education, apart from the increased remuneration levels it ensures, also reduces unemployment risk. As observed in Table 9.2, and in contrast to what is usually said about the potential of the Greek economy to absorb degree holders, the unemployment levels of graduates of higher and post-graduate education are clearly lower compared to those of graduates of secondary education. It is thus concluded that the investment in higher and post-graduate education reduces, but does not eliminate, unemployment risk.

Both post-graduate and doctoral studies, despite not ensuring lower unemployment levels (as compared to University/technological institutes studies), lead to higher remuneration levels and consequently reserve positive and significantly higher expected returns (ERORE).

In order to confirm this observation, the analysis also includes the unemployment risk by calculating the expected rate of return to education (ERORE), as shown in Tables 9.3 and 9.4.

From the analysis so far, it can be concluded that the returns promised by the investment in education are important because they ensure a significantly higher

Table 9.1 Private returns to every grade of education calculated according to the Psacharopoulos and Groot & Oosterbeek methods

Education level (i)	Indicative years of studies (S_i)	2003 Average income	$RORE_i$ Psacharopoulos method	Groot & Oosterbeek method	2004 Average income	$RORE_i$ Psacharopoulos method	Groot & Oosterbeek method	2005 Average income	$RORE_i$ Psacharopoulos method	Groot & Oosterbeek method
(1)	(2)	(3)	(4) (%)	(5) (%)	(6)	(7) (%)	(8) (%)	(9)	(10) (%)	(11) (%)
No education (1)	–	5,664	–	–	4,795	–	–	7,667	–	–
Primary school (2)	6	8,498	8.34	6.76	8,852	14.10	10.22	9,403	3.77	3.40
Junior high school (3)	3	9,080	2.28	2.21	9,574	2.72	2.61	9,720	1.12	1.11
High school (4)	3	10,185	4.06	3.83	10,992	4.94	4.60	11,203	5.09	4.73
University/ technological education institutes (5)	5	15,119	9.69	7.90	15,271	7.79	6.58	16,213	8.94	7.39
Master's degree/ doctorate (6)	4	26,301	18.49	13.84	22,772	12.28	9.99	24,076	12.12	9.89%

Source: Petrakis and Stratis (2008)

Table 9.2 Unemployment levels in all education grades

	2003 (%)	2004 (%)	2005 (%)
No education	4.3	13.4	9.3
Primary school	6.4	8.7	7.3
Junior high school	10.7	11.2	10.4
High school	11.8	11.6	11.1
University/technological education institutes	6.7	7.5	7.1
Master's degree/doctorate	7.2	5.9	8.5

Source: HEL. STAT. (Hellenic Statistical Authority)

level of income. More specifically, the investment in tertiary education further reduces the unemployment risk to a great extent. A study conducted by a consulting agency (Deloitte – Ethics & Workplace Survey Examines the Reputation Risk Implications of Social Networks, 2009) in the more competitive US economy reported a substantial differentiation in the remunerations of employees in the most innovative sectors of the economy as compared to those employed in other sectors (e.g., services, manual work) This differentiation, which is increasing (there is no reason not to assume that it will continue to grow in the future), demonstrates the level of returns of investments in human capital.

Figure 9.4 shows the average level of annual income by education grade and sector of economic activity.

From all of the above, we may safely conclude that the investment in human capital in Greece promises substantial returns beyond the real growth rate of the economy. Consequently, clear incentives exist for economically active individuals to further invest in human capital.

Thus, it is not by chance that the vast majority of secondary education graduates seek to continue their studies in a tertiary education institution. Then, a great part of tertiary education graduates seeks to further specialise by obtaining a master's degree or a doctorate.

9.9   Incentives and Economic Institutions

The preferences of economically active individuals are strongly affected by the economic institutions in every society that determine the "rules of the game". As already discussed, the most important of these institutions are the financial and the taxation systems as well as the social security system. The financial system affects the distribution of financing in the production process and the rights deriving from its results. The taxation and social security systems define, in common to a large extent, the returns in all expressions of the economic activity and consequently form the incentives favouring or discouraging the investment activity of the economy's production sector.

Table 9.3 The returns of the investment in education calculated in Table 9.1 according to the Groot & Oosterbeek method and the respective expected returns, taking into consideration the possibility of employment resulting from Table 9.2 (1-unemployment risk) for the same year

Education level (i)	Indicative years of studies (S_i)	2003			2004			2005		
		Employment possibility	$RORE_i$	$ERORE_i$	Employment possibility	$RORE_i$	$ERORE_i$	Employment possibility	$RORE_i$	$ERORE_i$
(1)	(2)	(3) (%)	(4) (%)	(5) = (3) × (4) (%)	(6) (%)	(7) (%)	(8) = (6) × (7) (%)	(9) (%)	(10) (%)	(11) = (9) × (10) (%)
No education	(1) -	95.70	-	-	86.60	-	-	90.70	-	-
Primary school	(2) 6	93.60	6.76	6.33	91.30	10.22	9.33	92.70	3.40	3.15
Junior high school	(3) 3	89.30	2.21	1.97	88.80	2.61	2.32	89.60	1.11	0.99
High school	(4) 3	88.20	3.83	3.38	88.40	4.60	4.07	88.90	4.73	4.20
University/ technological education institutes	(5) 5	93.30	7.90	7.37	92.50	6.58	6.09	92.90	7.39	6.87
Master's degree/ doctorate	(6) 4	92.80	13.84	12.84	94.10	9.99	9.40	91.50	9.89	9.05

Source: Petrakis and Stratis (2008)

Table 9.4 The returns of the investment in education calculated in Table 9.1 according to the Psacharopoulos method and the respective expected returns, taking into consideration the possibility of employment resulting from Table 9.2 (1-unemployment risk) for the same year

Education level (i)	Indicative years of studies (S_i)	2003			2004			2005		
		Employment possibility	$RORE_i$	$ERORE_i$	Employment possibility	$RORE_i$	$ERORE_i$	Employment possibility	$RORE_i$	$ERORE_i$
(1)	(2)	(3) (%)	(4) (%)	(5) = (3) × (4) (%)	(6) (%)	(7) (%)	(8) = (6) × (7) (%)	(9) (%)	(10) (%)	(11) = (9) × (10) (%)
No education	(1) –	95.70	–	–	86.60	–	–	90.70	–	–
Primary school	(2) 6	93.60	8.34	7.81	91.30	14.10	12.87	92.70	3.77	3.49
Junior high school	(3) 3	89.30	2.28	2.04	88.80	2.72	2.42	89.60	1.12	1.00
High school	(4) 3	88.20	4.06	3.58	88.40	4.94	4.37	88.90	5.09	4.53
University/ technological education institutes	(5) 5	93.30	9.69	9.04	92.50	7.79	7.21	92.90	8.94	8.31
Master's degree/ Doctorate	(6) 4	92.80	13.49	17.16	94.10	12.28	11.56	91.50	12.12	11.09

Source: Petrakis and Stratis (2008)

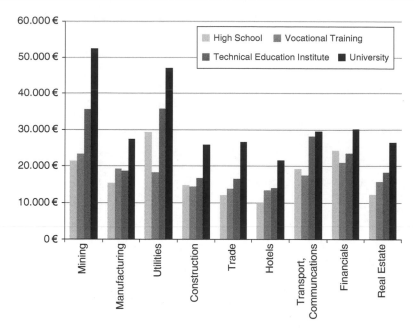

Fig. 9.4 Average level of annual income by education grade and sector of economic activity (2005 data). Source: HEL. STAT. (Hellenic Statistical Authority)

9.9.1 The Financial System

The bank-centred structure of the Greek financial system involves certain particularities concerning the incentive system of the business activity. The need to provide secured guarantees for ensuring credit loans renders bank financing prohibitive for a large subset of business efforts. More specifically, as regards the most dynamic part of the business action, that is, the innovative business schemes (which are infrequent anyway), the intangible assets do not allow the allocation of secured guarantees, rendering traditional bank loans almost impossible.

On the contrary, contracts flourishing in an environment regulated by the market enjoy a more adequate mechanism for financing new, innovative (and consequently more risky) schemes. This mechanism does not limit the expected returns of the funder in case the business attempt is successful and provides the possibility to liquidate a part (at least) of the funder's participation in the secondary market. However, the dominance of the banking system and the weakness of the market mechanism to provide alternative financing forms deprive the Greek economy's productive sector of the possibility to obtain funding using such contracts.

Consequently, the bank-centred features of the Greek financial system allow granting business loans only to persons who are able to provide the required guarantees. In other words, bank funding only reaches specific businessmen and isolated economic branches, reproducing in essence the model of economic activity and making things more difficult for those trying to introduce substantial innovations that will change the productive models in the direction of investments with more significant added value.

Besides, placing the banking system in the centre of the economic activity makes it easier to dissimulate taxable assets and to finance the business activity deriving from shadow (non-registered) activities. It is not by chance that Demirguc-Kunt and Levine (1999) highlight the fact that the financial systems presenting more bank-centred features are, at the same time, accompanied by higher rates of parallel economy.

9.9.2   Financial System, Crisis and Financial Managers' Incentives

A special matter concerning the financial system that became particularly evident from the current crisis is linked to the incentives of the financial managers.

The financial system, in an effort to deal with problems arising from the presence of moral hazard and the (economically rational) absence of confidence in it, has created processes and institutions through which these problems are limited, even though they are not eliminated. The best known method to avoid the moral hazard is creating the closest possible connection of a business manager's prosperity to the prosperity of the shareholders-owners of the business, which can be done by conditioning a great part of the business manager's remuneration to shares and options on the company's shares. The imperfection of this specific mechanism (i.e., that the options may be exercised and the shares may be liquidated long before the bad management by the outgoing administrators, among other issues, is perceived) was made known through the company scandals that saw the light long before the current crisis began. For this reason, arguments have started to be made for more careful connection of managers' remuneration with the company's long-term course.

The 2008 financial crisis, however, made the moral hazard levels underlying any investment activity widely known. Besides, the modern complex financial products (which, in many cases, were not understood by the parties involved) enhanced the existing weaknesses.

Perhaps the most typical example brought forward by the crisis is the securitisation products for claims, which were widely used by the banks in order to (re)finance their constant expansion. including in the real estate market. The securitisation process, however, transfers the risk from the underlying assets (loans) to the investors acquiring these securities without the latter necessarily knowing about it. Consequently, this practice impairs any incentive of the banking institutions to give an austere rating of the prospective borrowers. On the contrary, it enhances their incentives for rapid development of their activities to the detriment of those investing to such products, who are called to bear the cost in case the underlying loans are not serviced.

Moreover, the customary practice that the securities' issuers pay the rating companies seems to have moderated the rating companies' incentives for austere and complete analysis, which might turn out to be counterproductive for the development of their activities.

It is equally interesting to see the speculation example concerning the use of credit derivatives (for example, Credit Default Swaps – CDSs). These products, which are designed to balance the credit risk, render the underlying securities issuer's (company's or government entity's) bankruptcy profitable for investors holding positions in these financial instruments.

Finally, it should be noted that criticism (regardless of its political or ideological background) expressed about the bailing out of financial institutions (or even states) concerns the strengthening of the moral hazard problem by providing incentives for further undertaking excessive risks in the future. Proceeding to more risky investments in order to obtain higher returns (in case of success) becomes more attractive when there is a possibility of bail-out (in case of failure), which decreases possible future losses by transmitting the relevant cost to public funds.

9.9.3 The Tax System

The tax system's contribution to the formation of incentives for economically active individuals is at least equally critical. The provisions in force about the operation of the tax collection mechanism impact every legal transaction (for the non-registered, see the part of the chapter referring to tax evasion and the parallel economy) and, consequently, all aspects of economic activity. In this way, the tax system's structure and operation constitute the preferences of economically active people, with typical examples being the choice between labour or leisure and the decision to invest assets.

As regards the choice of economically active individuals between labour and leisure, the progressive nature of the tax system (see Sect. 8.1) often creates counter-incentives for labour. More specifically, as the taxable income from labour increases, a higher tax rate applies and, consequently, the average tax rate increases, i.e., to part of the income destined for the payback of the individual's fiscal burden. In this way, however, a series of rational individuals will choose less labour, even if this means less total income, because from a certain labour level onwards, the extra utility from income (from extra labour) is not enough to compensate the utility cost from the extra labour.

Similar counter-incentives for labour are likely to appear even in a proportional tax system (with a fixed tax rate that is not dependent on the income amount): In this case, at least some people will rationally choose lower labour levels and more leisure. As also analysed in Sect. 8.1, the only tax burden that does not alter the people's incentive for labour is the single and fixed tax rate (fixed amount tax or capitation tax) (Stiglitz 2000). Of course, this kind of provision would not be accepted by society because it raises issues of social injustice.

The impact of tax burden on company results is similar but perhaps more damaging. The reduction of real (after-tax) income from investment plans with low (but positive) current net value makes those plans prohibitive. In this way, however, the total investment levels will of course be lower (in relation to a case where there would be no taxes on company profits); this fact constitutes an impediment to the development process of the economy.

9.9.4 The Social Security System

The obligation of paying contributions and the right to social security benefits could be considered as a modern, complex financial tool. This financial instrument participates in the portfolios of economically active individuals at a disproportionately high rate as compared to other assets these people may hold (e.g., bank deposits, securities, share values, real estate property). Besides, for a small part of the population, the right to social security benefits constitutes the only element of their deposit/investment portfolio. Consequently, the importance of the social security system to the formation of incentives for economically active individuals becomes more evident. The basic features of the existing system (determined level of benefits and low rate of proportional justice) enhance the insured people's incentives to pay lower (or even zero) contributions.

Besides, the Greek social security system, in its current operational mode, creates counter-incentives for labour (including employment after the retirement age). In this way it turns out to be damaging to the Greek economy development effort.

Due to certain parameters in the operation of this system, abstinence from labour as well as non-registered (non-insured) employment constitute a rational decision for some economically active individuals, and an expected response to the institutional status has been formed. This is happening to a great extent because, in the context of retention and non-payment of the contributions, apart from the employer breaking the law (in some cases, at least), the employee is also favoured because, very often, the amount of the retirement depends less on the contributions paid by the insured person during his/her working life and much more on other factors (such as sex, activity branch that might justify premature retirement, or working in the public versus private sector). A typical example of the above is a low-wage worker who, after 15 years of insured work, is entitled to the same pension (minimum) as anyone having less than 32 years of insured work (Matsaganis, Sustainable and equitable retirement in an open society Athens Review of book, 2010). Consequently, many workers have the incentive to hide their labour for a significant number of years without greatly influencing their income at retirement.

Evidently, the excessive rise of uninsured labour is favoured by the particularly large size of the parallel economy as well as by the very high rate of uninsured labour of immigrants that has, from time to time, been considered as an antidote to the deficits of the social security funds. In any case, the nonpayment of the relevant contribution stems from the system's failure to provide adequate incentives. The preferences formed combined with the control mechanism's weakness to limit the contribution evasion phenomenon, explained to a great extent by the high levels of uninsured labour in Greece.

Finally, the prevalence of the view that the Greek social security system is only a few years away from collapsing further enhances incentives to avoid paying the corresponding contributions. People have no incentive to pay contributions if they consider that the collapse to come is almost certain and that the system is unable to provide the benefits they have consolidated.

Consequently, a reform that would modify the way in which benefits are calculated and would render them proportional to the contributions paid will increase the level of proportional justice in the system, reducing incentives for contribution evasion and creating preferences for staying in the labour market after the minimum retirement age. In this way, such a reform will contribute to the development and the growth of the Greek economy.

9.9.5 Parallel Economy and Incentives

Activation in parallel economies is mainly influenced by the tax and social security burdens, the rigidity of the regulatory framework, the possibility of tracing it, the severity of the punishment if caught and, finally, the unemployment levels.
(a) Tax and social security burdens.

The positive relation between the size of the parallel economy and the amount of the economic burden stemming from taxes and social security contributions has been highlighted by numerous studies.[5] The bigger the difference between the total labour cost (of the capital) in the official economy and the income after tax (from labour/capital), the bigger the incentive for tax/contribution evasion and consequently for a turn to the parallel economy. In other words, the profit from tax evasion increases proportionally to the tax burden, enhancing the tax evasion incentive. At this point, it is worth mentioning that the relation between the parallel economy and the amount of taxes is not necessarily reciprocal; i.e., while the increase of the tax burden means growth of the unofficial economic sector, a possible tax reduction through tax reforms may simply lead to stabilising and not reducing the parallel economy. This happens because there are factors, such as the high profitability related to unofficial activities or the investments (in real and human capital) resulting from it, that pose obstacles to the turn towards activities in the official economy.

According to the neoclassical examples of the economic theory, the marginal tax rate has a dominant place among the multitude of taxes affecting people's decisions about the allocation of their available time between labour and leisure (Hill and Kabir 1996). The lower the income after taxes from labour, due to the high tax rates, the more reluctant the people will become to sacrifice their leisure time for working in the official economy. Especially if we consider that people may replace the extra leisure hours with non-taxable labour in the unofficial economic sector, we can

---

[5] See indicatively Thomas (1992), Lippert and Walker (1997), Schneider (1994, 1997, 1998, 2000), Johnson et al. (1998a, b), Tanzi (1999) and Giles (1999).

realise why high taxes lead to an exchange of working hours from the official to the parallel economy.

(b) The rigidity of the regulatory framework.

An increase (quantitative, not qualitative) of the market regulations (as well as the size of the bureaucracy), such as regulations in the labour market, obstacles in the commercial transactions, working restrictions for foreigners, regulations in licensing new businesses, and so on, increases the size of the parallel economy.[6] Regulations lead to an increase of labour costs in the official economy. However, a significant part of these costs may be transmitted to the employees, leading to an increased incentive to work in the parallel economy, where such costs may be avoided. According to a study (Friedman et al. 1999) conducted in 76 countries classified as developing, in transition or developed, widening the regulations' scope by one point (on a five-point scale) is linked to a 10% increase in the size of the parallel economy. At this point it is worth noticing that the level of imposing these regulations, and not only their scope, plays perhaps the most significant part (Johnson et al. 1997; Friedman et al. 1999). The above analysis demonstrates the need to upgrade the market regulations qualitatively rather than increase them quantitatively. Nevertheless, many governments commit the "error" of following the second practice, which leads to the strengthening of bureaucrats and to a higher employment rate in the public sector. Greece seems to be a victim of this practice because, as shown in the comparative study conducted by the OECD in 2003 (Conway et al. 2005; Conway and Nicoletti 2006) on the levels of the regulation indicators in the production of products and services, Greece presents typically low performance, occupying the sixth worst ranking among a total of 30 countries.

(c) Possibility of tracking and severity of punishment.

The possibility of identifying these persons (legal or natural) as well as the severity of the punishment for tax evasion constitute critical determining factors for the size of the parallel economy. The relation between these two factors is interdependent because the effectiveness of the former depends on the existence of the latter. For instance, a combination of zero sentences and a high tracking possibility would obviously have a zero impact on people's tax conformity. It may easily be understood that if the tracking possibility is high and is accompanied by an equally severe sentence, then the incentive for non-conformity with the tax legislation in force is very small; moreover, according to Singh (1973), the more severe the sentence is, the lower the cost of tracking the tax evasion becomes. The possibility of tracking depends on: (a) the capacity for auditing (which is dependent on the criteria according to which those who will undergo the audit are chosen, on the fiscal audit policy of each country, and so on) and (b) the possibility that the audit will lead to the discovery of tax evasion phenomena (this possibility depends on the auditors' training, the organisation of the audits, the corruption and so on).

---

[6] See indicatively Johnson et al. (1998b), Deregulation Commission, Germany (1990/1991).

A critical question for policy-making aiming at tax evasion concerns the determination of the best relation between the tracking possibility and the severity of the sentence. Taking into consideration that the cost linked to the increase of the tracking possibility is much higher than the one of imposing sentences, a good answer to the above question would be to combine a policy of frequent and in-depth qualitative audits according to the income category and the tax history of the person and a sentence system where the sentence would depend on the size of the offense, while the type of sentence would be determined based on efficiency, as shown by experience. The negative relation between the size of tax evasion and the tracking possibility thereof is demonstrated in a study conducted in 2000 for the Foundation of Economic and Industrial Research (IOBE) through the use of a questionnaire (Tatsos 2001). A total of 74% of the interviewees thought the Greek tax collection mechanisms were efficient. The same study demonstrates the size of the sentence as the most important dissuasive factor for tax evasion.

(d) Unemployment levels.

Unemployment – mainly "long-term" unemployment – plays a significant part in the size of the parallel economy. A person's inability to find a job in the official economic sector leads him or her to the parallel economy, where usually this person is employed in worse working conditions (for instance, nonpayment of social security contributions). According to studies on the matter, Greece ranks first among the EU member states in long-term unemployment, which accounts for over 50% of the overall unemployment rate. This rate partly explains the very strong presence of the parallel economy in Greece.[7]

According to Schneider (2007), the increase of taxes or social security contributions is the basic cause pushing people towards becoming active in parallel economies. Moreover, parallel economies grow due to low GDP per capita, loose fiscal ethics, poor quality of service provision in the public corporations and severe regulatory interventions. People's incentives to maintain or to improve their economic situation result directly in an improvement of their quality of life even after the implementation of such measures and situations urges them to parallel economy activities.

The Greek Economic Chamber of Commerce, in collaboration with the Statistics Department of the Athens Economic University, conducted a study on tax evasion,[8] where 747 people above the age of 18 from Athens and Thessaloniki were asked to respond in an effort to reveal the incentives of those evading taxes. The most important factors that differentiated the answers of the evaders versus the non-evaders are sex, age, education level, economic situation and place of residence.

The interviewees seem divided as to what extent they would hide part of their income if they had the opportunity. Almost six out of ten interviewees stated that they did not like the idea of hiding income from the tax authorities. Graduates of

---

[7] See the newspaper "Vima tis Kyriakis", 1/10/2006.

[8] Greek Economic Chamber of Commerce (2010), http://www.oe-e.gr/publ/ecocr/res_for_20102702.pdf.

tertiary education seemed to express these views more extensively. Moreover, one in five people interviewed thought that if they were in a very difficult financial situation, they would be happy to take the risk of deceiving the tax authorities, even if doing so risked an audit. Nonetheless, almost six out of ten stated that they would not take the risk to deceive the tax authorities in an effort to pay fewer taxes; eight out of ten answered that they had not tried to deceive the tax authorities and considered that they have a moral obligation to declare all of their income and to pay all of their taxes.

As regards the tax evasion consequences, half of the people interviewed stated that they were fully informed on the subject; among the interviewed, men and those in a better economic situation stated that they had extensive information on the matter. Additionally, the subset of the interviewees agreeing that hiding income from the tax authorities is a serious offense, comparable to theft, drug dealing, issuing bounced checks or bribery, represented, respectively, 77%, 44%, 61% and 66%; the older interviewees agreed more with those views. The education level seems to play a part in responses to this type of question as well and relates positively to the view that hiding income is as serious as theft or drug dealing, while people with comparatively lower education levels tended to relate tax evasion to offenses such as issuing bounced checks or bribery.

The citizens' views on the tax evasion audit system led to significant conclusions. Forty-five percent of the interviewees thought that if they wanted to hide their income from the tax authorities, they would be able to do so. At the same time, more than half of the people interviewed thought there was a high or average possibility that the tax authorities would audit their financial data. Finally, almost half of the interviewees disagreed that state corruption justifies tax evasion, even though six out of ten secondary education graduates did not agree with the enhancement of tax evasion practices in areas with intense corruption phenomena.

A viable social security system presupposes an efficient mechanism to fight and prevent tax evasion. The most important consequence of contribution evasion in the operation of state mechanisms is related to excessive budget deficits, often resulting in borrowing or in adopting the wrong policy due to falsified data. These consequences generally threaten the viability of the social security system. Additionally, the rehabilitation measures taken by the state, such as increased contributions, have a direct impact on the workers and the employers. At the same time, a large percentage of workers remains uninsured, have intense feelings of uncertainty about their medical care, and feel insecurity in the work environment and about their particularly low pensions.

An important cause for contribution evasion is the loose connection between benefit and contribution levels. An increase in the return would provide the insured people with a strong incentive to ensure their coverage, while even the institution of minimum pensions may create a moral hazard for refusing social security. The insured people know they will enjoy a minimum pension anyway, and consequently, they have reduced motivation not to lose insurance years. The incentives that lead to contribution evasion are identified as the increase in business profits, the absence of efficient prevention, surveillance and suppression mechanisms, the lack of an insurance mentality and confidence in the state's efficiency, the financial difficulties faced by the citizens or the businesses (such as starting a family or ensuring a satisfactory level of life), avoiding bankruptcy and extending viability of the company, the existing institutional framework on labour and social security and other economic reasons, such as low salaries and high social security contributions.

9.9.6   Incentives and Capital Returns

In order for an economic environment to attract new investments, the return margins of the invested capital should constitute a strong incentive. Consequently, the return on capital constitutes an indicator of major importance because it marks the dynamics and the potential of the economy as a whole, its attractiveness compared to other economies and the perspective created by committing funds on a macroeconomic level. The high returns lead to incentives for investments, business activity and innovative action, establishing perhaps the most important pillar of growth.

The most noteworthy indicator concerning the return of natural capital (profitability) is the relation of profits (net operational surplus) to the net capital stock, i.e., the indicator of net returns of the net capital stock.

The net capital stock is defined as "the difference between gross capital stock[9] and the expenditure/amortisation of the fixed capital."

The returns on capital presented in Table 9.5 result from the ratio of the net operational surplus to the capital stock[10] (Harvey, OECD – National Accounts and Economic Statistics: Comparability of Saving and Profit Ratios, 2003). It is observed that the relative returns at the beginning of the decency are at higher

Table 9.5 Returns on capital in Greece and in other European countries

	2000 (%)	2001 (%)	2002 (%)	2003 (%)	2004 (%)	2005 (%)	2006 (%)	2007 (%)	2008 (%)	2009 (%)
Greece	12	12	12	13	14	14	15	16	16	16
Italy	11	12	12	12	12	12	11	12	12	11
Spain	9	10	10	10	10	11	11	11	11	11
Portugal	9	9	9	8	9	8	8	9	9	8
Denmark	8	7	7	7	7	8	8	7	7	4
Sweden	6	5	5	6	6	7	7	7	6	6
Finland	10	10	11	10	11	10	11	12	11	9
Netherlands	9	9	9	9	9	10	10	11	11	9

Source: European Commission (AMECO Database)

---

[9] The gross capital stock is in turn defined as the acquisition value/price of assets, calculated as new, regardless of their age and their actual condition.

[10] The net operation surplus and the capital stock result from European Commission data (http://ec.europa.eu/economy_finance/ameco/user/serie/ResultSerie.cfm).

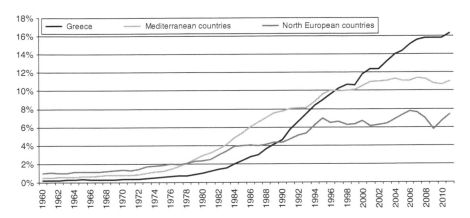

Fig. 9.5 Time evolution of capital returns in Greece, the Mediterranean countries and the Northern European countries (Source: European Commission (AMECO Database). Note: The 2011 data are estimations made by EC)

levels in all Mediterranean countries compared to all members of the European Union. At the same time, the relative indicator both for Greece and for the rest of the countries of the Mediterranean region approaches high levels as compared to the Northern European countries (Fig. 9.5).

Based on these findings, it is ascertained that in terms of capital returns, there are noteworthy incentives for making investments, primarily in the Mediterranean countries, and in particular in Greece, as compared to the Northern European countries. This finding is also explained to some extent by the different development levels. Nevertheless, the creation of investment incentives in a geographical area is not only dependent on capital returns but also includes much broader issues such as communication capacity, infrastructure use and corruption levels.

9.10   Incentives and Entrepreneurial Activity

The definition of "entrepreneurship" refers to the creation, primarily, of a small business. The emphasis of the concept seems to be placed on the private individual who initiates a business or innovates, undertaking some risk in his action. The analysis of the incentives leading individuals to establish a business is particularly important because entrepreneurship contributes significantly to economic development.

The tax policy has a determinative and multifaceted impact on the private individual's decision to establish a business. Consequently, the tax system may render entrepreneurship more or less attractive. The result of the business activity is taxable in different ways as compared to the income generated from dependent labour.

As highlighted in the previous chapter, incentives directly impact human behaviour relating to future actions. Under this scope, the incentive mechanisms in the economy, despite being numerous, do not exclusively relate to the process of optimising benefits when the latter takes into consideration only the maximisation of growth.

Entrepreneurship refers to a process including all of the operations, activities and actions linked to identifying opportunities and to creating an entity that will exploit them. In this sense, behind all risks undertaken and all resource investments lays the activation of the entrepreneurial mind.

The incentives behind entrepreneurial action are highly variable and determine its goals. These incentives relate to the profit capacity for subsistence by identifying and exploiting business opportunities and also to reasons directly linked to creativity and innovation.

Economic remuneration is one of the most significant incentives in any work relation and in particular in the case of entrepreneurship, where there is high uncertainty as to the result of the production process. Businessmen expect investment returns that will not only compensate their initial capital (natural and human) but will also offer satisfactory remuneration for the risks and the initiatives taken in their business activity.

The freedom of independent work is also a significant incentive for entrepreneurship. The expressions, "I want to be my own boss" or "I don't want anyone supervising me" are very common. This particular incentive always relates to the person's psychological status as well and to his or her personality and mentality. Table 9.6 presents the classification of incentives for business activity in the Southern and Northern EU countries. Greece, with 23.7% of businessmen stating that their incentive for establishing a business is labour independence, is ranked much lower than the European average (33.5%).

Another very significant incentive directly linked to the creation of a new business operation is to ensure employment and income. Entrepreneurship out of need is created mainly when individuals face low or nonexistent wages and try to increase their income, or in case they are unemployed and wish to do so, to find

Table 9.6 Business activity incentives (2007)

	Need/ maintaining of income	Income increase	Labour independence	Opportunity entrepreneurship	Combination of opportunity and need
Denmark	6.3	38.8	42.3	81.1	12.6
Sweden	12.6	37.3	41.7	79.1	8.3
Netherlands	20.1	18.7	47.3	66.0	14.0
Italy	20.7	32.1	38.1	70.2	9.1
Portugal	22.7	39.4	16.8	56.2	21.1
Spain	21.1	24.0	30.4	54.4	24.5
Greece	12.9	39.7	23.7	63.4	23.7
EU average	20.8	27.1	33.5	60.5	18.7

Source: Foundation for Economic and Industrial Research (IOBE), Data Process: GEM

work. In Greece – according to research by the Foundation of Economic and Industrial Researches (Enterpreneurship in Greece 2007–2008, Athens, November 2008) – the percentage of young and aspiring businessmen stating need as their exclusive incentive for business establishment was 13% (2007).

The possibility of an alternative choice to an unsatisfactory job, either for reasons related to wages or for other reasons, is also a significant incentive. Many businessmen worked as executives in other companies before establishing their own businesses. While they did not risk unemployment, at a certain point they realised that their job was no longer satisfactory to them. Others realised that their potential both for evolution and for increases of their remuneration was very limited, and obviously, this could in no case be an important incentive to make them stay. In Greece, as shown in Table 9.6, the income increase of businessmen is a very significant incentive for starting a business activity.

Moreover, the incentives linked to entrepreneurship contribute to the possibility of developing personal skills. Quite often, business action is led by the need for personal development and self-actualisation stemming from the creation of an integrated and productive entity; a typical example is a properly structured business with solid bases. The development of a business primarily requires the businessman's personal development. The most important skills for business success include, among others, uncertainty and psychological pressure created by the entrepreneurship, management skills, talent in interpersonal relations at all levels and the optimal management given the availability of resources and the business goals.

Besides, in Greece, the business opportunity incentive (63.4%) is higher than in Spain (54.4%) and Portugal (56.2%); it is also higher than the European average (60.5%). Nevertheless, it remains rather weak as compared to the Northern European countries (see Table 9.6).

Finally, another very significant incentive is the opportunity for creativity and innovation. Innovation leads to improvements in the production of the product or the service, and this results in reducing production costs, increasing productivity and limiting production time for a product unit. The final result is to form monopolistic or oligopolistic profits, which are the ultimate business goal.

According to Table 9.7, the incentives inciting business activity concentrate in three categories: primary stage entrepreneurship, "novelty" of product in the market and absence of competitors. For Greece, only 12.8% of new businessmen consider that their products offered are entirely new for all of the customers to whom they are addressed. This performance is marginally below the European average and situates Greece in the middle of the European ranking along with Portugal (12.7%). The majority of efforts identified by the research (64%) have no innovation element whatsoever, and as a result, the businessmen believes that none of the potential customers will consider that the products he/she buys are new in concept or in content. In any case, it should be noted that this percentage has been shrinking over the last years since reaching 70% in 2005; this change shows that new businessmen demonstrate a more creative attitude and that the innovation incentive of new businessmen is stronger now than in the recent past.

Table 9.7 Incentives for innovative activity (2007)

	Primary stage entrepreneurship	Percentage of consumers considering the product as entirely new in the market:			No competition
		All customers	Some customers	No customer	
Denmark	5.4	22.8	32.7	44.5	19.4
Netherlands	5.2	18.4	21.1	60.5	7.9
Italy	5.0	19.3	30.3	50.4	7.2
Portugal	8.8	12.7	23.1	64.1	9.5
Spain	7.6	20.3	28.3	51.4	9.4
Greece	5.7	12.8	23.4	63.8	5.4
EU average	6.0	13.0	26.2	60.8	9.0

Source: Foundation for Economic and Industrial Research, Data Process: GEM

Table 9.8 Duration and characteristics of the investment and the investor

Indicators	Average
1 Estimated ideal duration of the investment (1–10 years)	5.57
2 Estimated ideal duration of the investment in an economy where there will be higher growth rates (1–10 years)	4.34
3 Estimated ideal duration of the investment if the government takes serious measures to reduce bureaucracy, corruption, etc.	4.86

Source: Petrakis (2005)

Finally, only 5.4% of businessmen enter a truly new market where there is no other competitor, creating a new market islet. This is very low performance as compared to the other countries.

The amount of business investments is dependent on the macroeconomic conditions, which have an economic but also a social background; it also depends on business opportunities (Christiansen 1997) and on features of the human behaviour relating to business incentives (Shane et al. 2003) and knowledge thereof (Mitchell et al. 2002).

The concept of time, from the businessman's point of view, affects business activity in two ways. On one hand, it differentiates the value of the present in relation to the future, while on the other it affects the time span of the business project.

According to data deriving from the answers to the questionnaires given to 120 businessmen of SMEs active in the Greek economy (Petrakis 2005), the ideal duration of the investment seems to be as follows:

Based on the answers to the questionnaires, the average ideal duration of the investment commitment is 5.57 years (Petrakis 2007). This duration is interpreted as the average desirable time among businessmen for the paying back of their capital. This time may be considered as "short in business" because it does not allow a substantial commitment of a large volume of own funds. It is also observed, from points two and three of the Table 9.8, that the overall economic and institutional situation is significantly detrimental to the ideal time duration of the investment, as confirmed by the businessmen.

According to Petrakis' (2005) research, it is characteristic that while the average ideal duration of committing own funds, as discussed above, is 5.57 years, the average desired payback period of funds is only 3.91 years. This means that the businessmen's expectations are pessimistic. In other words, the investor expects that his funds will be committed for a longer period of time than they really are, but this does not create incentives to increase the nature of the business investment in volume and to widen its time span.

References

Ando A, Modigliani F (1963) The "Life Cycle" hypothesis of saving: aggregate implications and tests. Am Econ Rev 53(1):55–84, http://www.jstor.org/stable/1817129

Bird B, West P (1997) Time and entrepreneurship. Entrep Theory Pract 22(2):925–950

Christiansen C (1997) The innovator's dilemma. Harvard Business School Press, Cambridge

Conway P, Nicoletti G (2006) Product market regulation in the non-manufacturing sectors of O.E.C.D. countries: measurement and highlights. Econ. Dep. Work. Pap. 530

Conway P, Janod V, Nicoletti G (2005) Product market regulation in O.E.C.D. countries: 1998 to 2003. O.E.C.D., Econ. Dep. Work. Pap. 419

Das T, Teng B (1997) Time and entrepreneurial risk behaviour. Entrep Theory Pract 22(2):69–88

Demirgüç-Kunt, Levine R (1999) Bank-based and market-based financial systems: cross-country comparisons. World Bank Policy Res. Work. Pap. 2143

Derman E (2002) The perception of time, risk and return during periods of speculation. Quant Finance 2:282–296

Epstein L, Zin S (1989) Substitution, risk aversion and the temporal behavior of consumption and asset returns: a theoretical framework. Econometrica 57:937–969

Epstein L, Zin S (1991) Substitution, risk aversion and the temporal behavior of consumption and asset returns: an empirical analysis. J Polit Economy 99:269–286

Friedman E, Johnson S, Kaufmann D, Zoido-Labton P (1999) Dodging the grabbing hand: the determinants of unofficial activity in 69 countries. Discuss. Pap. Washington DC, World Bank

Friedman M (1957) A theory of the consumption function. National Bureau of Economic Research Princeton, New Jersey

Giles D (1999) Measuring the hidden economy: implications for econometric modelling. Econ J 109(456):370–380

Groot W, Oosterbeek H (1992) Optimal investment in human capital under uncertainty. Econ Educ Rev 11:41–49

Hill R, Kabir M (1996) Tax rates, the tax mix, and the growth of the underground economy in Canada: what can we infer? Can Tax J/Revue Fiscale Canadienne 44(6):1552–1583

House RJ, Hanges PJ, Javidan M, Dorfman PW, Gupta V (2004) Culture, leadership and organisations – the GLOBE study of 62 societies. Sage Publications, Thousand Oaks

Johnson S, Kaufmann D, Zoido-Lobatón P (1998a) Regulatory discretion and the unofficial economy. Am Econ Rev 88(2):387–392

Johnson S, Kaufmann D, Zoido-Lobatón P (1998b) Corruption, public finances and the unofficial economy. Discuss. Pap. Washington DC, World Bank

Johnson S, Kaufmann D, Shleifer A (1997) The unofficial economy in transition. Brook. Pap. on Econ. Activity, Fall, Washington DC

Lagrange J (1797) Theorie de Fonctions Analytiques. Imprimerie de la Republique, Paris

Lefley F (1996) The payback method of investment appraisal: a review and synthesis. Int J Prod Econ 32(12):2751–2776

Lefley F (1994) Capital investment appraisal of advanced manufacturing technology. Int J Prod Res 32(12):2751–2776

Lippert O, Walker M (1997) The underground economy: global evidences of its size and impact. The Frazer Institute, Vancouver, BC

Maslow AH (1954) Motivation and personality. Harper, New York

Mitchell R, Smith B, Morse E, Seawright K, Peredo A, McKenzie B (2002) Are entrepreneurial cognitions universal? Assessing entrepreneurial cognitions across cultures. Entrep Theory Pract 26(4):9–32

Petrakis P (2007) The effects of risk and time on entrepreneurship. Int Entrep Manag J 3(3):277–291

Petrakis P (2005) Factors influencing the ideal duration of entrepreneurial commitment: the greek case. Econ Bus Rev 7(2):101–118

Petrakis P (1997) Entrepreneurship and growth: creative and equilibrating events. Small Bus Econ 9:383–402

Petrakis P, Stratis K (2008) Rates of return to education, recent evidence from Greece, 2003–2005. Paper presented in the Second Int. Conf. on Educational Econ., Athens, 29/08/2008

Psacharopoulos G (2008) Funding universities for efficiency and equity: research findings versus petty politics. Education Econ Taylor and Francis J 16(3):245–260

Psacharopoulos G (1994) Returns to investment in education: a global update. World Dev 22(9): 1325–1343

Psacharopoulos G, Patrinos H (2002) Returns to investment in education: a further update. World Bank Policy Res. Work. Pap. 2881

Schleicher A (2006) The Economics of knowledge: why education is key to europe's success. lisbon council, Policy Brief.

Schneider F (2007) Shadow economies and corruption all over the world: new estimates for 145 countries. Open Access J 1(9):1–66

Schneider F (2000) The increase of the size of the informal economy of 18 OECD countries: some preliminary explanations. Paper presented at the Annu. Public Choice Meet. Charleston, SC

Schneider F (1998) Further empirical results of the size of the informal economy of 17 OECD-countries over time. Paper to be presented at the 54 Congress of the IIPF Cordowa, Argentina and Discuss. Pap. Dept. of Econ. Univ. of Linz, Linz, Austria

Schneider F (1997) The informal economies of western europe. J Inst Econ Aff 17(3):42–48

Schneider F (1994) Can the informal economy be reduced through major tax reforms? An empirical investigation for Austria. Public Financ 49:137–152

Shane S, Locke E, Collins C (2003) Entrepreneurial motivation. Hum Resour Manage R 13(2):257–279

Singh B (1973) Making honesty the best policy. J Public Econ 2(3):257–263

Stiglitz J (2000) Economics of the public sector, 3rd edn. W. W. Norton & Company, New York

Tanzi V (1999) Uses and abuses of estimates of the underground economy. Econ J 109 (456):338–340

Tatsos N (2001) Underground economy and tax evasion in Greece. Papazisis, Athens

Tay A (2008) Time – varying incentives in the mutual fund industry. Finance work. Pap., East Asia Bureau of Econ. Res.

Thomas J (1992) Informal economic activity. LSE, Handb. in Econ. Harvester Wheatsheaf, London

Vroom V (1964) Work and motivation. John Wiley, New York

Weil P (1990) Nonexpected utility in macroeconomics. Q J Econ 105:29–42

The 2008–2010 Crisis and the European Stability Mechanism[*]

10

The study of this particular crisis, always from a medium-term perspective, should be emphasised for various reasons.

(a) The most important of these is the intensity of the crisis, which created criticalities in several basic operational sectors of the economy; since 1929, this is the largest crisis for the global and by extension, the Greek economy.

(b) The 2008 crisis demonstrated the Greek economy's weaknesses in a most profound way. Thus, the changes proposed by the economic policy, which sought to intervene more actively in the activities of the Greek economy, clashed with the high budget deficit. The negative impact of high budget deficits will be crucial not only for establishing the conditions that will lead the way out of the crisis but also for the future of the Greek economy.

(c) Some aggregates of the Greek economy, such as public debt and the labour market, are particularly affected. The critical state of these aggregates creates qualitative situations that will necessitate unprecedented restructuring.

(d) The intensity of global imbalances has reached a point that promises constant future fluctuations in the medium term (5–8 years). Consequently, it is necessary to pay particular attention to identifying possible ways of emerging from the crisis with both international and domestic involvement.

(e) Methodologically, it is necessary to distinguish between the long-term view of the evolution of growth and the short-term, acute nature of some economic phenomena. Unfortunately, economic policy makers tend to exploit the social realisation of the general economic problems and suggest measures that may be effective in the long run but have absolutely no effect on the current situation (crisis therapy) or measures that may even have a concentric impact, i.e., they intensify the crisis. The opposite may occur; policy makers may exploit the social realisation of a short-term crisis and suggest restructuring measures that

---

[*]Greece entered the European Stability Mechanism (ESM) in May 2010. Therefore, this chapter contains information relevant up to that date. Chapter 12 includesupdates until December 2010, when the partial amendment of the Lisbon Treaty was decided, focusing on the restructuring of the rescue mechanisms for excessively indebted European economies.

P. Petrakis, *The Greek Economy and the Crisis*,
DOI 10.1007/978-3-642-21175-1_10, © Springer-Verlag Berlin Heidelberg 2012

will have no effect on the short-term growth of the economy. Indeed, it is possible that these measures could be socially defeated, and consequently, the society might miss the opportunity to adopt them under normal circumstances.

Section 10.1 describes the greatest financial crises of the global economy. Section 10.2 studies the emergence and major global effects of the crisis, which started in 2008. Section 10.3 analyses the crisis in the Greek economy for the year 2008 and the changing phases of the crisis from 2007 until today. Section 10.4 discusses the chronological evolution of the crisis (e.g., political developments and exchange rates). Section 10.5 analyses the internal conditions of the crisis (public debt, financial system, spreads, CDSs (Credit Default Swaps), credit rating agencies, and government borrowing). Section 10.6 presents the external conditions, and Sect. 10.7 describes the integration of the Greek economy into the European Stability Mechanism. Finally, Sect. 10.8 describes the history of various economies and the basic global imbalances.

10.1   Financial Crises in the Global Economy

Table 10.1 presents the four major post-war[1] crises of the global economy as reflected by the basic aggregates. These peaked in 1975, 1982, 1991 and 2009. We observe that the most substantial peak (in 1982) prior to the 2008 crisis was only 1/3 to 1/2 as large, based on GDP changes.

Major financial crises in the global economy occurred between 1975–1977 and 1992. Five of these crises seem to have been particularly serious (Reinhart and Rogoff 2008): in Spain in 1977, in Norway in 1987, in Finland and in Sweden in 1989 and in Japan in 1992.

The 1970–2007 period was associated with 42 systematic bank crises in 37 countries (Laeven and Valencia 2008). In Greece, only one crisis that occurred in 1983 was primarily monetary.

Table 10.1 International recessions (percentage changes in global aggregates)

	1975	1982	1991	2009
Production per capita	−0.13	−0.89	−0.18	−2.5
Industrial production	−1.6	−4.33	−0.09	−6.23
Total trade	−1.87	−0.69	4.01	−11.75
Capital flux	0.56	−0.76	−2.07	−6.18
Unemployment rate increase	1.19	1.61	0.72	2.56
Consumption per capita	0.41	−0.18	0.62	−1.11
Investments per capita	−2.04	−4.72	−0.15	−8.74

Source: IMF-World Economic Outlook, April 2010, p. 14

---

[1] A longer-term perspective (covering the last two centuries) of the evolution of the global financial crisis is mainly found in Chap. 11.

The sequence of the economic impacts is almost identical in all financial crises (Furceri and Mourougane 2009). A crisis reduces the incentives for capital investment as the demand for products decreases while uncertainty and risk increase. Simultaneously, the financial system reduces funding to the private sector. The labour market is weakened, and thus, unemployment increases and further aggravates demand conditions.

Recessions usually lead to a permanent production loss, estimated by Furceri and Mourougane (2009) to be approximately 1.5–2.5% of the GDP for ordinary crises and approximately 4% for more significant crises, such as the current one. Based on a global GDP of approximately $54.5 tr, the current crisis created a loss in GDP of approximately $2.2 tr. Considering that the removal of securities from the financial system has reached $4 tr,[2] it seems that the value lost from the removal of securities is almost double the value lost in the real economy.

10.2 The 2008 Crisis and the Real Global Economy

Towards the end of 2007, a 6-year period of continuous economic growth appears to be coming to an end. The widely expected decline in the U.S. real estate market[3] was threatening to end a prolonged period of prosperity in the developed world and slow the rapid economic growth of emerging economies.

International investors were alarmed by the further delay in the repayment of housing loans, which was first noted at the end of 2006 (Fig. 10.1). The increased repayment delays were accompanied by an increase in the number of borrowers who went bankrupt, whereas, to avoid the negative consequences of such an event, other borrowers witnessed the repossession of their real estate.

However, this decline not only had the short-term consequence of a correction in the market but threatened to sink the global economy into a recession. Moreover, the direct or indirect exposure of several banking and investment giants in the US residential market made investors particularly hesitant towards the assets of these institutions.[4] In addition, the depreciation of commercial and investment banks was threatening the global financial system with chain reactions. Holders of financial products from these institutions and those who had concluded OTC transactions

---

[2] IMF, World Economic Outlook, April 2009.

[3] In the USA, the transformation of investments in property from a means of ensuring one's housing into an investment vehicle began in the previous decade with the relief of the real estate buying and selling and tax levies from interest rates in the housing loans by President Clinton as an answer to the Republican program for tax coefficient reduction. This fiscal background has particularly favoured the housing boom during the current decade.

[4] American bank and investment giants were involved in the "subprimes" issue mainly due to the financial reform introduced by President Clinton in cooperation with the Republican Party in 1999 that overthrew the 1933 rules, according to which investment activities were prohibited for commercial banks.

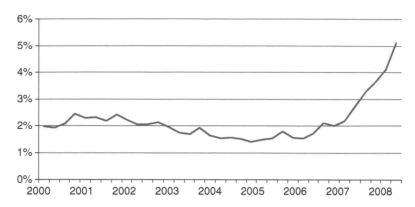

Fig. 10.1 The longitudinal course of single-family residential mortgages, where payment delays are observed (Source: US Federal Reserve)

with them risked financial losses, as did entities that insured investors in the international credit markets.

Investor insecurity increased as no one was able to predict which institutions succumb to the economic situation and to what extent. In fact, the exact size of the "toxic financial products" was still unknown. The adverse selection cost[5] that accompanies similar situations of asymmetric information appeared in the form of high interest rate loans in the inter-bank market because no one was willing to entrust funds to any credit institution, even for a brief period. In other words, once again the international financial system demonstrated pre-circular behaviour, increasing the problem of economic and credit shrinkage.

At the same time, the insurance cost for bankruptcy increased, even for company bonds of business giants with excellent credit standing (in the USA, Xerox and IBM; in Europe, Siemens and others). This fact was reflected in the course of indexes monitoring international credit markets.

However, the crisis affected production structures both in the US and in the rest of the world. The fall of the inter-bank interest rate did not translate into a lower lending cost for enterprises and consumers, as banking institutions were trying to reduce their credit expansion and improve the image of their assets. The high

---

[5] The adverse selection is due to the existence of asymmetric information in a given market. In the case of inter-bank loans, borrowers may not evaluate the quality (risk) of the bank's assets *before* being granted the loans. Because they are not able to determine the difference between "good" banks (those with the highest-quality portfolios) and "bad" banks (those with the most risky assets), lenders charge a higher than normal interest rate that corresponds to the average risk of the inter-bank market. The additional loan costs of banks with the highest-quality portfolios (which, in the case of perfect information, would have a lower lending cost) comprise the average selection cost. This situation leads to the dominance of high interest rates and segmentation in capital markets. The importance of asymmetrical information was first introduced in Akerlof's study (1970), while its part in the banking system operation is discussed in Mishkin's (1997) book, "The economics of money, banking and financial markets."

lending cost to the business world weakened the desire to undertake investment risk and led to some efforts aimed at reducing operating costs. These efforts, which usually included staff reduction, led to higher unemployment rates. Uncertainty about future employment along with borrowing difficulties for households (when borrowing was possible, its cost was high) led to a decrease in consumption demand.

Beyond the sectors that are usually affected by consumers' effort to reduce spending (e.g., retail, and services such as tourism), the crisis seemed to directly threaten the already problematic American automobile industry. Political disagreements and ideological conflicts developed as to whether there should be an effort to provide state support to the enterprises in trouble or whether the industries should seek protection from their lenders by filing for bankruptcy and passing on their restructuring costs to shareholders, suppliers and employees. Finally, it was decided to grant conditioned loans to the automobile industry (including General Motors, which had declared partial bankruptcy) and to announce an investment plan to stimulate economic activity and restore trust in the American economy.

In the financial sector, state support was deemed necessary to avoid bankruptcy. Some opposed the state rescue plan for investment banks, proposing the moral hazard argument.[6] According to opponents, rescuing the investment enterprises with taxpayers' money would mean rewarding those who participated unwisely in risky investment schemes and encouraging similar practices in the future.

Nevertheless, it was widely accepted that the financial system required a capital boost to reduce the adverse selection cost, which had led to the skyrocketing of lending costs and could only negatively affect the "real economy" on a global level.

In this context and to avoid any opportunistic behaviour in the future, it was made clear that not all institutions that had demonstrated unwise investment policies should be supported, but only those whose survival was judged necessary for the financial system's stability. Thus, no effort was made to rescue the Lehman Brothers investment bank, which went bankrupt in September 2008. However, when the size of the problem and the extent of the risk it posed for the global economic system became obvious, it was understood that it was necessary to conduct a large-scale[7] bailout.

---

[6] Moral hazard concerns the existence of asymmetrical information on undesirable actions that could take place *after* a transaction is completed. In the case of providing state support to banking institutions, there is a risk that the administrators of the financial institutions will not act in accordance with the public sector's interests, i.e., by participating in extremely risky investments to achieve higher profits, considering that the public sector would cover possible losses.

[7] The amount of the initial Paulson plan (named after the Secretary of the Treasury of the USA at the time; its official name was Troubled Asset Relief Program, or TARP) for supporting the US financial system in the autumn of 2008 exceeded $700 bn. It was followed by a similarly sized second round of support by the Obama administration in the beginning of 2009. More recent estimates (July 2009) set the support cost for American banks to the inconceivable amount of $23.7 tr, against $3 tr already spent by July 2009 (see deposition of N. Barofski before the Committee on Oversight and Government Reform. U.S. House of Representatives, Kathimerini, 26/7/2009). However, such a development (although possibly exaggerated) would reverse every-thing we currently know on the subject.

The British bank, Northern Rock, is a typical example. This bank faced long queues of depositors who were worried about their deposits (bank panic). To avoid the worst outcome, the British authorities had to resort to a capital grant, placing the bank under state control. Additionally, after rescuing its largest financial institutions, Iceland had to resort to international borrowing to avoid bankruptcy, and even EU member states (such as Hungary) turned to the International Monetary Fund for loans (after the crisis begun).

In the context of this international effort, the central banks announced repeated interest rate reductions with the aim of decreasing lending costs. At the same time, the swapping of depreciated bank asset instruments for easily liquidated state securities from the central banks was commonly allowed for a short period. This movement enhanced the liquidity of credit institutions because the instruments they acquired could be used as a pledge for borrowing in the inter-bank market. Finally, the public sector acquired stakes in several financial institutions in the form of preference shares, whereas in some cases, the state capital grants led to buyouts of problematic banks by other institutions.[8] The above actions managed to significantly restore investor trust in the financial system, as reflected in the disinflation of the inter-bank lending cost.

Another important issue that raised concerns was the real impact of the crisis on the basic aggregates of the global economy. Specifically, as we see in Table 10.1, the rate of change in real GDP of developed countries decreased from 2.7%, in 2007 to −3.2% in 2009, whereas for 2010 and 2011, it is projected to be 2.7% and 2.2%, respectively. This slowdown manifested as a decrease in consumer confidence, which was reflected in the reduction of total domestic demand from 2.3% in 2007 to 0.1% in 2008 and −2.7% in 2009. We also find that private consumption (2.5% in 2007, 0.2% in 2008 and −1% in 2009) declined much more than public consumption did (1.9% in 2007, 2.3% in 2008 and 2.3% in 2009). This difference is attributed to economic policy efforts to stimulate economic activity to alleviate the serious consequences of the crisis. However, these efforts led to increasing deficits in public budgets. Another "treatment" applied was the reduction in interest rates, but this did not prevent a serious decline in private loans.

The serious consequences of the crisis were reflected in the reduction of the imports of developed countries (from 6.6% in 2007 to 1.9% in 2008 and −12.4% in 2009) and of course exports (from 5% in 2007 to 0.4% in 2008 and −12.7% in 2009). Due to the decrease in global demand, product prices, including oil (which had increased by 10.7% in 2007 and by 36.4% in 2007 and 2008, but decreased by 46.4% in 2009), decreased dramatically, and deflation appeared (the indexes of consumer prices decreased to −0.1% in 2009, down from 2.2% and 3.4% for 2007 and 2008, respectively).

Perhaps the crisis of 2008 is the first global financial crisis whose evolution and diffusion of consequences were so rapid. The crucial question that arises relates to

---

[8] For instance, the buyouts of Wachovia by Wells Fargo and of the investment banks Merrill Lynch and Bear Sterns by Bank of America and J.P. Morgan, respectively.

Table 10.2 Rates of change in key aggregates of developed countries

	2007	2008	2009	2010[a]	2011[a]
Growth rate of real GDP	2.7	0.2	−3.2	2.7	2.2
Domestic demand	2.3	0.1	−2.7	1.6	1.8
Private consumption demand	2.5	0.2	−1.0	1.6	1.7
Public consumption	1.9	2.3	2.3	1.4	−0.5
Investments	2.2	−2.4	−12.3	1.8	4.4
Imports	6.6	1.9	−12.4	11.0	6.0
Exports	5.0	0.4	−12.7	10.1	5.2
Oil price	10.7	36.4	−36.3	23.3	3.3
CPI	2.2	3.4	0.1	1.4	1.3

Source: IMF-World Economic Outlook, 2009
[a]Forecasts

the systemic production of systemic[9] crises by the banking system, which we have just examined. Essentially, the capitalist system is now dominated by the interweaving of the financial capital and political administration, which "follows" the continued banking practices and behaviours that create continuous minor or major crises (Table 10.2).

10.3   The 2008 Crisis and the Greek Economy

The 2008 crisis[10] hit an already weak Greek economy that had largely exhausted the traditional means of facing a classic recession; these means included an expansionary fiscal policy, as the fiscal deficit had achieved very high levels in the preceding years. The situation caused a decrease in domestic demand, threatening the banking sector and further aggravating public finances.

Evidence for the weakening of the Greek economy had already appeared in 2007, mainly through the reduction in investments as a result of inflated private investment in housing in 2006. This excessive growth of investments in residential property was consistent with the international economy but was also a result of the government policy (in the context of the political cycle that ended in September 2007 with the national elections), mainly through the creation of a climate that "rushed" the purchase of residential properties due to the expected introduction of VAT[11] for these transactions. The excessive demand for real estate was further enhanced by the low interest rates offered by banks until 2007. Thus, in 2007, 250,000 apartments were listed for sale in Greece. The 15.6% decrease in

---

[9] The same word is deliberately used twice.

[10] Termed thus here because it appeared during the last months of 2008, even though its maximum impact in the domestic economy was felt mainly in 2009.

[11] According to Law 3427/2005.

construction in the first semester of 2009 was expected due to both excessive supply and decreasing demand because of the crisis.

Law 3296/2004 introduced a policy to reduce taxation of personal business profits (from 25% to 20% in 2007). The same policy was also introduced to allow individuals to apply a reduction of tax coefficients over the period of 2007–2009. Finally, the same law introduced a gradual reduction of company tax coefficients from 35% in 2004 to 25% in 2007.[12] These reductions had an obvious negative impact on government revenues.

At the same time, the public finances relaxed in terms of the function of the collection mechanisms, mainly through a "popular" policy of fiscal "book closure," which in fact resulted in the inadequate operation of tax collection mechanisms. Nevertheless, the reduced number of audits by the governing bodies (SDOE and YPEE)[13] during the years 2000–2007 had a medium-term scope.

As a result, until 2008, government revenue grew at a slower rate than public spending. This directly caused a dramatic increase in the cash deficit of the general government. It is significant that in 2008, the cash deficit increased to €18.25 bn (representing 7.5% of GDP), which is even higher than the deficit of €16 bn recorded in 2004, the year of the Athens Olympics.[14] Consequently, the financial exhaustion of the economy has been apparent since 2008. A deficit of 10% at the end of 2008 was accompanied by a cash deficit at the end of 2009, which approached 15% of GDP.

These aggregates should be added to the already high debt levels, maintaining the high borrowing costs of the Greek government. In absolute terms, the debt of the Greek government began at €183,157 bn[15] in the 2001–2004 period, increased to €262,071 bn during the 2005–2008 period and reached €292,000 bn in 2009. The budget deficit at the end of 2009 was €32.3 bn and was adjusted by Eurostat to €36.1 bn (15 November 2010). Table 10.3 is presented here as drafted in September 2009 as a contribution to the debate about whether the true size of the deficit was known in 2009, or whether it could be assessed accurately and in a timely manner.

The 2008 crisis became apparent in the Greek society mainly through the informational deluge about developments in the USA and then in Europe. It was initially noticed in the Greek economy after a rapid decrease in the Athens Stock Exchange prices due to the liquidation of positions by foreign investors who controlled approximately 50% of the total value of the Greek money market. The "upcoming recession" reduced consumer confidence and reduced investment plans. The situation of public finances also decreased public investments, whereas the crisis directly affected the demand for exported products (the demand for imports was also reduced, and consequently, trade was affected; we have seen that the latter

---

[12] See OECD, Economic Surveys: Greece (2007).

[13] Service for Special Audits (ΥPEE) of the Ministry of Economy. It is the evolution of SDOE (Body against Financial Crime).

[14] Bank of Greece.

[15] Bulletin of Conjunctural Indicators of the Bank of Greece, December 2008, p. 128.

Table 10.3 Evolution of public debt (billion euros) and similar indicators[a]

	Public debt	Public debt	Change	Change per year	Average balance	Service estimation with 5%	Participation of annual service in the annual debt increase (%)
2001–2004	140,971[b]	183,157[c]	42,182	10,545	162,064	8,103	76.9
2005–2008	183,157	262,071[d]	78,914	19,729	222,614	11,131	56.2
2009	262,071	292,000[e]	29,929	29,929	277,035	13,851	46.3

[a] Written in September 2009 and was included in the trial edition of this book in November 2009 (ISBN: 978-960-92491-5-7, SET: 978-960-92491-4-0, 10/12/09)
[b]Statistical Bulletin of Conjuctural Indicators, Bank of Greece, December 2006, p. 122
[c]Statistical Bulletin of Conjuctural Indicators, Bank of Greece, December 2008, p. 128
[d]Communication of the Minister of Finance G. Papathanasiou, 9/16/2009
[e]"Vima" newspaper and other sources 9/17/2009

Table 10.4 Growth rate estimates

	2009	2010[a]
Eurozone	−4.2	1.7
Germany	−4.7	3.3
France	−2.5	1.6
Italy	−5.0	1.0
Spain	−3.7	−0.3
Netherlands	−3.9	1.8
Belgium	−2.7	1.6
Greece	−2.0	−4.0
Austria	−3.9	1.6
Portugal	2.6	1.1
Finland	−8.0	2.4
Ireland	−7.6	−0.3
Slovakia	−4.7	4.1
Slovenia	−7.8	0.8
Cyprus	−1.7	0.4
Japan	−5.2	2.8
Great Britain	−4.9	1.7
Canada	−2.5	3.1

Source: IMF-World Economic Outlook, October 2009
[a]Projections

constitutes a structural sector of the Greek economy) and decreased receipts from tourism. As a result, unemployment started to increase.

Table 10.4, showing the rate of change in real GDP for 2009 and the forecast for 2010, demonstrated that the crisis was slow to affect the Greek economy, which showed some resistance.

This development occurred for the following reasons:

1. The degree of openness of the economy is relatively low, so the impact of external factors is limited.

2. The parallel economy and the parallel financial system, which operate as inhibitors in the event of a recession, are particularly extensive in Greece.
3. The result of the high share of real estate property in the personal portfolio does not have a particularly negative impact because:
   (a) Real estate prices did not decrease significantly due to the valuable consideration system, where the plot (in cities with short offer) is a significant factor in determining the property price, and due to the low dependence of homebuilders on bank credits (i.e., instead relying on their own assets and funds from the shadow economy).
   (b) The real estate market of the Greek economy is not an investment choice but rather a means of assurance against uncertainty, and therefore, it is financed by it own assets. Consequently, the nature of real estate property as a "non-tradable good" that eventually increases its value in a crisis and as a means of supporting personal economic planning is enhanced.

We should also note the dependence of Greek economic activity on domestic demand. The latter feature poses risks in the event of a reduction in public expenditure and increasing taxation.

The Greek financial system, with its four large players (National bank, EFG Eurobank, Alpha bank, Piraeus bank), developed rapidly after the country joined the Eurozone (2001) (Fig. 10.2).

This development was based, to some extent (10% of banks' total assets), on the banks' penetration into the countries of Southeastern Europe, including Turkey.[16] It

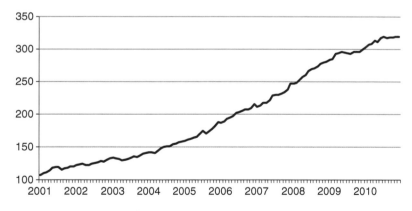

Fig. 10.2 Evolution of financing by Greek banking institutions (in million euros) (Source: Bank of Greece, Statistical Bulletin of Conjuctural Indicators)

---

[16] This percentage varies between 5% in Turkey and 27% in Bulgaria and Albania (OECD, Economic Surveys: Greece, July 2009, page 41.) More precisely, the National Bank of Greece, in February 2009 (Vima 2/22/2009), granted 30% of its financing towards these countries, Alpha bank 13%, Eurobank 26% and Piraeus bank 17.4%.

Table 10.5 Irish and Greek bank institutions' claims in foreign countries (amounts in millions of dollars)

Irish banks' claims		Greek banks' claims	
Country	Amount ($ million)	Country	Amount ($ million)
United Kingdom	272,965	Turkey	20,823
USA	124,199	Romania	18,689
Italy	52,146	Bulgaria	10,358
Germany	46,477	United Kingdom	10,277
Spain	34,539	Cyprus	8,605
Developing countries	41,919	Developing countries	67,042
Offshore centres	20,885	Offshore centres	2,725
Total	738,686	Total	101,177
Total (as % of GDP)	259.2%	Total (as % of GDP)	27.1%

Source: Bank for International Settlements (http://www.bis.org/statistics/consstats.htm)

is estimated that 17% of 2008 profits for these banks were obtained from these countries (OECD, Economic Survey: Greece, July 2009).

As the US, British and other financial institutions invested their assets in "toxic" products, Greek banks expanded their activities in Eastern Europe. The comparison of Ireland (as a country of similar size to Greece but with opposing economic characteristics) with Greece in terms of the claims of its banking system abroad (Table 10.5) is revealing. For an entire year, and even until September 2010, it was widely thought that the Greek banking system had not funded significant off-balance-sheet transactions. However, since June 2010 (coinciding with the entry into the Economic Adjustment Program), credit institutions have begun to follow the International Accounting Standards and have begun to recognise securitised claims in their assets. Therefore, on the Comparative Balance Sheets of financial institutions outside of the Bank of Greece, these accounts are no longer removed from the assets. These amounts total approximately €67 bn, or 25% of the deposits for non-MFIs in the banking system. Liabilities indicate the respective obligations in the item "deposits from non-MFIs of other countries."

However, the development of the 2008 crisis led to the collapse in inter-bank confidence (in Greece and abroad), which ended credit liquidity. As a result, the confidence of enterprises and the broader public in the banking system was negatively affected.

10.4   The Phases of the Crisis over Time

The international economic crisis of 2008 may be divided into three different periods. The first lasted from 2007 and until September 2008. This period began with a new, mild recession cycle in 2007 and lasted until the collapse of Lehman Brothers. The second period began in September 2008 and lasted until November 2009, when the debt crisis in Dubai occurred. During this period, the crisis mainly affected the financial sector of the Southern Eurozone countries. From November

2009 until May 2010, the crisis mutated into a mainly financial crisis. The exchange rate issue played a very important part in this third phase.

In the first two sections of this chapter, we discussed the first and the second phases of the crisis; this section presents the third phase. This third phase started with a "shock" in the money markets due to the fear of collapse of the construction company Dubai World in Dubai, which is an international centre for investments (November 2009). The Emirate economy depended exclusively on financial services, tourism and the real estate market. However, when the credit crisis began, at the end of 2007, the real estate market collapsed (−50% according to Deutsche bank), international tourist flows decreased dramatically, and foreign investments stopped. The Dubai government asked for a 6-month freeze for repaying its loan liabilities as the fall of real estate prices and the international recession had caused an added $59 bn burden for Dubai World (November 2007). The Emirate's total debt was between $80 and $90 bn.[17] The failure of top groups to repay their debts created great anxiety amongst investors worldwide, while the indicators in big markets faced significant pressure. The possibility of bankruptcies in emerging markets began to appear as real possibilities. More specifically, following the news that a very large company was failing to repay its debts, the biggest stock exchanges worldwide recorded the largest daily drop in last months in terms of percentage; however, the biggest losses by comparison were suffered by banks and enterprises with a business or share relation to the Emirates. Additionally, the six main state enterprises of the Emirates were immediately ranked in inferior positions by Standard & Poor's and Moody's, which increased their borrowing costs. Over the next 3 years, these enterprises must repay $50 bn in liabilities, which corresponds to three quarters of the state GDP.

The ensuing debate in the international economic media highlighted the expansion of public debts, which increased due to counter-cyclical policies.

At this time, the European Commission published the Sustainability Report 2009, which marked the intensification of the considerations of the medium-term budget difficulties that the European Union was about to face. Table 10.6, which presents the adverse financial perspectives in the Eurozone, is revealing.

According to Table 10.6, all countries except for Denmark were expected to face serious problems with their public debt, which, according to the forecasts, was expected to increase significantly in the subsequent years. For 2009, public debt exceeded 100% of the GDP both in Greece and in Italy (103.3% and 113%, respectively), and it was expected that the same would happen in Belgium in 2010. From 2020 onwards, forecasts are unfavourable for countries such as Greece, Ireland, Spain, the United Kingdom and France, whose debt is expected to increase dramatically.

---

[17] The company, Nakheel, Dubai World's subsidiary that constructed the famous artificial islands in the form of palm tree leaves, also failed to repay an Islamic bond amounting to $3.5 bn by December 14. Limitless, another construction subsidiary, could not pay another bond amounting to $1.2 bn that was to reach its term in spring.

Table 10.6 Forecasts for public debt evolution in Eurozone countries (as a percentage of GDP)

Countries/years	2008	2009	Forecasts						
			2010	2020	2025	2030	2040	2050	2060
Austria	62.5	70.4	75.2	84.8	97.4	116.7	170.4	245.3	337.8
Belgium	89.6	95.7	100.9	103.1	116.3	137.8	199.0	278.1	372.4
Denmark	33.3	32.5	33.7	12.2	10.3	11.3	17.4	21.3	18.3
Finland	33.4	39.7	45.7	35.5	44.4	61.3	111.1	172.6	248.7
France	68.0	79.7	86.0	122.4	147.4	177.4	250.5	336.5	431.3
Germany	65.9	73.4	78.7	77.7	86.8	102.5	152.1	222.1	318.9
Greece	97.6	103.3	107.9	133.7	160.3	205.9	360.5	596.5	884.0
Ireland	43.2	61.2	79.7	154.7	203.8	260.8	403.8	606.3	848.5
Italy	105.8	113.0	116.1	109.9	109.0	112.2	136.6	173.1	205.9
Netherlands	58.2	57.0	63.1	75.5	93.9	121.0	202.2	312.1	450.3
Portugal	66.4	75.4	81.5	113.6	134.2	156.1	203.9	282.9	389.9
Spain	39.5	50.8	62.3	111.0	144.5	188.2	320.2	528.0	766.6
Sweden	38.0	44.0	47.2	31.4	29.9	32.2	45.7	64.0	93.1
United Kingdom	52.0	68.4	81.7	159.8	212.7	271.3	406.1	559.9	759.2

Source: European Commission, Sustainability Report (2009)

These considerations regarding public financial problems highlight the issue of liquidity in the banking system. The linkage is relatively simple. The Greek banking system used Greek bonds to improve its liquidity. Consequently, their potential downgrading directly affected the liquidity of the banking system.

A debate started at the end of 2009 on the problem of bond evaluation and on the ECB's ability to accept these as guaranties for refinancing banking liquidity.[18]

This was the beginning of an intense period of discussion that addressed the Greek issue and lasted until May 2010.

Figure 10.3 presents a timeline based on the most significant events and with reference to several economic indexes capturing the evolution of the spreads for 10-year Greek bonds compared to German bonds and the euro-dollar exchange rate. The period depicted is referred to as the third phase of the crisis and lasted from December until 9 May 2010. Particular attention should be paid to the increase in the spreads for Greek bonds compared to German bonds and the decrease in the euro-dollar exchange rate during this period.

Just after the Panhellenic Social Party came to power, it announced an income support plan for the economically weaker individuals amounting to approximately

---

[18] This position was completely reversed by an ECB decision (03/05/2010) that suspended "indefinitely" the minimum credit rating required for eligibility for security requirements of the Eurosystem for the cases of marketable securities guaranteed by the Greek government. This means that there was no risk of further downgrading of Greek bonds by international rating agencies and that the increase in performance of Greek bonds over German benchmark bonds was expected to be slowed.

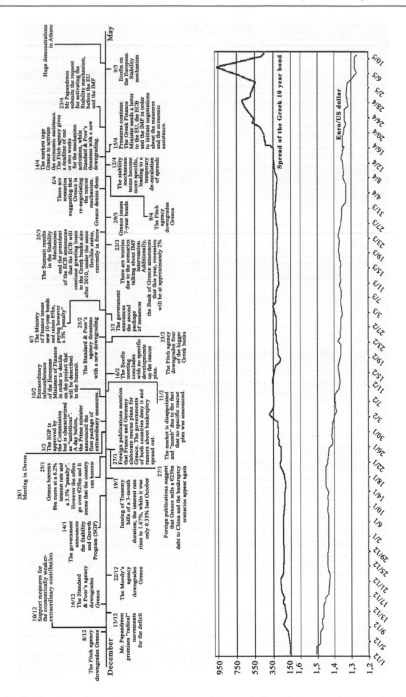

Fig. 10.3 Timeline of developments. Events and the evolution of the spread of Greek 10-year bonds compared with German bonds (base points) and the euro/dollar exchange rate (Sources: Newspaper "Kathimerni" (03/07/2010) and (04/18/2010), newspaper "To Vinna" (03/07/2010), Bloomerg, Naftermporiki)

€1 bn. This plan was in fact financed by an equivalent emergency contribution paid by SAs that were profitable as of early December 2009.

On December 8, 2009, the Fitch rating agency downgraded Greece's credit rating from "A−" to "BBB+"; 8 days later, Standard & Poor's downgraded Greece to the same level, stressing that the measures announced by the Greek government were unlikely to lead to a sustainable decrease in the public debt burden. Interestingly, a day after these announcements, the spreads of the Greek 10-year bonds increased by 25 and 22 base points, respectively. Moreover, the two enterprises confirmed that the rating of the Greek economy remained at a Credit Watch status, with possible negative consequences. They stressed that the government's efforts to reform public finances faced domestic obstacles that could require serious efforts over several years to overcome. Due to the upward revision of forecasts for the general debt of the Greek government and the deficit levels and the estimated cost for serving these liabilities, the credit rating agencies predicted a further decrease from the initial forecast in the Greek public financial flexibility.

On December 22, 2009, Moody's was the third major credit rating agency to downgrade the Greek economy, albeit by only one grade, from A1 to A2. This mild downgrading, which kept the rating two levels above the ratings of other two agencies, meant that Greek bonds would be accepted by the European Central bank. Following this development, the general index of the Athens Stock Exchange recorded an increase of more than 4%, while the spreads of Greek bonds compared to German bonds decreased significantly (eight base points). The A2 rating balanced the very limited liquidity risk faced by the Greek government in the short-, medium- and long-term solvency risks.

On January 14th, 2010, the Minister of Finance presented the Stability and Growth Program (SGP) to the Council of Ministers; that program was subject to approval by the European Commission. The program provided for the return of the Greek economy to positive growth in 2011. 5 days later, the issuing of 3-month Treasury Bills in view of the issuing of bond loans caused serious concern. The reason for the concern was that the issuing interest rate was 1.67%, five times higher than the last such interest rate (0.35%). Indeed, for the first time in a long time, the 3-month Treasury Bills' interest rate was higher than even that of 6-month Treasury Bills. This development led directly to the increase of the spread of Greek bonds by 19.9 base points over German bonds.

On January 25, 2010, there was an oversupply of tenders for 5-year Greek bonds that exceeded €25 bn. This amount is five times higher than the capital originally targeted by the Greek government (the target was €5 bn). As a result of this oversupply, the Greek government finally secured €8 bn, while the pricing of the new issuing reached the lower part of its expected range, close to 6.2%.

On January 27, 2010, the foreign press reported that Greece was selling a debt of €25 bn to China and that Germany and France had started working on rescue plans for Greece. These reports led to rumours about Greece's bankruptcy. The Greek Minister of Finance denied these rumours, and stressed that Greece did not have an "alternative plan" in case the Stability and Growth Program did not achieve the expected results in reducing the budget deficit and restoring investors' confidence.

The increase in the spread of Greek bonds continued, reaching approximately 300 base points.

However, on 28 January 2010, on his way back from the Davos Summit, Prime Minister G. Papandreou inaugurated a period of successive austerity measures.

On February 3, 2010, the European Commission approved the Greek SGP, which included fiscal measures and structural reforms aimed at the drastic and immediate reduction of the fiscal deficit. On the previous day, the Prime Minister had announced the first series of emergency measures. The President of the European Commission, Mr. Barroso stated, "The Commission has processed the plan. The predicted deficit correction is possible, but not without risks. If these risks are not confirmed, due to the timely implementation of the structural measures, then the deficit will indeed decrease. And we believe that this will be the case. The Greek government is determined to take such measures. A successful correction of excessive deficit is important not only for Greece but also for the entire EU". The acceptance of the SGP by the European Commission affected the evolution of the spreads for 10-year Greek bonds, which increased by 41 additional base points, reaching 369 points on the day of the adoption of the SGP.

On February 10, 2010, the Eurozone ministers of Economy and Finance (Ecofin) held an unplanned teleconference to decide on the rescue plan that would be presented to the Summit. They did not decide on a specific plan, which filled the Greek market with pessimism on the following day. However, they decided that their countries would take "decisive and coordinated action" to support Greece. This action would be debated at the Ecofin meeting 5 days later using the IMF's expertise but not its funds. The support package would depend on Greece's commitment to take additional measures to deal with its financial problems. On February 16, the Ecofin meeting ended without any further developments in the rescue plan.

On February 23, 2010, the Fitch credit rating agency, proceeded to downgrade four major Greek banks. Fitch downgraded its ratings of the long-term credit capacities of National bank, Alpha bank, EFG and Piraeus bank from "BBB+" to "BBB" with negative prospects. According to Fitch, the already weakened capital quality and profitability of banks were expected to be under great pressure from the significant public financial adjustments expected in Greece. The profitability of the banks was expected to be affected by the higher financing cost as the markets felt that the risks surrounding the Greek debt had increased. This downgrading caused the 10-year Greek bond spread to increase from 304.9 to 320.4 base points just after its announcement, compared to the German benchmark. Two days later, S&P referred to downside risks to growth that could jeopardise the stability program, which further increased the Greek bond spread. A similar statement was made by Moody's, emphasising that any change in Greece's rating would depend on whether the country could apply the public financial restructuring measures smoothly, consistent with its commitments.

On March 3, 2010, the government announced a second set of emergency measures to raise €4.8 bn (2% of the GDP) to reduce the deficit. On the following day, the Ministry of Finance issued new 10-year bonds, which earned €5 bn. The successful issuing of state bonds created optimism about the management of the country's financial problems and was an indication that the set of new austerity measures announced by the Greek government on the previous day would bring the desired results. As a direct consequence, the Greek bonds spread decreased from 355.1 to 326.1 base points.

On March 22, several rumours suggested that Greece would seek assistance from the IMF; however, the market had shown that this solution was not welcome. If Greece did not receive assistance and did not manage, through borrowing, to reduce Greek bond spreads, suspension of payments would most probably result. Such a development would have dire consequences for stocks and bonds. In fact, the model that Greece was to adopt after the EU Summit of 25 and 26 March seemed to entail a combined solution, with the EU contributing guaranties and the IMF providing loan and technical support. However, the Finance Minister was optimistic about the Summit's decisions, which suggested, at least at that time, that the need to resort to help from the IMF seemed less likely. At the same time, according to a report by the governor of the Bank of Greece, the events of the recent months had confirmed the bleak forecasts and were undermining confidence in the future of the Greek economy. The timely promotion and implementation of structural policy measures was thus of critical importance because the Greek economy was shrinking by 2% in 2010. On March 25, 2010, the EU Summit adopted the stability mechanism, and the ECB president announced that the ECB would continue lending to Greek banks after 2010 through the same flexible scheme. Additionally, the partners stated that if Greece did not manage to get money into the market (even at a high cost), then the member states would, jointly with the IMF, finance the Greek government, but at market interest rates with no "discount." The next day, the spread of Greek bonds stood at approximately 314 base points.

On March 29, the Greek government raised €5 bn from the auction of 7-year bonds at an interest rate of 6%. Total bids amounted to €7 bn; although the auction's success was judged to be mediocre, the fact that Greece, despite its financial problems, managed to raise this amount was encouraging. The spread rose from 313.7 to 323.9 base points.

On April 6, 2010, rumours spread that Greece was renegotiating the rescue mechanism. According to these rumours, after the Summit, the Prime Minister received information from the IMF on possible measures and reforms that would be requested in exchange for the economic support; the measures would be harsh and could cause social and political unrest. Several members of the Council of Ministers were opposed to the contribution of the IMF, opting for a European stability mechanism with no IMF participation, which would be faster and immediately activated if the country officially asked for economic assistance. The Greek government denied these scenarios, and the spread of Greek bonds over the German bonds decreased from 328 to approximately 313 basis points.

On April 12, 2010, after announcing the details of the stability mechanism, it became clear that, at least for the next 12 months, there was no bankruptcy risk for Greece. This development led to a temporary decline of the spreads.

On April 14, 2010, the Greek government began to feel pressure from the markets to proceed with the activation of the economic assistance mechanism. It was thought that this action would ensure the implementation of the announced reforms and would reduce interest rates. The Fitch rating agency that earlier (April 9, 2010) had again downgraded the Greek economy by two levels (from BBB+ to BBB−) estimated that for Greece to avoid failure in the market, it would have to seek assistance from the EU within 1–2 weeks. At the same time, Standard & Poor's was threatening a new downgrading. The following day, under persistent pressure, the Greek Finance Minister sent a letter to the EU, the ECB and the IMF to initiate negotiations for the measures and the economic assistance. This letter was deemed necessary to involve the IMF in the consultations to be held with the European Commission and the European Central Bank. That day, the spread of Greek bonds reached 345.2 points, but from then on, the spread skyrocketed.

On April 23, 2010, as the markets continued to exert pressure on Greece, and following the deficit's revision to 13.7% of GDP, the Greek Prime Minister submitted a request to activate the stability mechanism for the Greek economy to the EU and the IMF. The spread of Greek bonds reached 559.5 base points.

On May 9, 2010, in an emergency meeting in Brussels, the EU-27 Finance Ministers agreed to create a European stability mechanism with the participation of the IMF. These developments marked the beginning of a fourth phase of the international financial crisis. It is telling, however, that a day before the Ecofin conference, the spread of Greek bonds compared with the German benchmark reached the all-time high of 965.2 base points, whereas a day after the conference it decreased to 481.1 base points. This enormous drop of the spread reflected the satisfaction and the sense of security provided to the markets by the conference decisions.

In May, large demonstrations occurred in Athens against the adopted measures, resulting in the deaths of three people. This incident heralded (Wall Street Journal, 27/11/2010) a period of "tolerance" of successive waves of adjustment measures by Greek society.

10.5   Internal Conditions of the Crisis

The internal conditions of the crisis can be better understood when they are distinguished based on their reference sectors. These sectors include the following: (1) the public debt and its maturity; (2) the evolution of the spread, mainly of 10-year bonds; (3) the evolution of derivative prices based on these bonds; and (4) the role of ratings by the three rating agencies. Another critical reference sector was the issue of the financial system and the new public lending.

10.5.1 Public Debt and its Maturity

Figure 10.4 presents details of the maturity dates of the Greek public debt already concluded with 7 year average maturity. In each year, if we add the claims of the budget deficit that are related to the coverage of the current public financial needs (for 2010, these were calculated at approximately €25 bn), a very difficult picture of public financial claims emerges.

The critical issue of the national financial borrowing crisis did not appear suddenly; there were forecasts about its importance from the beginning of 2009.

The following excerpt from the World Economic Outlook Crisis Recovery (IMF, April 2009, p. 23) is enlightening: "Yield spreads and prices on credit default swaps on government securities have moved upward across a range of countries, even as yields on debt issued by major economies such as the United States, Germany, and Japan have declined. In the advanced economies, among the most affected have been those with a large and vulnerable banking sector, whether from excessive leverage (for example, Iceland), exposure to emerging Europe (Austria), or exposure to housing corrections (Ireland, Spain), although concerns over the impact of a prolonged downturn on already weak fiscal positions have also played a part (for example, Greece)."

What changed in the international economy was the perception of the capacity of certain economies to repay their debts.

Table 10.7 shows clearly that the Greek economy may face problems with debt repayment, but other may face problems as well. Similar significant problems are

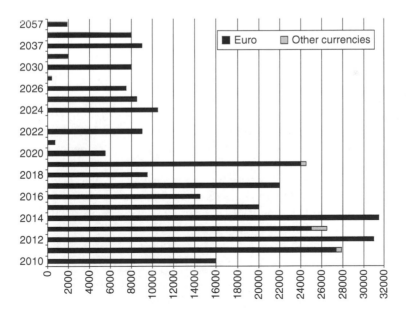

Fig. 10.4 Greek public debt expiry dates (in million euros) (Source: PDMA (Public Dept Management Agency, www.pdma.gr))

Table 10.7 Difference between bond yields on debt (middle maturity) and OECD forecasts on growth for the 2010–2011 period

	GDP %, forecast for 2010 Primary balance of payments	Net debt	Difference between GDP growth and financial cost (%)
Austria	−0.9	42.9	−0.6
Belgium	1.3	85.4	−0.6
Denmark	−1.4	1.6	0.1
Finland	−0.9	−46.4	0.9
France	−3.8	60.7	−0.7
Germany	−1.2	54.7	−0.5
Greece	−4.6	94.6	−3.2
Ireland	−7.0	38.0	−5.1
Italy	2.2	100.8	−1.0
Netherlands	−1.4	36.5	−0.6
Portugal	−2.7	62.6	−2.3
Spain	−4.3	41.6	−3.0
Sweden	−0.3	−13.1	1.5
Switzerland	0.4	11.0	0.5
United Kingdom	−6.7	59.0	−1.5
USA	−7.0	65.2	1.4

Source: The Economist, 13/02/2010

faced by Ireland, Spain and Portugal. More specifically, the governments' capacity to repay their debts depends on the following factors: (a) the size of the debt in relation to the country's GDP; (b) the interest rate of the debt in relation to the economy's growth rate and (c) the size of the primary deficit or surplus in the balance of payments. When the economy's growth rate is smaller than the loan interest rate a country has to repay, this leads directly to an increase in the deficit as a percentage of GDP. The only case that may not exist is when an economy has a primary surplus in the balance of payments that is capable of preventing the public debt from increasing. Yet, even if the primary deficit is zero (i.e., there are no new government loans), the ratio of public debt to GDP may continue to increase (avalanche effect).

Since 2009, a similar phenomenon has existed in the Greek economy. The difference between the interest rate on loans and the rate of change of GDP led to a decrease in the ratio of public debt to GDP by 0.9 percentage points per year on average beginning in 2000. The year 2009 was the first year during which the debt to GDP ratio increased by 4.7 percentage points due to the avalanche effect (Eurobank, 2010).[19] According to the same analysis, if the Greek economy remains

---

[19] Eurobank EFG Economic Research (2010) The Dynamic of Greek public debt and why bankruptcy is not the option, February, V: 9.

in a situation of low growth for a sufficient duration of time, the avalanche effect may assume threatening dimensions.

10.5.2 Spreads

As shown in Fig. 10.3, the evolution of spreads (i.e., the difference between the 10-year Greek bonds and the 10-year German bonds) is perhaps the most sensitive index linked to the developments of the period under consideration.

Several negative developments in Autumn 2009 and Spring 2010 led to massive liquidations of Greek bonds and consequently to a significant increase in yields required by international investors to hold onto these securities. The downgrading of the country's credit rating by foreign rating agencies, the adverse estimates of the growth rate of the Greek economy and the negative context that persisted for months in the international headlines intensified the worries of investors and kept the yields of Greek bonds particularly high. The evolution of the interest rates of Greek bonds indicates that interested investors were not convinced (and speculators were not "scared off") by the potential of the Greek SGP submitted to the European authorities (January 2010) or by the stability mechanism adopted by the EU and the IMF (World Economic Outlook, April 2010). Indicatively, even after the Ecofin agreement to provide support to Greece (and the first set of financial adjustment measures), reports on a possible restructuring of the Greek debt were enough to widen the gap with German bonds once again (May 2010).

Only after the European Commission clarified that it intended to provide assistance to any European country that might need support in a total amount of approximately €750 bn (i.e., at levels similar to the first stability program of the US financial system provided by the G.W. Bush administration) did the yields of Greek state bonds begin to decline.

Possibly, it was not only the political will of European governments that led to the decline of the interest rates. Perhaps the most important contributing factor was the ECB's decision, for the first time in its history, to proceed with purchasing state securities from the secondary market (May 2010).

10.5.3 Credit Default Swaps

The developments in the Credit Default Swaps (CDSs) market at the end of 2009 and the beginning of 2010 also negatively affected the market for Greek state financial instruments. The speculative game in relation to the possible (initial) suspension of payments or (then) to debt restructuring greatly increased demand for credit derivatives on Greek state securities. This development led to a decrease in the value of Greek bonds in the secondary market, rendering the required yields prohibitively high, even for newly issued securities. Essentially, the international markets closed for the Greek loan program, and the EU and IMF stability mechanism was the only option.

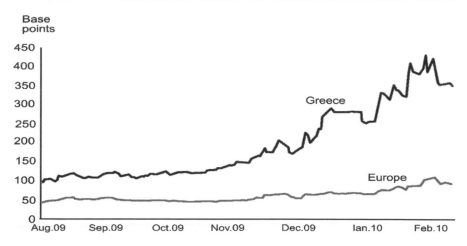

Fig. 10.5 Average insurance costs of Greek and European bonds (Markit iTraxx SovX Western Europe) (Source: Markit Magazine, Issue 7, Spring 2010. Note: The line for Europe represents the index Markit iTraxx SovX Western Europe, calculated by Markit (www.markit.com). It is the primary reference index for these products, and its publication begun in September 2009)

The total amount of transactions in this market manifests the interest of CDSs in Greek state securities. In February 2010, it amounted to €80 bn. This is not a representative amount because it includes intermediate transactions in related products. The "net value" is estimated at €10 bn, whereas the corresponding amount in the beginning of 2009 was approximately €7 bn (Mantikidis, article in newspaper To Vima 02/28/2010).

According to estimates by investment banks published in the International Financial Press,[20] the size of the CDS market on Greek state bonds corresponds to only 8% of the market of the underlying bonds. Consequently, the high spreads were formed by small transactions (in relation to the total negotiable bonds) and could not constitute substantial indications for the true conditions of bankruptcy or declaration of payment suspension by the Greek government.

The bets based on the Greek debt and the single European currency, combined with the raising of the basic stock exchange indexes (and the commodity indexes) led to a sharp increase in the profits of hedge fund managers, which exceeded $25 bn[21] (for 2009).

---

[20] Financial Times: Short view Greek CDS, 02/15/2010, and the digital edition of Reuters news agency.

[21] Among the managers with the higher profits for 2009 are: D. Tepper (with total profits estimated around $4 bn), G. Sorros (with profits around $3.3 bn), J. Simons (with profits of $2.5 bn), J. Paulson (who maintained high positions against the euro and Greek debt, with profits of around $2.3 bn), S. Cohen (estimates place his profits at $1.4 bn) and C. Icahn (with profits of around $1.3 bn).

The derivative products on credit instruments are usually negotiated directly over-the-counter (OTC) and not within organised capital markets. In their simplest form, they are a type of security provided by the protection seller to the protection buyer against any possible negative credit events (for example, bankruptcy, debt rescheduling) affecting the issuer of the underlying security.

Nevertheless, the possibility of buying CDSs for investors who are not exposed to the underlying instruments may cause negative developments in the markets of these instruments. Similar investment strategies allow "bets" in favour of the appearance of negative credit events. Due to the interconnection of this specific market with the market of underlying instruments (through arbitrage investment strategies), the developments in the CDS market affect the prices in the secondary bond market. In turn, these developments directly affect the issuer's capacity to borrow additional funds by issuing new instruments and also mainly, the cost of this borrowing.

10.5.4 The Three Credit Rating Agencies

The 2008 financial crisis and the collapse in the value of securities linked to the American real estate market (even those with the highest possible ranking) was a serious blow to the credibility of the three[22] credit rating agencies.

Nevertheless, the rating of the credit capacity of enterprises as well as sovereigns is still a necessary procedure for the smooth operation of the modern financial system. Current financial instruments are so complicated that rating by expert analysts becomes necessary.

The particularly negative developments in the Greek economy in general, and in the public finances in particular, that began to become apparent in late 2009 led to negative reports and to the downgrading of the country's credit capacity by the credit rating agencies (the development of the credit rating of Greece is shown in Fig. 10.6). The negative developments in the bond market in the spring of 2010 led to an additional downgrading of the credit rating of the Greek state bonds that resulted in even higher yields for Greek bonds.

The adverse consequences of the negative ratings again favoured several arguments about the establishment of a European Agency of Credit Rating that had been proposed in the past.

More specifically, in terms of the European financial system, the positive evaluation of securities constitutes a necessary condition for the acceptance of securities by the European Central Bank and the supply of liquidity to their holders at a low cost. This directly affects the smooth operation of the Greek banking system. The recent levy of the related restriction by the central bank was an equally

---

[22] The companies Standard & Poor's, Moody's and Fitch.

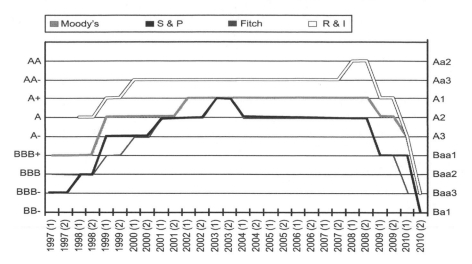

Fig. 10.6 The evolution of credit ratings of the Greek state (Source: PDMA)

important development in the European agreement for the provision of support to the Greek economy (April 2010).

10.5.5 The Problem of the Financial System

As the financial crisis has affected the banking system through pressure on lending to banks, to enhance the liquidity of banks and to limit the extent of the economic suffocation of the market, the state offered a "support package" to the banks. As shown in Table 10.8, it offered guarantees up to €15 bn (by March 2010, €3 bn had already been raised), special bonds (structured finance instruments, international bonds, ETFs) of €8 bn (€4.67 bn had already been raised) and support of €5 bn through the issuance of preference shares by the banks that were bought by the Greek government (which has already bought €3.75 bn).[23]

The provision of the "support package" led to the restoration of the relationship between capital and reserves to total liabilities in April 2009, which had already been affected in April 2008.

This relationship was threatened again in March 2010, and only the evolution of the economic program of liquidation in May 2010 reversed this trend.

---

[23] According to the law, the guarantees and bonds provided entail commissions for the government, while, for preference shares, a 10% yield is foreseen for the government. According to the new provisions, the yields of preference shares are predicted to rise from 10% to a higher percentages that has not yet been defined so that the cost will act as an inhibitor and they will not rest on the support package.

Table 10.8 The state support package to the Greek banks (in million euros) as of March 2009

Financial institution	Preferential shares	Government guarantees	Special instruments
Piraeus bank	–	–	865
Attica bank	100	–	200
Agricultural bank	675	–	807
Alpha bank	940	2,000	1,138
Proton bank	80	–	78
Post bank	225	–	–
EFG Eurobank	950	500	1,025
National bank	350	500	–
Millennium bank	–	–	98
General bank	–	–	158
FBB	50	–	60
Panellinia bank	28	–	41
Aspis bank	–	–	86
Achaiki Cooper. bank	–	–	11
Pankritia Cooper. bank	–	–	50
Total	3,768	3,000	4,617

Source: "Ta Nea" 15/03/2010

Despite the assurances of bank and government agents about the stability of the Greek banking sector, the uncertainty that prevailed from the autumn of 2009 until the activation of the support mechanism of the Greek economy (May 2010) affected the domestic banking system.

The various arguments heard about a possible "bankruptcy" and the possible imposition of "asset and funds-source declarations" for all assets (including deposits) with retrospective effect led to the flight of capital to "safer" destinations abroad. Undoubtedly, this flight of capital was driven by the need of financing the individuals and the enterprises after the crisis (Fig. 10.7).

The mass flight of deposits demonstrated in Fig. 10.8 illustrates the uncertainty that persisted. In the first quarter of 2010, business and household deposits decreased by more than €10 bn, which was equivalent to a size reduction of approximately 5%.

This development occurred in a period where the stability of the banking sector was perhaps tested by the contraction of economic activity. The lower production levels and the subsequent high unemployment rates were expected to further aggravate the already high levels of non-serviced loans. It is not by chance that the IMF predicted the creation of a "fund" at the time the Greek economy stability mechanism was adopted (May 2010) in order to strengthen the domestic financial system if necessary. This would prevent the further shrinking of the credit expansion that occurred with the outbreak of the 2008 crisis, which continued unabated in 2010.

The liquidity of the Greek banking system deteriorated considerably during 2009 and 2010, prompting the European Central Bank to intervene to strengthen it.

Specifically, Fig. 10.9 shows that the ECB strengthened the liquidity of the Greek banking system with €89.8 bn as of March 2010. The liquidity support was

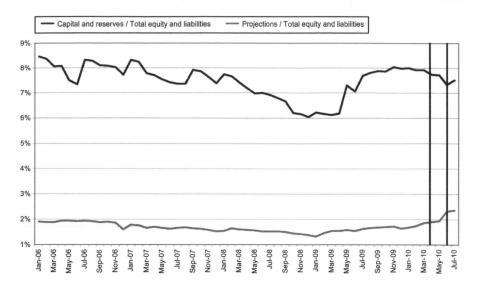

Fig. 10.7 Relationship between the equity, reserves and provisions for doubtful debts to total liabilities (Source: Bank of Greece (balance sheets) 2010)

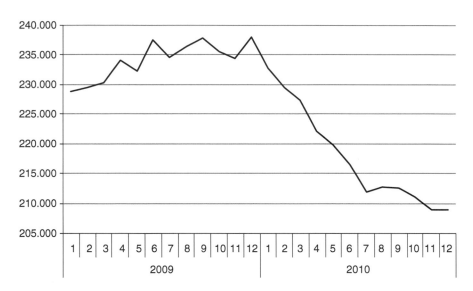

Fig. 10.8 Total amount of business and household deposits at the end of each month (Source: Bank of Greece (2010))

implemented through the pledge of securitisation packages offered by banks to the ECB and the Greek government bonds in their possession. Notably, in January 2010, the Greek government bonds held by banks amounted to €55.7 bn (see Table 12.12, Chap. 13).

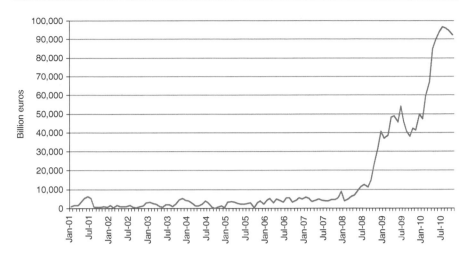

Fig. 10.9 Obligations of Greek credit institutions towards the ECB (Source: Bank of Greece (balance sheets) 2010)

Table 10.9 Issuing of new Greek government securities (October 2009–April 2010) (amounts in million euros)

Auction day	Maturity	Auctioned amount	Bid amount	Subscription index	Acceptable amount	Yield (%)
10/13/2009	26 weeks	800	4,795	5.99	1,280	0.59
10/13/2009	52 weeks	800	3,550	4.44	1,280	0.91
10/20/2009	13 weeks	1,500	7,040	4.69	2,400	0.35
1/12/2010	26 weeks	800	3,894	4.87	1,040	1.38
1/12/2010	52 weeks	800	2,442	3.05	1,040	2.20
1/19/2010	13 weeks	1,200	3,870	3.23	1,585	1.67
2/2/2010	5 years	8,000	25,000	3.13	8000	6.10
3/11/2010	10 years	5,000	16,145	3.23	5,000	6.25
3/29/2010	7 years	5,000	7,000	1.40	5,000	5.90
4/13/2010	26 weeks	600	4,602	7.67	960	4.55
4/13/2010	52 weeks	600	3,925	6.54	960	4.85
Total		25,100	82,263	3.28	28,545	4.47

Source: PDMA
Note: The total yield of new securities derives from the average weighted yield of the individual financial instruments

10.5.6 Public Lending

Table 10.9 presents the new securities issued by the Greek government. Despite the increase in required yields, international investor interest in the Greek debt did not decrease. On the contrary, the high yields in the secondary market attracted several investors, even to the new securities. Interestingly, almost all issues, except 7-year instruments (end of March 2010), were heavily oversubscribed.

Table 10.10   Structure of the Greek public debt ownership

By country (%)		By type of institution (%)	
United Kingdom/Ireland	23	Banks	45
France	11	Institutional Investors	19
Germany/Switzerland/Austria	9	Retirement Funds	14
Italy	6	Capital Management Groups	10
Scandinavian countries	3	Hedge Funds	5
USA	3	Central Banks/Governments	5

Source: Janssen (2010)

Moreover, bids for the issue of Treasury Bills (April 2010) were oversubscribed by more than six times the auctioned amount. However, the particularly high interest rate that accompanied the offered funds may have complicated the coverage of a significant part of the government's loan needs through these securities. Nevertheless, by April 2010, no insurmountable obstacles to national borrowing had been identified.

The biggest part (almost 80%) of the Greek public debt at the end of 2009, approximately €240 bn, was primarily owned by German, French and British banks (Table 10.10). These banks consequently were exposed to significant risk in the event of a crisis in the Greek state.

Interestingly, the international banking system held not only Greek instruments (Fig. 10.8) but also instruments of other problematic countries (Spain, Portugal and Ireland) (Fig. 10.10).

Essentially, the case of Greece could result in a second "Lehman Brothers," but the consequences of bankruptcy would be disastrous not only because the portfolios themselves would suffer the depreciation of Greek bonds but also because the "disease" could be transmitted to the portfolios of the other "problematic" countries (Spain, Portugal and Ireland).

10.6   External Conditions of the Crisis

The external conditions of the Greek crisis from November 2009 until May 2010, when Greece joined the European Stability Mechanism (ESM), are characterised by three components: (a) Germany's attitude, (b) the USA's attitude and economic policies and (c) the results of the international efforts to develop a policy for ensuring economic stability in Europe.

10.6.1 Germany's Role

Germany's role in the developments within the European Union and in the Greek crisis in general may be fully understood if we consider that Germany exported a large part of its funds after the creation of the euro. These funds were transferred

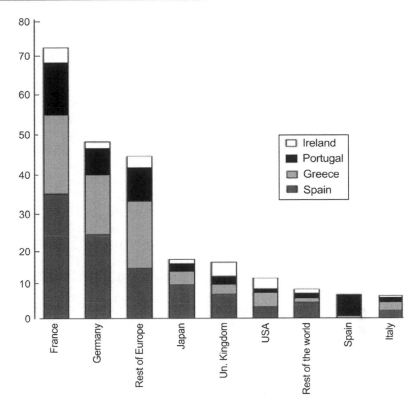

Fig. 10.10 Ownership of public sector claims in Spain, Greece, Portugal and Ireland by foreign banks (in billion euros) (Source: Hans-Werner Sinn (2010))

mainly to the USA but were also transferred to all other Eurozone countries, especially those in Southern Europe (see Fig. 2.2, Chap. 2). They were, of course, derived from exports to those same countries.

This export of capital from the German economy occurred because it was assumed (risk lover) that placements in these areas offered satisfactory yields to holders. However, the export of funds is not necessarily positive for the German people, who, in the opposite case, would have the opportunity either to participate in profit distribution via wage raises or to benefit through an increase in employment. The movement of these funds led to a convergence of interest rates and to the real convergence of several indexes in the European economy.

Elections (on 9 May 2010) in the most populous state of Germany, which occurred 7 months after the German general elections and after 5 years of governance by the centre-right coalition of the Christian Democrats and the Free Democratic party, played a role in the evolution of the crisis that affected the Greek economy through their impact on the policies of Prime Minister A. Merkel.

Germany's attitude changed, showing evidence of introversion. Although the Greek economy experienced pressure through its borrowing costs, the German leadership was initially slow to grasp the magnitude of the crisis, thus effectively intensifying it. The German delay highlighted the responsibility of the Greek factor and subsequently spearheaded the creation of a European mechanism with a strong IMF presence.[24]

Germany's continuous scepticism and objections regarding the creation of a European mechanism in March 2010 theoretically paved the way for the bankruptcy of the Greek economy and for transmitting the Greek problem to the European financial system. Simultaneously, the value of the euro against the dollar steadily decreased, even though the euro was already at its lowest exchange rate with the dollar in the last year. This development largely favoured the highly extroverted German heavy industrial infrastructure; Rhineland in particular now turned towards Russia to supply its production equipment and away from the declining demand of the economically weakened Southern Europe. Therefore, on May 11, 2010, the German Central bank announced that the German current transactions balance had shown a surplus of €18 bn in March 2010, whereas the initial forecast was €12 bn. Of course, at this point we should also consider the increased demand from the rapidly resurgent economies of the USA and China.

Overall, in the Eurozone, the decrease of the euro against the dollar increased exports (seasonally adjusted) in March 2010 by 7.5% in comparison to February, marking the largest increase since January 2008. At the same time, the rate of imported products (energy) also increased, as did the general price levels. However, in a deflationary environment, this does not seem to be the problem for now.[25]

However, the predominance of German exporters' interests was not the only factor responsible for Germany's attitude towards the Eurozone's problems and especially those of the Southern European countries.

During the last decade, the limitation wage increases and the weakening of some aspects of social welfare (e.g., reduction of unemployment benefits) contributed to increasing the competitiveness of the German economy while also creating, through the strong euro, an image of strong purchasing power in the German public opinion. In addition, the high saving behaviour that reached an extraordinary 12% of GDP further expanded the self-financing capacity and the strong surpluses in the current account balance. Therefore, it would not have been at all acceptable if this image had been threatened by the "imprudence" of Southern Europeans, and especially Greeks, who were the focus of the debate.

---

[24] The lack of an efficient response to the crisis from Germany, and essentially the entire EU, reflects an EU institutional weakness that constitutes one of the two basic factors determining the features of the international financial crisis of the 2010s. The second factor is the peculiar institutional structure of the Chinese economy that has resulted in a constantly growing economy with a depreciated currency (Yuan).

[25] However, it should be noted that, "at the end of the day", the reduction of the euro's price against the dollar is a particularly welcome result, especially for the weakest economies.

10.6.2 The Obama Administration's Policy and the US Financial System

The conflict in the US between the Washington political capital represented by the Obama administration and the most aggressive funds of the Wall Street financial capital likely had many indirect consequences for the formation of the global environment around the Greek crisis.

The linkage of the US conflict with the Greek crisis (which came to light in February 2010) took the form of involvement of Goldman Sachs in "hiding" part of the Greek debt by using the (legal, according to the European Standards at the time) method of derivative financial products[26] to overcome the Maastricht terms related to national deficits and to obtain the green light for Greece to join the Eurozone (around 2002). Of course, the achieved debt dissimulation is estimated at around €5.3 bn, which does not dramatically change the image of Greek debt. However, at the time, it was probably particularly important.

In early December 2009, legislation was passed by the US Congress that forced large banks and Wall Street firms to set higher capital reserves. At the same time, an emergency fund ($150 bn) was established to support risky financial operations. Furthermore, the US Congress set some conditions on the management of derivatives. Nevertheless, the problems and calls for regulating the financial markets remained. These can be summarised[27] as follows: the existence of a central authority that would monitor the evolution of systematic risk; the isolation of investment risks from the process of accumulating savings (a return to the oldest rule of separation of financial activities); the existence of lower leverage in the financial institutions; addressing the growing moral risk by imposing severe penalties on capital managers; the "disclosure" of the volume of derivatives (at the end of 2009, according to the International Swaps and Derivatives Association, there were $30.4 tr in credit default swaps outstanding and another $426.8 tr in seasonal derivatives); and changing the bankruptcy rules in the financial sector, especially when bankruptcies are caused by derivative management.

In early May 2010, the Obama administration tried to pass a bill through the Senate that was supposed to address several of the above points (The Washington Times, April 23, 2010). However, with only 41 votes for the bill and 57 against, this legislative initiative was rejected by the Senate (April 26, 2010).

This failure of the U.S. President to pass needed legislation came at a time when a very serious conflict between the United States Securities and Exchange Commission (SEC) and Goldman Sachs was in progress concerning the latter's intentional dissimulation of "important information" to investors in relation to the

---

[26] These are cross-currency swaps, by which the government debt issued in dollars and yen was exchanged in euros for a specific period of time, to return to the initial currencies at a specific date.

[27] Based on journalistic and scientific references.

financial product Abacus[28] of the capital management company Paulson and Co. Victims appear to include the Royal Bank of Scotland, the Dutch ABN AMPO and the German IKB.

In this context, the Obama administration developed a strategy of general settlement and global intervention in capital markets through the IMF (where the US influence is very significant), which came to play an enhanced role in the international crisis as a "last resort band" in the crises of over-indebted states. The reasoning of the Obama administration at an international level reflected its logic guiding the management of the domestic crisis, but also, and mainly, the need to avoid destabilising international transaction relations. In addition, a failure to deal with the European problems could have caused the collapse of the euro and the dollar's revaluation. This situation would have a hugely negative impact for export opportunities in the US.

10.6.3 Creation of Rescue Packages in Europe

Thus, the US (F.T. 11/10/2010), via communication of A. Merkel with Obama and via the meeting of Obama with the Greek Prime Minister G. Papandreou in the US (March 2010), participated in the establishment of a three-party (EU, IMF, ECB) scheme of the European Financial Stability Facility and the European Financial Stability Mechanism.[29]

A rescue mechanism for the Greek economy was also created. All of this consultation resulted in raising €920 bn, of which 23.3% represented Germany's contribution, 17.7% came from France and 27.5% from the IMF (except from France and Germany, with significant US participation). In fact, the IMF (mainly the USA), Germany and France contributed 70% to the Euro rescue package (and for Greece) (Table 10.11).

10.7   The Creation of the ESM and the Entrance of the Greek Economy

The deterioration of the Greek economy in the autumn of 2009 coincided with a change of government, which exacerbated the problem as a result of the political conflict. Additionally, the upwards revision of the debt, the downgrading of the country's credit rating and the revelation of extensive corruption further complicated the situation. The complications also resulted from the strong external

---

[28] Hedge fund that had a dominant role in the Greek bond crisis of March 2010, specifically with the use of credit default swaps subject to Greek bonds.

[29] The decisions were made in the period from 22/04/2010 to 7–9/8/2010 and began 2 days before the spring summit of the IMF, on April 24, 2010, with the participation of ministers and central bankers of the G-7.

Table 10.11 Rescue packages for the Euro and for the Greek economy (in million euros)

	All countries	Germany	France
European financial stability facility	440	147.4	110.7
European financial stability mechanism	60	12	9.7
IMF (euro rescue plan)	250	14.9	12.3
EU (rescue plan for Greece)	80	22.3	16.8
IMF (rescue plan for Greece)	30	1.8	1.5
ECB state bonds purchase (until 30/7/2010)	60	16.4	12.3
Total	920	214.9	163.3

Source: Hans-Werner Sinn, Rescuing Europe (2010)

pressure from the wider international community for immediate cross-sectional measures that required direct implementation and absolute discipline.

The Greek government, in an effort to manage the situation promptly and at the lowest possible social cost, made "responsive" decisions address the adverse public financial evolution in late 2009 in three consecutive phases. The time sequence of the decisions and measures taken is presented in three stages: December 2009, March 2010 and May 2010.

10.7.1 Measures of December 2009 (Stability and Growth Program, SGP)

Three main priority axes determined the measures taken in late 2009: (a) improving the quality of the public finances, (b) ensuring their sustainability and (c) the program of reforms and stability that aimed to improve individual indicators. More specifically, the conclusion resulting from the study of these measures is that they constitute an overall response of the government to the country's economic and general needs, with omissions in particular targeted proposals based on a timetable and assessment of potential and expected results.

The independence of Eurostat, the creation of an Office of State Budget Control and the adoption of fiscal rules for its observance were suggested to take first priority. This initiative provided 3-year spending plans for ministries, mergers, a decrease in employment in the public sector and an improvement of public procurement practices. Moreover, it provided for a tax reform to ensure fairer taxation and the reduction of tax evasion and tax avoidance, increase the efficiency of the tax collection mechanisms, enact anti-corruption measures, enable management of the existing liabilities to the budget and improve compliance.

The following options to improve the sustainability of public finances were suggested: rationalisation of spending, increase in the income base, implementation of policies against evasion of social security contributions and a reduction of health care spending. For the public health reform, the possibilities envisaged included the strengthening of state regulation, the restructuring of public procurements and reinforcement of accountability, attention to money wastage and omissions.

The implementation of the third priority axis (implementation program of the stability program) included assigning priority to the green economy and development through public investments in health, education, research, innovative entrepreneurship and natural resource management. National and European funds were reoriented in this direction. An increase in public investments from 3.9% in 2009 to 5% in 2013 and a revision and efficient implementation of the NSRF 2007–2013 with the acceleration of fund absorption were also agreed upon. Moreover, priority was given to investments in energy saving, tourism and culture and to the promotion of research and development. Moreover, the government prioritised the containment of inflationary pressures, active employment policies, the promotion of entrepreneurship through the acceleration of licensing processes and the simplification of procedures and bureaucracy. The need to improve competitiveness and to provide sufficient liquidity and financing for development (through public-private association, establishment of the Greek Development Fund and enlargement of the Credit Guarantee Fund for Small and Very Small Enterprises (TEMPME), suspension of recruitment in the public sector for 2010, and from 2011, creation of one new employment position for every five new retirements) was highlighted. For education, the proposal was aimed at increasing pupil/student performance at the national and international levels with the concurrent incorporation of information technology. Finally, it provided for ending privatisations of public enterprises that were not related to public goods or to national security and prioritised environmental policies.

10.7.2 March 2010: The Result of Aggressive Market Pressure and the Additional Corrective-Supplementary Decisions of the Greek Government

The additional government measures that were implemented during the second phase focused on a direct revenue increase and spending cuts. These measures were estimated to draw €4.8 bn (2% of GDP) from the budget and were expected to raise an equal amount from revenue and from spending cuts.

The measures relating to revenue growth included the following:

- Increase of the VAT rates from 4.5% to 5%, from 9% to 10% and from 19% to 21% (expected income €1.3 bn).
- Further increase the excise taxes on fuel (except fuel oil), tobacco and alcohol (expected income: €1.1 bn, or 0.45% of GDP).
- Introduction of excise duty for luxury items (such as yachts, precious stones, precious metals and leather).
- Abolishment of tax exemption of the special oil tax for the PPC (Public Power Corporation).
  The overall increase in income was estimated at €2.4 bn (1% of the GDP).
  Spending cuts:
- 30% reductions in the Christmas, Easter and holiday allowances in the public sector.

- 12% reductions in all allowances and compensations in the public sector.
- 7% reductions in incomes, compensations, and allowances subsidised by the government budget; these measures were implemented with no exceptions to all members of the government, the ministries and the parliament.
- The above cuts did not apply to public- or private-sector pensions.
- The financing percentages of the insurance funds of OAP-PPC and TAP-OTE by the state budget were reduced by 10%.
- A 5% reduction (€500 m) in the national part of the Program for Public Investments, which included €100 m from part of the Public Investments of the Ministry of Education, and €100 m from the credits for new programs by the Ministry of Education.

The spending cuts from the additional measures announced on this date that were related to incomes and pensions were equivalent to €1.7 bn (0.7% of the GDP). An additional decrease arising from a reduction in public investments was estimated at €700 m (0.3% of the GDP).

Moreover, all paid committees of the public sector were abolished, and all compensations of collective management entities were cut by 50%. A cap was set on remuneration from the public sector, the use of bonuses for public sector management executives was prohibited and compensation for overtime and transport was reduced. Finally, additional taxation was imposed, on a case-by-case basis, to individuals with high incomes, real estate property with offshore enterprises, and real estate properties of great value; in addition, measures were taken to reduce prescription drug prices and to subsidise insurance contributions, mainly for unemployed youth, to facilitate the job search process.

10.7.3 May 2010: Inclusion in the European Stability Mechanism

Under pressure from its financial problems and the limited liquidity of the Greek financial system (conditions that caused explosive instability situations much bigger than those caused by the financial conditions[30]), on April 24, 2010, the Greek government required the activation of the European Stability Mechanism (ESM).

The measures taken in May 2010 set out three basic priority axes.

(a) Budgetary adjustment.
(b) Competitiveness and development.
(c) Financial system.

The measures for fiscal adjustment in Greece were both corrective and structural and essentially supplemented the decisions made in March in a determinative way

---

[30] It is estimated that when Greece entered the ESM, the liquidity of the Greek banking system provided by the ECB reached €90 bn from approximately €40 bn that it was during the period of the financial crisis.

in terms of their strength and their immediate intervention. The Greek government took the following actions to increase its income:

- Further increases in the VAT from 21% to 23% and from 10% to 11%.
- Further increase in the excise tax on fuel, tobacco and alcohol.
- Taxation of unauthorised buildings and a duty for maintaining semi-outdoor areas.
- Increase in luxury item duties.
- Special tax on very profitable enterprises.
- Moreover, an accounting assessment of incomes was applied, taxes were imposed and licenses were granted for technical and gambling games, the VAT fiscal base was enlarged, green duties were imposed, objective values of real estate properties were increased, and finally, remuneration in kind was also subject to taxation.

In relation to spending, the following actions were taken:

- Replacement of the 13th and 14th wages in the public sector with fixed bonuses at Christmas (€500), at Easter (€250) and at holiday leave (€250) per employee with a wage less than €3,000. For employees with income exceeding €3,000 per month, the 13th and 14th salaries were abolished.
- Further decrease in allowances in the public sector by 8%.
- The 13th and 14th pensions for retired people receiving less than €2,500 were replaced according to the schedule above, while they were abolished for pensions exceeding €2,500 a month.
- Reduction of high pensions.

Moreover, it was decided to further decrease consumption spending, to suspend the payment of solidarity allowances, to reduce public investments, to grant no raises of salaries and pensions during the 3-year period of the programme and to save on resources by implementing the Kallikratis project.

Additionally, the age limit for public-sector pensions rose to 65 years for women, the minimum contribution period increased from 37 to 40 years, premature retirement was limited and the minimum age limit was increased to 60 years. Pensions began to be assessed based on a person's income during his or her entire working life, and the return of contributions in pensions was enhanced.

In addition to measures already taken to stimulate competitiveness and entrepreneurial action, it was also decided to deregulate closed professions and transports, restructure the public railway company (OSE), deregulate the energy sector, attract foreign investments and increase the absorption of resources provided by the EU structural finds.

In terms of the financial system, it was decided to create a Financial Stability Fund (of an amount of €10 bn) and to enhance the monitoring of banks by the Bank of Greece. This monitoring of banks is one of the most critical issues for the entry of the Greek economy into the ESM. The amount of €10 bn is not related to the liquidity guarantee for the Greek banking system but is rather a means to reinforce the capital adequacy and thus the control of banking institutions. Consequently, the road is open for ownership restructuring in the banking sector.

The estimated contribution of the additional measures taken in May 2010 for the public finances concerns the period of 2010–2014 and is calculated as €30 bn, in total (13% of the GDP). This contribution is estimated at €5,800 m for the year 2010, €9,650 m for 2011, €5,575 m for 2012, €4,775 m for 2013 and €4,700 m for 2014.

10.8   The Evolution of Economies: The Unbalanced Recovery and the Global Imbalances

The course of the global economy in the period from November 2009 until May 2010 was characterised by a generic confirmation and in many cases, improvement of the earlier forecasts by global institutions (IMF, World Bank). However, in reality, two main differentiations should be highlighted. The first differentiation is related to the growth rate in the developed economies and in developing countries in Asia. These rates were better than expected, especially given the trade volumes transferred. The second differentiation is related to the emergence of imbalances between the external flow and the internal demand in developed economies, particularly in Europe. This involves the weakness of financial markets, particularly those in Europe (European Economic Forecast – Spring 2010). Essentially, the question remains whether the "repair" of financial accounts is sufficient to support growth. The sector that seems to be the most affected is the labour market. Moreover, the differences within the European Union have grown, widening the gap between North and South. In any case, the EU presents a phase lag in its development because it is foreseen that it will present a growth rate of approximately 1–1.5% for 2010–2011. This rate is much lower than in the rest of the developed world.

However, the growth rates and the other indicators reveal significant variations among economies and groups of countries. These discrepancies in growth rates are mainly identified among developed countries and BRIC countries (Brazil, Russia, India and China), where on one hand, in the developed economies the average growth rate for 2010 and 2011 is ≈2.3%, while on the other hand, in BRIC countries it is between 4% (Russia) and 10% (China) (IMF, World Economic Outlook, April 2010).

It is obvious that if the growth discrepancies in the Greek economy vary at approximately −4% for 2010 and −2% for 2011, Greece's difference from the rest of the world will be very significant. Nevertheless, even discrepancies between developed and developing regions are higher, in favour of the latter.

The global imbalances that dominated the international economic scene during the first months of 2010 have two major, closely-interwoven effects. The first is related to the need to finance budget deficits. The second is related to the movement of global capital flows and the exchange rates.

Globally, the crisis essentially increased the risks linked to national budget deficits as it increased the national budget burdens, which, combined with the low growth rates, worsened the dynamic repayment of debts. This situation increased the destabilisation risk of financial systems, eventually creating short-term funding difficulties (Greece) (Fig. 10.11).

As shown in Fig. 10.9, the interconnections and mutual influences of aggregates move in both directions, dynamically complicating the situation.

Because of the interconnections of the above parameters, the cost of public borrowing developed differently across countries. Figure 10.12 presents the yields of state 10-year bonds on 11/1/2009 and for the next 4 months for Greece in comparison to other countries.

The explosion of government debt, of course, took a heavy toll and exerted too much pressure on the bond funds markets.

These national debts were funded by an apparent increase in international liquidity (from approximately $4,500 bn in 2000 to approximately $9,300 bn in 2009), which after a fall in 2008, returned to their previous condition.

The need for new borrowing in the major economies of the Western world created strong competition to attract capital.

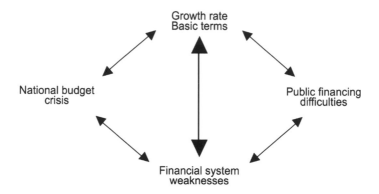

Fig. 10.11   Interaction of basic problems

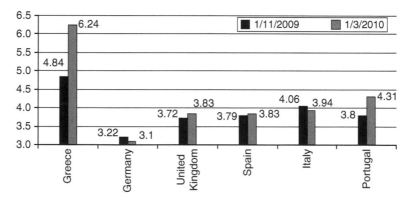

Fig. 10.12   State 10-year bond yields (Source: European Central Bank, www.tradingeconomics. com)

Table 10.12 Net borrowing at a global level (percentages of GDP)

Countries/years	Average 1994–2003	2006	2007	2008	2009	Forecasts		
						2010	2011	2015
Basic developed economies	−3.6	−2.3	−2.1	−4.7	−10.0	−9.5	−7.6	−5.4
EU	−2.7	−1.3	−0.6	−2.0	−6.3	−6.8	−6.1	−4.0
Germany	−2.5	−1.6	0.2	0.0	−3.3	−5.7	−5.1	−1.7
France	−3.3	−2.3	−2.7	−3.4	−7.9	−8.2	−7.0	−4.1
Japan	−6.0	−4.0	−2.4	−4.2	−10.3	−9.8	−9.1	−7.3
United Kingdom	−2.1	−2.6	−2.7	−4.8	−10.9	−11.4	−9.4	−4.3

Source: IMF, World Economic Outlook, April 2010

Table 10.12 shows the evolution of fiscal balances of central government debt in the various countries in the world.

Table 10.10 clearly shows that the budget deficit in key developed economies will most probably increase in 2010 as a result of the global debt crisis, whereas from 2011 until 2015, it is estimated that the problem will gradually decline. The budget deficit in key developed economies is at historically high levels, and the United Kingdom's deficit has also been very high since 2009.

However, the needs for financing national budget deficits in 2010 were not particularly higher than they were in 2009. For the years 2009 and 2010, the net and short-term borrowing in the EU increased by 3.2% and 20.4%, respectively, while the medium-term borrowing decreased by 11.1%.[31]

Meanwhile, the ratio of debt capital concentration within and outside Europe did not change dramatically (Table 10.13).

Furthermore, as we saw earlier, the fundamental characteristics of the economies and their productive orientations have created conditions for an unbalanced recovery, leading the global economy to the expansion of the already existing growth inequalities.

The countries that presented the best performances in this international, dynamic, and changing scenery are still China, Germany and Japan, which presented the highest current account surpluses.

In fact, forced by competition, all economies saw a devaluation of their currencies. However, international pressure for revaluation of the yuan as a method of reducing the competitiveness of Chinese products increased.[32]

The US seeks a stronger dollar to attract international financing but understands that this process reduces their export expectations for the recovery of their economy.

---

[31] Kathimerini, March 2010.

[32] As already noted, the yuan's reevaluation is one of the basic demonstrations of institutional particularity of the Chinese economy, which is also one of the two most important destabilisation factors of the global economy. The other destabilisation factor, as previously mentioned, is the weak institutional organisation within the EU.

Table 10.13 State need for borrowing in 2010 (amounts in billion euros)

	Gross borrowing	Net borrowing	Net borrowing (%)
Austria	30.3	14.3	1.68
Belgium	86.8	16.9	1.98
Denmark	18.3	9.4	1.10
Finland	33	14.2	1.67
France	454	155.5	18.24
Germany	385.8	141.1	16.55
Greece	51.1	24	2.81
Ireland	38.3	19	2.23
Italy	393.5	79.8	9.36
Luxembourg	3.2	2.9	0.34
Netherlands	115.6	37.4	4.39
Portugal	36.9	12.3	1.44
Spain	228.4	108.1	12.68
Sweden	25.1	13.2	1.55
Switzerland	21.3	10.8	1.27
Great Britain	278.5	193.7	22.72
Total	2,200.1	852.6	100.00

Source: Kathimerini, March 2010

In essence, we observe a conflict of interests. The financial sector wants a strong dollar to attract international capital surplus, but the productive sector wants a cheap dollar to increase exports.

Another serious medium- and long-term impact of exchange rate changes is associated with the role of the euro as a reserve currency. It is true that, since its creation, the euro has been particularly favoured by the management of central banks because in their effort to avoid strengthening their own currencies against the euro, they bought dollars that they then converted into euros. It is quite typical that China, with its $2.5 tr reserve, was holding 20–30% of its reserves in euros.

Of course, weakening of the euro would render it less attractive as a reserve currency and would have medium- and long-term financial (i.e., reduction of its value) and political implications.

At this point, it should be noted that this chapter was last updated in May 2010. More recent developments up to December 2010 will be included in Chap. 12.

References

Akerlof G (1970) The market for lemons: quality uncertainty and the market mechanism. Q J Econ 84:488–500

Furceri D, Mourougane A (2009) The effect of financial crises on potential output: new empirical evidence from OECD countries. OECD Econ. Dep. Work. Pap. 699

Hans-Werner Sinn (2010) Rescuing Europe. Cent. for Econ. and Policy Res. Vol. 11.

Janssen R (2010) Greece and the IMF: who exactly is being saved? Cent. for Econ. and Policy Res. 1611, Conn. Ave. NW, Suite 400, Washington.

Laeven L, Valencia F (2008) Systemic banking crises: a new database. IMF Work. Pap. 08/224

Mishkin F (1997) The economics of money, banking and financial markets, 5th edn. Addison-Wesley, England

Reinhart C, Rogoff K (2008) Is the 2007 US sub-prime financial crisis so different? An international historical comparison. Am Econ Rev 98(2):339–344

The Deeper Causes of the Greek Economic and Social Problems

11

The deeper causes of the Greek economic problem should be understood through the features of Greece's long-term economic and social organisation.

The comprehensive study of the Greek social development and political economy highlights five main deeper explanations (Table 11.1) for the Greek economic evolution. The reasons are of primary importance, do not relate to each other (as causes or as causal through common generative causes) and belong to different spheres of human activity. Obviously, we are not looking for long-term causes in the lack of raw materials, the size of the market, or the lack of innovative activity because we consider these factors to be secondary. Several countries had none of the above factors and nonetheless presented systematic and significant growth rates.

The deeper causes of Greece's social and economic problems display several features significantly affecting the permanence and repeatability of the Greek problem.

1. They have a long-term dimension (i.e., they date back to the creation of the Greek state), and in essence, they characterise the existence of the social and economic formation in the Greek territory.
2. They have a general impact on the entire (or almost) spectrum of social and economic activity.
3. They have a significant impact on society and economy in the sense that they are not related to secondary, marginal activities, but instead they enter the core of the economic activity and are related to the bigger part thereof.
4. They are related to the remaining inputs of growth, or the Total Productivity Factor, resulting in the following:
   (a) Determining the effectiveness of the basic growth inputs. As addressed in the next chapter, it should be considered that a significant part of the envisaged future growth is expected to derive from this factor.
   (b) Determining the features of the basic operational economic model. Thus, whereas this model has the basic operational features of a capitalistic system, it actually bears particular qualities that prevent it from having a more flexible response to the economic policy. The financial system case is a typical one: the increasing change in the deposits' interest rate (e.g., during the last crisis) had a smaller effect than the crisis of confidence due to the

Table 11.1 The deeper causes of the Greek economic and social problems

1. Institutional background
1.1 Special features of the cultural background
1.2 Property rights obscurity
1.3 Political institutions and restructuring of economic institutions
2. Common resources (land, environment) as a main source of wealth
3. The moral hazard in the international financial system and the institutional weakness within the EU
4. The long-term choice of expanding the public sector as a means to absorb the excess workforce
5. High levels of systematic risk

"unexpected consequences of the fears for bankruptcy of the economy." As a result, the increase in the deposits and grant interest rates was accompanied by a capital outflow. At the same time, the model generates particular features that are related to capital accumulation and thus the future potential of its operation and expansion.

5. Some dimensions of the deeper causes are also related to the available quantity of the basic growth factors:

    (a) The characteristics of the cultural background have a (negative) impact on nativity and possibly on the need to formulate a productive immigration policy.

    (b) Some features also impact the capital availability as a primary growth factor. Therefore, the long-term choice to maintain high levels of public employment and the existence of high systematic risk (capital cost), as well as the impact of moral hazard on the operation of international capital, are directly related to the offer of capital in the Greek economy.

The primary causes of the Greek economic and social problems are described in this chapter. Section 11.1 presents three special features of the institutional background (11.1.1), the particular features of the cultural background, the obscurity of property rights (11.1.2) and the political institutions as a determining factor for restructuring economic institutions (11.1.3). In Sect. 11.2, it is proven that the main wealth source of the Greek economy derives from common resources that include land and environment. Section 11.3 describes certain external circumstances and, more specifically, the moral hazard in the management of the global financial system and the general features of the overall external economic environment. Section 11.4 presents the long-term social choice to expand the public sector as a means of absorbing the excessive workforce in the Greek economy. Finally, Sect. 11.5 identifies the existence of high systematic risk levels in the Greek society and economy.

11.1 Special Features of the Institutional Background

The institutions in a society and an economy are human constructions that function as rules and restrictions to the formation of human, economic and social behaviour. As a result, they organise the incentive framework for human transactions, regardless of whether the transactions occur at a political, social or economic level. In fact, the institutional framework reduces the uncertainty that is inherent in everyday life, offering a structure for its operation, although this structure is not necessarily effective. Nevertheless, it is obvious that the same transaction is surrounded by different institutional situations in various parts of the world. The background of institutional transactions mostly includes the issue of property rights and the contract terms referring to transactions.

Undoubtedly, capital, labour, technology and institutions are the main factors that generate development and growth in an economy. However, emphasis is often placed on the first group of factors (capital, labour and technology) while ignoring the importance of institutions. This should only happen in situations where the institutional framework, including incentives, would not play a part or would remain stable over time, which is not realistic.

It is thus obvious and well understood, even by the most hesitant neoclassical economists, that institutions play a significant role, especially if we wish to comprehend the long- and short-term performance of economies, drawing typical examples, such as Eastern Europe and China. Currently, the importance of institutional changes has become even more critical because it is acknowledged that in most of the developed world, the process of accumulating basic growth factors has been significantly disrupted. Consequently, institutions remain the most appropriate possible source for new development processes.

Institutional change indicates the existence of a leading factor that can act as the source of change. The leading factor of the change is the person conducting business, i.e., the entrepreneur.[1]

If institutions are the rules of the game in a society (North 1990), then the players are the organisations and people who make the decisions. These players consist of groups of people, such as companies, political parties, banks, or universities. The organisations develop (by investing and remunerating) adequate skills and knowledge to achieve the organisation's objectives (e.g., cost maximising, winning elections, financial intermediary operation), which are considered to be an important incentive for the operation of their model. Therefore, it is obvious that there is a direct correlation between the institutional framework and the skills developed in an economy. If the institutional framework promotes piracy of other people's wealth, then it cultivates skills and knowledge serving this cause, providing incentives for committing such actions and being indifferent to the protection of the intellectual operation. However, if the institutional framework places the emphasis on the development of technological capacities, then it cultivates the potential to produce innovation and protect intellectual rights.

---

[1] In the Greek language, the "entrepreneur" is usually identified as the owner or the manager of a private enterprise. In fact, an entrepreneur is a person generally trying to change an institution. Of course, the entrepreneur-owner of an enterprise (producing products or services) is a sub-group of the ensemble of entrepreneurs.

People transact with each other, and institutions provide the framework for these transactions. They include formal and informal restrictions as well as enforcement procedures. The informal rules include behaviour rules, assumptions and self-restrictions. All of these elements stem from the cultural background of the society. The effectiveness of the enforcement of regulations also defines the relationship between the objectives of the institutions and the ways in which the transactions are conducted. The enforcement of regulations may stem from the disposition of self-restricting one of the two leading factors in the transactions, by the imposition of the will of a second actor (compensatory behaviour), or finally from a third party, such as the state rules. The institutions affect the economic performance of the system, impacting transactions and transaction costs.

Institutional change originates from the opportunities perceived by the entrepreneurs and may be associated with the external environment (technology, change of relative prices, policy and change of preferences), the knowledge and the skills. Usually, a change in the institutions is a mixture of external changes and internal conquest of the relevant knowledge. Consequently, the entrepreneur continually calculates the benefits of maintaining the existing situation and of the changes in the institutional framework. The change process is always gradual and slow. The role of the transactions relates to the fact that every institutional situation has winners and losers. Every change in the situation creates new winners and new losers and is thus accompanied by the creation of opposing forces. In addition, complementarity in the institutions' operations, economies of scope and external economies created from the networks developed, always operate in favour of the existing status and against the new, upcoming situation.

Based on the above analysis, institutions are a dominant source for defining the individuals' incentives in an economy or a society in terms of the economic development and growth, which influences the degree to which these individuals innovate and invest.

In addition, because institutions remain stable for long periods of time, they are responsible for the historic evolution of societies and economies.

Moreover, we observe a particularly close relationship between institutions and cultural background. Both concepts affect human behaviour and human incentives. However, there is a significant difference between these two concepts. Institutions are under the full control of the members of society in that social institutions may also be modified when changing the distribution resources, the constitution, the laws and their policies. On the contrary, cultural background demonstrates a long-term persistence. Perhaps we should accept that education influences the structure of the cultural background to some degree.

However, whereas institutions may be considered to be entities of social balance, this is not the case for cultural background. In this sense, a change in the institutions may also modify the elements of the cultural background.

Acemoglu et al. (2001) proved that institutions have seriously influenced the current performance of economies. In essence, they introduce the question of whether improved institutions favour development or if development helps improve institutions. They concluded that the historic institutions come first and thus influence the economic development.

Historic institutions   ⟶   Economic development

In any case, the perception that the cultural background is the basic determining factor for economic development is not new. Greif (1994) clearly shows that the cultural background and institutions affect each other and also that this mutual influence leads to specific development paths.

Tabellini (Culture and institutions: economic development in the regions of Europe, 2005) discusses the entire issue and attempts to identify the actual relationship between institutions and development: do institutions influence development or does development form the institutions? It shall be noted that this question is particularly difficult to address in practice. Tabellini comes to the conclusion that historic institutions precede economic development, which is formed by introducing the element of cultural background as an intermediate factor.

Historic institutions   ⟶   Cultural background   ⟶   Economic development

Of course, cultural background is an intrinsic phenomenon of economic development, and for this reason, it is very difficult to isolate and quantify its impact independently of the economic result. An approach to the problem is developed through the use of human capital indexes (e.g., literacy rate).

11.1.1 Cultural Background and Its Significance

Cultural background is a determining component of the institutional construction and derives from a basic generator of behaviours and structures: the human mind. The human mind processes information and comprehends situations. However, the information is incomplete, and the capacity of the information process is limited. Thus, there is not one point or level of balance, but multiple ones, if we consider the cost of processing information and the operation of transactions.

The cultural background influences the economic results mainly through two channels. First, it may influence the incentives and desires of individuals to become involved in different employment activities and in the organisation of the markets, and it may influence the desire to accumulate natural and human capital. The second channel concerns the degree of cooperation with and confidence in the economy.

Institutional   ⟶   Rules of   ⟶   Incentives   ⟶   Transactions   ⟶   Economic
framework (Cultural   the game   performance
background)

The cultural dimensions and the social psychological stereotypes that prevail in Greek society have been present for a long time, long before the formation of the Modern Greek state. This does not indicate that the dimensions and stereotypes are immobilised and fixed in time, even though it is generally observed that they have a systematic presence not only in the Greek economy but also in all societies of the world, although not yet those that are defined by national borders. Generally they concern the knowledge structures that connect the past to the present and define the future.

The cultural characteristics of societies reflect psychological and social stereotypes that were created in the distant past and constitute the factors forming institutions and transactions in the present. The cultural values represent stability in the course of time. Different societies and political processes that form the cultural background in every society guide the character of the parties involved. Generally, cultural stereotypes present a great resistance to change and to their redefinition (Johnston 1996).

The long-term nature of social stereotypes that form the cultural background is mainly due to two causes. The first cause relates to the extrinsic nature of powers that define the creation of stereotypes (e.g., climate, environment) (Schwatrz 2009). This view includes references to the external environment (McClelland 1961; Triandis 1995) and the correlation of the natural environment of humans and the external environment through "homeostasis" (Tavassoli 2009). Contrary to this view, there is the opinion that the cultural background is formed by intrinsic (for human culture) processes (Hong 2009; Oyserman and Sorensen 2009). In essence, this view considers the cultural background as an ensemble of "common knowledge" consisting of (a) thinking processes that are taught, (b) constructions of beliefs, behaviours and values, and (c) latent theories on the natural and social world. This is the second reason for the long-term nature of the cultural background. Because cultural background consists of the cultural syndromes that may be considered to be intermediary mental constructions coming from the long past and connecting it with the present (Hong 2009), even if they are intrinsically reproduced, it should be considered to be steadily and extrinsically reproductive until the present.

In Chap. 6, it was demonstrated that in the Greek society, eight social psychological stereotypes prevail. These stereotypes are considered to have noteworthy social and economic reflections on the productive and social environments of the Greek economy and are directly linked to its particularities.

It should be stressed that a noteworthy impact of the prevailing social model is related to the reduction in the population growth rate. It is obvious that the population growth rate changes for economic and realistic reasons. We refer to the level of economic development and its impact on the overall environment, formed by the development thereof (e.g., protection of motherhood, perspectives of the economy), and constitutes a general attitude that exists in developed countries. However, even these purely realistic economic reasons have been incorporated as elements of the Greek cultural background and affect child bearing decisions, which are personal. Therefore, evidently, the prevailing social stereotypes and more specifically, the orientation towards the present, the dominance of uncertainty and the lack of confidence (low social capital), contribute to low birth rates (Table 11.2).

Table 11.2 Hierarchy of prevailing social psychological stereotypes in Greek society

Prevailing stereotypes	Non-prevailing stereotypes
1 Collectivism	Privacy
2 Orientation towards the present	Orientation towards the future
3 Uncertainty prevalence	Risk undertaking and active uncertainty management
4 Non-orientation to performance	Orientation to performance
5 Acceptance of inequalities	Equality pursuit
6 Non-confidence	Confidence
7 Masculinity	Femininity
8 Religious impact neutral to negative	Religious propulsive factors

The analysis in Chap. 6 also demonstrated that the impact of this specific cultural background extends to a series of economic sectors that in general, function in a counter-development way. These sectors lead to insistence on whatever is familiar (even tourism, the most significant extrovert sector of the economy, has an intrinsic demarcation), a lack of willingness to compete and to control, the prevalence of paralysis due to uncertainty and consequently the stress for undertaking risky positions (entrepreneurship) and finally to lower levels of social capital.

The cultural background has a long-term counter-circular development impact or circular counter-development impact. In the prosperity phase of the economy, there are certain "development" aspects of social values. For example, strong family cohesion has the following impact: (a) it reduces the options for the future careers of children's and (b) influences the time constraints on professional decisions. For instance, parents who are medical doctors or lawyers, even though they are aware of the saturation in these fields, influence the perception of these professions to prevent the over-saturation "signals" (unemployment, reduced remunerations) from affecting the choices of younger generations. Additionally, a lack of orientation towards performance contributes to the creation of social organisations that include excessive spending of resources without evaluation. The dominance of uncertainty leads to reductions in the investment spectrum and consequently to the inhibition of innovation. In a recession phase, this social model "creates" defence mechanisms that oppose its modification. Thus, during the current crisis, it is obvious that collectivism and especially intra-group collectivism (family) functions absolutely positively for the reduction in the negative impact created by the crisis, as in the case of unemployment or salary caps. In the very difficult phase of recession, cultural background functions as a "rescue mechanism," providing the model with the possibility to survive and even to become stronger.

From a cultural dimension point of view, a special emphasis is placed on the lack of orientation towards the future in the sense that the equally significant dimensions of (a) collectivism protection, (b) uncertainty avoidance, (c) lack of orientation towards performance and (d) lack of confidence are easily understood.

A special emphasis should be placed on the impact of this cultural background model on Greek society in the existing incentive framework. In Chap. 9, it was determined that when a society is not characterised as oriented to the future (as is the case in the Greek society), there is no organisation of "goals and objectives," and consequently, there is no incentive activation. Thus, the basic framework of human needs remains the only incentive-forming factor; this framework corresponds to more primary development levels, and as a result, development incentives cannot be activated. At the same time, Orthodox Christianity that dominate in the Greek society seems to be moving in the opposite direction from the process of maximising profits, i.e., the necessary motivation needed to activate the growth process.

11.1.2 Property Rights Obscurity

The obscurity around the nature and thus the ownership of property rights is a basic feature of the quality of economic institutions (property rights and contracting conditions). Fundamentally, there is confusion in many sectors of economic activity, either in the material or the immaterial world, as to who is entitled to the property rights on certain assets.

The modern expressions of this phenomenon (see Chap. 7) are numerous and may refer to construction in areas outside of the urban planning and building lines, including intellectual property piracy, constant modification of the tax system or the re-selling of registration licences of public means of transportation.

However, the causes of the obscurity phenomenon's prevalence in the property rights context should not be sought exclusively in terms of economic facts but also in basic cultural characteristics; these characteristics include the prevalence of collectivism stereotypes versus privacy (which, in essence, provides the possibility to every new authority to question the structures of the previous one), the basic features in the nature of transactions within a society (mainly expressed by uncertainty and non-repeatability) and finally, the basic wealth-producing resources, which constitute common resources for the entire economy (see Sect. 11.3).

However, obscurity of rights favours the counter-productive organisation of the formal economic activity and encourages the growth of the shadow economy because most of the transactions related to rights of a similar nature begin in the official economy and end in the parallel economy.

More specifically, it is obvious that when non-specified property rights are at stake in transactions, the operation of both the formal and the shadow economy is affected (Table 11.3). For the formal economy, unclear property rights have as a primary consequence the increased frequency of non-productive economic transactions because the necessity of the procedures is decisive, and consequently, transactions concerning the circulation framework of those rights are equally necessary (e.g., procedures for legalisation, protection, processing). As a result, there is a trend towards developing an economic framework characterised by procedure transactions. This framework is not necessarily oriented towards operational efficiency of the economic system. Subsequently, all attempts to control an economy's operational procedures appear to lead to the control of the economy

Table 11.3 Property rights obscurity

Formal economy	Shadow economy
Increased frequency of non-productive economic transactions	Expansion of transactions in shadow economy
(Procedure vs. efficiency)	Increased frequency of non-productive economic transactions in the shadow economy
Particular non-repetitive transactions	Increase of transactions in the shadow financial system
Uncertainty of transactions	Intellectual property rights circulation and lack of innovative investments
Expansion of corruption	
Avoidance of innovation and of investments in intellectual property	
Lower level of information circulation speed	
Transactions requiring lender-borrower relations in the banking system and not market development based on information circulation (arms' length systems)	

itself and thus to a distribution of the surplus. Thus, instead of developing an economic and social system aimed at creating surpluses, the main economic and social system mainly deals with its operational procedures, and its control constitutes the objective of the social and political system (government, trade unions and pressure groups). The concept of efficiency follows.

However, precisely because of the cloudy nature of intellectual rights, peculiar transactions with very low repeatability are developed. In addition, repeatability would also lead to a better description of property rights that would shed light on their exact nature. Therefore, those performing transactions aim at the non-existence of precise repeatability, and this is usually assisted by the single-sided structure of transactions in a non-rational way (e.g., multiple overlapping laws), *ensuring* the preservation of property rights obscurity.

The above conditions obviously increase uncertainty in transactions, add an uncertainty and risk premium to transactions and, of course, constitute a scheme that favours corruption. Under these circumstances, it is very difficult to discuss consolidating innovation and promoting intellectual property production.

In addition, the information regarding the market operation either does not circulate on purpose among the participants (so that the obscurity in property rights is extended) or encounters structures designed to create obscurity. Therefore, asymmetrical information is both a product and a result of property rights obscurity.

The formation of arm's length financial systems (i.e., systems based on information circulation) is opposed to the circulation of unclear property rights and favours the expansion of banking-type systems having as a main characteristic the relationship between the lender and the borrower.

However, the property rights obscurity mainly favours the shadow economy. The issue of correlating the property rights with the shadow economy is a renowned and theoretically founded view (Torgler and Schneider 2009). The most evident example is, of course, the frequent (and almost always increasing) change in the tax and insurance coefficients resulting in the expansion of the parallel economy. The above is also valid for the additional reason that obscurity is usually based on the existence of "semi-illegal" procedures, markets, etc. that could in no way be part of the formal economy.

It is obvious that under similar circumstances a great deal of the intellectual creation (which is the cornerstone of productive innovation) would trade in the shadow rather than in the official economy. Besides, according to all evidence, this is a way of preserving and managing exclusively (by the holder) the property rights deriving thereof.

11.1.3 Political Institutions as a Defining Factor for Restructuring Economic Institutions

The system of political institutions is the main formatting factor of resource distribution in the economy, which in turn forms the new political and consequently economic institutions in an economy.

The political institutions influence to a great extent the way in which the political system will be organised and the acceptance it will have within the society. The acceptance of political institutions by the majority of the society creates an adequate basis to reduce pressure from different interest groups, intervening both at the creation of a positive investment environment and at income distribution and, by extension, at economic development. Of course, the way public administration is exercised and its efficiency also play a very significant part.

The problem of internal cohesion between political and economic institutions is distinct because the political institutions express the society's balance of forces and consequently influence the distributions of wealth and income.

In the distant past (time 0), there was a certain distribution of resources, a basic cultural background and several basic features in transactions. These formed, in the present time t, the transactions' characteristics, the cultural background, the political institutions and the distribution of resources. These basic situations of the society dispose both a de jure and a de facto political force. Finally, the overall framework formed the economic institutions (property rights and contracting procedures). The political institutions, in turn, shaped and are still shaping the relative prices in the economy and consequently form the operational incentives of its actors (individuals and enterprises). Eventually, the economic performance of the entire system depends on how incentives are formed.

However, the entire system has a dynamic character, and the image of its performance constitutes only one moment in the time evolution. In the next moment, two situations are re-evaluated and restructured: the political institutions of the society and the distribution of resources. Both situations are restructured in period t + 1 to form the new evolution conditions in the society and in the economy.

The political institutions function to sum up or, alternatively, to accumulate individual preferences and conflicts covering the entire society. Different political institutions form different winners and losers and represent different power balances as a result. This leads to the eternal existence of social tension in terms of the formation of institutions. The political institutions comprise the decision-making procedures, including control of the administrators (e.g., governments, administrations), of the representatives, and the election systems.

There are two main issues related to the formation of collective balance choices for political institutions. These are the type and the form of the political institutions and the power of different groups acting in the society. When individuals or groups of individuals act, they form institutions encouraging opinion change in the direction of their preference. The way and the intensity with which political authority is distributed within society depend on political institutions. The comparison between an oligarchy and a democracy is a typical example that clearly and vividly demonstrates the value of this view.

However, the distribution of political power as well as the capacity of forming the institutions is not only shaped by the pressures of the interested parties. It is also formed by the existing technology level, the accumulation of wealth and the income and wealth distributions. For instance, if these issues are related to a rural, an industrial or a post-industrial society (technology) or an oil economy, this knowledge will be particularly important for understanding the type and the nature of institutions to be formed. It should be noted that the social preferences are not only related to the results of political institutions, but they may also be related to the institutions themselves. Therefore, democracy itself, as a political system that expresses society's views, offers benefits to the individual, and most probably, people are not awaiting the results of its operation to decide whether it is desirable.

The major question is why societies do not chose to have the most efficient political institutions and the most effective policies. Three basic answers have been suggested (Acemoglu 2009):

(a) There is an intense social conflict, creating losers and winners.

(b) There is a problem of engaged obligations. In other words, when political decisions are made by those having the authority to do so at a given time, there is a plexus of undertaking obligations formed, which does not remain unchanged in time. Therefore, an important source that introduces distortions in the society's preferences is created because there decisions are continuously based on older schemes of political power.

(c) Those having the political authority consciously form institutions and make political decisions that are far from the optimal resource distribution, favouring or displeasing certain groups of individuals. This happens mainly because a policy of appropriation of incomes of other members of the society is applied, through a conflict with other members of the society.

As also demonstrated in Chap. 8, the political institutions in the Greek economy, at least in the recent period, are characterised by the gap between program declarations and the applied government policy; this gap is bridged through the programmatic conversion of the parties in power. However, the political parties lose their reform capacity. For the Greek economy in particular, we consider that among other problems created (e.g., lack of confidence, devaluation of the political system) the time lag that characterises the (election) order of the political authority in relation to the problems that need to be resolved constitutes a permanent obstacle in the development process.

However, along with the negative impact that stems from the reform weakness of the political system, mainly due to lack of time and quantity coincidence between the political order and the responsibility of implementing the policy, it should be highlighted that the pressure groups also impact the society's adjustment capacity. As discussed in Chap. 8, the strong impact of pressure groups contributes to reducing the society's and the economy's adjustment capacity to external influences.

The impact of pressure groups on the adjustment capacity mainly derives from their influence on the economy's operational systems, affecting principally the cost of transactions. This is why, in the Greek economy as well, although the trade union density in the private sector is rather low, key activity sectors in the operation of the economy are influenced by professional groups exercising pressure (e.g., lawyers, engineers, medical doctors, clergy) and are remarkably effective at controlling developments. The fact that these pressure groups included dynamic elements that, due to ideological restrictions (dominance of post-civil war right-wing parties), could not find a way to the public sector also contributed to the above situation.

In addition, it has been stated (Thomadakis, lecture at Hellenic Open University, 2010) that the adjustment capacity is weakened by over-indebtedness of national economies or their components (e.g., companies, organisations). Thus, the reform and adjustment potential, but also the capacity to manage sudden external shocks in the Greek society, is significantly reduced. Therefore, it is possible to explain the fact that even though the Greek economy is very small in size compared to the global economy and changes in the international economy are significant and rapid, in Greece, those changes encountered much slower adjustment rhythms. The society itself would rather adjust in the context of an external obligation than in the direction of an internally deriving order. It is worth noting that only during the post-war era did Greek history have three periods of serious external supervising: the post-civil war period (1950–1960) of the Marshall plan, the dictatorship period (1967–1974) and the implementation of the Economic Adjustment Program after 2010. It shall be noted that in the 2005–2009 period, another two "supervising" periods by the EU can be identified. Of course, relying on the external factor for determining the evolutions creates many significant possibilities but also entails risks. Every time the adjustment effectiveness is doubtful because it mainly depends on (a) the intentions of the external factor and (b) the quantity and the quality of knowledge the latter has on the Greek reality.

11.2 Common Resources as the Main Source of Wealth

The problems related to the optimal management of natural resources utilised in common by many individuals have not been resolved either theoretically or politically (Ostrom 2002). Two different concepts regarding their management are perceived. According to the first concept, their management should be the responsibility of the state, whereas, according to the second concept, the problem may be resolved by privatising these resources. Nevertheless, it is certain that neither the state nor the market have helped so far to maintain the long-term, efficient use of the natural resources systems.

Ostrom (2002) supports that the considerations on the nature of the common resources management problems originates with Aristotle, who, in his "Politics," observed that if one thinks mainly of his own interest, then he has a minimum concern for common interest.

The tragedy of common resources (Hardin 1968) as a description of environmental degradation is the inevitable result of the fact that many individuals commonly use a scarce resource. This results in destruction, i.e., when every individual looks out for his personal interest in a society that believes in the freedom of common goods.

However, common resources have as their main feature absolute obscurity in terms of the nature of their property rights. To be more precise, the problem is not only related to their exact nature and their owner, but also to the procedure of their contracting. Therefore, it becomes obvious that it is difficult to clarify to whom the fresh air, the sea or the shining sun belongs, and even more difficult to determine how one may obtain (and from whom?) their usage rights.

Given that a society is characterised by an intense presence, first, of the construction sector and second of the tourist industry, its primary production source is the environment. Therefore, it is obvious that it will be influenced by a complicated plexus of relations between property rights and contracting processes. As a result, finally the whole economy will be characterised by a high transaction cost, evident or not. It goes without saying that the confusion in the property rights sector is also intensifying the impact of the parallel economy (e.g., through construction outside of urban planning areas, appropriation of beaches, destruction of the environment, tax evasion).

As also shown in Table 11.4, the participation of the tourist industry in the domestic product is around 7% of the GDP. The construction industry has an equivalent share. If we also consider the indirect contributions of those two industries to the domestic produced product, both sectors of economic activity represent 31% of the GDP, while their contribution to employment is even higher, approaching 37%.

Table 11.4 Direct and indirect contributions of the tourist and construction industries in the GDP (2008)

	Share in the GDP (%)			Share in employment (%)		
	Directly	Indirectly	Total	Directly	Indirectly	Total
Tourism	7	9	16	10	9	20
Construction	7	8	15	8	9	17
Total	14	17	31	18	18	37

Source: Eurostat, Hellenic Chamber of Hotels, "Greek Tourism Exhibition" (2009) and Association of Greek Contracting Companies, "The Greek construction industry" (July 2010)

From the data below it is clear that a great part of the product produced in the Greek economy is linked to common resources. It should be noted that construction includes a significant and unspecified part relating to infrastructure works and not only to housing projects. Nevertheless, even the big infrastructure projects include aspects where issues of property rights obscurity are raised, such as expropriations and undeclared employment.

An interesting extension of the fact that (a) in the Greek state, land ownership has been a basic source of wealth, while at the same time (b) society is surrounded by the cloudy concept of the property rights obscurity is reflected in the way the Greek banking system operates. Just because entrepreneurship on its own could not provide generations of property rights a precise result, the Greek banking system, at least until the early 1990s (but in essence until today), to secure its loan-granting activities requires a mortgage on the owned property. Thus, only those owning real estate property could establish business activity, and as a result, the nature of the quality and the quantity of entrepreneurship in the Greek economy was significantly affected.

11.3   The Moral Hazard in the International Financial System and the Institutional Weakness Within the EU

The fact that elements of external origin are included in the deeper causes of the Greek economic and social problem may perhaps be surprising in the sense that it poses questions on how many external conditions are responsible in a long-term scope for the internal developments of a country. Similar assumptions appear in the concepts of global economic development, from the Lenin concept on the role of Imperialism until the dimension of the relation between Center and Regions by Samir Amin (1973–2010) and from the dimensions of the differences between North and South in European integration.

However, in this book, the reference on extrinsic factors has a whole different meaning. The external factor is responsible for creating an environment that provides the opportunity for permanent pathologic conditions of the Greek economy to be transformed into severe crises incidents. Additionally, it seems that the regularly repeated severe national crises have an individual, negative character of causality in terms of the development conditions of the Greek society. This is mainly due to the fact that these crises present a periodicity of 50–60 years and consequently do not allow for a period of unimpeded development.

The creation of a long-term concept based on the appearance and the evolution of financial crises in the global economy provides an excellent opportunity to place the current crisis in the global evolution concept. Therefore, the real parameters of the current reality may be better assessed.

The studies by Reinhart and Rogoff (2009, 2010) and by the IMF Department of Public Economics (Abbas et al. 2010) provide similar long-term views on the evolution of financial crises. Of course, the question of what characterises a financial crisis is perhaps the most important issue that these studies address.

Here, we will not participate in that discussion, but we will accept the views of the initial researchers. Reinhart and Rogoff discuss these crises as national bankruptcy crises or as situations approaching bankruptcy of a county's external debt that include the government bankruptcy either because of its own debts or because of private-sector budgetary deficits.

According to Reinhart and Rogoff (2008), from 1800 until 2010, there were five such incidents at a global level. The first occurred during the Napoleonic wars. The second comprised the period from the 1820s until the late 1840s, when almost half of the countries in the world could not service their debts (including all Latin American countries). The third incident lasted for two decades and began in the 1870s. The fourth began with the big recession of 1930 and lasted until the early 1950s when, again, almost half of the countries of the world could not repay their debts. The most recent incident included the debt crisis in the emerging economies during the 1980s and 1990s. To these five incidents the 2008–2010 crisis should be added, given that many countries, even developed ones, demonstrated excessive debt symptoms (Island, Greece, Ireland, Portugal, Great Britain and USA). This incident is depicted in Fig. 11.1 with the indication.⊕

According to Bulow and Rogoff (1990), Mauro et al. (2006) and Reinhart and Rogoff (2008), the economic reasons generating these international crises should be sought in global economic factors, such as product prices and capital prices (interest rates), in the basic global economies. The periodic growth of securities in the global economy was accompanied by sheer increases in the monetary values and in capital mobility (Obstfeld and Taylor 2003) that sought ways to investment, even under reduced assurance terms and repayment promises (moral hazard).

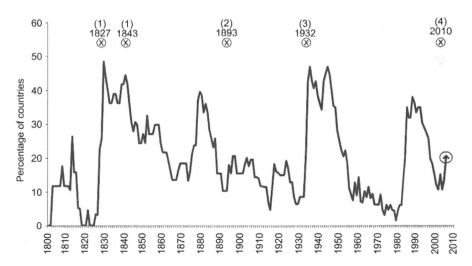

Fig. 11.1 Percentage of countries in a state of bankruptcy or debt restructuring (Source: Reinhart and Rogoff (2008). Note: The analysis includes countries representing 90% of the global GDP)

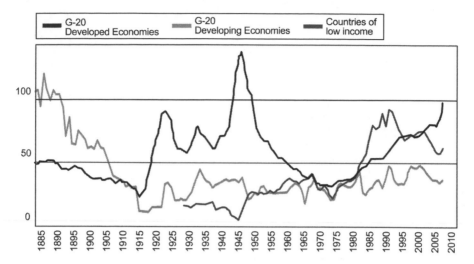

Fig. 11.2 Debt as a percentage of GDP in developed, emerging and low-income countries, 1880–2009 (Source: Abbas et al. (2010))

However, Abbas et al.'s (2010) estimates provide a similar picture, even though the depicting means vary (debt-to-GDP ratio) for different country groups (G-20 developed, G-20 developing economies, countries of low income (Fig. 11.2)).

Reinhart and Rogoff (2008, p.155) have gone a step further: they ascertained that "periods of high mobility in international capital have repeatedly produced international economic banking crises."

In fact, Reinhart and Rogoff's (2010) research on the long-term vision of the financial crises has concluded that there is a repeated sequence of facts relating to the crises:

(a) The private and public debt increase as a primary indication of the upcoming crisis.
(b) The banking crises (domestic and international) make their appearance or accompany financial crises.
(c) Public debt is growing excessively, revealing "hidden, individual public debts" (Fig. 11.3).

In the first incidence of global over-indebtedness, there was no Greek state. However, in the four other incidents of "global over-indebtedness," Greece was present! The relevant years are 1827–1843, 1893, 1932 and 2010 (Table 11.5); perhaps, except for the global over-indebtedness incident of 1990–2000, although even then, the ratio of interest rates to GDP in Greece reached its peak in the post-war era. It should be noted that in 1993, this ratio reached a level higher than the one estimated for 2014, which will be the peak level for Greece's financial obligations under the present circumstances.

The moral hazard inherent in the separation of monetary funds in the global capitalistic system (Sinn 2010) does not acknowledge geographic or national borders. Therefore, the moral hazard also appears in the international fund managers established in the domestic banking system and in the public management positions

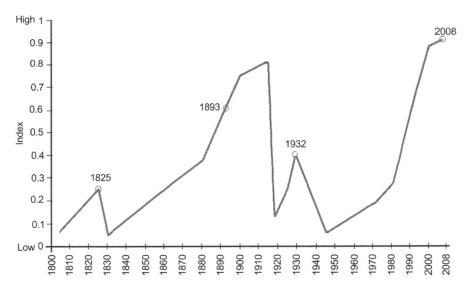

Fig. 11.3   Capital mobility 1800–2007 (Source: Reinhart and Rogoff (2008))

Table 11.5   Bankruptcies of the Greek state

	Year	Cause	Regulation
1.	1827 1843	Impossibility to repay credit amortisation for two loans granted by England of a nominal value of £2.8 m. Interruption in instalment repayment of a syndicated loan of 60 m French francs (for the repayment of the "Independence Loans," buy-out from the Turks of the Attica, Evia and part of the Fthiotida provinces and maintenance of the Bavarian armies)	Battle of Navarino (creation of a state entity with an accountability capacity) – Interruption of credit lines from abroad, turn to internal borrowing for financing the debt
2.	1893	Impossibility to service loans of a total value of 585.4 m gold francs (for servicing old loans, infrastructure development, buy-out of more provinces in Thessaly, financing of the "Cretan Cause" and supplies of war material)	In 1897 placement under International economic control, collection on behalf of the lenders of taxes on monopoly articles (salt, matches, oil), granting of a new loan of 150 m francs in 1898. Levy of the International Economic Control in 1978
3.	1932	Speculative attacks against drachma after the fall of the gold standard, loss of exchange reserves of $3.6 m, declaration of payments standstill (total value of accumulated loans 2,868.1 m gold francs)	Final settlement of all pre-war debts of Greece by Spyros Markezinis in 1952–1953. The final payments of those loans were completed in 1967
4.	2010	Fiscal crisis Financial crisis	European stability mechanism – International monetary fund

Sources: Eurobank Research, V. 9 (9/2/2010)

of the public debt and guaranties of the Greek public sector. In addition, the development of cross-border banking transactions seems to constitute one of the factors that created the complicated situation of control absence in the inter-banking transactions during the last crisis (OECD-Economic Surveys: Euro Area, December 2010). Perhaps it might also constitute a determining factor in shaping the European economic governance system after 2010.

However, as previously mentioned, the regularly repeated major national crises are very much responsible for the economic and social problem itself in Greece. That is, not only do they mark its outbreak, but they also function as a potential cause, establishing an intrinsic relation of cause and causality.

This involves the relation between debt and growth, as discussed and analysed by Reinhart and Rogoff (2010). It seems that when the ratio of debt to GDP exceeds 90%, the average growth rate drops by more than 1%. The main reasons for this situation are related to issues of financing flow operations, budget burdens, reduced budget expenses, and so on. When discussing the specific case of the Greek economy, it is worth mentioning that due to the repeated national crises, the Greek economy has been excluded from the international money markets for decades; the influx of capital resources was restricted.

However, the causes of periodic appearance of problems in the Greek economy do not only include long-term factors. The most recent evolution presents new sources of risk (and, of course, of opportunities as well). The institutional weakness of the EU is perhaps the most serious source of problems. The analysis in Chap. 10 demonstrated that the operation and the decision-making process in the EU played a significant role in the management of the Greek and the European crises. The core of the problem is not related to the differences in competitiveness, productivity etc., which are of course present and play an equally important role; the attention is rather drawn to the deficit of cultural and thus communicational cohesion observed in the EU.

The problem of different languages and mentalities and the issue of differences in the existing cultural stereotypes are sources of consideration. Moreover, when these relate to the management of marginal situations between the interested parties, the communication and coordination issues become much more important.

Nevertheless, we consider that the institutional issue of cultural background cohesion in the EU, along with the paradoxical matter of the relation between the political and economic system in China, are the most important institutional generators of primary and very serious problems in the global economy.

11.4   The Long-Term Social Choice of Expanding the Public Sector as a Means to Absorb the Excessive Workforce

The social choice of expanding the public sector as a means to absorb the excessive workforce is one possibility not applicable in all economies of the world; when this choice is activated although it is not necessarily preserved over the years. We distinguish two applications of this choice. The first is of a pure, counter-cyclical budget nature; that is, every time a Keynesian counter-cyclical policy is about to be implemented, an expansion of the public sector is observed. The second application has more permanent features and is preserved for long periods of time, regardless of the phases of the economic cycle. Its activation usually requires the existence of an adequate cultural background that is mainly characterised by the acceptance of collectivism in all of its expressions. Similar backgrounds are observed in the developed Northern European countries but also in the less economically developed areas, such as some countries of the Southern European region.

The social excuse base for expanding the public sector is to provide employment possibilities to the population of the country, given that the available workforce exceeds the capacities of the demand.

In the Greek economy, the increase in the workforce offer depends on two factors: the evolution of population, which is not necessarily an intrinsic phenomenon (increase of the space territory with addition of new territories), and the evolution of pure immigration movements, which, again, is not necessarily an intrinsic phenomenon (increase of immigrants, legal or not). Nevertheless, the increase of work offered, depending on and relating to the management of public spending, is also linked to the shrinking of the agricultural sector and to the dropping of the number of workers in cities.

The fall of the agricultural sector during the last three decades, the entrance of women into the production process and the replacement of the low-skilled workforce by economic immigrants have created surpluses of the workforce that, during the post-war period, found their professional way through immigration.

However, the return of democracy during the change of the regime in 1974 was accompanied by a promise to society by the political parties, as if they needed to promise something in order to convince people that democracy was better than dictatorship. The promise mainly concerned full-time employment. Fundamentally, the budget deficit appeared just after 1974 and then became uncontrollable (see Fig. 11.4).

This choice is deeply rooted in the society and its political advocates. Even when the 2008–2010 crisis occurred, which was of a purely budgetary nature, the political authorities were not willing to reduce the number of people employed in the public sector. Even though salaries in the Greek economy are rather low (as in the case of Portugal) compared to other countries, salary cut-offs were accepted much more easily from a political and social point of view than the reduction of the number of public servants would have been. In essence, this held the political and social choice of preserving employment in the public sector intact, resulting in (due, of course, to the provoked recession) the generation of rather high unemployment rates in the private sector.

Of course, the increase in public debt in Greece, and in the entire Greek economic history, should not be related only to the objectives of the employment policies. Obviously, wars and international economic crises have played a very significant part. In the Greek economy, however, there are several indications of the fact that the political leadership was using and is still using the public sector to provide employment. There is a typical case of a central square in Athens (Klafthmonos square, which in Greek means "square of crying"); the square

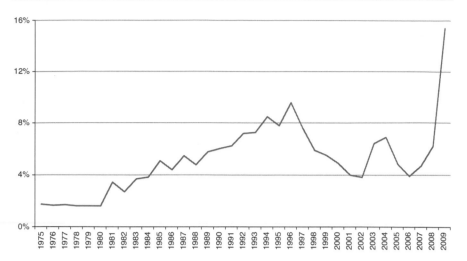

Fig. 11.4 State budget deficit (% of GDP) (Source: Bank of Greece, Monthly Statistical Bulletin (1975–1998), and Statistical Bulletin of Economic Conjuncture. Note: The deficit for the period 1975–1995 has been readjusted based on the available common years (Monthly Statistic Bulletin and Statistical Bulletin of Economic Conjuncture) to avoid differentiations in the way it is calculated)

adopted this popular name in 1878 because the public servants who were fired every time there was a political change would go there and cry. This phenomenon faded after the "urban revolution" of 1909, when it was established that civil servants would hold permanent positions as a modernisation means to restructure and render independent the public administration.

11.5   Systematic Existence of High Risk Levels in the Greek Society and Economy

When, in October 2009, Prof. C. Reinhart (University of Maryland) was asked about the situation of the Greek debt and the perspectives that lie ahead, she replied: "Greece, since its independence in 1830, is in a state of bankruptcy almost 50% of the time. Does this tell you something?".

Obviously, this tells us a lot of things; more specifically, it tells us that the Greek society is constantly under the pressure of a restricted funding capacity for what the society itself perceives as its needs. In fact, the reality is much gloomier. In Chap. 6, it was found that since the early twentieth century (110 years), only the periods 1953–1973 and 2000–2007 could be qualified as periods not subject to intensive inflationary pressures or high risk.

In essence, only one generation (in the existence of the Greek nation), the one born and raised in the 1960s and 1970s, did not experience during its upbringing (the first 15 years of their lives) a serious social or economic turbulence. This conclusion would have a certain value if we assumed that the upbringing of this generation did not bear the marks of the parents' experiences, an assumption that is, of course, implausible. Consequently, the risk as a component of the economic reality is also a component of the personal, social and economic lives of Greeks, from the creation of the Greek state until today.

Fundamentally, the economically active individuals understood that the society's survival terms were opposed to its development terms.

In addition, due to the existence of high risk levels, in Chap. 6 it was ascertained that the economically active individuals avoid engagement with investments requiring significant funds. This results in the prevalence of the model small and medium traditional enterprises, leading to: (a) absence of innovation in the business activities, (b) prevalence of a small peak (in size) business activity and (c) prevalence, from time to time, of conditions of "banking liquidity panic" (years 1931, 1991, 2009–2010).

In conclusion, it shall be noted that the regular existence of systematic risk levels within a society, and especially in the Greek society, also influences other sectors, such as foreign policy and economic relations (Fey and Ramsay 2010). These influences generally result in the failure to achieve balance in external relations or in the fixation on low balance levels. Similar developments impact the availability of economic resources in all economies and, of course, in the Greek economy as well.

References

Abbas A, Belhocine N, ElGanainy A, Horton M (2010) A historical public debt database. Int. Monetary Fund, IMF Work. Pap. 10/245

Acemoglu D (2009) Introduction to modern economic growth. Princeton University Press, Princeton

Acemoglu D, Johnson S, Robinson J (2001) The colonial origins of comparative development. Am Econ Rev 91:1369–1401

Bulow J, Rogoff K (1990) Cleaning up third – world debt without getting taken to the cleaners. J Econ Perspect 4:31–42

Fey M, Ramsay KW (2010) Uncertainty and incentives in crisis bargaining games. Am J Polit Sci. 55(1): 149–169

Greif A (1994) Cultural beliefs and the organization of society: a historical and theoretical reflection on collectivist and individualist societies. J Polit Econ 102:912–950

Hardin G (1968) The tragedy of the commons. J Sci 162:1243–1248

Hong Y (2009) A dynamic constructivist approach to culture: moving from describing culture to explaining culture. In: Wyer RS, Chiu C, Hong Y (eds) Understanding culture: theory, research and application. Psychology Press, New York

Johnston L (1996) Resisting change: information-seeking and stereotype change. Eur J Soc Psychol 26:799–825

Mauro P, Nathan S, Yishay Y (2006) Emerging markets and financial globalization: sovereign bond spreads in 1870–1913 and today. Oxford University Press, London

McClelland DC (1961) The achieving society. Van Nostrand, New Jersey

North D (1990) Institutions, institutional change and economic performance. Cambridge University Press, Cambridge

Obstfeld M, Taylor AM (2003) Globalization and capital markets. In: Bordo M, Taylor AM, Williamson J (eds) Globalization in historical perspective. University of Chicago Press, Chicago, pp 121–190

Ostrom E (2002) Policy analysis in the future of good societies. PEGS: Good Soc 11(1)

Oyserman D, Sorensen N (2009) Understanding cultural syndrome effects on what and how we think: a situated cognition model. In: Wyer RS, Chiu C, Hong Y (eds) Understanding culture: theory, research and application. Psychology Press, New York, pp 25–52

Reinhart C, Rogoff K (2008) Is the 2007 US sub-prime financial crisis so different? an international historical comparison. Am Econ Rev 98(2):339–344

Reinhart C, Rogoff K (2009) This time is different: eight centuries of financial folly. Princeton University Press, USA

Reinhart C, Rogoff K (2010) From financial crash to debt crisis. Univ. of Maryland, NBER and CEPR

Schwatrz SH (2009) Culture matters: national value cultures, sources and consequences. In: Wyer RS, Chiu C, Hong Y (eds) Understanding culture: theory, research and application. Taylor and Francis group, New York, pp 127–150

Sinn HW (2010) Rescuing Europe. Forum, Special Issue, CESifo, Munich.

Tavassoli TN (2009) Climate, psychological homeostasis and individual behaviours across cultures. In: Wyer RS, Chiu C, Hong Y (eds) Understanding culture: theory, research and application. Psychology Press, New York, pp 211–222

Torgler B, Schneider F (2009) The impact of tax morale and institutional quality on the shadow economy. J Econ Psychol 30(2):228–245

Triandis HC (1995) Individualism and collectivism. Westview Press, Boulder

The Greek Economy and the Crisis

12

The Greek economy was integrated into the Economic Adjustment Program (EAP) in May 2010 (see Chap. 10). The way in which the Greek economy entered the period after May 2010, was determined by the integration of the economy into the EAP itself and the medium-to-long term impact of this integration, whose implications extend across both economic and social structures.

Thus, the first section of this chapter discusses the way in which the crisis was felt in society, namely, the social perception of the crisis (Sect. 12.1). Section 12.2 presents the medium-term perspective of the international and European economies. Section 12.3 presents the classic market model, which was based on the working assumption of the EAP, the features of the peculiar market model (the Greek case) and the peculiar market model in a crisis. Section 12.4 discusses the logic of the actions to convert the peculiar market model, the role of politics in that decision and the impact on income distribution. Finally, Sect. 12.5 links the EAP with cultural background, incentives, and social and venture capital.

12.1 The Social Perception of the Crisis

Throughout the book, we have highlighted the important role of social perceptions of economic developments, primarily because these perceptions relate to the following: (a) the transactional conditions by degree of uncertainty, (b) the cost of capital through the risk premium, (c) the desired form of involvement of investments, (d) human motivations associated with many activities, and (e) the relations of the public and the state regarding economic growth and other issues.

By definition, the implementation of the EAP aimed to restore confidence. This confidence relates to: (a) the relations of individuals with each other and with banks, businesses, and the state, (b) intermediary relations, such as the relationship between banks at the domestic and international levels and the relationship between banks and business and (c) the relations between service agencies (especially the Greek Statistical Office and Eurostat).

P. Petrakis, *The Greek Economy and the Crisis*,
DOI 10.1007/978-3-642-21175-1_12, © Springer-Verlag Berlin Heidelberg 2012

In this section, we will see how the Greek society perceived the crisis, evaluating its attitude towards the reforms of the EAP.

We investigate two main issues concerning the acceptance of reforms introduced by the EAP and the question of the perception of "economic developments." In fact, more or less important reforms are currently being implemented in all European countries. Table 12.1 presents the views of Greek society and the Eurozone in general (16 countries) on the outcome of reforms in various fields of application.

Table 12.1 shows that the public sees labour market and insurance system reforms as negative. Conversely, health system and product market reforms are viewed positively. In other sectors, the public feeling is ambivalent.

In total (all sectors combined), reforms in the Greek economy are deemed marginally positive (Fig. 12.1). A similar situation is seen in the Netherlands, and by far the most positive attitudes are observed in Finland. However, in other Mediterranean countries, societies believe that the reforms will have a negative effect.

Europeans (September 2010) clearly believe that 2010 would mark a serious decline in the income of their households. Figure 12.2 is revealing. Based on this figure it is evident that approximately 66% of Greek households expect that their income will decrease in 2010. This number is double that of other countries.

Table 12.1 Evaluation of reform results by implementation sector

Sectors	Rather negative result (%)		Rather positive result (%)	
	Eurozone	Greece	Eurozone	Greece
Labour market	40	57	35	25
Health system	38	32	26	44
Insurance system	41	63	24	25
Product markets	30	31	39	59
Taxation	41	44	30	47
Education system	38	34	25	32
General reforms	27	34	37	43

Source: Flash Eurobarometer, December 2010

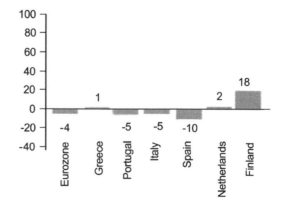

Fig. 12.1 Overall assessment of attitudes and perceptions about reforms (Source: Flash Eurobarometer, December 2010)

Fig. 12.2 Expectations on household income for the same year (Source: Flash Eurobarometer (December 2010))

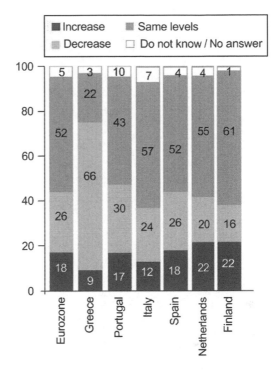

Fig. 12.3 Expectations of the financial situations for households over the next 12 months (Source: Flash Eurobarometer (June 2010))

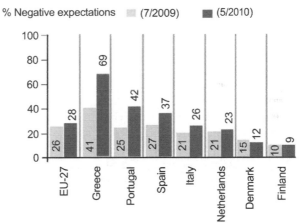

The most serious indication of the perception of changing economic conditions is recorded in the changing perceptions of citizens about the financial situation of households over the next 12 months (after May 2010). This rapid deterioration is observed from March 2010 onwards (Fig. 12.3).

However, the fear of the future is seen more clearly when people are asked whether they believe that their income in old age will be sufficient for a decent life.

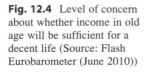

Fig. 12.4 Level of concern about whether income in old age will be sufficient for a decent life (Source: Flash Eurobarometer (June 2010))

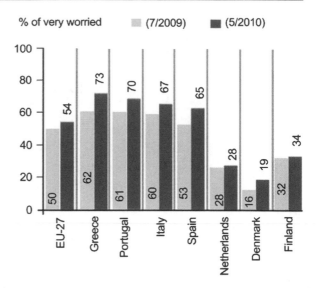

We note that doubt about the future, which has been a traditional feature of Greece and Portugal, is now also particularly pronounced in other countries (Fig. 12.4).

Greeks' general concerns about the future have been incorporated into their perceptions about the "probability of bankruptcy" of the Greek state. Specifically, 50% of the Greek society (KAPA Research – November 2010) considers an eventual bankruptcy likely and 39% unlikely.

This evolution in perceptions of the future resulted in the collapse of national self-esteem. Answers to the question "How do you imagine Greece after 10 or 20 years?" (KAPA Research), submitted in December 2001 and again in December 2010, is revealing (Fig. 12.5).

The findings of this analysis have led us to some observations:

1. As we have seen in previous chapters (Chaps. 4 and 5), Greek society has always been plagued by a major problem of increased pessimism and fear for the future. According to all indications, these attitudes have grown significantly.
2. Greek society is convinced that certain reforms are required, particularly those related to the products market. Furthermore, some other very important reforms, such as those in taxation, are largely acceptable.

12.2 The Medium-Term Perspective in the International and European Economy

Over the past two centuries, especially in the second half of the twentieth century, the world economy has grown exponentially. This development was interrupted by the deep recession of 1930. The reorganisation of certain agencies in the 1950s (the General Agreement on Tariffs and Trade, the predecessor of the World Trade

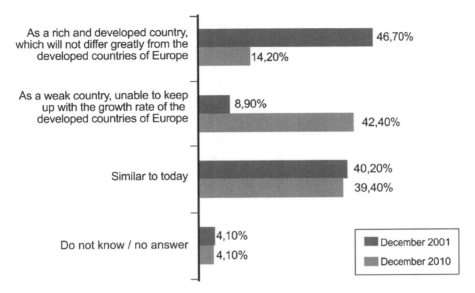

Fig. 12.5 Expectations on the economic situation of Greece in the next 10 or 20 years (Source: Survey by KAPA research: What do Greeks expect of the future and what do they think about the consequences of economic crisis?)

Organisation; the International Monetary Fund; the World Bank and the United Nations) shaped the global institutional framework. Globalisation accelerated with the assistance of a changing legal framework (isolation of tariffs and relaxation of regulations on the movement of capital) and changes in technology (reduced transport costs and the facilitation of communication).

Globalisation has broadened the possibilities for the transfer of technology and expertise to less developed regions, which can assimilate these faster than they are recycled in their countries of origin. Thus, less developed regions are approaching wealthier areas, whereas, in contrast, income disparities within and between states grow (Fig. 12.6).

The long history of global development has shown that the global economy has been marked by periods of scarcity and periods of abundance. The period 1975–2005 was a period of relative abundance. Global development was supported by relatively cheap and accessible energy, and the global financial system provided cheap and abundant credit. The role of the state declined. The period of abundance ended in 2005–2010. Thus, interbank transactions and credit to the business sector shrunk due to the tightening of funding criteria.

By all indications, the period 2010–2050 will be noted by shortages of all resources. First and worst, of course, is the crisis of confidence (financial and business) which resulted from the 2008 crisis. The resurgence of the state in the financial system only partially corrected this problem. The second decade (2010–2020) of the twenty-first century will be marked by international efforts to

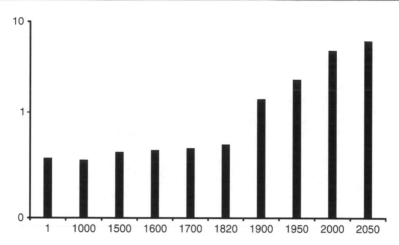

Fig. 12.6 The evolution of global per capita GDP over the last 2000 years (Source: For the years until 2020, commission on growth and development (2008), the world bank. Note: For the year 2050, estimate)

restore confidence and thus to recover the fragile flow of credit. Therefore, the key feature of this period will be the shortage of credit (capital "indigence").

However, as the financial system is gradually restored (by 2020), the world will begin to face the implications of increasing demand for commodities, mainly due to population growth. The increase in demand (which can be calculated as approximately at 1/3 above current levels) will concern both industrial raw materials and food and will have an initially upward effect on the prices and availability of food. According to an announcement of the UN's Food and Agriculture Organisation (FAO) (05/01/2011), the International Food Index prepared by the agency reached a record high in December 2010. These trends are expected to emerge more strongly in 2030.

Of course, these trends will be reflected mainly in the technology sector, which will strive to develop the efficiency of input use, spearheaded by environmental (green) development.

The shortage period (until approximately 2050) will give way to a new period of abundance based on completely different principles, especially in terms of the operation of the economic and social system (changes in technology, aiming for the abundance of energy resources and change in the operation of the economy).

The period of resource scarcity will be reflected in the growth rates of economies as well as in per capita product, whose development is expected, in general, to be lower than in previous decades. This scarcity of resources will mainly manifest through the available quantities of capital. Curiously, but not inexplicably (as compared to the rest of the world), the European economy will also suffer from a deficit of its available workforce.

To gain a clearer picture of the future, however, we should make some explicit working assumptions concerning the key factors of growth, in particular capital

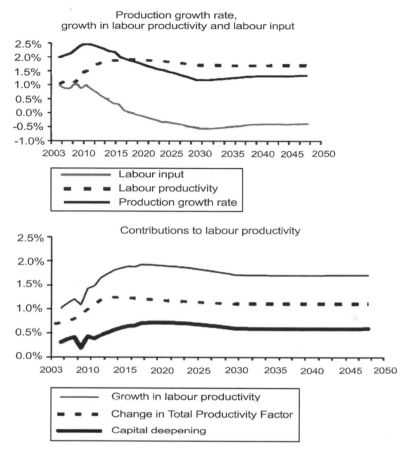

Fig. 12.7 Change in productivity and labour productivity in the EU-15 (projections) (Source: Carone et al. (2006))

deepening, the availability of labour (population capable of labour and labour participation rates) and, finally, the Total Productivity Factor (Carone et al. 2006). Estimates on the evolution of these factors for the EU-15 are shown in Fig. 12.7.

The main feature of the above projections is the confirmation of the trends shown in Fig. 12.7. More specifically, they confirm the following:

1. The contribution of the labour factor will decrease over time, though labour productivity will increase.
2. The growth rate of production will decrease, thus becoming a major economic policy issue.
3. The change in labour productivity will derive mainly from the Total Productivity Factor and less from capital deepening.

To these trends we should add a purely intra-European territorial issue: the differences between Northern and Southern countries. Essentially, the landscape of structural imbalances within the European Union assumes the following form:

1. In Northern Europe, labour markets require structural changes, whereas they present a shortage of labour supply.
2. Labour productivity, especially in southern countries, requires an improvement, which obviously can derive either through structural changes or through investments (capital deepening).

The issue of population dynamics deserves closer attention. Indeed, the question raised concerns about the evolution of the working population. Overall, the trend is towards a reduction of population in developed countries. However, the main problem observed is the reduction of the working population in some countries, which is expected to become particularly severe. Additionally, there are countries where the demographic problem is already evident. Interestingly, if growth in Japan for 1990–2008 is isolated from demographic trends (Ward 2011), we find that its performance is not so bad over this "lost" period.

Demographic trends are thus expected to play an important role. Table 12.2, which shows the estimated average annual change in the labour population of various developed countries by 2050, is enlightening.

Referring to medium-term projections until 2050, we note that the crisis of 2008–2010 does not drastically change the medium-term picture of growth rates because according to all realisation estimates (reported in the present chapter as forecasts), the crisis will cause a potential output decrease of about 3% (OECD – Economic Outlook, 2010), which will affect future growth rates.

Thus, according to more recent estimates (Roeger and Jan in't Velt 2010), the medium-term picture until 2050 remains the same, marked by decreased growth rates (Table 12.3).

The medium-to-long term perspective also encounters two other issues: the development of significant points of tension across the world and the shaping of the European Support Mechanism (ESM). This section will conclude with a short-term analysis of developments in the monetary war because its results relate directly to the Greek economy.

The creation of the ESM is part of a relatively organised policy of the European Commission (EC, 12/1/2011) in effect until 2020 12/1/2011 and described by the following points:

1. Basic conditions for growth:
   (a) Application of strict fiscal consolidation.
   (b) Correction of macroeconomic imbalances.
   (c) Ensuring the stability of the financial sector.
2. Mobilisation of labour markets, creation of employment opportunities:
   (a) Improving incentives to work.
   (b) Reform of pension systems.
   (c) Return of the unemployed to the labour market.
   (d) Balancing flexibility and security.

Table 12.2 Projected average change in the labour population

	2010–2020 (%)	2020–2030 (%)	2030–2040 (%)	2040–2050 (%)
Egypt	1.9	1.6	1.1	0.5
Australia	0.6	0.4	0.4	0.4
Austria	0.0	−0.6	−0.6	−0.3
Belgium	−0.1	−0.3	−0.2	0.0
Brazil	1.1	0.2	−0.2	−0.7
France	−0.1	−0.1	−0.2	0.0
Germany	−0.4	−1.1	−1.0	−0.7
Denmark	−0.2	−0.3	−0.4	0.2
Greece	−0.2	−0.4	−0.8	−0.8
UK	0.2	0.1	0.2	0.3
USA	0.5	0.3	0.4	0.3
Japan	−0.9	−0.7	−1.4	−1.2%
India	1.7	1.2	0.7	0.1
Indonesia	1.3	0.6	0.0	−0.2
Ireland	0.9	0.9	0.2	−0.1
Spain	0.4	−0.1	−0.7	−0.7
Italy	−0.2	−0.6	−1.1	−0.6
China	0.2	−0.1	−0.7	−0.5
Malaysia	1.7	1.1	0.7	0.2
Mexico	1.2	0.5	−0.3	−0.5
Norway	0.4	0.2	0.1	0.3
Netherlands	−0.2	−0.5	−0.4	0.1
Poland	−0.8	−0.7	−0.7	1.5
Russia	−0.9	−0.8	−0.6	−1.1
Sweden	−0.1	0.1	0.1	0.2
Turkey	1.4	0.7	0.2	−0.2
Finland	−0.5	−0.3	0.0	−0.2

Source: Ward (2011)

3. Acceleration of development:
   (a) Realising the potential of the single market.
   (b) Attracting private capital to finance growth.
   (c) Cost-efficient access to energy.

However, the application of this fiscal consolidation is closely interrelated with the implementation of growth policies, as the target variable is the relationship between GDP and public debt. It is significant that the return to the traditional conditions of Stability Pacts (annual reduction of primary deficit in the EU member countries by 0.5% of GDP) is no longer enough (Scenario 2, Fig. 12.8) and a further reduction by 1% is required (Scenario 3, Fig. 12.8). This European policy framework has been heavily criticised by several analysts (J. Stiglitz, 2/2/2011) on the basis that austerity in the Eurozone is a "disastrous experiment, which, if not leading to double dip, will clearly lead to slower growth."

Table 12.3 Annual change rate of potential GDP and potential GDP per capita for the EU-15

EU-15	Potential GDP – annual GDP change (%)			Potential per capita GDP – annual change (%)	Hourly labour productivity (potential)			Per capita labour input (hours) (potential)			Percentage of working age population (%)
Potential development	Total	Total population change	Per capita growth	Total	Total (in pps per hour worked)	Total productivity factor	Capital intensity (in pps per hour worked)	Total (average annual number of hours per capita)	Average annual number of hours per worker	Employment index	
1991–2000	2.2	0.3	1.9	1.9	1.9	1.3	0.6	0.0	-0.4	0.5	0.0
2001–2005	2.1	0.6	1.5	1.5	1.4	0.9	0.5	0.1	-0.4	0.6	-0.1
2006–2010	1.4	0.5	0.9	0.9	1.2	0.6	0.6	-0.3	-0.3	0.1	-0.1
2011–2015	1.1	0.2	0.8	0.8	1.3	0.7	0.6	-0.4	-0.1	0.0	-0.3
2016–2020	1.4	0.2	1.2	1.2	1.3	0.7	0.6	-0.1	0.0	0.3	-0.3
2011–2020	1.2	0.2	1.0	1.0	1.3	0.7	0.6	-0.3	0.0	0.1	-0.3

Source: Roeger and Jan in't Velt (2010)

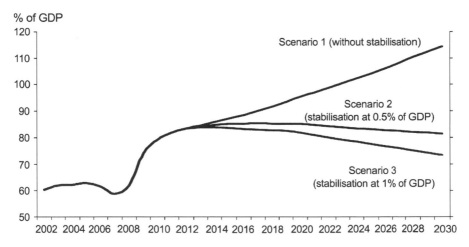

% of GDP

Fig. 12.8 Projected trends in EU public debt (Source: EC, 12.1.2011 (Annual Growth Survey))

Any conflicts at these points of tension across the world can reverse the medium-to-long term prospects for future growth. However, for the consequences of a conflict to be felt in the long-run, it must be very serious, which is rather unlikely.

The global points of tension that show a tendency for deterioration (Roubini, 29/12/2010) are as follows: tension in the Korean peninsula; tension in relations between China and the USA (especially on the issue of the Yuan exchange rate, although this tension has decreased); the destabilisation of Pakistan and the reappearance of Al-Qaeda; the issue of nuclear power in Iran (in the form of unilateral action by Israel); and the situation in the Eurozone, with Italy and Belgium included in the "dangerous" countries (along with Greece, Portugal and Spain). However, the turn of events proved that instability in a crisis could come from unlikely sources, such as the Middle East and North Africa in the beginning of 2011.

Returning to the medium term, 2010 was a year in which exchange rates finally succumbed to "forced devaluations," resulting in the Euro reaching $1.40 (October 2010) and the Yuan reaching €0.10 (Fig. 12.9a and b).

Three factors contributed to the formulation of exchange rate depreciation policies:

- The relatively weak recovery of the US, though avoiding a double dip scenario (W-type development), has not led to satisfactory growth rates. Therefore, the Fed announced its intentions to support demand rather than keeping interest rates low and, possibly, to buy U.S. bonds, leading rigid currencies (Europe, Brazil, India, South Korea, etc.) to become more expensive. Thus, the possibility of a demand bubble in developing countries (BRIC) increased dramatically, and the values of the portfolios of creditors were threatened to the extent it consisted of dollars.
- Despite intense pressure, the Chinese government did not devalue the Yuan, which, as early as October 2010, was estimated to be artificially devalued by

Fig. 12.9 (**a**) Evolution of the Euro-Yuan exchange rate (April–December 2010) (Source: Naftemporiki [www.naftemporiki.gr]). (**b**) Evolution of the Euro-USD exchange rate (April–December 2010) (Source: Naftemporiki [www.naftemporiki.gr])

20%. However, annual Chinese exports to the U.S. now reached $296 bn, whereas Chinese imports were $69 bn.

– Germany's consistently tough attitude towards the Euro exchange rate (which, at least at this stage, moved in the direction of a stable euro) was mainly reflected in the European summit, where, together with France, Germany imposed a very organised fiscal austerity plan and allowed only small changes in the Lisbon Treaty.

We could conclude that Germany, having enjoyed the benefits of a dramatically undervalued currency (all its economic indicators increased spectacularly) in 2010 (the crucial year of the Germany's repositioning in the international economy), organised its behaviour through medium-term planning. This planning clarified that Germany was willing to support the fiscal problems of European economies, but would not accept any real threat to the Euro.

On 16 and 17 December 2010, the European Council decided to establish a "permanent Eurozone structure, called the European Stability Mechanism (ESM), to replace the European Financial Stability Facility (EFSF) and the European Financial Stabilisation Mechanism (EFSM), which would operate until June 2013." The European Council (EUCO 30/10) decided that this mechanism would operate from 1 January 2013, and its legal framework would be agreed upon by June 2013. The aim of this mechanism was to ensure the implementation of the strategy of 2020.

Therefore, the years 2013–2014 are considered to be a threshold for the situation across Europe, particularly in relation to the Greek economy. This fact provides for a mechanism to manage indebted national economies, adopted probably in the first months of 2011. During these years, Greek debt will reach a record percentage of GDP and thus will create intense pressure from those expecting the bankruptcy of the Greek economy. Of course, the big question is under what conditions this new mechanism will manage debt-ridden economies. The question raised is how the temporary mechanisms that already exist at the European level, such as the EFSF (European Financial Stability Facility), will manage the Greek problem before it reaches the threshold date; the creation of the ESM relies on the crucial question of the participation of private capital in the potential costs (haircut) resulting from the restructuring of the national debt of a heavily indebted economy.

Germany raised an issue regarding the involvement of the private sector in this cost, justified through the principle of the control of moral risk, i.e., the impunity of the banking capital following risky practices of excessive lending to indebted countries. During the crisis of 2008–2010, the rewarding of this risk became a usual practice. On the other hand, the opposite sides point to the risk that private capital may assess the default risk of borrowing costs at current levels and thus excessively increase the cost of national debt. Therefore, there is a clear trade-off between moral risk and the cost of national debt that should be reflected in the ESM. In conclusion, the period 2011–2013 is considered to be extremely critical for the Greek economy.

12.3   The IMF, Growth and Adjustment

The most important event in the Greek economy after May 2010 is of course the implementation of the economic adjustment program. This implementation developed under the influence of the IMF's experience of intervention in the economies of countries with severe economic problems – usually developing countries. In general, the Greek economy is classified as a developed country.

However, the Greek economy is directly affected not only by the discussion of the role of the IMF in developing countries but also by the experience of developed countries with the implementation of economic adjustment programs. This is because, though in terms of nominal economic aggregates the Greek economy is classified as a developed country with a classic market model, in terms of the function of the financial system (institutions) the economy could be considered more akin to the peculiar institutional economic systems mainly seen in developing economies. However, the experience of the IMF, which we will discuss here, is the experience of its executives and probably relates more to developing countries.

Subsequently, we will discuss experiences from the implementation of such programs in developed economies. Immediately after the major crises of 1970 (oil) and 1980 (debt), the IMF began to play an important role in the international arena, particularly in correcting external imbalances through a devaluation policy. Its intervened by imposing conditions (conditionality) for the issue of loans and soon included institutional reforms and sectoral interventions. This formed the ultimate interventional role for the IMF in development and growth.

This expanded policy, particularly conditionality, was criticised (Bird and Willet 2004, IEO – Fiscal Adjustment in IMF-Supported Programs, 2007) by the left as incompetent and by the right as incompletely applicable (Abbott et al. 2010). A more centrist criticism (Stiglitz 2004; Vreeland 2006) focused on the issue of "a suit to fit all," and thus demonstrated its inefficiency. This situation led to the emergence of extensive debate, which concluded that interventions by the IMF should be flexible and based on local knowledge (Easterly 2008). In this light, the new guidelines issued by the IMF (Conditionality Guidelines 2002) indicate that the IMF guidelines on cooperation with recipient countries should be drawn up by local authorities with the help of the IMF and should reflect the objectives of the country in which the IMF intervenes. Essentially, the IMF began to feel that the goal of external balances and macroeconomic stability are milestones that serve the ultimate goal of economic growth (IEO – Fiscal Adjustment in IMF-Supported Programs, 2007).

Has the IMF achieved this last goal, or would national economies experience better growth without its intervention? Obviously, this is an extremely complex issue (Przeworski and Vreeland 2000; Barro and Lee 2005). Summarizing this discussion, Abbott et al. (2010) concludes that the findings do not favour a positive response.

Instead of being distracted by a discussion on the overall effectiveness of IMF interventions, it is preferable to focus on an area of particular interest, especially for the Greek case: the institutional modernisation and binding constraints of development capabilities. Essentially, this entails a conceptual difference that separates the classical market model from the peculiar market model that appears to prevail in the Greek economy. Of course, the discussion on institutional modernisation and release from development constraints raises a question regarding the primacy of the market model (the classical model) that incorporates these features in relation to the peculiar market model, which does not.

Ultimately, however, the whole issue (of the degree of desirability of the classic over the peculiar model) is deeply political and linked to the structure of interests in society. It should be noted that often the political debate about the desirability of one model over another can lead to the initiation of a restructuring process of the structure of interests in the existing model, without achieving the goal of restoring the classical market model. The structure of restructuring can only lead to a simple reordering of these interests. The classical market model has an internal consistency of operation that is crucial to achieving effectiveness. Over time, however, the peculiar market model also develops an internal consistency of operation with concrete results in terms of efficiency. Obviously, these results are inferior to the classic market model; otherwise, we would not discuss its deviation. However, the peculiar market model produces results that society (political system, pressure groups, etc.) considers positive – otherwise it would not organise the system in this way.

The issue of institutional modernisation derives from the original Washington Consensus, formed under the influence of the World Bank and the IMF. The Washington Consensus contains mainly neoliberal ideas that support the free market, the reduction of fiscal deficits, the liberalisation of international trade, international capital movement and the strengthening of growth policies based on the promotion of exports ("Stabilise, privatise and liberalise," Rodrik 2006). The main aim of this view was the correct display of relative prices in economies showing signs of administrative determination of prices and changes in the mechanisms used to display these. The subsequently developed concept of "institutional fundamentalism" (Rodrik 2006) included, besides the initial discussion of the Washington Consensus, issues of corporate governance, flexible labour market policies, reduction of corruption, etc. All of these changes are summarised in what Rodrik called the "Augmented Washington Consensus," which is the typical perception that prevailed in the 1990s. The Augmented Washington Consensus constitutes the ideological platform that formulates the measures imposed as mandatory conditions (conditionality) for providing loans to economies that accept the help of the IMF. It is generally believed that the dominance of the Washington Consensus, established in the late 1970s and replacing Keynesian perceptions, lasted until the 2008–2010 crisis. It seems to have been abandoned, however, under the pressure of the extensive activation of the public sector to meet the demand gaps created in global economic activity. In fact, the G-20 meeting in Seoul (November 2010) is seen as establishing the Seoul Development Consensus, which covers the new economic needs and aims to replace the Washington Consensus. The Seoul Consensus leans towards the promotion of strong, sustainable and balanced growth. Similar objectives, beyond immediate goals, are improving institutions, restoring the price mechanism, etc.

Such packages of measures from the Washington Consensus allow two main criticisms. The first concerns the now commonly accepted fact that miracles of growth feature "strange" institutional organisations (Rodrik 2005) primarily created by human incentives conducive to the functioning of the markets (China is one example). Indeed, Hausmann et al. (2005a), who studied 80 cases of strong growth, found that 85% of these were not linked to institutional reforms but caused by specific, small-scale changes that appear to be imposed on a very small number of institutional functions. This last issue brings us to the second main criticism, which stems from the Second Best Theory.

The second best theory simply states that when individual markets malfunction under restraints, the removal of some and not all of these leads the system to reduced efficiency. The policy implemented in economies where the IMF intervenes is based on the opposite perception, which is composed of the following

(Hausmann et al. 2005b): (a) any reform is good, (b) the more reforms introduced the better, (c) radical changes are preferred. Thus, a model for the diagnosis of growth problems can detect the most important reforms needed. However, on neither the empirical (econometric) nor theoretical (mathematical) level has this approach shown to have positive effects on welfare.

Under the pressure of changing perceptions internationally regarding the manner of intervention in "problem countries" (e.g., the Seoul Consensus), the nature of the IMF changes (IMF Factsheet, March 2010), assume specific features, such as new terms for loans from the IMF, more flexibility, fewer mandatory conditions, focus on the social protection of disadvantaged groups, etc.

12.4   The Classical and Peculiar Market Models, the Crisis and the Economic Adjustment Program (EAP)

Across the world, the market model is applied with specific adjustments that correspond to local conditions. From the perspective of analysing conditions of growth, three questions are raised: (a) whether the particularities of the Greek economy are systematic, thus establishing a more specific market model, (b) whether these particularities play a role in the exercise of economic policy and, in particular, in the implementation of the EAP and (c) whether the classical market model, especially as presented in the literature and as it operates primarily in the developed economies of Europe and America, has so many advantages in terms of allocative efficiency that the adjustment of the peculiar market model to this is by itself a desirable and necessary process.

To answer these questions, we briefly and concisely present the classical and peculiar models. These will be presented in two stages. In the first stage, we will present the main differences between the two models based on the following methodological distinctions: (a) whether its features concern the economic nature or social of the model and (b) whether these features are formed and change in the medium- or long-term. As part of this second stage, we will present the issues related to the peculiar market model in a crisis (with reference to the Greek case). In addition, we will distinguish three temporal levels of reference: the short, medium and long term. The presentation compares the targets of the peculiar market model and the measures contained in the Economic Adjustment Program as supplemented by domestic economic policy.

The peculiar market system, with particular reference to the Greek economy, has already been discussed in the past. On an international level, its origins can be sought in the theoretical understanding developed in the literature regarding relations between the centre and the periphery (Amin 1976). On the Greek level, we may refer to the discussion in the early 1970s on "Malformed Capitalism" (Amin and Vergopoulos 1975) and on "Retail Capitalism" (Moskof 1972). However, both in Greece and internationally, this debate was pushed aside due to the increase in efficiency of the global financial system and the acceleration of globalisation. Nonetheless, the main problem in this discussion was that it never reached a satisfactory longitudinal explanatory framework, but remained focused on perceptions that mainly concerned observations on the trans-border movement of surpluses. These analyses did not bear the test of economic developments and changes. In addition, the theoretical perceptions had relied on the analytical importance of theoretical constructions such as the "retail bourgeoisie vs. the national class," which albeit useful in analysis, were and remain unable to comprehensively interpret the observed economic and social changes.

The peculiar market model (PMM) is not approached to produce one or more new theoretical tools; it is presented as a note on the deviations from the classical model.

Table 12.4 shows the features of the two models. Information on the compilation of the table is provided in previous chapters. Therefore, at this point, we do not justify its compilation further; some comments, however, are necessary. In general, we believe that the classical market model is linked to the effectiveness of resource allocation, and this requires a series of conditions. Incomplete markets or limited information both act as deterrents for the efficient allocation of resources. To the extent that it is marked by a number of shortcomings as regards the efficient allocation of resources, the peculiar market model presents deviations in this respect. Indeed, its overall operation leads us to form the view that it is a system geared more toward controlling the operation of the market and less toward improving efficiency. Moreover, the classical market model has capital either because it is consistently in surplus, or because it offers financial reliability. Usually the peculiar market model is based on borrowed funds, leading to fluctuations in its borrowing reliability.

The main usefulness of Table 12.4, apart from its illustrative nature, is that it contributes to the formulation of Table 12.5, which compares the target issues of policy interventions in the peculiar market model in crisis. At this point, the crisis (with special reference to the Greek case) is analysed based on three factors: the fiscal issue (debt to GDP ratio), the financial issue (cash flow – confidence) and the question of the economic model of the Greek economy. Thus, it is a national debt crisis and a problem of sustainability of the financial system that can stem from the reduction of performing loans or liquidity problems, or both, or from a functionality problem of the financial system.

The peculiar market model of Greece deviates from the classical market model. However, in a crisis (fiscal/financial), the PMM presents even greater deviations. Indeed, these additional deviations are critical. Therefore, the management problems of the PMM grow. The new image of the PMM is presented in Table 12.5. This Section presents a critical comparative analysis of the PMM and the Economic Adjustment Program (EAP) adopted in May 2010. The presentation evolves based on the duration of the effectiveness of policy measures that can be applied to correct these deviations.

The EAP is the text governing the borrowing conditions of the Greek government, while describing the conditions governing this loan relationship (Conditionality agreement). The EAP is formed as a cooperation Stand-By Arrangement with the IMF and is strongly influenced by the Augmented Washington Consensus we

Table 12.4 Comparison of CMA and PMM (labels contain only differences)

Economic and social character	Time horizon	Basic inputs for growth	Sectors of activity	Issues	Classic market model	Peculiar market model
Economic status	Long term				Effective resource allocation	Deviation
	Medium term	Capital			Capital surplus (real or debt) flows	Excess or deficit debt flows
		Labour			–	Parallel economy
		Human capital	Education	Nursery education	High	Very low
				Overall efficiency of higher education	High	Low
				Orientation of higher education specialisations	–	Deviations
				Lifelong learning	High	Low
				Linking of research and production	Yes	Absence
			Innovation		Activity	Absence
			Health		–	–
			Property rights		High vesting	Low vesting
			Characteristics of transactions	Frequency	High	Low
				Fund specialisation	Analysis required	Analysis required
				Uncertainty	Low	High
			Markets	Extroversion	High	Low
				Oligopoly	Low for Cost of Living Index products	High
				Domestic – foreign	–	–
				Transfer pricing	Countries of input and output	Countries of output
				Labour market	Functionality	Interventions
				Products – services	Functionality	Interventions
		Financial institutions	Systems	Taxation	Support for direct taxes	Support for indirect taxes – parallel economy
				Financial intermediation	–	–
				Insurance systems	Common problems	Common problems

Social status				Representation – program implementation	Lag of representation and implementation
	Medium term	Political institutions	Political representation system		
			Pressure groups	Consensus building	Intense controversy
			Administrative mechanism	Effective	Ineffective
		Incentives		Use of excessive growth	Non-use – regulatory operation
	Long term	Cultural background	Psychological – social stereotypes	Assistance in growth	Mediterranean character
				Privacy	Collectivity
				Future orientation	Orientation to the present
				Undertaking of risk and active management of uncertainty	Domination of uncertainty
				Performance orientation	Non-performance orientation
				Pursuit of gender equality	Acceptance of inequality
				Trust	Lack of trust
				Femininity	Masculinity
				Religious promotional factors	Neutral to negative religious impact

examined in the previous section. Perhaps the Greek EAP may be one of the last loan agreement texts of the IMF with such a strong influence from the Washington Consensus and so little influence from the Seoul Consensus.

Essentially, a crisis creates short-term criticality and thus alters the PMM, lending it a short-term feature.

But how did the EAP (or the so-called memorandum[1]), which is the main economic policy document covering the period 2010–2013, emerge? Essentially, the EAP was formed within 2 months (April–May 2010) by Greek technocrats and their peers, who were mainly from the IMF, the European Commission (EC) and the ECB. In fact, it resulted from the application of the common observations of the technocratic staffs, mainly of the IMF and the European Commission (EC-DG ECFIN). The works of these two technocratic staffs typically ran in parallel with similar work by the OECD and were at times reflected in the publication of Greek Economic Outlooks.

The work of these technocratic staffs was based on a composed methodology, which usually involves the production of specialised research by researchers and scientists. These works are usually published in leading financial journals. The research findings are processed and transformed into policy guidelines and usually included in the monthly reports of the IMF, the OECD, and the European Commission (EC-DG ECFIN). Finally, the main findings are included in the EAP in the form of a political decision. It is worth noting three observations with regard to the points included in the EAP.

First, the policy conclusions included in the EAP usually undergo a mutation, characterised by the strengthening of their positivism, from their birth as research texts until their inclusion in the EAP. There have been instances of serious policy decisions which, although "suffering" at the original research level from extensive (cautious and rational) uncertainty regarding their effectiveness, even at the level of results (positive or negative) or even supporting complete agnosticism (we do not know what will happen), are included in the EAP in the form of simple command (e.g., "such and such must happen!"). In fact, the "invisible hand" policy has lent a specific character to the policy measures included in the EAP.

The second point concerns the timing of the measures included in the EAP in relation to their effectiveness. According to Table 12.5, many of the EAP measures have long-term effectiveness. However, as we saw in the previous section, they have been included in the EAP for political reasons in order to be used in conjunction with the disbursements of the lending plan (Conditionality).

The third point relates to the quality of experience (or empirical data) included in the text of the scientists and technocrats that have been used as raw material for the EAP. In this wave of applied IMF adjustment policies, experience probably originates mainly from countries using the CMM, and not the PMM.

The study of the macroeconomic effects of fiscal adjustment, which is reflected in a series of texts, as we shall see in more detail later (Chap. 13), is enlightening.

---

[1] The monitoring of the EAP's evolution requires the study of a series of texts, the most important of which are:

Table 12.5 The PMM in a crisis and the intervention policies, as reflected in the EAP (May 2010) and the domestic economic policy (2010–2011)

Time scale	Economic and social character	Peculiar market model in a crisis (Greek case)			EAP and DEP
Short term horizon	Economic status	Fiscal problem			Implementation of EAP
		Debt to GDP ratio			Reduction of costs
		Increased cost of public expenditure			Increase of revenue
		Financial system			Establishment of financial stability fund
		Interbank confidence			Intervention by the ECB to provide liquidity – €96 bn (December 2010).
		Banking system liquidity problem			Intervention by the EFSF in the secondary bond market – €46 bn (December 2010).
		Stricter funding criteria for the economy			–
		Labour: Increased unemployment / Parallel economy			Shrinking of the parallel economy
	Social status	–			–
Mid-term–long-term horizon	Economic status	Capital: deficit			–
		Labour: parallel economy			Shrinking of the parallel economy
		Human capital	Education	Nursery education (very low)	–
				Overall effectiveness of higher education (low)	–
				Orientation of higher education specialisations (deviation)	–
				Lifelong education (low)	–
				Linking of research and production (deviation)	–
			Society		–
			Health	–	Rationalisation program for health services

(continued)

Table 12.5 (continued)

Time scale	Economic and social character		Peculiar market model in a crisis (Greek case)		EAP and DEP
		Financial institutions	Property rights	Low consolidation	–
			Characteristics of transactions	Uncertainty	–
			Markets	Extroversion	Weak (DEP)
				Oligopolies	Weak intervention (DEP)
				Bank pricing	–
				Labour (Administrative regulations)	Strong intervention
				Products + Services (Administrative regulations)	Strong intervention
			Systems	Taxation (Tax evasion)	Intervention
				Insurance system (ageing)	Strong intervention
	Social status	Political institutions	Political representation system		–
			Pressure groups		–
			Administrative mechanism		Intervention
		Incentives			–
		Cultural background			–

One of the most recent key works on this is that of the IMF (IMF – Global Financial Stability Report, October 2010). The study included 15 countries, while data covered the period 1980–2009 for Australia, Belgium, Canada, Denmark, Finland, France, Germany, Ireland, Italy, Japan, Portugal, Spain, Sweden, UK, and the USA. Perhaps an observant researcher can identify one or two countries applying a CMM, but the overall sample of countries mainly applies a PMM.

According to all evidence (literature, Table 12.6), the basic working hypothesis of the EAP (the implemented economic policy plan of the EAP) is as follows.

Table 12.5 clearly shows that some features of the PMM were subjected to stronger adjustment interventions, whereas others were not intervened with at all. This selective choice concerns both short- and medium-term implementations. Thus, though the EAP established the Financial Stability Fund to disable the financial system with a short- (and long-) term implementation horizon, and although the disabling of the financing of the economy is a key point of the

Table 12.6 The working hypothesis of the EAP

1. Policy decision to implement the EAP, with four main objectives: (a) fiscal contraction, (b) financial stability, (c) change of the operating model of the economy, (d) decreased global systematic financial risk

2. Creation of positive expectations, increased confidence (due to the EAP) and reduction of uncertainty

3. Fiscal adjustment and depression, in particular revenue growth and, secondarily, reduction of costs with the expected results of:

   (a) Reduction of domestic demand and hence lower prices

   (b) Reduction of the fiscal deficit and public debt

   (c) Reduction of the balance deficit

   (d) Reduction of the shadow economy

   (e) Reduction of the attractiveness of the public sector

   (f) Adjustment of the insurance system for budgetary reasons

   (g) Decrease of unemployment

4. Currency depreciation and internal devaluation, which are expected to lead to:

   (a) The increase of competitiveness and hence export growth

   (b) The stabilisation (non- increase) of prices in a deflationary environment

   (c) Reduction of the balance of payments deficit

5. Monetary policy: lowering of interest rates, which are expected to lead to:

   (a) Increase of funding to the economy to balance public demand

   (b) Increase of savings for the future financing of the economy

6. Structural measures to increase supply in the economy:

   (a) Structural interventions

   (b) Financial system (reorganisation of the banking system): restoration of the supply of credit in the economy

   (c) Reduction of transaction costs

7. Sectoral changes:

   (a) Reduction of the importance of retail and wholesale trade

   (b) Reduction of the size of the construction sector

   (c) Reduction of the parallel economy

   (d) Promotion of the export sector

EAP's application, no activity was noted (until December 2010). In addition, there is a lack of substantial medium-to-long term interventions in the area of human capital (education), innovation and the control of transfer pricing.

To be completely accurate, we should mention that there are verbal references in the EAP to all these issues for which we note substantial interventions. Thus, there is the following reference to the issue of human capital, especially in the field of education: "The government shall establish, by February 2011, an independent education policy, to improve the efficiency of the public education system (primary, secondary, tertiary education) and allow the more efficient use of resources". In practice, however, the intervention in the field of education (from mid-2010) was translated as follows: (a) the bill to change the administration of universities and institutes of technology and (b) the establishment of e-learning for primary and secondary education. Neither issue appears to be directly related to the needs of the

EAP to increase the supply of human capital in the economy, which should (see next section on the relative effectiveness of measures), for example, ensure the interlinking of research and production and improve the efficiency of spending on secondary education (see Chap. 5).

In addition, the EAP contains several references to lack of competition in the markets, but at least until the January 2010, policy actions mainly assumed the form of increasing the supply of professional services. Moreover, we note the almost complete absence of policies to manage markup policies and transfer pricing.

This selective process in setting priorities, organizing, and implementing the EAP raises the suspicion of the presence of political priorities. It is therefore obvious that, due to their huge costs under normal conditions, the application of reforms (as contained in the EAP, aiming to adjust the PMM to the CMM) requires political debate and a political command for change. In other words, though the avoidance of national bankruptcy and the rescue of the financial system (due to conjuncture), the change of the operating conditions of the insurance system (due to longitudinal demographic data) and the change of the political system (due to the longitudinal improvement of representation) are functions that can be executed by the government regardless of the nature of the mandate, the adjustment of the PMM to the CMM is clearly a social and long-term politic, requiring political choice. It is, however, in the nature of the PMM to be administrated by a poor mandate. In this way, the system itself essentially ensures its rescue and perpetuation, in different forms. In practice, the reason the need for change is ignored is that society would never consent, in a pre-election period, to the potential change of the PMM, and thus would not elect the party that proposed it. Moreover, it is widely believed that significant changes are made under the pressure of crises, including the crisis of representation. However, given the poor political mandate, the economic and social system cannot be substantially changed, thereby reproducing its major crises with almost certain frequency.

The Economic Adjustment Program is not certain to lead to the restoration of the classical market model and the feeing of its growth potential. It can lead to the formation of a new peculiar market model. This, however, (a) may contain the inherent weaknesses of the older PMM, at least as regards the production of major crises if, for example, it does not create forces of new value production or (b) is merely an expression of the political forces that dominate at the time of its formulation. These forces may be the product of the process of domestic society, the product of external interventions or the product of the dominance of specific interest groups.

In addition to interventions aimed to rescue the economy from bankruptcy and create the conditions for its medium-term growth, the Economic Adjustment Program had another objective or, at least, its application had a clear result: the reorientation of the Greek debt from private sources to public entities; reduction in global financial risk. This point has enabled many to argue that what was finally saved by the intervention was not the Greek economy but large foreign creditors (Jansen 2010). This view is based on Table 12.7, which compares the structure of the Greek public debt between December 2007 and June 2010. It appears that during this period the structure of claims has changed dramatically. Most importantly, the claims of foreign banks have decreased by €153 bn. In addition, some

Table 12.7 Claims of foreign banks in Greece, by country of origin

	December 2007	June 2010
France	64,495	53,469
Germany	41,835	36,840
Netherlands	20,387	4,716
Belgium	14,338	2,020
United Kingdom	13,753	11,980
Ireland	9,301	7,801
Italy	8,128	5,347
Portugal	6,501	10,031
Austria	5,949	3,103
Spain	958	925
Sweden	477	479
Denmark	136	108
EU	240,833	141,564
USA	8,497	7,500
Japan	7,108	1,957
Switzerland	52,595	2,403
Turkey	62	404
Total	309,095	153,828

Source: Bank for International Settlements (BIS)
Note: Amounts in million of dollars

countries (Netherlands, Switzerland) have "disappeared from the picture," while others have reduced their claims.

This observation leads us to consider another dimension of the financial nature of the EAP. This is an analysis of input–output in the Greek economy in terms of the final recipient of funds. A complete analysis should also extend to the entire spectrum of relations between the Greek economy and the European Union (ECB, EC, EFSF, EFSM) and the IMF.

Table 12.8 covers the period 2010–2015 (according to the EAP, the financial assistance of €110 bn will be paid in 2016) and shows the extent of the mobilisation of capital resources to manage the Greek economic problem. Its analysis can provide information on many levels of operating and decision-making. We distinguish five of these: first is the field that formulates the fiscal result, i.e., the primary deficit of the state prior to the payment of interest. For the 6-year period of 2010–2015, the primary surplus barely reaches €32 bn (line 1a). Interest payments (line 2) are almost €107 bn, from which it is estimated that €32 bn goes to domestic investors (mainly banks and institutional investors) and €75 bn goes to foreign investors.[2] The second level concerns the large volume of financing needs created by the maturities of securities (line 3) of nearly €332 bn. Of these, €152 bn are bonds as these existed before the intervention of the EAP, Treasury bills estimated

---

[2] Readers understand that the concept of domestic, as opposed to foreign, investors is relative because domestic and foreign destinations are hardly distinguishable on the basis of proprietary features.

Table 12.8 Inflows/outflows to domestic and foreign destinations, for the Greek case (amounts in billions of euro): 2/2011

		2010	2011	2012	2013	2014	2015	Total	Source
1	Public deficit (Primary result + payment of interest) (the (−) indicates surplus)[a]	22	17	15	11	6	3	75	EC (2011)
1a	Of which primary surplus (the (−) indicates surplus)	7	2	−2	−8	−14	−18	−32	(1) − (2)
2	Of which interest payments	15	15	17	19	20	21	107	EC (2011)
2a	Interest payments to domestic investors[b]	4	4	5	6	6	6	32	(2) × 30%
2b	Interest payments to foreign investors[b]	10	10	12	13	14	15	75	(2) × 70%
3	Maturity of securities	31	42	46	52	78	73	322	(3a) + (3b) + (3c)
3a	Bond maturities	16	27	31	27	31	20	152	PDMA (2009)
3b	Maturity of treasury bills	15	15	15	15	15	15	90	Estimates
3c	EAP payments	-	-	-	10	32	38	110	European Commission (2011), the total includes payments of €32 bn in 2016
4a	Maturities of securities held by domestic investors	14	17	18	17	18	15	100	Note[b]
4b	Maturities of securities held foreign investors	17	25	28	35	60	58	222	Note[b]
5	Total financing needs	53	59	61	63	84	76	397	(1) + (3)
6	Issue of short-term securities	15	15	15	15	15	15	90	Estimates
6a	Placement of domestic investors in issues of short-term securities[c]	9	9	9	9	9	9	54	(6) × 60%
6b	Placement of foreign investors in issues of short-term securities[c]	6	6	6	6	6	6	36	(6) × 40%
7	Funded by the EAP (foreign origin)	32	47	24	8	0	0	110	EC (2010)
8	Need of financing from the markets (excluding short-term securities and the EAP)	7	−2	22	40	69	61	197	(5) − (6) − (7)
9	Purchase of Greek bonds by the ECB on the secondary market	45	-	-	-	-	-	45	BoG
9a	Purchase of Greek bonds from ECB by domestic investors[b]	14	-	-	-	-	-	14	(11) × 30%

9b Purchase of Greek bonds from ECB by foreign investors[b]	32	–	–	–	–	32	$(11) \times 70\%$
10 Financing of Greek banks by the ECB (inflow in the domestic economy, including 2009)	96	–	–	–	–	96	Estimates
11 Outflow of deposits from Greek banks abroad (to foreign investors)[d]	31	–	–	–	–	31	BoG
12 Grand total of financing instruments used	225	59	61	63	84	76	569	$(5) + (9) + (10) + (11)$
13 Domestic destinations of capital	166	24	21	15	11	3	240	$(1) - (2) + (2a) + (4a) + (10) + (9a) + (11)$
14 Foreign destinations of capital	59	35	40	48	74	73	329	$(12) - (13)$

Source: European Commission, Evaluation of EAP (December 2010, February 2011), PDMA, Aggregate financial statements BoG

[a] According to the Medium-term Fiscal Frame 2012–2015

[b] It is assumed that the long-term securities of the Greek government are held by domestic and foreign investors at a ratio of 30/70% (Source: PDMA)

[c] It is assumed that domestic and foreign investors participate in the issuance of new short-term Greek government securities at a ratio of 60/40% (Source: International Press)

[d] It is assumed that the total outflow of deposits was directed inside the economy

at €15 bn per year and the repayment of the EAP's assistance, which according to this, will take place between 2013 and 2016. These can be divided into bonds estimated to be held by domestic (line 4a) and foreign investors (line 4b).

Greece's overall financial needs for the period 2010–2015 (line 5), amounting to €397 bn, are formed based on these two reference levels. In other words, in practice, the problem of Greek bankruptcy in 2010 was transferred to after 2013, culminating in 2014 and 2015, while the demands of foreign banks in Greece until June 2010 had decreased by €55 bn (Table 12.7).[3]

The question raised refers to the financing of these financial demands. This is accomplished through short-term securities (T-Bills, line 6) divided according to whether they are held by domestic (line 6a) or foreign investors (line 6b), through the EAP (line 7) or through the markets (line 8). This figure reached €197 bn for the period 2010–2015 including the €32 bn (last dose of the EAP) that concern 2016. €165 bn concern strictly the period 2010–2015.

However, there are three further reference levels related to the management of the Greek problem: this third level concerns the ECB's interventions in the Greek secondary bond market, which, in December 2010 stood at €45 bn (line 9). These can be divided into Greek bond markets and domestic investors (line 9a) and foreign investors (line 9b). The fourth level refers to the inability of the Greek banking system to exit to the interbank market. Thus, the ECB was forced to fund it with capital of €96 bn (line 10). Finally, the fifth and last level refers to the outflow of deposits from the Greek banking system to the internal of the economy, which, in December 2010, amounted to €31 bn (line 11).

The grand total of used financial instruments amounted to €569 bn (line 12). If we add all domestic destinations of capital (line 13), these reach €240 bn, while, if we include foreign destinations, they reach €329 bn (line 14).

These estimates relate to the specific point in time in which they were made and are based on assumptions whose change will differentiate them. Furthermore, it should be stressed that this is just a snapshot and will vary over time. However, the general direction of the main conclusions will not change. These are as follows:

(a) The outputs of the international system are too high compared to the nominal value of the EAP. This justified the criticism received by A. Merkel (Gerhard Schröder, 2/2/2011) that if Germany had reacted sooner (6 weeks) to the Greek crisis, "Germany would have saved lots of money."

(b) A very large share of outflows went to foreign destinations.

Under these conditions, we cannot understand how it is possible to develop an "unfriendly" settlement on the Greek issue between creditors and the Greek economy, provided that the promises made between the parties shall be kept, since the international system has been "exposed" though the outflow of substantial capital. On the other hand, this process has freed foreign investors from "bondage," thereby changing Greece's bargaining power (stronger or weaker?).

---

[3] At this point we must agree that the design of the EAP, in May 2010, was unsustainable from the beginning.

The following chart shows the five reference issues of the Greek financing problem. The length of arrows reflects the size and intensity of issues.

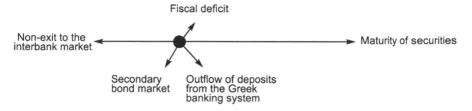

12.5   The Economic Adjustment Program, Policy and Income Distribution

In the previous section, we saw that there is a clear distinction between the classic market model and the peculiar market model of the Greek case.

Before we discuss the adaptation processes of the peculiar model to the specifications of the CMM, we should answer the key question of the point of this adaptation. This is important because the economic and social cost of this adaption is enormous. Moreover, such programs are usually expected to be effective in the long term. The peculiar market model was developed over time and according to certain power, need, and demand correlations of society and its elements. For example, it is clear that minimum wages for engineers or lawyers were imposed due to their strong relative position in society and due to the strong historic character of those professions. It also expresses, though, the social will to share the small surplus produced administratively, because the expectations for future large production surpluses is limited mainly due to the weak economy. It is also evident that the post-civil-war Greek society itself (after 1950) allowed social strata that were forbidden access to the public sector to operate on the fringes of the economy, namely, in the shadow economy (all types of professionals, etc.). Nowadays, of course, external conditions have changed dramatically because of increased financial needs. Nevertheless, this model of economic functioning is deeply rooted in the transactional and social habits of Greek society. Moreover, the shrinkage of the shadow economy is directly related to an upward impact on unemployment.

The adjustment process through the EAP is in itself a process of redistribution of power and wealth in society. The question of the impact of IMF policies on income distribution has already been discussed based on international experience (Vreelend 2003; Gabor 2010). Can we trace these trends through data in the Greek economy? The answer is yes, to a certain extent: we can analyse the changes at least as concerns greater categories of production factors, such as capital and employment. It is, however, difficult to conduct more detailed analyses, such as analyses on population group capitation, pressure groups, etc. Through those categories, we can see the remuneration of capital connected to the public debt.

Figure 12.10a (data 1995–2012) presents the course of remuneration of production factors. The compensation of employees line concerns employment remuneration "de-inflated" by the number of employees. The self employment compensation

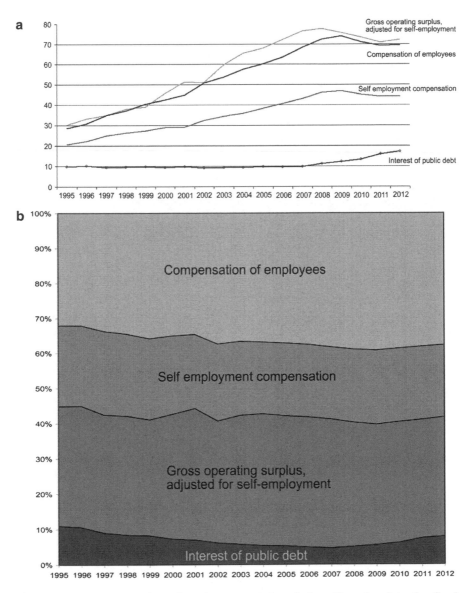

Fig. 12.10 (a) Compensation of employees, capital, and the self-employed in the Greek Economy: 1995–2010 (in billion euros) (Forecast) (Source: EC (AMECO Database). Note: The public debt interest rates resulted from the statistic reports of economic conjuncture of the bank of Greece. For 2009–2012 the amounts resulted from the EAP (2nd Review, December 2010).) (**b**) The course of the percentile structure

(presented in a separate line) is taken out of the line of "gross operating surplus." Lastly, it presents the course of the public debt rates.

If we sum these numbers and analyse their percentile contribution, we can monitor the course of the percentile contribution of productive factors (Fig. 12.10b).

We observe that compensation of employees steadily and significantly increases from 1995 to 2009, up to €74.16 bn from €28.54 bn. After that, it falls (following the implementation of the EAP) and is estimated to drop by €4.59 bn by 2012. A smaller but equally important increase is noted in the self employment compensation. Since 1995 (€20.56 bn), it steadily increases until 2009 (€46.97 bn) and then decreases. More specifically, in 2010 it drops by roughly €2 bn (compared to 2009), in 2011 it reaches €44.08 bn, whereas in 2012 it is estimated to reach €44.12 bn (reduced in total by €2.85 bn for the period 2009–2012). The recovery tendency is more evident in the gross operating surplus. Therefore, future consequences (2012–2015) will be of great importance. The course of the gross operating surplus (without the self employment compensation) is similar; from €30.15 bn in 1995, it more than doubled by 2008, reaching €77.69 bn. As of 2008, it follows a decreasing trend. The European Commission estimates that by 2011 it will reach €70.73 bn, while for the second year of implementation of the EAP (2012), it is estimated to reach €72.29 bn. The total decrease for the period 2009–2012 will be €3.49 bn. Finally, regarding the course of public debt interest rates, we observe a stable course until year 2007 (roughly €10 bn). Following the financial crisis in 2008, the rates started a stable upwards course and it is estimated that by 2012 they will amount to €17.07 bn (EAP Evaluation, December 2010).

In essence, we conclude that from 2008 onwards, the public debt rates exert decreasing pressure on all three categories of remuneration of productive factors (capital, employment and self-employed). Here we detect the most serious change in the allocation of income that, to a certain extent, is reminiscent of the structure of percentile remuneration of productive factors at the start of the 15-year period beginning in 1995. In practice, the remuneration of productive factors is compressed in favour of the public debt service rates. Therefore, the EAP has an impact on the allocation of income.

12.6 Economic Adjustment Program, Cultural Background, Motivation, Social Capital and Business Capital

When the EAP was created, its organisation focused on the fiscal aspect and financial stability. However, in this book, as elsewhere, the importance of cultural background and social capital has been stressed as agents of production. Indeed, the literature on the formation of their input in the magnification procedure has not been sufficiently proven to easily underline the connection of measures of financial policy to the concepts of cultural background and social capital. This weakness usually leads to the disregarding of the consequences of financial policy in both of these sectors.

However, the analysis so far has proven the following: (a) in crisis conditions and in the implementation of the EAP, Greek society has recreated an intense background of uncertainty and risk, (b) the concept of trust in the economy and of expectations play a very important role in the reaction of a real economy in the short-term and medium-long term, (c) the grave matter of liquidity of the banking system is largely due to issues of trust and (d) the formation of an environment of trust constitutes a key element of the basic working hypothesis of the EAP. Therefore, the disregarding of consequences in these sectors is erroneous. At the same time, the consequences of the EAP in the so-called Business Capital must be investigated.

The definition of business capital arises mainly from the research of Audretsch et al. (2006) and Audretsch (2007, 2009), who claimed "the business capital in addition to employment, to the natural capital and the educational capital, also consists a factor that contributes to the creation of an economic magnification." The business capital refers to the institutions, cultural background, and historical framework that lead to the creation of new businesses. This concept includes elements such as the social approval of business behaviour and the existence of people who are willing to share risks and profits. Thus, the business capital reflects a number of different legal, institutional, and social factors and forces. Audretsch names some of the above "remaining inflow" as business capital. These are the forces used for the creation of a "cognitive filter" that intercedes in the relation between the products of educational process and science and the ideas towards commercialisation. The activation of that filter leads to the selection of those ideas that lead to economic magnification (Audretsch 2007). In conclusion, the business capital includes the institutions, cultural background and wider social background necessary for the creation of new businesses. It includes a series of aspects of social life, such as the social approval of business behaviour but also includes behaviours available to manage the business risk. Thus, the business capital reflects legal institutions as well as social factors and forces.

At this point, we should remind the reader that the longitudinal development of the density of business incidents in relation to per capita GDP shows that, in the Greek Economy, an increase of per capita GDP correlates with an increase of the percentages of business activity (see Chap. 3). However, for business activity to take a form based on innovation and not just on the need for survival "cognitive filters" (Audretsch 2007, 2009), it must develop personal or institutional abilities to detect which products of knowledge and science that can be turned into business opportunities. "Cognitive filters" are fundamental components of business capital. However, for this aiding of filters function to be meaningful, there must be a real innovative background, i.e., research ideas that can be turned into business opportunities. This, however, is a matter of education and research growth.

The EAP came into contact with the cultural background in its elementary components: (a) the element of collectiveness and privacy, (b) the element of longitudinal development and (c) the element of uncertainty and risk management.

In the issue of collectiveness and privacy, the crisis and the EAP enhanced the elements of in-group collectiveness as the broader financial circumstances deteriorated in a society that has not developed social protection mechanisms and networks. However, in parallel, the economic sector where the in-group collectiveness finds expression, i.e., SMEs, suffered a blow because of the recession and the shrinkage of economic activity. At the same time, collectiveness suffered a severe blow because of the collapse of the capacities of the government. This collapse led to the classic symptoms of loss of stable backgrounds of personal and social function. The first stage of reaction in this condition is the instability of economic orientation, given that the public sector ceases to be an attractive area of work. Yet, during the implementation period of the EAP, the private sector also suffered, due to interventions in the labour market. Thus, the symptoms of initial shock are much greater. It will take at least 3–5 years for labour reorientation to the private sector to be effective, mainly through the creation of new businesses.

Longitudinal development suffered the greatest impact. Whilst the EAP should be a framework of enhancement of the economic orientation towards the future, the fear of "bankruptcy" increased (also facilitating the approval of reforms), leading to a situation that strengthened orientation to the present. This is an extremely worrying situation for the Greek economy, affecting the possibilities of recovery. However, the EAP is not solely responsible for this situation; the overall policy of "seeing how it goes" followed in Europe also shares responsibility. Only when the monitoring mechanisms of economic policy at the European level were formalised in early February 2011, and a more stable operational framework for the medium-term horizon thus started emerging, were similar expectations created for the Greek economy. Thus, we hope that uncertainty will start to decrease. The management of uncertainty and risk appetite is an important issue. Besides the historical significance of the value of a cultural background, this also demonstrates an additional feature. A series of factors, such as capital costs, the bankruptcy risk premium of the national debt and the time of bonding of investment funds, have grave consequences. Of course, it should be noted that when developmental aspects of the cultural background are affected, they might take many years to recover.

The same considerations relate to the core issue of social capital, i.e., trust in society and the economy. Trust suffered a blow as suddenly conditions in the economy worsened. On the other hand, the potential to implement an organised course in the future within the framework of a wider stable organisation increases the level of trust and creates potential of improvement of the financial climate. The conditions of improvement of accumulation of social capital in an environment of trust are necessary for a developmental procedure. However, we don't know if this happened in the Greek economy.

Finally, the cumulative increase of uncertainty, the increased focus on the present and the restructure of collectiveness had three results in the field of human behaviour incentives:

1. Given the weak relation of the time horizon of human behaviour to the future, the process of target-setting (essentially an effort of personal motivation) is not particularly active. Indeed, if we consider that the implementation of the EAP increased (at least on a first level) the focus on the present, this tendency averts even more the setting of aims and goals, thus decreasing the availability of labour supply.

2. A decrease on the returns of private investments either in personal or natural capital resulted in increased abstinence from savings and investments.
3. The scale of active hierarchy of incentives has migrated to lower levels, where personal survival is stronger than personal fulfilment, with a negative impact for individual ambitious activation.

References

Abbott P, Andersen TB, Tarp F (2010) IMF and economic reform in developing countries. Q Rev Econ Financ 50:17–26

Amin S (1976) Unequal development. Monthly Review Press, USA

Amin S, Vergopoulos K (1975) The ugly face of capitalism: its dominance over agriculture. Papazissi, Athens

Audretsch DB (2007) The entrepreneurial society. Oxford University Press, New York

Audretsch DB (2009) The entrepreneurial society. J Technol Transf 34:245–254

Audretsch DB, Keilbach MC, Lehmann EE (2006) Entrepreneurship and economic growth. Oxford University Press, New York

Barro RJ, Lee JW (2005) IMF programs: who is chosen and what are the effects? J Monet Econ 52 (7):1245–1269

Bird G, Willet TD (2004) IMF conditionality and the new political economy of ownership. Comp Econ Stud 46(3):423–450

Carone G, Denis C, Mc Morrow K, Mourre G, Roger W (2006) Long-term labour productivity and GDP projections for the EU25 member states: a production function framework. Eur. Comm. DG ECFIN, 253:1–92

Easterly W (2008) Institutions: top down or bottom up? Am Econ Rev 98(2):95–99

Gabor D (2010) The IMF and its new economics of crisis. Dev Change 41(5):805–830

Hausmann R, Pritchett L, Rodrik D (2005a) Growth accelerations. Harvard University, Cambridge

Hausmann R, Rodrik D, Velasco A (2005b) Growth diagnostics. Harvard University, Cambridge

Jansen R (2010) Greece and the IMF: who exactly is being saved? CEPR, 1611

Moskof K (1972) The national and social consciousness in Greece 1830–1909 ideology of resale space. Thessaloniki

Przeworski A, Vreeland JR (2000) The effect of IMF programs on economic growth. J Dev Econ 62:385–421

Rodrik D (2005) Growth strategies. In: Aghion P, Durlauf S (eds) Handbook of economic growth. North-Holland, Amsterdam, pp 967–1014

Rodrik D (2006) Goodbye Washington consensus, hello Washington confusion? A review of the world bank's economic growth in the 1990s: learning from a decade of reform. J Econ Lit 44 (4):973–987

Roeger W, Jan in't Velt (2010) Fiscal stimulus and exit strategies in the EU: a model-based analysis. Eur. Commission for Economic and Financial Affairs

Stiglitz J (2004) The parties' flip-flops on deficit spending: economics or politics? The Economists' Voice. 1(1)2. DOI: 10.2202/1553-3832.1001

Vreeland JR (2006) Self reform: The IMF strategy. Wall Street J p.10

Vreelend JR (2003) The IMFand economic development. Cambridge University Press, New York

Ward K (2011) The world in 2050. Quantifying the shift in the global economy. HSBC.

The Effectiveness of Economic Adjustment Interventions

13

Under the Economic Adjustment Program (EAP) and the accompanying Domestic Economic Policy (DEP), two intervention methods were selected:

- Fiscal adjustment.
- Structural interventions in labour, human capital, products, services and the banking system.

Unfortunately, the intervention into the financial system have not been fully implemented yet (January 2011). Three key questions arise regarding both modes of intervention: How deep should the interventions be in theory, and how deep are they in practice? What are their basic effects? And, how much time is required to produce the results? These questions involve both the negative and positive effects of these interventions.

Section 13.1 discusses the fiscal adjustment process and the resulting economic developments, while Sect. 13.2 analyses the implemented structural interventions. Section 13.3 presents the financial system intervention together with the state of the real economy. Section 13.4 describes the education and innovation sectors as areas suitable for development intervention, while Sect. 13.5 discusses the viability of the EAP's working hypothesis.

13.1 Fiscal Adjustments and Economic Developments

Fiscal adjustments involve two important issues: (a) the relationship between debt and growth (in other words, whether and how excessive debt reduces growth) and (b) the best way to reduce the debt to facilitate future growth (i.e., whether it should be compared with spending cuts or tax increases and to what extent).

The notion that there is a negative relationship between excessive debt (i.e., over 90% of GDP) and future growth (Reinhart and Rogoff 2010) has been adopted over

P. Petrakis, *The Greek Economy and the Crisis*,
DOI 10.1007/978-3-642-21175-1_13, © Springer-Verlag Berlin Heidelberg 2012

earlier perception of mutual independence.[1] In fact, in societies such as Greece with an excellent orientation to the present (for example, they do not believe they will live forever), taxation consists of consumption taxes; as such, there is a distinct probability that the country may go bankrupt. While the debt-to-GDP ratio is high, individuals maintain reduced savings, which reduces growth potential for the future. Thus, there is good reason for a society to reduce its national debt. However, as long as these conditions prevail, the social conditions needed to mobilise debt reductions are lacking. The relationship between fear of bankruptcy and the amount of deposits is instructive with respect to the present state of Greek society. In other words, as long as Greek society focuses debate on the possibility of bankruptcy, no recovery in terms of additional savings is possible. Therefore, the prospects for future growth will be doomed. As such, a society that constantly discusses the prospect of bankruptcy is in fact likely to go bankrupt (Table 13.1).

Of course, a society (particularly its political leaders and media) may inflate the risk of bankruptcy, ultimately encouraging this outcome. This scenario sounds absurd, but it is possible if (a) a society has opted to adopt adjustment measures that presuppose a crisis, (b) the crisis obscures the true state of affairs, and (c) the real impact of such "bankruptcy talk" is ignored.

Debates regarding the ideal composition of a fiscal adjustment portfolio boomed in late 2009 and early 2010, primarily because of theoretical conflicts between Alesina and Ardanga (2009) and Alesina (2010) and Krugman with respect to the latter's column in the New York Times entitled "The Conscience of a Liberal" during February 2010 and October 2010. Articulating a viewpoint subsequently adopted by the IMF, Alesina and Ardanga argued that to have a minimum impact on growth, a fiscal portfolio should be based more on spending cuts (i.e., a spending base) than on raising taxes (i.e., a tax base). On his part, Krugman argued that "if you're in a liquidity trap simultaneously (zero rates) and face a global recession, the negative effects of fiscal discipline will be much worse".

Interestingly, the views of Alesina, Ardanga and the IMF did not apply to the Greek case, as this case involved an increase in interest rates and a decrease in private-sector funding; nor did the views of Krugman apply, as the Greek economy was not in a liquidity trap with zero interest rates. Rather, a different model altogether applied to the Greek case, as fiscal and monetary policy presented concentric behaviour. However, we focus on the so-called "Alesina-IMF" model because its principles formed the basis of the EAP.

According to the results from a study of 15 countries that applied fiscal adjustments from 1980 to 2009 (IMF-Global Financial Stability Report, October 2010), a fiscal adjustment (that is, a reduction) of 1% of GDP typically decreases real GDP by 0.22% 1 year later and 0.5% 2 years later (Table 13.2). It also increases unemployment by 0.2% 1year later and 0.3% 2 years later. Of course, fiscal

---

[1] This is the Barro-Ricardo equivalence theorem (Barro 1974) that proposes that how a government decides to finance its costs (i.e., debt or taxes) does not play a role in the overall level of economic activity.

Table 13.1 The Greek economy, 2007–2010

Annual data	2007	2008	2009	2010[a]
GDP (constant prices)	4.5	1.3	−2.3	−3.7
Private consumption	3.1	3.2	−1.8	−3.7
Public consumption	9.2	1.0	7.6	−9.0
Gross investment	4.3	−7.6	−11.4	−16.3
Processing	2.2	−4.7	−11.2	−5.0
Unemployment (%)	8.0	7.4	9.5	12.5
Total employment	1.3	1.2	−1.1	−2.6
CPI (average levels)	2.9	4.2	1.2	4.5
Labour costs per unit	3.5	3.9	5.8	1.4
Credit expansion (to the private sector)	20.0	15.9	3.3	−1.5
General government deficit (% GDP)	−3.6	−7.8	−13.6	−9.0
Current accounts balance (capital transfers, % GDP)	−12.4	−12.6	−9.9	−8.0
Quarterly data	2007	2008	2009	2010[a]
Economic activity				
Volume of retail sales (excluding vehicle fuel and lubricants)	2.3	−1.4	−9.3	−4.5
Industrial production (manufacturing)	2.2	−4.7	−11.2	−4.6
Economic sentiment indicator	107.9	93.4	70.6	67.0
Business climate index in industry	102.8	91.9	72.1	74.6
Consumer confidence index	−28	−46	−46	−69
Credit expansion				
Private sector	21.5	15.9	4.2	0.4
Prices				
Consumer price indices	2.9	4.2	1.2	4.9
Interest rates				
Savings	1.14	1.17	0.56	0.42
Company subsidies (up to 1 year)	6.57	6.82	4.62	5.96
Yield of 10-year bond	4.50	4.80	5.17	9.57
GDP at constant prices	4.5	2.0	−2.0	−4.6
Final consumption	3.9	2.0	0.3	−5.5
Fixed capital investments	4.9	−7.4	−13.9	−20.0
Exports of goods and services	5.8	4.0	−18.1	−1.1
Imports of goods and services	7.1	0.2	−14.1	−17.8
Balance of payments (in billion euros)				
Trade balance	−41.5	−44.1	−30.8	−24.5
Balance of invisibles	13.5	13.2	6.1	5.8
Current accounts balance (capital transfers)	−28.1	−30.9	−24.7	−18.7

Source: Alpha bank (December 2010).
[a]Forecasts

contraction has not short-term positive effects on GDP and unemployment (NBG-Greece: Monthly Macroeconomic Outlook, January 2010). These effects depend on three factors: (a) the role of interest rates and exchange rates, (b) the composition of the fiscal package (i.e., costs versus revenues) and (c) the role of public perceptions

Table 13.2 Theoretical expectations based on international experience, expected results and actual results

		Theoretical expectations based on the experience[a] of 15 countries (%)	Expectations based on the EAP and EAP implementations (May 2010) (%)	Expectations based on the EAP and EAP implementations (December 2010) (%)
First year of fiscal adjustment	Reduction in primary outcome	4.6	5.4	4.6
	Change in GDP	−1.4	−4.0	(−4.5%)[b]−4.2
	Increase in unemployment	0.9	2.1	2.1
	Change in real exchange rate	−4.5		
	Contribution of domestic demand	−3.9	−5.6	−8.0
	Change in imports	−3.1	−10.3	−8.4
	Change in exports	4.4	1.5	5.7
Second year of fiscal adjustment	Reduction in primary outcome	3.9		2.1
	Change in GDP	−1.7	−2.6	(−3.47)[b]−3.0
	Increase in unemployment	0.9	2.1	2.9
	Change in real exchange rate	−2.3		
	Contribution of domestic demand	−3.8	−5.9	−6.0
	Change in imports	−3.7	−6.6	−5.4
	Change in exports	2.7	6.1	6.5

Source: EAP assessment, August and December 2010
[a]Estimates based on the theoretical model of the IMF (IMF, World Economic Outlook, October 2010)
[b]Estimates January 2011

on the development of risk in national debt, after the adoption of fiscal adjustment. The first factor, which involves interest rates and the depreciation of domestic currency, should be analysed by introducing the effect of exports and imports. Under normal circumstances, fiscal adjustment is associated with a reduction in interest rates by 20% for each 1% change in GDP. At the same time, as price levels are not expected to change, the decline in real interest rates is similar. The same applies to long-term interest rates on government bonds. More specifically, 2 years later, a decrease of 15% for every 1% decrease in GDP is expected. That is to say, under normal circumstances, a reduction in current and future interest rates, which is partially due to a reduction in the risk premium due to fiscal adjustments, leads to a reduction in interest rates on 10-year bonds. In addition, fiscal contraction is usually associated with a reduction in the real exchange rate of about 1.1%. Essentially, three very important changes take place, at least in theory: (a) fiscal contraction, (b) a reduction in real interest rates and (c) a reduction in the real exchange rate. Moreover, these changes lead to: (a) a reduction in the budget deficit, (b) an increase in consumption and investment due to the drop in interest rates and (c) real depreciation that in turn increases exports. Regarding this latter point, it should be noted that the contribution of net exports to GDP normally increases by 0.5% and thus increases economic activity. Here, we emphasise net exports since imports decrease because of the reduction in domestic purchasing power. In fact, a 1% reduction in GDP reduces the contribution of domestic demand by 1% 2 years later. Export growth is critical, or else the negative effect on GDP would be double that described above.

In the Greek economy, real devaluation was addressed by cuts in production costs using wage reductions in the public and, consequently, private sectors. Furthermore, real lending rates fell from 3.42 in 2009 to 1.06 in 2010 for loans in the private sector, mainly because of rising inflation (see Table 13.1). However, in reality, businesses faced interest rates of 7–8%, representing an increase in real interest rates as compared with 2009 by around 1%.

However, these changes in the interest rate mask a significant deterioration in the financial conditions of the private sector (see Table 13.1). Credit growth decreased to 0.4% in 2010 from 4.2% in 2009 (October 2010). The 10-year bond yield skyrocketed to 9.57% in 2010 from 5.17% in 2009. The labour cost per unit is expected to increase by 1.4% in 2010 versus 5.8% in 2009.

In Greece, as throughout the developed world, the crisis of 2008–2010 affected the external balance. The deficit in goods and services declined dramatically because of a significant reduction in imports and an increase in exports. The trade deficit shrank from 20% to 10%, while the current account deficit decreased from 15% to about 6% (Fig. 13.1).

Before proceeding further, it should be noted that Greece's recovery is expected to have negative effects on current account balances on a global level. The forecast for 2005–2015 by ECB (European Central Bank) President M. Constâncio (3/12/2010) is enlightening. Therefore, improvement on a global scale (and thus in Greece) is temporary.

Importantly, these developments in the Greek economy have been accompanied by a decrease in deposits. This decrease was due to two main reasons: (a) the

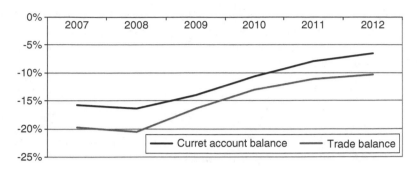

Fig. 13.1 Current transactions and trade balance as a percentage of GDP (Source: European commission [European Economic Forecast, autumn 2010])

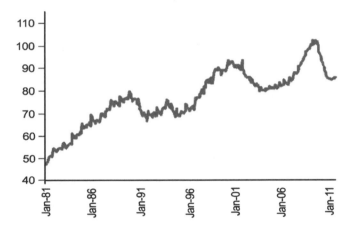

Fig. 13.2 Total deposits in the Greek banking system (% of GDP) (Source: National Bank of Greece (November 2010))

long-cycle behaviour of deposits (Fig. 13.2) and (b) the issue of trust in the Greek economy.

This evolution in deposits is outside the expected aggregate behaviour as compared with the classical market model.

What is interesting in relation to the above figures is that despite the adjustment process (i.e., downward pressure on wages), competitiveness indicators have shown an impressive recovery, at least up to now. In any case, unit labour costs have declined, both in absolute terms and in comparison with other Mediterranean countries. In fact, the Greek economy's contraction in 2011 may prove greater than AMECO[2] forecasts (Fig. 13.3 and Table 13.3).

---

[2] AMECO is the annual macro-economic database of the European Commission's Directorate General for Economic and Financial Affairs.

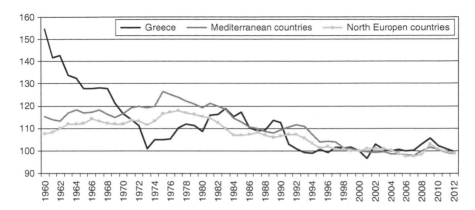

Fig. 13.3 Changes in unit labour costs (Source: European commission (AMECO database). Note: Mediterranean countries (Spain, Italy, Portugal) and Nordic countries (Netherlands, Finland and Sweden) are weighted based on the overall labour force for the examined period)

Table 13.3 Annual percentage change in real unit labour costs

	1992–1995	2007	2008	2009	2010	2011	2012
Germany	−0.6	−1.9	1.3	3.7	−1.4	−0.2	−0.1
Greece	−0.2	0.6	2.4	2.7	−3.2	−1.4	−1.3

Source: European commission (European Economic Forecast, autumn 2010)

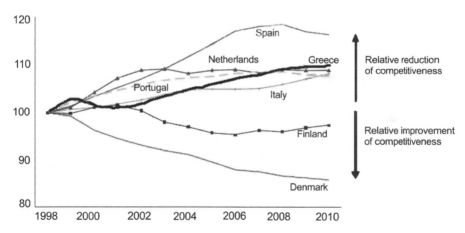

Fig. 13.4 Development in price comparisons as compared with the rest of Europe (Source: European commission (Annual Growth Survey, 12.1.2011))

This decline in unit labour costs in Greece is comparable to that of the most dynamic Nordic countries, but the gaps in competitiveness based on price comparisons (i.e., price competitiveness) between these countries have not been bridged (Fig. 13.4).

Table 13.4 Annual percentage change in the export-to-import ratio

	1992–2005	2007	2008	2009	2010	2011	2012
Greece	0.0	0.8	−3.3	1.0	1.0	0.1	−0.6
Spain	0.4	0.1	−2.3	4.1	−3.7	0.4	0.4
Italy	−0.4	1.5	−2.8	7.6	−2.4	0.3	−0.1
Portugal	0.4	0.4	−2.2	5.1	−1.8	0.2	−0.4
France	0.0	1.5	−1.2	2.3	−3.5	0.5	−0.2
Ireland	−0.3	−2.0	−5.9	4.9	−0.1	0.0	0.0
Germany	0.3	0.7	−1.5	6.1	−3.2	−0.1	−0.3

Source: European commission (European Economic Forecast, autumn 2010)

This trend will probably continue until 2012, if we take into account the expected change in the Terms of Trade for goods, as shown in Table 13.4.

Thus, it seems that the EAP interventions do not greatly change the competitiveness of the Greek economy.

Because of these deviations in the model of international experience of fiscal adjustment programs, the observed effects of the EAP on GDP and unemployment in the Greek economy are much larger than would be expected based on the 15 countries studied by the IMF (see Table 13.2).

The overview shown in Table 13.2 displays an even more interesting conclusion. The impact from the implementation of fiscal adjustments in the Greek economy is severe both in the first year and the second year of adjustment, as compared with the experience of the 15 countries studied by the IMF. This can be attributed to the monetary policy and to administrative ankylosis.

Will the Greek economy exhibit a positive growth rate of 1.1% in 2012, as predicted by the EAP? This expectation requires a 4.57% (= 3.47% + 1.1%) change in the growth rate; if this happens, it will be particularly impressive, as it is more realistic to expect a negative to zero growth rate. This scenario will be accompanied by a great (higher than expected) increase in unemployment, particularly if the shadow economy is affected. This will lead to a rise in unemployment without a decrease of the reportable product. Thus, this will lead to the "destruction" rather than the "unveiling" of the shadow economy.

The second factor relates to the composition of the financial package (i.e., revenues and costs). The IMF's 15-country model (October 2010) shows that spending cuts (i.e., the spending base) play a less negative role in the contraction of the real economy than raising taxes (i.e., the tax base). More specifically, when the fiscal adjustment is 1% of GDP, the contraction of the real economy 2 years later is 0.3% (assuming all else constant), while in the case of increasing taxes, it is −1.3%. However, what is this finding based on? When fiscal limitations are addressed using credit, there are negative consequences. Essentially, the real interest rates and the value of a currency (if depreciation is allowed) seem to fall even more so in the case of spending cuts than under tax increases. Indeed, it appears that net exports respond much better to spending cuts.

However, the character of these costs and revenues is of importance, particularly as to whether they refer to costs related to fiscal transfers, public investment or public consumption. Analysis shows that the impact of public investment is the greatest, followed by public consumption. Changes in public consumption have the slightest impact. In any case, these results are based on classical assumptions related to the role of monetary policy and real exchange rates, which requires the introduction of the concept of fiscal multipliers. To effectively determine the intensity and timing of fiscal adjustment interventions, we must assess the size of these adjustments, that is, the extent of the impact of aggregate charges on the real economy. Research based mainly on endogenous growth (Roeger and Velt 2010) focused on the European Union has found that fiscal multipliers have been found to be greater in the following cases:

1. For direct government spending and targeted transfers.
2. For households that cannot be financed from the banking system.
3. For monetary policies that do not counterbalance the effect of fiscal contraction.
4. For introverted economies.
5. For permanent, rather than temporary, budget changes.

Therefore, a reduction in direct government spending and targeted transfers with higher interest rates given credit-starved households and businesses in an inward-looking economy (as in Greece) will have very negative effects on economic activity, resulting in greater fiscal multipliers. Unfortunately, we cannot reconstruct these conditions (especially the scenario of an increased interest rate). However, studying available data on fiscal multipliers in conditions similar to those of Greece can lead to interesting insights for the Greek case (Table 13.5).

In any case, the contraction in costs proposed by the fiscal policy should follow the ranking below to minimise the impact on economic activity.

Table 13.5 Fiscal multipliers with credit restrictions and zero interest rates

	EU	World
	(1)	(2)
Investment grants	2.0	2.6
Government investment	1.1	1.2
Government purchases	1.0	1.2
Government salaries	1.4	1.5
General transfers	0.5	0.6
Transfers for credit constraints	0.9	1.0
Transfers for liquidity constraints	0.9	1.1
Labour tax	0.6	0.6
Excise tax	0.7	0.8
Property taxes	0.2	0.2
Corporate income taxes	0.0	0.1

Source: European commission (European Economic Forecast, autumn 2010)
Note: This can only be approximated for Greece, assuming that the Greek case lies between the two cases but with increased aggregates due to the increase in interest rates and the reduction in credits. In other words, monetary policy augments the effects of fiscal policy and is not neutral or compensatory

Indeed, the decline in the use of salaries has a 14-times higher negative effect on economic activity as compared with the contraction due to an increase in corporate profits. If indeed these results were combined with an increase in interest rates, then there would be an even greater differential effect on the two instruments. We note once again that the measures do not aim to reduce economic activity but to reduce public expenditure with minimal impact on economic activity.

Because of the EAP, the investment sector suffered extensive cuts, although Table 13.6 shows that it appears to have the lowest priority. The evolution of real public investment (Fig. 13.5) is enlightening.

The decrease in fiscal investment spending came by reducing state participation in the implementation of the full NSRF, in which, as is well-known, the Greek government participates at a level of 25%. It is significant that this program, which amounts to €24.3 bn with public participation of €6 bn, should be implemented from 2007 to 2013. At the end of 2010, the absorption rate was around 18%. The solution chosen by the government in 2010 to absorb the NSRF took the form of

Table 13.6 Estimation of ideal priority in fiscal actions in the Greek case

Corporate income tax	1
Property tax	2
General transfers	3
Excise tax	4
Transfers to households with credit constraints	5
Government consumption	6
Government investment	7
Government salaries	8
Investment incentives	9

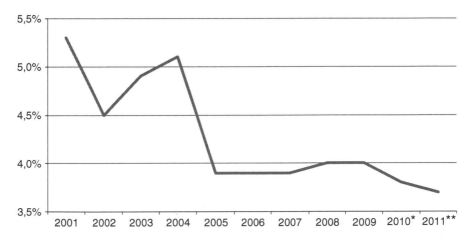

Fig. 13.5 Expenditure of the public investment program as compared with GDP (Source: Draft budget 2011. Notes: (*) Figures for 2010 estimates during the submission of the budget. (**) Figures for 2011 projections during the submission of the budget)

a new law. The new law allowed the conversion of the Managing Authorities of the Ministries into Program Implementation Authorities, thus dampening any results on the poor efficiency of the public sector, especially under the shock of fiscal adjustment. We attribute the failure to implement the NSRF – which is the largest observed implementation for the Community Support Framework in Greece since the 1980s – largely to this development.

We especially note that while the costs of the NSRF breakdown over time, which normally boosts the transfers of the balance of payments by an amount that can reach up to €4 bn per year, they actually have a much higher impact on domestic economic activity. In fact, after Portugal, Greece exhibited the greatest positive impact on the rate of growth because of EU budget interventions (Schneider 2007).

Using the HERMIN model to calculate the effects of structural funds, Bradley et al. (2003) assessed their impact on growth and unemployment for the period from 1993 to 2010 in Greece, Ireland, Portugal and Spain (Table 13.7).

This table shows that the costs of structural funds increase GDP growth by up to 2% and reduce employment by 1.4% over the reporting period from 1994 to 1999. It should be noted that this beneficial effect of structural funds remains until 2010, when the effect of structural funds in the period from 1994 to 1999 on the GDP reached an average of 0.44%. Essentially, the rest of this effect is greater than the effect of almost any other structural change.

In practice, these findings show that only a similar program with a positive influence on the Greek economy (which implies an annual financial burden of around €1 bn in public participation out of the €4 bn inflow) could support a growth rate of around 2%. However, it is not certain that the conditions from 1994 to 1999 are applicable to the period from 2010 to 2015 and, as such, would lead to a similar level of effectiveness with respect to structural costs.

Therefore, according to all indications, the most positive structural intervention could be the activation of the NSRF.

In the Greek economy, the mixture of income and expenditures in the fiscal adjustment package changed during the first year of implementation. The reason for this change refers to the weakness of collection procedures and the general institutional framework that shifted the mixture's emphasis on tax increases to cost cuts. Table 13.8, which contains a breakdown of the individual VAT liability for January–June 2009 and January–June 2010, is revealing, as it shows that the tax base of the economy has not widened, at least as regards VAT payers. In other words, although measures were introduced in the EAP Greek economic policy that would increase the number of those who submitted VAT statements (including specific measures for receipts and invoices), this did not happen (Table 13.9 and 13.10).

The effect of the change in revenue growth on reducing primary expenditures in the first year of the EAP implementation is twofold. The first aspect involves the severity of its impact on the real economy, and the second involves the socio-political aspects of the announced intervention of the EAP in relation to the implementation of this package. More specifically, the first effect refers to the views formed in society when politically sensitive spending is cut (Alesina and

Table 13.7 The effect of structural funds on GDP and unemployment, 1994–1999

	Greece		Ireland		Portugal		Spain	
	GDP	Unemployment	GDP	Unemployment	GDP	Unemployment	GDP	Unemployment
1994	2.01	−1.38	1.61	−0.96	2.72	−2.21	1.10	−0.98
1995	1.94	−1.19	2.02	−1.07	2.78	−1.76	1.18	−0.83
1996	1.95	−0.97	2.17	−0.92	2.87	−1.31	1.25	−0.57
1997	1.90	−0.68	2.34	−0.73	3.30	−0.73	1.32	−0.19
1998	2.03	−0.40	2.76	−0.51	4.04	−0.16	1.39	+0.30
1999	2.16	−0.31	2.83	−0.35	4.66	−0.05	1.39	+0.60
2000	0.44	+1.00	1.56	+0.53	2.20	+1.93	0.18	+1.78
2005	0.71	+0.68	1.20	+0.49	2.40	+1.09	0.63	+0.38
2010	0.66	+0.58	1.00	+0.40	2.06	+0.82	0.58	+0.35

Source: Bradley et al. (2003)

Table 13.8 Distribution of quarterly VAT statements (January–June 2009) in euros

Debit amount range (€)	Class C		Class B		Class A	
	Number of statements	Amount of VAT (€)	Number of statements	Amount of VAT (€)	Number of statements	Amount of VAT (€)
0–10000	525,357	345,309,101.93	1,694,909	750,040,463.49	43,375	4,872,479.01
10001–20000	19,409	273,728,472.85	10,018	136,106,188.51	7	97,182.85
20001–30000	8,134	198,688,455.25	2,377	57,278,927.46	1	25,744.81
30001–50000	7,220	277,022,832.52	1,230	46,053,092.04	–	–
50001–100000	5,703	398,092,626.95	394	26,242,327.92	–	–
100001–150000	2,070	251,200,512.45	86	10,156,247.31	–	–
150001<	3,973	2,325,059,052.87	95	63,215,338.64	–	–

Table 13.9 Distribution of quarterly VAT statements (January–June 2010) in euros

Range of debit amount (€)	Class C		Class B		Class A	
	Number of statements	Amount of VAT (€)	Number of statements	VAT amount (€)	Number of statements	VAT amount (€)
0–10000	515,729	355,116,001.77	1,637,995	883,872,325.19	39,682	4,506,509.77
10001–20000	20,253	285,485,980.11	12,246	165,766,431.15	8	116,819.62
20001–30000	8,192	200,457,415.26	2,669	64,109,804.91	1	29,924.65
30001–50000	7,418	284,821,302.22	1,372	51,241,018.37	–	–
50001–100000	5,658	394,604,224.21	451	29,826,238.63	–	–
100001–150000	2,001	242,379,870.25	53	6,444,226.86	–	–
150001<	3,933	2,280,220,246.31	104	82,161,851.63	–	–

Source: Ministry of Economy and Finance

Table 13.10 The fiscal adjustment package mix for the Greek economy

Year	Increase in revenue	Reduction in primary spending	Primary balance/GDP (%)
2009	–	–	−10.1
2010	22.0% (60)[a]	78.0% (60)[a]	−3.2
2011	86.0%	14.0%	−0.8
2012	−57.6%	157.6%	−0.2
2013	183.8%	−83.8%	0.1
2014	80.9%	19.1%	0.3

Source: EAP Assessment, December 2010
[a]As originally planned (June 2010) in the EAP

Perotti 1994). This effect emphasises the political nature of the decision to end financial excesses and curb budget deficits. As a result, it is created a real confidence about the future of the economy, and therefore, the reducing effect on economic activity is smaller. But, what if the political nature of this decision is fully understood, but confidence in the future nevertheless decreases, either because it is already limited or because the risk of fiscal bankruptcy has increased?

In this case, the negative impact of politically sensitive spending is perceived as a genuine political weakness and therefore a factor encouraging a dismal future. Thus, the impact of this decision on the current level of economic activity will be higher due mainly to decreased consumption.

The second effect concerns the fact that ultimately, the weakness of the state to perform the announced program of fiscal adjustment affects the economic outcome. Therefore, (a) if we adopt the opinion of the IMF, lower effects are eventually expected, while (b) if we adopt the opinion of the European Commission, a greater impact is expected. With respect to the issue of multipliers, we should probably rely on the European Commission because in reality, the impact of the EAP was greater than expected (although this finding may be due to other reasons that those outlined here).

Finally, the perception of fiscal bankruptcy risk plays a very important role in shaping the impact of fiscal adjustment. The assessment of the effects of potential bankruptcy on the effectiveness of fiscal adjustment is grounded in simply reasoning. If there is increased confidence regarding the future, the possibilities for managing the negative impact of fiscal adjustment are greater, and therefore, the impact on the real economy is smaller. The opposite happens in an environment of reduced confidence (as in the case of Greece). This dynamic, which acts in a direction opposite from theoretical expectations, can worsen the effects of the EAP intervention.

More generally, any action that increases confidence in the future (IMF – Global Financial Stability Report, October 2010) and improves expectations should enhance economic activity during fiscal adjustment. The opposite occurs in an environment with lack of confidence in the future.

13.2   Structural Interventions

The structural changes proposed by the EAP (organised in 2005[3] into a proposal to OECD and G-20 countries), aimed to augment potential growth. That is why they are often divided by their scope of application with respect to growth, namely, capital, labour, human capital, innovation and the institutional framework, with particular emphasis on financial institutions such as product and service markets, the banking system and the insurance system.

Structural changes affect the (future) capacity of legislation via two essential channels: the effect of structural changes on labour and human capital and the improvement of the economy's productivity, i.e., the Total Factor Productivity (TFP), due to structural changes.

It is certainly very difficult to appreciate the positive efficacy of a single change as compared with the costs incurred. Let us not forget that "contrary to long-term benefits, in the short-term the effects of structural change are sometimes questionable and should not be overestimated. Especially the existing approaches to assessing the effect of the reforms may not capture all short-term costs associated with these changes" (European Commission – European Economic Forecast, autumn 2010). However, in the above quote, the European Commission makes reference to the desirability of these policies through three examples. If public expenditure on research and development (R&D) is 0.6% for the EU-27, the three top-performing European countries have expenditures of 0.8% and the U.S. has an expenditure of 0.7%, then there is obviously room for improvement. In addition, if the mark-up[4] for final products is 24.2, this figure is 17.8 for the three top-performing European countries, and it is 20.5 for the U.S., then there is obviously room to enhance competition in final product markets

To evaluate the impact of structural interventions, we use multipliers, that is, the relationship between the quantity of intervention in a specific area and the GDP or

---

[3] OECD, Going for Growth, 2005–2010.

[4] Mark-up is the difference between production cost and selling price. This difference creates profit.

the GDP per capita as a whole. These multipliers refer to different time scales and are derived from general endogenous equilibrium models (such as QUEST III for the European Commission).

Table 13.11 summarises some conclusions concerning the effect of speed of adjustments in different areas of structural change. It is obvious that strengthening research and development through tax exemptions or salary payments to research staff can bear results at best a decade from the present. The same applies to higher educational policies that affect the supply of specialists. However, as the private rates of return of these investments are particularly important, it is obvious that

Table 13.11 Effects of GDP on structural reforms

Policy	Effects of GDP on standard reform simulations				Steady state
	2 years	5 years	10 years	20 years	
Availability of labour coefficient					
Reduction in replacement rate	0.8	1.3	1.5/1.0	1.7/1.5	
Reduction in salary revaluation	0.4	0.7	0.8	0.9	
Transfer of taxes from labour to VAT	0.1	0.2	0.2	0.3	
Transfer of taxes from low-skill to high-skill labour	0.1	0.2	0.2	0.2	
Reduction in the average tax margin			3.3	5.2	
Reduction in regulations on labour			0.3	0.4	
Increase in the percentage of medium-skilled labour protection	0.0	0.0	0.1	0.2	0.6
Increase in the percentage of high-skilled labour	0.0	0.1	0.1	0.3	0.1
Productivity					
Human capital[a]					
Infant care			0.0		0.0
Effectiveness of secondary education (PISA)			0.1		2.0
Average years of education			0.6		8.1
Innovation[b]					
Tax subsidies for R&D	0.0	−0.1	0.0	0.1	
Wage subsidies for R&D	−0.1	−0.1	0.0	0.1	
Product markets					
Reduction in mark-up (finished goods)	0.3	0.4	0.5	0.6	
Reduction in mark-up (intermediate goods)	0.2	0.3	0.3	0.3	
Reduction in administrative burden	0.5	0.6	0.6	0.6	
Reduction in barriers to entry (for high-tech companies)	0.0	0.0	0.0	0.0	
Reduction in tangible capital cost	0.1	0.3	0.5	0.9	
Reduction in intangible capital cost	−0.1	−0.1	0.0	0.1	
Decrease in regulations on industry of networks			0.6	0.3	

Sources: [a]Luiz de Mello and Padoan (2010)
[b]European Commission (European Economic Forecast, autumn 2010)

such investments are also desirable in the short term. In conclusion, although investments in education have a long-term performance and thus low priority, their absence would cause deterioration in the future. During the crisis, Greece had a significant amount (€2 bn) invested in education, of which 75% came from European structural funds. The effectiveness of investing this amount remains questionable, due to the time of completion of the present book.

According to all indications, final product markets present a high potential for intervention to strengthen hypothetical dynamic growth. Measures such as the easing of administrative restrictions to entry and the reduction of the administrative burden are commonly used for assistance in these markets. These conditions improve the allocation of resources between goods and services sectors as well as within these sectors. Some of the effects of these measures are direct, but their overall positive impact extends over time. For example, Table 13.11 shows that the reduction of the mark-up on finished products by 1% increases GDP by about 0.2% in 2 years, 0.5% in 5 years and 0.5% in 10 years. The same applies for the mark-up on intermediate goods and the adoption of measures that would reduce administrative burden.

One question that arises concerns product mark-ups in the Greek economy. Recall that in Chap. 7, which analyses the situation of its oligopolistic organisation, we highlighted the presence of strong oligopolistic concentrations, which suggested strong performance in the formulation of rates of return. Figure 13.6 shows the relationship between net operating profit (adjusted for the compensation of employees) and net capital in the Greek as economy compared with other Mediterranean countries (MEDC) and Nordic countries (NEC). It shows that in the Greek economy, the ratio of profit to capital, which was especially high in the period from

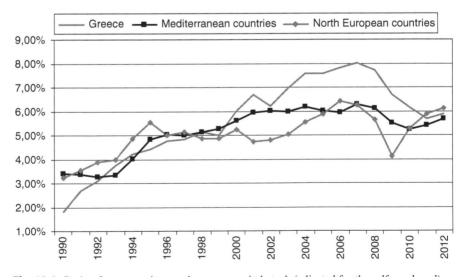

Fig. 13.6 Ratio of net operating surplus to net capital stock (adjusted for the self-employed)

2002 to 2008, fell sharply after 2008, not a result of structural policies but of the financial crisis.

When an increase in tax rates was attempted, the Greek production system applied a practice of maintaining mark-up policies (i.e., profit margin retention) coupled with oligopolistic competition. That is, according to both the EAP and bibliography, part of this increase was expected to be absorbed by profits based on forecasted inflation at around 1%; however, the inflation turned out to be 4.9% in 2010, with a downward trend in the future. It should be noted that this development occurred when the capacity utilisation gap was very high. This development depressed incomes and demand even more; as such, it did not prevent a decline in profit margins.

Interestingly, this decrease in net profit rates is observed despite reduced labour costs; the change in work pay in 2010 was −1.8%, and it is estimated to be −0.2% in 2011 and 0.1% in 2012 (European Commission – European Economic Forecast, autumn 2010).

This effect on the labour markets may emerge either from the increase in labour supply or the reduction in structural unemployment. Obviously, the top priority is to increase workforce expansion policies either by adopting measures to increase the labour supply (i.e., tax incentives) or by protecting the most vulnerable groups from long-term unemployment. The prohibition on older employees, which is achieved through administrative and fiscal measures, is a typical example of the latter approach. These legislative initiatives ignore the human capital invested in people aged 50–60 years old, who are encouraged to retire relatively young because of the available pension systems. These initiatives in turn impose crippling disincentives for older employees to return to the labour market. Most commonly, they resort to the underground economy, even if they end up working for the same companies that just let them go.

Mourougane and Vogel (2008) have found a very high correlation between unemployment and structural reforms, on the one hand, with the taxation of work immediately after the application of such policies. All other correlations and policy measures, however, were found to be statistically insignificant. However, there is a general agreement that labour market reforms can create significant short-term problems in terms of the growth rate.

The European Commission (European Economic Forecast, Autumn 2010) concludes with a table showing the expected macroeconomic effects of structural policies on GDP and employment in the EU during from 2012 to 2030 (Table 13.12).

Table 13.12 shows that the improvement in competition (i.e., the reduction in mark-ups) would result in a 0.2% increase in the GDP in 2012, a 0.7% increase in 2015, a 0.9% increase in 2020 and a 0.6% increase in 2030. Bearing in mind, however, that these increases relate to growth rates, the cumulative increases in economic growth are extremely important.

It appears that perhaps the intervention with the greatest impact on GDP is an improvement in product market competition, followed by a reduction in the administrative burden of businesses. In terms of employment, an improvement in

Table 13.12 Macroeconomic effects of specific structural reforms

	2012	2015	2020	2030
GDP effects				
Reduction in mark-ups	0.2	0.7	0.9	0.6
Reduction in administrative burden	0.1	0.3	0.3	0.6
Tax subsidies for R&D	0.0	0.0	0.0	0.1
Decrease in replacement rate profit[a]	0.1	0.3	0.5	1.7
Transfer taxes from labour to VAT	0.1	0.3	0.5	0.3
Total	0.4	1.5	2.2	3.3
Effects of employment				
Reduction in mark–ups	0.2	0.4	0.2	0.1
Reduction in administrative burden	−0.1	−0.1	−0.1	−0.1
Tax subsidies for R&D	0.0	0.0	0.0	0.0
Decrease in replacement rate profit[a]	0.1	0.5	0.8	0.8
Transfer taxes from labour to VAT	0.1	0.4	0.6	0.7
Total	0.3	1.2	1.5	1.4

Source: European Commission – European Economic Forecast, autumn 2010
[a]Refers to the replacement rate of labour wages by pensions. When the replacement rate is high, it acts as an incentive for retirement

efficiency again has the greatest impact, followed by an increase in the labour supply through incentives such as insurance and tax systems that move the tax burden from labour to VAT.

On the basis of the above analysis, we find that although structural changes are found to have positive effects on GDP and employment, (a) these extend over time, and (b) in the Greek case, the economic system does not react exactly as expected. Aghion and Cage (2010) note that the promotion of competition (i.e., a decrease in mark-ups) and an improvement in the functionality (i.e., competitiveness) of labour markets make sense to the extent the effected areas are technologically advanced. In other words, reaping the benefits of enhanced competition requires high-level players (in terms of production and technology). As such, these measures may help the most (technologically) powerful players in the economy while negatively affecting weaker players (and not only in the Greek economy).

The next aspect to be considered carefully is the social cost of these changes and, consequently, the order in which changes are adopted.

The horizontal approach, for example, to labour market intervention involves increasing the supply of services. As such, it can entail a high social cost and be highly inefficient, for example, if the number of professionals is very high despite administrative constraints. In this case, the real problem is the existence of mandatory minimum wages, not the number of those who offer their services.

Moreover, a crisis of confidence may cause more extensive restructuring in the financial system. Focusing on the period from 2008 to 2010, Aghion and Cage (2010) proposed that "we should all become Scandinavians" as a response to the crisis.

The last issue in the analysis of structural changes involves sectoral preference policies. Theoretically, sectoral policies favoured by the state should not be adopted by the EU mainly because of concerns regarding competition. However, since its establishment, the EAP has induced an indirect negative impact on certain sectors of the economy. Thus, if demand is reduced in Greek economy which is 80% based on domestic markets, then certain sectors will suffer the greatest burden, particularly retail, wholesale trade and construction. We note that the agricultural sector will also suffer the negative consequences of recent developments. Alternatively, under this policy, export industries and businesses that would enjoy an innovative and competitive advantage. This latter group though is very small and non-significant. Thus, we emphasise that this policy's differential effects on various sectors is such that the negative consequences are far greater than the positive. Therefore, a policy of structural interventions in such an economy would have to develop a compensation policy that addressed sectoral variations to develop new sectors for comparative advantage.

The crisis of 2008–2010 showed that focusing on the safety of individual banks is not enough; however, it may be important from a systemic perspective. Implemented policies must take into account the extensive connections throughout the financial system and the numerous problematic financial positions across a wide variety of economic activities, including the non-financial sector (Rehn 30/11/2010). In other words, emphasis should be placed on the issue of liquidity.

Indeed, the restoration of financial stability must treat two main negative Consequences: (a) the development of systematic risk and (b) concentric conduct (Viñals et al. 2010). In other words, policy makers should be concerned with the tendency of banks to boost expansionist forces in an economy during economic expansion and decrease them when the economy contracts. This is why the EU developed a European System of Financial Supervision that appointed the European Supervisory Authority to implement microeconomic control and the European Systematic Risk Board (ESRB) to implement macroeconomic control.

Before concluding this section, we should refer to the relationship between fiscal deficits and income inequality because these will likely be magnified during periods of fiscal adjustment. Therefore, if there is a positive correlation between income inequality and fiscal deficits, then fiscal adjustment itself is a self-defeating mechanism. In contrast, the reduction of income inequality is likely to restrict fiscal deficits.

So-called persistent deficits are typically accumulated by creating a large public debt and using government borrowing to finance this debt. The recent upsurge in these deficits is mainly due to two political factors. First, voters often do not consider that economic deficits must be covered by future tax increases and spending cuts. Second, those in power favour policies and reforms that benefit their own voters but ignore the tax burden over the entire economy (von Hagen 1992; von Hagen and Harden 1994; von Hagen and Poterba 1999).

According to Atkinson (1997), for several years now, the unequal distribution of income has been considered a political and social issue rather than a question of neoclassical economics. However, as Meltzer and Richards (1981) and Dixit and

Londregan (1996) have noted, an unequal economic distribution creates the conditions for a voting majority in favour of redistributive tax and spending programs. So the greater the economic imbalance is, the greater is the level of redistributive spending and, hence, the need for government borrowing. At the same time, Alesina and Drazen (1991) have argued that the more unequal is the distribution of the burdens of reform, the greater is the resistance to new changes. In other words, there is a delay in efforts aimed at fiscal stabilisation, which increases with an unequal distribution of the burdens of fiscal intervention. Moreover, Larch (2010) has argued that unequal distributions of income outweigh the effectiveness of interventions, which create deficits. More specifically, the political differences between the rich and the poor may lead to delays in fiscal adjustment, accelerating the accumulation of debt for future generations. This debt can be easily accumulated because future generations are not present when this new public debt is created (Ozler and Tabellini 1991). The uneven distribution of income can lead to increases in costs that do not correspond with the increases in revenue, nor do they prevent growth from affecting the budget. Eventually, this imbalance impedes economic growth (Aghion and Howitt 1998). Past research has only approached this issue theoretically; indeed, Larch's study (2010) represents a first attempt at empirical analysis.[5] It places special emphasis on the political factors that play a role in shaping the relations between politics and economics, concluding that: (a) an increase in inequality leads to lower levels of fiscal discipline, (b) political instability coupled with an unequal distribution of income may result in additional budget costs and (c) the positive effects of growth decrease as this imbalance increases, as the political pressure to distribute revenue resulting from increases in growth.

13.3   The Financial System and the Real Economy

Given that this portion of the research was completed in January 2011, when very few efforts to reactivate the Greek financial system had started, its appropriate title would be "(Non)-intervention in the financial system."

At the end of 2010, Greece's four largest banks held 80% of total loans and 83% of deposits (Table 13.13).

Despite the clear intent of the EAP (European Commission – European Economic Forecast, autumn 2010, p. 87) to increase confidence in the Greek economy, a number of negative developments emerged.

---

[5] Larch (2010) uses data for 30 industrial and middle-income OECD countries for the period 1960–2008.

Table 13.13 Selected figures on Greece's four largest banks

		Amount (in million euros)					Percentage of total			
		National bank	EFG Eurobank Ergasias	Alpha bank	Piraeus bank	Total	National bank (%)	EFG Eurobank Ergasias (%)	Alpha bank (%)	Piraeus bank (%)
2010/09	Assets	123.517	86.490	65.004	57.559	467.661	26	18	14	12
	Loans	74.414	55.583	40.594	39.257	261.380	28	21	16	15
	Deposits	70.134	43.590	32.525	30.027	212.545	33	21	15	14
2009/09	Assets	112.240	84.269	67.848	52.252	481.295	23	18	14	11
	Loans	69.877	55.837	41.811	38.335	251.471	28	22	17	15
	Deposits	69.939	46.808	35.258	31.410	237.824	29	20	15	13

Source: BoG, Consolidated MFI balance sheets and CI balance sheet statements, September 2010

1. A wave of distrust, indicated by a flow of bank withdrawals, meant that liquidity relied exclusively on the ECB. Importantly, this phenomenon did not take place exclusively in Greece. It is estimated that in December 2010, the ECB's financing of the Eurozone reached €500 bn, of which €100 bn went to Greece, suggesting that Greek's economic plight was particularly severe.
2. We argue that this crisis of confidence in the banking system relates to the following five main issues.
   - The Greek fiscal problem.
   - The expansion of the Greek banking sector to southeastern Europe coupled with the crisis of confidence regarding the Greek fiscal problem. Note that when the crisis began, activities in southeastern Europe accounted for close to 20–30% of the entire Greek banking system. This expansion also increased the obligations of the Greek banking system towards other financial institutions, which aggravated (to what extent?) their status and Greece's position during the crisis (May 2010).
   - The refinancing needs of the banks themselves due to their excessive expansion in recent years (see Fig. 13.7).
   - The need to fund public sector and the forced investment of available bank funds into Greek bonds (see Table 13.14).
   - The exclusion of Greek banks from the international capital markets, which resulted from the factors above.

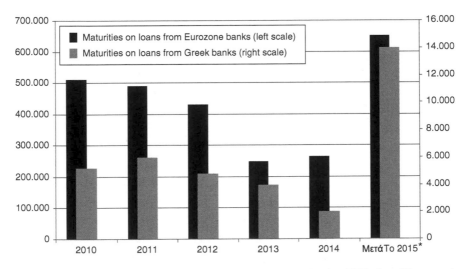

Fig. 13.7 Maturities on loans from Greek banks and Eurozone banks (2009) (in million euros). Note: *For European banks, the amounts are from the period 2015–2019, while for Greek banks, the period is 2015–2049 (Source: ECB and credit institution statements)

Table 13.14 Bank equity
and value of bonds held
(January 2011)

	Capital	Bonds
National bank	11	15
Alpha bank	5.2	4.6
EFG Eurobank-Ergasias	5.5	7.45
Piraeus bank	4.2	8.8
Agrotiki bank	1.3	4.4
Hellenic Postbank	0.8	5.3
Bank of Cyprus	3.2	1.9
Marfin Popular bank	4.6	2.9
Total	35.8	55.7

Source: Credit institution announcements
Note: Amounts in billion euros

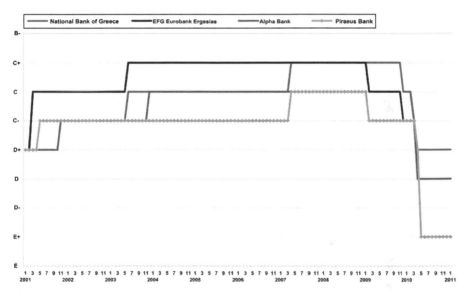

Fig. 13.8 Changes in the Moody's bank financial strength rating for the four major Greek banks
(Source: Moody's)

This crisis was indicated through the continuous downgrading of the banking
system's creditworthiness by three international rating firms (see Fig. 13.8).

These conditions would have had highly negative effects on the core capital ratio
of banks if the Greek government's plan for bank recapitalisation had not been
implemented.

When the time for the bank stress tests (summer 2010) arrived, all Greek banks
were in fairly good condition, with the exception of Agrotiki bank; Piraeus bank
was marked as a borderline case (Table 13.15).

However, the stress tests from last summer reflected the condition of banks with
respect to their ability to withstand adverse developments due to late payments.
Problems related to the confidence crisis and risk liquidity risk were not covered by
the stress tests in summer 2010.

Table 13.15 Core capital ratio of Greek and Cypriot banks in December 2009 and estimates for late 2011

	Equity capital ratio (December 2009) (%)	Estimates of equity capital ratio for December 2011		
		Reference scenario (%)	Worst-case scenario (%)	Worst-case scenario and additional financial turmoil (%)
National bank	11.3	11.7	9.6	7.4
EFG Eurobank	11.2	11.7	10.2	8.2
Alpha bank	11.6	12.3	10.9	8.2
Piraeus bank	9.1	10.9	8.3	6.0
Hellenic Postbank	17.1	17.0	15.0	10.1
Agrotiki bank	8.4	10.7	8.9	4.4
Bank of Cyprus	10.5	10.9	9.4	8.0
Marfin Popular bank	9.4	10.0	8.5	7.1

Source: CESB, BoG and CI announcements.
Notes: The equity capital ratio results from the relation of equity to weighted risk assets. The price of the index should not be less than 4% (Basel II), and from 2015 to 2019 (Basel III), the minimum threshold is projected to grow to 6% and gradually reach 8.5% if the strict suggestions proposed are accepted. This estimate includes a further provision for periods of credit expansion in the banking system
The basic scenario involves the contraction of the Greek GDP by 4.1% and 2.6% in 2010 and 2011, respectively, and an unemployment rate of 11.7% and 14.1%, respectively. The worst-case scenario assumes that GDP will shrink by 4.6% and 4.3% in 2010 and 2011, respectively, while unemployment will reach 11.8% and 14.8% in those years, respectively. In the event of adverse macroeconomic developments and financial turmoil, it is assumed that the nominal value of Greek government bonds will drop by 20.1% and 23.1% in 2010 and 2011, respectively.

The EAP's provisions included a line of €10 bn that could be used to support Greece's financial system.

It should be noted that the amount of €10 bn sufficed for the capitalisation of the Greek banking system (i.e., the four big banks) as of the end of December 2010.

However, as of January 2011, the Financial Stability Fund was still not activated, possibly because of difficult political issues associated with the major shareholders of these banks. After all, the activation of the Fund may lead to loss of private ownership. To compensate for this loss, NBG, Pisteos, Piraeus, Cyprus, Marfin and Agrotiki proceeded to implement a total of €4 bn in capital increases. The National Bank also announced its intention to sell its 20% shareholding in Finasbank Turkey.

At the same time, the issuance of guarantees by the Greek government to the banking system to ensure that the European Central Bank would continue to provide liquidity gained momentum. Unfortunately, we cannot accurately differentiate between the announcements regarding these support packages and their actual utilisation. According to all indications, the guarantees shown in Table 13.16 should apply as of January 2011.

Table 13.16 Guarantees
to the banking system

	Guarantees	Preferred shares
April 2009	€25 bn	€3.7 bn
June 2010	€25 bn	
January 2011 (announcement)	€30 bn	
Total	€78 bn	€3.7 bn

If we also take into account that the portfolios of Greek banks included Greek government bonds (investments) of €55.7 bn and that €140 bn had been deposited as collateral securities to the ECB, it appears that the figures in Table 13.16 are correct if we include the securitisation of loans, which amount to approximately €76 bn (see Chap. 10, Section 10.3).

These findings reveal yet again that this is a banking system with an extremely severe liquidity problem. This is apparently true if we consider that by the end of December 2010, the German system had absorbed €64 bn from the ECB, while this figure was €100 bn for Greek banking system. Meanwhile, the fund designated to stabilise the German financial sector (SoFFin)[6] had stakes amounting to €29 bn in four German banks.

The long-term seasonal movement of deposits (see Fig. 13.2) and the crisis of confidence in the Greek banking system culminated in January 2011, without immediate prospects of recovery. This is why the provision of a new €30 bn securities package to the banks was announced by the Greek government in January 2011; this was not included in the above calculations. This package will cover the new projected liquidity needs of the Greek banking system for 2011, which are estimated at €15 bn. As such, this is the context in which we should evaluate the merger proposal made by the NBG to Alpha to create a Greek super-bank; this new bank would be the 27th bank in the Greek economy. Undoubtedly, though this would address NBG's business objectives, this move essentially serves to restore a climate of confidence.

The conditions described above have resulted in a serious reduction in funding opportunities for the Greek economy. Indeed, similar phenomena related to contracted private-sector funding have emerged worldwide, particularly in the U.S. However, the contraction of bank financing was much more severe in the Greek economy than in the Eurozone, and mid-2010 and 2011 estimates remain negative (Fig. 13.9).

Note that the creditworthiness of the productive economy (i.e., the non-financial sector) already began to deteriorate significantly in 2009. The growth in sector defaults in 2009 as compared with 2008 for a sample of 21,743 SAs and LTDs examined by ICAP (2010) is revealing; see Table 13.17.

Of course, the key problem of the Greek economy concerns its production sector. If systematic risk of economies across the globe clearly affected the respective banking systems, which was the main characteristic of the crisis period of

---

[6] SoFFin: Sonderfonds Finanzmarktstabilisierung – Financial Market Stabilization Fund.

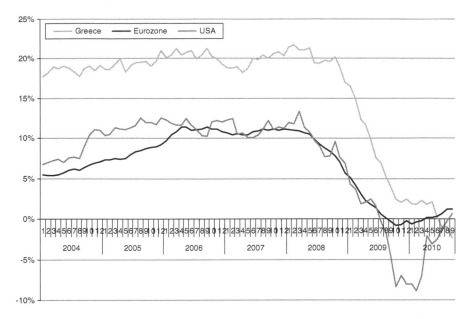

Fig. 13.9 Bank lending to the private sector (excluding financial institutions). Percentage indicates change as compared with the same period 1 year ago (Source: BoG and OECD (Economic Surveys, Euro Area, December 2010))

Table 13.17 Percentage of defaulted companies by sector

	Industry (%)	Trade (%)	Services (%)	Total (%)
Avg 2003–2008	4.43	2.82	2.80	3.37
2009	6.04	4.65	3.08	4.70
Percentage change	36.34	64.89	10.00	39.47

Source: ICAP (2010).

2008–2010, does it not also follow that systematic risk would involve the entire production system? In other words, the means chosen by politicians and policy makers to solve the problem emphasised the financial system rather than the production sector insofar as they aimed to strengthen the equity of banks rather than the production units that suffered from the crisis. In the U.S., the TARP, which was an economic rescue program developed after the crisis, included generous aid to the productive sector in straightforward ways, including commercial paper purchases, capital injections and so on. In Europe, such solutions were ignored, or they were only selected as a supplementary option. This also applies to the Greek economy. This economy, however, was and is "bank-oriented" in the sense that the mediating function of banks, which largely determines the functionality of the capital markets, presents multiple problems when (a) the intermediary system (i.e., the banking system) faces increased liquidity problems and (b) corrective interventions are delayed. Hence, the choice to strengthen the financial system as a means to solve problems related to the real economy leads to interventions in the relevant fields of economic power. In addition, this move has caused property restructuring within the production sector itself in unknown directions, with particular benefits to the strongest financial and manufacturing centres. These interventions have thus had a purely political purpose.

However, the decision to withhold the so-called "horizontal" support through the financing of the banking system, at the European level, no one imagined that providing liquidity to the banking system of an economy could reach such levels. These liquidity injections sometimes almost equalled 40% of all other loans to the private sector, without actually directly benefitting the private sector (at least in 2010 and 2011). Therefore, it is necessary to address at the outset the funding situation of Greece's banking and production sectors from a different perspective. On the basis of the EPA estimates', there is no reason that the Greek economic crisis should have been so intense.

13.4 Education and Innovation

According to all indications, both education and innovation are suitable areas for development interventions, as they are key elements in forming an effective production system. Indeed, their key feature as TFP factors is their long-term effects.

Interventions in these two areas face significantly different implementation contexts. Apart from financial costs, interventions in education usually have short-term multiplier effects that are not related directly to improvements in the economic growth rate, including: (a) improvement of the intellectual level and maturity of the recipients of higher levels of education inflows and (b) increases in the private investments of recipients of higher levels of inflows.

Interventions in the field of innovation should be divided into two main categories, namely, (a) those that use research to boost production and (b) those that facilitate the use of innovations by companies.

One typical example is the effort made in Greece to create spin-off companies in collaboration with universities and research centres from 2002 to 2007 through the implementation of strong financial incentives. As a result, 36 spin-off companies with a total budget of €45 m were created (first, second, third round of calls for interest). Moreover, from 2007 to 2010, 112 companies with a total budget of €99 m applied for funding (third, fourth round of production). This applicant pool should result in a similar number of approvals as in first three cycles (Data 2010, General Secretariat for Research and Technology, Ministry of Education). We estimate that in a best-case scenario, all of the efforts described above may lead to the creation of perhaps a dozen dynamic spin-off companies. This is a very poor result.

This approach to entrepreneurship involves collaboration with universities and research centres in the sphere of knowledge production. In reality, Greece's implementation of this approach is at a similar stage as the U.S. was in the period before the Second World War and then from 1940 to 1960 (Mowery 2005) before the Bayh-Dole Act in 1983. Even then, the U.S. was afraid of changing in the non-profit character of institutions. Of course, this fear subsequently gave way to an explosive growth in approvals for economic exploitation from 1980 to 2000 (as indeed happens up to now).

In conclusion, the economic exploitation of research results requires the following conditions.

1. Universities and the research system (including publications and citations) should operate reasonably well.
2. Research results do not immediately result in patent registrations. This may occur for two main reasons.
    2.1. There may be social factors that separate production and research; for example, in Greece, while science, mathematics and technology degrees may be important in starting a scientific career, these degrees are irrelevant for careers in the production sector.
    2.2. The benefits of the economic exploitation of research results must outweigh a number of factors, as follows.
        (a) A social environment hostile entrepreneurship.
        (b) Any negative social perceptions (usually emerging from the university) on the economic exploitation of research results, and
        (c) The poor salaries and personal motivations of researchers, which together are not conducive to the development of intellectual innovation. Characteristically, researchers must pay a 23% VAT on income from intellectual creations. Essentially, it is treated as a luxury item such as luxury goods and jewellery, which accumulate value, in contrast to intellectual creation, which produces value. Interestingly, if someone were to exempt intellectual creation from VAT as a tax incentive, the impact on public finances would initially be almost null, given the currently limited contribution of this tax to Greek government revenues.

Some additional comments are relevant on the issue of intellectual property. The treatment of the production of intellectual goods should be uniform, regardless of the scientific field from which they originate (e.g., natural, literary or computational sciences). This is especially important in an economy in which the cultural sector and the education system deviate from the human sciences. It is obvious that there is great potential for value production in these disciplines.

The EAP references educational interventions that focus on improving the efficiency of public spending while emphasising higher education. The European Commission's research in this area (Miguel et al. 2009) reached some key conclusions, which should set the main priorities for educational interventions. The priorities relating to efficiency improvements include the following.

(a) Good-quality secondary education.
(b) Financing arrangements that rely on results.
(c) Independent institutions for evaluation.
(d) Self-governing operation authorities.

The implementation of initiatives would improve the efficiency of the education system, enabling it to contribute more effectively to economic growth. This is confirmed by a number of observations. Table 13.18, which describes the monetary benefit in terms of current values and OECD economic growth, is revealing.

Interestingly, if Greece managed to increase its overall PISA performance by 25 points, the overall positive result of this change by 2070 would equal $996 bn at

Table 13.18 Benefit from reforms in secondary education and their performance

Countries	Scenario 1: Increase in the average performance in PISA scores by 25 points	Scenario 2: All countries on average reach Finland's PISA score (546 points)	
	Benefit from reform (billion $) (at current values)	Benefit from reform (billion $) (at current values)	Performance of reform (long-term growth) (%)
Australia	2,527	2,011	0.35
Austria	899	1,430	0.67
Belgium	1,108	1,452	0.56
France	6,043	10,424	0.72
Germany	8,088	15,743	0.80
Denmark	586	1,181	0.82
Switzerland	792	1,120	0.60
Greece	996	3,996	1.48
UK	6,374	7,326	0.49
US	40,647	103,073	1.01
Japan	11,640	2,526	0.10
Ireland	514	870	0.71
Iceland	40	74	0.76
Spain	4,147	11,289	1.07
Italy	5,223	18,094	1.31
Canada	3,743	2,524	0.30
Korea	4,054	746	0.08
Luxembourg	116	383	1.26
Mexico	4,812	38,756	2.50
New Zealand	338	258	0.34
Norway	841	1,956	0.94
Netherlands	1,889	1,251	0.29
Hungary	587	1,282	0.88
Poland	2,029	5,061	0.99
Portugal	680	2,588	1.42
Slovakia	311	709	0.92
Sweden	1,019	1,657	0.68
Turkey	3,416	21,365	2.08
Czech Rep.	918	1,060	0.50
Finland	553	0	0.00
Total	114,930	260,204	0.87

Source: The High Cost of Low Educational Performance (OECD 2010)

current prices. If it increased the efficiency of its education system to that of Finland, it would create new wealth of about \$3.996 bn, which is approximately equal to 14 times its current GDP.

These figures are so compelling that they led Hanushek and Woessmann (2010) to investigate whether reforms aimed at developing institutional property rights frameworks and encouraging degree of openness of economies or the performance in understanding capabilities (PISA results in mathematics, sciences and reading) are the most significant reforms from 1960 to 2000. Their conclusion is clear: property rights and an economy's degree of openness encourages long-term growth, but differences understanding capability imply differences in the resulting growth across countries.

This is also confirmed by Glaeser et al.'s (2004) conclusion that human capital may be a more important inflow than institutional restructuring.

Hanushek and Woessmann (2010) expanded their study to include structural measures usually recommended to improve medium- to long-term growth opportunities, including (a) market arrangements, (b) administrative arrangements, (c) government controls, (d) barriers to entrepreneurship, (e) barriers to trade and investments and (f) arrangements in collective agreements. Their conclusion is very clear: "Not even one from this large arsenal of measures concerning either the product or labour markets is even remotely relevant to differences in long-term growth in OECD countries". However, the results on education are noted to be strong indicators of differences in long-term growth across OECD countries.

In conclusion, efficient structural policies in education and innovation are among the most pressing problem of all structural policies, despite their mid- to long-term performance expectations. Their absence in the Greek economy from period 2009 to 2010, which is to some extent explained by a lack of public participation, had multiple negative effects. In any case, one cannot help but wonder why the benefits of education and innovation have been ignored to such an extent.

13.5 The EAP's Working Hypothesis and the Greek Economy

The previous chapter contained a brief description of the EAP's working hypothesis. Table 13.18 describes its implementation and summarises details on the viability of the EAP's working hypothesis with respect to the Greek economy.

We can draw a number of conclusions for the Greek case by considering the EAP's basic working hypothesis (Table 11.6) as compared with its implementation (Table 13.19) together with the previous conclusions of the IMF's Independent Evaluation Office (2003) on the implementation of SBA/EFF[7] fiscal adjustment programs of form.

---

[7] SBA/EFF: Stand – By Arrangement/Extended Find Facility Arrangement.

Table 13.19 The EAP implementation

1. The political decision to implement the EAP was clear (as in the case study; see Table 11.6) with the following caveats.

   (a) The political mandate was incomplete, resulting in a decreased ability to implement reforms.

   (b) The reforms were easier to introduce during crisis (i.e., the threat of bankruptcy). This climate was first created by the way in which the financial rescue plan itself was designed, which estimated that the debt-to-GDP ratio would culminate at extremely high levels by 2013–2014. This climate was eventually exacerbated by the media and by institutions that were invested in the prospect of bankruptcy.

   (c) Thus, the ease with which the reforms were introduced and the creation of uncertainty were at a trade-off situation. There was an attempt to resolve this conflict by using so-called "social engineering," i.e., by applying laws that would mechanically cause the expected effects but without sustainable success. Typical examples were the public revenue management mechanisms, ranging from complete tightening of procedures (i.e., asset means declaration control and so on) to absolute amnesty on a decade's worth of taxation (i.e., tax self-assessment). Obviously, a large part of the amount collected from tax self-assessment came from a reduction in the regular tax liabilities of entrepreneurs in November and December 2010.

   (d) In repeated cases, the administration sent out mixed messages. In some cases, it supported a peculiar market model (establishing minimum wages for engineers and legal regulations for "semi-outdoor areas" and "green buildings.") and in other cases, the administration promoted the opposite promoting a ban on engineer minimum wages and encouraging legislation that would release "closed-off" professions. The policy of reducing the global financial risk, was satisfactorily materialized.

2. Trust was neither domestically nor internationally generated. On the contrary, uncertainty grew. These trends may begin to reverse after February 2011 because of greater stability at the European level. However, the state's over-indebtedness reduces its capability to adapt to new conditions.

3. Fiscal adjustment expenditures were reduced, while revenues did not appear to significantly increase. The EAP thus shifted from a revenue-based to an expenditure-based structure. The economic recession is evident. However, because of (albeit declining) profit retention policies, increases in indirect taxes have shifted to increases in prices, initially causing a significant general increase. This was an unexpected development, although prices are expected to return to a much lower rate of change. This development, however, increased the public perception that revenues are shrinking, thereby exacerbating the recession. The debt-to-GDP ratios developed as expected. The deficit in terms of balance of payments showed the expected decline mainly because of the decline in domestic demand. Since the decline in the balance of payments deficit is not a result of improved competition, imbalances are expected as economic activity improves. There is evidence that the tax base has not increased. The potential reduction in the underground economy has taken the form of a "disaster" and rather than its "revelation" and its integration to "white economy" The insurance sector was reorganised by reducing its financial burden. Essentially, the reorganization of the insurance sector due to the reduced financial burden has resulted in longer employment of manpower at work. These developments, however, do not help reverse the expected reduced contribution of the employment rate to growth. The increase in unemployment came mainly from the private sector. The fiscal adjustment is expected to be around €12 bn or 5% of GDP from 2012 to 2014.

4. Domestic devaluation took mainly the form of reduced wages due to the reduction of wages in the public sector. However, improved competition due to reductions in the unit labour cost does not seem to be important. Nevertheless, exports showed a substantial recovery mainly because of the recovery of global demand for goods and services from key Eurozone economies.

5. Monetary policy (i.e., reducing interest rates and increasing allowances) did not work towards offsetting the financial decline, but it did work co-cyclically to intensify the negative effects of fiscal adjustment. This development contrasted the predictions of the classic IPP working

(continued)

Table 13.19 (continued)

hypothesis (see the IMF's experience), but it was expected since the financial system's problems became known. The recession, however, was sharper than expected for two reasons. First, there was a sharper decline in private-sector financing and deposits, and second, confidence in the Greek economy was reduced.

6. In terms of structural interventions, the delay in reactivating the financial system has been very serious. Meanwhile, in a number of other areas such as education and innovation, there is a lack of intervention altogether. It should be particularly noted that since the authorities had improved competition, this should emphasis should be extended to areas that had hitherto been excluded from competition (e.g., "closed-off" professions or oligopolies). Also particularly significant was the failure to take actions to reduce transaction costs; some initiatives even led to its increase (e.g., the operational control of transactions aimed at reducing the parallel economy or initiatives aimed at the mandatory use of checks by entrepreneurs). The structural reforms for the period from 2012 to 2014 are characterised by expectations of reduced public organisations, linkage between wages and productivity in the public sector, changes in taxation aimed at broadening the tax base and reductions in social and defence expenditure.

7. Sectoral changes have developed almost as expected, while some sectors (particularly in retail, the media and so on) suffered more than expected. Also, the positive developments in the export sector were better than expected, though they were not significant enough to offset the negative effects of declining sectors.

The EAP's primary objective is fiscal adjustment in societies where, for various reasons, financial expenditure is excessively inflated in relation to GDP. Its working hypothesis is based on a very simple choice. That is, the necessary contraction in the public sector will be replaced by an expansion in private-sector activities. This obviously means that there is potential for a "technical" substitution of the public sector by the private sector. However, when private-sector activity is predominantly regulated and administratively controlled, substitution possibilities are limited. When the financial system also malfunctions, then the private sector has even more reasons to become activated. Thus, if we include multipliers, any shrinkage in the public sector leads to a very significant decline in the overall level of economic activity, without any prospect for a strong recovery of the global economy.

What is the political significance of these findings for the future implementation of intervention policies?

(a) All crisis interventions should be implemented in ways that generate trust among citizens from the onset (November 2009). We note that (1) the occurrence of political elections just before the outbreak of crisis was fortuitous for the Greek economy and (2) the positive attitude of foreign markets to finance the Greek State in early 2010 was also advantageous (see Table 9.8, Chap.10).

(b) What was of essence, was the administrative liberation and the liberation of the capability to substitute the public sector economic activity by the private sector. At this point, it should be stressed that when discussing the conditions that make possible the substitution of public-sector activity by the private sector, we basically refer to the substitution of economic activity rates rather than specific activities. The latter may only play a secondary role in a context of crisis because it simply intensifies social tensions. This form of substitution should occur in a modern state, where private-sector intervention promises greater socio-economic returns than those achieved by the public sector.

(c) Next, it is necessary to restore the functionality of the financial system.

(d) Shortly thereafter, EAP implementation should be the priority.

Despite all of these theoretical considerations, reality is imperative. In the Greek economy a critical time was created in early 2010 because of its excessive public debt and financial instability. The main reason was the peculiar economic model. The only way out of the crisis was to turn to IMF and EU for loans. But how could the loan conditions be guaranteed? On the basis of the above, these conditions could be guaranteed by implementing measures to address the financial problem that had created the need for loans in the first place. Given the rapid reduction in public expenditures and revenues since December 2009, these interventions would require an emphasis on the ratio between deficit and debt to GDP and financial stability. Given (a) with the huge social cost of the economic interventions and (b) the uncertainty it engendered, it could not be reasonable to apply in these circumstances. In addition, the Washington consensus had already started to be abandoned at the global level (see Chap. 12); we imagine that there is no coincidence in the emergence of these events.

Changing the market's peculiar financial model represents a significance challenge for Greek society; as such, it is the main theme of the next chapter of this book.

References

Aghion P, Cage J (2010) Crisis Exit Strategies and Crutch, Workshop of Structural Reforms, OECD/Bisque de France, 9–10 December

Aghion P, Howitt P (1998) Endogenous growth theory. MIT Press, Cambridge

Alesina A (2010) Tax cuts vs. 'stimulus': the evidence is in. Wall Street J

Alesina A, Ardanga S (2009) Large changes in fiscal policy: taxes versus spending. NBER Work. Pap. 15438

Alesina A, Drazen A (1991) Why are stabilizations delayed? Am Econ Rev 81(5):1170–1189

Alesina A, Perotti R (1994) The political economy of growth: a critical survey of the recent literature. World Bank Econ Rev 8:351–371

Atkinson AB (1997) Bringing income distribution in from the cold. Econ J Royal Econ Soc 107 (441):297–321

Aubyn SM, Pina A, Garcia F, Pais J (2009) Study on the efficiency and effectiveness of public spending on tertiary education. European Economy - Economic Papers 390, Directorate General Economic and Monetary Affairs, European Commission

Barro R (1974) Are government bonds net wealth? J Polit Econ 82:1095–1117

Bradley D, Huber E, Moller S, Nielsen F, Stephens JD (2003) Distribution and redistribution in post-industrial democracies. World Polit 55(2):193–228

Dixit A, Londregan J (1996) The determinants of success of special interests in redistributive politics. J Politics 58(4):1132–1155

Glaeser EL, La Porta R, Lopez-De-Silanes F, Shleifer A (2004) Do institutions cause growth? J Econ Growth 9:271–303

Hanushek EA, Woessmann L (2010) How much do educational outcomes matter in OECD countries? NBER Working Papers 16515, National Bureau of Economic Research, Inc.

Larch M (2010) Fiscal performance and income inequality: are unequal societies more deficit – prone? Some cross – country evidence. Eur. Comm. for Econ. Financial Aff.

Luiz de Mello, Padoan PC (2010) Promoting potential growth: the role of structural reform. OECD Econ. Dep. Work. Pap. 793

Meltzer AH, Richards SF (1981) A rational theory of the size of government. J Polit Econ 89:914–927

Mourougane A, Vogel L (2008) Speed of adjustment to selected labour market and tax reforms. OECD Econ. Dep. Work. Pap. 647

Mowery DC (2005) The Bayh Dole Act and High Technology Entrepreneurship in US Universities: Chicken, Egg or Someone Else? Available at: Entrepreneurship.eller.arizona.edu/docs/conferences/2005/colloquium/ D_Mowery.pdf

Ozler S, Tabellini G (1991) External debt and political instability. CEPR discuss. Pap. 582, C.E.P.R. Discuss. Pap.

Rehn O (2010) Next steps for securing financial stability in Europe. Eur. Comm. for Econ. and Monet. Aff.

Reinhart C, Rogoff K (2010) From financial crash to debt crisis. NBER and CEPR, University of Maryland, College Park, MD

Roeger W, Jan in't Velt (2010) Fiscal stimulus and exit strategies in the EU: a model-based analysis. Eur. Comm. for Econ. and Financial Aff.

Schneider O (2007) The EU budget dispute a blessing in disguise? CESifo Work. Pap. Ser. 1986, CESifo Group Munich

Viñals J, Fiechter J, Pazarbasioglu C, Kodres L, Narain A, Moretti M (2010) Shaping the new financial system. IMF Staff Position Note 2010/15

Von Hagen J (1992) German unification: economic problems and consequences: a comment. Carnegie-Rochester Conf Ser Public Pol 36(1):211–221

Von Hagen J, Harden I (1994) Budget processes and commitment to fiscal discipline. Eur Econ Rev 39:771–779

Von Hagen J, Poterba J (1999) Fiscal institutions and fiscal performance. University of Chicago Press, Chicago, pp 13–36

The Medium-Long Term Outlook of the Greek Economy

14

The medium- to long-term outlook of the Greek economy depends on the sources that can generate growth. These sources, however, are dictated by the basic growth model that will be adopted and implemented. First, a medium-long term perspective of possible developments should be formed giving consideration to the current Greek economy and projecting its long-term prospects up to 2050 (Sect. 14.1). Section 14.2 discusses the relationship of the main sources of growth and other factors (Total Factor Productivity – TFP). Section 14.3 discusses the conditions and possibilities to overcome the tendency observed in the evolution of growth, given that even the best development scenario promises relatively low growth rates. Finally, to overcome this tendency, a development model and its objective, instruments and temporal efficiency is presented in Sect. 14.4.

14.1 The Medium-Long Term Perspective on the Greek Economy and the Sources of New Growth

The development of the medium-long term prospects of the Greek economy is expected to be affected by the evolution of the financial problems that peaked between 2008 and 2010. Any development that would lead the Greek economy away from international capital markets would have a serious medium-long term impact on growth rates.

As we established in the previous chapter, Europe is facing a significant problem of fiscal adjustment along with the implementation of a restrictive economic policy. This method, it is argued, will ensure a return to strong growth rates. Essentially, the economic entity (European Economy), which includes the Greek economy, implements a policy of economic adjustment to achieve the goals of "Europe of 2020". The development of the European economic policy framework is expected to be accompanied by the particularisation of the European Support Mechanism

P. Petrakis, *The Greek Economy and the Crisis*,
DOI 10.1007/978-3-642-21175-1_14, © Springer-Verlag Berlin Heidelberg 2012

(ESM) to manage the situation in countries with broader fiscal problems. Therefore, developments in the Greek economy occur within this broader framework.

By all indications, the decision-makers in the Eurozone are not prepared to deal with a sovereign credit event. A sovereign credit event activates legal consequences that are marked by bankruptcy processes in a country. Such processes lead to long judicial and legal disputes at the international level. At the same time, "bankruptcy" usually leads to the exclusion of the affected country from international capital markets with serious negative consequences for the country's creditors and positive consequences for those who have invested in such events through Credit Default Swaps (CDSs).

Thus, to introduce the medium-term prospects of the Greek economy, we consider what the author posited in the introduction as his structural conception of what will occur in the future. The course of events in the Greek economy will not move along the bankruptcy-development axis but rather along the axis of 'good' and 'weak' growth. This is the prospect analysed in this section. We trace the course of economic growth and development of the Greek economy in the medium term. Our choice, of course, does not mean that we rule out the possibility of any form of restructuring of the national debt, such as the lengthening of repayment terms, the reduction of interest costs or the reduction of its value. Whatever form debt restructuring assumes, however, it will occur under conditions of voluntary cooperation between the parties, and its effects will spread to all involved.

In essence, nothing other than what is already happening today is expected because the Greek economy is already under capital restraints and its growth rate is negative or low. Additionally, its creditors bear the consequences of its fiscal problems as, in the secondary market, Greek bonds are being sold at 60–70% of their value, depending on their maturity. The only, though not negligible, expected outcome from the implementation of a general European mechanism of division and financial supervision would be the ability of the Greek private sector, especially the banking system, to be loaned by foreign sources. The implementation of any plan to improve fiscal management will not change the general trends described here. Change is possible only if a coordinated action plan is implemented (as described in Sect. 14.4).

In conclusion, in the context of the current trend of development, the fiscal scenery in the medium-term future will remain the same or similar. It is thus reasonable to expect that financial restructuring will be applied and that the restructuring will involve multiple forms/processes with the sole aim of establishing a GDP-to-fiscal debt ratio that can be served under more normal conditions.

Based on the above basic assumption of Greece's non-exclusion from international capital markets, we turn our attention to the main scenarios on the development of growth in the Greek economy in light of the scenarios established for the European and world economy in the previous chapter.

Three different sources will be referenced to determine medium-long term prospects:

Source		References	Period covered
(1)	Carone et al. (2006)	European commission (EC)	2003–2050
(2)	Economic Outlook, May 2010	OECD	2011–2025
(3)	The World in 2050, 2011	HSBC (Ward)	1990–2050

The data from all three sources are summarised in Table 14.1, and the data of the European Commission are shown in Fig. 14.1. The OECD and HSBC studies were published at the end of 2010, whereas that of the European Commission was published in 2006. However, the directions of the primary conclusions are similar. It is therefore evident that the crisis of 2008 does not alter the medium-long term picture of the growth rate and the contribution of key components in shaping this picture.

It appears that the growth rate of the Greek economy is expected to decline following the general decline of the corresponding rates in the European Union until approximately 2021. For Greece, as for the EU, this drop is due to the reduced positive effect of the employment coefficient. However, according to the European Commission, the negative effect of capital is much higher in Greece than in the EU. Any positive effect on the Greek economy is achieved by the increase in labour productivity and other economic factors (TFP), that is, the overall efficiency of the financial system. These factors, however, are unable to reverse the greater negative trend of growth of the Greek economy in comparison with the EU. Obviously, labour productivity and the overall efficiency of the financial system suffer from the reduction of the positive effects of capital deepening. This is evidenced by the fact that while labour productivity in Greece increases at approximately the same rate as the EU average – with the exception of 2011–2030, which suggests a very small difference of 0.1% – the Total Productivity Factor systematically deviates from the EU average.

This scenario for the future, in a sense, incorporates the probable medium-long term effects associated with the reduced capital flows to the Greek economy.

In addition, the negative impact from the increase of unemployment is greater in the Greek economy than in the EU. Indeed, estimates of employment levels do not present significant forecast errors as they are primarily based on population projections.

As a result of these trends, the growth of per capita GDP, despite the dampening effect of population dynamics, is much lower in Greece than in the EU, and thus, it is expected to deviate systematically from the EU-15 average (Table 14.1). What do these conclusions mean for the growth prospects of the Greek economy? Obviously, Greece's growth model should be based more on improving the efficiency of the financial system and less on the contribution of key growth variables (capital-employments). This issue is discussed further by the National Bank of Greece (NBG) (Greece: Economic and Market Analysis – November 2010) for the period 1998–2015. According to the calculations of the BoG,[1] in the medium term, it is likely to rely more on improving the efficiency of the financial system (see Fig. 14.2).

---

[1] According to the NBG, the differences are due to the fact that capital is only analysed to the degree it is used (adjustment for capital utilisation) and that employment figures are corrected for undeclared employment.

Table 14.1 Projected changes of aggregates in the Greek economy

	Source	2011–2020	2021–2030	2031–2040	2041–2050
GDP growth	OECD	3.3[a] [2.3][b]	1.7 [1.7][c]	0.8 [1.2]	1.5 [1.6]
	EC	2.0 [2.1]	1.2 [1.4]		
	HSBC	3.0 [3.0][d]	2.6 [3.5][d]	2.1 [3.8][d]	1.7 [4.1][d]
Capital deepening	EC	1.0 [0.7]	0.7 [0.7]	0.6 [0.6]	0.8 [0.6]
Growth in labour productivity	OECD	1.4 [1.5][a]			
	EC	1.8 [1.9]	1.8 [1.9]	1.7 [1.7]	1.8 [1.7]
Level of productivity EU-15 = 100	EC	80 (2010)	79 (2030)	79 (2040)	79 (2050)
Total Productivity Factor growth	EC	0.8 [1.2]	1.0 [1.1]	1.1 [1.1]	1.0 [1.1]
Dynamic growth of employment	EC	0.2 [0.2]	−0.6 [−0.4]	−0.9 [−0.5]	−0.3 [−0.1]
Growth in per capita GDP	EC	1.8 [1.9]	1.3 [1.4]	1.0 [1.3]	1.2 [1.6]
Per capita GDP EC15 = 100	EC	74 (2010)	72 (2030)	70 (2040)	68 (2050)
Inflation	OECD	0.3[a] [1.0][b] (2011)	2.0 (2015)		
	NBG	2.1[c] (2011)			
Unemployment	OECD	14.3 [10.1] (2011)	11.1 [8.6] (2015)		
			8.9 [7.6] (2025)		

Notes

[a] Covers the period 2012–2015

[b] Figures in brackets refer to the EU-15

[c] Covers the period 2016–2025

[d] Projections based on the assumption that the "economic infrastructure" will be improved as much as possible. The improvement of economic infrastructure means the improvement of coefficients relating to the total productivity factor (average years of secondary education, law enforcement, etc.). In a sense, this scenario could be regarded as describing the "overcoming of the tendency" discussed in this chapter

[e] The assessment relates to a forecast by the National Bank of Greece, November 2010 (Greece: Economic and Market Analysis)

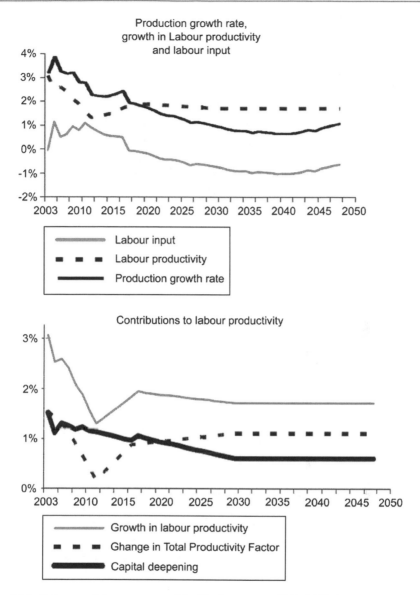

Fig. 14.1 Estimates of the aggregates of the Greek economy: 2003–2050 (Source: Carone et al. (2006))

The problem with the above estimates is that they do not refer to the forecast for the replacement of the positive effects of capital and labour in GDP growth for the period 2012–2015. The real issue raised is that, after this period (2021), these trends are magnified, and thus, the Greek economy suffers the observed long-term drop of growth (see Table 14.1).

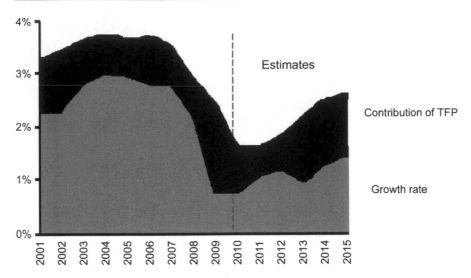

Fig. 14.2 Rate of growth and contribution of capital, labour, and TFP (Source: National bank of Greece, economic and market analysis, November 2010)

Is the relationship between key growth variables (capital and labour) and other factors (TFP) as "mechanical" as provided by the production function and contextual analysis? This is discussed in the next section, which provides interesting conclusions. Moreover, if the capacity utilisation gap is not absorbed, which in 2010 was the highest in the OECD, it will be difficult for other factors to boost economic growth in the medium term.

For the moment, let us concentrate on the main subject of this section, which is the deviation of the medium-long term prospects of the Greek economy based on the assumptions and trends already described.

Figure 14.3 has been formulated based on assumptions about the evolution of public debt to GDP after the implementation of the EAP for the period 2010–2014 and based on the data in Table 14.1 for the period 2015–2030 (Scenario 1). Scenario 2a has been formulated based on the assumption of the reduction of the average rate of debt servicing by 25%. Essentially, this means a decrease of 1 percentage point of the weighted average interest rate of debt servicing. Scenario 2b has been formulated based on the assumption of the repurchase of 33% of the existing debt at 75% of its nominal value.[2] Note that the second scenario is more efficient as regards the formulation of debt-to-GDP ratios but also more difficult to implement. Finally, we present forecasts about the course of the public debt-to-GDP ratio for the EU-27, according to the most stringent scenario (Fig. 12.8), which regards the annual reduction of primary deficit in the EU member states by 1% of the GDP.

---

[2] Scenarios 2a and 2b are associated with the so-called friendly public debt's restructuring scenarios.

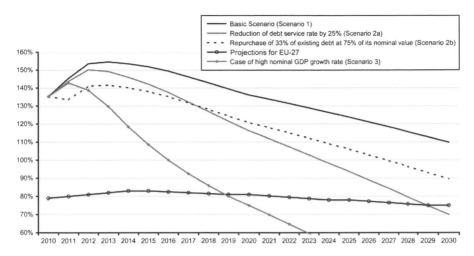

Fig. 14.3 Public debt-to-GDP ratio. Notes: For the creation of scenarios 1, 2a, 2b and 3, we have used the primary surplus for 2010–2014 as derived from the assessment of the EAP (December 2010 – second review), whereas for the period 2015–2030 it is considered stable, at approximately 5.5%. For the creation of Scenarios 1, 2a, and 2b, we have used the growth of GDP for 2010–2014 as derived from the assessment of the EAP (December 2010 – second review). We have used the forecasts of the European Commission (Table 14.1)

Figure 14.3 also reflects Scenario 3. This is a hypothetical scenario in which the nominal growth rates of GDP, that is, real GDP growth and inflation follow the following course: 4% in 2011, 7% in 2012, 9% in 2013, 10% in 2014, and a gradual decrease to 5% by 2010 and to 5% from 2011 onwards. Such a scenario is very positive and completely changes the Greek economy's ability to repay the public debt. Is such a scenario probable, however? The factors that support its feasibility include (a) the "aspect of scarcity" of food and oil expected in the next 15 years and the consequent increase of the general price level; (b) the social unrest in the Middle East that may exert additional pressure on oil prices and the general price level; (c) the possible rise of political forces – mainly in Central Europe (France, Germany) – that will promise and provide a higher prosperity dividend to their people and thus increase their demand; (d) the increased liquidity of the international economic system, mainly from the U.S. and (e) the accumulation of funds in surplus countries that will seek riskier and, therefore, more profitable investments. One of the factors that makes this seem less likely include the excess production capacity in terms of employed capital and labour, as well as the perspective of increased interest rates.

However, the educational importance of this scenario is not to indicate a positive development with respect to the abandonment of the effort to reorganise Greek public finances. This is not the interpretation of Scenario 3 intended by the author. It does offer, however, a useful application, as it stresses that there are realistic counter-arguments to the panic about the possibility of future bankruptcy and that the economic policy should be managed with composure and confidence in compliance with the prescribed and agreed to terms. In addition, the formation of primary budget surpluses after 2014 will automatically jump-start the discussion on debt restructuring on a pragmatic basis. If this occurs (conversation about the restructuring of public debt) in conjunction with a materialised version of Scenario 3, it will dramatically increase freedom in the economic policy.

The conclusions derived from the evolution of public debt (Scenario 1) to GDP (Fig. 14.3) and the data of Table 14.1 were inserted in Fig. 14.4. This figure depicts the Greek economy and social development from 1828 to 2050.

It appears that, in the Greek economy, significant changes in population growth and net migration are accompanied by periods of increase of the Greek public debt. The country's population grew greatly with the incorporation of the Ionian Islands in 1864. After the incorporation of Arta and Thessaly in 1881, it almost doubled. This period marked the beginning of high debt levels. At the beginning of the currant industry crisis, the central government debt began to grow rapidly, and the rural populations in the northern Peloponnese began migrating to America. Estimates for the period 1889–1911 suggest that approximately 370,000 people, 15–20% of the population, migrated. After the Balkan Wars (1912–1913), the population more than doubled and again increased significantly between 1920 and 1928 through a massive population exchange due to the Lausanne Treaty and the disaster in Asia Minor that created a wave of refugees. The subsequent German invasion and occupation combined with the civil war caused extensive population movement within the country as rural populations found refuge in larger urban or non-urban areas of the mainland or sought safety abroad, initially in the U.S., Canada and Australia and then in the industrialised countries of Europe, such as Germany. From 1940 to 1981, the population of Athens and Thessaloniki almost tripled. After 1980, emigration gave way to the return of Greek immigrants until 1990, along with the massive influx of foreigners from the former socialist countries and less developed Asian countries.

Figure 14.4 displays an increase of the population outflow from Greece, which the author assumed arbitrarily but is probably inevitable based on economic conditions. At the same time, it leads to the very simple hypothesis that a future period of prosperity would be combined with an increase in future population, which may be due to the legalisation of the existing immigrants. However, it also shows that there is no reason to believe that the public debt-to-GDP ratio will drop below 60%. It is thus reasonable to expect a new influx of loan funds in the future (long term).

14.2   The Relationship Between the Key Factors of Growth and Other Factors (TFP)

In the previous section, we saw that, according to existing data, the medium-long term growth of the Greek economy is expected to rely primarily on those factors that enhance the overall efficiency of the financial system (TFP) and less on key factors such as capital and labour. However, this implies the possibility of substituting the role of one group of factors by another in the process of growth,

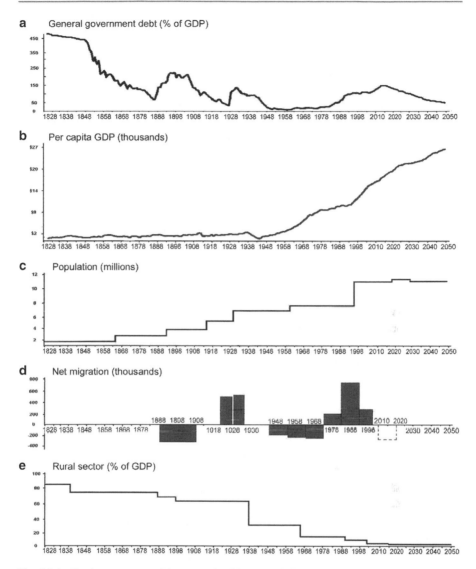

Fig. 14.4 Greek government debt per capita GDP, population, immigration and the agricultural sector Sources: (**a**) Reinhart and Rogoff (2010), EAP (second review) and Table 14.1. (**b**) Kostelenos et al. (2007), Groningen Growth and Development Centre, Total Economy Database, Table 14.1. (**c**) IMF (database), Kotzamanis and Androulaki (2009), statistical Yearbook of Greece (1931, 1939), Eurostat estimates. (**d**) Siampos (1973), Kotzamanis and Androulaki (2009), Statistical Yearbook of Greece (1931, 1939), Trading Economics (www.tradingeconomics.com). (**e**) Kostelenos et al. (2007), NSS Statistics Bulletins. Note: Figures (**c**) and (**e**) concern the most important dates of change of the Greek population and the Greek agricultural sector, respectively

which is open to questioning. Certainly, the theoretical establishment of the inter-relationship of key growth drivers within the context of a production function (a Cobb-Douglas function) resolves the issues of substitution. It is obvious, however, that the production function is an analytical tool that cannot replace reality, especially with respect to the "unexplored" other factors (TFP). It is not, however, only the peculiar nature and function of these other factors that hinders their in-depth analysis. It is also the problem of endogeneity concealed by the use of the simple production function. The endogeneity problem arises because key inputs affect production while production also affects the level and quality of production inputs. Therefore, we cannot be sure whether and how improving the flow of other factors will bring about growth or whether it is required to extend growth to improve the supply of other factors.

This issue is certainly not new. As Acemoglu (2009) noted, references to general environmental conditions that may affect human behaviours and conditions can be found in Montesquieu C (1748/1989), Machiavelli ([1519] 1987) and Marshall (1890/1997). References to institutions and their effects on growth can be found in Locke (1689/1988), Mill and (1848/1973) and, of course, in a more recent key contributor to the current understanding of institutions, North (1990). As for the role of religion, we should refer to the contribution of Weber (1930) and, much later, Harrison and Huntington (2000) as well as Acemoglu et al. (2005). Putnam (1993) extended the importance of cultural variables to the organisation and the concept of social capital. Similar research works, including quantifications, are those of (Knack and Keefer 1995 and Knack and Keefer 1997), Esfahani and Ramirez (2003) and Tabellini (2010) who noted the difficulties of quantifying the relationship between institutions and growth, thus positing the results related to endogeneity between the explanatory variables.

This section contributes to the extant literature because it distinguishes three diverse areas that form the "unexplained part" of growth, namely, the cultural background, the characteristics of transactions and the economic institutions. As a second contribution, we note the fact that we accept the obvious, namely, that the three areas cannot be completely distinct birthplaces of formative influences on levels of growth or isolated, mutually uninfluenced areas. These places, as well as financial and social environments, are shaped together, and the methodology used to quantify these effects must take account of this fact. As a third point of contribution, we examine the relationship between the unexplained part of growth combined with the key factors shaping growth (capital, labour and human capital). A fourth point of contribution concerns the fact that we attempt to quantify the qualitative variables that are responsible for growth, which are well known and accepted in this role but have not, until now, been quantified sufficiently to be submitted to analysis concerning the process of growth. A fifth point relates to the fact that while solving the issue of endogeneity between the annual change in GDP and the characteristics of trade and economic institutions (Acemoglu et al. 2001 and Acemoglu et al. 2002, Tabellini 2010 – "Culture and institutions: Economic development in the regions of Europe", etc.), we contribute to the debate about whether the "remaining inputs", especially the characteristics of transactions and economic institutions, affect growth (Acemoglu et al. 2001, Hall and Jones 1999, Knack and Keefer 1995) or if growth itself causes the improvement of economic institutions (Glaeser et al. 2004, Lipset 1960). Finally, as a sixth point, we consider the fact that we experimented with a "fantasy" world, which we constructed by affecting the levels of the variables we use whose main feature is that it is a "more secure" world. Essentially, it is a world where the other factors, such as a lack of risk and certainty, create an economic environment that logically favours growth. In this world, we observe the behaviour of the variables we study.

In the neoclassical theoretical foundation of Solow and Romer, the unexplained part of growth, the growth rate of "residual input" is the so-called Solow residual (Solow 1957) (see Sect. 2.2, Chap. 2). It is a part of growth not explained by the contribution of capital, labour, human capital and/or technology and is attributed to factors such as the cultural and institutional background of the growth process and the features of transactions that characterise a society. Here, we will only examine the effects of the cultural background, the economic institutions and the characteristics of transactions.

As we saw in Chap. 6, the different social and political processes forming the cultural background of each society guide human behaviour and the character of stakeholders and vice versa. This may also influence the growth process.

The behavioural features underlying the theory of transaction costs are summarised in the restricted rationale and possibility of searching opportunities (Williamson 1981) (see Sect. 7.1), characteristics that influence and are influenced by the cultural background of each society.

The general features of the theory of transactions are dominated by uncertainty, frequency and the particulars of the objects traded. However, its human aspects, such as bounded rationality and opportunism, constitute components of in-depth influence on what is known as active cultural background in a society.

As we noted, economic institutions are defined as the collective choices of society, which often reflect conflicting interests and which evolve under the influence of historical developments and cultural background. The book assumes institutional background to refer to those economic institutions that determine incentives in a society, including the incentives for physical capital, human capital, technology and production organisation (Economides and Egger 2009). Economic institutions are expressed in societies primarily through property rights, contracting conditions and through the influence of these characteristics on financial transactions (see Chap. 7).

The problem of observed endogeneity concerns the measurement of variables that reflect the characteristics of transactions, especially those that represent economic institutions. Those variables typically measure the individual results rather than the permanent features (Glaeser et al. 2004) and therefore increase as the income per capita increases, thus creating the problem of endogeneity. Of course, this conclusion is not true for all the variables that reflect the characteristics of transactions and economic institutions.

Several research studies have attempted to address the problem of endogeneity observed between growth and the institutional background using instrumental variables in order to determine if growth leads to better institutions.

However, as noted by Acemoglu et al. (2001), the use of these instrumental variables is not entirely appropriate in theory. Acemoglu et al. (2001, 2002) use the mortality of European settlers as an instrumental variable, as they consider the decision to colonise as a matter of mortality rates. Glaeser et al. (2004), using Acemoglu's model with the instrumental variable of settler mortality, conclude that this approach cannot ascertain exactly what causes growth.

We assume that the variables that reflect the cultural background can be used as exogenous variables in the model formulating the change in GDP for the 20–30 year period under analysis. In other words, the cultural characteristics of societies reflect psychological social stereotypes that were created in the distant past. Cultural values display stability over time. The different social and political processes that shape the cultural background of each society guide the character stakeholders, respectively, and in general, cultural stereotypes are extremely resistant to change and redefinition (Johnston 1996).

The durability of the social stereotypes that define the cultural background has two main causes (see details in Chap. 6). The first is linked to the exogenous nature of the forces that determine the construction of stereotypes (climate, environment, etc.) Schwatrz (2009). This view contains references to the external environment (McClelland 1961, Triandis 1995) and extends to the interrelationship of the physical condition of man and the external environment through "homeostasis" (Tavassoli 2009). At the opposite end of the spectrum is the concept of endogenous (for human civilisation) formation processes of cultural backgrounds (Hong 2009, Oyserman and Sorensen 2009). Essentially, this view considers the cultural background as a set of "common knowledge facts" that consists of (a) taught thinking processes; (b) beliefs, attitudes and value structures; and (c) latent theories about the natural and social world. This case provides the second reason for the durability of the cultural background over time. As this consists of intermediate cultural syndromes that are considered mental constructions originating in the distant past and linking it to the present (Hong 2009) for an analysis period of 20–30 years, they should be considered stable and inherently created.

The statistics used were those presented in Table 14.2.

From the manner in which the data are collected, it is evident that we regard the world as a typical country, assuming that the production process is homogeneous across the world because we do not allow for heterogeneous developmental experiences (Bos et al. 2010). This is because the limited number of degrees of freedom caused by the limited number of observations, which is primarily the result of a minimal number of observations for the variables of cultural background, does not allow a more in-depth analysis.

The methodology used to analyse the problem is as follows:

(a) We used the method of Principal Components Analysis (PCA) to summarise the effects of institutions, the cultural backgrounds and the transaction characteristics.
(b) We entered the "remaining inputs" (the PCs with the greater variations arising for the variables of cultural background, characteristics of transactions and economic institutions) in the classic Cobb-Douglas function, which contains capital, labour and human capital as explanatory variables. Essentially, we

Table 14.2 Sources and reference periods for the variables used[a]

	Variables	Reference period	Sources
Cultural background	Performance orientation		
	Future orientation		
	Gender equality		
	Imposition		
	Institutional collectivism	1995–1997	House et al. (2004)
	In-group collectivism		
	Power distance		
	Human orientation		
	Uncertainty avoidance		
Transaction characteristics	Composite risk	Avg for period 1997–2005	PRS Group (ICRG database) www.prsgroup.com
	Starting a business	Avg for 2004–2005	Doing business Reports, The World Bank Groups
	Happy life years	2000–2009	Veenhoven R., *World Database of Happiness 2009* worlddatabaseofhappiness.eur.nl
	Opportunity entrepreneurship	Avg for 2001–2006	Global Entrepreneurship Monitor (GEM) www.gemconsortium.org
Economic institutions	Property rights	Avg for 1997–2005	The Heritage Foundation, Index of Economic Freedom (HER) www.heritage.org/index/
	Rule of law	Avg for period 1997–2005	Business Environment Risk Intelligence (BRI), www.beri.com
Capital	Investment rate	Avg for period 2000–2004	Penn World Table Version 6.2, September 2006
Human capital	Literacy rate	1995–2005	UNESCO Institute for Statistics www.uis.unesco.org
Employment	Change in population	Avg for period 2000–2007	World Economic Outlook Database www.imf.org
Initial income	GDP per capita	1990	World Economic Outlook Database www.imf.org
Target variable	Annual change in GDP	Avg for 1990–2010	World Economic Outlook Database www.imf.org

[a]The 41 countries in the sample represent 90.44% of world GDP, 2007 (IMF database). These are Argentina, Australia, Austria, Brazil, Canada, China, Colombia, Denmark, Ecuador, Finland, France, Germany, Greece, Hong Kong, India, Indonesia, Ireland, Israel, Italy, Japan, Malaysia, Mexico, Netherlands, New Zealand, Philippines, Poland, Portugal, Russia, Singapore, Slovenia, South Africa, South Korea, Sweden, Switzerland, Thailand, Turkey, UK, USA, Venezuela

make an econometric estimation in which we analyse the influence of production factors (capital, labour and human capital) and of the remaining inputs (PCs) on the annual change in GDP.

(c) We conducted the sensitivity analysis, thus creating the more secure world. The value of the total risk variable dropped by 30% (i.e., risk is reduced equivalently), and the value of the uncertainty avoidance variable dropped by 30% for those countries below the average of the overall risk variable. Essentially, in our experiment, we created a more secure world where the most dangerous countries became more secure and, thus, their populations engaged in riskier practices. Our aim is to observe the effects of the cultural background, the nature of transactions and the economic institutions in shaping levels of growth in these changing societies.

(d) We reveal the problem of endogeneity between the annual change in GDP and the characteristics of transactions and economic institutions. To address this problem, using the three-stages least squares (3SLS) method, we assessed a system whose endogenous variables are the annual change in GDP and the variable that represents the characteristics of transactions and institutions and whose exogenous variables are the key growth drivers (capital, labour and human capital) as well as the variables that reflect the cultural background.

The full analysis of the relevant research and the variables used is available on-line at: http://elearn.elke.uoa.gr/growth/beyond_the_solow_romer.html

The main conclusions of the analysis are as follows:

(a) In today's (real) world, the factors that play a role in interpreting annual GDP growth are the key interpretative factors: capital and labour. A part of human behaviour, which centres on in-group collectivism, plays a negative role, as do the variables that reflect transactions and institutions along with a group of behavioural variables. In essence, today's world needs key inputs of growth.

(b) In the more secure world that we created, things change. The factors that played a role in the former world still exert a strong presence. Now, however, the factors that reflect the characteristics of transactions and institutions, as well as behavioural variables, also appear to play a role (Fig. 14.5).

Essentially, based on the above, we see that the factors that improve the efficiency of the system play an important role in promoting growth. However, this role is activated under conditions that pre-suppose the extensive use of the key inputs of capital and labour. In other words, a more secure world is required to activate the driving force of the cultural background. The formation of such a world can be the result of individual actions; however, we should logically expect that it will emerge in very advanced conditions of growth.

Thus, when discussing the growth model of an economy, we should clarify that the main driver of growth should be sought in the key inputs (capital – labour).

Our analysis certainly does not allow us to ignore the importance of improving the efficiency of the financial system as a factor for future growth. However, it does take us back to the basic needs arising from the critical scarcity of key variables (capital and labour) for promoting growth and place the relative role of other factors (TFP) on a more realistic basis with respect to their potential usefulness in the process of promoting growth.

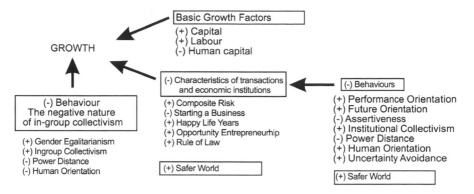

Fig. 14.5 Growth in the present and in the more secure world

14.3 Overcoming the Trend

In the previous sections of the book, readers were presented a picture of the medium-long term evolution of Greek economic growth. It is evident that the Greek economy has entered a long "low flying" period that is marked by low growth rates and the corresponding consequences for society. Indeed, this is not directly related to the 2008 crisis, nor is it exclusive to the Greek economy. Thus, the question raised regards the possibilities to overcome these trends. This section will identify the conditions for positive deviation from the medium-long term scenario.

The delineation of the implementation prospects for a medium-term growth scenario requires three stages of thinking:

The model's targets and implementation instruments are longitudinal. If we accept that the future can be divided into three periods, that is, short-term (1– 3 years), medium-term (3–15 years) and long-term (15–70 years), we should clarify that growth targets may require different time-scales. This is also true of their expected effectiveness. The instruments used to fund these targets can be similarly divided temporally.

14.3.1 The Political Conditions

Through the political institutions, policy introduces a hierarchy of social evaluations in the context of the real and the feasible, which are incorporated in the functioning of the economic and social systems and have specific effects and implications (Myrdal 1954). In this context, there are three basic political conditions for applying a long-term growth model:

(a) The enlargement of the reform capacity of the political system – The political system must resolve the question of its ability to propose the necessary reform initiatives, to receive the mandate to implement these and, then, to do so. For this to happen, however, it should be both willing and able to undertake political initiatives. Only then can the economic system's performance and allocation of managed resources overcome the perpetual "trap" of a certain level of political institutions as regards resource allocation and economic performance. This view is based on the simple observation that the allocation of resources in period t affects the allocation of resources in period t + 1, and economic institutions and certain financial performances are only an intermediate result thereof. The factors that can lead to the removal of this "trap" may relate to technology, to the emergence of charismatic political figures, to the occurrence of major changes in the international environment and to the improvement of the political system's capacity to reform. In a sense, the crisis of 2008 created for the Greek economy the conditions for revision of the factors that shape the political and economic institutions in the country due to the foreign "interruption" of the funding of the 30-year economic growth model.

(b) The convergence of the objectives of the political forces aiming not only to control functionality but also to promote economic efficiency – The model of the Greek economy that prevailed in recent decades, one which was based on the choice to finance full employment through public borrowing and one which focused on transaction procedures, ignoring the effectiveness of available resources, has apparently come to an end. The main feature of the creation of growth dynamics, that is, the business economy, requires a single objective: the effective use of available resources with the primary aim of reducing transaction costs. This requires the large-scale reorganisation of the relationship with pressure groups that have vested interests in society and that control transactions. The concept of social engineering should be replaced by the development of a system of motivational politics and organised systems for measuring the effects of policy.

(c) Agreement on the decision as to whether the public sector should exist – This concerns the dilemma of collectivity or privacy regarding the ownership of resources. In fact, what is being discussed is the competitive relationship between public and private wealth accumulation and, more specifically, the relationship between private wealth accumulation and the financing of fiscal deficits. However, the collapse of the insurance systems and the need for public finance administration, education, and health create demands that threaten the process of private wealth accumulation. Therefore, although it appears crucial, the decision regarding the existence of the public sector in Greek society cannot be taken for granted. If a tax rate cut or a hostile voluntary restructuring of debt are proposed and implemented while public finances collapse, this reveals the deliberate intention to reduce the public sector, thus creating a dilemma whose solution requires a political decision. For various reasons, political forces assume different views on the issue of collectivity and privacy. Indeed, it is not always the case that the so-called leftist forces favour the collective entity of the state while the right-wing forces favour privacy. This is due, on the one hand, to the different historical origins and relationships of each of these forces with the state entity (hostile or estranged state) and, on the other, to the very need of each political force for the existence of state power. It should be noted that this discussion is independent of the debate about the quality and efficiency of the public sector, which remains a topical problem.

(d) The method and the contents of the increased capacity of the political system, the promotion of economic efficiency as a criterion of its performance and the selected solution to the dilemma of the public or private sector form the bedrock of the political conditions regarding development issues – These all have specific implications for the distribution of income and wealth. For this reason, the process of balancing the political forces to achieve these goals is extremely difficult and complex. The structure of the final distribution of power, wealth and income forms the nature of the growth objectives and the instruments for their implementation. In other words, these objectives (for example, fiscal adjustment) are shaped differently in a society where the representatives of capital dominate than the objectives in a society dominated by the representatives of labour. The same applies to the implementation instruments for the growth problem, such as interventions in the product or labour markets or the reorganisation of the tax system.

(e) The basic social and political conditions that have already been developed have a common activation factor: the population's knowledge and level of awareness regarding the issues to be confronted. It is true that the financial crisis of 2008–2010 significantly increased awareness. Within 2 years of the crisis, the general level of public awareness on economic issues has increased significantly. An important role in this awareness was played by the media through their constant references and discussions of financial matters. Thus, we reach the critical relationship of policy options and the operation of the media. The latter are, of course, independent corporate entities that play a short-term strategic role in implementing policies. Therefore, the "developmental operation" of the relationship between politics and the media is a crucial political prerequisite.

14.3.2 The Specifications of the Growth Model

To evaluate the potential of a positive medium-term deviation from the trend of the Greek economy, we first prioritise the key issues of medium-long term growth. These consist of long-term problems (as we saw in Chap. 11), new issues that emerged after the economic crisis through the implementation of the Economic Adjustment Program and the Domestic Economic Policy, and the new problems posed by the changing world in which the Greek economy operates. At this point, it should be noted that when discussing issues of medium-term growth, these do not relate to changes in economic indicators, as these indicators reflect the occurrence of growth problems. We always speak of the forces that cause these medium-term trends.

The growth model has the following specifications:

1. It is to be implemented by a government with the corresponding mandate and capacity to reform.
2. It is to manage the long-term causes of the creation of the Greek economic problem. Particular emphasis is given to exploiting the recent political experiences of the past (from the application of EAP in Greek economy, see end of Chap. 12) and, in particular, to prioritising the organisation of the growth pattern. These priorities should be consistent with the new international growth assumptions as incorporated in the Seoul Agreement (Seoul Development Consensus for Shared Growth, Nov. 11, 2010) that may be summarised in the following signalling issues: infrastructure, private investment, job creation, human resource development and access to knowledge, commerce, financial stability and the providing of food and mobilisation of domestic capacities.
3. It is to be based on long-term trends, characteristics and developments related to the Greek and the global economy to achieve a development dynamic.
4. It is to take into account the real funding capacity of the anticipated growth rate and the actions required.
5. It is to take into account the characteristics of the next decade's (2010–2020) time horizon, as it is going to be a decade of economic turbulence.
6. It is to adjust to external management and regulation conditions (moral hazard) of the international financial system having as a main point the position of the Greek economy as a capital hosting country. This should be performed with the understanding that the lack of operational efficiency in the EU is primarily due to institutional differences in European social organisations. This framework is complemented by the features of resource scarcity and reduced capital deepening as well as by the final conflict between North and South in terms of population development and productivity differences.
7. It is to overcome one of the key features of society, that is, its longitudinal orientation to the present. It is difficult for such a society to initiate a dialogue on a new growth pattern with a time horizon of 10–15 years. In this section, we do not address the subject of cultural background in general (we will discuss this later), but we note that any attempt for growth will fail if this approach to the relationship of the preference for the present over the future is not reversed.
8. The social model that prevailed in Greek society, spearheaded by the expression of social solidarity, in-group collectivism, has affected economic growth and enhanced its introversion. These properties of the models undoubtedly act against growth. However, if the appropriate support structures (unemployment systems, support of family cohesion, etc.) are not developed during a crisis and the subsequent recovery due to a lack of resources, this should be assessed positively. In any case, these social trends may only change in the long-term.

9. The development approach should be based on the creation of a framework of behaviour incentives that deviates from the perception of administration through social engineering. Primary areas of attention are incentives such as willingness to work, entrepreneurship, and investments in human capital. This will foster a system of establishing incentives that correspond to higher levels of motivation (e.g., self-realisation vs. survival) and that will promote creativity and social cohesion.

10. The model should be based on the principle of optimal allocation of wealth and income. Furthermore, it should avoid the creation of deficits to the degree that inequality and deficient fiscal management interact.

11. The Greek economy does not appear capable of being supported by inputs of capital and labour in the context of productive organisation as provided by Solow (1957), but neither is it a knowledge-based economy as defined by Romer (1986), which would allow the dissemination of the impact of the widening of the knowledge base of the economy. Unfortunately, in the near future, we will be forced to depart from growth dynamics as defined by Romer because we found serious weaknesses in the relationship between education and innovation within the productive system. Moreover, because there has been no such organisation and investment in education in the last 15 years, we cannot expect any results, as it is estimated that investments in education yield result after approximately 15 years. Moreover, forecasts indicate a sharp drop in the number of graduates by 2030. This trend is intensified by the fact that many of the graduates in which the Greek society has invested will seek careers in other economies, increasing the economic outflow in the following years.

The ultimate deviation from the economies of Solow and Romer in the next decade gears the Greek economy towards the business economy and venture capital accumulation. The accumulation of venture capital should be the major priority of any new growth prospect. The implementation and effectiveness of capital accumulation evolve over a longer term. Along with the creation of venture capital, significant social capital, as described in Chap. 6, should be created. The effect of its operation will be felt throughout the long-term. Increased confidence leads to lower operational costs of the economy.

14.4   The Target, Instruments and Time Required to Overcome the Growth Trend

Tables 14.3 and 14.4 shows the development targets, the instruments for their implementation and the time required to overcome the trend in the long-term. The data constituting the two tables are the result of the analysis to date and are documented accordingly.

The definition of development goals is characterised by the fact that the sooner they are organised, the sooner they will be achieved. There are objectives and measures for the short-term (1–3 years) and for the medium-term future. Logically,

Table 14.3 Objectives, instruments and time efficiency to overcome the positive development trend. Time-scale for the adoption of measures

Short-term horizon (1-3 years)		Medium-term horizon (3–15 years)		Long-term horizon (15–70 years)	
Objectives and measures	Instruments	Objectives and measures	Instruments	Objectives and measures	Instruments
Political reorganisation				Political reorganisation	
Fiscal adjustment	————————————————————————————————⟶				
Financial reorganisation					
Sectoral preference	————————————————————————————————⟶				
Labour market					
		Creation of business and social capital	———————————⟶		
		Product markets			
		Investments in education & innovation			
		Property rights			
		Transaction costs			
		Population policy			
		Intervention in the cultural background	———————————⟶		

in the long-term horizon (15–20 years), we should incorporate the probability and potential for the reorganisation of the political system so that it may be able to follow the requirements of economic and social change.

Some of the objectives and measures are important (e.g., fiscal reorganisation), as are some constants (e.g., fiscal adjustment and austerity).

The activation arrows in Tables 14.3 and 14.4 indicate the duration of the activation of objectives and the activation of their implementation instruments.

14.4.1 The Objectives of the Growth Model

The objectives and measures to implement a development model designed to overcome the current trend can only begin by reforming the individual functioning of political institutions that are the source of any changes in the economic field. The top priority is to ensure the appropriate political mandates from the electorate to increase the capacity of reform. The reflection of the reorganisation of political institutions will be evidenced by the organisation of the state, the public sector and the public administration. The modern state contains a series of hierarchical stages of priorities: the minimum functions (provisions of public goods and protection of the indigent), fiduciary functions (the regulating of monopolies, the dealing with imperfect information, social security benefits) and, finally, the beneficial initiatives (the coordination of private activity and the redistribution of wealth). These functions are performed with the aim of managing market failures and improving the rule of law. The revitalisation of public institutions to increase the capacity of the state is associated with mechanisms such as the adoption of rules and restrictions, the provision of opportunities for expression and participation and the establishment of regulations to increase competition. The rules and restrictions establish barriers to arbitrariness and corruption by strengthening the institutional counterweights of state and administrative organisations. In turn, the more rational staffing of services with civil servants contributes to competitive services while the opening of the administration to society allows for the control and enhancement of efficiency. However, regardless of the manner of reorganisation of political institutions, the result must be to maintain political stability and improve all indicators regarding the functioning quality of institutions.

As has been previously discussed, fiscal adjustment through the effective abandonment of the use of the public sector as a means of ensuring full employment and the absorption of excess workforce is an ongoing goal.

Financial reorganisation is a direct short-term goal to support the growth process. The reorganisation of the financial system is, inter alia, imperative for two main reasons:

(a) To sustain the entrepreneurial expansion in S.E. Europe,
(b) To allow for the reorganisation of the financial system to attract capital from the private sector.

An attempt to overrun the current trend would be complemented by formulating a sectoral preference, which is expected to give rise to new development impetus for the Greek economy. In other words, it is an attempt to formulate an organised policy to promote problem solving and growth in economic sectors that should be regarded as particularly dynamic in the Greek economy. There are three major expressions of sectoral preference policies. These include the promotion of interests in the geographic area of southeast Europe (see Sect. 2.10), the promotion of the organised growth of tourism and culture as a driver of growth (see Appendix) and the promotion of the operational framework of the maritime sector whose main objective is to increase capital inflows from abroad and provide jobs for skilled staff.

It is significant that all three preference sectors are dynamically export-oriented. Despite its obvious positive effect, however, this point may come up against international competition, hence limiting the possibility of mobilising international resources to support them (for example, from the EU). These three sectors should be treated more as an internal affair that concerns the Greek economy and less as a guideline that fits, for example, in the logic of an EAP. We should stress here that the social mobilisation for the promotion of these sectors cannot be an isolated action regarding one support field (for example, finding capital or administrative

Table 14.4 Objectives, instruments and time efficiency to overcome the positive development trend. Time-scale for the effectiveness of measures

Short-term horizon (1–3 years)		Medium-term horizon (3–15 years)		Long-term horizon (15–70 years)	
Objectives and measures	Instruments	Objectives and measures	Instruments	Objectives and measures	Instruments
	Redistribution of wealth and power policy				
	Balance of payments surpluses, export growth				
	Increase in savings				
	Transfers				
	New special purpose public debt inflows				
	New private debt inflows				
			Business and social capital performance		
			Restructuring of the tax and insurance system. Increase in forced savings		
			Use of public property		
			Return on investment in education		
				Population and employment growth	

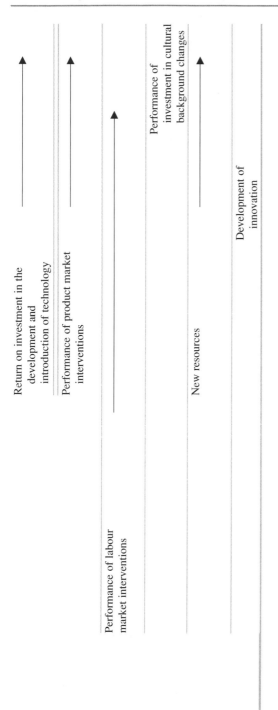

reorganisations such as the creation of a Ministry). Social mobilisation should concern and include the administrative level, the financial opportunities and the institutional cultural level (education, social mobilisation). Particular attention should be given to the fact that vertical sectoral preferences tend to favour the strongest units within these sectors and that they create competitive preferences and concentration of interests in areas or sectors that create the impression of being presented by this preference.

This book has adequately analysed the structural interventions in the labour and product markets with particular emphasis on the time-scale of their effectiveness. As effectiveness in the labour market appears sooner, it should be implemented first. Moreover, the implementation of reforms requires a complex and detailed preparation that takes time. For this reason, it is assumed that it can be implemented in the medium-term.

The creation and accumulation of business and social capital concerns the shaping of new business conditions and high levels of trust (social capital). This is an extremely laborious process that stretches across the long-term. The process of creating the business and social capital is more flexible in comparison with the process of intervention in the cultural background, as it concerns not only behaviour but also the procedures and systems of human incentives. The effectiveness of the accumulation of business and social capital depends on the effectiveness of interventions in education and innovation.

The interventions in education and innovation are expected in the long-term. Indeed, this is the field with the most promising returns in the medium-long term. Essentially, the improvement of labour productivity can be achieved by improving human resources and introducing innovation. We found, however, that despite the fact that there are indications, their efficiency is much higher than that of other structural interventions; both of these interventions are only efficient in the long-term. The improvement of the educational system should solve the problems already identified. Particular attention should be paid to the improvement of secondary education by creating conditions for lengthening the duration of education as a preliminary stage to entering university or as an extension of post-secondary education. Obviously, this is the measure with the highest and most immediate effect in the field of education. The adoption of instruments to introduce and produce innovation is a more complex process because it involves the logic of supply and demand. What must be clearly resolved, however, is the orientation of higher education towards serving the active (financial) needs of science and the linking of higher education with production.

Urgent interventions are required in the institutional background, particularly with respect to the issue of the consolidation of property rights. Because this is a major issue, provisions should be made across the entire range of their creation with emphasis on the following areas:

(a) Regulations for the management of commons, especially the environment,
(b) Rights to ownership of real estate, particularly in relation to public and private property,

(c) Rights to creations of intellectual property, especially with respect to the production of innovation,
(d) Rights to revenue generated, especially as regards the functionality of and changes to tax and insurance systems, with emphasis on the fact that both systems affect labour supply.

The intervention in transaction costs is an extremely important action that unleashes growth potential. There are two main components of this intervention. They include the reduction of the administrative burden of the economy's operation and the control of corruption in the public and private sector.

Obviously, the population policy is a key priority and one of the main factors of the future "growth landing". The population policy has three aspects. These include improving birth rates, developing a framework for immigration policy and developing a framework for domestic migration. This latter point should not be underestimated because if, for example, Greece produces scientists but they choose to migrate, this will lead to a significant long-term problem.

Interventions in the cultural background typically require a long time to bear results. The most important points on which these interventions should focus concern the following key issues of the cultural background:
(a) Collectivity and privacy.
(b) Orientation to the present and not to the future. A society that is not oriented towards the future will hardly agree to a mobilisation of resources in this direction. However, the absence of such interventions effectively amounts to a dead end.
(c) Management of uncertainty and risk.

As shown through the research, the sources forming the cultural background are experiences and education. The relationship between cultural values and growth is bidirectional. Furthermore, the role of education and the organisation of the educational system is critical in bridging the gap between the existing culture and the desire to change existing cultural values and, ultimately, to cultivate positive cultural aspects. Education is the most important change agent of culture, the mindset and the strategies to address problems. Therefore, the organisational structure and culture of the educational system catalytically affects the cultural background through spiritual culture and values. As such, education plays a crucial role in the development and growth of a society.

Although cultural values almost decisively determine the structure and function of education, they are largely determined by education. In particular, unconscious and irreversible perceptions are formed in the pre-pubertal stage, mainly under the influence of the family. However, more conscious and variable practices and values are formed in the post-pubertal stage, and these apply to education and work. It is interesting to see how these values are reflected in education and how education directs people's roles within the same field. This is particularly evidenced during the period when one's core values, underlying attitudes, behaviours, thinking and daily practices that define a person throughout his life are shaped.

Education can create individuals who will are willing to take risks and to think for the long-term and who are oriented towards performance and individual achievements or, in contrast, it may create individuals who will avoid uncertainty, be oriented towards the present, and will not engage in business activities or innovative enterprises. Education thus identifies the characteristics of the human capital that a society produces. The practices, methodology, content of curriculum and the teaching model adopted in education are tools that can reform the cultural values that, in other countries, appear to lead to economic growth and social prosperity.

Finally, we believe that, in the long-term, we should, and indeed will, see the activation of conditions triggering innovation that can be incorporated in production, which is of interest to the economy.

14.4.2 The Instruments for Implementing the Growth Model

The instruments for implementing the growth model can be divided into three major categories according to whether they result from the improvement of the supply of capital and labour or the productivity of the economic system.

The instruments for implementing a specific growth model have a set time-scale of activation. We could divide these into short-term (1–3 years), medium-term (3–15 years) and long-term (15–70 years) instruments. Those that can perform in the medium-term can also perform in the long-term while, of course, the opposite is not true.

Tables 14.3 and 14.4, which present a temporal classification of instruments for implementing objectives and Table 14.5, are useful mainly because they show, very clearly, that the problem of growth in an economy is not complex. Its sources are very clear and distinct. This allows for the development of specific action plans that

Table 14.5 The new sources of growth

Capital		Employment	Improved productivity of the financial system
Equity	Loans		
– Balance of payments surpluses, export growth	– New special purpose public debt inflows	– Population and employmen tgrowth	– Business and social capital performance
			– Redistribution of wealth and powerpolicy
– Increase in savings.	– New private debt inflows		– Return on investment in education
– Transfers			
– Restructuring of the tax and insurance systems. Increase in forced savings			– Return on investment in the development and introduction of technology
			– Performance of labour market interventions
			– Performance of product market interventions
			– Development of innovation
– New resources			– Performance of investment in culturalbackground changes
– Use of public property			

aim to enhance its growth. Certainly, the issue of increases in the balance of payment and export surpluses and the issue of increased savings are extremely complex and subject to many determinants. Furthermore, it is easy to understand that growth, especially when we demand the acceleration thereof, requires the intensified activation of some of its sources. Indeed, if one of these lags, another must replace it to whatever extent possible.

As regards the issue of transfers, these essentially relate to the inputs through the European Structural Funds.[3] In the next decade, we expect to see a change in the deviation of growth levels (per capita income) in the Greek economy compared to the European average (as reflected in Table), which creates the conditions for the repositioning of the Greek economy in relation to the European Structural Funds. However, the issue goes beyond the quantitative position of the Greek economy in relation to European support. The real question concerns the review of the functionality of this relationship and, more generally, the role of the Structural Funds in Greece and Southern Europe, in general. The case of the funds of the European Social Fund is typical in this respect. It is obvious that these funds serve as transfer mechanisms rather than as financing factors, for example, for systems to retrain the workforce. However, the problem is more complex. In areas where the funds require the cooperation of the national institutional framework, the effectiveness problems are greater. In areas where the funds are more directly related to the realisation of projects (participation in the construction of large engineering projects), effectiveness is more evident. Certainly, the EU should look into the formation of a new perception on how these funds are activated and review their usefulness and mode of activation in the host countries.

A developmental reorganisation of the tax and insurance system in the Greek economy should adhere to some simple guidelines:

(a) To improve the availability of labour supply without creating expectations concerning the extension of a parallel economy,

(b) To have final business tax and insurance rates that would be competitive at an international and interdisciplinary level, and

(c) To expand the possibilities of increasing the tax base as, by all indications (Alpha Bank, 27/1/2011), a gradual expansion of up to 3.5% of GDP is a realistic goal.

The new sources of wealth include the replacement of traditional energy inputs with corresponding inputs available in the Greek economy (renewable) and the exploitation of hydrocarbon and gas reserves within the Exclusive Economic Zone (EEZ) of the Greek territory. The new sources of wealth should be developed as soon as possible because they are of great importance to the economy and any technological change could threaten the conditions of their utilisation.

---

[3] The European Structural Funds are the European Regional Development Fund (ERDF), the European Social Fund (ESF), the European Agricultural Guidance and Guarantee Fund (EAGGF) and the Financial Instrument for Fisheries Guidance (FIFG).

Public property consists primarily of real estate, movable property and the value the presence of the state lends to certain actions, such as the licensing of business operations. A relatively cursory analysis of the value of immovable public property conducted within the framework of calculating state assets (Maglaras 2010)[4] estimated that out of a total real estate value of €272 bn, 18.11% of property value – that is, €49.4 bn – could be considered free and available for use. The participation of the state in public enterprises and its lending capacity could produce €5–€10 bn, depending on the development of prices in capital markets and the requisite policies. In any case, the use of public property over time (10–15 years) would yield an amount equal to the last EU support package (worth €25 bn). The creation of a leverage reserve could be of particular relevance to development policy.

We link the new special-purpose public debt inputs to the use of European federal bonds (E-Bonds).[5] Obviously, the debate about the use of E-Bonds contributes to the subject of this chapter as they are seen as a means of mobilising resources that reflect the wider European presence for investments in European regions with lower credit-worthiness. It is logical that, at some point, European Economic Governance will seek financial tools that will allow it to perform a better distribution of projects and a more extensive transfer of resources from surplus to deficit units. Combining this result with the use of an improved risk portfolio leads to the formation of new financial tools such as E-Bonds. It is evident that the issue of the €27 bn loan by the European Financial Stability Fund (EFSF) to finance the rescue package of Ireland (worth €85 bn) is a precursor to the use of E-Bonds. Of course, the problem lies in the conditions of moral hazard that may be incorporated into this new tool. Thus, pressure at the European level can lead to the decline of Franco-German opposition on the forming of a mechanism to integrate the risk of individuals in their investment practices. Although these new financial tools are necessary, their exact nature remains an open question.

The new private loan options are nothing more than the ability of the private sector to increase debt ratios in accordance with international standards. If this happens, it will not be affected by the indebtedness of the state as international practice during the crisis has revealed that this variable is not an objective of international markets. Certainly, national debt affects the cost of private sector lending. As we found in the beginning of the book, the indebtedness of private households is quite low at 50% household debt relative to GDP. This compares, as of the end of 2010, to 41% in Italy, 83% in Spain, 91% in Portugal, 56% in Finland, 123% in the Netherlands and 114% in Ireland (Bank for International Settlements, IBS). We note that the long-term burden of the Greek private business sector is even less, standing at just 38% in 2010 compared to 47% in Italy, 124% in Spain, 115% in Portugal, 100% in Finland, 60% in the Netherlands and 137% in Ireland.

The next source of growth that sets the trend for the Greek economy in the future is the development of population and employment. This is perhaps one of the major

---

[4] The complex problem of using the Public Property, ISTAME, November 2010, issue 9.

[5] We use the term European Federal Bond (E-Bond) because, in Banking Economics, the term Eurobond has a different meaning.

development issues in Greek society, which, to some extent, is manageable by domestic politics. Certainly, the issue of enhancing the birth rate is very difficult to manage, especially in a climate of financial stringency. However, the issue of workforce availability is very different; as we have seen, it depends on tax, insurance and staff retraining policies. These policies could be mobilised to reverse the future trend; however, the workforce availability may be affected by the migration balance. This result is based on the pressure of two variables: (a) the balance of the domestic population and (b) the balance of the foreign population. The balance of the domestic population will evolve under the medium-term pressure of the economic crisis in Greece; however, it is significant to note that the outflow of graduates to foreign destinations started much earlier.

The balance of the latest wave of immigrants mainly concerns unskilled workers. This does not contribute to the solution of the problem of population growth as a factor for future growth. In contrast, the Greek economy should see the future inflow of skilled labour in a very positive light provided that the economic conditions to attract skilled labour have been established.

Both concerns relating to the future available workforce encounter issues of cultural and political attitudes that often ignore the future needs of society. On the one hand, the workforce shrinks (wave of retirements), while on the other, the future needs of the economy are ignored. Thus, with regard to immigration, we note a broader issue of policy that could reverse the negative developments.

Finally, the medium and long-term improvements in productivity of the economic system through the performance of measures taken throughout the course of the growth model, contribute to new sources of growth that are in line with what we have already prescribed. These improvements will allow for the increased performance of business and social capital, investment in education and innovation, interventions in the labour and product markets, the development of innovation, and, finally, the complex effects of changes in the cultural background.

A final comment concerns the policy for the redistribution of wealth and power as a source of growth. Obviously, the problem is vast and extremely complex. We focus on the fact that various concentrations of power divert wealth from society, transferring the surplus for those who produce it (and, thus, possibly re-invest it) to those who have social and political power but are not targeted for investment and growth. A typical example concerns the action of pressure groups for the distribution of the budget and public procurements. Essentially, this source suggests that improving the allocation of resources improves the growth rate of the economy.

References

Acemoglu D (2009) Introduction to modern economic growth. Princeton University Press, New Jersey

Acemoglu D, Johnson S, Robinson J (2005) The rise of Europe: Atlantic trade, institutional change, and economic growth. Am Econ Rev 95(3):546–579

Acemoglu D, Johnson S, Robinson JA (2002) Reversal of fortune: geography and institutions in the making of the modern world income distribution. Q J Econ 117(4):1231–1293

Acemoglu D, Johnson S, Robinson JA (2001) The colonial origins of comparative development: an empirical investigation. Am Econ Rev 91:1369–1401

Bos JWB, Economidou C, Koetter M, Kolari JW (2010) Do all countries grow alike? J Dev Econ 91(1):113–127

Carone G, Denis C, Mc Morrow K, Mourre G, Röger W (2006) Long-term labour productivity and GDP projections for the EU-25 Member States: a production function framework

Economides G, Egger P (2009) The role of institutions in economic outcomes: editorial introduction. Eur J Polit Econ 25(3):277–279

Esfahani HS, Ramirez MT (2003) Institutions, infrastructure, and economic growth. J Dev Econ 70(2):443–477

Glaeser EL, Hanushek EA, Quigley JM (2004) Opportunities, race, and urban location: the influence of John Kain. J Urban Econ 56:70–79

Hall R, Jones C (1999) Why do some countries produce so much more output per worker than others? Q J Econ 114(1):83–116

Harrison LE, Huntington SP (2000) Culture matters: how values shape human progress. Basic Books, New York

Hong Y (2009) A dynamic constructivist approach to culture: moving @@from describing culture to explaining culture. In: Wyer RS, Chiu CY, Hong YY (eds) Understanding culture: theory, research and application. Psychology Press, New York

House RJ, Hanges PJ, Javidan M, Dorfman PW, Gupta V (2004) Culture, leadership and organisations – the GLOBE study of 62 societies. Sage Publication, Thousand Oaks, CA

Johnston L (1996) Resisting change: information-seeking and stereotype change. Eur J of Soc Psychol 26:799–825

Knack S, Keefer P (1997) Does social capital have an economic payoff? A Cross-Country Investigation. Q J Econ 112(4):1251–1288

Knack S, Keefer P (1995) Institutions and economic performance: crosscountry tests using alternative institutional measures. Econ Polit 7(3):207–228

Kostelenos G, Basileiou D, Kounaris E, Petmezas S, Sfakianakis M (2007) Gross domestic product 1830–1939. Centre of Planning and Economic Research, Athens

Kotzamanis B, Androulaki E (2009) The demography of modern Greece. In: Kotzamanis B (ed) The demographic challenge, facts and risks. University Press of Thessaly, Volos, pp 87–120

Lipset SM (1960) Political man: the social bases of politics. Heinemann, London

Locke J (1689/1988) Two treatises of government. Cambridge University Press, Cambridge

Machiavelli N (1519/1987) Discourses on livy. Oxford University Press, New York

Marshall A (1890/1997) Principles of economics. Prometheus Books, New York

McClelland DC (1961) The achieving society. Van Nostrand, New Jersey

Mill JS ([1848], 1973) Principles of political economy with some of their applications to social philosophy. William JA (ed) AM Kelley, New York

Montesquieu C ([1748], 1989) The spirit of the laws. Cohler AM, Miller BC, Stone HS (eds). Cambridge University Press, New York

Myrdal G (1954) An international economy: problems and prospects. Harper and Brothers, New York

North D (1990) Institutional change and economic performance. Cambridge University Press, Cambridge

Oyserman D, Sorensen N (2009) Understanding cultural syndrome effects on what and how we think: a situated cognition model. In: Wyer RS, Chiu CY, Hong YY (eds) Understanding culture: theory, research and application. Psychology Press, New York, pp 25–52

Putnam RD (1993) The prosperous community: social capital and public life. Am Prospect 4 (13):35–42

Reinhart CM , Rogoff KS (2010) From financial crash to debt crisis. NBER Working Paper 15795

Romer P (1986) Increasing returns and long-run growth. J Polit Econ 94(5):500–521; 1002–1037

Schwatrz SH (2009) Culture matters: national value cultures, sources and consequences. In: Wyer RS, Chiu CY, Hong YY (eds) Understanding culture: theory, research and application. Psychology Press, New York, p 127

Siampos G (1973) Demographic trends of modern Greece 1821–1985. Tzanetou, Athens

Solow RM (1957) Technical change and the aggregate production function. Rev Econ Stat 39:312–320

Tabellini G (2010) Culture and institutions: economic development in the regions of Europe. J Eur Econ Assoc 8(4):677–716

Tavassoli TN (2009) Climate, psychological homeostasis and individual behaviours across cultures. In: Wyer RS, Chiu CY, Hong YY (eds) Understanding culture: theory, research and application. Psychology Press, New York, pp 211–222

Triandis HC (1995) Individualism and collectivism. Westview Press, Boulder, CO

Weber M (1930) The protestant ethic and the spirit of capitalism. Unwin Hyman, London

Williamson O (1981) The economics of organization: the transaction cost approach. Am J Sociol 87:548–577

Appendix: A Sectoral Proposal for Potential Growth in the Greek Economy. Climate Change, Population Ageing, Tourism and Culture

This appendix briefly describes the two major developments that are (jointly) expected to largely shape the general environment of the Greek economy over the next few decades. These developments concern climate change and the ageing of the population. After considering recent estimates, we attempt to assess their impact on the key sectors of the Greek economy. We analyse their obvious impact on the demand for tourist services, due to changes in climatic conditions and demographic trends in the developed world. Moreover, we consider the importance of culture in the development of an innovative tourism concept, based on the interweaving of cultural resources and tourism development. We study the current situation and possible links with the sectors of health and agricultural production. Finally, as the developments mentioned create the need to strengthen and improve the existing infrastructure, we study the possible effects on the construction sector.

This appendix presents a brief sectoral proposal for potential growth in the Greek economy. The concept is very simple. The global climate change and population changes favour the development of tourist conditions. In the Greek economy, the tourism sector is particularly broad. If the expected climate change is used to lengthen the tourist season, the tourism sector will obviously benefit from these developments. A wide cultural field, however, characterises the Greek economy, with excellent competitive advantages in terms of accumulated capital and human resources. The interlinking between the two areas may prove to be highly effective. Moreover, as older tourists more systematically seek to connect with the cultural background, population ageing promotes this interlinking. The population change, however, promotes a new connection between the development of the health sector and of health tourism. In the last two sectors (culture and health), the Greek economy presents some significant comparative advantages in human resources, as it has an oversupply of graduates.

The development of key priority sectors (tourism, culture, and health) will lead to a broader sectoral mobilisation in the Greek economy. It is obvious that such a mobilisation directly concerns the areas of environment, agriculture, construction and, of course, communications and transport (Fig. A.1).

P. Petrakis, *The Greek Economy and the Crisis*,
DOI 10.1007/978-3-642-21175-1, © Springer-Verlag Berlin Heidelberg 2012

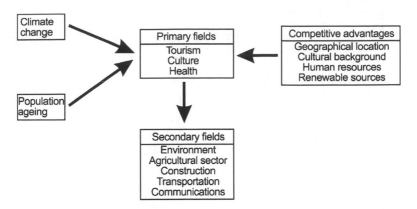

Fig. A.1 The main development proposal

1   Geophysical Components of the Long-Term Evolution of the Greek Economy

Two key developments will shape the conditions of economic activity in the oncoming decades. These are the climate change observed in recent decades and population ageing. These two mid-term developments seem unlikely to be reversed.

1.1   Climate Change and Its Effects

Today, climate change has become a hot topic, even beyond the scientific community. The European Commission[1] has classified the effects of climatic change among the larger political, social and economic challenges it will be called upon to address in the coming decades.

The term climate change refers to the long-term change in the distribution of the observed climatic parameters (e.g., temperature and precipitation), and it has become evident that it is directly related to the emission of greenhouse gases. The most obvious sign of climate change is global warming. The average temperature in early 2000 had increased by 0.5°C compared to the average for the period 1961–1990 (Dow and Downing 2006), and this trend is accelerating.

The increase in average global temperature is responsible for a series of events: The melting of the ice at the poles of the earth leads to a rise in the sea level, which creates significant risks for many coastal areas. Furthermore, climate change affects the flow of rivers, while it may lead to changes in the efficiency of agricultural production. Overall, in developing countries, agricultural productivity is expected to decline because of global warming, by between 9% and 21% (Rosegrant et al. 2008).

---

[1] For example, see http://ec.europa.eu/environment/climat/home_en.htm.

The social and economic impacts of climate change began to be more evident with the evermore frequent occurrence of extreme weather events. These phenomena (beyond the purely economic costs of addressing the resulting damage) have also created humanitarian disasters, thus highlighting social issues. The prevention of extreme weather events requires significant capital investment in infrastructure.

The positive or negative effects of climate change can differ in various geographic regions and across economic sectors. It is no coincidence that different national governments and international organisations do not show the same interest in climate change and in promoting cooperation and taking action to fight it.

Much like everywhere else, in Greece, the most obvious impact of climate change over the next few decades will concern the increase of the average temperature, which will increase the warmth of Greece's climate. Moreover, the expected increase in the sea level (which, as described above, is a consequence of global warming) poses some risks for island and coastal areas. The problems of water scarcity already faced by several areas of the country, at least on a seasonal basis, are expected to intensify. Furthermore, climate change is expected to significantly affect the agricultural production of the Greek countryside, creating new opportunities for business activity but also new risks.

In fact, the overall impact of climate change on the Greek economy and society cannot be easily measured with certainty. A typical example is that of the potential and hard-to-predict changes in energy demand and in the mix of energy inputs (for example, reduced demand for fossil fuels due to milder weather conditions during winter and increased consumption of electricity due to increased usage of air-conditioning equipment in warmer summers) with similar implications for the fuel balance deficit.

However, what interests us here is that climate change is expected to affect the country's tourism by substantially extending the summer holiday season.

1.2   Population Ageing

Population ageing is not a phenomenon limited to recent decades. On the contrary, the first occurrences were found in the developed societies of the nineteenth century. From the middle to the end of this century, we began to witness a simultaneous increase in life expectancy and a decrease of birth rates in developed countries.[2]

The even faster growth rates in life expectancy in the western world during the second half of the last century are primarily attributed to the rapid progress of medical science and technology. At the same time, the economic growth and development of the western world has enhanced the output produced, while political stability has allowed for access to the wealth produced for a large part of the population. Thus, a significant portion of the population has achieved higher levels of prosperity, further expanding life expectancy.

---

[2] E.g. for the case of Gr. Britain and Sweden, see Grundy (2003).

However, the decrease in birth rates is a social phenomenon associated with the modern way of life (e.g., a massive influx of women with education and in the labour market, cultural aspects and urbanisation) that accompanied the high rates of economic growth and development of that period.

All of the above clarifies why population ageing is observed exclusively in the developed world. In contrast to the ageing population of the western world, in less developed and developing countries, birth rates are clearly higher, while life expectancy remains lower, leading to a lower average age of the population.

Moreover, population ageing is not observed in all developed countries to the same extent. Societies that remain more tolerant towards migration (the most typical example is that of the US) accept a significant number of new workers, which automatically reduces the average age of their population and boosts their financial performance.

The phenomenon is not expected to reverse in the next few decades. However, all demographic studies predict a further escalation of ageing in Western societies (see Fig. A.2). Furthermore, the appearance of signs of population ageing will be more likely in developing countries as they begin to enjoy higher levels of development and their citizens begin to adopt the lifestyle of western societies.

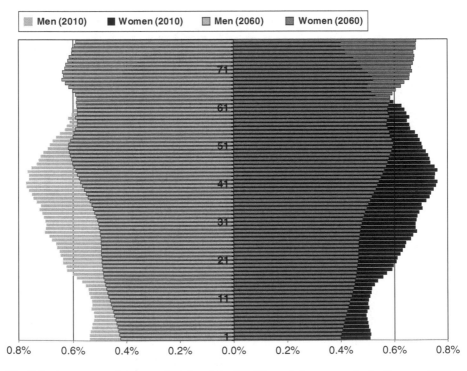

Fig. A.2 Assessment of the age allocation of the EU-27 population per gender for the years 2010 and 2060 (Source: Eurostat)

As it is easily understood, population ageing is connected to a series of economic developments. What interests us here is that demographic changes worldwide, and particularly in rich countries, increase the total time available for personal satisfaction (leisure time). In other words, they lead to a significant increase in tourist services.

2   The Tourism Sector and the Greek Economy

The tourism sector is rightly considered to be the important sector of the Greek economy, as, along with shipping, it represents the service sector with the most clear export orientation.

Total income from tourism-based foreign exchange represents a large proportion of total export revenues. Table A.1 below shows in more detail the contribution of tourism revenues in relation to the aggregates of the country's current transactions. It is indicative that tourism revenues are similar to the total exports of goods (column 5 of the table), forming 25% of total income from the export of goods and

Table A.1 The contribution of tourism in current account aggregates in Greece

	Revenue from exports	Revenue from exports and services	Current account balance	Revenue from tourism	Revenue from exports	Revenue from tourism compared to:		
						Revenue from exports and services	Current account balance	
	(1)	(2)	(3)	(4)	(5) = (4)/(1)	(6) = (4)/(2)	(7) = (4)/(3)	
2001	11,545.4	33,621.3	−10,585.5	10,579.9	0.92	0.31	1.00	
2002	10,433.6	31,565.0	−10,221.1	10,284.7	0.99	0.33	1.01	
2003	11,113.6	32,508.8	−9,886.9	9,460.1	0.85	0.29	0.96	
2004	12,653.3	39,395.8	−10,717.1	10,347.8	0.82	0.26	0.97	
2005	14,200.9	41,454.4	−14,743.4	10,729.5	0.76	0.26	0.73	
2006	16,154.3	44,518.4	−23,758.7	11,356.7	0.70	0.26	0.48	
2007	17,445.5	48,782.8	−32,602.2	11,319.2	0.65	0.23	0.35	
2008	19,812.9	53,879.1	−34,797.6	11,635.9	0.59	0.22	0.33	
2009	15,318.0	42,301.3	−26,630.9	10,400.3	0.68	0.25	0.39	

Source: BoG, SDOS, data processing

Note: The ratio of tourist revenue to the current account balance takes into account absolute figures

Table A.2 Contribution of the tourism sector to product output and employment in Greece and in competing countries

	Contribution to GDP (%)			Participation in employment (%)		
	Directly	Indirectly	Total	Directly	Indirectly	Total
Greece	7.49	8.79	16.28	10.42	9.34	19.76
Italy	4.02	5.81	9.83	4.35	6.63	10.98
Spain	8.17	11.76	19.93	8.93	12.84	21.77
Portugal	6.26	9.27	15.53	7.62	11.22	18.84
Cyprus	8.56	11.14	19.70	11.99	12.71	24.70
Croatia	12.14	13.48	25.62	13.66	15.15	28.81
Turkey	3.37	5.39	8.76	1.93	3.64	5.57

Source: Chamber of Tourism, Annual Report on Greek tourism, 2009, data processing

services (column 6 of the table). It also demonstrates that during the past decade, the ratio of tourism revenue to revenue from exports and services and the current account balance are decreasing. This, combined with the degree of the contribution of tourism to the Greek economy, necessitates the improvement of the current situation and long-term planning regarding the development of the tourism sector.

The total contribution of the Greek tourism sector to domestic economic activity becomes more evident in the Table A.2, which shows the direct and indirect contributions of the sector to total product output and employment in Greece and in a number of competing countries.

It is indicative that the direct contribution of tourism to GDP and employment in the case of Greece is quite high compared to the rest of the countries in the table. On the other hand, the indirect contribution of tourism to the Greek economy is not at the levels one would expect, given the direct involvement of the sector in the two examined indexes. This observation makes it clear that there is potential for further exploitation of the growth dynamics of the tourism sector for the development of the Greek economy.

The tourism sector in Greece is characterised by a very low concentration in many small and very small tourism businesses and the oversupply of services (Sampaniotis 2006; Dagkalidis 2008).

The emerging situation strengthens competition among small hotel businesses to attract tourists, mainly through pricing policies. By extension, the competition reduces the will of even large hotel enterprises to further invest and thus perpetuates a vicious cycle of low-quality services, low added value and low investments.

An important feature, however, of the tourism industry is the concentration of the tourist season during the summer months, leading several hotel companies, whether small or large, to underperform during the rest of the year, as they are limited to seasonal operation. The phenomenon of seasonality is present in all countries that attract tourists (including the other southern European countries, where there is a high turnout of tourists during the summer months). However, the phenomenon of Greek tourism seasonality is much more intense than in those countries. Fig. A.3, below, which shows the monthly average net utilisation

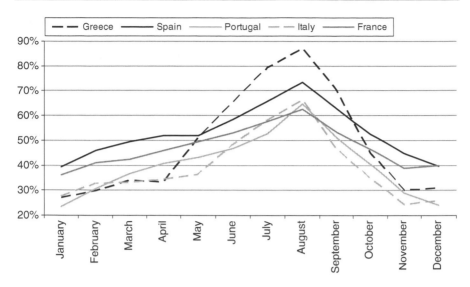

Fig. A.3 Average net utilisation of beds per month for the period 2001–2009 (figures for France concern the period 2004–2009) (Source: Eurostat)

of beds[3] for the period 2001–2009, is indicative of the seasonality of the Greek tourism industry.

The particularly high seasonality of Greek tourism makes investments in tourist facilities less attractive. However, the possibility of the profitable operation of units throughout the year would benefit entrepreneurs in the tourism sector. This would also enhance employment in this sector, which is largely temporary and seasonal because of the nature of the sector.

Despite the inherent weaknesses described above, the lengthening of the tourist season would act as a catalyst for companies in the tourism sector. Apart from the obvious positive effects of added value, achieving economies of scale and enhancing employment, the lengthening of the tourist season would create an environment more conducive to investments in the sector.

As already mentioned, the major impact of climate change is the warming of the planet. In this case, the particularly hot summers are likely to create an even hotter climate in the summer months. However, the structure of summer tourism in Greece is such that the flow of holidaymakers from northern countries seeking holidays in the sun will not be significantly affected. In other words, the "sun and sea" model is

---

[3] We arrive at similar conclusions by investigating the air passenger arrivals in these countries. However, this measurement probably underestimates the number of tourists in other countries, where a large number of tourists might not travel by air because of their proximity to the countries of central Europe.

not expected to be adversely affected by higher temperatures during the months with the highest demand for tourist services in Greece.

At the same time, however, temperature increases during spring and autumn are likely to create favourable conditions for tourism, attracting a larger number of holidaymakers during these periods. Thus, the increase in the average temperature in Greece might potentially extend the tourist season in spring and autumn, when demand is currently weak.

To the extent that visitors who arrive in Greece outside of the summer season seek higher quality services, it is very likely that the lengthening of the tourist season will lead to improved services and enhance the added value of the tourism industry.

This allows Greek tourist enterprises to reject the model of mass and seasonal tourism and turn to high-quality services, targeting market segments that can deliver more revenue and thus higher added value. Even if the mass tourism model is not fully rejected, in this way, the Greek tourism sector can reduce its exposure to this market and diversify its sources of income.

Finally, depending on the climate formed, it may be desirable to maintain this tourism model for the summer (for example, very hot summers that attract large numbers of visitors to Greek beaches), while turning to higher quality and added-value services in the remaining periods.

In addition, the attraction of tourists seeking more quality services, especially during the months in which demand is currently weak, will facilitate the exploitation of Greece's abundant cultural heritage as an additional element of the tourism product.

The strategic shift towards the higher quality of tourist services is expected to strengthen the incentives for protecting the natural environment (which is required, inter alia, to attract tourists to Greece), as "green growth" (e.g., an increase of energy produced by environmentally friendly methods, and utilisation of waste) and the support of the necessary infrastructure (e.g., prevention of fires and forest protection) indirectly but obviously enhance the country's tourism product.

Along with the changing weather conditions, the long-term trend of population ageing in Western societies is likely to cause significant changes in demand for the services of the Greek tourism industry. Specifically, as previously described, in the coming decades, the ageing population is expected to alter the absolute size of different age groups, shrinking the youth population and increasing the number of older people.

The developed countries that have already begun to feel the effects of ageing (which are expected to accelerate over the next few years) include several of the countries that traditionally support the Greek tourism sector. Thus, it is not unlikely that the next few years will mark a significant decline in demand for Greek tourism services by young people. Conversely, however, as the absolute size of the older population in these countries is expected to increase, this drop is likely to be offset by the increase in demand for tourism services by older tourists.

This creates new opportunities (but also new risks) for Greek tourist enterprises. The country's geographical position and the sunshine this ensures are insufficient to attract older tourists. Older visitors definitely demand higher quality services, even if they are accompanied by higher costs. In other words, the current model (sun & sea) of Greek tourism – apart from the other negative factors outlined above – does not seem to constitute a rational medium- or long-term strategic choice, given the demographic trends in the "client-countries" of the tourism sector. For this reason, the Greek tourism industry is again challenged to shift to higher quality tourism, which will provide higher added value and access to the numerous (and growing) older age groups in developed societies. This is expected to enhance the total (direct and indirect) contribution of tourism in the growth and development of the Greek economy.

Furthermore, the strategic shift of the tourism industry towards older visitors is likely to increase demand for tourist services for a longer period of the year, largely solving the industry's problem of seasonality. A typical example is pensioners, who, freed from the restrictions of working life, can remain in Greece for longer.

It is no coincidence that in recent years, there has been a significant demand from residents of northern Europe (mainly England and Germany) for housing in Mediterranean countries. Despite the fact that Greece benefited from this demand, it failed to reach the corresponding levels of Spain and Portugal.

At this point, it should be noted that the attraction of (mainly) older Europeans, and their longer sojourns in Greece, has a positive influence on the overall economy and strengthens the indirect contribution of tourism to all economic activity.

Specifically, some sectors, such as that of health, will enjoy significant positive effects. The expansion of an older population that chooses to remain in Greece allows public hospitals and private health companies to increase their turnover (and profit margins), expanding the number of customers supported by robust systems of social insurance.

Meanwhile, older holidaymakers are likely to show more interest in the Greek cultural heritage, reinforcing the relationship between and joint development of the tourism and cultural sectors. At the same time, the attraction of tourists for long periods of time to Greece and their familiarisation with Greek traditions and products will make Greece's exportable goods more attractive in the markets of the tourists' countries of origin.

In an attempt to summarise the above, we should reiterate that the strategic choice to attract the (ever increasing) older population to Greece will increase the added value of the industry and increase the indirect effect of tourism on a number of sectors of the Greek economy, which today lag behind those of other countries with a similarly developed tourism sector. This effort, however, is not simple and, in particular, cannot be achieved merely because of the country's geographic location.

Rather, it requires a series of substantial investments (public and private) in terms of available infrastructure. Apart from the purely tourist infrastructure, a series of investments in, e.g., transport infrastructure and health are necessary to make the Greek tourism product more attractive. As noted above, Greece has managed to reach Spain and Portugal with respect to the number of housing purchases by residents of Nordic countries. Obviously, the preference for the countries of the Iberian Peninsula is largely due to their proximity to the countries of residence of visitors. However, it is also due, to a significant extent, to the infrastructure and services offered there.

The contribution of agricultural production to tourism is particularly important. The existence of a close relationship between tourism and agricultural production increases the added value of the tourism product while promoting local agricultural products, in an effort to improve the competitive position of the country. The agricultural economy is closely linked to other economic activities and the development objectives of each region. This strengthens the country's other tourism targets and exploits to the fullest extent the advantages of agricultural production, leading to dynamic growth.

Recent years have witnessed declining interest in traditional forms of tourism, while visitors become more discerning about the level of services. Particular emphasis is placed on the quality of the tourist experience and sensitivity to the environment and local culture. In parallel, realizing these new conditions, local stakeholders and tourism professionals promote new types of recreation to highlight and maintain the characteristics of the natural environment of each region. This is achieved by linking the agricultural and tourism sectors, enhancing entrepreneurship and supporting the local economy.

The development of agricultural tourism in Greece is still in its early stages. However, there is a need for quality tourism and the creation of a specialised tourist product, which will highlight the special and original features of the country.

3   The Productive Sector of Culture

The fact that culture operates as a filter for the processing and formation of the identity of modern man in a market economy means that there is a need for the production and consumption of cultural goods and services, which have a distinct impact on the national economy. In this way, culture can boost employment and overall economic development.

Apart from the traditional sector of the creation and promotion of the arts (e.g., painting, theatre, literature, opera and dance), the broader sector related to the production of goods and services is of particular importance. The linking of the narrow concept of art with a range of high value-added service sectors (e.g., tourism and advertising) enhances the produced output and employment and contributes to overall economic growth.

Early research in different EU countries set the contribution of the wider cultural sector in the national economy at up to 9% of output, 12% of total employment and 14% of total exports. Regarding the core cultural sector and cultural tourism, the contribution to the national product reaches 3.1%, while the maximum contribution to employment stands at 3.6% (CIA World Factbook, 2003, 2004, 2005, European Commission – The Economy of Culture in Europe, 2006, Eurostat – Cultural Employment in Europe, 2004).

Greece's experience regarding the activities of the cultural industry places it in the middle of the EU scale. In 2004, the broader cultural sector in Greece showed a turnover of €6,875 m, while the added value to the national product was close to 1% (Table A.3); this is a very low rate compared to most European Union countries. This indicates the relative weakness of the broader cultural sector in Greece. In

Table A.3 Financial indexes of the cultural sector

	Turnover 2003	Value added to GDP (2003) (%)	Average turnover growth (1999–2003) (%)	Growth in value added to GDP (1999–2003) (%)	Level of investment in the wider cultural sector in relation to turnover, 2003 (%)
Greece	6,875	1.00	5.40	4.40	2.50
Italy	84,359	2.30	5.30	7.30	3.60
Spain	61,333	2.30	10.50	9.00	2.90
Portugal	6,358	1.40	6.00	6.30	1.50
Denmark	10,111	3.10	2.70	1.90	7.90
Netherlands	33,372	2.70	5.00	-	6.00
Norway	14,841	3.20	-	-	4.90
Sweden	18,155	2.40	78	2.60	4.40
Finland	10,677	3.10	7.10	11.10	4.70

Source: European Commission – The Economy of Culture in Europe, 2006

Table A.4 Classification of total employment in the cultural sector and cultural tourism

Country	Cultural employment	Percentage of total employment (%)	Cultural employment and employment of cultural tourism	Percentage of total employment (%)
Greece	97.4	2.2	139.4	3.2
Italy	466.9	2.1	622.9	2.8
Spain	379	2.1	558.9	3.1
Portugal	89.4	1.9	116.1	2.5
Denmark	80.6	3	89.6	3.3
Netherlands	296.4	3.6	343.1	4.2
Sweden	135.5	3.1	155.2	3.6
Finland	77.6	3.2	88.85	3.7

Source: European Commission – The Economy of Culture in Europe, 2006

addition, during the period 1999–2003, the added value increased to a satisfactory 5.4%, which is, however, still markedly lower than many other European countries. The level of investment in intangible assets in the wider cultural sector through the development of creativity and knowledge is very low in Greece, challenging the further development of the industry (Table A.3).

In the Greek economy, 97,400 workers are estimated to be employed in the cultural sector. If we include those employed in cultural tourism, employment in the wider cultural sector is estimated at 139,400 people (Table A.4), i.e., 3.2% of total employment (European Commission – The Economy of Culture in Europe, 2006).

The humanities consist of a wide cognitive field that includes literature, languages, philology, history of art and visual culture, communication and the media as well as musical, theatrical, cinematic and historical studies.

The employment opportunities for humanities graduates include options related directly or indirectly to the cultural sector (e.g., education, museums, management, editorial work, marketing, sales, and employment in libraries). Ultimately, however, an important percentage of these graduates select activities that are not related to the humanities (Nicholls 2005).

Especially in Greece, the employment opportunities for humanities graduates appear limited. Graduates of such schools face serious obstacles in entering the labour market and finding permanent jobs in a field related to their subject of study, thus leading to an oversupply of humanities graduates.

According to a study by the Liaison Office of the Democritus University of Thrace, humanities graduates (philosophy and literature) are employed with work contracts at a rate of 26.9%, which is higher than that for graduates of other schools. The study highlighted that only 17.7% of history graduates are employed in a job related to their subject of study, while a very high percentage of such graduates end up unemployed (42.9%).

In light of the international competitive environment in terms of cultural heritage attractions, copyrights and related products, Greece lags behind, both in developing specialised management and marketing personnel and in the financial reserves to develop the necessary infrastructure and use modern technologies. This is despite the easy access to cultural heritage sites and the familiarisation of the population through abundant cultural events.

At this point, it should be noted that the strengthening of cultural infrastructure contributes to the increased employment of skilled personnel of various specialties. According to a study (Deffner and Metaxas 2003), apart from qualified scientific staff, places of cultural interest also employ high-school graduates (e.g., security personnel and administrators). Unfortunately, a series of activities (e.g., improvement of cultural products, public relations, support and development of relationships with stakeholders, sponsors and activities related to copyrights) that can provide additional jobs to highly trained personnel have not been developed to the extent expected.

Apart from the training and practice of humanities graduates, a current trend concerns the formation of post-graduate programs specialising in cultural tourism and focusing on heritage tourism, which contributes to the convergence of the cultural and tourism sectors. Sample surveys of students in these programs show a clear preference for further work in the tourism industry (Hannam et al. 2004). The list of preferences is topped by e.g. research and academic work, staffing of relevant regional development agencies, local government and working at non-profit organisations (e.g., tourist chambers). Moreover, regarding the future (e.g. 10 years), there is a clear intention to conduct business in the area of cultural tourism.

As previously stated, culture creates synergies with tourism. The availability of cultural services is one of the most important criteria for selecting a tourist destination with many places of cultural interest (e.g., heritage sites, museums, exhibitions and festivals) that attract many tourists.

One particular study, which concludes that the ancillary jobs created in tourism near intellectual heritage attractions are double the net jobs relating to the operation and maintenance of these cultural sites (Brand et al. 2006), is enlightening.

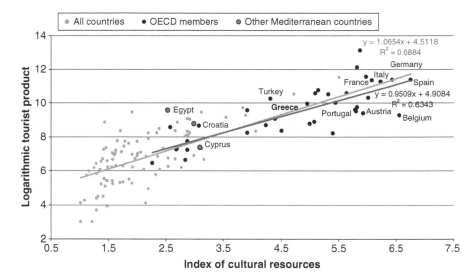

Fig. A.4 Correlation of direct tourism product and the cultural resources index calculated by the World Economic Forum (Source: World Economic Forum (2009), World Travel and Tourism Council)

In addition to the importance of cultural tourism, it is noted that many tourists visit destinations to experience the lifestyle, daily culture and customs of the people living there. Moreover, successful destinations are those that can create a positive interaction between culture and tourism. In an OECD report on culture and local development, Greffe (2005) identifies a number of criteria for the correlation between culture and tourism. These criteria consist of the continuity of cultural activities, the degree of involvement of locals and the country's ability to produce all the goods and services requested.

The obvious synergies between culture and tourism clearly emerge from the close relationship between the cultural wealth of a country and the size of the tourism sector. Fig. A.4 below shows the relationship between the tourism product (the picture that emerges when looking at the number of tourist arrivals is similar) and the index "cultural resources", prepared by the World Economic Forum.

Given the trend that seems to be emerging[4] in the developed world (OECD countries), we observe that an improvement in the index to the current levels of Portugal (increase of the index by approximately 17%) might increase Greece's tourism product by 63%. The image is identical with respect to tourist arrivals: an

---

[4] At this point, it is useful to mention that the correlation of the tourism product and the index of cultural resources (as well as the interpretation of the index) is stronger than that between the GDP of the industry and the general index of competitiveness of the tourism industry (Travel & Tourism Competitiveness Index) developed by the WEF (2009).

improvement in the cultural resources index of Greece by 17% would potentially lead to a 59% increase in visitors to the country.

At this point, we should examine exactly what the cultural resources index of the World Economic Forum records and, therefore, what actions lead to its increase. Already, readers might be surprised by the emerging classification of developed countries, as shown in the diagram, in which Greece is 23 rd, just behind Spain (first in the world), Italy, Portugal and a number of other European countries.

According to the WEF (2009), aside from the number of world heritage monuments (as recorded by UNESCO), the calculation of the index takes into account the capacity of sports stadiums and the number of international exhibitions held in a country. Finally, it includes the measurement of exports by creative industries as a measure to assess the cultural richness of a society.[5]

Given the (direct and indirect) contributions of the tourism and cultural sectors to GDP and employment in Greece, an improvement in relevant infrastructure would contribute significantly to the development efforts of the Greek economy.

Although Greece has traditionally relied on its physical assets, investing in the sun and sea model, a systematic effort to link culture and tourism while improving the necessary infrastructure will create opportunities for further development for both sectors.

4   Health

The health sector utilises the available production factors (e.g., economic resources, human resources, medical supplies, technology and infrastructure) to provide health services to the population. This is a key economic sector, contributing significantly to produced output and employment, as we shall observe further below.

The growth of expenditure in the health sector tends to be higher in relation to GDP than for OECD countries, except Finland (reference period 1995–2007), (OECD Health Data, June 2009). In 2007, the highest health spending as a percentage of GDP was recorded in the USA (15.3%) followed by Switzerland (10.8%). In Greece, the total health expenditure is 9.6% of GDP. Figure A.4 shows the temporal evolution of total health expenditures (as a percentage of GDP) in Greece, other Mediterranean countries of the European Union and some countries of northern Europe. The diagram shows the continued growth of the industry, with health expenditures amounting to 8.6% in 1995, 9% in 2002, and 9.6% in 2007. The rising expenditure in Greece after 1995 is justified by the economic growth recorded during the period 1995–2005, as, according to Smith et al. (2000), the growth rate of an economy directly affects increases in health spending (Fig. A.5).

---

[5] The last variable appears to reduce the performance of both Greece and other countries (e.g., Portugal). However, the same analysis, using WEF data (2008), excluding this variable results in very similar conclusions about the relationship between "cultural resources" and the size of the tourism sector (tourism GDP and foreign tourist arrivals).

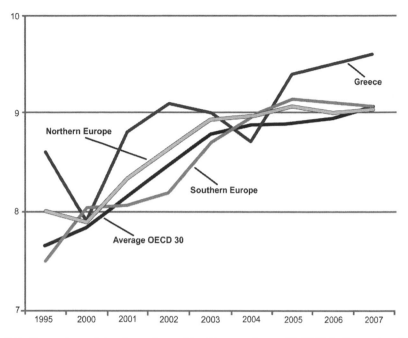

Fig. A.5 Comparison of the change in total health expenditures (% GDP) in Greece in relation to the average of the countries of southern and northern Europe (Source: OECD Health Data, June 2009)

The variations in the levels of health spending between countries (beyond the level of growth as outlined above) partly reflect the different policy decisions, the varied structures of financing and organisation of health systems and the value attached to health services compared to other goods and services (Katharaki 2006). In addition, the longitudinal change in health spending is also due to factors, such as advances in methods of prevention, diagnosis and treatment, as well as population ageing (Sturm 2002). In addition, the development and dissemination of new medical technologies and new drugs are consistent with the redefinition of decisions on the financing of new equipment and offered treatments.

According to EL.STAT.,[6] 313 hospitals, with 53,888 beds, operated in 2007, compared to 350 hospitals, with 52,474 beds, a decade earlier. The country currently has approximately 400 medical centres, many of which enter into contracts with public entities, such as pension funds. Furthermore, there are an estimated 20,000 private clinics and laboratories and 9,000 private dentists that employ about 20,000 specialty physicians and 13,744 dentists, respectively. The fundamentals of the public secondary and tertiary health services are as follows: on average, 10,000 admissions (scheduled and unscheduled), 4.5 m tests, and 150,000 drug

---

[6] EL.STAT: Hellenic Statistical Authority.

administrations annually per hospital. Health centres and regional NHS clinics employ 3,500 permanent doctors (of whom 2,500 are trainees), 2,000 nurses, and 3,000 support staff.

Regarding the medical staff employed by the sector, Greece has the highest ratio of doctors (5.35 practising doctors) per 1,000 inhabitants (figures for 2007), while Finland and Spain have 2.95 and 3.65, respectively. Moreover, the medical population increased in recent years compared with the Mediterranean countries of the European Union, the Nordic countries and the average of OECD-member countries. Thus, with 50,000 doctors, Greece suffers greatly from an oversupply of physicians (ratio of one doctor to 210 inhabitants). Despite this oversupply, a number of specialties are under-represented or completely absent in the Greek countryside, resulting in the uneven staffing of hospital units.

Furthermore, in contrast to the oversupply of medical personnel, the ratio of nurses to population is 3.21 nurses per 1,000 inhabitants, whereas, for example, in Finland, this ratio is 10.25 and in Norway, 31.92 (reference year 2007). There is thus a significant discrepancy in the ratios of doctors and nurses compared with the average of OECD countries, the Mediterranean countries of the European Union, and the countries of northern Europe.

The health services sector is facing new demands due to demographic trends (ageing population), disparities in healthcare levels, cross-border threats (e.g., pandemics), and other factors. To meet these demands, the European Union adopted a new health strategy to address the various problems in Europe and the world in general. This strategy emphasises not only primary, secondary, and tertiary healthcare but also prevention, health education, healthcare at home, rehabilitation services and the joint development of the health sector with other sectors, particularly health tourism.

Factors such as European integration, cultural evolution, demography (ageing and migration) and the state of the economy highlight the potential to expand the cooperation of the health sector with other economic sectors, with the ultimate aim of improving the quality of life and strengthening human capital, which, notably, is a determinant of a country's economic growth. Increasing the productivity of this sector contributes to the economic development of a country through the more efficient use of labour inputs (human capital) in the production process.

In addition, the factors that shape the demand for health services include patient mobility (within and outside of the Greek borders) and tourism. Greece's geographic particularities (islands and mountainous areas) increase internal mobility towards health services in large urban centres. Moreover, the influx of tourists during the holiday season reinforces the demand for health services and raises issues related to epidemics. These affect medical, nursing and pharmaceutical costs, both in the public and private sectors.

The term "health tourism" refers to visitors who, together with and complementary to tourist services, choose to make use of health services in their destination countries (Paparoidami and Katharaki 2009; Borman 2004). Interest has been expressed in this both by the medical field and tourism businesses, as medical tourism is a varied field (e.g., medical and dental tourism, spa, sports tourism and tourism for people in need of daily assistance). It should be noted that healthcare has evolved into an international market, where developed and developing countries compete for medical tourists (Cole and Razak 2008; Connell 2006; Lam and Hsu 2005; Lee 2007). Indeed, in 2012, India plans to secure \$2.3 bn from medical tourism services.

Health tourism and medical tourism are of particular interest for the Greek economy, given the level of development of the tourism and health sectors and the potential for their further co-development. This, however, once again highlights the issue of the necessary infrastructure and, therefore, the required (public and private) investments.

References

Borman E (2004) Health tourism. Where healthcare, ethics, and the state collide. BMJ 328:60–61

Brand S, Gripaios P, McVittie E (2006) The economic contributions of museums in the South West. South West economic centre, University of Plymouth Business Centre, Plymouth, U.K

Cole S, Razak V (2008) Tourism as future. Futures 41:335–345

Connell J (2006) Medical tourism: sea, sun, sand and...surgery. Tourism Manag 27:1093–1100

Dagkalidis A (2008) Hotel and tourism. Piraeus Bank, Econ Anal and Mark

Deffner A, Metaxas T (2003) The interrelationship of urban economic and cultural development: the case of Greek museums. Paper presented to the 43rd ERSA congress, Peripheries, centers, and spatial development in the new Europe, University of Jyväskylä, Finland

Dow K, Downing T (2006) The atlas of climate change: mapping the world's greatest challenge. University of California Press, Berkeley

Greffe X (2005) Culture and local development. OECD, Paris

Grundy E (2003) The epidemiology of ageing. In: Tallis R, Fillit H, Livingstone C (eds) Textbook of geriatric medicine. Churchill, Livingstone, London

Hannam K, Mitsche N, Stone C (2004) Tourism employability and the European social fund. In: Critical issues in tourism education, Proceedings of the 2004 conference of the association for tourism in higher education. Missenden Abbey, Buckinghamshire UK, 1999

Katharaki M (2006) The efficiency impact of telemedicine on obstetric and gynaecology services: effects on hospital units management. Discussion National and Kapodistrian. University of Athens, Greece

Lam T, Hsu C (2005) Predicting behavioral intention of choosing a travel destination. Tourism Manag 27:589–599

Lee C (2007) Medical tourism, an emerging international business. Monash Bus Rev 3(3):10–12

Nicholls D (2005) The employment of history graduates, A report to the higher education academy subject centre for history, classics and archaeology, University of Liverpool, Liverpool, United Kingdom

Paparoidami K, Katharaki M (2009) Investigating health tourism: current situation, key factors and future perspectives. Proceedings of the 7th InternationalConference. In: Information & communication technologies in healthcare (ICICTH '09), Greece, pp 299–305

Rosegrant MW, Ewing M, Yohe G, Burton I, Huq S, Valmonte-Santos R (2008) Climate change and agriculture: threats and opportunities. Eschborn, Deutsche Gesellschaft für Technische Zusammenarbeit (GTZ) GmbH

Sampaniotis T (2006) Greek tourism at the bound of international competitiveness. Eurobank Res Econ and Mark 8(10)

Smith SD, Heffler SK, Freeland MS (2000) The impact of technological change on health care cost increases: evaluation of the literature, Working Paper

Sturm R (2002) The effects of obesity, smoking, and drinking on medical problems and costs. Health Aff (Millwood) 21(2):245–53

WEF (2009) The Travel and Tourism Competitiveness Report. Managing in a Time of Turbulence, World Economic Forum, Geneva, Switzerland